Debating Human Rights in China

Debating Human Rights in China

A Conceptual and Political History

Marina Svensson

ROWMAN & LITTLEFIELD PUBLISHERS, INC.
Lanham • Boulder • New York • Oxford

ROWMAN & LITTLEFIELD PUBLISHERS, INC.

Published in the United States of America
by Rowman & Littlefield Publishers, Inc.
An Imprint of the Rowman & Littlefield Publishing Group
4720 Boston Way, Lanham, Maryland 20706
www.rowmanlittlefield.com

12 Hid's Copse Road
Cumnor Hill, Oxford OX2 9JJ, England

British Library Cataloguing in Publication Information Available

Library of Congress Cataloging-in-Publication Data

Svensson, Marina 1961–
    Debating human rights in China : a conceptual and political history /
Marina Svensson.
        p. cm.
Includes bibliographical references and index.
    ISBN 0-7425-1696-2 (cloth : alk. paper)—ISBN 0-7425-1697-0 (pbk. :
alk. paper)
1. Human rights—China. I. Title.

JC599.C6 S94 2002
323'.0951—dc21
                                        2002001199

Printed in the United States of America

♾™ The paper used in this publication meets the minimum requirements of American
National Standard for Information Sciences—Permanence of Paper for Printed Library
Materials, ANSI/NISO Z.39.48-1992.

Contents

Foreword

Marina Svensson's book makes a powerful impact not only on our understanding of the history of modern Chinese thought, but on our understanding of a contemporary issue, the so-called Asian values debate. This is the argument over whether human rights ideas are inconsistent with the values of Asian peoples. Since coming under concentrated criticism for its human rights record in 1989, the government of the People's Republic of China has mounted a counterattack, supported by other authoritarian Asian regimes and some thinkers East and West, that argues that human rights is a local Western idea without roots in Asia.

Svensson shows to the contrary that sympathetic discussions of human rights have been integral to Chinese thought throughout the modern period, more so than any previous scholar has demonstrated. Not that the authors whose thought Svensson analyzes were unknown until now. They include China's best-known modern thinkers. But no one else has brought the human rights themes in their thinking together in one place, to show how intense and continuous their conversation on this topic was across the decades.

The issues that animated Chinese debates over human rights were at bottom no different from those that entered into the Western discourse, which, although older, was also a creature of the modern period rather than a direct outgrowth of the Western tradition. What are the sources of rights? Which of them can be compromised and to what extent? And how should one balance them with the needs of the community? A strong, central set of answers among the many proposed to these questions in China was little different from an influential set of answers in the West—that human rights grow from human nature, that they are consistent with the ends of the good political community, and that some of them are absolute requirements for human dignity, while others must be balanced off against competing values that also contribute to that dignity.

With so much in common, no one who carefully reads Svensson's evidence can any longer doubt that the Chinese and Western discourses on rights partake of a common universality. Moreover, Svensson is persuasive not only in arguing, but more impressively in demonstrating, that a Westerner can describe the Chinese discourse with objectivity and sympathy.

To be sure, universality does not mean uniformity. Svensson's inquiry produces a rich sense of how the debate took on a particular cast from its embeddedness within the Chinese historical experience. Chinese thinkers faced a constant struggle over locating human rights within what was for many the more pressing claim of national salvation. Given that liberal and democratic forms of government were widely viewed as too ineffective and weak to save the nation, what kind of rights could one expect to enjoy under authoritarian government, and how could the advocate of rights defend their utility not just for the individuals who would enjoy them, but from the viewpoint of the authorities as well? How could the root idea of human dignity be made vivid to a society that lacked a religious tradition based on the idea of individual salvation, and which during much of the time discussed in this book confronted dehumanizing levels of poverty and violence? In a society where most people had more respect for justice than for law, how could rights be given a firmer basis than they could enjoy as mere legal or constitutional enactments? Chinese thinkers addressed all these issues and came up with answers that not only continue to influence the course of Chinese history, but remain worth pondering on their own terms, not only in the West but in the many other societies that are struggling over similar issues in the new century.

By relocating the Chinese human rights discourse away from the periphery and closer to the center of modern Chinese intellectual history, Svensson establishes another, equally important, revision of the conventional wisdom. If the "response to the West" paradigm has been displaced in the study of Chinese economic and social history, it remains influential in the study of cultural and intellectual history. But Svensson shows that the thinkers she writes about were not pressed into their intellectually painful, and often physically dangerous, inquiries by a desire to comment on remote foreign thinkers. Rather, they were driven to foreign thinkers for wisdom by the urgent need of their own society for guidance on how to face some of the most painful problems of modern politics.

Although carefully translating and studying what the foreign thinkers said, Chinese writers never limited their discussions within the ambit of debating received ideas. They used existing ideas as resources for resolving specific issues they perceived at home. As opposed to a "diffusion" model of how values change, this supports the idea that human rights principles are generated from within separate modern societies by the intrinsic needs of people living in them. If this is so, then these values' validity is truly universal, in the sense that they have sprung up virtually everywhere because of their widespread applicability to the modern condition. If the human rights idea had not already existed, then twentieth-century China would have had to invent it, to defend people whose traditionally rooted sense of human dignity came to be threatened by sweeping economic and social changes, and most of all, by the rise of the modern state. Indeed, in a real sense China did invent the human rights idea, in that Chinese thinkers invented and refined their own version of the idea for their own situation. That the Chinese version proved to have so much in common with the Western one demonstrates the independence of the central human rights concept from cultural differences.

As Svensson brings the story up to the near-present, an irony emerges. In one of the periods when human rights have been most under assault in China, the human rights idea has achieved near-hegemony in Chinese thought. It is not merely the platform of a persistent group of dissidents, not simply the demand of ordinary people who seek human rights in their dealings with authority even though they do not use the term, but also the justification that the ruling party uses in one form or another for its own actions—whether in suppressing deviant religious sects in order to defend the rights of those whom they allegedly manipulate, or in using harsh methods of control in order to better promote development for economic and social rights, or in criticizing American policy abroad that allegedly interferes with the equal rights of other countries. Even the abusers of human rights in practice, in short, cannot hope to legitimize what they do without having recourse to human rights as an idea.

Svensson's book is thus very much a treatise whose time has come, a reenvisioning of China's past that helps us make sense of the present. It is the work of a mature China scholar, insightfully interpreting a wide range of texts written in diverse and often difficult styles, against a series of complex historical backdrops arrayed over a long period of time. It is the product of wide reading, deep learning, and careful thought. We, the beneficiaries of Svensson's hard work, can draw from it not only much edification, but encouragement that the much-touted cultural gap between China and the West is hardly as wide as our earlier ignorance made it appear.

Andrew J. Nathan
Class of 1919 Professor of Political Science
Columbia University, New York

Acknowledgments

The origin of this book is to be found in my dissertation that covered the period 1898–1949. I defended the dissertation in 1996, and this much revised and expanded work has thus taken many years, too many years, to complete. During these years I have benefited greatly from readers of my dissertation, other works of mine, and several drafts of the present work, and from discussions and debates over human rights in both academic and nonacademic settings. It is pleasant to acknowledge the support and input of so many people who have offered insightful comments and new perspectives on human rights issues, but slightly embarrassing to admit that I haven't always heeded their advice and also probably overlooked many important views and arguments. I of course take full responsibility for all errors, weaknesses, and lapses of judgment that exist in the final product.

I'm very grateful to everybody at the East Asia Institute of Columbia University where I spent the academic year 1997–1998 as a postdoctoral fellow; special thanks are due Andrew Nathan and James Seymour whose works on human rights have been a source of constant inspiration. I would also like to thank the participants at the Modern China Seminar at Columbia University, in particular the discussant Michael Gasster, for their comments on a paper I presented at one of the seminars. I'm also grateful for an invitation to speak at the New England China Seminar at the Fairbank Center, Harvard University, and for comments and discussions with participants at this event. Parts of the following work have been presented in different incarnations at different conferences and at other settings. These include a conference on Asian values and human rights arranged by the Nordic Institute of Asian Studies, Copenhagen University, and the Danish Center for Human Rights in 1997, and a panel on human rights at the International Conference of Asian Studies in Leiden in 1998. I also presented papers on human rights at a conference on comparative legal cultures in Beijing in 2000, arranged by the Swedish Research Council and the Chinese Academy of Social Science, and at a conference on National Human Rights Commissions in Taipei in 2001, arranged by Soochow University. In recent years I have also benefited from participation in a couple of European Union–China human rights expert meetings and from being a member of the official Swedish human rights delegation to China in 2000.

Two people deserve special mention for their support and encouragement in the long, drawn out work of finishing this book: Jeff Wasserstrom and Steve Angle. Jeff has been very supportive of my work throughout, and it is very much thanks to him that this book is seeing the light of day. Steve has read both my dissertation and an earlier draft of the manuscript. I'm very grateful for his suggestions and comments and for our many discussions on human rights during the past few years. Steve and I have coedited an anthology of Chinese texts on human rights, *The Chinese Human Rights Reader* (Sharpe 2001), and this very fruitful and stimulating cooperation has also rubbed off on the present work. My readings of Jeff's and Steve's own works on human rights have also been a source of inspiration and have set me off on new periods and paths of reflection.

I'm very grateful for the careful reading of two anonymous readers whose comments and criticisms convinced me to fortify and rewrite some parts of the manuscript, although perhaps not as much as they would have liked. I would also like to thank Rune Svarverud, who read and commented on chapter 4, and whose own work on translation and the emergence of a new vocabulary has been very helpful for my own work. Heartfelt thanks are also due Anne-Marie Brady, who read an earlier draft of the manuscript, and Janet Sturgeon, who read parts of it at a later incarnation, for their valuable comments and help on language and style.

Human rights is not a topic that one can afford to discuss in the "ivory towers of academia," in splendid isolation from concrete human rights violations in the contemporary world. In my case human rights activism came first and academic work only later. This book owes much to the work and inspiration of human rights activists, and it is therefore dedicated to them in their continuing struggle for human rights. Many thanks to all friends in the human rights activists community: Peter Adler, Catherine Baber, Chine Chan, Chen Maiping, Daniel Eriksson, Maria Granefelt, Anna Gustafsson Chen, Mab Huang, Isabel Kelly, Arlette Laduguie, Beatrice Larouche, Liu Qing, Dominique Müller, Emma Nordlund, Peter Nässen, Louise Vischer, Per Wiktorsson, Sophia Woodman, Xiao Qiang, Yu Ping.

Last, but certainly not least, I would like to thank Susan McEachern and Renee Jardine at Rowman & Littlefield for their encouragement and interest in this work and for guiding the manuscript through the editorial process, and Rose Marye Boudreaux for her meticulous copyediting and hard work to improve my English.

Chapter One

Debating Human Rights in China:
Introductory Perspectives

A FORGOTTEN HISTORY

Since the crushing of the democracy movement in 1989, human rights has been a problematic topic for the People's Republic of China (PRC) in its relations with the international community, which is in stark contrast to the situation before 1989 when human rights did not feature very highly in bilateral and multilateral relations and the PRC was treated as something of a "human rights exception."[1] For most of the post-1949 period human rights had also been a taboo subject in domestic political discourse and labeled a bourgeois slogan (*zichan jieji kouhao*) that was inappropriate and irrelevant for a socialist society. It was the harsh critique that the PRC faced in 1989 that convinced its political leadership that it had to take a more proactive approach to human rights issues, both in order to ward off foreign criticism and with the more long-term goal of launching a systematic view of its own. In its first White Paper on human rights, published in 1991, the Chinese government proudly proclaimed that "Since the very day of its founding, the Communist Party of China [CCP] has been holding high the banner of democracy and human rights."[2] This is proof of a very selective memory on the CCP's part, but it also shows that the PRC now has come to embrace, or rather appropriate, the language of human rights. Thus, gone and forgotten are the days when the party criticized the concept of human rights as a mere bourgeois slogan; instead it has begun to push its own definition of "human rights with Chinese characteristics." Such a turnabout reveals that human rights today is a global language that no country can afford to ignore any longer.

The 1990s saw an upsurge of debates on human rights within the PRC, as well as numerous academic and diplomatic exchanges concerning human rights between China and other nations. China was hit by a human rights fever (*renquan re*) and experienced a boom in human rights work. To date, more than one thousand articles and one hundred books have been published since 1989, compared with a handful of articles and only two monographs during the previous decade.[3] It would be wrong, however, to think of China as a latecomer to the human rights discourse. To people with short historical memories, human rights only seem to have entered the Chinese political discourse after 1989. Nothing, however, could be further from the truth as China has had a rich and internally contested debate on human rights since the late Qing dynasty. In contrast to the official post-1989 human rights discourse, during most of the twentieth century human rights were the subject of indigenously motivated debates firmly anchored in domestic preoccupations. The concept of human rights was not imposed on China by outsiders, but actively and creatively taken up by the Chinese people themselves in answer to their own political needs.

Despite the recent scholarly attention to human rights issues in China, earlier domestic debates remain virtually forgotten and neglected by both Chinese and Western scholars.[4] This particularly refers to the pre-1949 period, but even the post-1949 debates remain seriously understudied. This study aims to remedy the prevalent historical amnesia and highlight the rich and diverse debates that have taken place in China throughout the twentieth century. It can therefore be regarded as an attempt to recover history, compared with the CCP's recent attempt to rewrite and invent a history in which the party is portrayed as having been a staunch defender of human rights all along.[5]

In view of today's highly charged political debates on human rights, it is instructive to take a historical approach and study how human rights have been discussed and debated de facto since the concept was introduced in China at the turn of the twentieth century. Knowledge of debates prior to the founding of the PRC in 1949 will provide us with a better understanding and broader perspective of the contemporary human rights discourse: When was the concept introduced in China, why, and by whom? What was the view among Chinese intellectuals during the late Qing, and how have Chinese people dealt with the concept since? Have there been any major turning points in the Chinese human rights discourse, and what factors, domestic and international, explain these shifts? One central question is whether, and to what extent, the Chinese view differs from that of the West and if there is a difference, why is this so and what does it imply? To what extent has the Chinese conception of human rights been shaped by people's different understandings of China's various cultural traditions, and to what extent does it reflect the domestic political situation at the time and debates and developments in the rest of the world? In this context it is also interesting to see if the arguments used in the Chinese debate are similar to those used elsewhere—thereby reaching an understanding either of the "Chineseness," or of the universality of the debate. It should of course be stressed, and I will come back to this point shortly, that there is no such thing as *one* Chinese conception of human rights any more than there is *one* Western conception of human rights.

In a cross-cultural study on such a controversial topic as human rights, one has to be aware of the potential charge of trying to impose the value standards of one's own society upon that of another; in this particular case the accusation would be "human rights imperialism." But by focusing on how the Chinese people themselves have discussed human rights, I believe that it is possible to refute such a charge. If it turns out that human rights have indeed been discussed in China, albeit differently from the West, charges of cultural imperialism are rendered irrelevant, or at least seriously weakened. I believe, however, that cultural imperialism might be the lesser of two evils, with an extreme culturally relativistic approach being far worse. It is important to stand up for the values you believe in. To claim for yourself rights you deny others smacks of hypocrisy and double standards, even though cultural relativism is usually motivated by a respect for other cultures.

IN DEFENSE OF A HISTORICAL APPROACH TO HUMAN RIGHTS STUDIES

It used to be the case that human rights was a topic more or less monopolized by philosophers and legal scholars, but other academic disciplines have of late also come to take an interest in the study of human rights. Jeffrey N. Wasserstrom has thus detected a "historical turn" in human rights studies, as historians increasingly have been attracted to the field.[6] My study can perhaps also best be described as that of a historian. A historical study is particularly fruitful since it enables us to investigate how human rights have been discussed in different societies and over time, and by whom. Although I address philosophical issues, my primary interest is the political ramifications of the debate. Therefore, this work could also be described as a piece of political history. Other historical approaches would have been of equal interest; social and legal historians thus take different approaches to the study of human rights.

But it is not only historians who recently have become engaged in human rights studies. Over the past ten to twenty years, political scientists, sociologists, and anthropologists in increasing numbers have made significant contributions that have broadened and enriched the study of human rights.[7] This scholarly shift illustrates the increasing importance of the human rights discourse as it now influences social movements and permeates political and legal institutions in countries all over the world. Building on recent scholarship in the human rights field, I understand human rights as a historically and politically constructed concept that reflects the concerns and interests of those who construct and invoke it. I therefore argue for a contextualized study of human rights that takes into consideration issues of power and agency, and that sees human rights debates as an area of fierce social and political contestations.

With reference to this latter aspect one could then also describe my study as an attempt at conceptual history.[8] Conceptual historians study the history of political concepts, tracing their emergence in the political discourse, attempts by competing individuals or groups to appropriate and control them, and their changing and contested meanings over time. The clearest sign of new concepts is the generation of a new vocabulary, but old concepts also undergo changes over time that radically change their meaning. Conceptual and political change, according to conceptual historians, is a single, complex, and interrelated process, so that the rate of new coinages of political concepts during a period indicates the increasing appropriation of new modes of thought and concomitant political changes.

Conceptual historians argue that in the West, 1750–1850 was a period of particularly rapid and radical conceptual and political changes. In the late nineteenth and early twentieth century, China experienced a time of equally revolutionary changes. During this period new political concepts reflecting new modes of thinking about self and society entered the Chinese language, while in some cases old concepts were imbued with new meanings. These developments were in many cases quite rapid and radically transformed the political landscape of China. Regardless of whether the new political concepts evolved from older Confucian terms or were imported from abroad, they have since in their turn evolved and been contested. The concept of human rights was but one of the new political concepts that entered the Chinese political discourse at the turn of the twentieth century. Other political concepts, such as nationalism and revolution, played even more important roles in the political transformation of China.[9]

In this study I will, however, focus on the concept of human rights and the political and linguistic contestations surrounding that particular concept. One aim is to trace the concept of human rights throughout the twentieth century and write "a history designed to provide both the contexts of [the concept of human rights] and [its] uses in argument, as well as to identify the different terms designating [this concept]."[10] In this context the identity of those taking part in the debate and the political background and ramifications of these debates are of particular importance. In order to analyze the contestations surrounding the concept of human rights, one has to grasp the discursive strategies of the participants involved. There have been both contestations over the human rights concept as such, as well as attempts to replace it with other concepts, for example, people's rights or citizens' rights. These contestations have usually taken place in a domestic context, but as human rights have come to occupy a prominent place in international relations these contestations now also cut across national borders. The globalization of human rights that began in the 1940s, but really took off only in the mid-1970s, has spurred different individuals, organizations, and governments to try to appropriate the human rights concept and influence or control the discourse. During the 1990s, for example, the PRC has challenged the West over the concept of human rights, but has also been challenged itself by dissidents at home and abroad.

In my analysis of the Chinese conception of human rights, I have used articles on politics and law published in various influential magazines, as well as collections of writings by leading intellectual and political figures. When studying a political concept, one could also make use of other materials, such as dictionaries, encyclopedias, and textbooks, as well as more literary works. I have, however, limited myself to more political and philosophical works, and only note in passing the appearance of human rights in literary works. Examples of the latter would include Su Qing's impromptu reference to human rights in her 1944 semiautobiographical novel, and the more self-conscious references to human rights in poems and short stories penned during the democracy movement of 1978–79. Since I focus on the written word and, in other words, a predominantly elite discourse, it is inevitable that I will be unable to probe the knowledge and understanding of human rights among Chinese people in general to any great extent. During the past few years, however, some surveys of Chinese citizens' perceptions of their rights and works that focus on the role of rights in legal and political struggles have appeared, which flesh out more theoretical studies such as my own.[11]

Writings on human rights can be either more political or more philosophical in character, or a combination of both. When all is said and done, however, the concept of human rights is more often than not invoked in a political context, as a way to criticize and attack the powers that be. Human rights debates in China, as elsewhere, have generally been motivated by political concerns and concrete human rights violations, so that writings on human rights, as a consequence, have a tendency to be very political and polemical in character. But there are also those who have been engaged in more theoretical studies of human rights and provided more philosophical work on the topic. An internal (or hermeneutical) reading of the texts therefore needs to be complemented by an external (or historical) reading, which attempts to locate the text within a broader sociopolitical framework. This study only deals with the conception of human rights and, as a result, does not venture into areas of legalization and institutionalization of human rights, issues that should be addressed in a fuller

treatment of human rights in China.¹² Nor do I focus in any great detail on
concrete human rights violations, other than as a background to and impetus
behind debates on human rights.¹³

In discussions on the historical origin of the concept of human rights, the
question has been raised of whether it is possible to imagine that societies (including the premodern West), which did not have a word for human rights (or
natural rights, or inherent rights), nevertheless could have had a concept of human rights. Some human rights scholars have argued that human rights ideas
did not emerge in the West but have been a feature of all societies in the world.
As one recent work on the history of human rights has it:

> Early ideas about general human rights . . . did not originate exclusively in one loca-
> tion like the West or even with any particular form of government like liberal de-
> mocracy, but were shared throughout the ages by visionaries from many cultures in
> many lands who *expressed themselves in different ways* [emphasis added].¹⁴

This author uses human rights in a very loose and broad sense to cover all
ideas of justice and human dignity. But whereas no one would deny that ideas
of justice and dignity constitute one important and central aspect of human
rights, or that humankind everywhere has fought against injustices in defense
of humanity, this does not signify that all cultures or societies therefore have
also had or formulated an explicit concept of human rights. On this point I
tend to agree with human rights scholars such as Jack Donnelly and others,
who argue that it is necessary to distinguish ideas of human dignity and justice
from the concept of human rights, although the former, of course, is embedded in the latter.¹⁵ One also has to distinguish between the historical origin of
a concept, its social and cultural legitimacy, and its actual realization in the contemporary world. In order to defend human rights as universal and applicable
in all societies, there is, in other words, no need to argue that the concept of
human rights also originally is found in all societies. To acknowledge the fact
that the concept of human rights has a history doesn't imply a rejection of the
universality of human rights, nor does it force us to step out on the slippery
slope of relativism.

While it is difficult to imagine that one can possess a concept without a corresponding vocabulary, it is important to note that a concept can be expressed
by different words and that the same words can carry quite different meanings.
It is a mistake to assume that words or concepts would carry exactly the same
meaning over time or across societies. It is obvious that they will take on somewhat different meanings depending on the historical, social, and political contexts in which they appear, or vary from individual to individual within one society at one particular point in time. What is touched upon here is also the
well-known problem of cross-cultural interpretation. In the process of translat-

ing and interpreting value-laden concepts and ideas into another language and another political and cultural context, the original concept will be understood and interpreted, either consciously or unconsciously, in a way that reflects the personality, cultural and social milieu, and political predicament of the translator and interpreter. The historical and cultural embeddedness of political and moral concepts has to be acknowledged. In this context it is instructive to remember that the first discussions on rights and natural rights in the West were configured differently from the discussions on human rights taking place today. But although there admittedly exist important differences between natural rights and human rights, it would be wrong to read too much into the use of different words and to argue that therefore they also constitute two fundamentally different concepts. The concept of natural rights is the predecessor to human rights, and they have more in common than separates them; they, so to speak, belong to the same semantic field.

BEYOND CULTURE TALK: POWER AND AGENCY IN HUMAN RIGHTS DISCOURSE

To acknowledge the historical and cultural embeddedness of political concepts does not mean that one has to reject the proposition that there can also be something universal and timeless about them. There is undeniably something transcendental and universal with respect to a great many moral and political concepts, as they can be shared and understood across cultures and over time. This is evident in the Chinese debates on human rights since the beginning of the twentieth century. The relative ease with which the human rights concept, originating in the West, became domesticated and accepted shows that it must have a strong universal and cross-cultural appeal. I thus disagree with the frequently heard assumption that the Chinese people, due to their different cultural background, would be unable to understand and grasp the meaning of human rights, or relate human rights to their own political struggles; the facts as presented in this study show otherwise. Nor does the fact that the Chinese language did not have any equivalent words for "rights" and "human rights" until the late nineteenth century pose any insurmountable difficulties. New words and concepts initially have to overcome many barriers, including generational, ideological, cultural, and linguistic, regardless of a domestic or foreign origin. In fact, the concept of human rights has met with considerable opposition in both the West and in China, and often for many of the same reasons.

Conventional wisdom, however, maintains that the concept of human rights is foreign and incomprehensible to the Chinese people because of their different cultural tradition. Since human rights is a foreign concept to the Chinese people, in the sense that it was first formulated in the West and later "imported" to China, many scholars have been preoccupied with questions regarding why the Chinese culture did not give rise to a concept of human rights. Additional questions concern whether the absence of an indigenous human rights tradition implies that human rights are incompatible with Chinese culture, and whether it also follows that human rights therefore are unrealizable in present-day China. To my mind, it is important not to reject the concept of human rights because of its (Western) historical origin, or to assume that an absence of a domestic tradition precludes its acceptance and realization in contemporary China. An absence of human rights thinking in the Chinese political tradition or on the political agenda are not sufficient grounds to dismiss the concept as irrelevant and inapplicable to China.

The fact that in the past neither the Nationalists, that is, the Guomindang (GMD), nor the Communists showed much interest in or respect for human rights (as a matter of fact their views have been quite similar) should not be taken as proof that human rights have never been discussed or advocated in China; still less, of course, should it be taken as proof that they are unrealizable. The days have passed when the GMD argued that human rights did not fit Chinese conditions and the CCP simply dismissed human rights as a bourgeois slogan. Today the language of human rights is embraced and appropriated by both of them. This indicates that politics and political expediency more than anything else inform and influence the human rights discourse, and that the globalization of human rights in addition has forced the GMD and the CCP to modify their earlier negative views. Rights and human rights have been debated in China since the beginning of the twentieth century and have since then become a part, however contested, of the Chinese political discourse. As Jeremy T. Paltiel so ingeniously has put it, "Rights are part of the contemporary Chinese vocabulary, which is as different from the classical Chinese lexicon as a Long March rocket is from a sedan chair."[16] Since China already has had a one-hundred-year-long history of human rights debates, one should think that the issue of whether human rights are compatible with the Chinese tradition could be laid to rest safely and finally.

Nonetheless, issues concerning culture, cultural legitimacy, and cultural compatibility continue to figure prominently in many works on the human rights discourse in China.[17] While it is easy to agree with the general proposition that culture shapes human rights discourse and, thus, to some extent, explains differences between societies, many scholars have tended to go one step further and argue that culture is all that matters. To establish the cultural legitimacy of human rights, or ground it in indigenous terms, is crucial, these scholars argue, because otherwise it is easy for opponents to dismiss human rights on the grounds that it is "unauthentic." Such a belief has prompted several scholars to engage in a cross-cultural search for equivalents to human rights or to analyze to what extent traditional values are compatible or at odds with human rights.[18] While I don't disagree with the view that human rights talk takes place in a cultural context, I harbor serious misgivings about some of these cultural approaches to the study of human rights, as they often seem to be based upon a crude and ahistorical understanding of culture.

A number of scholars have also criticized this, which they describe as a "tyranny of culture" in human rights studies.[19] Like Ken Booth they believe that the prevalent culturalism is guilty of a "reduction of social and political explanations to culture and to the black-boxing of cultures as exclusivist identity-referents."[20] One objection, in other words, is that culture in human rights studies often is essentialized and its multiple and contested faces ignored. Another major objection is that culture often is understood and referred to in a much too static and ahistorical way to be of much use as an explanatory factor. Many human rights scholars in addition are critical of the exclusive focus on cultural factors that neglect structural and political factors.

Recent works in cultural theory and anthropology have, however, enlightened us to the fact that culture is neither homogeneous, coherent, or timeless, nor deterministic or static.[21] It is inevitably contested, fragmented, evolving, and dynamic. People have multiple cultural identities deriving from gender, work, religious and political beliefs, and so on. These identities are so complex that one had better avoid any simple reference to a metacultural identity such as "Chinese culture" or "Asian values." Not only is culture contested and evolving, but the process of globalization in addition makes the proposition that culture is homogeneous, sharply delineated, and unique, outdated. No culture is self-contained or isolated, but interacts with and is influenced by other cultures and the global community. The globalization of human rights is an indisputable fact, and human rights has itself become a cultural practice lived and acted upon in many different societies in the world. At the beginning of the twenty-first century, we are witnessing the emergence of a human rights culture that transcends national, societal, and other cultural boundaries.

Issues of power and representativity are also all but absent from many cultural approaches to human rights, when, as a matter of fact, gender, class, and political power are crucial in shaping individuals' positions in society and therefore their perception of their culture and human rights. The power and position of the narrator is important and has to be taken into account. The crucial question is, Who interprets and speaks for that culture?[22] An analysis of power relations and sociopolitical factors serves to sensitize us to the fact that human rights conceptions might vary considerably within the same society.

Culture furthermore tends to be referred to in a way that obscures the fact that it is malleable and dynamic. Culture is much too vague, or used in a much too vague and sweeping way, to be used as an explanatory factor of human rights conceptions. While the anthropologist Adam Kuper might go too far, he has a point when he admonishes us to avoid the "hyper-referential" word *culture* altogether.[23] I have also become increasingly wary of the many general and sweeping references to Chinese culture when trying to explain, or defend, the Chinese position(s) on human rights. In this context it should also be mentioned that culture in human rights studies mostly seems to refer to a distant and unchanging culture (classical Confucianism in the case of China), without taking into account how and whether traditional values and practices still are relevant and practiced in contemporary society. Seldom has the task been to investigate how the concept of human rights was introduced in a new cultural setting, and how and to what extent cultural values shaped this encounter. I therefore agree with the anthropologist Richard A. Wilson, who argues that: "[I]nstead of hunting for conceptual similarities in different moral traditions, it might be better to look at how concepts are implanted in contexts from which they did not necessarily originate."[24] This is also the focus of the present work.

The emphasis on culture in human rights studies is also problematic for other reasons. Of late culture has begun to be referred to in a way that indicates that it has been elevated, or rather degenerated, to a political myth.[25] This culture talk basically takes two forms. On the one hand, there are those who use culture as a trump card to dismiss human rights critique and reject certain human rights for being at odds with their own societies; witness the Asian values debate.[26] Such an approach implies an advocacy of cultural relativism under the pretext of defending cultural pluralism. On the other hand, there are those, such as Samuel Huntington and others, who, although they also tend to see culture as a crucial factor that explains social and political behavior, instead reach the conclusion that some cultures, or, less bluntly put, some cultural values are better than others since they promote economic development, democracy, and respect for human rights.[27] Such an understanding has given rise to a belief in "the clash of civilisations" and views that can best be described as "cultural developmentalism."[28] In this case it is not a question of advocating cultural relativism but rather of promoting some cultural values as more "advanced" than others. The two forms of culture talk are, however, not so different as one might think at first glance but constitute two sides of the same coin. Both are guilty of essentializing culture and of presenting the West and Asia, the main areas of concern in my study, as two homogeneous and sharply delineated cultures.

I'm highly critical of both the advocacy of Asian values and of the thesis of a "clash of civilisations," especially given the strong political connotations surrounding these debates, which is one reason I caution against playing up the importance of culture in studies on human rights. The prevalent "tyranny of culture" in human rights work on China, and the Chinese government's own invocation of "national conditions" are cause for additional concern.

I would certainly not go so far as to deny that cultural factors play a role in human rights debates, but culture here refers to socially created legacies of values and practices that influence a people's world views and behaviors and by extension their social and political institutions. Furthermore, culture is neither a frozen past nor a singular destiny: it is created, changed, and abandoned by individuals who interact with each other, both within their own societies as well as with the global community. I believe not only that culture is dynamic and contested, but that one should focus more on structural factors, for example, the domestic and international political situation.[29] A study of human rights debates in addition needs to take issues such as agency and power seriously since human rights discourse takes the form of political struggles.[30] The identity of those speaking about human rights is significant since human rights, after all, are called for by those who feel that they are being deprived of them. Human rights are a weapon of the weak that challenges established authority, although in the hands of the power holders it also can become a propaganda slogan or even a tool of oppression.[31]

Although there are those who dismiss the relevance of the concept of human rights to China on the grounds of cultural differences, others, as mentioned above, try to explore the Confucian tradition in order to ascertain the common ground between Confucianism and the concept of human rights.[32] This approach often takes the form of a search for equivalents, such as ideas of equality and human dignity, which are found in the Chinese tradition and believed to either entail or nurture a concept of human rights. Some would therefore argue that, whereas the Chinese language lacked a word connoting "human rights" before the advent of the introduction of the Western concept around the turn of the twentieth century, the general notion of the idea, or at least elements of it, was served by indigenous concepts, which were loosely parallel or similar in character to, or, differently put, fulfilled the same functions as human rights.

I believe that the search for equivalents is wrongheaded and constitutes a dead end, as the acceptance and realization of human rights in contemporary China does not depend or hinge on the establishment or identification of Confucian equivalents. Furthermore, I tend to believe that the concept of human rights is in many ways qualitatively different from traditional concepts, thus implying not only the appearance of a new terminology but a different outlook frequently at odds with the Confucian worldview. In this context it should be remembered that for many Chinese intellectuals throughout the last century, it was precisely the many troubling aspects of Confucianism, such as its hierarchical nature and submission of women, that provoked their critique and led them to reject Confucianism for being at odds with human rights. It is also instructive to note that today's Chinese dissidents have not given much thought to the relationship between Confucianism and human rights—it seems mostly to be a topic of concern to scholars, especially those residing outside the PRC. Nor have Chinese dissidents tried to support their advocacy of human rights with references to Confucianism or Chinese tradition but rather they have sought support in universal proclamations of human rights. Their approach is not difficult to understand or unique for China. Human rights discourse develops in opposition to those in power and the ideology and belief system that they represent. To call for human rights and argue for their universality in a sense thus inevitably implies an attack on traditional values. I therefore concur with the legal scholar Martin Chanock, who writes that:

> Human rights have depended on the deliberate (bitterly opposed) active remaking of a new order, on a denial of the past, on a reinvention of political mythologies, not simply on an evolution of what had been historically and culturally acceptable. In doing this, the rights makers have specifically reached out towards universalism, and very often explicitly away from "culture" in a more specific sense. Rights may be claimed by their proponents as an inherent immanent virtue but they do not simply emerge and they do not proclaim compatibility with what "is" in a culture. They come from the fiercest of political contestation, from revolution and war.[33]

In this work I will argue, nonetheless, that one reason why the concept of human rights found fertile ground in China in the early twentieth century was that to some extent it could be related to or build upon Confucian discussions on the nature of man and human dignity. But it should be stressed that the human rights discourse in many ways signified a radically new understanding of self and human dignity and of the relationships between individuals and between the individual and the state. Lynn Hunt and Charles Taylor have both emphasized that in the West new conceptions of self paved the way for the concept of human rights.[34] In China, too, new ideas of self that emphasized self-autonomy, self-respect, and dignity went hand in hand with rights talk. The slave trope has been a standing feature of the Chinese rights discourse throughout the twentieth century. Rights, it has been said, enable the individual to establish an independent and autonomous personality whereas without them he would become dependent upon others and reduced to the position of a slave. Such an understanding of rights informed both the writings of Ma Junwu in the beginning of the twentieth century and Wei Jingsheng toward its close, and is also quite common among Western human rights scholars and activists.

Other scholars, when looking at the way tradition has shaped the Chinese human rights discourse, have instead focused on other, more negative traits of Confucianism. They argue that the contemporary focus on the collective over the individual and duties over rights in official discourse can be explained by the persistent influence of Confucianism and that communism has reinforced these indigenous trends of thought.[35] In this work I will attempt to show that this is a much too simplistic description of the Chinese discourse that ignores the wide range of views put forward during the twentieth century. I thus disagree with the often heard view that the West "emphasises the universal and abstract nature of the individual's civil and political rights, with social rights as secondary, concrete, non-universal and contingent, and that the latter [i.e., China] emphasises social and economic rights, but views all rights as collectively based, concrete, non-universal, and subordinate to state sovereignty."[36] The picture is much more complex, as quite different conceptions of human rights exist both in China and in the West. That being said, however, I would not completely dismiss the view that Chinese people have often emphasized the collective over the individual and harmony over rights. The reasons for this position cannot simply be sought in Chinese culture, however, but are found in a complex web of sociopolitical factors and specific political ideologies, in addition to being influenced by domestic crises and external threats to the nation.

To talk about a Chinese versus Western conception of human rights, as many have a tendency to do, is therefore a construct of limited value. Such an approach ignores the existence of different and conflicting views on human rights within the two societies. Neither China nor the West are monolithic societies, and the view of human rights in both societies has furthermore undergone significant changes over time. To simply juxtapose China and the West tends to exaggerate differences and overlook points of similarities. It also serves to prevent a meaningful dialogue and cross-cultural understanding. Those discussing the conception of human rights in China have been far too ready to submit to a monolithic view not only of China but also of the West. It would be a great mistake to assume that the Western conception of human rights is unproblematic and self-evident, as many different and conflicting views actually exist also within the West. Benjamin Schwartz early on called attention to the danger of assuming the West to be "a known quantity" in cross-cultural studies. As a matter of fact, he argued, we "are not dealing with a known and an unknown variable but with two vast, ever-changing, highly problematic areas of human experience. We undoubtedly 'know' infinitely more about the West, but the West remains as problematic as ever."[37] It is therefore imperative to question, not only the conventional wisdom regarding the conception of human rights in China, but also our own preconceived ideas regarding the conception of human rights in the West. One problem is that the West often has come to be identified with the United States when in reality the United States is but one country in the West. The West is a diverse and heterogeneous area, home to many different and conflicting ideas on human rights. To give

but two examples, the United States and European countries take quite different positions on the importance of social and economic rights, and they also
take opposite stands on the death penalty.[38]

A discussion of the conception of human rights in China does, however, require some kind of comparative framework. I have therefore chosen to compare the Chinese conception of human rights with that of the West. This does
not mean that I hold the Western view to be a universal standard against which
all other societies should be measured, nor does it mean that I regard the Western conception to be monolithic. I have instead opted for a more pluralistic approach and tried to identify a number of questions central to any discourse on
human rights, whether in the West or in China. The questions pertain to the
basis and origin of human rights, the subject of human rights, the substance
and scope of human rights, the justification and purpose of human rights, the
correlativity between rights and duties, and the relation between the individual and the state.

It is important not to see the introduction of Western concepts in terms of
a simple impact–response pattern, where the West is the provider and China
the receiver.[39] Although my analysis of the reception and understanding of
human rights only vaguely addresses the issue of whether Chinese tradition or
iconoclastic Chinese sources served as an inspiration and/or facilitated the reception of the concept of human rights, this is more due to my own shortcomings than a rejection of such an approach.[40] Even though the concept of
human rights, which undeniably originated in the West, was in part taken up
by the Chinese people as a response to the threat posed by the West, I prefer
to see this introduction as an example of cross-cultural borrowing rather than
as an example of a passive response or, for that matter, an imposition of foreign
values. It was not a question of a passive reception on the part of the Chinese
people but an active borrowing that reflected their preoccupations and concerns. Changes within China as well as external factors are the background
against which the debates on human rights should be set. Thus, differences exist between different generations of Chinese, due to changes in the political
and social environment, as well as within each generation, reflecting the pre-
disposition of each individual, his or her family background, education, ideological convictions, and so on.

THE GLOBALIZATION OF HUMAN RIGHTS

Although domestic changes and concerns have most influenced Chinese debates
on human rights, Chinese people have neither been immune to nor unaware of
international developments in the human rights field. Even before the adoption

of the Universal Declaration of Human Rights (UDHR) in 1948, many Chinese writers knew about and took part in the international human rights discourse. This trend has become stronger as the international human rights regime itself has been strengthened.

In the mid-1970s, human rights gained a new importance and dignity in international relations with the adoption of the International Covenant on Civil and Political Rights (ICCPR) and the International Covenant on Economic, Social, and Cultural Rights (ICESCR). During the 1970s human rights also became a central issue in the foreign policy of many countries. This new development owes much to the active role of national and international human rights organizations that have forcefully pushed the human rights issue. These developments in international human rights work also influenced the human rights situation and debate in Taiwan and on the Chinese mainland, as first reflected in the Kaoshiung Incident in Taiwan in 1979 and the Democracy Wall Movement on the mainland in 1978–79. In Taiwan, independent human rights organizations were established in the early 1980s and have since pushed the regime toward democracy, while on the mainland a similar development is yet to take place. Nonetheless, domestic developments in the PRC since the late 1970s have caused it to become more active in international human rights work, a development that has been reinforced since 1989. Chinese officials and human rights activists are increasingly aware of and engaged in the international human rights discourse and are active contributors to the globalization of human rights. Although they have different views, both are influenced by international human rights work and spurred on by foreign interest in the human rights situation in China.

VOICE AND POWER: THE QUESTION OF NARRATION

As has already been emphasized, agency and power are crucial factors in human rights debates. In the beginning of the twentieth century in China, human rights were invoked by both the revolutionaries and the constitutionalists against the Manchu regime, whereas the regime had no interest in such a language. During the decades before 1949, those who opposed the regime tended to invoke human rights, whereas the power holders, such as the Nationalists after 1927, were critical of the concept. The CCP would occasionally refer to human rights when criticizing the GMD, but after coming to power in 1949 more or less dropped human rights from its political rhetoric. When the CCP's critics, first in 1957 and then again in 1978–79, invoked human rights, they were rebutted and criticized as reactionary and antisocialist. In Taiwan, human rights discussions were initially more vibrant than on the mainland, but despite the Nationalists' affirmation of human rights internationally, they continued to violate human rights until the lifting of martial law in 1987.

Since the late 1970s it is possible to distinguish three different voices on human rights in the PRC, namely the government and its spokesmen; the establishment intellectuals, who, although they have become less and less homogeneous and put forward views differing from those of the regime, still belong to, and are dependent on the system; and dissidents, who, when they venture to discuss or demand human rights, without fail are silenced by the regime and therefore, in contrast to the establishment intellectuals, have limited resources and time to develop a counterdiscourse on human rights.[41] These groups are, however, by no means homogeneous. In 1978–79, for example, the more moderate democracy activists had more in common with the liberal establishment intellectuals than with the more radical democracy activists.

The language of human rights is spreading fast in the PRC. The fact that the Chinese government now affirms the concept of human rights and is willing to take part in international work on human rights has spurred a new interest that could prove difficult either to control or stop. The Chinese authorities may therefore, to their dismay, discover that they have opened a veritable Pandora's box of human rights talk. In this context it is interesting to note that Chinese citizens and dissidents to a greater extent than before are willing to invoke human rights in their open letters and petitions. Several studies also reveal a growing rights consciousness on the part of the Chinese citizenry since the late 1970s.[42] Chinese citizens refer to their legitimate rights and interest when protesting what they consider to be unjust policies, in the process making good use of the new legal and political institutions at their disposal.[43] Sometimes they directly invoke human rights, but more often than not they simply refer to the legal and political rights stipulated in the constitution and a whole range of new laws. If Chinese citizens continue to regard human rights as an issue of international politics and nothing that concerns them in their daily life, this reveals more the continuing impact of the government's propaganda than a lack of interest in human rights per se.[44] Be that as it may, it is obvious that Chinese citizens are becoming increasingly apt in using the regime's own human rights rhetoric against it. A good example of this can be found in an open letter sent to President Jiang Zemin in 1997 by a group of laid-off workers. The workers managed both to refute the official rhetoric on human rights as well as to take advantage of it, writing: "You said that human rights in China are the right to eat rice. This is an arbitrary justification for the sake of political agenda. This is not human rights, but rather animal rights. Anyway, according to your interpretation, when tens of millions of workers are deprived of their right to eat rice, doesn't this amount to the loss of their human rights?"[45]

OUTLINE OF THE BOOK

I begin this book with an overview of the development of the concept of human rights and current controversies in the West. The next chapter discusses the cultural dimensions of human rights debates: the issue of cultural relativism versus universalism, Chinese culture and human rights, and the recent Asian values debate. The following chapter discusses the intellectual setting and the introduction of the concept of human rights in China. For the rest of the book, the chapters follow a chronological arrangement. This includes chapters on the pre-1911 debates on human rights and the overriding goal of national salvation, the May Fourth Movement and early 1920s debates on human rights and individual liberation, the human rights debate and critique of the Nanking regime in 1927–37, and the fate of human rights discussions during the war against Japan and the Civil War.

I then proceed to the post-1949 period and devote one chapter to a discussion of the different human rights debates that took place in Taiwan and the mainland during the 1950s. Toward the end of the 1970s, human rights resurfaced in the political discourse on the mainland. In the next chapter, I describe this domestic challenge and the official response. The central and problematic question then was whether human rights should be dismissed as a mere bourgeois slogan, or whether human rights could actually be of relevance to a socialist society; this issue has now been laid to rest. In the following chapter I turn to the human rights debate in the late 1980s and the 1990s. This debate took place in a new domestic context and faced a different international environment. In contrast to the 1978–82 debate, the post-1989 debate was more a result of an international than a domestic challenge over human rights. The 1990s saw an official appropriation of the concept of human rights, which, however, was challenged by Chinese dissidents at home and abroad. The decade also witnessed the emergence of more profound and original discussions on human rights among Chinese establishment intellectuals. I end the book with a chapter summarizing the conceptual and political history of human rights in China and sketching the state of the debate on the eve of the twenty-first century.

It is my hope that this study will not only promote a better understanding of human rights in China and its future prospects, but that it will also deepen our understanding of the concept of human rights itself. Since human rights now is a global language, Chinese debates on human rights are a part of our common intellectual history. As has been said in honor of Benjamin Schwartz's intellectual approach to the study of China:

> [T]he value of China as an object of study does not rest in any qualities of exotic uniqueness it may possess; nor, certainly, is it of value as the West's "other" in some absolute sense.

Rather, China is valuable as an alternative repository of human experience, a vast labora-
tory (with its own distinctive furnishings) for the exploration of universal human dilem-
mas. The ultimate reason for studying China—or any other society/culture—is nothing
less than to deepen and enrich our understanding of the human condition.[46]

NOTES

1. This expression was coined by Cohen (1987) as a reaction to the fact that the Chinese government in the 1980s was exempted from human rights critique.

2. State Council (1991), p. 10.

3. For information on these works, see the 1995 White Paper, it can be accessed at
<www.chinaguide.org/e-white/> [accessed 14 July 2001]. See also the bibliography lists in
CASS (1992), Han Depei (1995), and Li Lin (1996a).

4. Even two recent works that offer a more historical study of human rights in China
have seriously ignored and distorted the pre-1949 debates. Both Müller (1997) and Weatherley (1999) fail to discuss these debates in any detail or provide an analysis of the process
whereby human rights entered the Chinese political discourse. They also fail to pay attention to some important post-1949 debates, such as the 1957, admittedly brief and scattered,
discussion on human rights on the mainland, and the more vibrant debate in Taiwan in the
1950s and later. In the case of Weatherley (1999), he also confines himself exclusively to the
contemporary official and academic debate and ignores the alternative views of dissidents,
for example the democracy movement of 1978–79. With respect to Chinese scholars, few
have tried to present a historical study of human rights ideas. For more academic works that
discuss the idea of human rights, see the articles by He Yimin (1991) for the pre-1911 period, and Liu Wenjuan (1993) and Xiong Yuezhi (1989) for the May Fourth period. For
more political works, see Xiao Jiabao and Liu Yingqi (1994), carrying a foreword by Yu
Quanyu, the chairman of the officially sponsored China Society for Human Rights Studies; and Zheng Hangsheng and Gu Chunde (1994), commissioned by the Beijing Municipal Propaganda Department. For a representative collection of Chinese texts on human
rights, see Angle and Svensson (2001).

5. I have found Bernard Lewis's (1975) distinction between remembered, recovered, and
invented history very useful for this study. A good example of the CCP's attempt to rewrite
history can be found in Liu Zhongheng and Tan Shuangchuan (1998). The issue of historical memory will be further discussed in chapter 12.

6. Wasserstrom (1997). For examples of more historical works, see Hufton (1995) and
Wasserstrom, Hunt, and Young (2000). Other authors try to trace the struggle for human
rights throughout the centuries; for a recent work, see Lauren (1998).

7. For the approach of political scientists, see Beetham (1995), Mendus (1995), and Bobbio (1996). For a sociologist's approach, see Howard (1995b), and for a peace researcher's approach see Galtung (1994). For a recent work on human rights by anthropologists, see Wilson (1997). And for contributions from several disciplines, see Dunne and Wheeler (1999).

8. I have found the methodological approach of the German school of *Begriffsgeschichte*,
as discussed by Richter (1995), and the works in Ball, Farr, and Hanson (1989) very stimulating and inspiring.

9. The "Keywords of the Chinese Revolution" project was initiated by Timothy Cheek,
Joshua Fogel, Elizabeth Perry, Michael Schoenhals, and Jeffrey Wasserstrom. The project has

analyzed a selection of political keywords and has thus far resulted in a number of working papers published by the East Asian Studies Center at Indiana University in Bloomington.

10. Richter (1995), p. 134.

11. For discussions on the role of rights talk in the social and political activities of Chinese people, see Xia Yong (1999a). And for a volume that addresses the issue of rights in various social and political protests, see Perry and Selden (2000).

12. For recent works that deal with China's incorporation in the international human rights regime, see Kent (1999) and Foot (2000).

13. For information on contemporary human rights violations in China, see reports by Amnesty International, Human Rights Watch, and Human Rights in China.

14. Lauren (1998), p. 11.

15. See Donnelly (1989). For more on the relationship between human dignity and human rights, see chapter 2.

16. Paltiel (1997), p. 25.

17. Examples include Kent (1993), Müller (1997), De Bary and Tu Weiming (1998), and Weatherley (1999).

18. See the contributions to An-Na'im (1995).

19. Booth (1999), Donnelly (1997), and Chanock (2000).

20. Booth (1999), p. 36.

21. Anthropologists apply their understanding of culture to a contextualized study of human rights. See Preis (1996) and the contributions to Wilson (1997).

22. For a volume that takes the issue of cultural representativeness seriously, see Jacobsen and Bruun (2000).

23. Kuper (1999).

24. Wilson (1997), p. 13. Jacobsen and Bruun (2000) also share Wilson's view.

25. See Booth (1999), Kuper (1999), and Chanock (2000).

26. For the Asian values debate, see chapter 3.

27. See Harrison and Huntington (2000) for the most recent and extreme view that "culture matters" and shapes human progress. Some articles in the book, it should be admitted, try to avoid the essentializing of culture.

28. On a critique and definition of cultural developmentalism, see Shweder (2000), p. 160.

29. On this point I agree with Donnelly (1997) and Booth (1999).

30. For the importance of power and agency in studies of human rights, see Wilson (1997), pp. 14–18; and Beetham (1995), p. 8.

31. In the PRC today, for example, we see the language of human rights being used in the propaganda war with the United States. The Chinese government has also come to exploit and refer to human rights when defending its crackdown of Falun Gong. These issues will be discussed in chapter 12.

32. A representative example of this approach is the volume edited by De Bary and Tu Wei-ming (1998).

33. Chanock (2000), p. 16. For a work that explores the relationship between revolutions and human rights discourse, see Wasserstrom, Hunt, and Young (2000).

34. Hunt (2000).

35. Kent (1993) and Weatherley (1999).

36. Kent (1993), p. 30.

37. Schwartz (1964), p. 2.

38. But, needless to say, different views also exist on some human rights issues within both the United States and the European countries, as well as between the European countries themselves.

39. For a work criticizing the earlier impact–response perspective in China studies and advocating a more China-centered history, see Cohen (1984).

40. For a work that further explores the neo-Confucian underpinnings of rights thinking in the early twentieth century, see Angle (2002).

41. I use the term *establishment intellectuals* to refer to all those Chinese intellectuals who write on human rights and are able to publish in China. Of course, this may be unfair since there are many differences among them; some are more independent, whereas others more or less echo the views of the regime. For a discussion on establishment intellectuals in China, see Hamrin and Cheek (1986).

42. See, for example, Gao Hongjun (1999).

43. On Chinese citizens' own invocation of rights, see O'Brien (1996).

44. When asked about the relationship between human rights and their everyday life, 33 percent of the peasants surveyed responded that human rights were of no relevance to them. See Xia Yong (1999b), p. 53. Xia Yong reflects that many of those who seem unaware of, or uninterested in human rights, are illiterate. This might be an important explanatory factor, although I tend to believe that the impact of propaganda is more important. Such a conclusion is also supported by the fact, which Xia also acknowledges, that the peasants, despite their lack of knowledge of human rights generally, are quite well aware of their rights and eager to protest heavy taxes and other injustices.

45. Quoted in Leung (1998), p. 12.

46. Cohen and Goldman (1990), pp. 6–7.

Chapter Two

The Conception of Human Rights in the West: Historical Origin and Contemporary Controversies

A HISTORICAL NOTE

It would be a great mistake to judge the concept of human rights by its historical origin since it is obvious that many tenets of the concept today were not part of earlier discussions. As clearly shown by several scholars, the history of the concept of human rights and its predecessor, natural rights, is highly complex and multifaceted.[1] Human rights has been and still is a very contested and debated concept that has been strongly refuted by many prominent Western philosophers. Nor are rights as deeply embedded in Western political thought as is often assumed. Most European languages, for instance, lacked a clear and unequivocal term for rights as we understand them today until the late Medieval period.[2] It is also important to be aware of the fact that early natural law philosophy actually placed more emphasis on duties than on rights: it was much less rights-oriented, individualistic, and antiauthoritarian than is generally assumed.[3]

We have, however, come to associate natural rights thinking with the attacks on absolutism and the belief in a natural hierarchy that occurred in Europe during the seventeenth century. Several institutional and intellectual developments, such as the advent of the modern nation–state and the rise of new conceptions of self, paved the way for a more individualistic and rights-oriented view of the relationship between individuals and between citizens and rulers.[4] John Locke is perhaps the most influential philosopher in the development of the idea of human rights (natural rights in his days). The natural rights theory held that all human beings were born with certain rights. In its classical form these rights were regarded as derived from God, but later the basis of rights was seen to be human nature or reason. Natural rights were described as inviolable and inalienable as they could neither be infringed upon nor voluntarily renounced or transferred. These rights were regarded as universal and thus applicable in all societies in the world. They were furthermore seen as pre-social since they existed anterior to and independently of the establishment of society; they derived their authority from nature (or morality), not from any legal or political institutions. The rights referred to were mainly civil and political rights, such as the rights to freedom of belief, speech, and association, and so forth.

The revolutionary potential of ideas on natural rights is well illustrated by their influence on the American and French revolutions. But this does not mean that the rights discourse at this time was unproblematic or uncontested; quite the contrary, it was surrounded by much confusion and heated debate on the origin of rights, as well as the subject and substance of these rights.[5] The two revolutionary rights discourses also exhibit interesting differences that undermine the appearance of a homogeneous West. The idea that women and slaves also should enjoy rights was anathema to many people during this period, although some, such as Marquis de Condorcet, wrote eloquently in defense of the universality of rights. "Either no individual in mankind has true rights, or all have the same ones; and whoever votes against the right of another, whatever be his religion, his colour, or his sex, has from that moment abjured his own rights."[6]

It is also interesting to note that not all people readily adopted the natural rights discourse but viewed it with some skepticism. For instance, many Americans at the time of the American Revolution complained that the general public did not fully understand the philosophical subtleties of rights. A Whig pamphleteer in 1775 thus "deplored the inability of persons of 'inferior condition' to form adequate conceptions of their rights."[7] A prominent French philosopher argued that while proclamations of rights could work in the American context, they would be disruptive and dangerous in France because of her specific historical and social circumstances.[8] The examples above are actually quite similar to some of the arguments in the Chinese debate today, such as that the Chinese people do not understand or care about human rights, and that human rights as understood in the West do not fit Chinese conditions. The fact that even such supposedly rights-oriented people as the American and French did not adopt the natural rights discourse unanimously or without difficulties should serve as a sobering reminder to those who argue that the concept of human rights is foreign to the Chinese people and, hence, inapplicable in China.

CRITIQUE OF THE CONCEPT OF NATURAL RIGHTS

The concept of natural rights met with strong criticism from various political thinkers and schools during the eighteenth and nineteenth centuries, and, as a result, lost much of its appeal in political discourse. Such diverse thinkers as Edmund Burke, Jeremy Bentham, and Karl Marx all attacked the idea for its high level of abstraction and lack of empirical backing.[9] These critics represented a range of political traditions from the conservative, to liberal-utilitarian, to socialist. One of the most influential critics of the idea of natural rights was Bentham, who criticized the idea of natural rights for, as he famously put it, being "nonsense upon stilts." According to Bentham, only legal rights laid down in positive law existed. Rights were furthermore subject to the test of utility; they were contingent upon whether they contributed to the happiness of the community. Utilitarianism became one of the major schools in the West and seriously weakened the influence of natural rights theories. John Stuart Mill, despite being an ardent advocate of liberty, thus rejected the idea of natural rights and proclaimed that rights were founded on utility.[10] Although Mill in *On Liberty* mostly argued the case for liberty and individuality as ends in themselves, certain passages read as if liberty were valued only as a means, the end being variously defined as truth, a fully developed person, or a progressive society. The belief that rights should be valued, not as an end in themselves but as a means either to individual self-development or for social progress, has played an important role in China as well, as we will see.

Marx, on the other hand, criticized human rights for being the rights of the egoistic man, man separated from other men and society. Marx made a distinction between human rights and citizens' rights, the latter being exercised in the community with other men. He denied the existence of any natural rights outside society and only accepted the existence of legal rights. But in a class society, these legal rights would have a class character and only serve the interests of the ruling class. In a future communist society, by contrast, rights would instead be rendered superfluous and irrelevant. In such a society people would willingly submit and identify themselves with the community; to give vent to interests and rights against others would be to act against one's own good as well as that of the community.

Different views of rights exist among Marxists but Richard Nordahl has argued that Marxists in general tend to see rights as instruments to satisfy needs.[11] Rights are not valued in themselves but are a means toward an end. They are furthermore relative since they are contingent upon the availability of necessary resources to satisfy people's needs, which means that there can be no absolute rights applicable in all societies. Nordahl also argues that, according to Marxists, rights can be curtailed, although only in the short term, for the sake of economic development.

Marxists more interested in the younger Marx and his humanistic writings, however, value rights in and by themselves. The German philosopher Ernst Bloch, for example, takes a more positive view of human rights. He believes that without human rights there would be no true liberation of humankind and vice versa. "[H]uman dignity is not possible without economic liberation, and this liberation is not possible without the cause of human rights. . . . There can be no true installation of human rights without the end of exploitation, no true end of exploitation without the installation of human rights."[12] Since human dignity and the liberation of man is central to Bloch, the idea of human rights plays an important role in his more humanistic interpretation of Marxism.

Be that as it may, the language of human rights has never been of the highest importance to orthodox Marxists in their efforts to change society, although at times they have used it as a strategic weapon in the political struggle. Whereas communists have not hesitated to accuse others of violating human rights, such as freedom of speech, it has not prevented them from curtailing or abolishing these very rights once in power. This is by no means inconsistent but quite logical from their point of view, as a strategy befitting different political circumstances.[13] If an orthodox Marxist would thus probably refrain from adopting the language of human rights, except as a tactical strategy, socialists of different persuasions have, however, come to embrace it. Although the socialist countries of the East bloc abstained during the balloting on the UDHR in 1948, they later signed and ratified several human rights conventions. They have tended, however, to place a priority on economic and social rights over civil and political rights. Furthermore, the rights stipulated in various socialist constitutions are seen as granted by the state, and not as something existing independently of, or before the establishment of the state. The exercise of rights in socialist countries has also been contingent upon the fulfillment of duties to society and the state. Political enemies and so-called counterrevolutionaries have been deprived of the rights stipulated in the constitutions because they are to be enjoyed only by those defined as the people. In socialist societies, correct political beliefs and belonging to a class, rather than a shared human nature, have been the criteria for enjoying rights. The Marxist and socialist understandings of rights and human rights, needless to say, have deeply shaped the human rights discourse in the PRC.

Other schools of thought in the nineteenth century served to further erode the influence of the concept of natural rights. The historical school, for example, disputed the notion that universal rights existed since the diverse notions of rights in the world show that they are a result of the specific culture and history of each particular society.[14] Legal positivism and social Darwinism, from different perspectives, also refuted the existence of universal human rights. But even within the liberal camp there was a tendency to abandon natural rights theories. This was, for example, the case with the British Idealists, the leading exponent of which was T. H. Green. Green and New Liberals, such as J. A. Hobson and L. T. Hobhouse, attempted to adapt traditional liberal ideas to changing circumstances. While rights remained central to their thinking, they emphasized their social and communitarian aspects, for example acknowledging welfare rights. These changes within the liberal camp influenced later political thinkers, such as Harold Laski, who presented a more society-oriented theory of rights. As will become apparent in the following chapters, not only have Chinese views on rights been influenced by Marxism, but the ideas of utilitarians, British Idealists, New Liberals, social liberals, and socialists have also found a fertile ground in China.

THE STRUGGLE FOR HUMAN RIGHTS IN THE TWENTIETH CENTURY

Human rights received little attention in the West in the beginning of the twentieth century and played hardly any role in international politics up to the Second World War. There was only some limited interest among scattered individuals and organizations, manifesting itself in declarations of human rights and academic works on the topic. Hannah Arendt has scathingly described the marginality of these people:

> [A]ll societies formed for the protection of the Rights of Man, all attempts to arrive at a new bill of human rights were sponsored by marginal figures—by a few international jurists without political experience or professional philanthropists supported by the uncertain sentiments of professional idealists. The groups they formed, the declarations they issued, showed an uncanny similarity in language and composition to that of societies for the prevention of cruelty to animals. No statesman, no political figure of any importance could possibly take them seriously; and none of the liberal or radical parties in Europe thought it necessary to incorporate into their program a new declaration of human rights.[15]

Whereas Arendt's description is perhaps a little exaggerated, it is beyond doubt that human rights was a fairly marginal issue in Western academia and politics before the Second World War. Despite the marginality of the issue, however, quite a few people still continued to refer to human rights and struggle for their protection.[16] In 1898, *La Ligue des Droits de l'Homme* was founded in France and in 1922, together with the German *Deutsche Liga für Menschenrechte* and fourteen other human rights organizations, it established the *Fédération Internationale des Ligues des Droits de l'Homme* (FIDH). The FIDH tried to promote human rights throughout the world and advocated a universal declaration of human rights. During the 1930s, other individuals and organizations were also active in trying to promote human rights within the League of Nations.

The outbreak of World War II and the atrocities committed by the Nazis brought the human rights issue back to the fore. One of those who then raised the human rights issue was the British writer H. G. Wells. In 1939, Wells wrote a letter to *The Times* suggesting a constructive aim for the war and a program for a lasting world peace.[17] He believed that this would best be served by proclaiming a universal declaration of human rights and in this context emphasized the importance of a de-Westernization and true universalization of human rights. Several people joined Wells in drafting a declaration of rights. A final version was published in February 1940 and then widely circulated and translated into several languages, including Chinese, influencing some of the Chinese thinkers who will be discussed in this work.

It is possible that President Roosevelt also was influenced by Wells's declaration; they at least knew each other and Roosevelt had commented on the 1939 draft declaration.[18] Be that as it may, in 1941 Roosevelt proclaimed the so-called Four Freedoms, that is, freedom of speech and expression, freedom of worship, freedom from want, and freedom from fear. In late 1942, the Allied powers declared that the protection of human rights was among their war aims. Thus, by the early 1940s, many individuals and organizations had taken up the cause of human rights, adopting declarations and publishing articles and books.[19] These efforts were not limited to the West, but, for example, involved countries in Latin America as well. At the United Nations Conference on International Organization in San Francisco in June 1945, Latin American countries and many nongovernmental organizations (NGOs) demanded that the UN Charter include a clear commitment to the protection of human rights and that the new organization should also adopt a bill of human rights. The first article of the charter, therefore, declared that UN member states should work to "achieve international cooperation . . . in promoting and encouraging respect for human rights and for fundamental freedoms for all without distinction as to race, sex, language or religion." All these various efforts and demands for human rights paved the way for a consensus that specific international instruments on human rights should be adopted by the United Nations. In 1946 the UN Human Rights Commission was established, and in 1947 work began on drafting the UDHR. The declaration, which was adopted in 1948, was drafted by people from different countries, including China, and can thus be said to have constituted a truly universal project. (For more on the drafting process and the Chinese involvement, see chapter 8.)

After World War II, the world has seen a revival of rights thinking, both in international politics and law and among philosophers and political thinkers. People no longer talk about natural rights, however, having lost faith in the possibility of justifying rights on the basis of human nature. Instead, we now speak about human rights, that is, rights we have as humans in order to uphold our humanity. It has become customary to speak of three conceptions, or generations, of human rights, namely the Western-liberal, the socialist, and the

Third World generations, which are rooted in different ideological and political realities and have developed during different periods.[20] The first generation of human rights, the Western-liberal conception of human rights that stresses civil and political rights, originated in Europe during the seventeenth and eighteenth centuries and reflects the aspirations of that time. The second generation of rights refers to economic and social rights and is closely associated with the political struggle of various socialist movements in the nineteenth century. Socialist thinkers pushed for social and economic rights, such as in the case of the socialist Anton Menger arguing for a right to subsistence.[21] Developments within the liberal camp also paved the way for economic and social rights.[22] Actually, a partial and embryonic defense of welfare rights already existed in the writings of Locke and, in particular, Thomas Paine. The depression in the 1930s conclusively turned people's attention to economic and social rights and gave rise to the development of the welfare state in the West.

The right to subsistence surfaced in human rights works during the 1930s and 1940s. The French *Ligue de Droits de l'Homme* in 1936 and Wells in 1940 both included the right to subsistence on their lists of human rights.[23] Wells thus talked about man being entitled to "nourishment, housing, covering, medical care and attention sufficient to realise his full possibilities of physic and mental development and to keep him in a state of health from his birth to death." Countries in Latin America had included social and economic rights early on in their constitutions. They also included these rights in the drafts for an international bill of human rights that some of them presented to the United Nations and from which John P. Humphrey drew upon when he wrote the first draft of the UDHR.[24] Given these developments, it was only natural that the UDHR and the ICCPR and the ICESCR also came to include economic and social rights.

The political independence of erstwhile colonies after the Second World War and their demands for a new economic world order that would ensure a fairer distribution of power and wealth between the First- and Third World have given rise to a third generation of rights, commonly referred to as developmental or solidarity rights.[25] First of all, these refer to rights that take the new states' interests and problems to heart, such as rights to national self-determination and economic and social development. They also include rights that make more demands on the international community and require cooperation and solidarity over national boundaries, such as the right to peace, the right to a healthy and balanced environment, and the right to humanitarian relief. Although the rights of the third generation also have the individual in focus they have mostly been formulated as collective rights—often being referred to as people's rights.

The concept of human rights as we know it today in many ways differs from that of its predecessor, natural rights. Human rights are generally much more egalitarian and universal in character; they are said to belong equally to all humans, not just white males, and apply in all societies in the world. They are also broader in scope, as they include social and economic rights besides the more traditional civil and political rights. In contrast to natural rights, human rights, furthermore, have a backing in international law and institutions. In the past few years human rights have become a global language that has been taken up by people in parts of the world where, until quite recently, the concept was foreign, if not completely unheard of. Nonetheless, many philosophical, political, and legal questions and controversies regarding human rights still exist, some of which will be discussed in the rest of this chapter.

CONTROVERSIES IN THE CONTEMPORARY DISCOURSE ON RIGHTS AND HUMAN RIGHTS

When discussing the conception of human rights it is useful to start with five basic questions, namely: what is the basis and justification of rights, who has rights, what is the substance of rights, what is the relationship between rights and duties, and what is the purpose and value of rights?[26] Not everyone discussing human rights takes up or provides answers to all these questions, but they are central to any meaningful discussion on rights. As Ian Shapiro has put it, someone who argued that rights did not belong to anybody, or who claimed that people have rights "not by virtue of any natural, rational, moral, or positive authority— they just have them in the same way as they have teeth," can hardly have understood the meaning of rights at all.[27] Not all Chinese writers discussing rights or human rights have probed so deeply into the more subtle, philosophical aspects of human rights, many having a more political interest in the topic. It should further be noted that in the following discussion I also draw on the contemporary Western debate; it would, of course, be highly unfair to Chinese thinkers at the beginning of the century to expect them to have anticipated these developments. Be that as it may, a brief discussion of the contemporary debate will nevertheless prove useful when we proceed to discuss the Chinese conception of human rights. It will then become clear that many of the aspects of human rights that Chinese thinkers have discussed and found problematic, such as the grounding of rights, whether or not utility can serve as a justification of rights, the relationship between individual rights and the general welfare, and so on, have been and are at the center of controversy also in the West.

THE BASIS AND JUSTIFICATION OF RIGHTS

Human rights, it has to be acknowledged, are essentially a universalistic project grounded in a presumed essential commonality of human beings that originated in the Enlightenment ideals of universalism, rationality, and modernity. Such a project has recently been criticized by postmodernists and poststructuralists. But despite the deep skepticism about the philosophical grounding of rights in the contemporary discourse, the language of human rights has never been more popular and widespread. This paradox can perhaps be explained by the fact that human rights discussions are no longer the monopoly of philosophers. Human rights talk today permeates political and legal institutions and is taken up by those who have a more practical and political interest in the issue.

In the modern debate, neither God or natural law, nor human nature or reason are any longer referred to as the basis or origin of rights. All attempts to provide a solid foundation for human rights seem to have failed. The idea that rights are based upon a universal, unchanging human nature and that man is endowed with natural rights before entering society was abandoned by the late nineteenth century, for example, by British Idealists such as Green.[28] Green rejected the idea that there could be any rights prior to and against society, and that it is only as members of society that people possess rights. "No one . . . can have a right except (1) as a member of a society, and (2) of a society in which some common good is recognised by the members of society as their own ideal good, as that which *should be* for each of them. The capacity for being determined by a good so recognised, is what constitutes *personality* in the ethical sense."[29] Even though Green still talked about natural rights, his understanding was quite different from that of earlier natural rights thinkers. "[Rights] are innate or natural . . . not in the sense that they actually exist when a man is born and that they have actually existed as long as the human race—but that they arise out of, and are necessary for the fulfilment of, a moral capacity without which a man would not be a man."[30]

The British Idealists' abandonment of classical natural rights theories led them, and subsequent generations, to see rights as historical and relative. According to this understanding, rights are historical and reflect people's needs in a specific society. But, if rights reflect the demands and needs of each society, can one then still argue the case for universal rights? Even though Green disputed the idea of rights outside and apart from society, he did not dispute the existence of universal rights, nor did he advocate moral relativism. Green argued that humankind constituted a universal society in which the true common good is common to all men. Following Immanuel Kant he argued that no man should be treated as a means but always as an end and as a moral agent.[31] "Natural rights . . . are universal rights, the rights of all persons, grounded on what is universal in men (moral agency) rather than on anything particular (being English, or a Lord, or a party to a contract). Each such right is a good for every person, and its possession is therefore a common good which is justified, and at the same time limited, by its being possessed by all."[32]

To some contemporary scholars, the lack of a foundation constitutes a serious problem and is therefore a reason to disparage the concept of human rights itself. Alasdair MacIntyre, for example, has dismissed human rights as fiction and no different from belief in witches and unicorns. "[T]he truth is plain; there are no such rights [as human rights], and the belief in them is one with belief in witches and in unicorns. The best reason for asserting so bluntly that there are no such rights is indeed of precisely the same type as the best reason which we possess for asserting that there are no unicorns: every attempt to give good reason for believing that there *are* such rights has failed . . . Natural or human rights then are fictions."[33] Richard Rorty takes a different approach and instead rejects the foundationalist approach itself.[34] On this point he agrees with the Argentinean philosopher Eduardo Rabossi, who argues that "human rights foundationalism [is] outmoded and irrelevant."[35] Rorty is content to advocate a "sentimental education," which he believes will increase our tolerance and sympathy for others, and, hence, promote respect for human rights.

The Italian political theorist Norberto Bobbio agrees that attempts to discover an absolute principle, or foundation, of human rights have proven fruitless, but his take on the issue is quite different from that of Rorty.[36] According to Bobbio, the lack of a foundation does not present a problem since human rights today are laid down in various international conventions and have obtained the status of positive law. The consensus on human rights serves to prove their universal validity. Bobbio also brings attention to the fact that opposition to human rights in the real world, that is, by authoritarian regimes, has never focused so much on their lack of a philosophical foundation as on their assumed infeasibility in a particular society and on perceived problems of implementation. (The PRC is a good case in point!) Our focus should therefore be shifted from the futile philosophical quest for the origin and basis of rights to the more pressing political task of implementing the human rights already acknowledged. Susan Mendus has somewhat similarly argued that "we may do better if we begin not with an account of how human rights may be justified, but rather with an account of what we stand to lose both politically and philosophically if we renounce the language of human rights. We should begin, not with a theoretical anxiety about the nature and origin of rights, but rather with a political question about what protection rights afford us."[37] It is not surprising that political scientists such as Bobbio and Mendus would be able to take the problem of the foundation of human rights so lightly; philosophers are much less likely to let go of the issue.

Bobbio's legal positivist position of course is vulnerable if the international human rights law would be contested and disputed. If we only accept positive rights as human rights, then we have no recourse in cases in which human rights are not laid down in law, or when their legal legitimacy is questioned.

Already in the 1950s, Leo Strauss worried that the rejection of natural rights left people without any recourse to moral standards independent of and higher than the legal order.[38] If the only rights that exist are those laid down in the law, people would be left without moral support in the face of totalitarian and despotic regimes that control and dominate the legal system. This is a very important point, and it constitutes the core of any defense of the idea of human rights as moral rights—albeit rights that should be laid down in the law—rather than mere legal rights.

Thomas Haskell, like Rorty and Bobbio, believes that human rights do not have, or indeed need any deeper justification.[39] Rights, according to Haskell, are not natural or metaphysical objects but conventions created by man. But like Strauss, and in contrast to Rorty and Bobbio, Haskell is sensitive to and disturbed by the explicit relativism of historicism and its negative implications for human rights. He worries that, if we give up the timelessness and universality of human rights, we will "slide all the way down the slippery slope of relativism."[40] If we were to deny that any transcultural and transhistorical moral standards exist, it would become impossible to condemn what we consider as inhuman practices across cultures and over time.

Strauss tried to dispute historicism by arguing that the existence of a variety of notions of rights did not disprove the existence of a true, objective, and universal notion of human rights, or, at least, the possibility of a consensus. Moreover, he argued that the historical school undermined its own existence because it is essentially self-contradictory. As he succinctly put it: "Historicism asserts that all human thought or beliefs are historical, and hence deservedly destined to perish; but historicism itself is a human thought; hence historicism can be of only temporary validity, or it cannot be simply true."[41] Bobbio argues along somewhat similar lines but manages to retain his faith in human rights as historical rights. He believes that we do not have to be so afraid of relativism because, as he cleverly puts it: "The evident plurality of religious and moral perceptions is a historical fact, and these too are subject to change. The relativism which derives from this pluralism is itself relative."[42] The view that the present relativism itself is relative may be comforting in the long run, but I cannot help worrying about authoritarian governments' exploitation of cultural relativism.

Strauss believed that human rights required a solid foundation, which had to be human nature, in order to uphold their universalism and fend off the relativism of historicism. Haskell, like most contemporary scholars, is not comfortable with the idea of an eternal human nature, nor is he prepared to deny that rights to some extent actually are historical and relative. His solution is to seek a compromise in the form of a moderate historicism. In this respect Haskell parts company with Strauss, who was a vehement and all-out critic of historicism. According to Haskell's moderate historicism, rights are neither eternal nor completely relative. They are durable in the sense that as conventions they are held over generations and across cultures, but at the same time they are also contingent upon changing historical circumstances and cultural differences. This compromise does not completely solve the problem, however, as it remains to be decided how, which, and to what extent, rights are historical and contingent. The question of how conventions are established, and by whom, also raises important questions regarding power and representativity in the human rights debate.

As described above, many scholars have thus abandoned the search for a foundation to human rights since they believe that a satisfactory justification is impossible and that one can do quite nicely without it. But in the contemporary human rights discourse, three foundations of rights are still often referred to, namely, human needs, human dignity, and consensus. These approaches, to varying degrees and in different ways, also attempt to retain and defend the idea that human rights are universal, or at least universalizable.

Some scholars have attempted to base human rights on the existence of certain fundamental and universal human needs.[43] For instance, Nordahl, as mentioned above, argues that Marxists view human needs as the basis of rights, or, differently worded, they view rights as instruments in order to satisfy needs.[44] Different scholars list different needs as basic and universal, but most often they tend to include the needs to subsistence, to physical security, and to be treated with respect as a person. The attractiveness of a needs-based foundation of human rights is that needs are less culturally variable. The belief in universal human needs, in other words, saves the idea of universal human rights and avoids the specter of relativism. An additional advantage of the needs-based approach is that it acknowledges economic and social rights. To derive human rights from human needs is, however, a minority view among Western human rights scholars. The human needs approach has been criticized for, among other things, being too vague and not covering all aspects of human life, but also for giving rise to too many and too arbitrary rights.[45] The functionalistic needs-oriented approach to human rights has however been quite common among Chinese intellectuals, as we will see.

Rather similar to the above approach is one that takes human dignity as its starting point and sees it as the basis of human rights and defines human rights as necessary in order to uphold one's humanity and live a dignified life. The difference with the needs-based approach is that those starting from human dignity emphasize man's common moral nature rather than his physical needs. The concept of human dignity is fairly recent in the West, and its association with human rights later still.[46] The appeal to human dignity in the rights discourse dates from Kant. The Kantian understanding of dignity is related to the categorical imperative according to which man is to be treated as an end in himself and not as a means.[47] Closely related to the notion of dignity, therefore, are ideas of personality, autonomy, and self-respect. The emergence of human rights talk in the West, it can be argued, was closely related to new ideas of self that stressed the individual's self-autonomy and self-respect.[48] As Taylor puts it, "To talk of universal, natural, or human rights is to connect respect for human life and integrity with the notion of autonomy. It is to conceive people as active cooperators in establishing and ensuring the respect which is due them."[49] Green, for example, argued that rights "arise out of, and are necessary for the fulfilment of, a moral capacity without which a man would not be a man."[50]

The tendency today is to justify human rights by referring to human dignity.[51] In the International Bill of Rights, for example, it is held that human rights arise from "the inherent dignity of the human person." Contemporary scholars like Joel Feinberg also believe that there is a close relation between human dignity and human rights. "[R]espect for persons . . . may simply be respect for their rights, so that there cannot be the one without the other; and what is called 'human dignity' may simply be the recognisable capacity to assert claims. To respect a person then, or to think of him as possessed of human dignity, simply *is* to think of him as a potential maker of claims."[52] Others turn the tables, however, arguing that rights and rights talk are at odds with, or undermine human dignity.[53] They regard the self-assertive emphasis on rights as degrading and dehumanizing because it makes people aggressive and litigious and gives rise to social conflicts.[54] But to others, to deprive a person of his rights is to violate his human dignity and deprive him of his self-respect and autonomy; it is to treat him as less than a human being, or, in other words, as a slave. The slave trope was very common during the American Revolution when, as Orlando Patterson has shown, it was used as the antithesis of liberty and thus deeply influenced and shaped the meaning of liberty.[55] The slave trope has played a similar role in the Chinese discourse on human rights. Most Chinese writers have argued that liberty is what distinguishes free men from slaves and that human rights are needed in order to uphold one's humanity.

Oscar Schachter has emphasized that the proposition that human rights derive from the inherent dignity of man is significant because it implies that these rights are not given by the state or any external authority.[56] It also follows that human rights are enjoyed by every person and one cannot be deprived of these rights. The focus on human dignity as the source of human rights has the additional advantage that notions of human dignity, however defined, can be found in all societies, which saves the universalism of human rights. Building on these understandings are those who would claim that all societies, therefore, have had conceptions of human rights.[57] Several China scholars start from the premise that since a notion of human dignity is embedded in Confucianism, it is possible to deduct that the concept of human rights at its minimum is compatible with Chinese culture or, at its maximum, latent or embryonic in Confucianism.[58]

I would, however, agree with Rhoda E. Howard and Donnelly, among others, who argue that this confuses ideas of dignity and justice with ideas of human rights.[59] All societies, of course, have the former concepts, whereas the latter is a modern concept that only originated with the development of the modern nation–state. Although human dignity is embedded in the concept of human rights it does not necessarily imply or lead to a conception of human rights. Furthermore, we also need to make clear what we understand by dignity. It would thus be useful to distinguish between intrinsic dignity, which pertains to every human being qua human being regardless of his or her behavior and status and is the dignity human rights advocates have in mind, and extrinsic dignity, which is the antithesis of human rights because it is not a general attribute but contingent upon one's behavior or status in society.[60] It is thus possible to imagine a society in which dignity of the extrinsic variety is respected without it giving rise to a concept of human rights. Dignity can be guaranteed and upheld by things other than rights, for example, by religious beliefs about the nature of man, ideas regarding how one should behave or treat people on the basis of their hierarchical status, or, in the case of China, by rites (*li*) that define people's status and, hence, their proper treatment and behavior. In fact, it could be argued that in traditional societies duties rather than rights guaranteed and protected human dignity. It has to be acknowledged that in traditional societies, whether Western or non-Western, the understanding of dignity has generally been at odds with the contemporary concept of human rights, which weakens the proposition that human dignity and human rights are equivalent or similar concepts.

Consensus, as manifested in international documents on human rights, is also often held to be able to solve the problem of the basis and justification of rights. This consensus shows that people from different cultures and societies share certain values. Bobbio realizes that consensus is not an absolute basis, but argues that it is the only one that can be factually proven.[61] Not too different from the consensus approach is the conventionalist approach advocated by Haskell. Those trying to seek the cultural legitimacy of human rights usually end up accepting the list of human rights as put forward in the International Bill of Rights and then proceed to retroactively justify these rights cross-culturally.[62] Consensus or conventions are, however, quite problematic as a basis and justification of human rights.[63] The fact that everybody agrees, or might eventually agree, about these rights does not explain why we have them in the first place. Whereas people from different societies and of different political persuasions have been able to agree on a list of human rights, it does not follow that they also would be able to agree on their theoretical conception. This is aptly brought out by Jacques Maritain, who, referring to the French discussions leading up to the adoption of the UDHR, wrote: "During one of the meetings of the French National Commission of UNESCO at which the Rights of Man were being discussed, someone was astonished that certain proponents of violently opposed ideologies had agreed on the draft of a list of rights. Yes, they replied, we agree on these rights, *providing we are not asked why*. With the 'why' the dispute begins."[64] Even with respect to the content of rights the debate has been fierce, especially regarding the order of priority of different rights.

The consensus approach also ignores the question of how a consensus is forged and maintained. According to some critics, to talk about a consensus on human rights as manifested in international covenants actually amounts to propagating Western values since they believe that the concept of human rights in these documents reflects the influence of the West; hence, their charge of cultural imperialism.[65] Others, however, reject this argument and point out that many different countries participated in and influenced the drafting of the UDHR.[66] Since the drafting of the UDHR and the adoption of subsequent covenants and conventions, many countries have furthermore adopted and accepted the international human rights regime. But the precariousness and danger of resting one's case for human rights on consensus has become apparent with the appearance of the Asian values debate. The UDHR has been questioned by some Asian governments, including China, which propose that it should be revised so as to better reflect the experiences of non-Western cultures, which, they mistakenly argue, did not participate in the drafting.[67]

While it may be the case that belief in human rights is on a par with belief in witches and unicorns, belief in human rights these days is much more widespread and accepted than belief in witches and unicorns ever was. Or as Haskell puts it:

> Rights not only survive but flourish after more than a century of skepticism about their timelessness and universality. The plainest meaning of the paradoxical persistence of rights in an age of interpretation is that Strauss was wrong, neither rights nor the practices they authorise need foundations sunk deep into the heart of nature. They evidently are so amply supported by the prevailing form of life that our inability to formulate an entirely satisfying theoretical justification for them has no direct bearing on their staying power.[68]

Despite the diversity and plurality of ideas and beliefs in the world, perhaps there really exists a consensus of sorts on human rights that reflects the existence of some cross-cultural values, or perhaps it could be that what we are seeing today is simply the globalization of human rights talk. The language of human rights has been taken up all over the world, including in societies in which, not long ago, it was a foreign and incomprehensible idea. This development is due to increasing contacts between societies and to the fact that human rights since the Second World War has enjoyed the backing of international law. In order to discover whether human rights actually is a shared and universal value, it is important to undertake empirical and historical investigations on how, and to what extent, different societies today discuss human rights, and compare these discussions with earlier ones in the same societies; this is also one of the intentions of this study.[69]

THE SUBJECT OF RIGHTS

A bone of contention in the human rights debate that dates from the French Revolution has been identifying the subject of rights. During the discussions leading up to the French declaration, heated debates took place on whether women, Jews, Calvinists, blacks, and slaves would also "merit" these rights. The contemporary debate is more centered on whether collectives can also enjoy rights, with liberals arguing that only individuals can be the subject of human rights. Socialist and Third World countries, on the other hand, have tried to extend human rights to collectives.[70] They believe that rights to self-determination and development are rights that can only be exercised by the collective. Furthermore, these rights are basic to the enjoyment of all other rights; without collective rights, even the exercise of individual rights is at risk. Among Western liberals, in contrast, the extension of rights to collectives has triggered a fear that instead of people having one extra right as a part of the collective, the rights of the collective might take precedence over the rights of individuals.[71]

There also exists other types of critique, one of which focuses on the supposedly individualistic orientation of rights thinking.[72] Communitarians criticize liberals for seeing the individual person as an atomistic and unencumbered self.[73] They stress that the person only can exist in a community with others. Individuals are furthermore not only rights-bearers, but also perform duties and shoulder different roles in the community. The communitarians in addition question the liberals' belief in universal rights because, they argue, people are products of and live in a specific social and cultural milieu. The advocacy of universal rights, to their minds, ignores this fact and "desocializes" and "deculturalizes" the human person.[74] Another critique concerns the view of some feminists that human rights is a male discourse that does not take into account women's specific concerns and interests.[75] The forms of oppression that women suffer in the family and society, these feminists argue, are not reflected in human rights talk, with its focus on the relationship between the individual and the state. Other feminists, however, try to incorporate women's issues in human rights discourse. They see women's rights as a part of the general category of human rights, only addressing the specific problems that pertain to women qua women.

THE SUBSTANCE OF RIGHTS

The debate has also run high on the substance of rights. In the modern debate, civil and political rights are often set against the other two generations of rights, that is, economic and social rights, and developmental or solidarity rights.[76] In this debate a distinction is being made between negative and positive rights. Negative rights refer to rights such as freedom of speech, press, assembly, and association, as well as the right not to be physically tortured; rights that are said only to require noninterference on the part of the state. Liberals stress that only negative rights are rights proper because they can be implemented in all societies regardless of the political system and level of economic development. Positive rights, on the other hand, referring to economic and social rights such as the right to health care and a decent standard of living, require action on the part of the state and are contingent upon the level of economic development. Some writers therefore object to economic and social rights on the grounds that they serve to undermine the universality of human rights and open the door to a relativistic approach to human rights.[77] To put economic and social rights on an equal footing with civil and political rights would thus, according to one liberal, only lead to "push *all* talk of human rights out of the clear realm of the morally compelling into the twilight world of utopian aspirations."[78] Others have criticized this distinction between negative and positive rights for being highly artificial and arbitrary. They argue that not all civil and political rights fall so nicely into the category of negative rights. The right to a fair trial, for instance, requires some positive action on the part of the government to establish an impartial and independent legal system. Nor do all economic and social rights fall into the category of positive rights; some simply require noninterference on the part of the government.

Socialists, for their part, tend to stress economic and social rights over civil and political rights in the belief that the former are the most basic.[79] According to their view, civil rights such as freedom of speech are of little use to those suffering from starvation, unemployment, and illiteracy. Many authoritarian regimes also tend to argue that certain rights are at present unrealizable in their societies for cultural, economic, or political reasons. Participants in the Asian values debate, for example, have argued that certain civil and political rights, such as freedom of speech and freedom of movement, are luxuries they can ill afford. But to let people put forward their grievances and demand a better standard of living, even if it cannot bring about changes overnight, can still go a very long way toward creating a better world. It is true that if you are illiterate and have no power or money, your ability to take advantage of the freedom of speech is severely undercut. But the best way to change this state of affairs cannot be to do away with the free press itself. "Even if bread comes first, since poverty is in large measure a social and political, not a natural product, civil and political rights may be the best, or at least the most peaceful way to get bread."[80] Whereas civil and political rights may be of little value to those who are deprived of the barest means to support themselves, the denial of these freedoms in the belief or, rather, under the pretext that this would promote economic development is a monstrous lie. As Louis Henkin so aptly puts it: "But how many hungry are fed, how much industry is built, by massacre, torture, and detention, by unfair trials and other injustices, by abuse of minorities, by denials of freedom of conscience, by suppression of political association and expression?"[81]

It is obvious that the right to freedom of speech is crucial in order to secure economic rights in the same way that it is important that people have the means with which to support themselves in order to be able to fully enjoy freedom of speech. All human rights are equally important and indispensable in order for man to live a dignified life. But such a statement perhaps obscures the fact that we sometimes are faced with difficult choices between different rights and freedoms.[82] One way of establishing priorities would be to place a priority on those rights that are prerequisites to the enjoyment of other rights.[83] While this theoretically would lead us to prioritize, let us say, the right to subsistence above the right to freedom of speech, the relationship between rights are much more complex. Freedom of speech could thus be regarded as a prerequisite to political participation, while the right to political participation in its turn could be regarded as a prerequisite to secure the right to subsistence, as the latter right might only be guaranteed through political means.

To say that human rights are universal is not to say that these rights are given for all time, they obviously evolve, or are being discovered over time, in response to new needs. In this respect they also often have to overcome bitter opposition before being accepted. Donnelly describes this development in the following terms: "Our list of human rights has evolved and expanded, and will continue to do so, in response to such factors as changing ideas of human dignity, the rise of new political forces, technological changes, new techniques of repression, and even past human rights successes, which allows attention and resources to be shifted to threats that previously were inadequately recognised or insufficiently addressed."[84] It is perhaps more accurate to argue that whereas one particular right, say freedom of speech, is universal, the dangers posed and the steps that have to be taken in order to safeguard that right differ between different societies depending on cultural and social factors and the level of economic development. It is thus the violations and the methods of safeguarding rights that are particular and relative, not the rights themselves.

THE RELATIONSHIP BETWEEN RIGHTS AND DUTIES

There has been a long and winding philosophical debate among Western philosophers on whether, or to what extent, rights and duties are correlative. The problem is whether statements of rights entail statements of other people's duties, and/or if statements of duties entail statements of other people's rights. Is it possible to imagine rights without concomitant duties, and/or duty-bearers? And can one be the recipient of a duty without being able to claim the correlative right? As already mentioned above, duties figured prominently in early natural law philosophy. In Feinberg's definition of rights as *claim-rights*, rights consist of two elements, claims to something and claims against someone.[85] Feinberg believes that people can have the right to something even though no duty-bearer has been identified. He calls rights in this weak sense *manifesto rights*. Rights in the stronger sense, that is claims against someone, would on the other hand also entail duties. Rights are thus prior to duties in his analysis, and he disputes the traditional view of a strict correlativity between rights and duties. H. J. McCloskey goes even further. Seeing rights as moral entitlements, he dispenses with the claims-against element in rights thinking, arguing that one does not have to be able to identify a duty-bearer, or even know exactly of what the duties would consist.[86]

Critics of economic and social rights often argue that these rights are mere aspirations since in many parts of the world the resources to ensure holidays with full pay, for example, are nonexistent. Maurice Cranston believes that one should abstain from talking about economic and social rights as human rights.[87] Underlying this argument is the belief that we can only have a right in as much as there exists the means to carry out the corresponding duty; or, differently put, that *ought* must imply *can*. But this is surely often as much a question of political will as of scarce economic resources. Discussing the can–ought implication of Cranston's view of human rights, Michael Freeden has pointed out that Cranston confuses the existence of a right with its implementation.[88] According to Cranston, we would not be able to claim a right prior to its potential implementation. This position is highly conservative and supports the status quo. In Cranston's eyes, rights seem to be more descriptive than normative in character. But the language of human rights is actually mostly invoked precisely when rights are being denied, or still have not been acknowledged or realized. Human rights are thus by their very nature always much more of aspirations than of reality.

Closely related to the issue of the relationship between rights and duties is the question of whether traditional, duty-based societies can be said to have entailed rights, albeit implicitly. This is an attractive idea whereby human rights would no longer be seen as an exclusively Western, or modern concept, except for its particular wording and the fact that rights were never explicitly spoken of, or claimed, in duty-based societies. Some scholars therefore argue that rights and duties are the flip sides of the same coin. As Alison Dundes Renteln puts it: "If, for example, the members of a given society have a duty to take care of the elderly, then the elderly could be said to have a right to proper care."[89] But it is important here to distinguish between the enjoyment of the substance of a right and enjoying the right itself. There is a big difference between enjoying goods and services as a result of benevolence and duty-fulfillment, calling forth feelings of gratitude, and enjoying goods and services that can be claimed as rightfully ours.[90] The former implies a life at the mercy of other people's benevolence, whereas only rights can bring about a life of dignity and self-respect. In many traditional societies, China being one of them, the rulers had a duty to secure the well-being of their subjects. But this duty did not entail any rights on the subjects' part, so that when the ruler failed in his duties, the subjects had to fall back on remonstrance rather than on rights talk.

The rights versus duties debate has taken on a new importance with the communitarians' attack on liberalism in the West and, of late, also because of the emergence of the so-called Asian values debate. As a reaction to, as they have put it, the "excessive rights-talk" in the United States (their main point of reference), communitarians and proponents of Asian values have emphasized the important and neglected role of duties in the West. Their conclusion is that the constant struggle in the West for ever more rights has made people there selfish and unconcerned about the community. But such an understanding of rights ignores the fact that human rights struggles, far from making people selfish and antagonistic, often take place on behalf of others in order to protect them from threats posed by the state or a hostile community. In societies that violate human rights, the problem is that instead of having too many rights people are regarded as having only duties and no rights, and are called upon to sacrifice their rights and interests for the sake of the community.

THE PURPOSE AND VALUE OF RIGHTS

The final point I would like to address concerns the purpose and value of rights, and involves questions such as, do rights exist for the individual or for the general interest? That is, do rights have intrinsic value or are they only a means to an end, and, if the answer is the latter, whose and which end? Very different and conflicting answers to this question exist within the Western tradition. Judith Shklar has made a distinction between a liberalism of rights and a liberalism of self-development.[91] The first stand focuses on rights in the tradition of Locke, whereas the second emphasizes the importance of freedom for personal and social progress in the tradition of Mill. In the case of Mill and the British Idealists, rights were regarded as teleological and they derived their authority by reference to an end. Although one could distinguish between individual ends, such as personal fulfillment, and more social ends, such as the common good, these two ends are often blurred, as in the case of the British Idealists or, for that matter, many Chinese intellectuals.

Rights have often been regarded as necessary and indispensable in order to live a life in self-respect and dignity.[92] This is also the view of contemporary philosophers such as Feinberg and Thomas E. Hill, who both argue that man needs rights in order to "stand up as a man." Feinberg has written that "Having rights enables us to 'stand up like men,' to look others in the eye, and to feel in some fundamental way the equal of anyone. To think of oneself as the holder of rights is not to be unduly but properly proud, to have that minimal self-respect that is necessary to be worthy of the love and esteem of others."[93] Hill also links rights to self-respect and argues that to undervalue one's rights is to manifest the vice of "servility."[94]

All along, a strong social and communitarian aspect to rights thinking has existed in the West. In early natural law philosophy, rights, being derived from duties, were perceived to contribute to moral order and the common good.[95] The British Idealists also stressed the communitarian aspect of rights. According to Green, the grounding and justification of rights was none other than their contribution to the common good, which was defined by him and other British Idealists as the perfecting of one's own character as well as that of others.[96] In Green's view, rights were not held irrespective of man's fulfilment of duties to society. Man could only claim rights that contributed to the common good; to claim rights against society would be a contradiction in terms. F. H. Bradley, another British Idealist, went one step further and rejected the idea of individual rights and emphasized the good of the community when, in 1894, he wrote that "The rights of the individual are today not worth serious consideration. . . . The welfare of the community is the end and is the ultimate standard."[97] Green and the other British Idealists did not value rights simply because of their contribution to the common good, but also because they were necessary in order to perfect one's moral personality. In their view there was a strong connection between being a person and being a rights-holder.[98] If someone was not treated as a person or could not realize himself because of being held in slavery, for example, it would be a loss, not only to the person in question, but to everybody else in society as well.

The British Idealists, like the communitarians, thus emphasized the social and historical character of the individual person, the importance of the common good, and the value of duties. Unlike them, however, the British Idealists did not abandon rights talk but attempted to historicize and socialize it. The need for rights in order to perfect one's personality and be a real person was also emphasized by later philosophers and scholars such as John Dewey and Laski. The influence of the British Idealists, directly in the case of Gao Yihan, but more often indirectly via Dewey and Laski, had a profound impact on Chinese intellectuals' understanding of rights and human rights in the early twentieth century. Chen Duxiu, for example, was deeply influenced by Dewey before becoming a Marxist, whereas Luo Longji and others in the 1920s and 1930s were influenced by and took up the ideas of Laski. In the 1990s, A. J. M. Milne has likewise greatly influenced some Chinese intellectuals. Milne, who himself has written on and is influenced by Kant and the British Idealists, emphasizes the social embeddedness of rights and takes a moderate, relativistic approach to human rights.[99] The linking of personality and moral fulfillment to human rights appeared much earlier in the Chinese debate, however, and cannot simply be attributed to the influence of the British Idealists and their disciplines. Moral fulfillment and self-cultivation is in a sense a very Confucian concern, which explains why the views of these Western scholars could later find a fertile ground in China.

Bentham and other utilitarians have been some of the most vociferous critics of the idea of natural rights. They also saw the enjoyment of rights, not as an end in itself, but as a means toward an end. Rights were evaluated on the merit of their usefulness and subordinated to the maximizing of the overall utility.[100] To take a utilitarian approach toward human rights need not be fatal. The consequences depend on who has the power to decide the definition and scope of the common good; they would therefore be quite different in democratic and authoritarian societies. In China, the common good and the national interest has often taken precedence over the interests of the individual, not because of any preordained or cultural characteristic of the Chinese people, but because power holders either have justified it by referring to the plight of the Chinese nation or demanded it out of political interests.

In this context one would also have to discuss whether rights, or which rights, are absolute and if they are not open to certain qualifications or can be overridden in certain circumstances. Most Western philosophers regard few, if any, rights as absolute, but instead speak of so-called *prima facie rights* that can be overridden in certain circumstances.[101] Even scholars who regard rights as trumps over the general interest, to adopt Ronald Dworkin's wording, do not believe that all rights have this status or that rights serve as trumps at all times and in all circumstances.[102] The right to freedom of speech is not generally regarded as absolute, although the question is, when can it be overridden? It does not entail the freedom to defame or slander others, although here one runs into the problem of how to identify what exactly constitutes defamation and who will define it. It is obvious that many governments try to undermine the right to freedom of expression by limiting its scope within certain boundaries. Chinese citizens can at present only exercise the right to freedom of speech within the constraints of the Four Cardinal Principles, that is, they have to acknowledge the leadership of the Communist Party, the supremacy of Marxism-Leninism-Mao Zedong thought, the dictatorship of the proletariat, and the socialist road. These constraints make the freedom of speech rather hollow, to say the least.

CONCLUSION

As briefly discussed in this chapter, the concept of human rights is complex, contested, and evolving. Many differences exist within the West itself on human rights and it would be wrong, as further elaborated upon in the next chapter, to succumb to a simple dichotomy of the West versus the non-West. As we will see, many Chinese scholars have been engaged in debates on the very same issues that have engaged scholars in the West. They have generally tended to regard rights as teleological, valuing them as necessary in order to realize one's humanity and be a complete and whole person. But rights have also been valued for their social utility, as a means toward the greater goal of social progress and national salvation. Chinese writers have been most influenced by the communitarian rights tradition in the West—the ideas of Jean-Jacques Rousseau, the utilitarians, and the British Idealists—rather than by the more individualistic Lockean rights tradition. In the contemporary debate, most Chinese writers on human rights still largely operate within a Marxist framework. But in their discussions on collective rights and the right to development they also reveal a close affinity to other socialist and radical trends of thought in the West. ·

NOTES

1. For historical studies, see inter alia Tuck (1979), Shapiro (1986), Strzelewicz (1983), Strauss (1953), and Lacey and Haakonssen (1991).
2. For a brief and lucid article on the history of the concept of rights, see Dagger (1989).
3. Lacey and Haakonssen (1991), p. 23; and Strauss (1953), p. 182.

4. For the view that human rights is a product of the rise of modern nation–states, see Donnelly (1989) and Wilson (1997). For the emphasis on new conceptions of self, see Hunt (2000).

5. A wealth of works exists on the French and American rights discourses; as an introduction to the topic see Hunt (1996), Lacey and Haakonssen (1991), and Rakove (1998).

6. Condorcet, reprinted in Hunt (1996), p. 120.

7. Huston (1991), p. 64, pp. 67–68. Since rights, it was complained, were undefined, any kind of desire or demand could be labeled a natural right. It is also evident that it was not necessarily a clear understanding of rights, or familiarity with rights theories, that prompted Americans to revolt against their British rulers. One soldier, when asked, said that he had never heard of either Locke or Paine. See Shain (1994), p. 79.

8. Pierre Victor Malouet as quoted by Bobbio (1996), p. 80.

9. For a very useful collection of these critical writings, see Waldron (1987).

10. Mill (1985), pp. 69–70.

11. See Nordahl (1995).

12. Bloch (1987), p. xxix.

13. Kolakowski (1983), p. 86. This tactical approach is something that the Chinese communists also have acknowledged. See discussion in chapter 10.

14. On the historical school and natural rights, see Strauss (1953), pp. 9–34.

15. Arendt (1973), p. 289. Arendt's view was shaped by the issue of stateless refugees during the war. She claimed that their treatment revealed the fiction of human rights and the supremacy of citizens' rights.

16. See Burgers (1992) and Lauren (1998).

17. See Wells (1940).

18. Burgers (1992), p. 470.

19. See Burgers (1992), Lauren (1998), and Morsink (1999) for these developments.

20. Vasak (1977) coined the term "three generations of human rights."

21. Menger (1899). The German original was published in 1886.

22. On the history of welfare rights in Western liberal thought, see Horne (1988).

23. Both reprinted in Wells (1940).

24. On this "Latin American connection," see Morsink (1999), chapter 4.

25. For a discussion of these rights, see Crawford (1988).

26. In my analysis I follow Shapiro (1986), who discusses rights from a fourfold relational schema: the subject of rights, the substance of rights, the basis of rights, and the purpose of rights. But I also add the question on the relationship between rights and duties, a major question in both the Western and Chinese discourse. Compare also the set of questions posed by Freeden (1991): who have rights, why do they have rights, what is the ground or basis of rights, and what kind of rights exist? Donnelly (1985) prefers to talk about three levels, namely, the nature, the source, and the substance of human rights, while Nickel (1987) asks questions regarding the analysis, content, and justification of human rights.

27. Shapiro (1986), p. 15.

28. On the British Idealists' view on rights generally, see Otter (1996), pp. 160–66; and Nicholson (1990), pp. 83–95.

29. Green (1986), para. 25.

30. Green (1986), para. 30.

31. Milne (1986a), p. 72.

32. Nicholson (1990), p. 93.

33. McIntyre (1981), p. 69.

34. Galston (1991), p. 222.
35. Quoted in Rorty (1993), p. 116.
36. Bobbio (1996).
37. Mendus (1995), p. 17.
38. Strauss (1953).
39. Haskell (1987).
40. Haskell (1987), pp. 1002–03.
41. Strauss (1953), p. 25.
42. Bobbio (1996), p. 6.
43. See, for example, Okin (1981).
44. Nordahl (1995), pp. 162–87.
45. For a critique of the needs-based approach, see Donnelly (1989), pp. 16–17.
46. Spigelberg (1970) has shown that it is no older than two hundred years.
47. For a Kantian understanding of human rights, see Milne (1986b).
48. See Hunt (2000).
49. Taylor, as quoted in Hunt (2000), p. 12.
50. Green (1986), para. 30.
51. This, for example, is the position of Donnelly (1989).
52. Feinberg (1980), p. 151.
53. Stetson (1998). See also Ames (1988), pp. 212–13, and (1997), p. 193.
54. See also Glendon (1991). Her critique is, however, directed against the excessive rights talk in American society and not against human rights talk per se. Human rights talk, after all, mostly takes place on behalf of others and thus is a manifestation of responsibility and concern about others.
55. See Patterson (1995).
56. Schachter (1983), p. 853.
57. Pollis and Schwab (1979), p. 15; and Lauren (1998), p. 11.
58. See, for example, Bloom (1998).
59. See Howard (1995a), p. 81, and (1995b), pp. 79–108; and Donnelly (1989), pp. 49–87. See also the anthropologist Wilson (1997), pp. 13–14.
60. For this distinction between intrinsic and extrinsic dignity, see Spigelberg (1970).
61. Bobbio (1996) describes three different ways of demonstrating human rights: deduction from an objective fact, such as human nature; their consideration as self-evident truths; and finally, consensus, which is his own choice.
62. See An-Na'im (1995).
63. Waldron (1987), p. 163.
64. Maritain (1952), p. 77.
65. See, for example, Pollis and Schwab (1979), p. 8; and Milne (1986b), p. 3.
66. See Lauren (1998), Morsink (1999), and Glendon (2001).
67. See Richardson (1997).
68. Haskell (1987), p. 1002.
69. Berlin (1969) argues for a historical and anthropological study of universal values, while the anthropologist Wilson (1997) argues for a similar approach with respect to human rights.
70. See Crawford (1988).
71. Howard (1995a), pp. 97–99. For a discussion on whether liberals can endorse collective rights, and what makes them hostile to the idea in the first place, see McDonald (1995), p. 141–54.
72. Waldron (1987), pp. 183–90.

73. See, for example, Leary (1995), Shapiro (1986), and Lee (1995).
74. See also Milne (1986b).
75. For discussions of feminists' critique of the contemporary human rights discourse, see Cook (1994).
76. For a critique of these polarisations, see Human Rights Watch (1993), and Sen (1999).
77. Ng (1995), p. 59.
78. Cranston (1973), p. 68.
79. Nordahl (1995).
80. Donnelly (1985), p. 46.
81. Henkin (1978), p. 130.
82. According to Berlin, for example, there is an incommensurable conflict between freedom and equality. Berlin (1969). See also Bobbio (1996), pp. 28–29.
83. Okin (1981), p. 244.
84. Donnelly (1989), p. 26.
85. Feinberg (1980).
86. McCloskey (1984).
87. Cranston (1973). See Donnelly (1989), pp. 31–34, for a critique of Cranston's position.
88. Freeden (1991), p. 33.
89. Renteln (1990), p. 12.
90. Feinberg (1980).
91. Shklar (1998), pp. 6–9.
92. Donnelly (1989), p.17.
93. Feinberg (1980), p. 151.
94. Hill (1973).
95. Lacey and Haakonssen (1991), p. 36, p. 52.
96. Green (1986), para. 16. Other British Idealists, such as Bernard Bosanquet and F. H. Bradley, also put forward ideas similar to Green's. On Bosanquet's view of rights, see Sweet (1993).
97. Quoted in Weston (1992), p. 16.
98. Nicholson (1990), pp. 87–89. See also Milne (1986b), p. 125.
99. Milne (1986b).
100. On the discussion of the relationship between utility and rights, see the articles in the anthology edited by Frey (1984). See also Hart (1979).
101. Mackie (1984).
102. Dworkin (1977).

Chapter Three

Culture and Human Rights: Between Universalism and Relativism

THE CHALLENGE OF CULTURAL RELATIVISM

In discussions on human rights, the question has often been raised of whether a concept of undisputable Western origin can be applied or rendered meaningful in other cultures and societies. Behind this question looms the larger issue of whether any moral values relevant for and applicable to all societies really exist, or, in other words, whether any universal values exist. Some are of the opinion that since moral values are culturally embedded and community based they will inevitably differ between different societies.[1] They go on to contend that all moral values, therefore, are relative and contingent and dispute the existence of universal human rights. This cultural relativistic view was first put forward by anthropologists in the 1930s, while today it is shared by both advocates of Asian values and communitarians in the West. According to the cultural relativists, the quest for universal human rights is misguided, or worse, an expression of Western cultural imperialism. Due to their Western historical origin, human rights would have to be regarded as foreign and incomprehensible to other societies. Human rights would thus be nothing more than a Western value masked as a universal value, hence a pseudo-universal, that the West tries to impose on the non-Western world.[2] This view and the assumptions it is based upon are open to many objections. One obvious objection is why should the historical origin of an idea be held against it? Another objection targets the implicit assumption that human rights somehow are deeply embedded in Western societies. Before I address these objections in more detail, I would like to discuss some other pitfalls of cultural relativism and its deeply flawed description of culture.

It is impossible to harbor any serious objections to a moderate descriptive version of cultural relativism, which holds that many values and practices differ between societies and therefore asks for caution on the part of outsiders when judging the values of another society. But such an understanding does not rule out the existence of some cross-cultural values, nor does it prevent external criticism. An extreme cultural relativism, on the other hand, is untenable since it seems to preclude the possibility of any form of cross-cultural communication and dialogue, something that clearly does take place. It can furthermore be seen as a moral commitment to the status quo, because it assumes that since value judgments differ between societies, they will and ought to remain different. In effect, however, values and beliefs are not given for all time, they are socially constructed and develop over time and in contact with other societies.

The consequences of an all-out acceptance of cultural relativism are devastating and amount to moral nihilism.[3] It is intellectually and morally irresponsible since it can be used in defense of, for example, the Holocaust, apartheid, ethnic cleansing, and so on, on the grounds that one has to respect the values of these societies. Not only is it a very specious argument to hold that these policies were/are deeply embedded in these societies, but even if they were, that is no reason why we should accept them or why they could not change. Cultural relativism taken to its extreme undermines our abilities to condemn repressive practices in other societies and cultures. It furthermore tends to essentialize culture and fails to take into account the existence of internal critique and fierce political contestations over cultural practices and values. Cultural relativism ignores the voices of the oppressed and reveals an utter disrespect for the victims of practices and policies such as those mentioned above. These victims naturally would neither agree that these policies are culturally embedded in their societies, nor that they should be accepted and upheld.

It must be emphasized that divergent standards of morality often exist within any given society, as well as over time, that give rise to an internal critique. People, furthermore, often inhabit more than one culture and thus have access to multiple and shifting, or even opposing and conflicting, cultural and social identities. This important aspect is missing in the cultural relativists' view of culture. The anthropologist Wilson has succinctly described the flawed understanding of culture upon which cultural relativism is based.

[Relativism] totalise[s] and reif[ies] "culture," constructing it as internally uniform and hermetically bounded. "Culture" is seen as shared and normative, not as cross-cut by social differences (age, caste, gender, etc.), or characterised as contested, fragmented, contextualised and emergent. . . . For their doctrine to be coherent, cultural relativists seem to hold a nineteenth-century notion of culture as discrete and homogeneous, as the product of isolation, and as the basis of all difference and similarity between human beings. Their relativism is predicated upon bounded conceptions of linguistic and cultural systems, but it falls apart in contexts of hybridity, creolisation, intermixture and the overlapping of political traditions.[4]

No culture or society is monolithic but often contains several conflicting value systems. Within a nation—state there are usually several distinct cultures or value systems, especially in a country as diverse as China. In an authoritarian country it would in addition be both dangerous and misleading to assume that the cultural mainstream is identical with the views of the power holders. It is not irrelevant who claims to be the "true" bearer of the culture and who dominates the debate on human rights. To respect cultural differences is applaudable, but cultural relativism can easily become a cover for all kinds of violations that are anything but culture specific. One should, for example, not accept the Asian governments' claim of cultural authenticity at face value since their advocacy of Asian values may have more to do with their own political interests than with cultural values as such.

When confronted with the argument that what we as outsiders consider to be human rights violations are not considered as such by a specific culture, we must ask ourselves if that really is the case and if an internal critique does not exist as well. Why should we accept that the Chinese leaders' opinions on human rights are more representative of the Chinese people than those of dissidents such as Wei Jingsheng? But although the existence of an internal critique is important, it is not a necessary precondition in order for outsiders to criticize what they consider to be unjust or cruel practices. Even without the present international human rights regime, which lays down universal standards agreed upon by the international community, we would still be entitled to criticize injustices taking place in our own and other societies. This is, after all, how the present International Bill of Rights came into being in the first place.

While it is true that our standards and moral values are shaped by the society in which we live, our values are also, and increasingly, shaped by our participation in and interaction with the global community. In recent years the language of human rights has become a global language that can be understood in parts of the world where it once was considered foreign and incomprehensible. The globalization of human rights talk is an indisputable fact. In many parts of the world disadvantaged groups of people are now making skillful use of human rights discourses to protect their rights and interests vis-à-vis other groups in society, domestic power holders, and multinational corporations.[5] Human rights, in other words, have itself become part and parcel of these societies' cultural practices.[6]

Some people also seem to object to universal human rights because they believe that such an advocacy "produces an unhealthy sameness" and has a totalitarian ring to it.[7] To advocate universal human rights, they claim, is to be guilty of dogmatism, monism, and cultural imperialism. They hold that human rights conceptions and standards inevitably vary between different societies, and that these differences should be accepted in the name of cultural pluralism.[8] This may on the surface seem like a rather harmless and even worthwhile proposition: who could possibly be against cultural pluralism! But to accept pluralism in the field of human rights conceptions is potentially dangerous and easily pushes one into the arms of cultural relativists. An advocacy of universal human rights and rejection of cultural relativism, I would contend, does not imply an attack on cultural diversity, nor does it rule out that cultural traditions to some extent influence both our understanding of human rights as well as their implementation.[9] It is not the advocacy of universal human rights that threatens cultural pluralism but, ironically enough, it is the acceptance of a pluralism of human rights conceptions. As a matter of fact, universal human rights actually serve to defend pluralism by protecting people's rights to hold different beliefs and opinions.

It is interesting to note that erstwhile proponents of cultural relativism, such as Admantia Pollis, who in 1979 disputed the universality of human rights and criticized the UDHR for being a "Western construct with limited applicability," felt compelled in 1996 to raise some warnings about the current fashion of cultural relativism.[10] Pollis warned that certain states, particularly some East Asian nations, had come to "exploit the language of cultural relativism to justify and rationalise [their] own repressive actions . . . [which] cannot be justified by claims of philosophic or cultural distinctiveness."[11] While in the past many academics in the West, such as Pollis, embraced some version of cultural relativism, often in reaction to Western ethnocentrism and colonialism, the recent Asian values debate has served to sensitize many of them to its inherent dangers and made them rethink their positions.

In a more recent work Pollis seems to have moved even closer to universalism, arguing that the dichotomy between universalism and culturalism has been overdrawn.[12] The past few years have in fact seen a general move away from cultural relativism to what some scholars have chosen to describe as a "reconstructed universalism" or a "chastened universalism."[13] These wordings underline that this new version of universalism acknowledges and takes into account cultural differences while not denying the universality of human rights. It is thus an attempt to stay clear both of the "arrogant universalism" found in the West in the past, and, on the other extreme, a "morally vacuous relativism."[14] Such a development is found among both anthropologists, the first advocates of cultural relativism, political scientists, and those engaged in area studies.[15]

THE HISTORICAL GENESIS OF HUMAN RIGHTS

The proposition that human rights are universal only refers to their applicability and not to their origin or recognition. It is important to distinguish between the historical genesis of the idea and its justification and realization in the contemporary world. The fact that the concept of human rights originated in the West does not undermine its universal applicability, nor do the obvious violations of human rights worldwide, including in the West, make their future realization impossible. Even though the concept was first formulated in the West, it does not follow that it reflects exclusive Western concerns. Totalitarianism and the denial of human rights is unfortunately as much a part of the West, both in theory and in practice, as are democracy and the respect for human rights. Nor are human rights as deeply embedded in Western thought as is often assumed. For those who dismiss human rights simply because of their Western origin, it should be pointed out that many schools of thought in the West have been highly critical of the concept, without making them any less Western. As Arthur Schlesinger Jr. has noted:

> As a historian, I confess to a certain amusement when I hear the Judeo-Christian tradition praised as the source of our concern for human rights. In fact, the great religious ages were notable for their indifference to human rights in the contemporary sense. They were notorious not only for acquiescence in poverty, inequality, exploitation and oppression but for enthusiastic justifications of slavery, persecution, abandonment of small children, torture, genocide.[16]

Although the concept of human rights was first formulated in the West, its development and acceptance has been far from smooth. Respect for human rights in non-Western societies is probably as realistic, or unrealistic, as is the respect for human rights in the West. Since the concept of human rights has gradually evolved in the West, it is not too farfetched to imagine a similar development in the rest of the world, especially in the contemporary world of cross-cultural communication and exchange of ideas. The concept of human rights was once equally foreign to traditional Western societies as it now may seem to some non-Western societies, but the development of the modern nation–state and market economy have made it relevant and indispensable. This should not be taken to mean that history only moves in one inevitable direction, or that developments in the rest of the world will mirror that of the West. Furthermore and unfortunately, it is not at all certain that democracy and respect for human rights will represent the "end of history," not even in the West.[17] The concept of human rights will no doubt continue to evolve in response to the appearance of new threats against humankind. In contrast to the early human rights debates, which were completely dominated by the West, different cultures and societies today play an equally important role in shaping the new global human rights discourse.

CHINESE CULTURE AND HUMAN RIGHTS

Many scholars discussing human rights in the Chinese context have focused on the question of whether it is possible to find indigenous roots to the concept of human rights in Chinese culture, and, if not, would that obstruct or rule out the acceptance and realization of human rights in contemporary China? This, of course, begs the questions of why indigenous values should be a prerequisite for acceptance, and why it would be impossible for foreign concepts to eventually become domesticated. As Paltiel has argued with respect to rights thinking, "So long as rights claims gain legitimacy in social practice, it may be irrelevant that certain practices and values have indigenous roots and others are imported."[18]

Those who discuss the relationship between Chinese culture (read Confucianism, usually) and human rights have taken very different positions. These range from claiming that Chinese culture is incompatible with human rights; to contending that certain human rights are more compatible with Chinese culture than others; to arguing that traditional thought entailed human rights, albeit implicitly; to pointing out that the Chinese culture contained within itself ideas that are congenial to and can nurture human rights ideas; to asserting that Confucian values could contribute to and enrich international human rights discourse; and, finally, to arguing that Confucian values are superior to Western rights discourse and should replace it.

It is quite revealing that so many different and contradictory views all can be derived by a simple reference to Chinese culture, which indicates that culture is problematic as an explanatory category and often referred to in a much too loose and sweeping way to be of much use. The focus on classical Confucianism, in addition, freezes Chinese culture and ignores the obvious cultural and political changes that have taken place since the late Qing dynasty. To equate Chinese culture with Confucianism, moreover, ignores other schools and aspects of Chinese culture, such as Buddhism and popular religions, which seem to have had as much, if not more, of a lasting influence on Chinese society.

Some scholars regard the Chinese cultural tradition as incompatible with the concept of human rights.[19] Since the Chinese tradition did not give rise to an explicit concept of human rights, this therefore precludes any acceptance of the concept today, or so this reasoning goes. Tradition furthermore explains the human rights violations that (in Western eyes) take place in China today. Criticizing China for these violations would not only be meaningless and ineffective but, worse, would be evidence of cultural imperialism. These scholars stress the huge differences that exist between a political system based on rites, and one based on rights. The former lends itself to authoritarianism and does not, or indeed cannot, give rise to ideas of democracy and human rights.

It has also been argued that the contemporary official view of human rights builds upon and reinforces traditional values found in the Chinese political culture; that the Communist state, in short, is simply an extension of the earlier authoritarian imperial state. As one scholar has put it, "In China, traditional concepts of the individual, the state and the law have reinforced Marxist concepts. The view of society as an organic whole whose collective rights prevail over the individual, the idea that man exists for the state rather than vice versa and that rights, rather than having any absolute value, derive from the state, have been themes prevailing in old as well as new China."[20] It is interesting to note the prevalent tendency to refer to an unchanging Chinese culture when trying to explain the official position on human rights in the PRC, whereas scholars of the former Soviet Union did not have the same urge and instead paid more attention to ideological and political factors. Despite the fact that these two countries' positions on human rights have been quite similar, the explanation has in the case of China singularly been sought in culture. This partly has to do with the focus on culture in today's international human rights debates, as exemplified by the Asian values issue, although cultural explanations have long been prominent in many other works on Chinese politics.

The above position on the negative influence of the Chinese culture on human rights discourse is open to dispute in several ways. First, it often tends to ignore the fact that the Chinese tradition is complex and consists of different strands of thought, of which Confucianism is but one. One cannot claim that Confucianism is all there is to Chinese culture.[21] Be that as it may, Confucianism in its turn is a rich tradition that not only contains authoritarian but also more liberal tenets and that, furthermore, has evolved over the centuries.[22] It is not accurate to argue that the Communist regime builds upon, and, even less, is an inevitable extension of the traditional political system; there are too many differences between the two political systems to warrant such a conclusion. Tradition, after all, has little to do with the human rights violations taking place in China today.

This static and negative approach to Chinese culture also fails to take into account, or explain, the different views of human rights among Chinese people from the end of the Qing dynasty up to the present.[23] How does one explain the fact that quite different and more positive views on human rights have existed if one regards the Chinese view of human rights as preordained by the Chinese political culture? It is not a satisfying answer to argue that since these views have only been minority views and never became predominant among the Chinese people, they were doomed and can be viewed as deviations. Their failures to take root, if that really is the case in view of recent developments, are contingent upon several factors, some of which may have been accidental or unrelated to cultural factors, for example, shaped by political and international developments. It is also misleading to read history backward and argue that the rejection of human rights on the mainland after 1949 was a logical and inevitable consequence of the Chinese political culture.

Another group of scholars, as well as the Chinese government itself, taking a somewhat different position, has instead contended that some rights are more compatible with the Chinese culture than others. They argue that the official emphasis on economic and social rights over civil and political rights, and the priority of collective rights over individual rights, reflect the persistent influence of Chinese tradition.[24] The paternalistic benevolence in imperial China, wherein the emperor had the duty to secure the well-being of his subjects, explain, they believe, the contemporary emphasis on economic rights.[25] But it is highly questionable whether tradition can explain the official emphasis on economic rights since it is obvious that the present view has a lot in common with that of other socialist and Third World countries.[26] In the following chapters it will also become clear that Chinese discussions on economic and social rights owe as much, or more, to the influence of Western social liberalism and Marxism, as to the Chinese tradition per se. Another objection to this view is that not all Chinese agree with the official list of priorities among different rights. Many Chinese throughout the twentieth century have forcefully argued the case for civil and political rights, and would not necessarily agree that collective rights trump individual rights.

One argument supporting the view of the Chinese, or Confucian, culture as being hostile to human rights, is that societies belonging to the Confucian cultural sphere, such as China, Taiwan, Korea, and Singapore, are not known for their respect of human rights. But from this fact alone one cannot draw the conclusion that an insurmountable incompatibility exists between Confucianism and human rights. It is highly debatable whether there is a causal correlation between the Confucian pasts of these societies and their present violations of human rights; there may very well be many other factors that help explain the latter. Such an approach also begs the question of how many, if any, of these societies rightly can be regarded as Confucian today. Furthermore, in many of them there have been significant improvements in the human rights situation over the past few years. The developments in Taiwan and South Korea in particular raise serious doubts as to whether Confucianism and traditional values really are incompatible with or obstruct the development of human rights and democracy. This serves to underline the fact that culture is not static but is evolving and contested. Instead of categorically dismissing the concept of human rights because of its alleged incompatibility with Chinese culture and tradition, it would be necessary to show which, if any, elements of the contemporary Chinese culture hinder or obstruct the acceptance and realization of human rights.

It should, however, be acknowledged that certain elements in Confucianism are indeed incompatible with the concept of human rights as we know it today, that is, the idea of universal rights belonging to all people regardless of sex, race, class, position in society, and political and religious beliefs. In Confucianism, the relationship between subjects and ruler, sons and fathers, women and

men, was strictly hierarchical and characterized by benevolence and righteousness from above, and loyalty and obedience from below. In this system people
did not possess any universal rights, nor could they expect equal treatment.[27]
But the hierarchical nature of Confucianism need not preclude the acceptance
of universal rights by a modified Confucianism since universal rights for all was
not a feature of classical natural rights theory either. Be that as it may, as I will
argue below, the question of whether Confucianism is compatible with human
rights seems quite academic and irrelevant as other factors shape the contemporary human rights discourse in China, and Chinese culture itself has undergone many changes.

Nonetheless, many Western scholars, who believe that it is necessary to establish an internal justification of human rights in order to make human rights
more acceptable to Chinese people, tend to pin their hopes on Confucianism.
They argue that even though Confucianism did not give rise to a concept of
human rights, it is compatible with human rights and contains within itself
ideas that are congenial to and can nurture human rights.[28] Sumner B. Twiss
has thus argued that even though Confucianism did not explicitly conceptual-
ize human rights, it has the resources necessary to "justify on internal grounds
and in [its] own moral idioms" its "agreement to participate in and abide by,
on pragmatic moral grounds, an international human rights consensus."[29] Several scholars claim that the Confucian humanist ethics, manifested in certain
ideals such as *ren* (benevolence or humaneness) and *yi* (righteousness), are quite
similar to, or contained in the concept of human rights. They therefore suggest
that the concept of human rights could build upon, or is entailed in these Confucian ideals.[30] Others, like Roger Ames, argue that the concept of rites (*li*) fulfilled some of the same functions as rights in the West, that is, guided the relations between persons and between a person and the state.[31]

I do not find the search for equivalences or congenial values to human rights
in Confucianism completely convincing or compelling. Even though I agree
with the view that there are no cultural impediments to human rights in China,
I find the stress on the existence of Confucian values similar to contemporary
conceptions of human rights far-fetched. This approach often seems to confuse
ideas of human dignity and justice with human rights. It is true that notions of
human dignity are found in Confucianism as well as contained in the concept
of human rights, but, as discussed in the previous chapter, it does not equal or
necessarily lead to a conception of human rights. There is quite a difference between a language of benevolence and a language of rights, between being the
beneficiary of a duty and being able to claim something as one's right. To simply engage in a search for traditional values akin to human rights in the Confucian classics furthermore ignores the question of whether these values were
ever applied and respected in the past and the question of whether they are of

relevance in the contemporary debate. Wm. Theodore de Bary seems to acknowledge as much when he writes: "[C]lassical statements serve only a limited purpose. They can illustrate traditional ideals or axial values—which are by no means insignificant—but they do not, in themselves, speak to the historical realities of China in later times or to the twentieth-century circumstances in which contemporary human rights issues are embedded."[32]

To argue the existence of "internal moral resources" in Confucianism that can support human rights could thus be more of an empty and scholarly exercise. This search for cultural resources may not be relevant for the realization of human rights in contemporary China. It is instructive to note that Chinese dissidents have not given much thought to the relationship between Confucianism and human rights.[33] Chinese dissidents and others before them have unabashedly turned to the West and universal human rights documents for inspiration in their struggles instead of trying to support their advocacy of human rights with references to tradition. I thus fully agree with Paltiel that for many Chinese people today, the Confucian tradition is more remote than either Western liberal discourse or Marxism.[34] It is also highly difficult to imagine that human rights would become more accepted and respected by the Chinese government if the human rights concept was to draw more explicitly on traditional Confucian values. That being said, however, as will also become obvious in my study, although most Chinese have not consciously tried to build upon traditional values, this has not prevented them from describing human rights in terms that carry some echoes of Confucian views on human dignity and self-cultivation. In this respect, I will concede, tradition indeed has and continues to permeate the Chinese human rights discourse.

Another problem I have with the position outlined above is that these scholars generally tend to ignore, or keep silent on, the more troubling aspects of Confucianism, such as its hierarchical nature and submission of women, which are at odds with the contemporary concept of human rights.[35] It was exactly these problematic aspects of Confucianism that were at the center of the Chinese debates on human rights in the early twentieth century when Confucianism still was a powerful ideology that people referred to or reacted against.

Other scholars turn the lack of an indigenous human rights tradition into an advantage instead of a liability. They argue that the reason why the concept of human rights did not exist in traditional China was because it was superfluous. Rights were not sought simply because they were not needed. Because of their belief in an underlying harmony in the Confucian system, people did not feel any urge to fight for rights and freedoms against each other or against the state.[36] Ames, in addition, argues that rights may not necessarily protect human dignity, since rights are grounded in the individual person and do not give due attention to his social embeddedness, something which, on the other hand, the

Confucian concept of the person does.[37] Some scholars, building on these understandings, go on to argue that to claim individual rights without consideration of others is detrimental to society. They believe that the attainment of human rights requires collaboration and consensus building. They also contend that duties have been sadly neglected in the West, something that accounts for many of its social ills.[38] Their conclusion is that certain Confucian values could enrich and contribute to human rights discourse and help redress some of its negative traits, in their view.

A more extreme version of this argument has been put forward by Henry Rosemont Jr.[39] Rosemont also contends that the lack of rights thinking in traditional China is not a weakness; quite the opposite, it is rather something positive and worth learning from in China itself and the West. Rosemont holds that the Confucian system is superior to that of the rights-focused system of the contemporary West, and sees at least some Confucian values as genuine alternatives to the rights discourse. He contrasts the rugged individualism and selfishness he finds in the West (read the United States) with the social relatedness and respect of community values that he believes exist in China (at least in the traditional society). The ills of the West, according to Rosemont, are partly due to its excessive emphasis on rights and neglect of duties. The West would thus do better to replace its focus on rights with an emphasis on duties and reciprocal social relationships in the Confucian manner. Rosemont's view resembles that of the communitarians and the advocates of Asian values, both of whom criticize the West for pretty much the same ills and advocate similar remedies.[40]

The weaknesses of the views discussed above, especially Rosemont's more extreme view, are all too obvious. First and foremost, the ideal Confucian system of righteous rulers was hardly ever realized in practice. These scholars seem to succumb to a romantic longing for a lost community, to use Howard's words, or, in the case of the Western scholars, an old tendency to romanticize a foreign society when facing problems in one's own.[41] Another objection is that people such as Rosemont tend to compare the best of an idealized and distant Confucian theory with the worst aspects of a liberal Western (read American) reality, which of course inevitably works to the former's favor.

Even if one agreed that human rights were not needed in the traditional, ideal society, it is obvious that the rise of the modern nation–state poses new challenges and threats to the individual. It is also highly questionable to claim that human rights are not applicable or relevant in China (or Asia) on the grounds that the indigenous tradition makes calls for human rights superfluous, since these traditions have long since been abandoned or seriously undermined by the current power holders. It is also obvious that today's authoritarian regimes in Asia use the common good, as defined by themselves, as a pretext to clamp down on individual dissent. In an authoritarian political system, to emphasize consensus and expect people to shoulder duties while ignoring their individual rights only serves to benefit the power holders. It is remarkable that these scholars can be so sensitive to the problems of excessive "rights talk" in the West, while not seeming to think twice about the dangers of excessive "duties talk" in China, especially given the present political system of the PRC.

THE ASIAN VALUES DEBATE

The demise of communism in Eastern Europe and the failed democracy movement in China served to bring about renewed attention to human rights issues. In the early 1990s, Asian values emerged as a hot topic in international human rights discourse. This debate was both a reaction to the increasing importance of human rights after the end of the Cold War, and an outcome of growing self-confidence on the part of the prospering Asian nations. The post–Cold War human rights debate is therefore configured somewhat differently from that of the Cold War period. It could be said that whereas during the Cold War the human rights discourse was more political-ideological in character, it is today more cultural-economic. Even so, many of the same arguments are still being voiced in the contemporary debate, for example, the argument that human rights are an internal affair.[42] The Asian economic crisis, which began in the fall of 1997, served to, if not silence the Asian values debate, at least take some of the heat out of it. Not only did it shatter the self-confidence among those Asian countries hardest hit by the crisis, but some of the reasons for it have also been attributed to these countries' political systems.[43] The very values that recently were hailed as being behind the East Asian miracle were instead described as the root of the problem.

Several Asian countries, notably China, Indonesia, Singapore, and Malaysia, have questioned both the West's exploitation of the human rights issue in international relations and the relevance of the prevalent human rights concept to their own societies. They charge that the concept of human rights has been influenced and shaped by the West and imposed on Asia without consideration of its different cultural and historical tradition. Differences with respect to human rights, they argue, are justified on the dual grounds of cultural and historical differences and on the priority of economic development. According to this understanding, human rights are not universal but historical and relative. Although reaffirming the universality of human rights at the Bangkok conference in 1993 (one of the regional meetings held in preparation for the UN World Conference on Human Rights in Vienna later the same year), the Asian governments at the same time stressed that "they must be considered in the context of a dynamic and evolving process of international norm-setting, bearing in mind the significance of national and regional particularities and various historical, cultural and religious backgrounds."[44]

It is interesting to note that the ideological conflicts characteristic of the Cold War human rights debate, at least partly and on the rhetorical level, have been replaced with arguments focusing on cultural distinctiveness. But even though cultural distinctiveness figures prominently in the Asian values debate, more political and economic issues seem to loom larger and inform the debate.[45] It was the increasing confidence brought about by economic success that moved some Asian countries, led by Singapore, to challenge the West over human rights; an analysis shared by Chinese scholars.[46] Nationalism has also been a crucial factor behind much of the Asian values debate. Many of the Asian countries that were colonized or threatened by the West in the past are particularly sensitive to what they perceive as the West's "preaching" on human rights and democracy.[47] They invoke these countries' imperialist pasts and accuse them of being hypocritical in their new-found concern about alleged human rights violations in Asia.[48] But while it is indeed true that many Western countries in the past grossly violated the very human rights of the Asian people that they today are criticizing Asian governments of violating, these historical injustices are being blatantly exploited by authoritarian Asian governments in order to divert attention or excuse their own human rights violations.

Although there has been much ado about Asian values, little has actually been written on their specific content, or on how and in what way they have shaped the understanding of human rights in Asia.[49] There does not, for example, exist much in the way of historical studies on how and when these societies first encountered the concept of human rights, or on how Asian people past and present have discussed the issue and struggled for human rights. By way of description of the supposedly distinctive Asian position on human rights, it is argued that people in Asia, in contrast to people in the West, emphasize collective rather than individual rights and place priority on economic and social rights over civil and political rights.[50] It is further argued that economic development is the most important and urgent concern of these societies and that it necessitates the sacrifice, however temporary, of individual political rights. But apart from general and vague notions such as these, proponents of a specific Asian approach to human rights have failed to provide a more detailed definition and analysis.

One of the strongest objections to the idea of so-called Asian values is the obvious fact of the cultural, religious, political, and economic diversity within Asia itself.[51] Can any common Asian values really exist given this diversity? Since the Asian values debate to some extent has been dominated by Singapore,

Asian values have often come to be identified with Confucian values. But Confucianism is by no means the only or dominating value system in Asia; it is quite foreign to most Asian societies. The question is not only whether there is such a thing as Asian values, but, even if there were, would they not then have to be described as regional values, which could also be criticized for not being grounded or local enough? The question, of course, is how local and particular should one have to get in order to satisfy the cultural relativists and others who believe in community-based values? Those who argue for community-based values, furthermore, often ignore the fact that people can belong to communities that transcend national and societal boundaries. Feminists in China and Sweden, for example, share many values and certainly have more in common than either of them have with male chauvinists in their respective societies.

Another crucial objection is that not all governments in Asia are in favor of or believe in a specific Asian approach to human rights. The attack on universal human rights has not been joined by Japan, for example. Lee Teng-hui, the former Taiwanese president, also supported the universality of human rights and criticized the advocacy of Asian values. The Asian concept of human rights has also been refuted by a number of local NGOs and individuals who refuse to adhere to the view that human rights are at odds with Asian culture. In the opinion of the NGOs, the governments' new-found concern about Asian values reflects more a need to defend their political power and the status quo than a genuine concern about cultural distinctiveness and pluralism. In their alternative Bangkok declaration, the NGOs for their part strongly stressed that human rights are universal and indivisible in character, challenging their governments' view that civil and political rights must be sacrificed for the sake of economic development.[52] In 1998, Asian NGOs published the Asian Human Rights Charter in defense of the universality of human rights, which criticized Asian governments' exhortation of Asian values as a "thin disguise for their authoritarianism."[53] Many Asian activists call for human rights and democracy and reject the notion that human rights are inapplicable to their societies. As Kim Dae Jung, the long-time democracy activist who was elected president of South Korea in 1997, has pointed out, "The biggest obstacle [to democracy and human rights] is not [Asia's] cultural heritage but the resistance of authoritarian rulers and their apologists."[54]

The advocates of Asian values, in addition, have a tendency to make an artificial dichotomy between Asia and the West. Not only should the existence of specific Asian values be questioned in light of the political and cultural diversity within the region, but, similarly, the existence of Western values must be considered an equally artificial and ahistorical construct. It is often claimed that the idea of human rights is deeply embedded in Western culture and tradition; a problematic assumption as already discussed. In the Asian values debate, the supposedly individualistic and adversarial West is juxtaposed with the communitarian and consensus-seeking Asia.[55] This is not only a highly questionable description, but it also misses the point: egoistic individuals claiming rights from society is not what human rights are all about.

Although the Chinese authorities now acknowledge that human rights to some extent are universal, they, like other Asian governments, at the same time also argue that human rights are contingent upon each society's level of economic development and historical and cultural conditions. At the UN World Conference on Human Rights in 1993, the head of the Chinese delegation, Liu Huaqiu, elaborating on his government's view on human rights, thus claimed that

> The concept of human rights is a product of historical development. It is closely associated with specific social, political and economic conditions and the specific history, culture and values of a particular country. Different historical development stages have different human rights requirements. Countries at different development stages or with different historical traditions and cultural backgrounds also have different understanding and practice of human rights.[56]

Even though references to culture and national conditions (*guoqing*) became more prominent in the official human rights discourse during the 1990s, Asian values never featured very prominently in the Chinese debate. The official position on human rights has not been informed by or relied on cultural arguments. As a socialist country, the PRC relies more on the argument that different economic systems and levels of economic development influence and shape the understanding and realization of human rights. In both the official rhetoric and among establishment intellectuals there are still more references to Marxism than to a distinctive Chinese culture.

China tends to perceive the world as divided into developed and developing countries, identifying itself with the latter, rather than see it as divided into different civilizations or cultural spheres. The official position is to identify itself with the Third World as a whole rather than with Asia.[57] There are few discussions on Asian values in either the official or the more academic discourse on human rights.[58] It is also instructive to note that when Chinese scholars describe Asian values, they focus more on the Asian nations' common economic and political experiences than on their supposedly shared cultural heritage. They stress these societies' struggle for economic development and self-determination and their resistance to Western hegemonism, but are hard pressed to come up with a list of shared cultural characteristics. Many Chinese scholars are also quite critical of Asian values that they see as posing a threat to the universality of human rights.[59] They are actually more likely to criticize traditional values and blame them for China's backwardness, in the tradition of the May Fourth Movement, than to give them credit for the more than twenty years of spectacular economic growth.[60]

Liu Junning is one of the Chinese scholars who has argued most forcefully against the idea of Asian values.[61] Liu offers a scathing critique of the view that democracy and human rights do not fit Asia, pointing out that this is only the view of the power holders and not shared by the Asian people themselves.

> Some people try to use the Asian values argument to prove that the values of human rights, freedom, and democracy are inappropriate for Asian societies. More precisely, it is not that freedom and democracy are inappropriate for Asian societies but rather that they are inappropriate for dictators like Suharto. If ordinary Asians were to advocate Asian values, the unique virtues of Asian people, or their unique cultural traditions, this would perhaps not be unreasonable. But when rulers talk loudly about Asian values, especially when they claim that Asian values mean that the state is above the individual, or insist that Asian values should replace both the respect for individual freedoms and rights and the necessity of building democracy in Asia, then we know that they are harbouring hidden intentions. . . . The invention of Asian values has provided those who would resist liberalism, democratic government, and human rights with the newest of ancient weapons, a weapon which has now been used to suppress internal critics and to incite fiercely anti-Western nationalism. . . . According to the views of some of East Asia's leaders, Asia's history and traditions preclude any need for democracy. Then why do so many people in so many Asian countries struggle and shed blood for democracy and human rights, and why are more and more Asian countries moving in the direction of democracy? From this point of view, it seems that the leaders of a few Asian countries have completely different values from Asian people, even to the extent of being fundamentally in conflict. Thus, Asian values seem more like the values of a few Asian leaders who do not like human rights and democracy, rather than the values of the people of Asia.[62]

Chinese dissidents are, as could be expected, even more critical of the Chinese government's attempts to defend its human rights position and excuse human rights violations by referring to cultural values and national conditions. They, like the literary critic Liu Xiaobo, describe this as an expedient strategy by a government facing international criticism: "Having come under international pressure over the human rights issue, the Chinese government . . . justify [*sic*] its trampling of human rights on the grounds that China differs from the West in national conditions, tradition, and human rights standards, and condemn the West for its hegemonism."[63] Wei Jingsheng concurs that the notion that different standards of human rights apply to different countries and cultural traditions is a dangerous fallacy used by authoritarian governments as an excuse to ·violate and disregard human rights.[64]

THE ORIENTALISM OF OCCIDENTALISM

It can be helpful to relate the Asian values debate to Edward Said's discourse on Orientalism. According to Said, Westerners have described the Orient as a homogeneous entity in a very stereotypical and negative fashion. Even though advocacy of cultural relativism and Asian values are generally motivated by respect for other cultures, they often tend to end up in very elitist, if not to say Orientalist, notions that human rights as advocated in the West are inappropriate and irrelevant for other societies, as well as in utter disrespect of those who are at odds with the cultural mainstream and/or power holders in their own societies. The notion that human rights are good for the West, or that certain human rights are only good for the West but not for Asia, is quite Orientalist in character, despite the fact that it is now put forward by Asian people themselves. But, as Liu Juning also argues above, it should be remembered that it is actually the power holders who put forward an Orientalist view of an unchanging Asia, where the idea of human rights is foreign and inappropriate. Their Orientalism should be seen as a manifestation of a repressive strategy and defense of the status quo. It is a manifestation of an elitist and paternalistic view according to which ordinary people cannot handle freedom and are not mature enough for human rights and democracy.

In this new Orientalism put forward by the advocates of Asian values, Asia, although still described as a homogeneous entity, is instead given positive characteristics, such as a commitment to the common good, duty fulfillment, reverence of authority, stability and order, economic vitality, and so on. Howard has described it as a "right-side-up" Orientalism, which does not criticize but rather idealizes the Orient.[65] The other side of this Orientalism, is that the West (the Occident) is nowadays demonized as Asia's "Other," and labeled with negative and stereotypical characteristics such as rampant individualism, lack of public morale, materialism, the breakdown of civil society, and economic stagnation.[66] The ills of the West are furthermore blamed on its excessive rights talk. It is therefore quite appropriate to speak about the emergence of Occidentalism in the human rights debate.

Chen Xiaomei has studied the use of an Occidentalist discourse in contemporary Chinese politics, and although she does not discuss human rights and the Asian values debate, her discussion is very helpful in understanding that particular debate.[67] Chen identifies two different strands of Occidentalism in contemporary China, one an official version that uses representations of the West to justify political repression at home, and the other an antiofficial version that serves as a counterdiscourse and uses the Western Other as a positive image in the fight against domestic oppression. It is the official Occidentalist discourse that is characteristic of the Asian values debate and the Chinese official position on human rights. The West is described in very negative terms as focusing on individual rights to the detriment of the collective and as violating economic and social rights.[68] The Occidentalist counterdiscourse, on the other hand, has been characteristic of much of the Chinese debates on human rights throughout the twentieth century. When Zou Rong and Chen Duxiu in the early twentieth century praised the West and the concept of human rights in no uncertain terms, their Occidentalism had a liberating effect and implied a critique of their own government. Later advocates of human rights, for example, during the democracy movement of 1978–79, have also hailed the West as a paragon of civilization. For Chinese activists it has been expedient to praise the West for respecting human rights when criticizing human rights violations at home.

CONCLUSION

Although I am not averse to trying to seek the cultural legitimacy of human rights within the Confucian tradition, which some scholars have attempted to do, I feel that this approach is a little off the mark for the majority of Chinese people today. It seems very roundabout to try to anchor human rights talk in Confucianism, as this would require a revival of Confucianism in order to promote human rights.[69] Confucianism, moreover, is not the only cultural tradition in China, and there are other possible ways of enhancing the cultural legitimacy of human rights. It is even possible that the Chinese authorities' own changing views on human rights, from a total rejection to a qualified acceptance, might open the way for a cultural legitimacy of sorts. In any case, as I hope to show in this work, the Chinese people have been so successful in relating the human rights concept to their own political problems that the issue of cultural compatibility could be laid safely to rest.

By way of anticipating the discussion later in the book, I would like to point out that most Chinese have responded directly to the Western concept of human rights instead of drawing on their own indigenous tradition and splicing human rights ideas onto it. This holds true of both the discussions in the beginning of the twentieth century and of the contemporary debate. Few contemporary Chinese scholars have attempted to relate their discussions on human rights to Confucian values, with exceptions such as Xia Yong, Du Gangjian, and Song Gang.[70] No Chinese dissident has yet attempted such an approach. In my opinion it is difficult to see any enduring or overwhelming Confucian influences on the contemporary Chinese human rights discourse, and even less to imagine the development of a viable conception of "human rights with Confucian characteristics." This is in sharp contrast to, for example, the Islamic world in which there have been numerous and profound attempts to establish the Islamic legitimacy of human rights ideas.[71] Since Islam and Buddhism, in contrast to Confucianism, are living religions, Buddhists, such as Aung San Suu Kyi and the Dalai Lama, and Muslim human rights scholars, such as Abdullahi Ahmed An-Na'im, have had more reason to relate their human rights demands to traditional concepts and ideas.

Although PRC spokespeople since the early 1990s often have referred to Chinese history and culture when claiming that the Chinese understanding of human rights differs from that of the West, this has been done in a very general and sweeping way without clearly explaining which cultural values are being referred to. In the official discourse more attention is being paid to economic than to cultural arguments, and there have as yet been no attempts to ground human rights discourse in indigenous terms. The new attention to Confucianism and criticism of certain human rights as being foreign to the Chinese tradition is more correctly understood as a rhetorical device and attempt to fill an ideological vacuum than as a genuine or all-out commitment to Confucian values. It should furthermore be noted that the Chinese regime focuses more on the authoritarian aspects of Confucianism, that is, its respect for authority, order, and stability, than its more humanistic and liberal aspects, which are the aspects to which Western scholars are attracted.[72] The Confucianism that these scholars want to see revived is thus very different from that which is praised and practiced by the Chinese and Singaporean authorities. It should also be noted that prior to the early 1990s, to the extent that the Chinese authorities affirmed human rights at all, they tended to put the blame on feudalism (another and more negative code word for the Chinese tradition) for any remaining human rights problems in Chinese society. And references to feudalism continue to play an important role in the CCP's political rhetoric when trying to explain practices such female infanticide, sale of women and children, and belief in Falun Gong or other religious or *qigong* groups.

The CCP exhibits a very ambivalent attitude to Chinese culture. On the one hand, it takes pride in China's alleged five thousand years of history, while, on the other hand, it regards so-called feudal practices and traditional beliefs as a cause of embarrassment and something to be discarded. To differentiate between cultural values and also want to preserve some while disregarding others of course makes perfect sense if the Chinese authorities only would be more clear and consistent on this issue. In order to make their cultural arguments more tenable they would have to let people decide for themselves which cultural values and traditional practices are of value and worth keeping.

If it was only a question of refuting all ideas originating in the West, the regime would have a hard time defending its socialist ideology. Although official China no longer dismisses human rights as a bourgeois slogan, its human rights rhetoric continues to be based on Marxism (another Western idea) rather than traditional values. It should also be pointed out that in the 1940s the CCP criticized the GMD for violating freedom of speech and other human rights, and obviously did not hesitate to make good use of a supposedly Western concept.

Cultural arguments and attempts to ground human rights in traditional language should not be accepted at face value; the political context of human rights debates always has to be kept in mind and analyzed. The GMD's position on human rights provides us with another telling illustration of why one should be cautious when those in power make use of cultural arguments or refer to cultural distinctiveness. In the 1940s, after having initially dismissed human rights as foreign and inappropriate to China, the GMD began to subscribe to the idea internationally, although still violating human rights at home. At this point its spokespeople consciously drew upon and sought parallels between the concept of human rights and Confucian values. Although this position could have reflected a genuine belief on the part of some of the individuals concerned, it cannot be denied that it also must have been influenced by the political considerations at the time. Toward the late 1970s, as the GMD was alerted to the new importance of human rights issues in international politics, it once again attempted to relate human rights to Confucian values. Here it should be noted that the GMD, since at least the 1930s, has seen itself as a defender of traditional Chinese values, in contrast to the CCP, which came to power through repudiating those very values; this also explains why the GMD has been more inclined than the CCP to refer to Confucian values in its human rights rhetoric. This being said, however, it should be noted that former president Lee Teng-hui in the 1990s distanced himself from other government heads in the Asian region when he criticized the idea of Asian values and supported the universality of human rights and democracy.

The fact that Chinese people generally have not tried to ground human rights in or relate them to traditional terms may be regarded as a problem, as the uncritical acceptance or imposition of a foreign concept. One could therefore argue that human rights, as a result, inevitably would experience difficulties in receiving cultural legitimacy and ultimately become domesticated.[73] To advocate human rights has, not surprisingly, also led to accusations of being a tool of the West. Wei Jingsheng and other advocates of human rights in the 1978–79 Democracy Wall Movement were thus often accused of being "the lackeys of the Americans" due to their invocation of human rights. Writing from prison in 1991, Wei still felt compelled to refute the government's accusation that he had been "incited or instigated by 'human rights diplomacy employed by hostile countries or hostile forces.'"[74] The CCP leveled the same kind of charges against the 1989 demonstrators.

Some Western scholars, arguing along somewhat similar lines as the Chinese government, have advanced the view that advocacy of human rights by non-Westerners is a sign of Westernization and therefore not authentic.[75] Such a dismissal is insulting to those in the Third World who are struggling for human rights, not as a result of alienation from their own culture and society but as a way to defend and protect it. As the Burmese democracy activist Aung San Suu Kyi so eloquently puts it:

It is a puzzlement to the Burmese how concepts which recognise the inherent dignity and the equal and inalienable rights of human beings, which accept that all men are endowed with reason and conscience and which recommend a universal spirit of brotherhood, can be inimical to indigenous values. It is also difficult for them to understand how any of the rights contained in the thirty articles of the Universal Declaration of Human Rights can be seen as anything but wholesome and good. That the declaration was not drawn up in Burma by the Burmese seems an inadequate reason, to say the least, for rejecting it, especially as Burma was one of the nations which voted for its adoption in December 1948. If ideas and beliefs are to be denied validity outside the geographical and cultural bounds of their origin, Buddhism would be confined to north India, Christianity to a narrow tract in the Middle East and Islam to Arabia. The proposition that the Burmese are not fit to enjoy as many rights and privileges as the citizens of democratic countries is insulting.[76]

I have not set for myself the task of providing a cultural legitimacy for human rights in China, but because I focus on the internal discourse on human rights, my study may be regarded as some kind of contribution toward that end. Some of the questions pertaining to cultural legitimacy that I pose are: do those discussing human rights feel that human rights are compatible with the Chinese culture; do they believe that human rights are realizable in China; which, if any, elements of the Chinese culture do they reject as harmful to the realization of human rights; and which human rights do they regard as the most useful and important? Needless to say, different individuals have expressed widely different and even contradictory views on these issues. In other words, there is no Chinese culture that either rejects or accepts human rights, but rather people of differing gender, age, and political conviction who adopt or invoke human rights in order to protect their own needs and interests.

NOTES

1. Cultural relativism and human rights has been discussed by many writers. See Renteln (1990), Donnelly (1989), Tesón (1992), and Booth (1999).
2. For a critique of the view that the universality of human rights is nothing but an imposition of Western values, see Booth (1999).
3. Booth (1999) for his part argues that "cultural relativism is the parent of ethical relativism," p. 50
4. Wilson (1997), p. 9.
5. For a useful volume on local human rights struggles, see Wilson (1997).
6. For an anthropological study of human rights as a cultural practice in Botswana, see Preis (1996).
7. See the discussion in Booth (1999), pp. 55–58.
8. For two examples, see Pollis (1992), p. 146; and Hsiung (1986), p. vii.
9. Donnelly (1989) in the end opts for a "weak cultural relativist" position, according to which deviations from universal human rights standards are permissible at the level of form.

10. Pollis and Schwab (1979).
11. Pollis (1996), p. 320.
12. Pollis (2000).
13. Pollis (2000), and Bell, Nathan, and Peleg (2001)
14. Bell, Nathan, and Peleg (2001), p. 4.
15. See Wilson (1997), Pollis and Schwab (2000), and Bell, Nathan, and Peleg (2001).
16. Quoted in Howard (1995a), p. 87.
17. On the end-of-history thesis, see Fukuyama (1992).
18. Paltiel (1997), p. 25. Compare Aung (1991), quoted below.
19. Such a view is evident in Müller (1997), Weatherley (1999), and Peerenboom (1998).
20. Kent (1993), pp. 30–31. See also Henkin (1986), p. 39.
21. Ames (1997) however seems to imply that "Chineseness" and Confucianism are inseparable, p. 193.
22. This point has been vigorously argued by Wm. Theodore de Bary in many of his works; see (1986), (1988), and (1998). Whereas most scholars focus on the repository of ideas in classical Confucianism, de Bary has also discussed neo-Confucianism. He argues that the reform proposals of certain neo-Confucians are quite congenial to social and economic rights, and that the ideas of Huang Zongxi would be favorable to civil and political rights as well.
23. Lucian Pye is perhaps the scholar who has gone the furthest in attempting to explain the current politics in China by referring to tradition; see, in particular, Pye (1988). For a good overview of the political culture approach and its weaknesses, see Clausen (1995). Wasserstrom (1992) has also argued that culture is a much more fluid and less deterministic force than scholars such as Pye would have it to be.
24. For exponents of this view, see Mab Huang (1979), p. 63; Nathan (1986c), pp. 153–54; and Weatherley (1999).
25. Xia Yong (1992) compares ideas of benevolent government with the contemporary second and third generations of human rights, p. 80.
26. See von Senger (1993), p. 310, and chapter 10 of this book.
27. People were treated differently in Chinese law depending on their position and status in society. A father who murdered his son was consequently sentenced more lightly than a son who committed parricide; the latter crime being regarded as one of the ten abominations.
28. See in particular the volume edited by Wm. Theodore de Bary and Tu Weiming (1998).
29. Twiss (1998a), p. 38, and p. 45.
30. See, for example, Copper (1985), De Bary (1988), Du Gangjian and Song Gang (1995), Xia Yong (1992) and (1999), as well as most of the contributors to the book edited by de Bary and Tu Weiming (1998).
31. Ames (1988). But Ames also argues that the idea of human rights in many ways is "incompatible with Chinese social considerations." For a similar view of the role of rites, see De Bary (1988). And for a critique of their views, see Peerenboom (1998).
32. De Bary (1998), pp. 10–11. In this work, De Bary shows a new awareness of the limitation of the approach to search the classics and also seems to modify his own position on the similarities between Confucian ideas and human rights. Angle (2002) also criticizes the attempts to compare classical Confucianism with human rights ideas for equating Confucianism with the whole of Chinese tradition and for interpreting Confucian values and rights much too loosely.

33. Ames is positive to a cultural approach as an alternative to the official rhetoric on human rights but seems dismissive of attempts to pay attention to dissidents' alternative views on human rights. See Ames (1997), p. 190 n. 79. For dissidents' views, see chapter 11 of this book.

34. Paltiel (1998), p. 271.

35. In a recent work De Bary (1998) has, however, drawn attention to this problem.

36. Woo (1980), p. 116.

37. Ames (1988), pp. 212–13, and (1997), p. 203.

38. See, for example, Hsiung (1986), p. 25; Xia Yong (1992), pp. 190–91; and Ames (1997), p. 192.

39. See Rosemont (1988) and (1998).

40. But some communitarians have argued that in countries such as China their main concern would still be the struggle for rights rather than duties. See Etzioni (1995), p. 1.

41. Howard (1995b).

42. Müllerson (1997) sees the Cold War confrontation over human rights as related to a dispute over different development patterns (market versus planned economy, liberal democracy versus state totalitarianism), whereas today's North–South confrontation is between countries on different levels of development. Xin Chunying (1996) sees the North–South conflict over human rights as standing between rich and poor countries, whereas the conflict between Asia and the West is a conflict between different cultures.

43. For such a critique, see Liu Junning (1998).

44. See Bangkok Declaration, in *Our Voice* (1993), pp. 244–45.

45. Tan (1996), p. 3. Rodan and Hewison (1996) also dismiss the claim that it is culture alone that underlines recent debates between Asia and the West. Instead, they detect the "harnessing of cultural arguments to ideological and political ends" p. 33.

46. Kishore Mahbuubani writes about "the growing realisation of East Asians that their moment in history has come," and "The growing realisation of East Asians that they can do anything as well as, if not better than, other cultures has led to an explosion of confidence," (1995, p. 103). Xin Chunying (1996) and Luo Yanhua (1997) also relate the rise of Asian values to the region's economic success.

47. In the case of China, see for example, "Our Delegate Strongly Refutes the Groundless Attack on China's Human Rights Situation Made by the Vice-Premier of the Netherlands," RMRB, March 14, 1997. See also the statement of the Chinese ambassador, Wu Jianmin, April 15, 1997, before the vote on the draft resolution in the Human Rights Commission. "Certain Western politicians have a bad habit—they have the propensity to lecture developing countries and make prescriptions for them." Statement issued by the permanent mission of the People's Republic of China in Geneva. See also Luo Yanhua (1997), p. 326.

48. See State Council (1991).

49. There is a wealth of works on the topic of Asian values but thus far no really good historical overviews of the debate. For recent works, see De Bary (1998), Bauer and Bell (1999), van Ness (1999), Bruun and Jacobsen (2000), and Bell, Nathan, and Peleg (2001).

50. For a Chinese discussion and analysis of Asian values, see Luo Yanhua (1997), and Xin Chunying (1996) and (1999).

51. On Asia's diversity, see Emmerson (1995), Ghai (1995), and Li Shenzhi (1995).

52. Bangkok NGO Declaration on Human Rights, in *Our Voice* (1993), p. 199.

53. For the charter, see the Asian Human Rights Commission Web site, <www.ahrchk.net>, 2001 [accessed 8 August 2001].

54. Kim (1994), p. 194.
55. See, for example, Kausikan (1993).
56. The statement is reprinted in Tang (1995), p. 214.
57. For an example of a Third World perspective rather than an Asian perspective on human rights, see Liu Nanlai (1994).
58. For a more official view, see "Commenting on the South-North Dispute over Human Rights," RMRB, March 17, 1997. Very few academic works have been devoted to the subject of Asian values. Xin Chunying has written some more descriptive pieces without endorsing the idea herself; see Xin Chunying (1996) and (1999), whereas Luo Yanhua (1997) and (1998) is more positive.
59. For two critical articles, see Li Shenzhi (1995) and Li Yonghui (1995).
60. See Xin Chunying (1999), p. 175.
61. Liu Junning (1998).
62. Liu Junning (1998). Translated in Angle and Svensson (2001), p. 410, p. 412.
63. Liu Xiaobo (1995), p. 18.
64. Wei Jingsheng (1997), pp. 166–68.
65. Howard (1995b), p. 69.
66. Roy makes the observation that Asia has "turned the tables" by making the West its Other, (1994), p. 232.
67. Chen Xiaomei (1995). A Chinese scholar, Li Yonghui (1995), has, however, tried to relate the debate on Asian values to an emerging Occidentalism. Li points out the ironic fact that whereas Westerners now have come to reject the earlier generalizations of Asia characteristic of the Orientalist discourse, Asians themselves have begun a similar endeavor; although they have replaced the earlier negative stereotypes of Asia with more positive ones of stability, vitality, and economic growth. Li makes the observation that emergent Occidentalism simplifies and distorts reality in the same way as Orientalism. Like Chen, Li argues that this takes the form of either vilifying or embellishing the Occident.
68. Such rhetoric is obvious in the Chinese reactions to the U.S. State Department's annual reports on human rights. For an example, see RMRB, March 2, 1999.
69. Chan (1999), in contrast, believes that Confucianism could fill the ideological vacuum left by Marxism, p. 213.
70. Xia Yong (1992) and Du Gangjian and Song Gang (1995).
71. See An-Na'im (1995).
72. This point is mentioned by De Bary in De Bary and Tu Weiming (1998), p. 4; as well as by Peerenboom (1998), pp. 252–53; and Chan (1999), p. 214.
73. He Zhaowu has argued that the reason why the idea of human rights did not take root in China was because it had not become sinicized, see He (1990), p. 18. The original article was published in Chinese in 1987.
74. Wei Jingsheng (1997), p. 164.
75. Pollis and Schwab (1979), p. 12. There is no hint of such an accusation in their most recent book, which reveals how much has changed in the field since then. See Pollis and Schwab (2000).
76. Aung (1991), p. 175.

Chapter Four

China and the Introduction
of Western Thought

THE INTELLECTUAL SETTING

During the late Qing dynasty knowledge of the West was encouraged and spread through different methods. One important source of information was newspapers and magazines, at first mostly established and edited by foreigners, usually missionaries.[1] These missionary writings, apart from focusing on religious affairs, also provided information on the West and its political institutions. They caught the attention of a number of Chinese officials whose interest in the West was provoked by the growing military threat it posed to China. Lin Zexu, the official appointed by the Qing court to handle the sensitive issue of the opium trade, was particularly active and farsighted in seeking information about the West, including commissioning the translation of Western works. The materials he collected were later used by Wei Yuan in his *Haiguo tuzhi* (Maps and Documents on Maritime Countries), published in 1844, the first significant work on the West to come out in China.[2]

The humiliating defeats in the two opium wars forced Chinese literati to reevaluate their view of the West and made them come to appreciate the need for more information about it. To this end, institutions such as the Interpreters' College and Jiangnan Arsenal were set up in the 1860s to provide for the translation and publication of Western works.[3] The majority of these translations were devoted to the natural sciences and to technical subjects, but given the Chinese interest in and need to understand international law, many works were also translated in this field. By the 1890s, the Chinese literati themselves began to run newspapers and magazines on a larger scale and also came to dominate translation work. Shanghai, which had been an early center for Western publishing activities, now also became a center for these indigenous publication activities. Progressive

Chinese individuals chose the city to establish publishing houses, newspapers, and magazines. The magazines *Shiwu bao* (founded in 1896) and *Shibao* (founded in 1904) were set up by reformers to introduce and spread new ideas.[4] These publications greatly influenced the political scene and public debate during the late Qing.

After the failure of the 1898 reform movement, which forced many progressive Chinese into exile, Japan became a new center for publishing and translation activities.[5] *Qingyi bao* (founded in 1898) and *Xinmin congbao* (founded in 1902) were the most important magazines associated with the reformers. When the revolutionaries in 1905 founded their mouthpiece, *Minbao*, heated debates took place on the pages of *Xinmin congbao* and *Minbao*. Other magazines, often with very short life spans, also vied for the readers' interest. Magazines such as *Yishu huibian*, and its successor *Zhengfa xuebao*, *Kaizhi lu*, *Guomin bao*, *Zhejiang chao*, *Jiangsu*, and *Hubei xuesheng jie*, to mention but a few, all carried articles on political events, new ideas, as well as translations of Western works.[6] These magazines were smuggled into China and avidly read and circulated among students and other progressive individuals. By this time many classical works in Western political thought had also begun to be translated into Chinese. A central figure in this endeavor was Yan Fu, who translated works by John Stuart Mill, Adam Smith, Aldous Huxley, Herbert Spencer, and Baron de Montesquieu, among others.[7]

The majority of the works translated from Japanese belonged to the field of social and political sciences.[8] It is interesting to note that many of these works were actually retranslations of Western works, so the Chinese understanding of the West took a roundabout route through Japan. After 1911 Japan's importance as a transmitter and mediator of Western thought diminished. As the Chinese people's own knowledge of Western languages improved, in many cases through prolonged years of study in the West, they were themselves able to make direct translations of Western works into Chinese.

It is no coincidence that demands for human rights would first be raised by individuals who found themselves abroad, partly released from the bonds of tradition and family, and exposed to new ideas and political institutions. These, at times, unsettling and disturbing experiences provided fertile ground for hitherto unheard of reflections on the relationship between the individual person and the state. The threat from the West in addition brought about intense soul-searching and the introduction of new political concepts, such as the nation–state, citizenship, democracy, and human rights. Their experiences in a rapidly changing social and political environment forced a whole generation of Chinese young people to redefine their roles as scholars and to acquire new identities as citizens (*guomin*) of a Chinese nation.[9] Student radicalism now became a feature of the Chinese political scene, manifesting itself both in political activism, such as the plotting of revolts to overthrow the Qing, and more intellectual endeavors, such as the publishing of magazines and translations of Western works.[10]

Within a very short time span, Chinese intellectuals were introduced to a whole range of political ideas that had developed over several centuries in the West.[11] They often encountered ideas from the nineteenth century at the same time as, and sometimes even before, ideas from the eighteenth century. They thus came across the concept of natural rights at the same time as, or after, ideas of democracy and nationalism, whereas in the West the concept of natural rights had preceded the latter. Many were introduced to nineteenth-century German statism, nationalism, social Darwinism, and the general attack on natural rights before being introduced to the concept itself. Furthermore, they encountered it at a time when it had lost much of its earlier attraction and was under attack in the West. Chinese students, in addition, went to Japan at a time when the earlier, more liberal intellectual climate of the Meiji period had given way to more conservative and imperialist trends of thought. Under such circumstances it was inevitable that the concept of natural rights could be rejected solely because it was regarded as outmoded, already abandoned both in the West and Japan. Liang Qichao, for example, seems to have been convinced that natural rights was an outmoded concept, already refuted by Darwinism.[12]

The discrepancy between the concept of natural rights and the actual behavior of the West, which aggressively and without consideration of the Chinese people's rights and freedoms was encroaching upon their territory, also served to make some of them highly skeptical of the concept. It is no wonder then that social Darwinism could seem to better explain the politics of the Western powers. The idea of might as right and rights of the strongest, which were then in vogue in the West and Japan, was regarded by some Chinese writers as holding more explanatory force in a world where the very survival of the Chinese nation was at risk because of foreign aggression, than the old concept of natural or human rights did.[13]

Despite all these negative circumstances, many Chinese writers were nonetheless very attracted to the idea of human rights and ready to embrace it. The concept of human rights was not imposed on China by the West. If anything, it must be admitted that by and large it had fallen out of favor with the major schools of thought in the West and that Western governments were hardly promoting human rights in their imperialistic endeavors. Indeed, the concept of human rights was embraced by Chinese writers as useful in their struggle to save China, although its primary target was the Chinese government. In contrast to the situation in the West in the early twentieth century, where it often was rejected, the concept of human rights could at times play a much greater role in Chinese political discourse because of its association with

the West, which to Chinese intellectuals symbolized for a long time everything
that was modern, progressive, and civilized. The concept of human rights was
attractive to Chinese intellectuals for some of the same reasons it had been
popular in the West. Chinese people were also faced with a despotic regime,
although the Chinese context was different from that of the West in that they
were also faced with foreign aggression and a very real and immediate threat
to national survival. It was therefore not only a question of securing respect for
individual rights; a more pressing concern throughout the pre-1949 period was
to safeguard national rights to sovereignty and natural resources. In the Chinese context, the importance placed on rights stemmed from a belief that
rights-bearing and rights-conscious citizens were needed in order for China to
be able to withstand foreign encroachment and ensure national freedom and
independence.

Mary Rankin has identified three dominant political themes among the revolutionary radicals during the period 1902–11.[14] The first is nationalism, which
in the beginning was anti-Manchu in character, only later to become more
anti-imperialistic. The second theme is individualism, interpreted as the personal need to escape from tradition and family, a theme that became stronger
during the May Fourth Movement. The third theme, which embraced the
other two, is modernization and change. This theme was the oldest of the three,
having been advocated to some extent already by some individuals in the
1860s, although their understanding of modernization differed considerably
from that of the reformers and revolutionaries in the early twentieth century.[15]
Human rights discourse in its turn, as we will see, was informed and shaped by
all three of these themes or concerns.

Where its advocates hailed human rights as a modern and progressive idea,
those opposing the idea saw it as already outmoded and passé. The belief in a
universal modernity was thus something that united advocates and opponents
of human rights alike. Given China's threatened position, Chinese intellectuals
searched for ideas and methods that could help save the nation. Among the
ideas that elicited the most interest at the turn of the century were those of nationalism and social Darwinism. As James Reeve Pusey has convincingly
shown, Darwinism seemed to explain the current dismal state of affairs and
show a way out, because it legitimized violent change and gave some hope for
the future if only the Chinese would become "fit."[16] If only the Chinese people could develop a feeling of nationalism, China would be able to stand up
and survive in the struggle among nations, or so it was believed. In this context, respect for individual rights and the implementation of broader political
participation could help unleash the energy of the citizenry to the benefit of
the nation. The fact that people in the West had struggled for their rights and
forced governments to protect them, was believed to help explain the strength

of the West. The concept of human rights and the struggle for rights were therefore advocated as a helpful antidote to the Chinese people's lethargy. In the minds of the advocates of human rights, there was a strong linkage and interdependence between nationalism and human rights. But human rights, such as freedom of speech and publication, were also sought for the individual in the belief that they would benefit personal development. This individualistic concern, however, which would come to the fore during May Fourth, was tempered by the strong social and nationalistic orientation of the rights discourse in the early twentieth century.

The problem with trying to analyze the early Chinese writings on human rights is that these essays were often written in a hurry and were, therefore, brief, superficial, and not always very rigorous in character. One never knows for sure whether things the author left unsaid or half-said were due to lack of time, were a willful exclusion, the result of an eclectic and idiosyncratic interpretation, or simply because of a lack of understanding of the original concept. As Michael Gasster has noted so perceptively regarding Wang Jingwei and others: "There is no sure way to ascertain when a man's understanding is limited and when his seeming lack of understanding is rather to be explained either by his attempt to modify other men's ideas and adapt them to different conditions and purposes or by an arbitrary but deliberate eclecticism that simply ignores the problem of faithfulness to the inner consistency and meaning of the original ideas."[17] Another reason writings on human rights are often weak on philosophical stringency, is that human rights language is used as a weapon in political struggles. Political rhetoric rather than philosophical or logical stringency is therefore more important to the writer and his audience. In view of the urgency these Chinese writers felt, it is no wonder that their writings were often long on emotional fervor but short on deeper analysis. Thus, the political context of the texts needs to be kept in mind when studying Chinese human rights discourse.

TRANSLATION AND THE
CREATION OF A NEW VOCABULARY

In order to study the concept of human rights in China, one has to examine how the concept was introduced there, and, consequently, how it was rendered into the Chinese language. In the late nineteenth and early twentieth centuries, China saw rapid conceptual and political changes that mutually influenced each other. New modes of thought on self and society were reflected in the creation of a new vocabulary. Some of these new words and concepts have indigenous roots in the Confucian political discourse, whereas others were neologisms imported from Japan or created by Chinese scholars themselves. The process whereby new words and concepts was created and adopted is extremely complex and still little understood.

Influenced by the work of Said, Lydia H. Liu has discussed the problems that arise when a theory or a concept not only travels across space and time but also from one language to another.[18] Said described his concept of a traveling theory in the following way:

> First, there is the point of origin, or what seems like one, a set of initial circumstances in which the idea came to birth or entered discourse. Second, there is a distance transversed, a passage through the pressure of various contexts as the idea moves from an earlier point to another time and place where it will come into a new prominence. Third, there is a set of conditions—call them conditions of acceptance or, as an inevitable part of acceptance, resistances—which then confronts the transplanted theory or idea, making possible its introduction or toleration, however alien it might appear to be. Fourth, the now full (or partly) accommodated (or incorporated) idea is to some extent transformed by its new uses, its new position in a new time and place.[19]

Liu has, however, criticized Said's concept of traveling theory for having abandoned the traveling aspect and, in particular, for omitting the problem of the vehicle of translation, that is, in which language and for what audience does the translation take place. She herself talks about "translingual practice," which she says allows us to understand the process through which concepts are translated, adapted, and appropriated in another language.

> Broadly defined, the study of translingual practice examines the process by which new words, meanings, discourses, and modes of representation arise, circulate, and acquire legitimacy within the host language due to, or in spite of, the latter's contact/collision with the guest language. Meanings, therefore, are not so much "transformed" when concepts pass from the guest language to the host language as invented within the local environment of the latter.[20]

Liu prefers to talk of translation from a guest language into a host language, rather than using the more conventional terms of source language and target language—a choice that is motivated by her emphasis on the active role played by Chinese writers and translators themselves in "inviting, selecting, combining, and reinventing words and texts from the guest language," and then determining the meaning and usefulness of these words and texts for their own needs and concerns. Liu thus focuses on how a concept is taken up in a new linguistic and political environment, taking into account the struggles over meaning that surround the domestication of new concepts.[21] This approach to translation and introduction of new concepts highlights the complex interaction between a process of discovering and interpreting foreign ideas, on the one hand, and building upon and relating them to native terms and domestic political concerns, on the other hand. It also bears some resemblance to the approach of conceptual historians, who, although they don't focus so much on the question of translation, nevertheless also draw attention to political and linguistic contestations over political concepts.

As already discussed in previous chapters, human rights is very much an evolving and contested concept. One could say that the concept of human rights already had been doing some considerable traveling both in time and space within the West, for example, from Europe to America and back, before it traveled to Asia. Chinese intellectuals have hence encountered different and conflicting conceptions of rights and human rights over the years. Even more important in our case, early on they also encountered ideas refuting or contesting the very concept of human rights. The introduction of Western political concepts, as already mentioned above, did not follow the temporal sequence of their evolution in the West: more recent concepts were introduced in China at the same time, or sometimes even before earlier ones. The concept of human rights, furthermore, did not travel on its own to China, but was accompanied by other concepts, such as democracy and nationalism among others, which informed its understanding. It also arrived with what one today would call strange bedfellows, such as social Darwinism. Furthermore, the concept did not travel to China just once and for all; it made the trip several times over the years under different circumstances, taking different routes and using different vehicles.

The process whereby new political concepts were rendered into Chinese is extremely complex and was in many cases influenced by choices already made in Japan. In the 1860s, however, China had led the way in translating Western works that were then translated by the Japanese, who thus took over words Chinese and Western writers had already coined. By the 1890s this trend was reversed. To complicate matters further, many of the perceived Japanese loan words introduced at the time had actually first been coined in Chinese.[22] Some of these originally Chinese inventions did not become widespread in China until they were reintroduced from Japan in the 1890s and early 1900s. Beginning in the 1870s the Japanese had been particularly active in studying and translating Western works, creating a new political vocabulary in the process. Japanese scholars used Chinese characters (*kanji*) to translate these new Western terms, creating neologisms.[23] Many words for Western concepts now widely used in China, such as society (*shehui*), economics (*jingji*), and human rights (*tianfu renquan*), were first coined in Japan and later introduced in China.[24]

In the beginning, different coinages could compete with each other as individual translators and scholars launched their own coinages for new words and

concepts. But gradually a consensus would emerge regarding the best translation; the other coinages were abandoned and the survivor became fixed in the
language and the general consciousness. This process of linguistic "survival of
the fittest" is seldom very transparent or clear. The eventual choice was not
necessarily because of linguistic or logical superiority but it was more often a
case of happenstance. It might have been that the coinage happened to be the
first around or that it had the backing of scholars with more influence, but
sometimes the outcome seems to have been purely arbitrary.

The character-compound still used today to translate "rights" (*kenri* in
Japanese and *quanli* in Chinese) was first coined in China. The compound was
first used by W. A. P. Martin in his 1864 translation of Henry Wheaton's *Elements of International Law*. It continued to be used in texts on international law
after that date but did not become firmly anchored in Chinese political discourse until the late 1890s under Japanese influence. Martin's translation of
Wheaton's work was translated into Japanese in 1865, and *kenri* was used by
Kato Hiroyuki as early as 1868. But before *kenri* became widely accepted in
Japan as the most appropriate rendering of the word "rights," other compounds
were also used and competed with each other.[25] During the 1870s, several
Japanese scholars who wrote in the liberal magazine *Meiroku zasshi* thus opted
to combine the first character of the Martin gloss with a homophone to the
second character, which has the more positive connotation of "ethical principles."[26] Fukuzawa Yukichi used several different character-compounds over the
years, including this second coinage.[27] This well illustrates how individual writers at first could waver on the most appropriate way to translate a term or a
concept, a process which no doubt both reflected the evolving nature of their
own understanding of the concept in question, as well as the influence of other
translations in vogue.

In 1887, the Japanese legal scholar Mitsukuri Rinsho, reflecting on the
process of translation, gave the following account of how difficult it had been
for him in the 1860s to translate Western works and find appropriate terms:

> There were, in fact, many parts which I didn't understand. And even when I did un-
> derstand, I was at [a] loss because there were no words to translate the terms. The
> words rights (*kenri*) and obligation (*gimu*)—today you use the words with ease—but
> it was a great strain for me to use them in translation. I didn't claim to have invented
> anything, however, so I wasn't able to get a patent. . . . Because the words *raito* (right)
> and *oburigeshyon* (obligation) were translated as *kenri gimu* in the Chinese version of
> International Law [i.e., Martin's translation] I took them, but I wasn't stealing
> anything.[28]

Thus, the compound used by Martin eventually won out in both Japan and
China. The Martin compound is found in the writings of Kang Youwei and

Liang Qichao in the late 1890s although Liang also briefly used the second homophone compound coined by the Japanese, as well as the single *quan*.

The character-compound *tianfu renquan* (literally, heaven-endowed human rights) was introduced in China from Japan, where scholars such as Kato Hiroyuki and others in the 1870s had been among the first to use it to connote natural rights. The first gloss of natural rights in Chinese, however, might have been *shiren ziran zhi quan* (literally, natural rights of humans), which Martin used in his translation of Wheaton's work.[29] And in the first Japanese translation of the French Declaration of the Rights of Man, which appeared in the magazine *Somo zasshi* in 1876, natural rights was translated as *tenzen no kengi* (*tianran zhi quanyi* in Chinese).[30] *Tianfu renquan* seems to have become fairly well established in the Chinese political lexicon at the turn of the twentieth century, judging by the various magazines published in Japan by Chinese students. Early usages appeared in *Qingyi bao* around 1899.[31] *Tianfu renquan* was, however, not the only word used to connote natural rights in the early twentieth century; other words were used interchangeably. Apart from *tianfu renquan* and *tianfu zhi quanli*, the Chinese also frequently used the words *tianran zhi quanli* and *ziran zhi quan/li*. Although *ziran zhi quan* was used quite often during the first decade of the twentieth century, it never entered Chinese people's consciousness to the same extent as did *tianfu renquan* and *renquan*. But *ziran quanli* seems to have made something of a comeback in the 1990s, as it is now preferred over *tianfu renquan* to connote natural rights.[32] The single compound *renquan* (human rights) was also used at an early stage as a synonym for *tianfu renquan*. This is evident in the writings of Kato Hiroyuki, who in 1882 used both words interchangeably in the same work, and of Liang Qichao, who in 1899 talked about *renquan* and in 1902 opted for *tianfu renquan*.

In conceptual history it is important to study all words that overlap semantically with the concept under study. In the case of human rights this includes a study of words such as natural rights, inherent rights, inalienable rights, human rights, and the like. In the Chinese context, this would include, apart from those mentioned above, words such as *you yingxiang zhi quanli* (rights that one ought to enjoy) and *guyou zhi quanli* (innate rights), which all were used to designate human rights and therefore functioned as synonyms. In this context it is also of interest to see how these rights were defined and described. As will become obvious later in this book, Chinese writers have generally described human rights as sacred (*shensheng*), inherent (*sheng ju lai, guyou*), inalienable (*buke yirang, buke paoqi*), and inviolable *(buke duo, buke qinfan)*, which reveal that they were treasured as necessary for a worthy human existence.

Not surprisingly, the wordings and contexts suggest that Chinese thinkers in the beginning of the twentieth century did not differentiate between natural rights and human rights. I will therefore speak about natural rights and human rights interchangeably when discussing the early Chinese human rights dis-course. In this context it should also be remembered that in the West people still talked about natural rights, or the rights of man, rather than human rights. The latter term did not come into frequent use in the West until after the Sec-ond World War, as a result of changes in views on the basis and nature of hu-man rights. In China, people such as Luo Longji later would go to great lengths to differentiate between natural rights and human rights. Luo consciously opted to use *renquan* to translate the latter to underline their differences and fend off the critique directed against the idea of natural rights (*tianfu renquan*).

When studying the Chinese conception of human rights, many scholars have tended to singularly focus on an etymological reading of words such as *quanli* and *tianfu renquan*. They have ignored the fact that different words have been used to designate the concept of human rights, and, furthermore, have not paid sufficient attention to the semantic field and the context in which they appear. Some scholars have thus argued that since the Chinese (and Japanese) used character-compounds found in Chinese classical texts or devised neologisms based on classical Chinese, these new words and concepts also came to be imbued with classical connotations that overshadowed or even stood in contradiction to the concepts they were supposed to convey.[33] *Quanli* is composed of two characters, which in classical Chinese have the meaning of power (*quan*) and profits (*li*). This character-compound, following the classical Chinese understanding, would thus give *quanli* a connotation lacking in the Western concept of rights.[34] Because of the classical Chinese meanings of *quan* and *li*, some contemporary scholars have argued that the Chinese inevitably, even today, would associate rights with power and interests, rather than with justice and as something inherent in man.[35]

But whereas it is probably true that *quanli* at first could have been perceived as a rather awkward and strange word, and also carried classical overtones, it seems to have rapidly become domesticated and accepted, as the quote from Mitsukuri above indicates. Martin and his Chinese collaborator reveal similar feelings when in 1878 they described their choice of *quanli* to convey the meaning of "rights."

> There were times when we could not find a proper Chinese term to render the orig-inal expression, so our choice of words would seem less than satisfactory. Take the character *quan*, for example. In this book the word means not only the kind of power one has over others, but something every person is entitled to. Occasionally, we would add a word *li* [to form a compound], as, for example, in the expression *quanli* mean-ing the born "rights" of the plebeian, etc. At first encounter, these words and expres-sions may seem odd and unwieldy, but after seeing them repeatedly, you will come to realise that the translators have really made the best of necessity.[36]

In view of the contemporary skepticism surrounding the choice of *quanli* to translate rights, it is also interesting to note that already in 1903 some Chinese

writers were sensitive to possible misunderstandings and warned against identifying rights with power. An article in *Zhejiang chao* explaining new terms and
translations of Western terms argued that it was necessary to clearly define the
term *quanli* (rights) since it otherwise easily could be interpreted as *quanli*
(power) and *quanshi* (might).[37]

Many contemporary scholars have also found fault with the choice of *tianfu*
(literally, heaven-endowed) to describe the idea that rights are natural and inherent in man.[38] Other scholars have suggested that the idea of "heaven-endowed
rights" was drafted onto very Confucian ideas of the nature of man, as illustrated
by the choice of the compound *tianfu*, and that thus it was a case of a Confu-
cianization of human rights.[39] Those who see a strong Confucian influence in
the word *tianfu renquan* should, however, take note of the fact that many of the
Chinese writers who used *tianfu renquan* at the same time would also use other
words, such as *renquan*, *ziran zhi quan*, and *guyou zhi quanli*, which do not carry
the same Confucian connotations, without differentiating in their usage of them.

Although I believe that the shared humanistic quality of Confucianism and
human rights facilitated the acceptance of the latter, when we look more
closely at how the concept of human rights actually was understood and put
to use, it becomes obvious that it actually was used to attack the hierarchical
Confucian system. Wang Guangwu has also put forward the view that the concept of rights had a strong anti-Confucian connotation, being the opposite of
the Confucian virtues of humaneness and righteousness (*ren* and *yi*), and that
its appeal was associated with an attack on tradition.[40] Supporting such a view,
an anonymous author in 1903 contrasted rights (*quanli*) with rites (*li*), arguing
that the former should replace the latter.[41] Liang Qichao, for his part, held that
the idea of rights stood in stark contrast to the Confucian concept of *ren* (humaneness), but believed that the concept of *yi* (righteousness) could be seen as
an embryo of a concept of rights.[42] Some contemporary scholars, in contrast,
have instead argued that there is an affinity between Confucian ideas, such as
ren, and the concept of human rights.[43]

It has also been suggested that the idea of rights was difficult to grasp for
Chinese people, not only because the characters gave it a "wrong" connotation, but because Chinese thought has emphasized duties and not recognized rights claimed for oneself against others. While there was no word for
rights in traditional China, Wang Guangwu has argued that the idea of duties (*yiwu*) could better fit Confucian morality since it is a compound of the
central Confucian term *yi* (righteousness) and the word for task (*wu*), thus
giving the word a very Confucian connotation of doing what is right.[44] Be
that as it may, of more importance is the fact that *yiwu* in the early twentieth century was used in a very un-Confucian way. It was used by Chinese
writers to encourage a new civic consciousness and public morality among
their fellow Chinese. It is tempting to speculate, as Wang Guangwu does,

that the generally assumed emphasis on duties over rights among Chinese people has something to do with its Confucian appeal. But such an understanding is not borne out by closer study. As I will discuss in the next chapter, many Chinese writers, instead of extolling duties, have actually more lamented the fact that they have only shouldered duties but not enjoyed any rights.

The above views on the problem of classical connotations informing or determining, or, as some would have it, even complicating and distorting the understanding of rights and human rights are much too simplistic and static. They fail to take into account the changing political and cultural environment into which these new words and concepts were introduced, domesticated, and contested. The fact that the Chinese language had no clear equivalents to "rights" and "human rights" before the creation of the neologisms *quanli* and *renquan*, or that they at first might have had strong Confucian overtones, tells us nothing about their subsequent fate and history, or of their cultural and political legitimacy; and even less, of course, about their realization in society. The group of neologisms to which *quanli* and *tianfu renquan* belong should be kept in mind: they were classical expressions that were given radically new meanings. It is therefore not possible to simply or directly derive their meaning from the constituting classical counterparts. Randall Peerenboom and others could thus be said to be guilty of etymological fallacy, that is the fallacy of assuming that the original or classical meaning of a word (or a character) is identical to and determines its present-day meaning.[45] They ignore the fact that the meanings of words and concepts change over time under the influence of social and political developments. In the case of the Chinese language, it is of course also a mistake to assume that a word is nothing but the sum total of its constituting characters.[46] Instead of tracing the origin and classical meanings of characters and words, it is more crucial to study the semantic field and the context in which they appear and are brought to life in political argument.

The crucial test of how the concept of human rights was understood in the early twentieth century must be to study how Chinese writers de facto discussed and made use of it, rather than to dismiss a priori any understanding on the grounds of a problem of translation or a lack of a domestic tradition. The ability to appropriate new and foreign concepts and relate them to the political issues of one's own day should be used as a criteria for successful acceptance and accommodation. This process of course took time and differed between different generations of Chinese people. We can get a clue of how this happened by looking at how and when the new concept appeared in writing, and if the author only casually referred to it without bothering to explain it in detail. It can be argued that when a concept enters the language of political rhetoric it has already become a part of everyday language, sufficiently familiar and agreed upon to serve as a political slogan—whether empty or not. A later amusing example of such a casual familiarity appears in a domestic quarrel scene between husband and wife in Su Qing's popular semiautobiographical 1944 novel, *My Ten Years of Marriage*. In the novel the protagonist accuses her lawyer-husband of only caring about money and not about human rights (*renquan*); the latter, she blurts out, should be the concern of lawyers.[47]

At the risk of anticipating the more detailed discussion later in my study, some things also need to be said on the definition and understanding of the concept of *minquan* and its relationship to human rights. Political concepts are often best understood when put in contrast with other competing or radically opposing concepts. The understanding and conception of *minquan* has differed considerably over time and between different Chinese generations. *Minquan* became a prominent feature of the Chinese political discourse at an earlier stage than any of the words connoting human rights. It was coined in Japan and first used in China by Chinese diplomats familiar both with Japanese and Western political institutions. In the 1890s, reformers in China then picked up the language of *minquan* when advocating reform of its political institutions. In the beginning, *minquan* referred to people's political power, mainly the right to political participation, and was contrasted with the power of the ruler (*junquan*). It was advocated by early reformers such as Zheng Guanying, Wang Kangnian, Liang Qichao, and He Qi, among others, and criticized by Zhang Zhidong. Although men such as Liang Qichao held that the power of the ruler was too strong and people's power too weak in China, the latter was by no means regarded as threatening or standing in opposition to the former. It was only if the latter was developed that the former would be preserved. *Minquan* were thus believed to promote the understanding and trust between ruler and subjects; advocacy of *minquan*, in other words, did not imply an advocacy of democracy. *Minquan* were not something that was demanded from the ruler or regarded as innate. But already in the early twentieth century there was a trend toward linking *minquan* to the idea of constitutional rights and citizens' rights. Several Chinese writers began to define *minquan* as civil rights. In 1907, Shen Qichang, for example, divided rights into *zhengquan* (political rights) and *minquan* (civil rights); the latter were then further divided into positive rights and negative rights. Negative rights, which he also referred to as the rights of freedom (*ziyou quan*), included freedom of speech, freedom of belief, freedom of association, freedom of movement, and so on.[48]

In the 1920s, Sun Yat-sen dismissed the concept of *tianfu renquan* (human rights) as metaphysical and chose to speak about *minquan* (people's power or people's rights), which left the GMD with a legacy that basically saw *renquan* and *minquan* as different, if not outright incompatible concepts.[49] The differences between human rights and people's rights were much debated by the GMD and its critics in the 1920s and 1930s. Although some writers were rather vague, those probing the subject in more detail made quite clear distinctions. They usually tended to refer to people's rights as rights that belong to citizens, which were contingent upon citizenship and at times political affinity, whereas human rights were described as rights that belong to all people regardless of citizenship and political beliefs. And while the former were granted by the state, the latter were regarded as innate and belonging to man before the establishment of the state.

An article published in *The Eastern Miscellany* in 1948 can be used to further illustrate the general understanding of the differences between *renquan* and *minquan*.[50] The author, historian Qian Shifu, defined human rights (*renquan*) as "rights which one enjoys by virtue of one's humanity [*yi renlei de zige er yingxiang de quanli*]," whereas nationals' rights (*guomin quanli*) are rights one has as a national of a particular country, and citizen's rights (*gongmin quanli*) are rights one enjoys as a citizen. Human rights were also described as natural and innate rights. (Qian used the words *tiansheng de guyou quanli* and *tianfu de ziran quanli*.) Qian refuted the idea of human rights because it held that people enjoyed rights from birth and that these rights could not be restricted by the state. Instead, he favored the concept of people's rights (*minquan*), which he felt were similar to nationals' rights and could also embrace citizen's rights. Qian's understanding of people's rights showed a close affinity with both the GMD's and the CCP's view of rights as conditional on people's political allegiance and given by the state with the national interest in mind.

Some writers in the 1930s and 1940s, in contrast, used *minquan* and *renquan* interchangeably or as synonyms, with the result that the two concepts more or less converged. As an example of this, Cai Yuanpei seems to have used them more or less as synonyms when discussing the *Zhongguo minquan baozhang tongmeng*, an organization set up in 1932 to protect people's civil and political rights and freedoms. The organization, interestingly enough, took the English name, China League for the Protection of Civil Rights, which shows that *minquan* here were understood as civil rights. To underscore that *minquan* and *renquan* at times and by some people could be understood as belonging to the same semantic field, Zhou Enlai, in a commemorative speech on the death of Cai Yuanpei, referred to the organization as the China League for the Protection of Human Rights, thus by "mistake" using the word *renquan* instead of *minquan*. (The organization is discussed in more detail in chapter 8.)

THE INTRODUCTION AND TRANSLATION OF WORKS ON HUMAN RIGHTS

It is impossible to say who first used the word human rights or discussed the concept in China, but it is probably safe to conclude that it was not until after

1898 that human rights really entered the Chinese political lexicon.[51] In the 1890s, people such as Kang Youwei, although not explicitly using the word human rights, expressed the view that man was endowed with life by heaven.[52] They furthermore stressed that all men were equal and had a right to autonomy (*zizhu zhi quan*).[53] The rather terse phrases of these authors on this subject make it difficult to analyze their thinking in any depth. It seems certain, however, that their thinking was a blend of traditional ideas and new ideas spread through missionary writings.[54] The idea that people were endowed with life and a right to autonomy might be said to have constituted the dawn of the concept of human rights in China, even though the actual word was not yet in use. This conclusion is warranted by the fact that human rights were later defined as encompassing the right to self-autonomy. Be that as it may, since these scholars did not develop their ideas further, I will not attempt any study of this early discourse. Suffice it here to say that the existence of these kinds of ideas served to facilitate the Chinese reception of the concept of human rights around the turn of the twentieth century.

The language of human rights seems to have become established and domesticated fairly quickly, judging by the various magazines published in Japan by Chinese students. For example, the purpose of *Guomin bao*, a magazine established in 1901, was said to be to inaugurate a national movement in China to defend the rights of the Chinese people. As the inaugural statement written in English put it: "We are liberal, unprejudiced and impartial reformers. We promise to tolerate all sorts of religions and we also promise to protect the life and property of all people living within our jurisdiction. What we are trying to do is to defend our inalienable rights, the rights of independence and of humanity. Self-defense is our justification; 'China for the Chinese' is our motto."[55]

A translation of Rousseau's *Social Contract* was available to the Chinese as early as 1898, and another translation, by Yang Tingdong, was published in *Yishu huibian* in 1901.[56] It was also Rousseau who was credited for having invented the concept of human rights.[57] It was thus Rousseau, rather than Locke, to whom Liang Qichao referred when mentioning human rights.[58] There were few references to Locke as the founder of the concept of human rights at this time. In one article from 1903, the author only mentions him without giving any details about his thinking and then rapidly moves on to Rousseau's idea of human rights, which he describes in more detail.[59] Although Rousseau was translated into Chinese, Locke and Thomas Hobbes were not, even though they were introduced and briefly discussed in magazines such as *Qingyi bao* and *Guomin bao*. In this context, an article in *Guomin bao* made some interesting observations on the differences between the two philosophers.[60] The author of the article, a Frenchman whom I have been unable to identify, was introduced as someone emphasizing freedom, equality, and human rights. According to this author, the main difference between Hobbes and Locke was that while the former argued that people gave up all their rights to the ruler when they entered society, the latter believed that man had not given up any of his innate rights (*guyou zhi quan*) after the establishment of a social contract. He also mentioned that Locke believed that man had a right to break the social contract if the government violated his rights. Of particular interest is the author's conclusion on the different views on freedom held by the English and the French. The English were said to value freedom because of its benefit (*liyi*) to the individual and the country, whereas the French were said to value freedom as an inviolable (*buke duo*) and innate right (*guyou zhi quan*), regardless of whether it was beneficial or not.

The French and American Revolutions were commonly referred to in these early discussions on human rights.[61] An article in *Yishu huibian* from 1902, for example, referred to the French Revolution, and mentioned that the Declaration of the Rights of Man (*Renquan zhi xuanbu*) had made a deep and lasting impression on people.[62] The American War of Independence was also well known and discussed in Chinese magazines around the turn of the century.[63] Zou Rong, who was one of the most ardent admirers of the American Revolution, was deeply influenced by American ideas and institutions. In his radical piece, *The Revolutionary Army*, published in 1903, he advocated a revolution modeled upon that of America.

It has been said that the French Declaration of the Rights of Man and the American Declaration of Independence were both available in 1903 in a Chinese translation by Xiao Pin, although I have been unable to obtain her work.[64] The American Declaration of Independence, however, had already been translated in *Guomin bao* in 1901.[65] The translation conveyed the original message that all human beings are equal and endowed by nature with certain rights, so-called natural rights (*tianfu zhi quanli*), which cannot be withheld. These rights were also described as "rights which people ought to enjoy [*renmin yingyou zhi quanli*]." A Chinese translation of *La Déclaration des droits de l'homme et du citoyen* (*Renquan zhi xuanyan*) appeared in the Shanghai daily *Shibao* in April 1907.[66] According to the introduction, human rights (*renquan*) were bestowed by nature and all people are entitled to enjoy them. Each article was followed by an explanation added by the translator. In some of the explanations, references were made to Chinese conditions. The explanation to article two, for example, mentioned that in China, as in France before the revolution, those in power had deprived ordinary people of their rights to liberty, property, safety, and the right to resistance against oppression.

Mill's ideas on the freedom of humankind were also well known among the Chinese at a fairly early stage. The first mention of Mill appeared in Liang

Qichao's "Notes on Freedom" in 1899, in which Liang emphasized the freedoms of thought, speech, and publication.[67] Feng Ziyou, in an article published in *Kai zhi lu* in 1900, also referred to Mill.[68] Feng said that, according to Mill, man has three freedoms: thought, speech, and action, which all are endowed and inherent in man's nature. Yan Fu translated Mill's *On Liberty* some time around 1899 or 1900, but it was not until 1903 that the translation was published; in that same year, Ma Junwu's translation of the work also appeared.[69] Ma Junwu, who also devoted several articles to introducing Mill's thinking, translated natural rights as *tianran quan* and *tianquan*.[70] He pointed out that Mill regarded freedoms of thought, speech, and publication as absolute and unrestricted freedoms to be enjoyed in all societies and by all people.[71]

George Jellinek, a German scholar who today occupies a more obscure position in the history of Western political thought, had some impact on the Chinese intellectuals in the early twentieth century by virtue of his fame in Japan. Jellinek's work *Die Erklärung der Menschen-und Bürgerrechte* was also translated into Chinese. In 1907, some chapters, appearing under the title *Renquan xuanyan lun*, were first published in *Minbao*, and in 1908 the work came out in book form.[72] This book attempted to dispute the originality of the French Declaration and credited the idea of natural rights to the earlier declarations of American states such as Virginia.[73] It is interesting to note that many other more central works on human rights in the Western political tradition were not translated or introduced in Chinese at this time. The important work on human rights, Thomas Paine's *The Rights of Man*, seems to have been virtually unknown to the Chinese at this time, only to be mentioned in the 1920s.[74]

It should also be noted that several works that painted a much more negative picture of the concept of human rights were also translated into Chinese and therefore came to influence Chinese intellectuals. It was not the works by Burke, Bentham, or Marx that were translated, however, nor do their attacks on human rights seem to have been known at this point. The works critical to human rights were either written by Japanese authors or were retranslations of Western works from the Japanese published by Chinese students in Japan. They include Rudolf von Jhering's *Der Kampf um's Recht*, Kato Hiroyuki's *On Competition and the Rights of the Strongest* (*Kyosha no kenri no kyoron*), and *A New Theory of Human Rights* (*Jinken shinsetsu*), which all were published by *Yishu huibian* between 1901 and 1903.[75] These works refuted the idea that rights are inherent in human nature. According to both Jhering and Kato, rights were not innate but something that people acquired through struggle. It should be stressed, however, that an understanding of rights that refutes their innateness and instead emphasizes that they are something to be fought for could play an equally powerful and progressive role as the idea of natural rights.[76] In China this understanding of rights legitimized the struggle for a whole range of rights, both vis-à-vis one's own government and vis-à-vis foreign powers.

In October 1882, Kato published his *Jinken shinsetsu*, which marked the beginning of a heated debate on human rights in Japan.[77] According to Kato, there were no natural rights, only acquired rights or, in other words, the rights of the strongest (*qiangquan*). Kato was influenced by German statism, the writings of Johann Bluntschli in particular, and social Darwinism, and he used the theories of evolution, the struggle for survival, and the survival of the fittest, to refute the idea of natural rights (*tianfu renquan*).[78] According to Kato, it was preposterous to believe that people were born with natural and inalienable rights. He compared the folly of those believing in human rights after the emergence of the theory of evolution with the folly of those persisting in believing that the sun revolved around the earth after the discoveries of Galileo and Newton. According to the concept of human rights as described by Kato, people were born with innate (*guyou*) rights of freedom, self-rule, and equality, which others could not infringe upon, or deprive them of. These rights were described as original rights (*yuanquan*), natural rights (*tianfu renquan*), or simply human rights (*renquan*).[79] But Kato argued that man was no different from animals in that he too had to fight for his existence. Rights originated from the struggle to secure one's existence, and they were therefore nothing but the spoils of the strongest. The enjoyment of rights, in other words, was the result of power struggles. Rights were not natural but obtained by man and then laid down in law.[80] In his view on the struggle for rights and the rights of the strongest, Kato was very influenced by Rudolf von Jhering's work.[81] Kato also believed that if one had rights, responsibilities (*zeren*) would follow, so that if people had the right to receive protection from the government, they also had a duty to obey it.[82]

It is revealing that none of Kato's earlier more positive works on human rights, or any of the works published by people such as Yano Fumio, Baba Tatsui, and Ueki Emori defending the idea of human rights after Kato's attack, were translated into Chinese. There were, however, some Chinese writers who disputed Kato's theory of the rights of the strongest, as shown in a book review published in *Jiangsu* in 1904.[83] The reviewer believed that Kato's opposition to the idea of human rights (*tianfu renquan*) and advocacy of the rights of the strongest (*qiangquan*) would make the world once more sink into a state of authoritarianism. Fortunately, according to the reviewer, Rousseau had in the twentieth century come forward to refute this mistaken doctrine. Once again Rousseau was referred to as the propagator and defender of human rights.

Kato's influence is clearest on Liang Qichao, who from an initial, however muted, belief in rights as something inherent in man's nature, later became convinced that it was an outmoded idea and turned against it. In 1899 Liang could thus write: "Man is given life by nature, and nature bestows him with abilities making him great and strong so as to fulfil his life. Thereupon he has popular rights [*minquan*]. These popular rights the ruler cannot deprive his vassal, the father cannot deprive his son, the older brother cannot deprive the younger brother, the husband cannot deprive his wife."[84] But the same year Liang also introduced Kato Hiroyuki and his theory that "might is right" in the essay "On the Rights of the Strongest."[85] In this article Liang mentioned that people tended to be negatively disposed toward the theory of the rights of the strongest and positive toward ideas of freedom and human rights (*renquan*).[86] He wrote that, according to the idealists, "people are born with rights to freedom and equality [*tian sheng ren er ren ren yi ziyou pingdeng zhi quanli*]." But in reality, people were no different from the animals and thus not born free and equal. According to Liang, the theory of the struggle for survival and the principle of evolution had proven that people have to struggle to obtain freedom and that rights are the rights of the strongest.[87]

In an article written in 1901, Liang described human rights and rights of the strongest as two different concepts or schools, and, furthermore, he contended that the former was outmoded.[88] He referred to the former as the "school of equal rights [*pingquan pai*]," whose main spokesman he regarded to be Rousseau. According to Liang, this school believed that rights are bestowed by heaven and belong equally to all and that the state was founded by an agreement among the people, that is through a social contract. Thus, people have unlimited rights and the government cannot suppress the will of the people. According to Liang, the positive aspect of this idea was that it could promote national strength by encouraging people's individual energy, but there also was a danger that it would lead to anarchy and chaos if the government's power was so restricted. The other school, which he called the "school of the rights of the strongest [*qiangquan pai*]," the main spokesman being Spencer, contended instead that there was no such thing as natural rights, only rights of the strongest. The government had unlimited power and the people had to obey it. Central to this thinking was the theory of evolution, that only the strong who acquire rights by force would survive in the struggle among people. While this idea could promote the interests of the collective within a country, Liang feared that it also could endanger world peace by promoting aggression on the international scene.

Liang thus seems to have been aware of the dangers associated with advocating the rights of the strongest, but since he was preoccupied with national survival it also held the most promise for China. That the advocacy of natural rights was a thing of the past was further stressed by Liang in an article written in 1902, in which he wrote: "Earlier generations believed in natural rights [*tianfu renquan*], that people are born with inalienable rights, but after Darwin people became aware of the struggle for existence and natural selection, [the principle] that the superior win and the inferior lose."[89] In "The New Citizen" in 1902, Liang devoted a whole chapter to a discussion on rights, like Kato referring to Jhering, which further reveals that he saw rights as obtained through struggle rather than as given by nature.[90]

Many authors made distinctions similar to Liang Qichao's between the concept of human rights and the concept of the rights of the strongest. In an article entitled "The [Two] Schools of Heaven Granted Rights and Rights of the Strongest," published in *Guomin bao* in 1901, human rights were associated with the French, and the rights of the strongest with the Germans. "The school of 'heaven granted rights' [*tianfu quan*] holds that people are born free and equal. Rights are natural and given by heaven. The school of 'rights of the strongest' holds that when people are born the strong wield rights, whereas the weak do not have any rights. Rights are acquired through struggle and through selection. According to the former school, people cannot infringe upon my freedom and equality, and according to the other school I cannot throw away my freedom and equality."[91]

Yan Fu was another influential Chinese who was skeptical of the concept of human rights. Like Liang Qichao, however, Yan Fu would at times also claim that freedom was endowed by nature and mention a right to autonomy. In his early articles from the late 1890s, for example, he wrote: "To kill, injure or steal another man's property are all an extreme violation of human freedom."[92] But this did not constitute or lead to an advocacy of human rights on his part. Yan Fu shared Liang Qichao's conviction that Darwin's theories had made the concept of human rights outmoded and unscientific.[93] In 1903, he wrote: "The principle stated at the beginning of Rousseau's *Social Contract*, that man is born free, has been rejected by later thinkers."[94] The fact that Yan Fu was an ardent advocate of social Darwinism and utilitarianism probably served to make him immune to the concept of human rights, as it is rejected by both these schools of thought.[95]

An article in *Zhi shuo* from 1903 reveals that the Chinese were aware of differences among Westerners on the nature of rights. The author contended that the English saw rights as interests (*liyi*), the Germans saw rights as power (*weili*), and the French saw rights as "one's natural position and duty in life [*benfen*]."[96] That the author regarded the German position as identifying rights with power or might seems rather plausible, given the predominant German schools of the late nineteenth century. And that he believed that the English focus on interests can be explained by the strength of the utilitarian school in England and the fact that works introducing Bentham and Mill were available in Chinese.[97] The author understood the French idea of rights as being inherent in man's nature and, in other words, as being derived from man's natural position in life. As we saw above, others had also voiced the view that the English valued freedom because of its benefits whereas the French regarded it as an innate and inviolable right and thus valued it for its own sake. Such an understanding of the French position on rights might perhaps also have informed the author in *Zhi shuo*. He obviously believed that the existence of rights derived from certain moral duties related to man's lot in society. "It is people's natural lot to preserve their physical and spiritual beings, and so they have material rights. It is people's natural lot to produce subsequent generations, and so they have the right of marriage. It is people's natural lot to play roles in national politics, and so they have the right of political participation. It is people's natural lot not to be controlled by others, and so they have the right of freedom."[98]

In this enumeration of rights, besides the rights to freedom and political participation, we also find the right to marry, which originated in the very Confucian duty to continue the family line. This article thus presents us with a mixture of Confucian tenets and Western ideas of rights belonging equally to all (both men and women) that cannot be infringed upon and that if lost makes man less of a man, as well as a Darwinian worldview of struggle between nations. It is a good example of how many, seemingly contradictory, ideas could be combined, and how human rights thinking, although explicitly stated to be in opposition to some Confucian values (the author juxtaposed rights with rites), nevertheless in the end could be grafted onto very Confucian ideas.

An article in *Fazheng xuebao* from 1907 also held that different opinions existed in the West on the nature of rights. Whereas in the past, the most influential had been the concept of natural rights (*tianfu quanli*), which held that "people are born to this world and thus enjoy the rights which are their due [*xiangyou quanli*]," the present view was that "there did not exist any rights outside of the law."[99] The idea that rights were a product of law was also put forward in an article in *Shen bao* in 1906.[100] The article stated that there were three different schools of rights. The first school saw rights as liberties (*yi quanli wei ziyou*), and stipulated that people have the right to any kind of action within the limits laid down by law. The second school saw rights as interests (*yi quanli wei liyi*) and held rights to be those interests that were protected by the law. The third school, finally, saw rights as power (*yi quanli wei li*).

CONCLUSION

At the beginning of the twentieth century the concept of human rights was mentioned and discussed by many Chinese writers, although these discussions often were quite brief and sketchy in character. It should, however, be noted that several of the most central Western works on human rights were not translated into Chinese, and that the Chinese from the beginning also were introduced to schools critical of the concept, such as German statism and legal positivism. But despite the fact that several works critical of the concept of human rights were available, many Chinese nonetheless embraced the concept, with notable exceptions such as Liang Qichao and Yan Fu.[101] As a matter of fact, to argue in the Chinese context that it was legitimate and necessary to struggle for one's rights was as equally revolutionary and liberating as was the belief in the innateness of rights.

It is interesting to note that it was not Locke but Rousseau who was referred to in these early discussions on human rights. It could, of course, be argued that the Rousseauian understanding of rights fits better with the Confucian emphasis on harmony between the individual and society; it is definitely more helpful when the goal of political affairs is national salvation. A utilitarian view of rights likewise is better in line with such a goal, which would help explain the influence of Mill's view that rights are needed for the progress of society. But this does not even begin to describe the late Qing understanding of human rights, or the reasons why so many Chinese writers found human rights talk attractive. It furthermore obscures the fact that many Chinese, as will become obvious in the following chapters, regarded human rights as necessary for human existence and, thus, a value in and of themselves.

NOTES

1. On the missionaries' publishing activities, see Cohen (1978).
2. For a discussion of the first translations of Western works on international law, see Svarverud (2000).
3. For the translations published by these institutions, see Biggerstaff (1961), Bennett (1967), and Xiong Yuezhi (1994).
4. For a fascinating study of *Shibao* and its influence on the political debate of the day, see Judge (1996).
5. On the publishing activities of Chinese students in Japan and their translations of Japanese works, see, for example, Saneto Keishu (1982), Tan Ruqian (1980), and Harrell (1992).
6. For information on these magazines, see Ding Shouhe (1982).
7. On Yan Fu, see Schwartz (1964).
8. Tan Ruqian (1980).
9. On the concept of citizenry in the Chinese revolution, see Zarrow (1998).
10. For a history of student radicalism during the early twentieth century, see Rankin (1971).
11. Yü Ying-shih has drawn attention to this special situation; see (1994), p. 133.
12. See Liang Qichao (1902a), p. 273.

13. For the sake of simplicity I will generally speak of human rights rather than natural rights in the following chapters. See my reasons for doing so farther down in this chapter.

14. Rankin (1971) pp. 227–28.

15. Reformers, here, refers loosely to those such as Liang Qichao and Kang Youwei who wanted to reform the political system but keep the emperor, whereas revolutionaries, men such as Zou Rong, Chen Tianhua, and Sun Yat-sen, wanted to overthrow the Manchus and establish a republic.

16. Pusey (1983).

17. Gasster (1969), p. 123.

18. See Liu (1996).

19. Said, as quoted in Liu (1996), p. 20.

20. Liu (1996), p. 26.

21. Although Liu mentions the issue of agency, I feel that her discussion leaves out the question of power. In the case of human rights in particular, it become obvious that sharp and heated domestic contestations have taken place in China during the twentieth century.

22. See Masini (1993).

23. These neologisms could take three different forms: (1) character-compounds found only in premodern Japanese, which did not appear in classical Chinese; (2) classical Chinese expressions that were given a radical change in meaning; and (3) modern Japanese compounds that had no equivalent in classical Chinese. Another important group of loan words were transliterations from Western languages, many of which eventually lost out against semantic translations. See Masini (1993) and Liu (1996) for examples and discussions.

24. The actual number of loan words from Japanese is not clear, and different scholars have presented slightly different figures. Early studies based on research by Saneto put the number of Japanese loan words at 844, where later studies have put the number at 1,063 or even higher. For a discussion on this issue, see Liu (1996).

25. See Suzuki (1996) and Tucker (1996) for the Japanese development.

26 Nishimura Shigeki used this latter character-compound, whereas Nishi Amane used both compounds, even within the same text. See the article by Nishimura Shigeki in *Meiroku Zasshi* from 1875, and that of Nishi Amane from 1874, translated in Braisted (1974), pp. 510–13 and p. 41, respectively.

27. See Tucker (1996) and Yanabu Akira (1996). See also Fukuzawa Yukichi (1969), p. 15.

28. Cited in Dudden (1999), p. 170.

29. See Masini (1993), p. 221.

30. See Tucker (1996), pp. 24–25.

31. Liang Qichao (1899).

32. In the human rights encyclopedia published by CASS in 1998, *ziran quanli* is used to connote natural rights. See CASS (1998), pp. 764–69.

33. See for example Wakabayashi (1984), p. 470, p. 491; Peerenboom (1995), p. 365; and Rosemont (1988), p. 173, and (1998), p. 60, and pp. 65–66.

34. In classical Chinese, *quan* has both a meaning of justice in the sense of measure and standards (*quanheng*), but it was also used in the sense of authority and power (*quanwei* and *quanli*). Wang Guangwu (1991), p. 176.

35. See Peerenboom (1995), pp. 365–66.

36. Quoted in Liu (1999), p. 149.

37. See Zhen Gui, "Translations of New Concepts" (1903), p. 1.

38. Xia Yong (1992), pp. 161–62 prefers *ziran quanli* to *tianfu renquan*.

39. This view is put forward by Wakabayashi (1984) and Tucker (1996).

40. Wang Guangwu (1991), p. 168.

41. Anon., "On Rights" (1903), pp. 479–84.

42. Liang Qichao, "On Rights Consciousness" in 'The New Citizen,' Liang Qichao (1902–1903), pp. 35–36.

43. Xia Yong (1992) and (1999b).

44. Wang Guangwu (1991).

45. Sir John Lyons has described the etymological fallacy as: "[T]he assumption that the original form or meaning of a word is, necessarily and by virtue of that fact, its correct form or meaning. How often do we meet the argument that because such and such word comes from Greek, Latin, Arabic . . . the correct meaning of the word must be what it was in the language of the original? The argument is fallacious because the tacit assumption of an original and true or appropriate correspondence between form and meaning, upon which the argument rests, cannot be substantiated. . . . [M]ost words in the vocabulary of any language cannot be traced back to their origin." Quoted in Richter (1995), p. 169 n. 5.

46. Others are also guilty of the same mistake. A myth has developed in the West around the Chinese word *weiji* meaning crisis. It has become a widespread "truth" that since it is made up of one character meaning danger and another meaning opportunity, Chinese people are wont to see opportunities in crises. This is not only a mistaken interpretation and an example of a trend to mystify China, but also completely misunderstands how Chinese words are constructed; their meaning is not just simply the sum total of their constituent characters. Furthermore, the character *ji* has a multitude of meanings, only one of which actually is opportunity. One word for opportunity in Chinese is *jihui*, made up of this *ji*, but *ji* is never used on its own to mean opportunity.

47. Su Qing (1989), p. 186. A woman who studied law in the late 1920s also described the purpose of lawyers as being to protect human rights (*renquan*). See Wang Zheng (1999), p. 192.

48. See Shen Qichang (1907a).

49. See Sun Yat-sen (1960).

50. Qian Shifu (1948).

51. This is also the view of Wang Ermin (1983), pp. 67–83.

52. Not much literature exists on the idea of human rights among the Chinese in the late eighteenth and early twentieth century. See, however, Wang Ermin (1983), Liu Guangjing (1994), Lin Qiyan (1989), and He Yimin (1991).

53. On the early usage of *zizhu zhi quan*, see Wang Ermin (1983) and (1995b), and Liu Guangjing (1994).

54. On the missionary influences, see Liu Guangjing (1994).

55. This statement was written in English in the inaugural issue of the magazine. *Guomin bao* was an important, albeit very short-lived, magazine that came out with only four issues in 1901 before publication ceased. The magazine was published under the auspices of the Chinese National Society in Tokyo. On the magazine, see Ding Shouhe (1982), vol. 1, pp. 98–113.

56. Yang Tingdong's translation was published in nos. 1, 2, 4, and 9. *Yishu huibian*, with the English title, *A Monthly Magazine of Translated Political Works*, started publication in 1900 in Tokyo. In 1903 the magazine was restructured under the new name *Zhengfa xuebao* and in 1904 publication stopped. During its few years of existence it was very active, and works by Rousseau, Montesquieu, Spencer, Jhering, Bluntschli, Fukuzawa Yukichi, and Kato Hiroyuki,

among others, were all published in the magazine. Their works were often first published as installments and later in book form. The majority of the Western works were retranslated from the Japanese. *Zhengfa xuebao* contained more original writings by the Chinese themselves. On the magazine, see Ding Shouhe (1982), vol. 1, pp. 55–68, and vol. 3, pp. 99–114.

57. On the translation and knowledge of Rousseau among the Chinese, see Bastid-Bruguière (1990).

58. See, for example, Liang Qichao (1901b), p. 189. Other references to Rousseau appeared in *Guomin bao*, *Yishu huibian*, and *Minbao*. Anarchists such as Liu Shipei also argued that Rousseau had founded the doctrine of natural rights (*tianfu renquan*). See Liu Shipei (1907a), p. 907.

59. Yang Dusheng (1903), p. 632.

60. The Frenchman's name is rendered as *Awuleituo* in Chinese; I have not been able to identify him. Awuleituo, "European modern philosophy" (1901).

61. See, for example, Anon., "Twentieth-Century China," (1901), pp. 70–71. The article stated that ideas of freedom and equality originated with the revolutions at the end of the eighteenth century, as did also *Shibao*. See Anon., "The Legal Status of Citizens," (1907).

62. Gong Fazi (1902a), p. 28–29.

63. On the influence and understanding of the American Revolution in China, see Yu Danchu (1987).

64. See Ma Zuyi (1984), p. 274.

65. *Guomin bao*, no. 1, 1901. The declaration had been translated into Japanese by Fukuzawa Yukichi in his *Conditions in the West*, published 1866–1870.

66. The translation appeared on 1, 3, and 4 April. The Shanghai daily *Shibao*, with the English title, *Eastern Times*, was founded in 1904, initially with the financial support of Kang Youwei and Liang Qichao. On the magazine, see Judge (1996).

67. Liang Qichao "Notes on Freedom," (1899–1902), p. 1.

68. Feng Ziyou (1900). *Kai zhi lu*, with the English title, *Wisdom Guide*, founded in 1900, was one of the earliest magazines in Japan. The magazine, which only came out with six issues before it was closed down in 1901, was a strong advocate of freedom and human rights. It was also engaged in publishing translations, mostly from the Japanese. See Ding Shouhe (1982), vol. 1, pp. 86–89; and Ning Shupan and Chen Kuangshi (1984).

69. On Yan Fu's translation, see Schwartz (1964). Ma Junwu (1881–1940) mentioned that he had seen the original work in 1901 and then began to read and translate it, but only had completed the first chapter before becoming preoccupied with other tasks. Later he was also introduced to a French translation and to Nakamura Masanao's Japanese translation (it had been translated into Japanese in 1872). It was not until in Japan that Ma found time to translate the whole work, which was done quite rapidly it seems because he writes that he spent less than twenty days translating the book. The translation was published by Shanghai-based *Kaiming shuju* in February 1903 and carried a foreword by none other than Liang Qichao. In contrast to Yan Fu's translation, Ma's was rendered into colloquial Chinese and does not seem to be all that well known today. The translation and Liang's foreword are reprinted in Mo Shixiang (1991). Ma was an ardent advocate of democracy and women's rights. He was at first associated with the reformers and also wrote several articles for *Xinmin congbao*, to which he briefly was appointed editor when Liang Qichao left Japan for a short period in 1902. In 1903 Ma distanced himself from the reformers and aligned himself with Sun Yat-sen. Ma was one in the group of people assigned to draw up a charter for the *Tongmeng hui* in 1905, and he later wrote for *Minbao*.

70. Ma Junwu (1903e), p. 138, and p. 141.

71. Ma Junwu (1903e), p. 136.

72. It was translated by Bo Yangzhong and appeared in no. 13, 1907. The *Minbao* translation only provided the first four chapters of Jellinek's work (1895), and neither it nor the book included any of the declarations found as an appendix in the original. I am grateful to Rune Svarverud for bringing my attention to the book.

73. Jellinek belonged to the school of conceptual jurisprudence, which was very influential in Germany in the period 1890–1910. Jellinek believed that rights were only meaningful when given objective expression in positive law. He was therefore more positive toward the guarantees laid down in the American declaration than to the vacuous phrases of the French document.

74. The first mention of Paine to my knowledge is in Wu Pinjin (1923). Mention of T. H. Green and D. G. Ritchie and their writings on natural rights also appeared around the same time. See chapter 6 of this book.

75. Jhering's work was published in the magazine *Yishu huibian* beginning with no. 1 in 1900. Kato's "On Struggle" was published beginning with no. 4 in 1901, and in book form in 1902. In 1903, Kato's "A New Theory of Human Rights" was published as a monograph by *Yishu huibian*.

76. It is interesting to note that a Swedish translation of Jhering's work was published in the 1940s by a liberal judge who saw it as a liberating piece of work in the struggle against conservative forces and against Nazism. I'm grateful to professor Kjell-Åke Modéer for bringing this to my attention.

77. On the human rights debate in Japan, see Pittau (1967), pp. 118–24.

78. Kato Hiroyuki (1903), p. 9.

79. Kato Hiroyuki (1903), p. 5.

80. Kato Hiroyuki (1903), pp. 32–34, and (1901), pp. 7–10.

81. See reference in Kato Hiroyuki (1903), p. 33, and (1901), p. 16.

82. Kato Hiroyuki (1901), p. 31.

83. Ya (1904), p. 3.

84. See Liang Qichao, "Notes on Freedom," (1899–1902), p. 12. A similar description is also found in "On Progress," in *The New Citizen* (1902–1903). "Nature gives birth to man and bestows him with rights and the knowledge to expand these rights, and the capabilities to protect these rights," p. 58. Liang's wordings echoes those of Fukuzawa Yukichi who wrote: "When heaven gives birth to man, it gives him faculties of body and mind and the powers to realise his rights in practice. Therefore under no circumstances should a man be deprived of his rights." Fukuzawa (1969), p. 11.

85. See Liang Qichao, "On the Rights of the Strongest," in *Notes on Freedom* (1899–1902), p. 29.

86. See Liang Qichao, "On the Rights of the Strongest," in *Notes on Freedom* (1899–1902), p. 30.

87. See Liang Qichao, "On the Rights of the Strongest," in *Notes on Freedom* (1899–1902), p. 31.

88. See Liang Qichao (1901b).

89. See Liang Qichao (1902a), p. 273.

90. See Liang Qichao, "On Rights Consciousness," in *The New Citizen* (1902–1903). For more on Liang's views on rights and this particular text, see Angle (2002).

91. Anon., "The [Two] Schools of Heaven Granted Rights and Rights of the Strongest," (1901), p. 4.

92. Yan Fu, reprinted in Wang Shi (1986), vol. 1, p. 2.

93. In 1914 Yan Fu returned to a critique of Rousseau's view of man being born free and equal. See Wang Shi (1986), vol. 2, p. 337.

94. Yan Fu, reprinted in Wang Shi (1986), vol. 1, p. 133.

95. Schwartz (1964), p. 145.

96. Anon., "On Rights" (1903), p. 484; the article is translated in Angle and Svensson (2002). It is a bit surprising to find the use of *benfen* in a Chinese article from 1903 in which the author also uses the compounds *quanli, tianran zhi quanli,* and *tianfu renquan.* It is possible that he might have been influenced by an early Japanese gloss for rights. In 1862, Tsuda Mamichi translated the Dutch word *naturregt* as *tenzen no honbun* (*tianran zhi benfen* in Chinese), although this gloss does not seem to have become widely used in Japan or in China. Fukuzawa had however, in a work written in 1878, discussed rights in relation to the notion of *bun* (*fen*), that is, "one's social position and duty." See Tucker (1996), p. 30. On *benfen,* see also Yanabu Akira (1996), pp. 2–3.

97. Liang Qichao, for example, had written on Bentham (1902e).

98. Anon., "On Rights," (1903), p. 484.

99. Shen Qichang (1907b), p. 85.

100. Anon., "On Rights," (1906).

101. But, for example, as Don Price has argued, Yan Fu and Liang Qichao do not represent the full spectrum of Chinese political views in the early twentieth century. Price (1990), p. 225.

Chapter Five

Ideas of Human Rights in the Early Twentieth Century: The Quest for National Salvation

A NEW INFATUATION

According to Feng Ziyou, the Chinese studying in Japan in the early twentieth century were "intoxicated with ideas of freedom, equality and natural rights [*tianfu renquan*]."[1] Feng Ziyou was himself one of those intoxicated with the new ideas, as his taken name Ziyou (freedom) also indicates. Another man who was deeply influenced by these ideas was Liu Yazi, who took the name Renquan (human rights) after having read Rousseau's *Social Contract*.[2] The Chinese who were writing on human rights invoked them against a despotic ruler, the Manchus, in much the same way as the Americans earlier had used the idea against the English, and the French against *l'ancien régime*. But although the idea of human rights was invoked in the struggle of the individual against a despotic state, the Chinese context was different from that of the West in that the main worry for most Chinese people was the encroachment of the Western powers and the possible extinction of their race and nation. National survival rather than the freedom of the individual from an oppressive state was the main preoccupation.

THE ORIGIN AND MEANING OF RIGHTS

Chinese intellectuals in the early twentieth century usually did not take up or embrace ideas of natural law and the social contract.[3] Although many acknowledged that human rights were inherent in man's nature and antecedent to the establishment of the state, others refuted the existence of natural rights and saw rights as the product of law or as the spoils of struggle. Many articles put forward the view that the only rights we have are those stipulated by the law. An article in *Zhejiang chao* in 1903, for example, argued that rights must be stipulated by the law and recognized by the state in order to count as rights.[4] The author held that only legal rights were to be regarded as rights proper and was adverse to the idea of natural rights before the establishment of society. But since Chinese law at the time of his writing did not stipulate any of the rights that he mentioned in the article (freedom of speech, thought, publication, assembly, and so forth), it was, of course, not in line with legal positivism to accuse the government, as he did, with violating rights that the Chinese people did not have in the first place. In the end, his argument could not avoid being distinctively normative in character since it referred to rights that one ought to have, rather than to those already stipulated in the law. The author thus ended up arguing that the Chinese people should recover the "rights which were their due [*yingxiang zhi quanli*]." Even though he had refuted the existence of natural rights outside of and prior to the law, he was, in the final analysis, unable to derive the origin or justification of rights from the law itself.

The majority of Chinese writers discussing human rights described them as due rights, rights that humans ought to enjoy by virtue of their human nature. In 1899, He Qi and Hu Liyuan, for example, stressed that all men were equally endowed with a right to autonomy (*zizhu zhi quan*), and that to deprive man of this right would be no different from killing him.[5] According to one of the earliest articles on human rights, published in Liang Qichao's *Qingyi bao* in 1900, man was endowed with certain rights. "Heaven [*tian*] gives birth to man and endows him with a brain and also with the freedom of thought. Man is endowed with an ability to speak and also with the freedom of speech. He is also endowed with intelligence and thus with a right to activity. All these rights are inherent [*sheng ju lai*], and the strong cannot deprive the weak of them."[6] An article in *Hubei xuesheng jie* in 1903 also emphasized that human rights were inherent in man's nature: "Human nature is given by heaven, and human rights [*renquan*] are likewise given by heaven."[7] An article in *Kai zhi lu* from 1901 described human rights (*renquan*) as rights that man possess as a human being and that are founded in his nature (*tianxing*); they were therefore described as original rights (*genyuan quanli*).[8] In the article it was argued that "that which makes human beings humans is all in their rights."[9] Although people were said to differ with respect to knowledge, wealth, and power, these were only differences in life circumstances and did not imply any difference with respect to their human rights (*tianfu quanli*).

Human rights were thus described as inherent and bestowed on humans as humans and not contingent upon their status or position in society; a belief that was at odds with the Confucian tradition. The Confucian worldview was strictly hierarchical and stipulated subservience and loyalty from below, and benevolence and propriety from above. People's rights and duties in the Confucian system differed depending on sex, age, and status in society. Those writing on human rights, in contrast, emphasized that people were equal with respect to rights. In the 1903 article "On Rights," it was explicitly stated that all human beings enjoy natural rights (the author used the words *tianran zhi quanli* and *tianfu renquan*). People were furthermore said to be equal with respect to rights. There were no differences between ruler and subject, father and son, husband and wife, man and woman.[10] Others also put forward similar views: "What is meant by rights? Heaven gives birth to humans and endows them with the rights of personal freedom and political participation. . . . Hence, the genuine rights of citizens cannot be suppressed by tyrants, cannot be infringed upon by oppressive officials, cannot be taken away by one's parents, and cannot be overstepped by one's friends."[11] Yang Du, for his part, criticized the fact that the subject of rights and duties in traditional China was the family and not the individual. He went on to emphasize that China, like the West, had to establish rule of law, which would take the individual as the basic unit and subject of rights and duties.[12]

The revolutionary Zou Rong, who later was imprisoned for his radical writings, also put forward the view that all human beings are free and equal at birth. "Everybody in the country, whether male or female, is equal. There is no distinction between upper and lower, base or noble. All inalienable rights are bestowed by nature. The freedom to life and all other privileges are natural rights."[13] Chen Tianhua, another revolutionary, who committed suicide in 1905 in an outburst of patriotism, described human rights (*renquan*) as rights that are "innate and that nobody can infringe upon, and which one oneself should not forsake."[14] He contended that it was the enjoyment of rights that defined man: "[I]f a man does not have any political thinking, if he does not understand how to fight for his rights, then he will not count as a man. Even though he has not died, he will be the same as dead."[15] Liu Yazi agreed that people are born with inherent (*sheng ju lai*) rights which they cannot be deprived of, and that people cannot part with these rights even for one single day.[16] Many others concurred with these views, for example, Wang Jingwei, who claimed that people were equal by nature (*tianran zhi pingdeng*) and that to make differences with regard to people's rights would violate the principle of justice (*tianli*).[17]

SLAVES, CITIZENS, AND RIGHTS: THE CONNECTION BETWEEN HUMAN DIGNITY AND HUMAN RIGHTS

In the early twentieth century, the Chinese made frequent use of the slave trope in political discourse. The American sociologist Patterson and others have argued that the practice of slavery played a crucial role in molding the conception and understanding of freedom in the West.[18] In the American political lexicon of the revolution, for instance, slavery was posited as the antithesis of liberty. W. J. F. Jenner has argued that in imperial China, in contrast to the West, the concept of freedom was absent and irrelevant when describing the differences between slavery and non-slavery. The opposite of "slave" was not a free person but a "respectable person [*liangmin*]."[19] This understanding of slavery, however, changed toward the end of the nineteenth century under the influence of ideas from the West. In the writings of Liang Qichao and others, slavery began to be juxtaposed with freedom.[20] Yan Fu, for instance, described freedom as the opposite of slavery, subjection, and bondage.[21] A view that others agreed with was: "Freedom is the opposite of slavery, therefore the one who has no freedom is but a slave."[22] Many Chinese writers, ranging from Liang Qichao to Li Dazaho, writing on the importance of freedom to human beings would explicitly refer to Patrick Henry's famous exclamation: "[I]s life so dear, or peace so sweet, as to be purchased at the price of chains and slavery? Forbid it, Almighty God!—I know not what course others may take; but as for me . . . give me liberty, or give me death."[23] Liang Qichao agreed with Henry that slavery was equal to unfreedom and argued that freedom was a universal value that also applied to China. "'Give me liberty or give me death'—these words expressed the basis on which the people in Europe and America established their nations in the eighteenth and nineteenth centuries. Is the principle of freedom applicable to China today? I say that freedom is a universal principle [*gongli*] and a necessity for human life; useful and applicable in all circumstances."[24]

Although slavery was not a reality in Chinese society, it came to play a powerful role in the political discourse. The Chinese were wont to describe themselves as being doubly enslaved, first by the Manchus and then also by Westerners.[25] The plight of women was even worse, as they were the slaves of slaves.[26] The slave trope was not so much a description of a factual state, however, as of a mental and moral one. Many Chinese writers lamented that China had a tradition of slavery and that the Chinese people had been nothing but slaves for thousands of years.[27] Zou Rong criticized the slave mentality of the Chinese people and charged that they actually enjoyed being slaves. He went on to lambaste his countrymen for their dependence, obedience, servility, and placidity.[28] In Zou's view, the slavishness of the Chinese people was a result of the Confucian teachings of loyalty and filial piety.

There was a strong nationalistic and civilizational element in these discussions on slavery and the slave mentality of the Chinese people. It was argued that in order for China to become a civilized and modern nation, Chinese people would have to throw off their slave mentality and fight for their rights.

Slaves were assigned negative characteristics that hindered the modernization and progress of China. As Mai Menghua so eloquently put it:

> A citizen [*guomin*] has an ability to rule himself, an independent character, a right to political participation, and enjoys the happiness of freedom. Regardless of his profession, he is not lacking in that which makes [him] a complete human being. But a slave has no power of self-rule and no independent mind. For all daily necessities he has to await the order of the master. His human rights [*tianfu zhi renquan*] and the happiness which should be his due are all something which are in his master's hand. He dresses in his master's clothes, eats his master's food, speaks his master's words, and does his master's deeds. He is dependent on others without any thoughts [of his own], and obeys others without any character [of his own].[29]

Instead of "respectable persons," the opposite of "slaves" came to be "citizens [*guomin*]" and "free people [*ziyou min*]."[30] The Chinese people were admonished to throw off their slave mentality and told to develop a sense of citizenry.[31] There were several discussions on what constituted a citizen apart from living in the same country and sharing the same language, history, and habits. Other characteristics such as patriotism and a concern with the affairs of the state and the general interest were regarded as crucial. "A citizen does not look to others for help but helps himself, he does not expect others to benefit him but looks after his own interests, he does not single-mindedly seek freedom without being capable of self-rule, he not only seeks rights but shoulders duties."[32]

Liang Qichao identified autocracy with slavery and argued that in order for people to shoulder their civic responsibilities it was imperative that they no longer be treated as slaves. If people were but given freedom, they would grow with the responsibility. The Chinese people's slave mentality, thus, was not completely their own fault but was a result of the lack of freedom in China.

> Nature gives birth to man and endows him with rights, the ability to exercise these rights and the capacity to protect them. If people are left alone to govern themselves in freedom, then the ability of the community to govern itself will steadily increase. . . . The reason why China does not progress in self-government is because the people have no regard for the common good; they have no regard for the common good because they have lived as slaves and thieves. The reason that people have lived as slaves and thieves is that tyrants have made the empire their private domain and property and turned my people into slaves and thieves.[33]

One of the crucial differences between citizens and slaves, as also pointed out in Mai Menghua's article above, was said to be that only the former enjoyed rights.[34] A slave would not fall in the category of citizen since "[he] has no rights nor does he shoulder any duties. [His] right to life is in the hands of the master, and to kill and hit [him] is the freedom of others."[35] Ma Junwu also claimed that a person without rights was no different from beasts of burden and slaves.[36] Whereas Liang Qichao wrote:

[I]n order for us who are called "human" to completely fulfil our self-responsibilities, we must preserve both our lives and our rights, which mutually rely on one another. If we do not do this, we will immediately lose our qualifications to be human and stand in the same position as the animals. Thus, the Roman Law's view of slaves as equivalent to animals was, according to logical theory, truly appropriate. If we use a logical syllogism to make the reasoning explicit, it would look like this: (1) those without rights are animals; (2) slaves have no rights; (3) thus, slaves are animals.[37]

One author argued that whereas earlier philosophers in the West, such as Aristotle, believed that slavery was a natural and unavoidable system, later thinkers such as Rousseau had disputed this. Ideas of human rights and freedom had swept the world and led to the abolition of slavery in countries such as America and Russia. The author only regretted that this tide of revolution against the slave system had not yet reached China.[38]

Chinese writers held that enjoyment of rights and freedoms signified a life in dignity and self-respect, whereas a life without rights was degrading and signified a slavelike existence. Xu Yucheng, discussing the situation of women, argued that rights and freedoms were needed in order to be a "complete human being [*wanquan ren*]."[39] Only if one enjoyed and fought for one's rights could one possess self-respect (*zizun*) and self-esteem (*zigui*). To be deprived of one's rights or to deny them oneself, on the other hand, would be a manifestation of self-contempt and self-degradation. The Chinese writers' understanding of human rights as that which makes men different from slaves, and the closely related notions of autonomy, human dignity, and self-respect, resembles views put forward by contemporary Western philosophers, such as Hill, who argue that to undervalue one's rights is to manifest the vice of "servility."[40]

Many Chinese thinkers thus saw rights as something indispensable in order to be a human being. In the article "On Rights" from 1903, man was described as having both physical needs that must be fulfilled as well as spiritual faculties to think and reflect.[41] The purpose of human existence is to complete and perfect one's human nature, and to this end rights are needed. As the author rhetorically asked: "Can we call those, whose rights are not protected, whose nature is incomplete, full-fledged persons?"[42] The author of an article in *Kai zhi lu* argued in a similar vein that human beings need rights in order to secure and protect happiness.[43] The close association between man's possession of rights and the realization of humanity also holds true of Yang Dusheng, who argued that a person who lost his rights would lose his personality (*renge*), whereas if he violated other people's rights he would harm their personality.[44] In his opinion, the enjoyment of human rights lent man his humanity.

Renge was one of the neologisms that entered the Chinese lexicon around the turn of the twentieth century. In modern Chinese it has two, related meanings, namely, "personality" and "the dignity of the human person."[45] In an article from 1903 introducing new concepts, "personality" was translated as *renge*.[46] In another article from the same year, it was argued that in order to be able to develop one's personality, it was necessary to enjoy rights and shoulder duties.[47] This could only come about in a society where rule of law is upheld, whereas in an authoritarian society people would lead slavelike existences. The relationship between personality and enjoyment of rights was sometimes reversed so that personality was said to be the subject or prerequisite for enjoying rights.[48] Personality was then defined as the root (*ben*) and rights as the branch (*mo*). Without personality, and hence rights, one would be no different from slaves or beasts. There is, in other words, a semantic field in which personality and enjoyment of rights are used to characterize citizens in contrast to slaves, who have no personality or rights and are completely at the mercy of their masters. Slavery was therefore described as anathema to people's inherent personality (*guyou zhi renge*).[49] Rights were said to belong equally to all people since nobody is born a slave, and in any case has the ability to throw off his slave mentality and stand up as a man and demand his human rights.[50] This line of thought would also prevail in later discussions on human rights, for example, in the writings of Chen Duxiu during the May Fourth Movement.

The moral element in these discussions on human rights shows an influence and affinity with Confucian tenets such as *zuoren* (to be a person) and *ren* (humaneness).[51] In Confucian thought, humanity is what distinguishes human beings from animals. Humanity is not something one is born with, though, but is achieved through self-cultivation. A person's level of humanity manifests itself in his understanding and performance of rites.[52] This emphasis on humanity in Confucian thought could be said to have facilitated the Chinese reception of the concept of human rights.[53] The notion that heaven, or nature, endows man with certain desires and faculties is found in the Confucian classics, although it does not postulate that these faculties also give rise to any corresponding rights.[54] Human rights and humanity were regarded as closely related and they would remain inseparable for the majority of later generations of Chinese writers discussing human rights. The explicit definition of human rights as those rights that are needed in order to be a person (*zuoren de quanli*) was later to be quite common in the Chinese human rights discourse.

The early twentieth-century discourse shows that the concept of human rights, to some extent, could build on Confucian notions of human dignity and human nature, while at the same time it was explicitly formulated as an attack on other aspects of the Confucian tradition, such as its hierarchical nature and submission of women. It was, however, a question of a new and interpretive understanding of what it meant to be a person, which emphasized equal rights for all rather than the observance of rites.

THE SUBJECT OF RIGHTS

Those discussing human rights believed that these rights belonged to all people, regardless of gender, position, and status, and thus refuted the Confucian hierarchical system. Many articles explicitly stated that women and men were equal and should enjoy equal rights.[55] "Men and women are both born to this world, they both enjoy natural rights [*tianfu zhi quanli*], and equally have abilities to fight for their existence."[56] In order to be fully human, people need rights and this principle also applied to women. "Why is it that women should have the same rights as men? In order to be a human being one has to have the rights which belong to humans, those which have been recognised by the world and which are protected by the law. Those who do not [have these rights] cannot be called human beings."[57] Women were regarded to be the group whose rights were the most violated in China; they were as unfortunate as slaves in this respect.[58] The culprit in this case was not only the state but the Confucian tradition, which stipulated inequality between men and women and made women dependent on their fathers, husbands, and sons. It was also said that it was men who had deprived women of their natural rights (*tianfu zhi quanli*).[59]

At the turn of the twentieth century, the plight of women became an important topic addressed and discussed by women activists and progressive individuals.[60] These concerns had precedents among iconoclastic Chinese thinkers, such as Yüan Mei and Li Ruzhen, but they were also shaped through the influx of Western ideas, both Christian and liberal. The writings of Mill and Spencer, for example, were known and referred to by many Chinese writers at this time.[61] One issue that caught the attention of progressive Chinese early on was the practice of foot binding. Opposition to this practice was voiced by a number of iconoclastic and radical Chinese as early as the end of the eighteenth and the beginning of the nineteenth century.[62] In the late nineteenth century many reformers, including Kang Youwei and Huang Zunxian, began to work for the abolition of foot binding. Missionaries also became engaged in this work and in their writings described the practice as unchristian and against God's will because God had created men's and women's feet alike.[63] Opposition to foot binding was also related to the idea of human rights. In an article published in the magazine *Nüzi shijie* in 1904, Du Qingfeng thus argued that the practice of foot binding violated the natural rights (*tianfu de quanli*) of women.[64] Since women were not born with small feet, he argued that it was against nature to bind them.

The struggles for national salvation and women's rights were closely related. Thus, as many scholars also have noted, there is a strong historical connection between the emergence of feminism and that of nationalism in China.[65] Women's rights were advocated in the belief that the contribution of women was needed in order to save China, a contribution that would not be forthcoming if women remained illiterate and with bound feet. As was the case with rights talk generally, the struggle for women's rights was for the most part motivated by and subordinated to nationalistic needs and considerations. Liang Qichao believed that only educated women could educate their children, and the country would become rich and strong only if women were active in the production of goods and services. One of the first organizations composed of Chinese women students, the Mutual Love Association of Overseas Students, founded in Japan in 1903 as a reaction to Russian imperialistic ambitions in Manchuria, declared that its aim was "rescuing [China's] 200 million women and recovering their innate rights; then, by instilling in them the sense of nation, they would be able to fulfil their divine obligations as women citizens of the nation."[66] Although the rights sought for women included the same rights of freedom of speech and publication that were advocated for men, they also included rights especially aimed at addressing specific problems affecting women qua women, for example, problems related to foot binding, education, and marriage.[67]

There does not seem to have existed much concern about the rights of workers and peasants during this period; I have only found one such reference. In an article in *Guomin bao* in 1901 it was stated that whereas workers in the West enjoyed the rights to establish organizations, make speeches, propagate socialism, and participate in national affairs to ensure the stipulation of laws protecting workers, workers in China did not enjoy any of these rights.[68] This lack of interest in workers' and peasants' rights is not surprising since the participants in these early discussions on human rights were members of a small and educated elite. Just as in the West, this meant that the rights that were advocated answered to this elite's demands and aspirations.[69]

THE CONTENT AND SCOPE OF RIGHTS

The rights discussed by Chinese writers were primarily civil and political rights. The rights to freedom of thought, freedom of speech, and freedom of publication were the most frequently mentioned. Liang Qichao thus pointed out that all civilized countries recognized freedoms of thought, belief, assembly and association, speech, publication, and movement.[70] Freedoms of thought, speech, and publication were often described as the three great freedoms.[71] In 1904, the magazine *Jiangsu* described these three freedoms as central in any civilized country, and as sacred (*shensheng*) and inviolable (*buke qinfan*).[72] In his work *The Revolutionary Army*, Zou Rong mentioned the right to life, and the freedoms of speech, thought, and the press, specifically arguing that these rights and freedoms should not be infringed upon.[73] The revolutionary Chen Tianhua devoted an article to exemplifying which rights the Chinese should have, ranging from the rights to life and property, freedoms of speech and association, to the right to participate in the government.[74] Chen explicitly defined the rights to freedom of life and property as natural rights (*tianfu de renquan*), rights that humans are born with and that cannot be withheld.[75]

Wu Yue, who tried to assassinate the participants of the imperial constitutional mission in 1906, argued that the most important rights were freedom of assembly, freedom of publication, freedom of the person, and the right to property.[76] Similar enumerations of rights can be found in the Shanghai daily *Shibao* during the years 1906–1908 and *Yunnan zazhi* after 1906.[77] Many writers claimed rights were sacred and inviolable and respected in all civilized societies, criticizing the fact that they were violated in China. It is significant that those discussing human rights during the period advocated classical liberal rights, including the right to property.[78] An article in *Kai zhi lu*, for instance, argued that without a right to property others would be eating the product of one's labor.[79] Chinese writers at that time put more emphasis on civil and political rights than on social and economic rights, which contradicts the view that the Chinese cultural tradition has prompted Chinese people to favor economic and social rights over civil and political rights.[80] Needless to say, the choice of, or priority among, rights is influenced by the interests and political ideology of those who dominate the human rights discourse. In the early twentieth century, the fact that a small elite controlled the debate explains the focus on civil and political rights. Economic and social rights only became an issue during the May Fourth Movement as a result of the radicalization of the political scene. The focus on economic and social rights in the PRC is also due more to the influence of socialism than resulting from any cultural legacy.

Those advocating human rights did not hold that all rights were absolute or that the exercise of rights was unrestricted. It was generally argued that one could not infringe upon other people's rights when exercising one's own.[81] This was also the view of Liu Shipei. Liu strongly argued the case for natural rights. "I firmly believe that humankind has three major rights: the rights to equality, independence, and liberty. Equality consists of everyone having the same rights and duties; independence consists of neither enslaving others nor depending on others; and liberty consists of neither being controlled of nor enslaved by others. These three rights we consider to be natural."[82] Liu believed that if liberty was used excessively, it could harm the liberty of others and thus come into conflict with the right of equality. This revealed an awareness of the fact that different rights might come into conflict with one another and that, in particular, liberty and equality could clash. In such a case, Liu believed that the liberty of the individual would have to be restrained in the interest of the liberty of others. This is an early example of the view that individual liberty could have to be curtailed with the interest of the majority in mind, although Liu didn't go so far as to argue that the rights of the individual would have to be sacrificed in the interest of the nation.

An article published in *Zhejiang chao* in 1903 revealed a similar awareness of potential conflicts between individual freedoms and the social interest.[83] The author stressed that the majority of rights was not absolute. Rights could only be exercised as long as they were not in violation of the law or threatened the stability and order of the country. While freedom of thought was unrestricted, freedom of speech, on the other hand, could only be exercised in accordance with the law. An article in *Shibao* from 1906, discussing the freedoms of assembly and association, also emphasized that in most constitutions these and other rights were restricted.[84] The limit on people's freedoms was so they did not violate the order of the country; this limit was to be laid down in the law. Although the author emphasized that the individual could not violate the interest of the whole nation (*guojia quanti*), he did not make the mistake of identifying the interest of the country with that of the government or the bureaucrats, but actually warned against such an identification. He argued that the government could not use its power to violate the interests of the people. Another article reprinted in *Shibao*, although stating that "the freedoms of the citizens were granted by heaven [*guomin zhi ziyou you yu tianfu*]," at the same time emphasized that the scope of these freedoms were laid down by the country and stipulated in the constitution.[85] The author claimed that only with a clearly defined scope of freedom would there be any real freedom; in a barbarian society the only freedom would be that of "the strong eating the weak." This article also argued that the power of the government and the freedom of the people were often at odds. Particularly in authoritarian countries the government would wield unlimited power and the people would be unable to fully enjoy the rights stipulated in the constitution. These early writings all indicate an awareness of the fact that the state could pose a threat to individual rights and freedoms but don't seem to imply or argue that the national interest could trump individual rights. This latter view, however, would come to be propagated in the 1920s by Sun Yat-sen and other political thinkers.

THE RELATIONSHIP BETWEEN RIGHTS AND DUTIES

The relationship and close correlation between rights and duties was often stressed in the early Chinese rights discourse. It was argued that people have a need to combine in groups such as the family, society, and the country, and that they have duties with respect to the group. If these duties are not upheld, the individual, as well as the group, is in danger. People's duties to the country were especially important because if they were not shouldered, the country would perish. The importance placed on duties was motivated by a concern about the perceived lack of public spirit among the Chinese people and by the ongoing effort to save the Chinese nation from extinction.[86] People had not only a duty to save China but a duty to fight for and restore their own inherent rights.[87] The Chinese word most commonly used to denote duties was *yiwu*, although a few articles used the words *zhi* and *tianzhi*. Some seem to have differentiated between *benfen* or *benwu* and *yiwu*, arguing that only the latter was held by the individual in relation to the state.[88]

One of the earliest discussions on the nature and character of rights and duties can be found in *Kai zhi lu* in 1901.[89] According to this article, people were born with both rights and feelings of duties. If one would exercise one's rights without restrictions, it was likely that one would infringe upon other people's rights and that strife would result. But since the exercise of rights was meant to secure people's happiness, infringement on others' rights and the resulting strife would violate the very purpose of rights. There had to exist some kind of restriction on the enjoyment of rights and, therefore, people had a duty (*yiwu*) not to infringe upon or hinder the exercise of other people's rights. To the author's mind, one individual's exercise of rights would always imply duties on the part of other people. Rights and duties furthermore arose in society; they could only be exercised in relation to others, so that an isolated man could not be said to have any rights or duties. An article in *Xinmin congbao* from 1902 put forth similar views.[90] It stressed that rights and duties were reciprocal, so that if A has a duty toward B, B has a right in exchange from A. To talk about rights or duties in the case of Robinson Crusoe would be out of place—at least until he met Friday.[91]

Rights and duties were often regarded as two sides of the same coin, as Zhang Baixi pointed out: "What the foreign countries call people's rights [*minquan*] is a term parallel to duties (*yiwu*); what is called freedom is a term parallel to law. The observation of law and duties is the obligation (*zhi*) of subordinates and subjects, while rights and freedoms are to be enjoyed by them. Without law and duties, how can there be rights and freedom?"[92] Zhang stressed duties, but pointed out that if one shouldered duties, one was entitled to enjoy rights as well. Other writers also claimed that duties were of primary importance if one wanted to enjoy rights.[93]

Liang Qichao emphasized the close relation between rights and duties, arguing that a person could not have one without the other.[94] According to Liang, rights originated with the individual's duties to society. The individual owes duty to society, rather than to other individuals, and it was this kind of duty to the community that Liang believed the Chinese people were lacking. In contrast to those today who see traditional China as a duty-based society, Liang lamented the lack of duty consciousness on the part of the Chinese people. His and others' emphasis on duties more reflected the imperative of national salvation than any traditional influences, while the emphasis on duties in today's official discourse likewise owes more to Marxism than to traditional values.

Rights and duties were often regarded to be of equal importance. The fact that the Chinese people had lived in an authoritarian society for more than two thousand years without knowing about their rights, only knowing about their duties, was something shameful that many writers strongly criticized.[95] They warned against an excessive emphasis on duties at the expense of rights and described those shouldering duties, but not enjoying any rights, as slaves. "Those in the world who are subjected to duties and do not enjoy any rights are simply slaves and beasts."[96] Once again we encounter the powerful slave trope in the Chinese rights discourse. A person who silently and placidly fulfilled his duties without demanding any rights was no more than a slave and had forfeited his demands to be treated as a human being. This kind of servile person was not only regarded with contempt but was also said to constitute a threat to the Chinese nation. A nation of slaves would be unable to stand up against the foreigners and the whole nation therefore risked sinking into a state of slavery. In order to save themselves and their nation, it was imperative that the Chinese people throw away their slave mentality and demand their rights as human beings and citizens.

When describing the differences between constitutional and nonconstitutional countries, some authors drew attention to the fact that it was only in the former that people had both rights and duties, whereas in the latter they would only shoulder duties.[97] Ya Cui argued that since society has been created by man out of mutual needs, people not only have rights but also duties toward society.[98] If people only talked about rights and did not contribute to society, it would amount to discarding all public morality (*gongde*). But, on the other hand, if they talked only about duties and did not have an independent spirit, then it would amount to discarding their human rights (*renquan*).Ya concluded that "Public morality is that which preserves society, whereas human rights are that which protect the elements of society."[99]

ATTACKS ON THE MANCHUS FOR VIOLATING HUMAN RIGHTS

The Chinese revolutionaries built upon a tradition of holding rulers responsible for the misfortunes that befell the people. Resentment against the Manchus, who were barbarian conquerors to boot, had existed from the earliest days of the dynasty. Earlier anti-Manchu writings, such as Wang Xiuqu's *An Account of Ten Days at Yangzhou* in which the atrocities committed by the Manchus at the beginning of the dynasty were forcefully described, were used by reformers in the 1890s in their propaganda against the regime.[100] When the Chinese came across the concept of human rights it was only natural that they would find it useful in their struggle against the Manchus. They made good use of the human rights language when attacking their own government and also saw it as useful in the struggle for national sovereignty.

Many Chinese intellectuals put forward quite liberal views regarding the relationship between the individual and the state. Zou Rong thus argued that the government was set up by public agreement and that one of its main responsibilities was to protect the rights of its citizens. If the government infringed upon these rights, the people had the right to overthrow it and regain their rights.[101] The purpose of the state was to protect people's rights. If it failed in this respect, it would lose the very reason for its existence and people would no longer have any duty to obey it. Many articles published at the beginning of the twentieth century dwelt on the perceived differences between democracy and authoritarianism. Authoritarian states were criticized for violating people's rights, while civilized countries, on the other hand, were said to have established a constitution in order to protect people's rights.[102] Nai Xuan described authoritarian political systems as wielding unlimited power and denying people the rights enjoyed in a constitutional system.[103] In an authoritarian system people only had duties but no rights. They had no right to political participation, and their other rights and freedoms were also violated. A country characterized by democracy (*pingmin zhengzhi*) and rule of law (*fazhi guo*), on the other hand, would by definition secure the happiness of its people and protect their rights.[104]

China was regarded as an authoritarian country and therefore the line between barbarian and civilized countries was drawn between China and the West. But it was emphasized that it was only with the development from authoritarianism to constitutionalism that people in the West had come to enjoy rights.[105] Chinese intellectuals were confident that China also would come to belong to the civilized world once a constitution had been adopted and a democratic system instituted. They believed that China was no exception to the universal development toward democracy, which shows their belief and faith in a universal and progressive history. But some, like Liang Qichao and Sun Yat-sen, however, argued that the Chinese people would have to go through a period of enlightened despotism or political tutelage before they would be prepared to enjoy democracy.

The Manchu government was often accused of violating human rights. *Guomin bao*, for instance, claimed that the government violated rights such as freedom of person and of association, speech and thought, religion, and correspondence.[106] *Zhejiang chao* described the situation in the following terms:

> Should our citizens desire to put into practice their freedom of assembly and association, and so gather a large number of people to form an organisation, the government would certainly label them as rebels, uprisings, or riots, and would employ its despotic force to dispel them, arrest them, imprison them, and would not stop until all are stamped out. Should our citizens desire to put into practice their freedom of thought and expression to make manifest the common principles of mankind, the government would definitely hold [the principles] to be rumours, heterodoxy, insults to the court, or sacrilege, and would proscribe them, destroy them, and would not be content until the principles can no longer be heard.[107]

Shibao also criticized the Qing government for curtailing and violating the freedoms of speech, publication, and association, and so on.[108] Similar charges against the Manchus were launched by Zou Rong and Chen Tianhua. Sun Yatsen accused the Manchus of infringing upon people's rights to life, liberty, and property, although this wording to some extent probably was influenced by the fact that the article in question was published in the United States.[109] The legal system was also criticized as deficient with respect to the protection of people's rights.[110]

In 1905, the Qing court sent two missions abroad to study foreign constitutions and when they returned the following year, it was announced that a constitution and a series of administrative reforms were being prepared. This development served to fuel the discussions on constitutionalism, since many, especially the revolutionaries, feared that a constitution established by the Manchus would provide little respect for the rights of the Han-Chinese.[111] After 1906, a number of constitutional organizations and many new newspapers and magazines, such as *Shibao* and *Dongfang zazhi*, that supported the constitutional movement appeared in China.[112] For those outside the government, the protection of people's rights and freedoms seems to have been of great concern and regarded as one of the main purposes of the constitution. According to Shen Qichang, the purpose of the constitution was twofold: on the one hand, it should uphold the power of the country, and, on the other hand, it should protect people's human rights (*renquan*).[113] That the purpose of the government was to protect people's rights was repeated in several articles in *Shibao* and *Yunnan zazhi*.[114] Ma Junwu likewise wrote that the purpose of a democratic country was to realize equality and to respect the freedom of the individual.[115]

But the concerns and priorities of the Qing government were quite different from those put forward in the magazines mentioned above. For the government, the constitution and the national assembly were acceptable because they would serve to strengthen the Chinese state. The idea that the people could need protection from the emperor was a foreign thought. When the constitution was promulgated in 1908, it was seen as a gift from the ruler to the people, and rights were seen, not as innate, but as granted by the emperor.[116]

THE PURPOSE OF HUMAN RIGHTS: THE QUEST FOR NATIONAL SALVATION

Although human rights were sought for the individual from the state, they were mostly invoked out of nationalistic concerns during this period, both as a means to strengthen the nation through unleashing the energy of the individual, and very often also as a weapon with which to attack the Manchus. The Chinese feared for the survival of their nation. One reason behind China's weakness was believed to be the Chinese lack of (human) rights thinking. Only if people were independent rights-bearing agents would they be able to shoulder the responsibilities pertaining to citizens and withstand the foreigners' encroachment on their land. A servile population, on the other hand, would bring about the downfall of China. Many, in addition, believed that in order to restore people's rights and save the nation it was first of all necessary to overthrow the authoritarian rule of the Manchus.

Utilitarian arguments appear at many different levels in the Chinese rights discourse. Rights were valued as a means toward social progress and, even more crucial, national salvation. Regarding the first of these social–utilitarian aspects, we can detect an influence from Mill. Freedom of thought and speech was thus defended as necessary for the progress of society and seen as a means to "enrich the country and benefit the people [*fu guo li min*]."[117] An article in *Guomin bao*, for instance, approvingly quoted Mill's view that the forbidding of thought would lead to the dulling of people's intellect.[118] It further held that the period of the Hundred Schools had been the most progressive period in China's history and criticized the subsequent burning of books, the supremacy of Confucianism, and the forbidding of all other thinking as heresy. Liang Qichao also argued that freedom of thought promoted the progress of civilization. It was only because the Warring States period had been a time of freedom of thought that Confucius had been able to develop his ideas.[119] Chen Tianhua likewise believed that freedom of speech was necessary for the progress of society, and argued that without freedom of association, the Chinese people would remain weak and unable to unite for the sake of the national interest.[120] Yan Fu, for his part, emphasized that freedom was necessary in order to release the energy of the individual so as to promote the wealth and power of the Chinese nation.[121]

The belief that rights and freedoms would promote progress and help strengthen the nation was a recurrent theme in much of the writings during this period. The language of rights and nationalism was closely related in the minds of many Chinese writers. According to Yang Dusheng, for example, China needed to adopt both nationalism and human rights if it was to stand up in the world.[122] If people enjoyed human rights, they would be able to stand on their own two feet and rule themselves. Only if the authoritarian power of the ruler were destroyed, human rights promoted, a parliament established, and the people were given the right of political participation, could the foreign powers be withstood. In order to save China it was therefore necessary to promote human rights, thus establishing a close connection between human rights and national salvation. Two articles in *Yishu huibian*, discussing the English and the Japanese conceptions of rights respectively, argued that the more developed a people's rights thinking is, the stronger the country.[123] The author believed that the English emphasized rights the most; they loved rights more than life itself. He mentioned that Europeans often criticized Asians for not knowing the meaning of rights and for having discarded their rights. But striking a positive note, the author claimed that Japan could be seen as a positive exception to that rule, internally in the struggle for a constitution and externally in the struggle to revise the unequal treaties. It is obvious that the Japanese awareness of the importance of rights was regarded to be closely associated with Japan's new-found ability to stand up to other nations and was heralded as something for China to emulate.

The struggle for rights, in other words, was regarded as being both internal and external in character.[124] One article in *Guomin bao* described the internal struggle as a struggle against the oppression of a domestic ruler, exemplified by the case of France, and the external struggle as a struggle against foreign oppressors, exemplified by the case of America. It argued that in order to overthrow these two forms of oppression, it was first of all necessary to throw away old customs, thinking, education, and knowledge and develop a spirit of freedom.[125] In the case of China, the authoritarian system had to be discarded to restore the Chinese people's natural rights (*tianfu zhi quanli*).[126] In this context, it was often pointed out that the present time was an era of fighting for one's rights (*zheng quan zhi shidai*), under-lining the social Darwinian element of much of Chinese rights thinking.[127] The view that the Chinese people lived in an age of struggle for rights was also put forward by Mai Menghua in an article in *Qingyi bao* in 1900. Mai argued that a close relationship existed between a people's enjoyment of human rights (*renquan*) and a country's enjoyment of national power or rights (*guoquan*).[128] In order to become an independent country and enjoy national rights, people first of all had to be able to enjoy their individual rights. Without rights thinking, the Chinese people would be unable to withstand foreign aggression, a view shared by Liang Qichao who wrote: "If people cannot obtain rights from the government, they have to fight for them. When the government sees people fighting for their rights they will give them their rights. If one wants the country to enjoy equal rights with other countries, then one first has to ensure that people's innate [*guyou*] rights are equally enjoyed and that the rights our people enjoy are equal to those, which people in other countries enjoy."[129]

This justification of rights was based on the premise that individuals enjoy-ing rights would promote national rights and national salvation. It seems that there were no concerns at that time that individual rights and a struggle for rights could lead to selfish and asocial behavior that would threaten the social fabric and stability and, by extension, national survival. Such concerns did not surface in the Chinese rights discourse until the 1920s, when a strong state be-came more of a possibility and new trends of thought reached China. The in-dividual would then be requested to sacrifice his freedom and rights for the sake of the nation, as argued, for example, by Sun Yat-sen in his *Three People's Principles*.[130]

Combining human rights demands with anti-Manchu attacks was also quite common among the revolutionaries at the beginning of the century. Chen Tianhua accused the Manchus of violating the freedoms of the Chinese peo-ple and of ruling in their own interest and not that of the whole people.[131] The anti-Manchu approach is perhaps best exemplified by Zou Rong's *The Revo-lutionary Army*, which Zou wrote in 1903 when he was only eighteen years old.[132] Zou Rong's work is an anti-Manchu tract and not a theoretical work. Since it contained a highly emotional call to drive out the Manchus and re-store human rights (*tianfu zhi renquan*), one cannot expect it to provide any deeper analysis. It was furthermore written by a youngster without any pro-found knowledge of Western political thought. Despite these shortcomings, it is interesting because the idea of human rights figures so prominently in the work. Since it caught the readers' imagination, the language and ideas must have fallen on fertile ground.[133] The Manchus were described as a barbarian and uncivilized lot who had usurped the rights of the Han-Chinese people.

Zou Rong identified despotism with Manchu rule and simultaneously attacked despotism and the Manchus. According to Zou, the overthrow of the Manchus was necessary if the Chinese would be able to recover their lost rights.[134] The following diatribe is very typical of Zou's style of writing: "Let us expand the nine generation vengeance, engage in a ten year bloody war, sharpen our knifes and raise our banners, and daringly face death in order to drive out the Manchu scoundrels who humiliate us, tyrannise us, slaughter us, and rape our women, in order to restore our cultured native land, recover our natural rights [*tianfu zhi quanli*], win back the freedom which is our birth right, and restore the happiness of freedom and equality of all."[135]

The fight against the Manchus was not only a fight against despotism, it was also a fight against a lowly and inferior barbarian race. Zou Rong's work is full of racist attacks on the Manchus. On the international scene he also perceived a struggle among different races, most notably between yellow and white. This focus on the struggle between races and an identification of superior and inferior races is something we find among other writers at the beginning of the twentieth century as well, for example, in the more vitriolic writings of Chen Tianhua.[136] Both Chen and Zou regarded the Han race as the most exceptional and outstanding of the yellow races and far superior to the black race. To a modern reader it might seem incongruous to link a concern for human rights with racial antagonism, but we need to remind ourselves that racism and human rights can serve the same end.[137] In this case they were equally powerful weapons against an oppressive ruler, who happened to be of a different nationality. Zou felt China to be doubly enslaved, first by the Manchus and then by the Western powers, and so he was also attacking imperialism. Chen Tianhua, for his part, forcefully described how Westerners treated Chinese as inferiors, exemplified by their powers of extraterritoriality that had enabled them to put up a sign in a park in Shanghai reading: "Dogs and Chinese are not admitted."[138] This was the first but not the last time this sign was referred to in the Chinese human rights debate; it was to be invoked again toward the late 1970s as the PRC became involved in international human rights work.

HUMAN RIGHTS AND CHINESE CULTURE

It is only possible to find isolated instances in the early twentieth century where human rights were explicitly described as at odds with Confucianism. In one of the more theoretical articles on human rights, published in 1903, the word rights was, for example, juxtaposed with rites (*li*).[139] The anonymous writer believed that one had to discard the teaching of rites and replace it with rights thinking in order for China to survive, a view that became widespread during the May Fourth Movement. Liang Qichao, for his part, argued that the Chinese lack of rights thinking was because of their emphasis on the Confucian concept of humaneness (*ren*) and neglect of the concept of righteousness (*yi*), the latter being critical to rights thinking.[140] Since Liang ended up seeing rights not as innate but obtained through struggle, he emphasized that it was important that people fought for their rights and not pin their hopes on benevolent rulers. In other words, Liang was very critical of the emphasis on *ren* in the Chinese traditional culture and saw it as obstructing the development of rights thinking in China. This was in contrast to some contemporary scholars who believe that the idea of *ren* is akin to and can nurture human rights.

By insisting that human rights should be enjoyed equally by all human beings regardless of their position and status in society, many writers, although not explicitly attacking Confucianism, were nevertheless refuting the Confucian hierarchical system. Confucianism was also generally attacked for violating women's rights. Even though the attack on the family for fettering the individual did not become prominent until the May Fourth Movement, some, at the beginning of the twentieth century, began to advocate a revolution of the family system on the grounds that the individual had no freedom within the family.[141] In 1907 Yang Du thus attacked familism (*jiazu zhuyi*) for hindering progress and the development of a spirit of citizenship and nationalism among the Chinese.[142] He contrasted the situation in the West, where the individual was the subject of rights and duties, with the situation in China where the family was the subject of rights and duties and where the individual had no human rights (*renquan*).[143] Anarchists, such as Li Shizeng, attacked Confucianism early on for violating the principles of equality and human rights.[144] In his opinion, science proved that all people were equal; therefore, Confucianism was also attacked for being unscientific.

Thus, already by the early twentieth century, there were elements within the Chinese cultural tradition that many Chinese writers criticized and that they believed explained the backward state of the Chinese nation. They felt that China lacked a tradition of rights thinking and a conception of a rule of law, and complained that for thousands of years the Chinese people had only shouldered duties without enjoying any rights. Ma Junwu was one of those who criticized the Chinese people's tendency to place their rights into the hands of a few people, in effect throwing away their freedoms; whereas those in power, in their turn, infringed upon people's freedoms.[145] Ma often made references to foreign sources to prove his point. For instance, he quoted Georg Hegel as saying that Asian people were unaware of freedom and human rights (*renquan*) and only knew how to respect their rulers.[146]

Criticism of the dependent character and lack of responsibility among the Chinese people was a general theme in the human rights discourse. In "The New Citizen," Liang Qichao strongly criticized his fellow Chinese for lacking public spirit, the ability to rule themselves, and feelings of nationalism. Chinese people were themselves responsible for the dismal state of their land since they neither had any rights thinking nor had they stood up for their rights and freedoms.[147] The opening article in *Guomin bao* stressed that the reason Western countries were strong was their development of the idea of human rights, while the reason China was weak was that the Chinese people had discarded their rights.[148] The Chinese were criticized for having lived under an authoritarian system for more than two thousand years and for having become used to being slaves. It was not the foreigners who had brought about the possible extinction of the country, but the Chinese themselves. In his "Notes on Freedom," Liang Qichao in a similar vein argued that the greatest crime was to throw away one's own freedom.[149] To resist the intrusion of rights and stand up for one's rights was a sign of self-respect and character, and to fail in this respect was a sign of weakness and servility.

Many Chinese writers, such as Liang Qichao and Yan Fu, in this context also criticized the Chinese for lacking a feeling of public morality (*gongde*), another central keyword in the political discourse at this time.[150] The Chinese lack of concern for the affairs of the country was contrasted with the public spiritedness and concern for the collective found in the West.[151] Before the Chinese people would be able to enjoy freedoms and rights in the same way as people in the West, it was argued that they had to cultivate an independent spirit and be able to rule themselves. Liang Qichao held that whether the Chinese would be able to enjoy rights and equality and be able to establish a constitution and a parliament or not, depended on the development of their ability to self-rule (*zizhi*).[152] Other writers expressed similar views: "If people want to talk about freedom they must first know how to rule themselves. If they want to talk about rights they must first know about duties."[153] *Shimin bao* argued that the reason Westerners could enjoy freedom (referring to freedoms of speech, assembly, and publication) was their ability to rule themselves and show concern for the public good.[154] Those lacking this ability were not qualified to speak about freedom.

It was further argued that Chinese people only thought about themselves but did not care about others.[155] They were described as "a sheet of loose sand [*yipan sansha*]," as individualistic and selfish without any sense for the collective and the country. "The Chinese think about the family, but they do not think about the country; they think about the individual, but they do not think about the collective."[156] It is interesting to note that many Chinese thinkers were troubled by the selfish individualism and lack of concern for the collective that they found among their fellow countrymen, which contradicts the conventional wisdom regarding the collective-oriented Chinese people as, for example, put forward in the recent Asian values debate.[157]

Respect for human rights served to distinguish civilized and democratic countries from authoritarian ones, and thus served as a hallmark of civilization. *Guangyi congbao* in 1905, for example, argued that England and America were the two countries in the world that most respected human rights and freedom (*zui zhong renquan, zun ziyou*).[158] It acknowledged that Germany had made some progress in this respect, although still falling short of England and America, but added that Russia still was an authoritarian country. The most advanced countries were said to be those in which people enjoyed the most rights. Chinese writers described their countrymen as servile, backward, and lacking in public spirit and rights thinking, whereas Westerners, in contrast, were said to be public spirit-minded, to take the interest of the nation to heart, and to be ever vigilant to protect their rights. The West was thus held as a paragon of civilization and a model for China. These descriptions could be described as a blatant example of Orientalism, but they were actually more of a tactical device intended to awaken the Chinese people rather than reflect an uncritical admiration of the West.

In contrast to the May Fourth period, those writing on human rights in the early twentieth century usually saw the authoritarian political system as the main enemy of human rights, rather than put the blame squarely on Confucianism. The majority seemed to have believed in the universality of human rights and did not question their applicability to China. Nai Xuan described how the idea of people's rights and freedoms had swept over Europe in the eighteenth century and criticized those who argued that since constitutionalism was a political system foreign to China, it would not fit China.[159] He pointed out that since foreignness and novelty had not hindered China from accepting and using technical innovations originating in the West, such as railways and firearms, the use of foreign political systems should not pose any problem either. When advocating women's rights, one author argued that if women in the West could have rights, Chinese women should likewise be able to enjoy them because, although they were of a different race, they too were women.[160] In the foreword to *Guomin bao*, it was pointed out that since the understanding of human rights once had been weak in the West, a growing rights consciousness could also very well occur in China.[161]

It is obvious that most writers believed human rights to be applicable to China, and that the question as to whether human rights was a foreign concept incompatible with Chinese culture never became an issue with them. They therefore did not feel any need to seek indigenous roots to the concept of human rights in order to make it more acceptable to their countrymen. Although Zou Rong and Chen Tianhua argued that the Chinese people had enjoyed human rights in the past, which the Manchus had deprived them of, they did not elaborate on whether a concept of human rights had also existed in the past, as this was not crucial to their argument. Wang Jingwei, on the other hand, argued that demands for liberty, equality, and fraternity could be found in all societies, including the Chinese.[162] Ideas conducive to democracy could be found in the Chinese past, for example, the idea to "take people as the basis," and the idea that the emperor had to obey Heaven and take people's well-being seriously, otherwise he would lose his mandate. But Yan Fu, who, on the other hand, never became an advocate of human rights, in contrast pointed out that the concept of human rights, as well as concepts such as freedom, equality, democracy, and constitutionalism had all been unknown in traditional China.

Hardly anyone attacked human rights for being a Western concept or a ploy that Westerners used in their dealings with other countries. An article in *Xin shiji*, however, criticized the imperialists for advocating liberty, equality, and fraternity while failing to uphold these principles in their policies concerning their colonies.[163] The anarchists did not criticize these ideas as such, however, but believed that they were universal ideas applicable to China. Yang Dusheng, who described in great detail the imperialists' scheme against China (how they divided the country between them, enjoyed extraterritoriality, and controlled railroads, mining, and business), nevertheless advocated the Western concept of human rights. Even though Yang emphasized that the thinking of different nationalities varied, he seems to have believed that the principles of nationalism and human rights (*tianfu renquan*) were universal principles applicable to all societies.[164] It is interesting to note that even those expressing a deep resentment of Western imperialism were not adverse to adopting the acknowledged Western concept of human rights.

CONCLUSION

Advocates of human rights can be found among both reformers and revolutionaries. And whereas reformers like Liang Qichao did not advocate human rights, other contributors to *Qingyi bao* and *Xinmin congbao*, such as Mai Menghua and Ma Junwu, wrote several articles taking a more positive approach to human rights than Liang himself; Ma Junwu later also became a contributor to the revolutionary magazine *Minbao*. The revolutionaries were also often positively disposed to the concept of human rights. It appealed to people such as Zou Rong and Chen Tianhua, who used it as a weapon against the Manchus. But human rights did not figure so prominently in the revolutionary discourse after 1905. Sun Yat-sen, the leader of *Tongmeng hui*, forerunner of the GMD, never became an advocate of human rights and later even argued that the concept of human rights was not applicable to China.

Many assumptions common today about the Chinese people's understanding of human rights in the early twentieth century turn out to have been mistaken. The concept of human rights obviously appealed to many Chinese people and was used in their struggle against the Manchus. Their understanding and use of the concept was also surprisingly similar to that which we find in the West. The human rights they invoked were mostly civil and political rights, such as freedom of speech, assembly, and publication. The differences between the Chinese and Western views that exist can mostly be explained by the precarious political situation in which the Chinese people found themselves rather than because of any cultural differences. National survival rather than individual freedom from an oppressive state was the main preoccupation, although many obviously also craved individual rights and freedoms. Rights and human rights were heralded as indispensable to a modern and civilized society, and as essential if China was to survive in the struggle among nations. Once the Qing dynasty was overthrown, the anti-Manchu attacks were replaced with attacks on Confucianism, and the concept of human rights began to be explicitly juxtaposed with traditional ideas.

NOTES

1. Feng Ziyou (1928), vol. 1, p. 54. In an article written at the time, he also mentioned that after the war with Japan, new ideas of nationalism and people's rights had gained influence among the Chinese. According to this new way of thinking, all people should enjoy human rights (*renquan*) and freedom. See Feng Ziyou (1906), p. 10.

2. Liu Yazi (1887–1958) mentions that he took the name Renquan in 1902 at the age of 16 after having read about Rousseau's theory of natural rights in *Xinmin congbao*. See Wang Jing and Wang Xuezhuang (1989), vol. 2, p. 1030, p. 1051, and p. 1076, respectively.

3. For a reference to Rosseau and the social contract when discussing human rights, see Yang Dusheng (1903), p. 633. Yang Shouren (1871–1911), as he was known after 1904, was, together with Huang Xing and Chen Tianhua, active in *Hunan youxue huibian,* a magazine published in Japan.

4. Zhina Zi (1903), p. 3. Translated in Angle and Svensson (2001).

5. He Qi and Hu Liyuan (1994), p. 410, p. 416, p. 419.

6. Mai Menghua (1900a), p. 1a.

7. Anon., "A Call to My Fellow Students" (1903), p. 2. See also Anon., "On China's Unity Starting from Local Self-Government," (1903), p. 2.

8. Anon., "On People," no. 6, 1901, p. 8b. This article was a translation but there is no mention of the author's name. The work appeared in nos. 4, 5, and 6, but publication of the magazine stopped before the whole work was printed.

9. Anon., "On People," no. 6, 1901, p. 7b.

10. Anon., "On Rights," (1903), p. 481, translated in Angle and Svensson (2001).

11. Anon., "On Citizens," (1901), p. 72, translated in Angle and Svensson (2001).

12. Yang Du (1907) in Liu Qingpo (1986), pp. 255–58, and p. 299.

13. Lust (1968) p. 123, Chinese text p. 43. See also, p. 101, Chinese text p. 28. I have used Lust's English translation of *The Revolutionary Army* and the Chinese version from his book.

14. Chen Tianhua (1982), p. 193.

15. Chen Tianhua (1982), p. 186.

16. Liu Yazi (1904), p. 935. An article in the magazine *Jiangsu* likewise argued that all people enjoy natural rights (*tianfu quan*) of which they cannot be deprived. Han Ju (1903), p. 584.

17. Wang Jingwei (1905), p. 83 and p. 101, respectively. Wang would later, however, distance himself from this view and make a distinction between certain freedoms, such as freedom of expression in academic work, which was held to be absolute, and other political freedoms, which were qualified.

18. Patterson (1995).

19. Jenner (1998), pp. 72–73. See also Kelly (1998) on the conception of freedom in China. In contrast to them, I would, however, argue that the slave trope has played an important role in China since the early twentieth century.

20. For examples by Liang Qichao, see his "On Rights Consciousness," in "The New Citizen" and "Notes on Freedom," reprinted in Liang Qichao (1978).

21. Yan Fu reprinted in Wang Shi (1986), p.132.

22. See Yuan Sun (1904), p. 1213.

23. Quoted in Shain (1994), p. 304.

24. Liang Qichao, "On Freedom," in "The New Citizen" (1902–1903), p. 40.

25. See, for example, Anon., "There Are No Differences between Being the Slaves of the Foreigners and of the Manchus," (1903), p. 527; and Lust (1968).

26. The description of women as the slaves of slaves is found in many works. See Jin Songzen's 1903 work, as quoted by Edwards (1994), p. 123, and Chen Xiefen's 1904 work in Dooling and Torgeson (1998), pp. 83–86. The anarchists went the furthest in their analysis; they also saw women as being the slaves of capitalists. See Beahan (1975), p. 412.

27. See, for example, Anon., "Admonishing Slaves," (1904), pp. 76–91.

28. Lust (1968) pp. 113–14, and Chinese text pp. 35–37. For another article stating that the Chinese enjoyed being slaves, see Anon., "The Bitterness of Slavery," (1903).

29. Mai Menghua (1900b), p. 1b.

30. See, for example, Anon., "On Citizens," (1901), pp. 72–73, the text is translated in Angle and Svensson (2001); and Anon., "On Rights," (1903), translated in Angle and Svensson (2001). According to Han Ju, there should only be citizens (*guomin*) and no subjects (*chenmin*) in a nation, only masters (*zhuren*) and no slaves (*nuli*). Han Ju (1903), pp. 579–93.

31. For a discussion on the development of a conception of citizenry in China, see Zarrow (1998).

32. Anon., "On China's Future and the Responsibilities of the Citizens," (1903), p. 463.

33. Liang Qichao, "On Progress," reprinted in "The New Citizen," (1902–1903), p. 58.

34. See, for example, Anon., "On Citizens," (1901), pp. 72–73, translated in Angle and Svensson (2001); Anon., "On Rights," (1903), translated in Angle and Svensson (2001); Ding Chuwo (1904), p. 926.

35. Anon., "On People," (1901), p. 2b.

36. Ma Junwu (1903a), p. 99.

37. Liang Qichao, "On Rights Consciousness," in "The New Citizen," (1902–1903), translated in Angle and Svensson (2001), p.?.

38. Anon., "Admonishing Slaves," (1904), p. 85.

39. Xu Yuchen (1907), translated in Angle and Svensson (2001).

40. Hill (1973).

41. Anon., "On Rights," (1903).

42. Anon., "On Rights," (1903), translated in Angle and Svensson (2001), p. 21.

43. Anon., "On People," no. 5, 1901, p. 5b.

44. Yang Dusheng (1903), p. 633.

45. *Renge* is often translated as human dignity, dignity, or humanity, see Ip (1994) and Schwarcz (1986). I am grateful to Stephen C. Angle for discussions on this term and agree with him that it is better to translate it as personality in most cases; this is also borne out by the articles referred to in the text. The kind of personality the Chinese had in mind, however, embodied self-respect and independence and was the opposite of a slave personality. In other words, notions of human dignity were clearly involved in their understanding of personality.

46. Zhen Gui (1903), pp. 183–84.

47. Long Chuan (1903), pp. 35–36.

48. Nai Xuan (1903b), pp. 85–86.

49. See Anon., "Admonishing Slaves," (1904), p. 89.

50. On nobody being born a slave, see Anon., "Admonishing Slaves," (1904), p. 76.

51. For a discussion of the meaning of *zuoren* in Confucian thought, see Kwok (1998), pp. 82–93.

52. On the meaning of humaneness in Confucianism, see, for example, Ames (1988), p. 202.

53. Wang Ermin (1983) has suggested that the Chinese people's reception of human rights was facilitated through their concern for *renge*, although he does not quote any references of texts explicitly linking *renge* and *renquan*, p. 74. For more on the Chinese consciousness of *renge* in the late Qing, see Wang Ermin (1995b), pp. 111–28.

54. For a discussion on how the idea of legitimate desires in Neo-Confucianism came to be linked with rights in the minds of Liang Qichao and Liu Shipei, see Angle (2002).

55. Wang Ermin (1983) has argued that discussions on human rights from the start were closely associated with the advocacy of women's rights, pp. 67–83. For a useful collection of articles on women issues, see Li Youning and Zhang Yufa (1975).

56. Zhu Zhuang (1904), p. 922. Ya Sheng (1904) also stated that: "Heaven gives birth to man and woman, they both have duties and also enjoy the rights that are their due," p. 931.

57. A translation by Ma Junwu of a program on women's rights adopted by socialists in Brussels in 1891, reprinted in Mo Shixiang (1991).

58. Liu Yazi (1904), p. 937.

59. Ding Chuwo (1904), p. 929.

60. On the Chinese women's press, see Beahan (1975), and on women's new role in politics, see Gipoulon (1989–90).

61. Ya Sheng (1904), p. 931, credited the new ideas to Mill and Spencer. Ma Junwu translated a piece by Spencer in 1902 and wrote an article in 1903 introducing Mill's "The Subjection of Women." See Mo Shixiang (1991).

62. See Rankin (1975), pp. 42–43; and Tao (1994).

63. See Tao (1994), p. 149.

64. Du Qingfeng (1904), p. 41. Huang Zunxian made a similar association in 1898, quoted in Wang Ermin (1983).

65. See Rankin (1975), Beahan (1975), Zarrow (1988), and Edwards (1994).

66. Quoted in Ono (1989), p. 214 n. 3.

67. On women's specific plights and their rights, see Ding Chuwo (1904), pp. 927–29; and the discussion of Jin Songzen's work in Edwards (1994), p. 135.

68. Anon., "On Citizens," (1901), p. 75. The article also mentioned that in colonies people were subjected to harsh labor. It enumerated three peoples subjected to this kind of treatment, namely Indians, Polynesians, and Chinese.

69. Anarchists such as He Zhen, however, paid more attention to the plight of poor women; see Zarrow (1988), p. 802.

70. Liang Qichao (1901a), p. 145, (1902b), p. 301, and (1902f), p. 335. On the freedom of belief see also (1902c), pp. 304–13. Yan Fu also particularly stressed the freedom of speech, reprinted in Wang Shi (1986), p.134.

71. See, for example, Li Shucheng (1903), p. 459. Freedoms of speech, assembly, and publication were referred to as the great freedoms in Anon., "To Talk About Freedom One Must First Have the Ability of Control," (1904), pp. 1147–49. Whereas an article in *Beiyang xuebao* mentioned the freedom of belief (*zunxin ziyou*), the freedom of publication, and the freedom of assembly. See Anon,. "On the Character of Monarchic Constitutionalism," (1906), pp. 1105–7.

72. Anon., "The Closure of *Su bao*," (1904), pp. 120–21

73. Lust (1968) p. 123, Chinese text p. 43.

74. Chen Tianhua (1982), pp. 185–96.

75. Chen Tianhua (1982), p. 193.

76. Wu Yue (1906), p. 5.

77. See the following articles from *Shibao*: Anon., "The Freedoms of Assembly and Association and Their Restriction," (1906); Lei Fen (1906); Anon., "The Legal Status of Citizens," (1907); Xue Hong (1908). My view of the understanding of human rights in *Shibao* differs to some extent from Joan Judge. In contrast to her, I believe that many of the writers in the magazine were quite knowledgeable and supportive of human rights. See Judge (1996), pp. 66–67, and p. 75. For an example from *Yunnan zazhi*, see Si Hui (1906).

78. Apart from the example of the right to property given in the text, see also Anon., "The Education of Citizens," (1903), p. 16.

79. Anon., "On People," (1901), no. 5, p. 6b. For an isolated reference implying a criticism of the French Declaration of the Rights of Man on the grounds that it stipulated the right to private property and that the French Revolution therefore could not be regarded as a social revolution, see Xian Jie (1906), p. 23.

80. For the view that Chinese tradition has given rise to the primacy of social and economic rights in Chinese rights thinking, see Nathan (1986c), pp. 153–54.

81. Ma Junwu, for example, wrote on Mill's understanding of the relationship between two individual's rights; see Mo Shixiang (1991).

82. Liu Shipei (1907b), p. 918. On Liu Shipei's understanding of rights I have benefited from the works by Angle (2002) and Zarrow (1998).

83. Zhina Zi (1903), the text is translated in Angle and Svensson (2001).

84. Anon., "The Freedoms of Assembly and Association and their Restriction," (1906).

85. Lei Fen (1906). Compare with another article in which it was argued that although human rights were bestowed by heaven, their implementation was laid down by the people (*renquan zhi shou chu yu tian, er renquan zhi li ze zai yu ren*). Anon., "On China's Unity Starting from Local Self-Government," (1903).

86. See Anon., "In Order to Save China It Is First Necessary to Develop the Public Morality of People," (1906). See also Anon., "On Rights," (1903), translated in Angle and Svensson (2001).

87. See, for example, Lust (1968), pp. 99, and 124, Chinese text pp. 25 and 44; Xue Jinjiang (1903), p. 528; and Wu Yue (1906), p. 2. Resistance to tyrannical oppression had also been considered as both a right and a duty during the American revolution.

88. In contemporary usage, *yiwu* is mostly associated with duties stipulated by law and of an objective character, whereas *benfen* has more of a moral connotation and refers to duties that are more subjective in character and dependent on social relationships. In an article reprinted in *Dongfang zazhi* in 1906, a distinction was made between *yiwu*, referring to duties held toward the public, and *benwu*, which were understood as duties of the individual. See Anon., "A Distinction of People's Duties," (1906). See also Zhen Gui, "Translations of New Concepts," (1903), p. 4, who translated duties as *benfen*, and obligations as *yiwu*, although without being explicit about the difference. It seems, however, as if the former referred to the realm of morals (*lunli*), whereas the latter referred to the realm of law. Another article took a different approach; the author argued that only if one has rights will one shoulder duties (*yiwu*), but, on the other hand, he also argued that rights were derived from one's *benfen* (one's natural position and duty in society); see Anon., "On Rights," (1903), p. 484.

89. Anon., "On People," (1901), nos. 4, 5, and 6.

90. Feng Banggan (1902).

91. The allusion to Robinson Crusoe is found in the original, but the reference to Friday is mine.

92. Zhang Baixi (1904), p. 104.

93. Quan Liang (1903), p. 6. See also Xin Hua (1904).

94. Liang Qichao, "On Duty Consciousness," in "The New Citizen" (1902–1903), pp. 104–8. See also the discussion in Hao Chang (1971), p. 275.

95. Xue Hong (1908).

96 Zhina Zi (1903), p. 8. In another article it was likewise argued that "Those having duties but no rights are no more than slaves, whereas those enjoying rights but not shouldering any duties are but robbers." See Anon., "The Legal Status of Citizens," (1907). The argument that those without rights were slaves and those not shouldering duties were thieves is also found in Jian Hongyi (1907), p. 10092, and Si Hui (1906), p. 13.

97. See Anon., "The Freedoms of Assembly and Association and Their Restriction," (1906), and Xue Hong (1908).

98. Ya Cui (1903).

99. Ya Cui, p. 45.

100 Hao Chang (1971), p. 126.

101. Lust (1968), pp. 123–24, Chinese text pp. 43–44.

102. Yang Du reprinted in Liu Qingpo (1986), pp. 255–58, and p. 347. See also Quan Liang (1903); and Wang Jingwei (1905), p. 111.

103. Nai Xuan (1903a).

104. See Han Ju (1903).

105. See, for example, Ya Cui (1903), p. 42.

106. Anon., "Freedom Cannot Die," (1901). A charge repeated in Anon., "On Citizens," (1901), p. 76.

107. Zhina Zi (1903), p. 7. In another article in the same magazine it was also pointed out that people's rights were violated by the authorities; see Da Wo (1903), p. 509.

108. See, for example, Jian He (1908). For a critique of illegal arrests, see also Anon., "On the Right to Life," (1907).

109. The English title of the article published in 1904 was "The True Solution of the Chi-

nese Question: An Appeal to the People of the United States." Two different Chinese texts of this piece, originally in English, now exist; both are reprinted in Sun Zhongshan (Sun Yat-sen) (1981), vol. 1, pp. 243–55. Only in the second text are the rights to life, liberty, and property mentioned together, whereas the first text only mentions the rights to life and property.

110. See Wu Yue (1906), p. 6; and Yang Dusheng (1903), p. 636. Wang Jingwei (1905) also accused the Manchus for discriminating against the Han-Chinese and violating their rights.

111. See Hen Hai (1906), Huai Jiang (1906), and Liu Yazi (1907).

112. See P'eng-yüan Chang (1968).

113. Shen Qichang (1907a), p. 193.

114. See Anon., "The Right to Life," (1907), and Si Hui (1906).

115. Ma Junwu (1906), p. 230. A view that he reiterated five years later in Ma Junwu (1911), p. 243.

116. On the work on the constitution, see Meienberger (1980).

117. Chang Yu (1910), pp. 205–12. Others also argued that a vigorous public opinion was important for the development of the nation. See Ma Weilong, translated in Angle and Svensson (2001).

118. See Anon., "The Harm of Identical Opinions," (1901), pp. 180–81.

119. See Liang Qichao (1902c).

120. Chen Tianhua (1982), pp. 194–96.

121. On Yan Fu's view of freedom, see Schwartz (1964).

122. Yang Dusheng (1903), pp. 612–48.

123. Gong Fazi (1902b), pp. 117–18.

124. In *Shibao* the view was also put forward that externally one had to fight for sovereignty rights whereas internally one should fight for rights against the government, that is, the Manchus. See Anon., "On the Citizens' Enthusiasm for Rights," (1908).

125. Anon., "On Citizens," (1901), p. 73, translated in Angle and Svensson (2001).

126. See another article in *Guomin bao*, anon. "The Extinction of the Country," (1901), p. 82.

127. See, for example, Anon., "On Citizens' Enthusiasm for Rights," (1908).

128. Mai Menghua (1900a).

129. Liang Qichao, "Rights Consciousness," in "The New Citizen" (1902–1903), p. 40.

130. Sun Yat-sen (1960).

131. Chen Tianhua (1982), p. 208. Chen argued that the country had a duty to protect its citizens' rights and that it was a great shame that the Chinese government could not protect its citizens at home or abroad, p. 192.

132. For biographical details on Zou Rong, see Lust (1968). For the context of his writings, see also Rankin (1971).

133. Hu Shi has written about how strongly Zou Rong's work moved him in his autobiography (1992), p. 49.

134. Similar opinions were also put forward by Wu Yue, who argued that the principle for establishing a state based on nationality was to restore the Han-Chinese rights (*huifu wo Hanzu zhi quanli*) and overthrow the authoritarian government of foreign nationality, that is, the Manchus. See Wu Yue (1906), p. 2.

135. Lust (1968) p. 82, and Chinese text pp. 24–25. I have made some small changes in Lust's English translation.

136. To drive out the Manchus was also the first goal for the *Tongmeng hui*. On racial themes in the revolutionary struggle, see Gasster (1969), chapter 3; and Rankin (1971), pp.

26–28. On the discussion on race among the Chinese in general, see Dikötter (1992).

137. In this context we also need to remind ourselves that the advocates of human rights in America willfully excluded slaves from enjoying the same rights for which they themselves had fought. Those who were ardent advocates of human rights did not necessarily perceive any contradiction in denying these rights to other groups of people, thus combining human rights and racism. In the 1980s, Chinese students attached slogans about human rights to anti-black exhortations; for example, during the late 1988 anti-African protests in Nanjing preceding the 1989 pro-democracy movement.

138. Chen Tianhua (1982), p 37, and p. 70, respectively. For the history and myth regarding this sign, see Bickers and Wasserstrom (1995).

139. Anon., "On Rights," (1903), the text is translated in Angle and Svensson (2001).

140. Liang Qichao, "Rights consciousness," in "The New Citizen" (1902–1903), pp. 35–36; see also "Protect China," in "Notes on Freedom," (1899–1902), pp. 40–41.

141. See Ding Chuwo (1904), p. 926.

142. Yang Du (1907) in Liu Qingpo (1986).

143. Yang Du (1907) in Liu Qingpo (1986), p. 256.

144. See, for example, Zhen (Li Shizeng) (1907a) and (1907b); reference to human rights on p. 146.

145. Ma Junwu (1903f), p. 152f. In another article published the same year he also lamented the fact that the Chinese had no rights thinking; see (1903a), p. 94.

146. Ma Junwu (1903b), p. 107.

147. This theme was very common during this period; see Zhina Zi (1903), p. 7; Anon., "On Violating Other's Freedom and Renouncing One's Own," (1904); Liu Yazi (1904), p. 937; and Xu Yucheng (1907), p. 445.

148. See also Anon., "On Citizens," (1901), p. 73. In an article in *Han sheng*, the successor to *Hubei xuesheng jie*, it was stated that the reason for China's weakness was that the Chinese did not know the theory of human rights. Anon., "On China's Unity Starting from Local Self-Government," (1903), p. 2. Feng Ziyou also argued that the reason the West was so strong was its concern with people's rights and freedom, and that the reason for China's weakness was her lack of this kind of political thinking. Feng Ziyou (1900), p. 5a.

149. Liang Qichao, "The Crime of Letting Go of Freedom," in "Notes on Freedom" (1899–1902), pp. 23–24; and "National Rights and People's Rights," in "Notes on Freedom" (1899–1902), pp. 24–25.

150. Liang Qichao, "On Public Morality," in "The New Citizen" (1902–1903), pp. 12–16.

151. Ma Junwu also complained that the Chinese lacked a sense of public spirit. He quoted Robert Hart as having said that "the Chinese are a people naturally devoid of any public morality." See (1903f), p. 161. On the importance of public morality in order to save China, see also Anon., "In Order to Save China it is First Necessary to Develop the Public Morality of the People," (1906), and Anon., "On the Weak Points of the Chinese Society," (1907), p. 10082f.

152. Liang Qichao, "On Self-Rule," in "The New Citizen," (1902–1903), p. 54.

153. Quan Liang (1903), p. 6.

154. Anon., "In Order to Talk about Freedom One Must First Have the Ability of Control," (1904), pp. 1147. On the Chinese lack of a public spirit (*gonggong xin*), inability to rule themselves, and selfishness, see also Zhina Zi (1903), p. 7.

155. See, for example, Anon., "The Danger of the Chinese Having Lost Their Consciousness," (1906). That the Chinese only knew about themselves and were unaware of oth-

ers was regarded as the major ill of China; see Jian Hongyi (1907), p. 10086.

156. Anon., "In Order to Talk about Freedom One Must First Have the Ability of Control," (1904), p. 1148.

157. Schwartz (1964) also noted the puzzling fact that the public spirit of the West was contrasted with the narrow selfishness of Confucian China, p. 70.

158. Anon., "On the Future Major Powers in the World," (1905), p. 6a.

159. Nai Xuan (1903b).

160. Lian Shi (1907), p. 433.

161. In another article in the same magazine a similar argument was given. It was argued that before the French Revolution, the French had also been submissive to authority and not developed a sense of citizenry. See Anon., "On Citizens," (1901), p. 77. Another article also pointed out that the authoritarianism in Europe before the eighteenth century was similar to that in China at that time, but that after Rousseau had laid down the idea of a social contract, ideas of human rights and constitutionalism had spread in the West. Sun Lou (1910), p. 216.

162. Wang Jingwei (1906b), p. 413. Others also regarded freedom, equality, and fraternity as universal ideas; see, for example, Fen Min (1911), pp. 116–17.

163. Anon., "The Results of Imperialism," (1908), pp. 1307–9. Liu Yazi (1907) also referred to the fact that even though England was a constitutional monarchy, people in India still did not enjoy any rights, p. 81.

164. See Yang Dusheng (1903), p. 632–33.

Chapter Six

The New Culture Movement and Beyond: Human Rights and the Liberation of the Individual

CULTURAL ICONOCLASM AND POLITICAL RADICALISM

The New Culture Movement signified an all-out attack on Confucianism under the two catchwords of science and democracy. The participants sought the emancipation of the individual from the stifling constraints of Confucianism and advocated the Enlightenment ideal of critical and independent thinking. The movement was initially liberal and cosmopolitan in character, only to become more radical and nationalistic as a consequence of the May Fourth incident in 1919, when demonstrations broke out in protest of the Paris Peace Conference's decision to transfer the German concessions in Shandong to Japan. The May Fourth Movement can be said to have continued and developed the spirit of the New Culture Movement and it therefore came to exhibit a multiple and somewhat ambiguous nature.[1] Its double character of cultural enlightenment and national awakening is important to keep in mind when discussing the role of human rights in political discourse during this period.[2]

Peking University played a particularly important role at the time, being home to several of the central figures of the intellectual and political debate. The chancellor of the university, Cai Yuanpei, gathered around him a number of China's brightest and most progressive scholars, such as Hu Shi, Chen Duxiu, Li Dazhao, and Lu Xun.[3] Cai Yuanpei tried to uphold the principle of academic freedom at the university, and his liberal attitude showed both in his hiring policy and his tolerance of the faculty members' political views and extracurricular activities.[4] During these years, liberalism, pragmatism, utilitarianism, anarchism, and socialism were all discussed and debated, both at the university and in society at large.[5] Many of the faculty members at Peking

University became involved in different publishing activities. The most important of these was the magazine *New Youth*, founded by Chen Duxiu in Shanghai in 1915.[6] The magazine, which became the symbol of the spirit of the period, was a vehicle of both liberal and more radical writings and contained
both academic as well as more political and polemical articles. In late 1918, the
students at the university founded the New Tide Society, and in January 1919,
also a magazine of their own, *New Tide* (*Xin chao*).[7] A wealth of other magazines also saw the light of day during these years, focusing on issues ranging
from literature to women's rights to political affairs.

The Allies' decision at the Paris Peace Conference served to radicalize Chinese intellectuals and disillusion them with the West, which hitherto had been
their chief source of inspiration. Nationalistic feelings made communism and
the political system of Soviet Russia a more viable alternative. Discussions on
socialism had been rather sparse up to 1919, but attracted more interest after
the May Fourth protest.[8] After his release from prison for having distributed
pamphlets in opposition to the peace treaty, Chen Duxiu decided to leave
Peking and in 1920 moved *New Youth* to Shanghai. In Shanghai Chen became
more involved in socialist activities, which eventually led to the founding of
the CCP in July 1921. Chen later moved *New Youth* to Canton and converted
it to a communist organ. From then on the ideological gulf between liberals
and socialists gradually widened, although they were still able to unite from
time to time to criticize human rights violations committed by various power
holders.

The May Fourth generation devoted much of its time and energy to attacking Confucianism, especially the family system and the notion of filial
piety. A central concern was the liberation of the individual person and humankind in general.[9] The May Fourthers sought the liberation of the individual from the demands of the family, demands that were seen as stifling individual autonomy and crushing all sense of individuality. Hu Shi later stressed
that the May Fourth Movement had aimed itself at the liberation of thought
(*sixiang jiefang*) and the liberation of the individual (*geren jiefang*).[10] Henrik Ibsen's *A Doll's House* caught the imagination of a whole generation of Chinese
precisely because it advocated, not only the emancipation of women, but, more
generally, the liberation of the individual from family and traditional shackles.
In his preface to the special Ibsen issue of *New Youth*, Hu Shi underlined the
need for freedom for both the development of individual personality and for
social well-being.

> If the individual does not have any right to freedom, he will not shoulder responsi-
> bility and will become like a slave. Regardless of how much fun he has or how happy
> he is, he will in the final analysis not experience any real happiness or be able to de-
> velop his personality. . . . If the family is like this, society and the nation will also be

like this. A self-governing society and a republican nation require that the individual
has the right to choose freely, and that he furthermore bears the responsibility for his
own conduct and actions. If this is not the case, he will absolutely not be able to create his own independent personality [*duli renge*].[11]

The preoccupation with seeking liberation from the family loomed larger in
most people's minds during this period than any need to seek freedom from
the hand of the state; there was no strong state to speak of in the first place and
the hand of the family weighed heavier. Nonetheless the May Fourthers, like
Hu Shi, considered that there was a strong linkage between the situation in the
family and in society at large. The struggle for an independent personality, human dignity, and self-respect therefore came to be closely connected to calls for
human rights and democracy. When the Chinese government suppressed freedom of speech and so on, it inevitably provoked demands for the respect of individual rights and freedoms.

FOREIGN INFLUENCES AND INSPIRATIONS

One important characteristic of the May Fourthers, despite all of their individual differences, is that they were generally more influenced by and knowledgeable of Western political and philosophical ideas than earlier Chinese generations. This was in many cases due to prolonged years of studies abroad,
including in the West itself, and better language capabilities that enabled many
Chinese intellectuals to read Western works in the original. But it also had to
do with developments and improvements of the Chinese academic system;
many new universities had been established and new subjects were now taught
by teachers who themselves had studied abroad. China also became more integrated in the international academic and political community through its returned students and through foreign visitors to China. Several well-known
Western scholars visited China and spent some time teaching and lecturing in
the country. Dewey spent two years and Bertrand Russell spent one during
1919–21, crucial years in the history of modern China.[12]

Dewey in particular had a wide following in China consisting of his former
students, including Hu Shi, among others, and it was at their invitation that he
visited the country.[13] Both Dewey and Russell lectured widely, not only in
Peking but in the provinces as well. Their lectures were often translated into Chinese and published in magazines such as *New Youth* and in book form. Although
several of Russell's works had been translated before he arrived in China, and he
was better known, Russell did not have the same kind of following as Dewey,
nor did he influence Chinese intellectuals to the same extent.[14] Alan Ryan has
suggested that one of the reasons Dewey was more attractive to the Chinese had

to do with the fact that his liberalism was less individualistic than that of Russell. "Dewey's liberalism was holistic; it stressed community values, emphasised the child's ties to his or her local culture and community, and saw the school as a natural extension of the family. To an audience brought up on Confucian ideals of family and community loyalty, Dewey's liberalism was much more attractive than the fiercely individualistic liberalism of someone like Russell."[15]

It would indeed seem as if Dewey, as Laski later, was particularly attractive to Chinese intellectuals since his liberalism was a social liberalism that stressed community values. For all of their differences, both Dewey and Laski put a high value on the community and emphasized the importance of duties. Both of them had been greatly influenced by Green, another Westerner who was to have some influence on the Chinese during this period, albeit more limited and largely indirect. British Idealism was very congenial to the Chinese, with its emphasis on moral fulfillment and obligations toward society. It is interesting to note that Anglo-Saxon thinkers, in contrast to the pre-1911 period, exerted a much greater influence than either French or German thinkers. During the period 1915–17, for example, there were sixteen articles on Anglo-Saxon thinkers in *New Youth*, compared with five on French thinkers. *Tiger Magazine*, edited by Zhang Shizhao, was another publication deeply influenced by Anglo-Saxon political thought.[16]

Dewey exerted a particularly great influence, not only on his student Hu Shi, but on people as different as Chen Duxiu and Gao Yihan. Gao Yihan was perhaps the May Fourther who was the most knowledgeable about Western political thought.[17] He wrote extensively on Western philosophers such as Mill, Albert Dicey, Rousseau, and the social contract theory of Hobbes, Locke, and Rousseau. He was also well aware of the criticism directed against these thinkers. In his own political writings, Gao referred to a wide range of Western scholars, in particular Anglo-Saxon scholars, ranging from the two Americans John William Burgess and Dewey, to British idealists such as Green, Bernard Bosanquet, and Ritchie, to New Liberals such as Hobhouse, and to socialists such as Laski.[18] Laski, as we will see, exerted a particularly great influence on the Chinese human rights discourse toward the late 1920s. Although Laski never visited China, he, like Dewey, had several prominent Chinese students who actively promoted his ideas and translated his works.

Although Dewey was a strong advocate of democracy, he was opposed to laissez-faire individualism.[19] Dewey's view on democracy was spelled out more fully only after he returned to the United States, but in China he gave several lectures on the history of political thought and the development of democracy in the West.[20] In one of his lectures Dewey pointed out that the West had passed through two stages of political development. The first was the struggle for individual freedom, and the second was the struggle for social equality brought about as a response to unrestrained individualism.[21] Dewey argued that China might be able to take the two stages in one step. To this end he believed that the Mencian tradition of social protection could be democratized. Since Dewey knew all too well the problems that unrestrained individualism could bring, he was eager to advocate that China should not follow the same route as in the West but emphasize equality from the start. This was a suggestion, however, that could easily lead to a slighting of individual rights and freedoms, especially in a country such as China, which lacked a strong tradition of individual rights.

The concept of human rights does not figure so prominently in Dewey's thinking.[22] But throughout his life, Dewey was a strong supporter of academic freedom and the freedom of speech; he was one of the founders of the American Civil Liberties Union (ACLU). When the China League for the Protection of Civil Rights was founded in the early 1930s, Dewey and the ACLU were cited by Chinese liberals as a source of inspiration. While in China, Dewey spoke on natural rights (*tianfu de quanli*) and individual freedoms in several of his lectures.[23] Dewey did not regard rights as existing before or outside of society. Only as a member of society could an individual have rights, and only in as much as rights were supported and upheld by the law. "The individual can have these rights only so long as he is a member of his society and his state; there are no such things as individual rights until and unless they are supported and maintained by society, through law. It is absolutely fundamental that the concept of individual rights be considered with reference to the society which grants them and to the state, which, through the agency of law, enforces them."[24] Dewey thus believed that the only rights we have are those given by law.[25] For Dewey, every right also had as its obverse an obligation.

Dewey's view on rights thus differed from the traditional natural rights theory and owed much to the British Idealists. According to Dewey, rights had originally been sought in the West in reaction to the suppression of individuals by despotic governments, but this was no longer a problem—a rather premature assertion one is forced to conclude; instead, the problem in the West was how to provide people with opportunities to exercise rights already acknowledged. As an example Dewey mentioned the right to property, which would remain a rather empty right for those who did not own any property. Although Dewey was not to write much on the need for a welfare state, he supported the idea that the government should provide old-age pensions and unemployment relief; throughout his life he was active in efforts to provide education for socially disadvantaged people.

Russell's experiences and outlook were quite different from those of Dewey. His visit to Soviet Russia, shortly before coming to China, had left him deeply disappointed with the lack of individual freedom in that country.

This disillusionment was made known to his Chinese audience through articles in *New Tide* and in the *Eastern Miscellany*.[26] Russell himself was troubled by the fact that people's freedoms of thought and speech were restricted to the point that communism had become a new faith. But the Chinese commentator in the article in *New Tide* tried to defend the situation in Soviet Russia by putting the blame for all the sufferings and problems on hostile foreign forces.[27] Russell, who was disillusioned with the materialism and strife in the contemporary West, also had a tendency to see the Chinese tradition in a much more positive light than did most Chinese intellectuals at the time.[28] Dewey later objected to Russell's romantic view of China and tendency to idealize Chinese ideas, such as its pacifism, while ignoring problems of political corruption and economic stagnation. Not only did Dewey and Russell leave different impressions among Chinese intellectuals, they returned home with different impressions of China.

THE PARTICIPANTS: LIBERALS AND COMMUNISTS-TO-BE

The teachers' generation, people such as Chen Duxiu, Li Dazhao, and Gao Yi-han, seems to have been more concerned with the issue of human rights than the students writing in *New Tide*.[29] Both Communists-to-be and liberals discussed human rights during the May Fourth period. One of the undisputed leaders of the New Culture and May Fourth Movements was Chen Duxiu.[30] In his first articles in *New Youth*, Chen gave view to a belief in liberal values such as human rights and individual freedom, which later, under the influence of Marxism, he abandoned, although he never explicitly repudiated them. Toward the end of his life, he seems to have returned to some of his former liberal ideals, probably as a reaction to the harsh treatment meted out to him by both the GMD and the CCP.[31] Wang Fanxi, Chen's old disciple, claims that Chen then returned to his "intellectual first love, 'pure' democracy."[32] According to Wang, Chen was appalled by the Moscow trials and this event made him reappraise bourgeois democracy and individual rights.

During the period 1915–19, Chen published his most liberal and individualistic-oriented articles. Chen then also emerged as something of a champion of human rights.[33] Whether this advocacy was a reflection of his iconoclasm more than a genuine concern is a matter open to dispute.[34] It must be acknowledged, however, that Chen had emphasized already in his earliest writings that the protection of people's rights was a basic concern of the state, a view he reiterated after his expulsion from the CCP.[35] Chen's interest in human rights, in other words, was by no means only confined to the New Culture period, which shows that one cannot simply dismiss his advocacy of human rights as having been brought about by political expediency and iconoclasm. It is also worth remembering that Chen was not alone in advocating human rights during this period; his views and priorities were shared by others at the time, both Communists-to-be and liberals.

Li Dazhao, another founder of the CCP, differed from Chen Duxiu in many respects.[36] Being younger than Chen he seems not to have had the same need to distance himself from tradition; he did not spend so much time and energy attacking Confucianism and was also able to take some pride in it. Li's early writings reflect a belief in constitutional government and civil and political rights and a familiarity with Western philosophers, such as Rousseau, Montesquieu, Mill, and others. It has been argued that Li's nationalism was much stronger than Chen's, and that he therefore was more critical of the West and much more readily adopted Marxism. Be that as it may, in comparison with Chen, Li was much less preoccupied with the concept of human rights, although he showed a strong interest in individual rights and freedoms.

Together with Chen Duxiu, Gao Yihan contributed the majority of articles discussing human rights in *New Youth*. Gao served as professor of political science at Peking University during May Fourth and he was also a member of the editorial board of *New Youth*. Gao's articles were quite theoretical and elaborate; it is evident that he was more knowledgeable about Western political thought, including human rights, than many of his contemporaries. It is thus appropriate to let Gao represent the liberals writing on human rights during May Fourth. Gao later published articles on human rights, rule of law, and constitutionalism in magazines such as *Nuli zhoukan*, *Dongfang zazhi*, and *Xiandai pinglun*. He also published a book on Western political thought in 1920 and one on political science in 1930.

HUMAN RIGHTS, HUMAN DIGNITY, AND THE LIBERATION OF THE INDIVIDUAL

Chen Duxiu and Li Dazhao did not provide any systematic or in-depth discussions of the origin and basis of human rights in their articles, while Gao Yihan discussed the question in greater detail. Gao argued that the old belief that rights exist prior to the state had been refuted by many Westerners; rights were instead regarded as given by the state and stipulated in the law.[37] One of Gao Yihan's main authorities on this point was Burgess, an American political scientist who only acknowledged legal rights, arguing that people's rights and freedoms originated from the state.[38] In his book on political science in 1930, Gao Yihan further developed his views on human rights. He wrote that in the past, the idea of natural rights had been useful, because if rights had been regarded as simply derived from the state, the establishment and scope of rights would have been left in the hands of despotic rulers. People had had to seek the basis of rights outside the state, leading to the formulation of the idea of natural rights (*tianfu renquan*). But since the legislative power, Gao contended, was then in the hands of the people, conflicts between the state and the people no longer existed. As a result, people did not have to be afraid of being deprived of their rights, and the concept of natural rights had consequently lost its value.[39] This conclusion, albeit premature, shows that Gao realized that demands for human rights were basically directed against despotic regimes. To only acknowledge legal rights would deprive rights of their necessary and compelling moral force. Gao went on to argue that people had reached a new and different understanding, not only of the origin of rights, but of their nature and justification as well. Whereas people used to regard rights as innate (*sheng ju lai*) and inalienable (*buke gerang*), they now saw them as necessary preconditions for individual development and the advancement of social welfare. The progress of society depended on people having opportunities to develop themselves, and to this end they needed certain rights and freedoms. The state did not acknowledge rights because they were inherent in man's nature (*tiansheng*), but because they were beneficial to society.

Chen Duxiu is never explicit on whether he believes that human rights actually exist before or independently of the establishment of society, but he seems to tend toward such a view through his insistence that human rights are essential in order to realize one's humanity—that which distinguishes men from slaves. There is hardly anything in Chen's writings on rights and freedoms that indicates that he regarded them to be bestowed on people by the state.[40] It is beyond doubt that Chen Duxiu regarded human rights as indispensable for human existence. People were equal and endowed with rights that the law cannot deprive them of. "Individuals are equal before the law. The individual's rights and freedoms are proclaimed in the constitution, and the laws of the country cannot deprive [him] of them; this is what is called human rights [*renquan*]. Human rights are that which makes man a man; nobody is a slave and all enjoy these rights without difference."[41] Humans, Chen believed, needed to have a personality (*renge*) that embodied self-mastery, independence, freedom, self-respect, and equality, and to this end, rights were indispensable.[42] Li Dazhao would also argue the importance of freedom for an existence worthy of a human being, claiming that "Freedom is necessary for humankind's existence; without freedom life has no value."[43]

This belief in the importance of rights and freedoms for individual development and the realization of man's true humanity was shared by other May Fourthers. Gao Yihan thus argued that the enjoyment of human rights was necessary for human existence: "From Rousseau we know that man is born free and equal; in order to be a human being we also have to enjoy natural

[*tianran*] freedoms and equality."[44] Human dignity and personality were regarded as closely related to the enjoyment of rights. If one lost one's personality one also lost one's rights and would become no different from the birds and
beasts. Whereas people could be asked to sacrifice their lives for the country,
they could never be asked to sacrifice their personalities.[45]

The idea of human dignity and personality was central not only to *New
Youth* writers such as Chen Duxiu and Gao Yihan, but also to *New Tide* writers such as Ye Shengtao and Luo Jialun. Luo Jialun put forward the view that
there were certain conditions that needed to be fulfilled in order to be a person (*zuoren*). Among these conditions were the possession of personality, the
possession of one's own will, and the possession of rights.[46] Luo's article was
written as a critique of the fact that women in Chinese society were reduced
to the status of dependent creatures. When women were deprived of their
rights to equal education and political participation they were also in effect being denied their human dignity.[47] Human dignity was also stressed by Gao
Yuan, who wanted to abolish the Confucian hierarchical system and replace it
with the idea of personality (*renge*).[48] According to Gao Yuan, personality manifested itself in the development of the self. In order to realize one's potential,
humans had to be free and have a sense of autonomy and be able to make their
own choices. Gao Yuan criticized Chinese society for having failed to permit
the individual to develop a sense of self-consciousness (*zijue*) and independence. The individual had no sense of himself in the Confucian system, he
complained, but was identified solely in relation to his parents and ancestors.

In 1925, the short-lived magazine *Human Rights* (*Renquan*) likewise argued
that human rights were needed in order to be a person (*zuoren*); without human rights, humans would be reduced to the level of beasts.[49] According to Hu
Shiqing, one of the main contributors, there were three criteria that characterized human beings: life (*shengming*), reason (*lizhi*), and feelings (*qinggan*).[50] From
this description of man's nature, Hu inferred that man also has certain needs,
such as the need to preserve his life and develop his personality and intellect.
Human rights were based on these needs and included economic, political, and
educational rights. According to Chen Zhushan, the other main contributor of
the magazine, human rights were essential for the protection of people's personalities.[51] To discard one's human rights would therefore amount to denying
one's personality; this would be equal to suicide, or, differently put, to reduce
human existence to a mere physical existence.

There was both a moral and a political dimension to the May Fourthers' concern with man's personality, dignity, and autonomy. Democracy was often discussed in moral terms and seen as closely intertwined or even synonymous with
individual fulfillment and liberation. Many people argued that one of the purposes of democracy was to promote the development of individual personality.[52]

In the *Peking University Monthly*, for example, one could thus read that the meaning of democracy, broadly speaking, was: "[T]o respect the personality [*renge*] of all individuals in the world, help all individuals to develop a complete personality, and undertake activities beneficial to humankind in order to promote world culture."[53]

It is interesting to note that this concern with developing an independent personality actually resembles the Confucian notion of self-cultivation, despite the often strong anti-Confucian views of these authors. The concern with the moral purpose of the state also resembles the view of the British Idealists, who were concerned with self-realization and linked the possession of rights to the perfection of moral character. Chen Duxiu saw rights as inherent in man's moral nature: not necessarily man as he is, but man as he ought to be when his potential as a human being is fully realized. In this respect Chen's understanding of human rights also resembles that of modern human rights scholars, such as Donnelly, who see humanity or human nature as the source of human rights and argue that "nature" in this case refers to "a moral posit, a moral account of human possibility."[54] According to Donnelly: "Human rights point beyond actual conditions of existence; they are less about the way that people are, in the sense of what has already been realised, than about how people *might* live, a possibility that is viewed as a deeper moral reality."[55]

The slave trope, which was so central in the pre-1911 discussions on rights, remained a prominent feature of the human rights discourse during May Fourth. Slavery was not only defined as submission to others but also as a loss of rights. In the article "A Call to Youth," Chen Duxiu admonished China's youths to throw away their slave character and develop an independent character.[56] Chen's urging carries echoes of Liang Qichao and Zou Rong, who both invoked similar pictures of the Chinese people as servile and dependent. Chen argued that the development of an independent and free individual could only be accomplished through adopting the ideas of human rights and equality and throwing away the shackles of slavery. "Since the rise of the ideas of human rights and equality, nobody of courage and uprightness would stand being called a slave any longer."[57] It is the enjoyment of human rights that, according to Chen, makes men different from slaves.[58] Chen therefore contrasted free people (*ziyou min*) with slaves (*nuli*).[59] In order to be a human being and complete one's personality one has to have a right to self-mastery (*zizhu quan*), whereas a slave, on the other hand, has lost his rights to self-mastery and freedom. Li Dazhao would also occasionally use similar wording in his early writings, talking about people having lost their personality of self-mastery (*zizhu zhi renge*) and sinking into slavery and dependency.[60]

Chen Duxiu, in addition, stressed that nobody has the right to enslave others, and that all people have the capacity and right to make decisions regarding their own lives.[61] A person who oppresses others, or who is oppressed himself, cannot be a true or complete person.[62] It was not only the oppressed who would lose their personality and human dignity, the oppressors would also lose their human dignity in the process.[63] Chen's view resembles that of Dewey, who had been influenced by the British Idealists. Dewey thus spoke about the negative impact of the master–slave relationship, both for society at large and for the individual.[64]

The concern with human dignity and individual personality did not completely disappear from Chen Duxiu's writing when he became more radical; perhaps one could even say that this concern led him to socialism when he realized that man's dignity and personality could not be protected in a capitalist society.[65] Chen's concern about the dignity and self-respect associated with being in control of one's own life and destiny is thus very much in evidence in his early articles on workers' issues. Chen argued that only if the workers had management rights would they truly be their own masters, whereas to demand a better treatment from the capitalists was to be like a slave begging for food and depending on others for favors.[66] Once again we encounter the powerful slave trope.

> Regardless of how the treatment improves, it would never be the same as being in the position of a free master. It is the same, and of as little use for a worker to ask the capitalist for an improvement in treatment, as it is for people to ask the ruler to implement benevolent government; one would to no avail lose one's dignity [*shenfen*]. Excessive tenderheartedness, regardless of whether in the political or in the economic sphere, is a kind of favor without a guarantee that the master bestows on his slave. We are ashamed to ask for it and, moreover, will not receive it; it is suffering a gibe in vain and really adds insult to injury.[67]

Li Dazhao expressed similar sentiments about respecting and protecting the human dignity of workers when he called for a democratic system in which the worker's personality would be respected and protected.

> We should demand a kind of democratic production system which gives the workers equal opportunities to divide the results of production. Not only that, humankind, apart from clothes and food, also values and demands knowledge, and apart from material needs also has spiritual needs. A person who toils in his sweat and blood the whole day does not have energy to develop his knowledge and cultivate his character, and is just like a machine or a cattle [*sic*]. As time passes, his humanity [*renxing*] will completely disappear and he will be no different from a material thing.[68]

In another article, Li similarly defined democracy as a system in which people, regardless of race, gender, class, and regional belonging, have equal opportunities to develop their personalities and enjoy their rights.[69] It was their concern with protecting people's dignity and personality that moved Chen and Li toward socialism when they came to feel that these things inevitably would be violated under capitalism. This understanding can also be compared with Western Marxists such as Bloch, who saw the end of economic exploitation as the only guarantee for the protection of human dignity and human rights.[70]

The liberation of the individual figured prominently in Chen Duxiu's and other May Fourthers' writings as we have seen already. Generally speaking, it was a question of breaking free from the shackles of slavery and becoming independent in all aspects of one's life.[71] According to Chen, the West had seen different stages of liberation, involving different subjects and having different adversaries. At first it was a question of political liberation from the oppression of rulers and aristocrats and a religious liberation from religious powers. Later, it evolved into movements seeking the economic liberation from capitalists and women's liberation from male oppression. Initially, Chen seems to have believed that socialism simply continued the earlier political liberation movements, but focused on economic rather than on political inequalities and shackles.[72] As he became more radical Chen came to believe that the individual could not be liberated unless the whole society was liberated. He then stressed that it was economic liberation that was the most important in order to become a truly free and independent individual.[73] If one was not economically independent, one would never attain an independent personality. But economic independence was impossible in the capitalist system and, Chen contended, only socialism could liberate the whole of humankind.

HUMAN RIGHTS, CHINESE CULTURE, AND THE WEST

In contrast to earlier discussions on human rights, the May Fourth period is characterized by its attacks on Confucianism and its claim that Confucianism and human rights are incompatible. Chen Duxiu was one of the most vociferous in criticizing Confucianism for violating people's human rights, whereas Gao Yihan was not really preoccupied with attacking tradition. Chen had no qualms about proclaiming the Western origin of the idea of human rights. He obviously felt no need to try to find any origins to the idea in the Chinese tradition, nor to engage in a search for equivalences in order to make it more acceptable to his countrymen. In fact, as in earlier periods, the very foreignness of the idea seemed to work in its favor and guarantee its acceptance, as Western ideas were valued as representing everything modern and progressive. This is quite obvious in Chen's description of the origin of human rights. "Since *La declaration des droits de l'hommes* was published in 1789 by the Frenchman Lafayette, the author of the American *Declaration of Independence*, the Europeans awakened as if from a dream or a drunken stupor, and recognised the value of human rights [*renquan*]. They rose up and fought against the monarchs, threw down the aristocrats and established a constitution."[74] Chen held that human rights, evolutionism, and socialism, all ideas for which he gave the French credit, were characteristic of a modern civilization. It is worth noting that Chen here regarded human rights and socialism to be of equal importance in the history of humankind.

In the article "A Call to Youth," Chen argued that the reason Europe was superior to China was its respect for science and human rights, and that in order to change China it would be necessary for her, too, to adopt these two principles.[75] In this article Chen put science and human rights on a par, whereas he was later to pair science (Mr Sai) and democracy (Mr De).[76] Chen believed that the spirit of human rights and equality had to be developed in a modern state, which shows his belief in the universality of human rights.[77] "[I]f we want to establish a new state and society of the Western model in order to be fit to exist in the contemporary world, then the fundamental question must first of all be to import the foundation of the Western societies, that is the belief in equality and human rights. We must be thoroughly aware that Confucianism cannot be tolerated at the same time as this new society, new state, and new belief."[78] As can be seen from this quotation, Chen Duxiu believed that human rights was incompatible with Confucianism. Chen advocated the total rejection of the Confucian way and a wholesale Westernization. In contrast to Chen, Li Dazhao did not focus so much on criticizing Confucianism for being incompatible with the idea of human rights, nor was he as harsh as Chen in his verdict on Chinese culture. Li could even casually write that if Confucius had been alive then (i.e., 1917), he would have advocated freedom and people's rights (*minquan*).[79] But Li was certainly no adherent of Confucianism and, for example, criticized the Temple of Heaven Draft of 1913, in which article 19 stated that Confucianism was to be the basis of all teachings. To his mind, this stipulation undermined the freedoms of speech, publication, and belief, which all were guaranteed by the constitution.[80] But Li's critique was more directed at Yuan Shikai's elevation of Confucianism to a state religion than at the Chinese tradition itself.

Both Chen Duxiu and Li Dazhao, and others with them, wrote about the differences between China and the West, much as Liang Qichao and others had done previously.[81] Chen Duxiu quoted extensively from Confucian sources to show how the Confucian teachings of filial piety and obedience deprived people of their independence and self-respect and turned them into slaves. According to Chen, the Confucian morality of filial piety and loyalty was in essence nothing but a slave morality.[82] The Confucian morality harmed the individual's personality of independence and self-respect (*geren duli zizun zhi renge*), obstructed his freedom of thought, deprived him of equal rights before the law, gave rise to a dependent mind, and undermined his productivity.[83]

Chen Duxiu's view of Confucianism as incompatible with the idea of human rights was shared by other May Fourthers. Guang Sheng, for example, held that although the Confucian and Legalist schools of thought had very different views on the best methods to rule the country, they both failed to recognize the idea of rights and freedoms.[84] According to the Legalists, people only existed for the benefit of the country and were not entitled to any individual freedoms. In contrast to the Legalists, the Confucians advocated benevolent rule. But in this system people were dependent on others for their welfare and therefore did not have, or indeed need, any rights. Guang concluded that the main difference between the West and China was that the former stresses rights and the rule of law, whereas the latter stresses moral teachings, virtue, and giving precedence to others out of courtesy. Wu Yu was another vociferous critic of the Confucian tradition, especially its hierarchical system that denied the Chinese people equality and freedom.[85] He also criticized the lack of freedom of speech and publication in Chinese history as exemplified with the burning of books during the Qin dynasty. Gao Yihan, in contrast, did not spend much time attacking Confucianism, although he criticized the Confucian hierarchical system and ethical code for stifling people's minds and for having prevented the development of individualism.[86]

The May Fourthers thus argued that the Confucian tradition suppressed the Chinese people and deprived them of their rights as human beings. In the West, on the other hand, people were equal before the law and could not be deprived of their rights and freedoms, which explained their independent nature. It would be wrong, however, to describe this critique of the Chinese tradition as self-loathing or a manifestation of self-orientalization. In fact, I would argue that it was an example of a conscious and deliberate Occidentalism, in which the purpose was to attack tradition and those in power rather than to slavishly copy the West.[87] This kind of Occidentalism thus had a strong liberating and universalistic quality.

THE SUBJECT OF RIGHTS:
INDIVIDUALS, WOMEN, AND WORKERS

The liberation of the individual was the primary concern and focus during this period. The Chinese who demanded liberation were young men and women who rebelled against their elders and fathers. They were first and foremost seeking personal liberty: the freedom to seek an education, to choose a spouse, to have space to grow and develop without being bound by duties to family and ancestors. It was youth and women who were the main subjects of this liberation from the family. But the young people and their teachers were not self-

ish and asocial individuals only concerned about their own well-being and liberation; they also sought the liberation of humankind. And like the generation
before them, they felt a strong responsibility toward society and the Chinese
nation. They believed that the creation of an independent and free individual
was also beneficial to the progress of society and civilization. To some Chinese
writers the emancipation of the individual was as much a means as an end in
itself. It was advocated in the belief that only an independent and free individual would be able to contribute to the progress of society. The liberation of the
individual and salvation of humankind (*jiuren*) was thus closely connected with
the salvation of the nation (*jiuguo*).[88]

After the May Fourth incident, and under the influence of social and political changes, Chinese intellectuals became more radical, and the labor issue appeared on their agenda. The oppression of workers had hitherto been virtually
ignored, but when workers took part side by side with students during May
Fourth, the latter became increasingly aware of the workers' plight at the hands
of foreign and domestic capitalists. The demands for liberation became more
radical and addressed social and economic injustices, and calls for the liberation
of workers from capitalist oppression became frequent. The concept of class
struggle, which the Chinese initially seem to have been rather reluctant to embrace, became a feature of the Chinese political discourse.[89] The introduction
and acceptance of the idea of class struggle meant that the idea of human rights
began to be either neglected or attacked outright by Chinese radicals. Although human rights would continue to play a role in radical discourse from
time to time, after 1921 it became more of an issue addressed by liberals than
by communists. Another result of the May Fourth incident was an increasing
awareness of racial oppression, which provoked calls for global racial equality
and an end to racial discrimination. Chen Duxiu and Li Dazhao spoke out
against racial prejudice and advocated racial equality, strongly criticizing the
oppression of non-whites by Westerners.[90] Chen divided humankind into people who were oppressed and those who oppressed others. He believed that
women were oppressed by men, non-white races by white people, and Han-
Chinese by Mongols, Manchus, and Japanese.[91] He later added the category of
workers who were oppressed by capitalists.[92] Chen's and Li's interest in racial
equality was provoked by discussions on this topic raised by Japan at the Paris
peace conference, an issue that was blocked by the Western powers.[93] This development from a concern about family and gender oppression to economic
and national oppression also influenced the human rights discourse, both with
respect to subject and content.

The May Fourthers' concern with the liberation of women predated their
concern with the situation of workers.[94] The May Fourth period saw the publication of several magazines devoted to the struggle for women rights. These

magazines also helped spread information on important feminist works such as Olympe de Gouges's *Déclaration des droits de la femme et de la citoyenne* and Mary Wollstonecraft's *A Vindication of the Rights of Women*, as well as on more contemporary suffragist works in the West.[95] In the early 1920s, Chinese women also became engaged in different activities to promote women's rights, for example, setting up organizations demanding equal political rights.[96]

The interest in the woman issue during May Fourth was closely related to the attack on Confucianism.[97] Women were seen as suffering the most in the Confucian system; they were deprived of their independence and human dignity and lived inhuman lives (*feiren de shenghuo*), subjugated and oppressed by men.[98] In order to realize their autonomous and independent personalities, Chinese women had to throw off this yoke of slavery. Calls for equality between the sexes, respect for women's independent personality, and for women's liberation informed the feminist discourse during May Fourth.[99] As in the pre-1911 period, the concept of human rights was linked to feminism and served as a driving force behind women's liberation. The May Fourthers advocated women's rights and criticized the fact that women in the past had been excluded from enjoying human rights. They were well aware of the fact that the rights discourse in the past had been quite male-centered, and argued that women were entitled to the same respect and rights as men. Ye Shengtao thus pointed out that the fact that those advocating human rights (*tianfu renquan*) had denied women the right to political participation revealed that they were not really concerned about human rights (*renquan*), only about men's rights (*nanquan*).[100] Wei Fang also drew the conclusion that although human rights (*tianfu renquan*) did not allow for any distinction between men and women, in reality only men's human rights (*tianfu nanquan*) had thus far been recognized.[101] He therefore stressed that it was necessary to restore and realize human rights (*renquan*) for all people, both men and women.

The May Fourth language of independent personality (*duli renge*), women's rights (*nüquan*), and human rights (*renquan*) deeply influenced those women who came of age during May Fourth. In a recent work, Wang Zheng has convincingly shown how these ideas shaped their identities and life choices and that, with ease, they continue to use the same kind of language today.[102]

ON OLD RIGHTS AND NEW: THE EMERGENCE OF THE RIGHT TO SUBSISTENCE

The rights most frequently discussed during this period continued to be civil and political rights, such as freedom of thought, speech, publication, belief, association, and assembly. Freedom of thought, speech, and publication were especially high on the agenda. Chen Duxiu thus argued that the freedoms of thought and speech were necessary for the development of one's personality, describing them as necessary things in life (*shenghuo bixu pin*).[103] Even though Chen was later to criticize the idea of absolute freedom, he advocated the absolute freedom of speech in "A Manifesto of the Citizens of Peking," distributed during the height of the May Fourth Movement.[104] He further reiterated his advocacy of freedom of speech in the article "The Law and Freedom of Speech," in which he wrote that the law should restrict people's activities but not their speech.[105] Chen also argued that freedom of speech was necessary in order to reveal the shortcomings of society; without it progress would be all but impossible.

Freedom of thought and speech was also high on the rights agenda of Li Dazhao, as can be gathered from several of his articles. To Li, the most important of all freedoms was the freedom of thought, which he held to be absolute.[106] In an article published in 1919, Li argued that man was free to believe in and study any kind of thought and idea, and that nobody could forbid or restrict his thinking. "In the world there are no such things as indisputably correct thinking or heresy. Even if there were, people should still be free to seek knowledge, and they should still enjoy freedom of belief."[107] According to Li, there was no such thing as dangerous thinking; what was really dangerous was ignorance, falsehood, and attempts to forbid people to think freely. To try to suppress freedom of speech was not only wrong, but would also prove impossible as thought has a way of transcending all boundaries and surmounting all difficulties, so that imprisonment, punishment, suffering, and even death cannot restrain or hinder thought from surviving and flourishing.[108] Similarly to Li Dazhao's article, Zhang Shenfu ventured his view on this topic in an article published on the eve of May Fourth.[109] But whereas Li had argued that there is no such thing as dangerous thinking, Zhang argued that all thinking by its very nature is dangerous since it is wont to threaten all established truths and authorities. Their conclusion was the same, however: it is impossible to restrain or suppress people's thoughts.

But in 1922, Li Dazhao retracted his earlier commitment to freedom of thought and belief in a most revealing way. He contended that since religion meant that one believed in what one regarded was an indisputable truth, religious belief by its very nature implied a negation of the freedom of thought.[110] Since religion shackles people's minds, real freedom of thought could not exist unless people were liberated from religion itself. Li therefore felt that he and other atheists were not interfering with people's freedom of thought when attacking religion, but actually defending it. This conclusion is at variance with his earlier insistence that people have the freedom to believe in whatever they want to, however dangerous or absurd this thought or belief might seem to others.

Other May Fourthers differed from Li Dazhao and argued against trying to limit or restrict freedom of thought. Gao Yihan, for example, criticized the attempt to seek unity of thinking and advocated that one should be allowed the freedom to dispute everything. One should never believe anything a priori but question everything and develop a critical mind.[111] To develop a questioning and critical mind was very much the essence of the May Fourth enlightenment, and to this end, freedom of thought was needed. Gao also argued that one could not confine freedom of speech only to people and magazines belonging to one's own political camp, but that one had to allow opponents and opposition magazines the same degree of freedom.[112] The magazine *Peking University Students' Weekly* also defended freedom of thought and criticized the arrest of Chen Duxiu who only had tried to exercise his freedom of speech.[113] The students opposed all attempts to unify thinking and the dominance of any ism or theory in society.[114] Luo Jialun, writing in *New Tide,* was also a strong advocate of freedom of thought. He emphasized that it did not imply that one had only the freedom to sit and think by oneself, but that one also should have the freedom to communicate one's thinking to others.[115] Luo's defense of the freedom of thought and speech was based on a utilitarian justification, as he believed that these freedoms would be of benefit to society as well as to the individual. Luo's interest in the freedom of thought led him to translate John Bagwell Bury's *History of Freedom of Thought*, and it was from Bury that he derived his utilitarian understanding of the concept.[116]

Communists-to-be were initially very concerned about the freedoms of speech and belief. But both Li Dazhao, who from a unequivocal advocacy later came to argue for the restriction of the freedom of belief in the interest of the individual, and Chen Duxiu, who at one point was prepared to accept the restriction of freedom of speech in times of crisis, showed some ambivalence with respect to the question of whether this freedom was absolute and, if not, when, how, and by whom it could be restricted. Several writers were careful to point out that freedom of speech was not unrestricted but had to be exercised with the general interest in mind.[117] Others were more radical and explicitly argued for the restriction of freedom of speech for certain groups of people, a view that later was to become the standard and practiced in the PRC. Zhou Fohai, one of the founding members of the CCP, for example, argued that if the bourgeoisie were allowed freedom of speech and association, it would continue spreading its old ideas to the detriment of the proletariat and the revolution.[118] This danger prompted him to advocate that the freedoms of this group of people had to be restricted.

The May Fourth generation generally focused on civil and political rights to the neglect of economic rights. It was only in the early 1920s that economic rights, such as the right to subsistence, entered the Chinese rights discourse. In

Chen Duxiu's early articles there are no discussions on economic rights. But Chen was later to argue that social and economic democracy were more important than political democracy. He also became more adamant in demanding that workers should get the whole produce of their labor, arguing that they should have management rights and no longer be dependent on the graces of the capitalists for a living. Although Li Dazhao, as far as I know, did not specifically discuss economic rights, or criticize the earlier human rights movement for having focused exclusively on civil and political rights, he nevertheless summed up the differences between the French and the Russian revolutions by saying that whereas the former had been seeking spiritual liberation, with "freedom" as its slogan, the latter was seeking the satisfaction of material needs, with "bread" as its slogan.[119]

Interestingly enough, the liberal Gao Yihan spoke out more clearly in defense of economic rights. Gao Yihan was probably one of the first in China to talk about a specific right to subsistence (*shengcun quan*). In an article on rights in the provincial constitutions, published in *New Youth* in 1921, Gao elaborated on the various rights that, to his mind, were essential for human existence.[120] In this article he also expressed a critique of the limitations hampering the enjoyment of human rights in the West. Gao pointed out that since it was the bourgeoisie who in the seventeenth and eighteenth centuries had been fighting for rights, the constitutions had not stipulated the economic rights needed by the proletariat. Gao's view on economic rights was shaped by his more positive view of the state as an active agent. The state should not only protect people's rights through noninterference, but also had the duty to actively interfere to prevent people from ruining their own or other people's lives. The state should, for example, stipulate laws on working conditions and also have the right and duty to guarantee people's livelihood.

Gao argued that in order to be able to enjoy civil and political rights, some essential conditions had to be fulfilled. If people's lives were not protected, the stipulation of political rights would be quite meaningless. Gao talked about fundamental economic rights, which he divided into the right to full compensation for one's work, the right to subsistence (*shengcun quan*), and the right to work. Whereas the first right was associated with Marxism and only realizable in a communist society, and the last was only applicable in an economy dominated by private ownership, Gao argued that the right to subsistence was applicable in both societies. It was consequently the right to subsistence to which Gao devoted the most attention. He argued that this right should be acknowledged by law and stipulated by the constitution. To his mind it included the right to education and the right to economic help for the old, the handicapped, and those who had lost their ability to work. If people did not enjoy rights to economic equality, they would also be unable to enjoy political rights and freedoms. As an example, Gao mentioned the freedoms of thought and speech, which would be empty if people did not enjoy the right to education. But even this right was not sufficient if there were no libraries and nothing to induce people to study, or if the industrial system or other social factors obstructed man's opportunity to study. Gao later made a distinction between negative fundamental rights, that is, civil and political rights such as the freedom of the person, of speech, and belief; and positive fundamental rights, that is, economic rights such as the right to economic help and the right to education.[121]

Dai Jitao, together with Gao Yihan, was one of the first Chinese writers to mention a right to subsistence, and he had also earlier occasionally invoked the concept of human rights.[122] A political activist as much as a scholar, Dai was a GMD ideologist with close ties to Sun Yat-sen.[123] In contrast to Gao, Dai was strongly influenced by both Marxism and Confucianism. Like many of those who were interested in Marxism and responsible for introducing it in China, he later refused to join the CCP and became an ardent anti-Communist.[124] Dai expressed a strong concern about the plight of workers and the effects of capitalism on Chinese society. He criticized economic inequalities and believed that the government had a responsibility to improve people's livelihood. Although Dai discussed human rights and invoked the French Declaration on Human Rights in his early writings and in his May Fourth writings in *Xingqi pinglun*, his main concern was national salvation rather than individual freedom. Dai did not advocate Western individualism but rather criticized it, arguing for unity, harmony, and the individual's subordination to the common interest. In 1919, Dai began to edit and write for *Xingqi pinglun* and *Jianshe zazhi*. The first mention, to my knowledge, by Dai of a right to subsistence appeared in an article published in *Xingqi pinglun* in 1919, two years before Gao Yihan's more elaborate piece appeared.[125] Dai argued that people have a right to subsistence that includes rights to food, clothing, and shelter, and that the government has a duty to protect this right. Dai went on to argue that since food and clothes were not bestowed by nature but produced through labor, people were expected to work for them. But the problem was that people often lacked the opportunity to work and Dai therefore also strongly argued for a right to work. Dai was later to emphasize the crucial role of the Confucian concept of "mutual social responsibility" and argue that Sun Yat-sen's idea of people's livelihood (*minsheng*) originated in Confucianism, but in his 1919 discussion of the right to subsistence there were no references to traditional ideas.

By the early 1920s, the right to subsistence seems to have entered the Chinese rights discourse; it was thereafter embraced by people of different political persuasions, ranging from social liberals to socialists. The content of rights was a hot topic during debates on a new constitution that took place in

1922–23. Several writers pointed out that earlier constitutions had omitted many important rights, in particular economic rights such as the right to subsistence and the right to work. Following Gao Yihan's example in 1921, Wei Fang, Shi Weihuan, Lin Keyi, and others advocated that the right to subsistence be stipulated in the constitution.[126] Similarly to Gao, they argued that without a right to subsistence, people would be unable to enjoy the civil and political rights stipulated in the constitution. Shi Weihuan credited the right to subsistence to men such as Goodwin and Fourier, but also argued that it originated in the *French Declaration of the Rights of Man*.[127] He also referred to the principle of securing people's livelihood (*minsheng*) in traditional China, something that none of the others had done. Shi provided several quotations from Confucius, Mencius, and Guanzi, among others, to prove his point, but was careful to stop short of suggesting that they had actually recognized a right to subsistence.[128] The magazine *Renquan*, founded in 1925, also had a broad definition of human rights (*tianfu renquan*) that included the right to subsistence (*shengcun quan*), the right to freedom (*ziyou quan*), and the right to equality (*pingdeng quan*).[129] The government, it argued, had a duty not only to protect people's lives by punishing those who hurt or killed others, but to take active measures against the forces and circumstances that deprive people of the means of existence and leave them to die from starvation.

THE PURPOSE OF RIGHTS: INDIVIDUAL DEVELOPMENT AND SOCIAL PROGRESS

The May Fourthers heralded the concept of human rights as synonymous with progress and civilization. According to the magazine *Renquan*, human rights were applicable in all countries and characteristic of a civilized (*wenming*) and just society.[130] The world was said to have seen a development from divine rights (*shenquan*) to rulers' rights (*junquan*), then to people's rights (*minquan*), and finally to human rights (*renquan*), which represented the most civilized and advanced stage.[131] A society without human rights could not be regarded as civilized. In order for China to catch up with the West and become modern and civilized, it, as Chen Duxiu also argued, had to adopt the concept of human rights. The Shanghai weekly *Xingqi pinglun* also associated civilization with respect for human rights, arguing that members of society should promote the progress of civilization, the protection of human rights (*renquan*), the development of equal happiness, and a lasting world peace.[132] This association of human rights with civilization and progress reflects a persistent belief in a progressive, teleological, and universal history.[133] Most May Fourthers seem to have believed that the idea of human rights was of universal application and therefore of relevance to China. At least none of them openly criticized the idea of human rights for being unsuitable to China's national conditions.

The May Fourthers' justification of rights and freedoms was quite similar in character to that of earlier and later generations of Chinese intellectuals. Gao Yi-han thus argued that rights were necessary preconditions for both individual development and social progress. The progress of society depended on people having opportunities to develop themselves, and to this end they needed rights and freedoms. The state did not acknowledge rights because they were inherent in man's nature, but because they were beneficial to society.[134] The justification or purpose of rights, in other words, had come to be their social utility. Taking this proposition to its logical conclusion, Gao argued that rights, to some extent, had been transformed into duties toward society.[135] Chen Duxiu's discussions on human rights also at times carry a very pragmatic and utilitarian tone. Chen believed that freedom of speech was needed for social progress and like others before him valued the liberation of women as a precondition for women to better contribute to society.[136] In some May Fourth articles there was also an echo of the pre-1911 tendency to associate the individual's enjoyment of rights with national strength, as a citizenry enjoying rights and shouldering duties was still desperately needed in China. Chen Duxiu for instance argued that if people's rights were strengthened and consolidated, the country's rights would also be strengthened.[137] But this concern with national salvation was much weaker during May Fourth than during the pre-1911 period.

Even more striking than this social evaluation of rights was the insistence that rights were needed in order to fulfill one's personality and realize one's humanity. This view was not new—it already existed in the pre-1911 period— but became more pronounced during May Fourth. Rights were associated with dignity and self-respect so that the enjoyment of rights, in other words, was regarded as a value in and of itself. In fact, I would argue that in the case of Chen Duxiu, for example, rights and freedoms were valued mostly because of their importance for a dignified existence and for the development of one's personality, rather than out of narrow social and nationalistic concerns.

CRITIQUE OF HUMAN RIGHTS IDEAS

Given the radicalization of Chinese political discourse, it is somewhat surprising to find so little in the form of a more explicit and elaborate critique of the concept of human rights during this period. Marx's critique of human rights, for example, does not seem to have been known or discussed by the Chinese. Some authors were, however, aware of the critique directed against the idea of natural rights by other thinkers, such as Burke, Bentham, and Comte.[138] Some of the critique voiced against the concept of human rights seems to have been made more in passing, which prevents a more in-depth analysis. In an article on anarchism, for example, the idea of natural rights (*tianfu de quanli*) was simply disparaged as a metaphysical idea advocated by utopian thinkers.[139]

As mentioned above, Gao Yihan criticized the neglect of economic rights in earlier rights discussions and the fact that rights thus far only had been enjoyed by the bourgeoisie. In an article published in *New Tide* in 1920, one year before Gao's piece, Tan Mingqian, later a founder of the CCP, reached the same conclusion.[140] Tan wrote that the bourgeoisie during the French Revolution had struggled against aristocratic privileges and religious authorities in order to attain civil and political rights and freedoms but that the *French Declaration of the Rights of Man*, in effect, only had made these rights a monopoly of the bourgeoisie. The proletariat thus continued to be deprived of all rights. But to replace the hegemony of others with one's own was a negation of the freedom and equality of all so proudly proclaimed in the declaration, as nobody had the right to only concern themselves with their own rights while violating other people's rights.

HUMAN RIGHTS ACTIVISM IN THE 1920S

Chen Duxiu and Li Dazhao criticized Yuan Shikai for violating human rights, whereas they believed that the kingdom of freedom would arrive with the future socialist society and make calls for human rights superfluous. As they became more radical, Chen and Li abandoned the language of rights and freedoms. Instead of seeking the protection of rights and freedoms within the existent political system, they argued for its overthrow. Chen lived long enough to realize that it was naive to believe that calls for human rights would be superfluous in a socialist society. Toward the end of his life, he again more strongly advocated individual rights and freedoms, and specifically stressed the importance of the freedoms of assembly, association, speech, publication, and the right to strike.[141] In some letters to friends, Chen in 1940 went so far as to criticize the political system of the Soviet Union, placing the blame not on Stalin personally but on the system as such.[142] He took a more positive view toward the West and criticized the fact that the Russian people were unable to enjoy civil and political rights to the same extent as people did in the West.[143]

Throughout the 1920s, liberals such as Gao Yihan and others kept up the human rights talk. In 1920, Hu Shi, Jiang Menglin, Tao Menghe, Gao Yihan, Wang Zheng, Zhang Zixun, and Li Dazhao published a "Manifesto for the Struggle for Freedom."[144] This manifesto denounced the tyranny of the warlords, and demanded freedom of speech, publication, assembly and association, and secrecy of correspondence. It criticized oppressive laws on press and publication and the widespread practice of illegal arrests. The manifesto was followed two years later with "Our Political Proposal."[145] The proposal argued for the establishment of a "good government," which would look after the welfare of all people. These manifestos were feeble and ineffective attempts to try to influence the political environment, but they show that a concern existed among Chinese intellectuals (and not only among the liberals, as we find Li Dazhao among the signatories) with violations of civil rights such as freedom of speech, publication, assembly, and association.

Human rights were also referred to in discussions on the drafting of a new constitution; the new constitution was finally promulgated in 1923.[146] In these discussions it was pointed out that the purpose of the constitution was to protect people's rights and freedoms. Great efforts were made to exemplify which rights should be stipulated and how they should be protected. Two of the signatories of the political manifestos, Gao Yihan and Tao Menghe, continued to express concern about human rights as the 1920s proceeded, writing in the magazine *Xiandai pinglun*.[147] The magazine published several editorials criticizing human rights violations committed by the warlords, explicitly using the word *renquan*. The press laws and censorship practiced by the authorities were strongly criticized, as were the arrests of journalists and closures of newspapers.[148] Human rights issues also appeared on the pages of other magazines. The short-lived and less influential magazine *Renquan* took as its task to raise people's awareness of the concept of human rights, advocating a society based on respect for human rights.[149]

CONCLUSION

By May Fourth the Chinese discourse on human rights had become more radical in character, as manifested in both the subject and content of rights. There was an increasing awareness that human rights thus far had only been enjoyed by certain privileged groups in society. Groups such as women and workers received increasing attention as groups that were suppressed and deprived of their human rights. Although the human rights discussed during this period were still predominantly rights such as freedom of thought, speech, and publication, Chinese intellectuals also began to talk about economic rights, including the right to subsistence. In contrast to the early twentieth century, many came to see Confucianism and human rights as incompatible, although this did not mean that they also believed that the concept of human rights was inapplicable to China. Even though the ideological differences between liberals, Nationalists, and Communists had not yet become so clear and sharp, some of the future conflicts regarding the subject, content, and scope of rights were already beginning to become apparent. The language of human rights was not a monopoly of the liberals but it had a much stronger and lasting influence on them. The Communists, in contrast, came to adopt a different and more radical terminology of class struggle and social revolution, although they, for tactical reasons, would still continue to invoke human rights from time to time.

NOTES

1. It is possible to take 1915, the founding date of *New Youth*, as the starting point of the New Culture Movement, which then was followed and encompassed by the May Fourth Movement. Grieder (1981) talks about the New Culture Movement for the whole period 1915–1927. It has become customary to let the term May Fourth Movement include the years before as well as after the actual event. Chow Tse-tsung (1960), for example, laid down the time span as stretching between 1917 and 1921.

2. The Communists have tended to see May Fourth as a predominantly patriotic and socialist movement that helped spread communism, eventually leading to the establishment of the CCP. Whereas the GMD, on the other hand, has hailed it as a patriotic student movement and downplayed its iconoclasm and criticism of Confucianism. See Schwarcz (1986).

3. On Cai Yuanpei, see Duiker (1977).

4. For Cai's view on the policy of Peking University, see a letter written as a response to criticism from Lin Shu, reprinted in Fairbank and Ssu-yü Teng (1954), pp. 238–39.

5. For the intellectual debate during this period, see Chow Tse-Tsung (1960) and Schwarcz (1986).

6. It was first called *Youth Magazine* (*Qingnian zazhi*) but later renamed *New Youth* (*Xin qingnian*). It was edited by Chen Duxiu alone until January 1918 when a board of editors took over. See Chow Tse-tung (1960), pp. 42ff.

7. On the members of New Tide Society, which included Luo Jialun and Fu Sinian, see Schwarcz (1986).

8. On the history of communism in China, see Dirlik (1989).

9. On discussions on the liberation of the individual, see Schwarcz (1986).

10. Hu Shi (1935b).

11. Hu Shi (1918), p. 170.

12. Dewey stayed in China from May 1919 to July 1921, whereas Russell arrived in October 1920 and left almost one year later. On Dewey in China, see Keenan (1977) and Clapton and Tsuin-Chen Ou (1973). On Russell, see Ogden (1982).

13. According to Hu Shi, no Westerner had influenced the Chinese to the same extent as Dewey. See Hu Shi (1921).

14. For Russell's failure to influence the Chinese, see Ogden (1982). Russell, however, exerted an influence on Zhang Shenfu; see Schwarcz (1986).

15. Ryan (1995), p. 206.

16. See Weston (1998).

17. Gao Yihan (1884–1968) graduated from Meiji University in 1916. He served as professor of political science at Peking University 1918–26, and at the Law School of China

National Institute of Shanghai 1928–30. During the 1930s and 1940s he held posts in the civil administration. He later became a member of the Central Committee of the Democratic League. After 1949 he was dean of the Law School of Nanjing University, and served for some time as vice-chairman of the Jiangsu Province Political Consultative Conference. Judging by Gao Yihan's writings from the May Fourth period up to 1930, I think one can characterize him as a social liberal. In an article in *Xiandai pinglun*, Gao mentioned that he had been mistaken for a Communist with a similar name and refuted that he himself was a Communist, see Gao Yihan (1929).

18. See the bibliography in Gao Yihan (1930).

19. Several good works exist on Dewey's political thinking, I have found Ryan (1995) and Westbrook (1991) particularly useful.

20. One series of lectures appeared in *New Youth*. They were translated back into English by Clapton and Tsuin-Chen Ou (1973). I refer to the English translation but give the Chinese words for crucial terms.

21. See Clapton and Tsuin-Chen Ou (1973), p. 154f.

22. Westbrook (1991) has nothing to say about Dewey's view on rights, whereas Ryan (1995) mentions only in passing that Dewey did not believe in natural rights and that his liberalism was not of the rights "obsessed" version.

23. "The Rights of Individuals," reprinted in Clapton and Tsuin-Chen Ou (1973) pp. 147–155. This chapter appeared in *New Youth*, vol. 8, no. 1, 1920. He also discussed human rights while lecturing in Fujian, see Du Wei (John Dewey), n.d., pp. 82–84.

24. Clapton and Tsuin-Chen Ou (1973), p. 151.

25. Clapton and Tsuin-Chen Ou (1973), p. 148.

26. He Siyuan (1920), p. 107.

27. He Siyuan (1920), p. 112.

28. On the eve of his departure from China, Russell published an article venturing some thoughts on China's future, and in 1922, after his return to England, he also wrote a book, *The Problem of China*.

29. Schwarcz (1986) has brought attention to the differences between the teacher and student generations. I will, however, loosely refer to both teachers and students when talking about the May Fourthers.

30. For biographical details on Chen Duxiu, see Kuo (1975) and Feigon (1983). See also Chen's autobiography in Kagan (1969).

31. Benjamin Schwartz has described Chen's development after his release from prison in 1937 as a "softening and mellowing," whereas Hu Shi regarded Chen as a "late-in-life reconvert to democracy." Schwartz (1951), p. 71, and Hu Shi as quoted in Feigon (1983), p. 225.

32. Wang Fanxi in Benton (1998), p. 141.

33. There are not many materials on Chen Duxiu's view of human rights, or on the human rights discourse in general during May Fourth. For Chen, see Zarrow (1996). For the May Fourth period generally, see Liu Wenjuan (1993) and Xiong Yuezhi (1989).

34. It could be possible to see Chen's advocacy of human rights in *New Youth* as nothing but window dressing or lip service. It is obvious that Chen used the idea of human rights to criticize the Manchus and Yuan Shikai and that it later proved useful in the attack on the Confucian order, but it may not have been of primary interest in and of itself. This seems to be Feigon's (1983) reading of Chen, although he does not explicitly discuss Chen's view on human rights. I believe that Chen's preoccupation with the idea of human rights during the New Culture period, and his return to the idea toward the end of his life, show that his

commitment may have been genuine. Feigon is also critical of Schwartz's view of Chen as a Westernizer, and takes both Grieder (1981) and Lin Yü-sheng (1972) to task for seeing Chen as the key representative of Western liberalism and cosmopolitanism in China between 1915 and 1919. Wang Fanxi, Chen's disciple, however, disagrees with Feigon on this point. See Benton (1998), p. 137.

35. See Chen Duxiu (1914), and (1919e).

36. For a biography and study of Li Dazhao's thinking, see Meisner (1967).

37. Gao Yihan (1916b), p. 5, and (1918a), p. 8.

38. Gao Yihan (1915a), p. 5. Burgess (1844–1931) is regarded as the father of American political science. Gao Yihan referred to his work *Political Science and Constitutional Law.*

39. Gao Yihan (1930), pp. 132f.

40. Chen Duxiu (1919g), p. 43.

41. Chen Duxiu (1915c), p. 166.

42. Chen talked interchangeably about a *zizhu ziyou zhi renge, duli zizhu zhi renge, duli pingdeng zhi renge, duli zizun zhi renge,* and *duli ziyou zhi renge.*

43. Li Dazhao (1916b), p. 62. Li also quoted Henry's famous words "Give me liberty or give me death."

44. Gao Yihan (1915a), p. 6.

45. Gao Yihan (1915c), p. 4, and (1915b), p. 6.

46. Luo Jialun (1919a), p. 3.

47. Kang Baiqing (1919) also criticized the fact that women were deprived of their personalities (*renge*) as well as of their human rights (*renquan*).

48. Gao Yuan (1919).

49. The magazine came out with five issues in 1925. I have been unable to find anything about the magazine or its editors, Chen Zhushan and Hu Shiqing. From its content, it is possible to conclude that it had fairly radical views, leaning toward socialism but being critical of communism. It is possible that Hu Shiqing was the same Hu Shiqing who later was one of the founders of the National Socialist Party of China. This would be quite interesting since Zhang Junmai and Luo Longji, two leading figures of the party, also were ardent advocates of human rights.

50. Hu Shiqing (1925).

51. Chen Zhushan (1925b).

52. See Zhong Jiu (1919), p. 21.

53. Chen Qixiu (1919), p. 29.

54. Donnelly (1989), p. 17.

55. Donnelly (1989), p. 18.

56. Chen Duxiu (1915b), pp. 130–31. Compare also the discussion in an article on his hope for the new year, in which he urges people to stop being the appendage (*fushupin*) of others and to restore their independent and autonomous personality (*duli zizhu zhi renge*). Chen Duxiu (1915e), p. 172.

57. Chen Duxiu (1915b), p. 130.

58. Chen Duxiu (1915b), p. 130, see also (1915a), p. 137.

59. For example, in Chen Duxiu (1919f), p. 29.

60. See Li Dazhao (1916a), p. 31. In the same article he also writes about the importance of respecting the worth of the individual (*zunzhong ren zhi jiazhi*), p. 37.

61. Chen Duxiu (1915b), p. 130.

62. Chen Duxiu (1921a), pp. 265–66.

63. Chen Duxiu (1921b), p. 268.
64. Reprinted in Clapton and Tsuin-Chen Ou (1973), p. 92.
65. Ip (1994), who first drew my attention to this line of reasoning, has argued, convincingly in my opinion, that both Chen Duxiu and Li Dazhao were partly attracted to socialism because of their concern with individual liberty and dignity, which they felt were better protected under socialism.
66. For the phrase begging for food, see Chen Duxiu (1920a), p. 136.
67. Chen Duxiu (1920b), p. 138.
68. Li Dazhao (1919a), p. 632.
69. Li Dazhao (1919b), p. 635.
70. Bloch (1987).
71. Chen Duxiu (1915b), p. 130.
72. Chen Duxiu (1915a), p. 138.
73. Chen Duxiu (1921b), pp. 267–70.
74. Chen Duxiu (1915a), pp. 136–37, translated in Angle and Svensson (2001).
75. Chen Duxiu (1915a), p. 136.
76. Chen Duxiu (1919a), pp. 442–43.
77. Chen Duxiu (1916c), p. 240.
78. Chen Duxiu (1916a), p. 229.
79. Li Dazhao (1917a), p. 74.
80. Li Dazhao (1916b), p. 62.
81. Chen Duxiu (1915c), pp. 165–69; Li Dazhao (1918a), pp. 150–64.
82. See Chen Duxiu (1915b), p. 130. To bring strength to his argument, here he quoted Nietzsche's idea of slave morality.
83. Chen Duxiu (1915c), pp. 165–69.
84. Guang Sheng (1917).
85. Wu Yu (1917).
86. See Gao Yihan (1918b) and (1915c).
87. See Chen Xiaomei (1995) for a definition of Occidentalism. Compare also Feigon, who writes: "Chen's use of Western ideas and examples in the New Culture movement was clearly as much an attempt to break down the authority of the old society as a real desire to have China look like France or Germany," Feigon (1983), p. 135.
88. On the relationship between *jiuren* and *jiuguo*, see Schwarcz (1986), p. 6. Lin Yüsheng (1972) has downplayed the importance of liberal and individualist values during May Fourth and argued that they were only used as a tool in the attack on the family and Confucianism. But such an understanding, in my view, needs to be modified and nuanced.
89. See Dirlik (1989).
90. See Chen Duxiu (1919c) and Li Dazhao (1917b).
91. Chen Duxiu (1915e), p. 172.
92. Chen Duxiu (1921a), pp. 265–66.
93. On the debate on racial equality in the League of Nations, see von Senger (1993), pp. 66–87, and pp. 287–89.
94. Chen had been influenced by Chinese iconoclasts such as Yüan Mei on the woman issue; see Feigon (1983), p. 29. For a collection of writings on women's issues by the May Fourthers, see Lan and Fong (1999).
95. See, for example, Shang Yi (1922).
96. See Wang Zheng (1999), pp. 99–111.

97. For one of Chen Duxiu's earliest discussion on women, see (1916b).
98. Chen Duxiu (1921b).
99. For the feminist discourse during May Fourth, see Wang Zheng (1999).
100. Ye Shengtao (Ye Shaotao) (1919), p. 257.
101. Wei Fang (1922), p. 52437.
102. See Wang Zheng's (1999) fascinating account of some Chinese women's life stories.
103. See Chen Duxiu (1915c), p. 166, and (1919f), p. 29.
104. See Chen Duxiu (1919d), p. 25.
105. Chen Duxiu (1919g), p. 43.
106. Li Dazhao (1916b), p. 63.
107. Li Dazhao (1919c), p. 191.
108. Li Dazhao (1919c), p. 192.
109. Zhang Shenfu (1919), pp. 551–53.
110. Li Dazhao (1922), p. 392.
111. Gao Yihan (1918b), p. 255, see also (1915a), p. 7.
112. Gao Yihan (1926b), pp. 224–25.
113. Anon., "A Call to Teachers and Staff," (1920), p. 4.
114. For a sample of their views, see Anon., "The View of the New Man in the New Thought," (1920); Anon., "Our New Faith," (1920); Anon., "The Coming Three Freedoms," (1920); and Anon., "The Price of Freedom," (1920).
115. Luo Jialun (1919b), p. 231.
116. The first five chapters of Bury's work were translated by Luo Jialun in the spring of 1919 and published in successive numbers of *Chen bao*. Luo later continued to translate and revise the work while studying abroad, and in 1927 the whole book was finally published in China. The original work had been published in 1913.
117. See, for example, Wang Shijie (1924).
118. Zhou Fohai (1922), p. 776.
119. Li Dazhao (1918b), pp. 164–67.
120. Gao Yihan (1921).
121. Gao Yihan (1930), pp. 130–31.
122. See, for example, Dai Jitao in Tang Wenquan and Sang Bing (1990), pp. 195–96.
123. On Dai Jitao (1891–1949), see Tan (1971), pp. 176–84.
124. Many of those responsible for introducing Marxism in China were associated with the GMD, and Dai was one of them. Dai's contribution, in fact, was very important during the period 1919–21. He wrote extensively himself but was also responsible for many translations. See Dirlik (1989), pp. 99–103.
125. Dai Jitao in Tang Wenquan and Sang Bing (1990), pp. 964–73.
126. See Wei Fang (1922), Shi Weihuan (1922), Lin Keyi (1922), and Gao Yihan (1922).
127. Shi Weihuan (1922), p. 52446.
128. Shi Weihuan (1922), p. 52449.
129. Chen Zhushan (1925a), pp. 2–4. See also Hu Shiqing (1925), p. 9.
130. Chen Zhushan (1925a), p. 4.
131. An earlier, very brief article in *The Eastern Miscellany* gave a similar historical description of the development from divine rights to human rights. It described the stage of human rights in terms of brightness (*guangming*) and universal peace (*datong*). See Hua Lin (1913), pp. 24079–80.
132. Anon., "On the Policy of the Construction of the Republic," (1919), p. 1.

133. For a discussion of the Chinese view of history as linear, see Duara (1995).

134. Gao Yihan (1930), pp. 133–134. Guang Sheng (1917) also believed that if people were not given freedom and opportunities to develop themselves, the progress of society would be impaired.

135. As an example, Gao gave the right to work that had been reformulated as a duty in the Soviet Union. See Gao Yihan (1930), p. 134.

136. Chen Duxiu (1919h), pp. 41–42.

137. See Chen Duxiu (1915e), p. 172.

138. Wu Pinjin (1923) and Zeng Qi (1920).

139. Ye Lin (1919), p. 440.

140. Tan Mingqian (1920).

141. See Chen Duxiu (1940c), pp. 559–63. A collection of Chen's last articles and letters have now been translated; see Benton (1998).

142. Chen Duxiu (1940b), pp. 552–58, and (1940a), pp. 547–49.

143. Chen Duxiu (1940b), pp. 552–58.

144. For the manifesto, see Hu Shi (1920), translated in Angle and Svensson (2001).

145. Originally published in *The Eastern Miscellany*, vol. 19, no. 8, 1922, reprinted in, for example, Gao Pingshu (1985), pp. 220–25.

146. The republic had promulgated a provisional constitution in 1912, and in 1913 the Constitutional Commission of the Parliament prepared a draft constitution known as the Temple of Heaven Draft, which was never enacted. In 1914 Yuan Shikai promulgated a provisional constitution, and in 1919 the Anfu Parliament also prepared a draft constitution. See the list of constitutions and drafts listed by Ch'ien Tuan-Sheng (1961), p. 435. On the provisions for political rights in the republican constitutions, see Nathan (1986b), pp. 86–89.

147. Tao Menghe had studied in Japan and in Britain, where he graduated from London University in 1913. He served as a professor at Peking University 1914–21 and became director of the Institute of Social Sciences at Academia Sinica in 1934. *Xiandai pinglun* was published between 1924 and 1928, and edited by two professors from Peking University, Chen Yuan and Zhou Gengsheng.

148. See Anon., "The Freedom of Speech in Beijing," (1924), Tao Menghe (1924), and Gao Yihan (1925b). On arrests, et cetera, see Anon., "Where is there Protection of Human Rights?" (1925), and Anon., "Another Human Rights Question," (1926).

149. Chen Zhushan (1925a), p. 5.

Chapter Seven

The Nanking Decade, 1927–1937: Liberal and Radical Voices on Human Rights

REPRESSION UNDER THE NATIONALISTS

Demands for human rights and the rule of law reached new heights after the establishment of the Nationalist government in Nanking in 1927. These demands were fueled by the GMD's tightening grip on ideology and politics, guided by Sun Yat-sen's Three Principles of the People of nationalism, democracy, and people's livelihood. As Hu Shi so acidly pointed out: "It is possible to deny God, but not to criticize Sun Yat-sen. One need not go to church, but one must not fail to read the Great Leader's 'Last Will and Testament,' or observe the weekly memorial service."[1] After the proclamation of the period of political tutelage in 1928, several liberals, including Hu Shi and Luo Longji, were active in demanding institutional checks on GMD rule and the promulgation of a constitution. The constitutional protection of people's rights remained a much debated topic during the first half of the 1930s. But in the early 1930s, the GMD became less and less tolerant of dissent. The new press law of 1930 gave the authorities considerable powers of censorship. Postal privileges for critical magazines were sporadically withdrawn, issues occasionally confiscated, and editors and journalists arrested and even executed.[2]

Although both liberals and Communists were victims of GMD's repression, the more radical critics of the GMD bore the brunt of this repression. In 1927, the First United Front between the GMD and the CCP fell apart and the GMD turned against its erstwhile allies. The Nationalists launched a manhunt on suspected Communists and during this so-called White Terror thousands of people were arrested and killed. This suppression forced the Communists underground and into the countryside, where at first they established base areas in Jiangxi province. After successfully defending themselves against the Nationalists' attacks, the Communists finally had to leave their base area and embark on the famous Long March in 1934, eventually establishing the Yan'an Soviet in Shaanxi province. Many left-wing intellectuals and Communists continued to be rounded up throughout the 1930s until the Second United Front in 1937 again gave them some respite. One case that received much attention was that of Chen Duxiu, who was arrested in Shanghai in October 1932 and in April of the following year, he was sentenced to thirteen years imprisonment.

The GMD's repression was criticized by both liberals and Communists during the Nanking decade. But their critique was usually configured differently and had a different content and aim. From time to time, however, the two groups were able to unite in criticizing the GMD. In late 1932, they thus united in establishing the China League for the Protection of Civil Rights. But their different perspectives and political programs soon led to a split and the end of the organization. The liberals tried to influence the GMD to become more democratic and respect human rights and the rule of law. But their efforts were almost exclusively confined to intellectual activities aimed at reforming the system from within. Faced with Japanese aggression and a very real threat to national survival, many liberals came to take a less critical stance toward the GMD as the 1930s proceeded, in the process severely compromising their own ideals.[3] The need for a strongly centralized state in a time of national crisis seemed to justify the sacrifice of some individual liberties. The growing disillusion among many Chinese liberals with Western democracy and liberalism was also a result of the political situation in the West during this time. Fascism and authoritarian solutions to social and economic problems in Germany and Italy inspired some Chinese to take the same road.[4] This shift in the liberals' position can be seen in the heated debate on democracy versus dictatorship that dominated the pages of influential liberal magazines in 1933–35.

THE XINYUE GROUP AND
HUMAN RIGHTS: THE LIBERAL VIEW

The most vociferous liberal attack on the Nationalists for suppressing freedom of speech and other civil liberties in the late 1920s came from the Shanghai monthly *Xinyue (The Crescent)*.[5] The loose group of liberal intellectuals who wrote in the magazine came to be referred to as the "*Xinyue* group," or the "human rights group."[6] Founded in 1928 in Shanghai, *Xinyue* had started out as a purely literary magazine. It was edited by such legendary literary figures as Hu Shi, Xu Zhimo, Wen Yiduo, and the literary critic Liang Shiqiu.[7] The editors believed they had a mission to end the dark period in China and create a bright new future. *Xinyue* did not have any well-formulated program or organization. It consisted of friends who shared the same convictions and liberal ideals and were united around the demands for freedom of thought and freedom of publication.[8] To them, human rights were rights that belonged to the individual person qua human being; they were not given by the state and therefore could not be infringed upon by it. They were also in agreement in their opposition to one-party dictatorship and in their advocacy of rule of law and constitutionalism. National needs, they argued, should never be used as an excuse to suppress individual freedoms; furthermore, there did not exist any necessary correlation between the sacrifice of individual freedom and the realization of national freedom.[9]

Starting with Hu Shi's article "Human Rights and the Provisional Constitution," published in April 1929, *Xinyue* began to comment on the political issues of the day.[10] The new direction was strongly influenced by the literary critic Liang Shiqiu and the political scientist Luo Longji. Together with Hu Shi, these two wrote the majority of the magazine's articles on human rights, freedom of speech, and the rule of law.[11] In 1932, *Xinyue* reverted to its former stance as a purely literary magazine. Even though no formal explanation was given for this change, it is probably not incorrect to conjecture that it was partly due to GMD's displeasure with some of the magazine's articles and a growing pressure on the part of the regime. But there were also underlying political differences among the editors themselves on the preferable position of the magazine that could explain this shift in direction.[12]

Hu Shi's demands for human rights sprung from a belief that human rights were held by people against the state and that the state must not infringe upon these rights. Citizens should be protected from arbitrary actions by the government and, to this end, legal protection in the form of a constitution and other laws were needed. Hu Shi was highly critical of the GMD's work in this respect. When the Nationalist government issued a decree on April 20, 1929, regarding the protection of human rights, he was provoked to write an article criticizing the content and implication of the decree. The decree read as follows: "Human rights are protected by law in every country in the world. Now that our tutelage government is in existence, a foundation for the rule of law definitely needs to be established. All those entities within the Republic of China's legal jurisdiction, whether individuals or organisations, shall not engage in illegal behaviour which harms the physical being, freedom, or property of others. Those who violate this order shall be harshly punished according to the law."[13] Hu Shi's main criticism was that the decree failed to realize the possibility that the government and its organizations could be the real culprits, which, Hu Shi pointed out, was the case in the majority of human rights violations. He cited several cases in which people had been arrested after having been randomly labeled "a counterrevolutionary" or "communist suspect" and deprived of their human rights. Hu Shi also faulted the decree for failing to explain the kind of legal protection people enjoyed in the exercise of their rights. In order to address these problems and truly protect people's human rights, Hu Shi believed that it was necessary to quickly promulgate a constitution.

It was left to Luo Longji in his article "On Human Rights" to provide a more theoretical discussion on the nature of human rights.[14] Luo had an intimate knowledge of the West after many years of studies abroad, during which he earned a Ph.D. in political science at Columbia University.[15] His conceptual framework, therefore, owed much more to Western political thought than to Chinese thought; in this respect he resembled Gao Yihan. As a political scientist Luo had a much deeper insight into Western political thought and institutions than Hu Shi, and he put forth his political views in a much more coherent and systematic way. Luo was a disciple of the British political scientist Laski, who came to exert a strong influence on his thinking.[16] Laski was also quite popular with many other Chinese intellectuals. Both Xu Zhimo and Wang Zaoshi had been students of Laski at the London School of Economics, and after returning to China they, like Luo Longji, were instrumental in introducing his works and ideas to their fellow countrymen. Laski also exerted a considerable influence on Zhang Junmai (Carsun Chang) and Ding Wenjiang. Ding, for instance, named Laski as his favorite British author, besides Russell and Wells.[17] Laski never visited China but many of his works were translated and published in China in the late 1920s and early 1930s. His major opus, *A Grammar of Politics*, widely used as a textbook in political science in the West, was translated into Chinese by Zhang Junmai in 1927 and published in 1930.[18]

Laski's rights thinking was heavily influenced by Green and the British Idealists and also owed much to Fabianism and a socialized Benthamism. But the economic depression and the emergence of fascism ultimately radicalized his thinking and turned him into an advocate of Marxism, which also influenced his view of and interest in rights.[19] The writings of Laski's Fabian period, culminating with *A Grammar*, most influenced Luo Longji and other Chinese writers. It is interesting to speculate that Laski's more Marxist writings would not have impressed his Chinese disciples to the same extent, given their well-known critical views of communism. Laski's social liberal ideas and more socialized conception of human rights, however, seem to have fallen on fertile soil in China. According to Zhang Foquan, many Chinese appreciated Laski precisely because he emphasized rights, although Zhang himself at this time was critical of this emphasis on rights at the expense of duties; Zhang was later to change his mind and become a staunch advocate of human rights in the 1950s.[20] Zhang's view is quite interesting since what is striking about Laski and the British Idealists is that they emphasized duties to a much greater extent than many other Western thinkers, albeit without neglecting the importance of rights.

In his article "On Human Rights," Luo Longji set himself the task of defining and defending human rights against those who regarded it as an excessively abstract concept not applicable to China.[21] This article clearly shows Luo's debt to Laski, and Luo often quotes from *A Grammar*.[22] Luo was also influenced by Paine and human rights manifestos like the *French Declaration of the Rights of Man and Citizen*. The point of origin of Laski's and Luo's rights theory was the human personality and the needs that have to be fulfilled in order for man's personality to be fully realized. As Luo Longji wrote: "Human rights, to put it simply, are all those rights that enable one to be a person [*zuoren*]. Human rights are those necessary conditions in order to be a human being."[23] Luo shared with Laski a functionalistic approach to human rights according to which human rights simply are all those rights that enable one to be a person. They not only include rights to material goods like food, clothing, and shelter in order to preserve life, but also those rights that give people the opportunity to develop their individuality and personality, such as freedom of speech. Luo argued that as a human being, he must be given the opportunity to "be myself at my best."[24] This was a phrase he borrowed from Laski, which Laski took from the British Idealists.[25]

Luo Longji and Laski derived the justification of rights from their function (*gongyong*) as a necessary means for human existence.[26] In this context their concern with rights was as much due to an interest in the social welfare as with the individual's well-being. Rights were no license to do as one liked without concern of the collective. Luo stressed the social side of rights when he wrote that one individual's happiness could not be attained in isolation from that of one's fellow men. Human rights, according to Luo, must be instrumental in promoting "the greatest happiness of the greatest number."[27] Though the individual may have rights against the state, they could by definition not be used against the "public welfare." Rights were not one individual's rights against society. Because all individuals share the same goal, rights against the common end were impossible to imagine. An individual who claimed rights against the common welfare was not only acting unsocially and irresponsibly, but also against his own good.

Implicit in the thinking of Luo Longji and Laski is therefore a close correlation between rights and duties. The opposite side of the coin of rights are duties, which Laski emphasized time and again. "I have . . . rights which are inherent in me as a member of society. . . . They are, of course, counterbalanced by the duties I owe in return. I am given rights that I may enrich the common life."[28] This phrase lends itself to the interpretation that the enjoyment of rights depends on the fulfillment of one's duties, and that one enjoys rights in order to enrich society. Luo Longji was not prepared, however, to let talk of duties supersede rights talk. He was acutely aware of the fact that many governments, the Chinese included, were apt to use people's duties to the state as an excuse to clamp down on their rights. Luo was highly critical of the GMD, which saw the state as a goal in itself and seemed to believe that the people existed for the benefit of the state and not vice versa. "They [i.e., the GMD] do not ask what rights the state gives the people, but believe that 'save the nation,' 'love the nation' are the unconditional obligations of the people."[29]

Luo was sensitive to the fact that national goals, as defined by one person or one party, can and have been used as an excuse to suppress people's rights. To Luo, the state and the general welfare were two different things that should not be confused. In his view rights were claims that the individual has upon the state. Rights belong to individuals and the primary responsibility of the state is to safeguard these rights. Following Laski, Luo thus argued that the function of the state was to protect human rights.[30] He went on to argue that if a state fails to protect, or itself violates people's rights, it would lose its justification and moral claim to allegiance. This view of the state was at odds with the predominant view of both the GMD and the CCP.[31]

Rights, according to Luo, were not only claimed against the state, but held prior to the establishment of the state. Rights, in other words, were not granted by the state, as Wu Jingxiong, for example, and others later would contend, but existed prior to and independently of the state. "The state, to put it simply, does not create human rights, it can only recognise them, its merits at any given point of time are decided by using its recognition of human rights as a standard."[32] Both Luo and Laski opposed the legal positivist view on rights that rejects any rights except those stipulated by the law. As Luo so aptly put it: "From the law I can at the most know my present rights, but I cannot know what kind of rights I ought to have."[33] This distinction between *is* and *ought*, between positive and normative rights, clearly shows that Luo believed human rights to belong to the category of moral rather than positive rights. Human rights were thus not confined to the rights stipulated by the law at that time.

Luo was also aware of the fact that the law could be devoid of meaning and be but a sheet of paper without any real value.[34] But his skepticism regarding legal stipulations did not prevent him, like Hu Shi, from insisting that legal safeguards and the implementation of a constitution were crucial so that people's rights at least would have the prospect of being protected. The provisional constitution, which was promulgated in 1931, was, however, a disappointment in this respect. Luo's critique of it went completely unheeded and, furthermore, led to political problems for the magazine. When a constitution finally was promulgated in 1946, it was obvious, as Luo had feared, that mere stipulations of constitutional rights could not guarantee that they also would be respected and protected.

Given Luo's belief in the existence of human rights prior to and independent of the state and the law, what was then the basis of his rights theory? Despite his belief in human rights prior to and independent of the state, Luo did not believe in the existence of rights in the state of nature. He refuted Rousseau's belief in a Golden Age when people were free and equal, which he seems to have believed to be an indispensable part of a natural rights theory.[35] Luo was also very troubled by and critical of the concept of natural rights.[36] In order to avoid being associated with advocates of natural rights, Luo was careful not to use the term *tianfu renquan* and instead insisted on using the word *renquan*. Rights, according to Luo, were needed in order to be a human being; in this sense they were also seen as pre-social and as an outcome of man's moral and physical needs. It could therefore be apt to describe Luo's view of human rights as a needs-based theory of rights. And although rights inevitably, to some extent, would be universal, Luo stressed that they also had a historical and relative aspect.[37] Human rights were not eternal and universal as natural rights advocates would contend, he argued, but changed with differing needs and circumstances. Or, as Laski, echoing Green, put it: "They [i.e. human rights] are not historical in the sense that they have at some time won their recognition. They are not natural, in the sense that a permanent and unchanging catalogue of them can be compiled. They are historical in the sense that, at some given period and place, they are demanded by the character of its civilisation; and they are natural in the sense that, under those same limitations, the facts demand their recognition."[38]

Given their emphasis on the historical character of human rights, the rights Laski and Luo enumerated differed to some extent. Luo provided a list of no less than thirty-five rights, some of which reflected specific Chinese conditions.[39] Similarly to Laski, Luo included civil and political rights on his list, such as freedoms of thought, speech, belief, the press, and association.[40] He also included social and economic rights, such as the right to work, the right to protection against disaster and illness, and the right to education. These rights indicate Laski's influence and, by extension, the influence of Fabianism and socialism. But whereas Laski was doubtful about the right to property, Luo also included the right to private ownership on his list.

Luo Longji insisted on the importance of free speech in order to develop one's personality and as a means to enable people to contribute to society.[41] He furthermore regarded this freedom to be absolute, arguing that it should not be subjected to any infringements whatsoever. Consequently, one had the right to advocate all kinds of political ideas, ranging from monarchism to communism. The *Xinyue* group generally held freedom of speech and publication to be very important and criticized the GMD for suppressing freedom of thought.[42] Although they were very critical of communism, as true liberals they were nevertheless prepared to grant the Communists freedom of speech, which was more than the GMD was prepared to do.[43] Luo acknowledged the danger of absolute freedom but contended that suppression of speech was even more dangerous. He argued that this would only result in driving dissenting views underground. Open and free discussions, on the other hand, could serve to strengthen and democratize the GMD.

A TWO-WAY CRITIQUE OF THE XINYUE GROUP

Hu Shi's first article on human rights was widely read and republished in various Chinese and foreign magazines.[44] It received both praise, from Cai Yuanpei, for example, and criticism, mainly from the GMD. This and other articles by him led party members, such as Zhang Zhenzhi and others, to publish critical articles in the GMD-controlled press. In 1929, these were compiled into a book entitled *Criticising Hu Shi for Violating the Party Spirit*.[45] And in 1930 Chen Dezheng then published *On Human Rights and Other Subjects*, specifically devoted to an attack on Hu Shi's views on human rights.[46] Hu Shi was criticized for worshipping the idea of "natural rights," and accused of opposing the GMD and being under the influence of the CCP.[47] The only attempt by the *Xinyue* group to answer these criticisms, as far as I know, was Luo's replies to Zhang Yuanruo, another GMD ideologist who criticized the group.[48]

Although the CCP was extremely critical of the GMD and its suppression of people's rights and freedoms, itself being the main victim, it interestingly enough concurred with GMD in its critique of the *Xinyue* group. Even though their perspectives differed, the CCP and the GMD were in agreement in rejecting human rights as an excessively abstract idea that did not fit China's revolutionary needs. The CCP, as could be expected, however, focused on the political and class standpoint of the group. CCP spokesmen, people such as Peng Kang and Qu Qiubai, in addition argued that Hu Shi and the others were not honest in their critique of the GMD and that they were bourgeois liberals unconcerned about the suffering of the laboring masses.[49]

Some of those criticizing the *Xinyue* group dismissed the concept of natural rights as old and out of date, or, in other words, lacking historical and scientific backing.[50] Zhang Yuanruo dismissed the concept of human rights as outmoded, pointing out that Western constitutions no longer mentioned human rights but preferred to speak of *guomin zhi quanli* (citizen's rights) or *renmin zhi quanli* (people's rights).[51] The most trivial part of Zhang's criticism was the charge that if one talked about *renquan*, that is, "the rights of man" or *droits de l'homme*, then one would exclude women from enjoying these rights, whereas *minquan* (people's rights) made no such distinction between the sexes, a charge that Luo had no trouble refuting. Luo acknowledged that Western philosophers no longer talked about *tianfu renquan* (natural rights), but argued that they still acknowledged the existence of *renquan* (human rights). According to Luo, to say that people are born with human rights, rights that exist independently of the state, was not the same as to say that people have lived and enjoyed rights in a natural state.[52] His critics, however, failed to see any difference between an advocacy of natural rights and of human rights, a distinction that Luo tried to uphold. Chen Dezheng, for example, criticized Hu Shi for worshipping the idea of *tianfu renquan* (natural rights). (Hu Shi himself generally preferred to use the word *renquan*.)

The real conflict between the *Xinyue* group and their critics was not between an advocacy of *tianfu renquan* versus *renquan*, however, but between *renquan* versus *minquan*. The GMD thus dismissed human rights and instead advocated people's rights. Sun Yat-sen himself had rejected the idea that the individual possesses certain inherent and inalienable rights, in addition to dismissing the concept of human rights as unsuitable to China.[53] Sun was convinced that the Chinese people, in contrast to Westerners, had excessive freedom. This excessive freedom was dangerous, as it resulted in the Chinese people becoming like "a sheet of loose sand," unable to unite for the sake of the nation. Sun therefore argued that instead of fighting for individual freedoms, the Chinese people's task was to fight for national freedom, and, not only that, in order for this to succeed, they were also expected to sacrifice their individual freedoms.

Chiang Kai-shek later argued against the language of human rights, drawing on the same arguments that Sun Yat-sen had used earlier.[54] Chiang criticized those who regarded the idea of natural rights as a useful theoretical basis for the Chinese revolution, describing it as not only inconsistent with historical facts but also as unsuitable to the Chinese situation. Chiang emphasized with Sun that in the current crisis the Chinese people would have to sacrifice their individual freedoms for the greater goal of national freedom. And he went on to suggest that people had both a right and a duty to take part in the GMD. He justified this by arguing that only membership in the GMD and participation in the revolution could bring about national salvation and the welfare of all people. Criticism of the GMD, on the other hand, would equal opposition to the revolutionary cause and be detrimental to the national welfare.

In the declaration of the GMD's First National Congress, adopted in 1924, it was explicitly stated that the concept of people's rights was different from the concept of "so-called natural rights [*suowei tianfu renquan*]."[55] It was emphasized that the former rights were enjoyed by citizens opposing imperialism, whereas they would be denied to those opposing the republic. People's rights, thus, were not only derived from citizenship but were dependent upon political allegiance.

The difference between people's rights and human rights was further developed by Zhou Fohai in 1928.[56] Zhou argued that even though the goal of the GMD was political rights for all, it could deny some people their rights in order to reach this goal. In fact, to deprive those who opposed the republic of their rights was necessary if this goal would ever be realized. This argument was reiterated by Sa Mengwu, another GMD ideologist, who argued that before the counter-revolutionary forces had been destroyed, those who did not follow the Three Principles of the People would not be allowed any political rights.[57] Another reason the GMD opposed the idea of natural rights, according to Zhou Fohai, was that if they acknowledged the idea of natural rights, everyone, including counterrevolutionaries, could demand rights, as even counterrevolutionaries were human beings and therefore, by definition, endowed with human rights.[58] People's rights, on the other hand, were only enjoyed by the people, that is, those supporting the revolution, which excluded counterrevolutionaries.

The critics of *Xinyue* built on the understandings of the differences between human rights and people's rights prevalent in GMD theoretical work. In addition, they criticized human rights for being the rights of the bourgeoisie, whereas people's rights were the rights of all people, albeit excluding counterrevolutionaries.[59] Like the Communists were wont to do, the GMD argued that only the bourgeoisie enjoyed human rights in the West. Where the Chinese liberals were only fighting for the human rights of the minority, the GMD proclaimed itself to be fighting for the true rights of all people. Thus, the conflict also concerned the subject of rights and how people came to enjoy them, that is, the issue of whether people were born with rights or whether they were granted by the state. Luo Longji regarded human rights to be broader in scope and more fundamental than people's rights. People's rights were only one part of the wider rights of man, he argued; they only pertained to man qua citizen of a specific country. But, according to Luo, people were first and foremost members of society and only second were they citizens of a particular nation. Human rights therefore belonged to man as an individual rather than man as a citizen. "[H]uman rights are the rights which enables one to be a person [*zuoren*], whereas the rights of a citizen are the rights to be citizen in a political state. . . . There are people who are not citizens, but there are no citizens who are not human beings. From this it is easy to see that the scope of human rights is wider and more basic than that of the rights of citizens."[60]

One fundamental difference was that whereas the advocates of human rights believed that people were born with these rights, the advocates of people's rights insisted that rights were derived from citizenship and thus given by the state. Human rights, according to Luo and other liberals, were not created by the state, they were only recognized by it. But this was a preposterous assumption according to their critics, who instead argued that neither were rights and freedoms enjoyed outside of society, nor were they inherent; they only came into existence through the recognition of law or customs.[61] The human rights advocates believed that the function of the law was to protect people's rights, and that was why they demanded rule of law and a constitution. But Pan Gongzhan ridiculed this demand, pointing out that if they believed human rights to be innate there would be no need for them to demand the implementation of a constitution.[62] Behind these differences lay a completely different understanding of the purpose and role of the state. According to the human rights advocates, the state was created by and for the people as a tool to protect their rights.[63] The critics of the *Xinyue* group, on the other hand, regarded rights as granted by the state with the safety and prosperity of the society and the nation in mind.[64] Rights were a mere means toward an end and not an end in and of themselves. Pan Guangzhan argued that rights were only bestowed so that the individual could help promote the progress of society and, therefore, he could not use his rights to violate this purpose.[65] The GMD demanded that people fight for the freedom of the nation rather than for their own freedoms, arguing that a curtailment of individual rights was inevitable at a time of national crisis.[66]

On the surface, Pan Guangzhan's view of the purpose of rights was not all that different from that of Luo's, as both saw rights as necessary for self-development and for the progress of society. But whereas Pan concluded that rights could be curtailed or restricted in the interest of society, Luo accepted no such restriction regarding the enjoyment of rights and refused to see any conflicts between the rights of the individual and the social or national interest. He and the other liberals writing in *Xinyue* disputed the view that there was a causal correlation between the sacrifice of individual freedom and the realization of national freedom.

Another type of critique concerned whether human rights were applicable or suitable to China. This critique was not posed as a question of cultural compatibility but framed as a question of political needs and expediency. Zhou Fohai argued that whereas the theory of natural rights had been suitable to the circumstances in revolutionary France, it did not match the present needs of China.[67] Zhou's sentiments were shared by other critics of the *Xinyue* group who stressed that advocacy of individual human rights was not in keeping with the "revolutionary needs" of China, as imperialist forces and internal enemies threatened the very survival of the Chinese nation.[68] In order to secure national freedom people would have to sacrifice some of their individual freedoms. In this context, the GMD critics also emphasized that people were born with duties toward society and the state.[69] Duties were said to be more important to society than were individual rights in the struggle for national survival.[70] Another political argument against the concept of human rights was that counterrevolutionaries would have been encompassed by it, since, by definition, they were human beings also. But by talking about people's rights and excluding counterrevolutionaries from the category of the people, it was possible to deny them rights.

The Communists' critique of the *Xinyue* group centered on its political and class standpoint. Communists such as Peng Kang criticized Hu Shi and the others for advocating abstract (*chouxiang*) and imprescriptible human rights (*yong bu momie de renquan*).[71] Luo Longji had the following to say about this kind of critique in his essay on the nature and character of human rights:

> There are some people . . . who have deceived themselves into saying that human rights is an "abstract term." They use slogans like "starving and unable to eat, freezing, and unclothed" to claim that the human rights movement cannot be compared to the reality of the materialist, class revolution. Those people have completely failed to realise what human rights are. Of course human rights encompass clothing and food; they also include many things still more important than clothing and food. Consider, after all, that if in his day Germany had enjoyed complete freedom of thought, speech, and publication, Marx would not have had to flee to London's British Museum in order to write *Das Kapital*! Those who criticise human rights as an abstract term have completely failed to realise what human rights are.[72]

Peng Kang, following Marx, argued that man is a social animal who belongs to a certain class and that laws and rights are a product of existing social relationships that reflect the interests of those in power. Following this analysis, the *Xinyue* group was accused of only fighting for the freedoms of the individual and the bourgeoisie. Their human rights movement was nothing but a reactionary movement, whereas the Communists claimed to be fighting for the rights of the proletariat. Qu Qiubai, furthermore, questioned the motives behind the *Xinyue* group's struggle for human rights.[73] He claimed that its criticism of the GMD's violations of human rights was not convincing but just a cover-up. Taking Luo Longji's articles on communism as evidence of this, Qu argued that Luo and his friends did not really oppose the GMD; but only criticized it for not fighting the CCP sufficiently resolutely. The Communists also questioned the liberals' belief that respect for human rights could be brought about through the establishment of laws and a constitution. Rights and freedoms, they argued, could only be secured through political struggles, which called for a political revolution rather than reform of the present political system. Although Peng Kang did not venture into a discussion on the actual content of human rights, he nonetheless affirmed the value of freedom of thought and speech and didn't focus exclusively on social and economic rights.

THE CHINA LEAGUE FOR THE PROTECTION OF CIVIL RIGHTS: THE CLASH BETWEEN LIBERALS AND RADICALS OVER HUMAN RIGHTS

In the early 1930s, the GMD became increasingly repressive, resorting to arrests and executions of its political opponents and critics. Those arrested were mostly alleged Communists and left-wing supporters, but liberal journalists were also a target. These cases were reported in the Chinese press and provided the impetus behind the founding of the China League for the Protection of Civil Rights.[74] Song Qingling, the driving force behind the league, had become more and more critical of Chiang Kai-shek, feeling that he had betrayed the ideas of her late husband, Sun Yat-sen. Cai Yuanpei, the other central figure of the league, had also become increasingly concerned about the GMD's ruthlessness toward its critics. Song Qingling initially suggested a committee under the GMD to solve the problem of political prisoners but failed to receive any support for this idea.[75] She then put forward the idea of founding an independent organization and solicited support among Chinese intellectuals.[76] The idea was favorably taken up by a broad spectrum of Chinese intellectuals, who, despite their different political views, shared her concern with human rights violations under the GMD. On December 18, 1932, Song Qingling, together with Cai Yuanpei, Yang Quan, Lin Yutang, and others, published a statement declaring the founding of the China League for the Protection of Civil Rights (*Zhongguo minquan baozhang tongmeng*).[77] The league declared that it had three tasks: (1) to work for the release of political prisoners and for the abolishment of torture and other cruel treatments; (2) to give political prisoners legal and other assistance, investigate prison conditions, and publish facts about the suppression of civil rights; and (3) to work for the freedom of association and assembly, the freedom of expression, and the freedom of the press.[78]

When a constituting meeting was held in Shanghai on January 17, 1933, Song Qingling was elected chairperson; Cai Yuanpei, vice-chairman; Yang Quan, secretary; and Lin Yutang was made responsible for the league's publicity work.[79] The members of the league came from a broad spectrum of the Chinese political scene and included famous writers such as Lu Xun, Yu Dafu, Zhou Jianren, Zao Taofen, and Mao Dun. Two foreigners also became active members, namely, Harold Isaacs, a young American journalist for *China Forum*, and Agnes Smedley, an American journalist who served as Song Qingling's English secretary. The original plan had been to set up sections in other major Chinese cities, but in the end this was successful only in Beiping (the name for Peking at that time). On January 30, 1933, the Beiping section was established with Hu Shi as chairman.[80] Other members in Beiping included Jiang Menglin and Tao Menghe. John and Wilma Fairbank, who were then staying in Beiping, also became members, although it seems they were not very active.[81]

The political cases that Song Qingling and Cai Yuanpei had taken an interest in continued to preoccupy the league, which also took up the cases of students and teachers who had been arrested for protesting Japanese aggression.[82] The league tried to provide political prisoners with legal assistance and also investigated prison conditions. Hu Shi and Yang Quan, for example, visited several prisons in Beiping in early 1933.[83] The league also advocated resistance to Japanese aggression and participated in an umbrella organization with the same purpose.[84] Not only concerned with human rights violations in China, the league also became engaged in the fight against Nazism and protested the treatment of Jews and workers in Germany.[85] These activities received ample coverage in the Chinese press, notably in Isaac's *China Forum*. The league came to an abrupt and tragic end after only six months, however, when Yang Quan was assassinated on June 18, 1933.[86] He and the other members had repeatedly received letters containing warnings and threats, but Cai Yuanpei and Song Qingling were protected by their high standing within the GMD and so it was Yang Quan who became the victim of its wrath. Although no formal evidence exists, it has been alleged that it was Dai Li's infamous "secret service," or the Blue Shirt Society, that was responsible for the assassination.[87] Even though Song Qingling vowed that the assassination would not stop the league from carrying out its work, it nevertheless meant the end of the league.[88]

It is interesting to note that the league chose the word *minquan* instead of *renquan* in its name. But from this fact alone one should not conclude that the league shared the GMD's understanding of *minquan*. This is revealed by the fact that the league opted for "civil rights" as the English translation of *minquan*. From this choice of word and the discussions in the league's manifesto and other statements, we can conclude that *minquan* had a radically different meaning from that of Sun Yat-sen and the GMD ideologists. It should also be pointed out that when referring to the league, some people would waver between the words *minquan* and *renquan*.[89] Cai Yuanpei, for his part, seems to have used *renquan* and *minquan* interchangeably in his writings.

Cai Yuanpei understood human rights (*renquan*) as rights belonging to the individual person and transcending the boundaries of national and party affiliations.[90] Cai furthermore described the purpose of the league to be the protection of human rights (*renquan*) and the rule of law.[91] In a speech in Shanghai, later published in *Xinwen bao*, Cai Yuanpei further developed his view, this time opting for the word *minquan*.[92] In this speech he pointed out that even though *minquan* was a new concept, its meaning had been known to the Chinese people for thousands of years. Although they had not then conceptualized rights, they had been very concerned about the protection of life and the freedom of speech.[93] Cai quoted several Chinese sources, including Confucius and Zhuang Zi, to prove his point; he was the only one of the league's members to consciously search the Chinese tradition for precedents to the concept of *renquan* or *minquan*. Cai also mentioned incidents in Chinese history that showed that those who had tried to suppress rights such as the freedom of thought had come to bitter ends. Cai believed that the freedoms of speech and publication were crucial in order to save the country, and he criticized those who argued that in a time of crisis people should not be allowed any rights but only asked to shoulder duties. Cai, in contrast, held that if people were deprived of the freedoms of life, property, and speech, they would be unable to shoulder any duties.

Wang Zaoshi, another member of the league, also presented some more theoretical discussions on *minquan*. Wang was a political scientist who received his doctoral degree from the University of Wisconsin. Like Luo Longji, Wang had also been a student of Laski and was a follower of Fabianism, which is reflected in his discussions on human rights.[94] According to Wang, the concept of *minquan* was different from the concept of natural rights put forward by Locke and others in the seventeenth and eighteenth centuries.[95] They believed rights to be endowed by nature (*tianfu*) and inherent (*sheng ju lai de*). Although Wang rejected this idea of inherent rights, he nevertheless argued that rights were attached to man's moral nature. Without rights people's human dignity would be violated and meaningful existence rendered impossible; in other words, without rights man could hardly be said to be a person (*zuoren*). Or, as Wang also put it to emphasize the central value of rights: people need rights as much as fish need water. *Minquan* were defined by Wang as those fundamental rights necessary in order to develop the individual, protect his interests, and promote the progress of society; a definition that implies a rather utilitarian evaluation of rights in the tradition of Mill.

It was obvious from the start that people had different motivations for participating in the league, as well as different ideas about the purpose and aim of the organization. From a cursory glance at the league's statutes and demands, it is tempting to draw the conclusion that it fell well within the liberal camp. The fact that it drew many of its members from among the world of Chinese liberals could support this view. People such as Hu Shi, Lin Yutang, Jiang Menglin, and Tao Menghe were all members. The expulsion of Hu Shi and the debate on the legalistic approach to human rights, however, reveals the existence of more radical views.[96] Song Qingling's appeal for the establishment of an organization for political prisoners had been motivated by a concern with the terror waged by the GMD against "the Chinese working class, the peasants, and against students and revolutionary intellectuals."[97] She ridiculed those who only came to the defense of Chen Duxiu because he had disassociated himself from the Communists. This kind of criticism was not far off the mark, as can be gathered from some editorials in the *China Critic*. The magazine thus emphasized that it was to Chen Duxiu's "credit that he denounced the present communist party in no uncertain terms."[98] It is obvious that their concerns were very different from those of Song Qingling and other radical members of the league.[99]

When the *China Critic* endorsed Song Qingling's proposal, the editorial pointed out that such an organization should take as its task the defense of "people's civic rights as such, without respect to any particular political faction, and even without limitation to political prisoners only."[100] The magazine and the league's liberal members seem to have taken the American Civil Liberties Union as their point of inspiration. Lin Yutang thus advocated the establishment of "a non-partisan Chinese Civic Liberties Union, along the same lines as the American Civic [*sic*] Liberties Union headed by John Dewey."[101] In the manifesto adopted at the founding of the league, there were also references to organizations for the protection of civil rights led by people such as Dewey.[102] Lin Yutang also referred to earlier discussions on human rights and the rule of law in China by people such as Hu Shi, Luo Longji, and Luo Wengan, and suggested that Luo Wengan should become the head of the organization. Lin quoted with approval Luo Wengan's opinion that "Civic rights should come before political rights. When the people's life and property are not protected, one has no time to talk about politics. Our people may be shot, imprisoned and our property may be confiscated at any time."[103] Lin also stressed that the organization should work for all prisoners and not only for political prisoners. Lin later contributed an article on freedom of speech to the *China Critic* based on a lecture he had delivered at a meeting of the league, which also shows his view on human rights. In his usual ironical style he argued with Bernard Shaw "that the only kind of liberty worth having is the liberty of the oppressed to squeal when hurt and the liberty to remove the conditions which hurt them."[104]

When the *China Critic* announced the formation of the league in an editorial, it also revealed its liberal approach to human rights. Criticizing those, that is, the GMD, who believed that people's obligations to the state rather than their rights should be given priority in view of the precarious times in which China found herself, the editorial continued:

> Unless our rights are safeguarded, we shall not be able to fulfil our duties. Rights and duties are after all reciprocal. Duties without rights make for tyranny; rights without duties make for anarchism. Rights, however, are not liberties to act in general, for they are not absolute possessions of individuals irrespective of conditions. To struggle for civil rights is therefore really to demand that we may be given the freedom to act in ways consistent with, or conducive to the common good. It is, in other words, not freedom to do as we choose that we wish to gain, but freedom to do as the welfare of our nation may require of us.[105]

It is obvious that the writers of the *China Critic*, like Luo Longji and many other Chinese writers, believed that rights were no license to do as one wanted; rights could not be exercised to the detriment of the common good. But the above passage does nonetheless set the magazine apart from the GMD, which believed that the individual's rights had to be sacrificed for the sake of the nation. In a satirical essay giving advice to journalists wanting to stay clear of trouble, T. K. Chuan questioned the GMD on this point:

> The question of civil rights is a ticklish one, but one can always put forth the argument that at the present time when China is facing a national crisis, her citizens should strive for national rights instead of civil rights—that is, for the emancipation of the race instead of the individual. Such an argument is of course based on the following premises, the truth of which, however, must never be called into question: A. Civil rights are rights of the individual, B. The possession of individual rights and liberties is incompatible with the welfare of the nation as a whole.[106]

Mainland official historians have alleged that the league was inaugurated under the auspices of the CCP, but no substantial or conclusive evidence to that effect has been presented.[107] There is, however, a possibility that it could have been inspired by the *Zhongguo jinan hui*, an organization founded in 1925 by the CCP to secure the release of imprisoned revolutionaries and provide financial aid to their families; this organization was finally dispersed in 1934–35. Lending credence to this view is the fact that among the league's members are also members of the *Jinan hui*, such as Lu Xun, Yang Quan, and Zhou Jianren. That the *Jinan hui* might have been a source of inspiration to the establishment of the league has also been suggested by league members such as Zhou Jianren and Hu Yuzhi.[108]

I would, however, venture to speculate that liberals and radicals could have had very different motivations and inspirations for their participation in the league, which helps explain the conflicts that later erupted. Song Qingling obviously took a more radical approach, arguing that the reason the league was fighting for civil rights and the release of political prisoners was that such an approach would gather broader support and make the fight for the revolution easier.[109] She believed that revolution was the only path to take for China, otherwise the imperialists would conquer and split the country. In this struggle the league was but one instrument. It is also evident that Song Qingling harbored no hopes whatsoever about the possibilities to reform the GMD. She regarded it as corrupt and beyond reform, in contrast to Hu Shi who still believed in loyal remonstrance. Song Qingling's more radical views were shared by others in the league, for example, Zao Taofen.[110] Where Song Qingling argued that violations of human rights were fundamentally a political question, Hu Shi, in line with his earlier position, adopted a narrowly legalistic approach to human rights and the league's work. Since he regarded the GMD as the legitimate ruler of China, especially so, since the adoption of the provisional constitution that he had demanded, he advocated that the league confine itself to seeking the legal protection of human rights.[111]

The expulsion of Hu Shi from the league is one indication of the rift between liberals and radicals over human rights. In January 1933, Hu Shi and

Yang Quan undertook an investigation of prison conditions in Beiping. When political prisoners in one prison later sent an appeal to the league, which Song Qingling and Smedley endorsed on behalf of the league, Hu Shi questioned the authenticity of the prisoners' letter and voiced the opinion that the conditions described by the letter did not match the findings of his and Yang's investigation.[112] The bone of contention soon shifted from being a question of whether the letter described the true conditions in the prison, to whether an unconditional release of all political prisoners would constitute a legitimate demand on the government. According to Hu Shi, unconditional release was too much to ask of the government, or any government. The league's task should instead be confined to help individuals, supervise the government, and promote people's understanding of law and rights. All that the league should do, in other words, was to seek the legal protection of political prisoners; anything else would signify revolution.

Because Hu Shi openly questioned the league's policy, he was accused of violating its statutes. He was repeatedly requested to alter his position and comply with the league's policy, but to no avail. As a consequence, he was expelled from the league.[113] Hu Shi received some support from other members of the league, for example, from Jiang Menglin and others of the Beiping section, who criticized the lack of freedom of speech within the league.[114] Although Cai Yuanpei and Lin Yutang at first had voiced their criticism of Hu Shi's public disagreement with the league in no uncertain terms, Cai later expressed his and Lin's disappointment with the league and announced their decision to withdraw gradually from the organization.[115] They also found an excuse for not attending the meeting of the league at which Hu Shi was formally expelled. Lin later alleged that he and Cai had been "exploited without their knowledge," and that they had not realized the leftist nature of the league.[116]

POLITICAL DEBATES IN THE EARLY 1930S

Two of the most hotly contested political issues during the early 1930s were the drafting of a constitution and the debate on democracy versus dictatorship; they are also directly related to the issue of human rights. In 1928, the GMD announced that it intended to complete the period of political tutelage within six years, or by 1935, and in 1931 a provisional constitution for the tutelage period was promulgated. Already by 1932, factions within and outside the GMD were demanding that preparations for the adoption of a constitution should begin immediately.[117] This work did not go smoothly; the draft underwent many revisions and changes and received much criticism from independent observers. A draft constitution was eventually presented on May 5, 1936, and in 1946 the Constitution of the Republic of China was finally adopted. Hu Shi and Luo Longji had rested their argument for the establishment of a constitution on its ability to protect human rights. But Luo had acknowledged that a constitution by itself was rather useless and would be nothing but a scrap of paper if the authorities did not abide by it, which turned out to be the case. The promulgation of the tutelage constitution hardly made any difference, and respect for human rights continued to be a distant reality. Discussing Hu Shi's and Luo Longji's earlier struggle for a constitution, Zhong Yi, writing in 1933, argued that a constitution instituted from above could not ensure the protection of people's rights if people did not also fight for their protection.[118] He pointed out that Hu Shi and others had now realized the truth of this, as manifested in their involvement in the China League for the Protection of Civil Rights. According to Zhong Yi, this kind of people's movement was more crucial for the factual protection of human rights than any governmentally organized constitutional movement could ever be. But not even the league managed to bring about any fundamental changes or improve the situation for human rights.

Some scholars have argued that the demand for a constitution was used as a tool in the GMD's internal struggles and that it did not reflect any genuine commitment to constitutionalism.[119] This observation, however, should not detract from the fact that some people, both within the legislative Yuan and outside of it, were quite sincere in their appreciation of the constitution as an important vehicle to protect people's rights and freedoms. Zhang Zhiben, vice-chairman of the drafting committee, thus regarded the committee's task to be to lay down a constitution that would protect people's freedoms.[120] But his concern was not shared by Wu Jingxiong, chairman of the drafting committee, who emphasized that national interests could justify the restriction and even curtailment of people's rights. Their disagreement prompted Zhang to resign from his post. Qiu Hanping agreed with Zhang that the most central section of the constitution, and the part that had the most effect upon people's lives was the chapter dealing with people's rights.[121] Regarding the content of human rights, he believed that there had been a development from individual, mostly negative rights, with which the government could not interfere (the dominant position before the end of the nineteenth century), to positive, more concrete rights, such as the rights to education and help for the needy. This change had come about through the realization that unrestrained individual freedom could be harmful to the progress of society and the interest of the majority.[122]

Wu Jingxiong's view on rights differed radically from that of Zhang Zhiben and Qiu Hanping. Wu, an American-trained lawyer and jurist, was responsible for the draft constitution of 1933, also called the "Wu draft," as well as one of those responsible for the final constitution adopted in 1946.[123] According to Wu, people did not have any rights prior to or outside of society. "Rights are given to the individual by society. Society is the source of rights. If the individual leaves society he will have no rights. Since society bestows rights, it can also in times of need deprive [the individual of his] rights, or at least restrict the scope of rights."[124] This view was in line with that of the GMD, namely, that rights were given by the state to a select group of people who were expected to use their rights for the benefit of the nation. Wu furthermore held that the advocacy of innate (*tianfu*) and absolute (*juedui*) rights in the West had proved harmful and resulted in the aggressive assertion of individual rights that he found there. He contrasted this individualistic-oriented rights thinking of the West with the more social-oriented rights thinking of Sun Yat-sen. Wu also argued that the political situation in China was very different from that in the West, which explained their different approaches to rights. Where the constitutional movement in the West had begun as a struggle for individual salvation (*jiu ziji*) and freedom against feudalism and authoritarianism, the Chinese, on the other hand, took the struggle for national freedom and national salvation (*jiu guo*) as their starting point.[125] Since national freedom took precedence over individual freedom, the individual was requested to sacrifice his freedom for the interests of the collective. And since rights were derived from society, they could also be restricted or curtailed with the interests of society in mind.

Wu subscribed to a relativistic view of rights, believing that rights reflected different social and political circumstances. "In philosophical parlance, rights of man are not given *a priori* but acquired *a posteriori* and therefore subject to modification with the change of circumstances. This may be called a theory of relativity of rights. With Dr Sun [Yat-sen], as with [Justice] Holmes, rights are no longer conceived as solid substances existing from eternity to eternity with invariable size and weight, but as little creatures born out of the bowels of history and subject to all the vicissitudes of mortality."[126] Wu was influenced, as Thomas E. Greiff has clearly shown, by "a particular kind of 'modern', utilitarian, anti-natural law, historicist liberalism" that he encountered in America in the 1920s, which would have authoritarian implications in the Chinese political environment of the 1930s.[127] Wu rejected the conception of rights as it had originally been formulated in the West, not because of its Western origin or out of a belief that rights as such were incompatible with Chinese culture, but because he saw rights as historical and relative to each particular society. Eighteenth-century notions of rights, therefore, could not possibly fit contemporary Chinese conditions, nor contemporary Western societies.

It was not so much the Chinese tradition as such that shaped Wu's understanding of rights, as the precarious political situation in China at the time, and the fact that the West provided him with ideas that refuted the idea of natural rights. For all of his historicism and relativism, however, Wu believed that it was possible to achieve a synthesis between Western rights ideas and Chinese circumstances. Although he argued that rights were relative, he nevertheless seems to have believed that values, to some extent at least, were universal. He thus argued that Sun Yat-sen's Three Principles of the People constituted a combination or blend of the best of Chinese and Western ideas. "[The Three Principles of the People] is broad and cosmopolitan in spirit, and at the same time, it is deeply rooted in the native soil. It represents a magnificent harmony between the one and the many, doing justice at once to the urgent claims of unity and universality and to the vital urges of diversity and uniqueness."[128] Wu himself is a good example of such a cultural cross-breeding. As a cosmopolitan and a Catholic, he wrote with insight and great knowledge about American jurisprudence and corresponded with many of its brightest minds.

Toward the end of 1933, a debate on democracy versus dictatorship broke out on the pages of Chinese magazines and journals.[129] The debate raged for two years, which reveals that it was an issue that deeply engaged many Chinese writers. Those who took part in the debate were mostly liberal intellectuals, many of whom had been educated in the West. Jiang Tingfu, Zhang Xiruo, and Chen Zhimai had, for example, all obtained doctorates at Columbia University.[130] But interestingly enough, they chose to take quite different sides in the debate and drew quite different conclusions from their Western educations, which once again shows that the West could provide widely different lessons to people of different dispositions and persuasions. The debate on democracy versus dictatorship was prompted by many factors. On the international scene the Chinese people could not fail to notice that several countries in the West had moved away from democracy. They also repeatedly referred to totalitarian countries, such as the Soviet Union, Italy, and Germany, which, they felt, provided important lessons for China. Many of those advocating dictatorship argued that since China lacked democratic experiences and the necessary preconditions for democracy, such as a literate and politically interested citizenry, it should follow the example of other democratically inexperienced countries. Behind this view loomed a deeper, more general disillusion with China's aborted attempts at democracy since 1911. Dictatorship, furthermore, seemed like an attractive option, or at least as the second-best choice, since a strong government was felt to be necessary in order to withstand Japanese aggression. The GMD was regarded as the only savior of China, but the support was qualified, since many who advocated dictatorship also felt that the GMD did not live up to the demands of an enlightened dictatorship. Those who argued for a dictatorship did so quite reluctantly as the only way out of the national crisis, only temporarily rejecting democracy as infeasible. It was, in other words, the imperative of national salvation that prompted many Chinese liberals to reject democracy. This was, for example, the case with Ding Wenjiang, Qian Duansheng, and Jiang Tingfu, to varying degrees.

In this debate the differences between democracy and dictatorship were brought up for discussion and analysis. Several authors, including those rejecting democracy, pointed out that the advantage of democracy was that it protected the rights and freedoms of the individual. Echoing his earlier views, Luo Longji argued that people needed certain basic rights in order to be persons (*zuoren*) and "be themselves at their best."[131] These rights, Luo contended, were only respected in democracies, whereas they were denied and violated in dictatorships. His indictment of dictatorship was harsh: "If people lose their freedoms, their personalities lose their nourishment, their brains become machines, and they turn into walking corpses."[132] Other writers likewise argued that in order to promote "the greatest happiness of the greatest majority," it was necessary to allow a citizen the right to be a person (*zuoren de quanli*).[133] Qian Duansheng, albeit himself advocating dictatorship, also described democracy as a system that protects human rights (*renquan*).[134] But for Qian, it was the very tendency of dictatorships to curtail individual freedoms in the interest of society that earned it its support. Chen Zhimai also argued that people would not begrudge the sacrifice of individual freedoms if it was in the interest of society.[135] Zhang Foquan took exception to an advocacy of unrestricted individual freedom and agreed with James Stephen that infringements on individual freedoms could be justified on utilitarian grounds if it could be showed that the purpose was good and that the benefits to society outweighed the costs to the individual.[136] It is, however, obvious that a clear understanding existed among Chinese liberals that only a democracy would actually guarantee the full protection of human rights. It is difficult not to draw the conclusion that many Chinese intellectuals advocated dictatorship less out of conviction than out of despair; the sacrifice of individual rights was justified with reference to China's desperate situation and believed necessary in order to solve the national crisis.[137]

CONCLUSION

Both liberals and Communists denounced the human rights violations committed by the Nationalists during the Nanking decade. Although their political and ideological visions differed, they could at times put these differences aside and unite in an effort to speak out for the victims of these human rights violations. But their's was a fragile and brief alliance that, as the case of the league clearly shows, inevitably would break down over differences in conceptions of rights as well as on the best method to ensure respect for human rights. The liberals opted to work through democratic and legal methods, believing that the regime would be responsive to their critique, whereas the Communists harbored no such hopes and therefore advocated revolutionary methods. It should be noted, however, that the GMD and the CCP during this period actually voiced very similar views on human rights, which reveals that the two parties had the same Leninist background. Both parties thus dismissed human rights as a bourgeois idea ill suited to the revolutionary needs of Chinese society, which required the individual to sacrifice his rights and freedoms for the interest of the nation or the party in question. The GMD and the CCP were also uneasy about the idea that all people, regardless of their class or political views, should enjoy rights; they wanted instead to confine rights to those showing them political allegiance.

Although many liberals became more muted in their critique of the GMD as the 1930s proceeded, many of them still continued to criticize it for violating human rights. *Duli pinglun*, the main liberal magazine during this period, published several articles in defense of freedom of thought and speech, and so forth.[138] It also condemned the arbitrary arrest of people on suspicion of counterrevolutionary views.[139] During the 1940s, and despite war and civil war, human rights talk would continue among both liberals and Communists. The latter found it useful in their struggle of words with the GMD, as a way to win the sympathy and support of the liberals. Even the GMD itself would come to embrace the language and rhetoric of human rights, at least on the international scene, as human rights became a central concern for the United Nations.

NOTES

1. Hu Shi (1929c), p. 4.

2. On the oppression of the press by the GMD, see Ting (1974).

3. On the liberals' gravitation toward the government, see Lubot (1982), pp. 95–114.

4. On the discussion of fascism in China, see Eastman (1974).

5. The group's view on human rights has been briefly treated by Narramore (1985), Spar (1992), and Fung (2000).

6. The labeling of it as a "human rights group" was common among their contemporaries; see, for example, Qu Qiubai (1931).

7. The magazine was an offspring of *Xinyue Society*, founded in 1923 in Peking by Xu Zhimo and Hu Shi. In 1927, Hu Shi, Xu Zhimo, Wen Yiduo, Pan Guangdan, and others started *Xinyue Bookstore* in Shanghai, and the following year saw the birth of the magazine. Because of the influence of Xu Zhimo and Wen Yiduo, who both preferred to remain aloof from politics, the first year of *Xinyue* was almost entirely devoted to literary works.

8. See the "discussion" column in *Xinyue*, vol. 3, nos. 5–6, 1930.

9. See Liang Shiqiu (1929b).

10. Hu Shi (1929a). The article was eventually republished in 1930, with other political essays from the magazine, in a volume edited by Hu Shi, *A Collection of Essays on Human Rights.*

11. The new direction was explained and defended in the editors' postscript in volume 2, number 3. Discussing Hu Shi's article, the editors stated their intention to publish an article on ideology in every number of the magazine and expressed their hope that the readers would offer criticisms and suggestions. A special announcement on the new policy was also included in an insert in nos. 6–7. I have not seen this insert, but it is mentioned by Lubot (1982), p. 158 n. 4.

12. That different views existed among the editors was quite obvious. Xu Zhimo, for example, advocated that the magazine should stop talking about politics, whereas Luo Longji argued that the magazine should not abandon its stance of fighting for freedom of thought and speech. See, for example, Luo's letter to Hu Shi of August 6, 1931, and Xu Zhimo's letter to Hu Shi of September 9, 1931, both reprinted in Liang Xihua (1982), vol. 1, pp. 376–78.

13. The text as reprinted in Hu Shi (1929a), p. 1.

14. Luo Longji's article was published in 1929 and later reprinted both in Hu Shi (1930) and in Luo Longji (1932). In the following, I will refer to the 1930 volume.

15. Luo Longji (1898–1965), a native of Anfu, Jiangxi province, graduated from Qinghua University in 1921. He then spent seven years studying in England and America. Upon his return to China in 1928 he became a teacher of political science at Guanghua University in Shanghai and one of the editors of *Xinyue.* Luo Longji later held posts at Nankai University and the Southwest Association University. He continued writing, first as editor of *Yishi bao* in Tianjin and later in *Chen bao* in Peking. In the 1930s and 1940s he became involved in the attempt to create a "third force" between the Nationalists and the Communists. He was active with Zhang Junmai in organizing the China Nationalist Socialist Party in 1932. He was also instrumental in forming the Democratic League in 1941 and remained one of its leading figures, eventually becoming its vice-chairman. After the Communist victory in 1949, Luo held different posts, eventually becoming minister of the timber industry. But, given his earlier criticism of communism in *Xinyue,* it comes as no surprise that he was one of the most prominent victims of the 1957 antirightist movement. For biographical details on Luo, see Boorman (1967), pp. 435–38, and Spar (1992).

16. On Laski, see the biography by Martin (1953).

17. See Furth (1970), p. 216.

18. I have not been able to make a full assessment of Laski's influence on Chinese intellectuals and the political discourse at the time. Many of his works were translated into Chinese and continued to be translated after 1949. Luo Longji translated his articles "The Danger of Obedience" and "A Plea For Equality," whereas the article "Teacher and Student" was translated by Hu Yi; they all appeared in *Xinyue.* The *Xinyue* book company published his book *Communism* in 1930, and Wang Zaoshi translated *The State in Theory and Practice* in 1937. Other articles by Laski were also published in *The Eastern Miscellany* and *Guowen bao.*

19. On Laski's political ideas, see Zylstra (1968).

20. Zhang Foquan (1933), p. 8.

21. Luo Longji in Hu Shi (1930), p. 35.

22. Laski devoted chapter three of *A Grammar* to a discussion of rights.

23. Luo Longji in Hu Shi (1930), p. 37.

24. Luo Longji in Hu Shi (1930), p. 39.
25. Laski (1948), p. 91.
26. Luo Longji in Hu Shi (1930), p. 94.
27. Luo Longji in Hu Shi (1930), p. 40.
28. Laski (1948), pp. 39–40.
29. Luo Longji (1930g), p. 6.
30. Luo Longji in Hu Shi (1930), p. 44.
31. For his view on the state, see also Luo Longji (1930g).
32. Laski (1948), p. 89, quoted by Luo Longji in Hu Shi (1930), p. 49.
33. Luo Longji in Hu Shi (1930), p. 41.
34. Luo Longji (1930b).
35. Luo Longji in Hu Shi (1930), p. 40–41.
36. Luo Longji (1930e).
37. Luo Longji in Hu Shi (1930), pp. 55–60.
38. Laski (1948), p. 91.
39. Oddly enough, right number twenty-six is missing from the list. Among the rights enumerated by Luo Longji that most clearly bear the stamp of China's political problems in the late 1920s were those pertaining to separating civil and military powers, and those attacking corruption and nepotism in the Chinese bureaucracy; see Luo Longji in Hu Shi (1930), pp. 60–73.
40. In the late 1940s, Laski contributed an article to a volume on human rights edited by UNESCO (1949). By the time Laski wrote this article, his understanding of human rights was more radical than in *A Grammar*. He now put a much stronger emphasis on economic and social rights and argued that civil and political rights, such as freedom of speech and freedom of association were largely a function of economic power. Without economic security, freedom of speech could not be realized. He was also critical of the right to private property, which he believed made it increasingly impossible to maintain freedom and democracy. In this article he did not provide any discussion on the origin and basis of rights so it is difficult to say whether his thinking also had undergone changes on this point.
41. On freedom of speech, see also Luo Longji (1929b).
42. See Hu Shi (1929c), and Liang Shiqiu (1929a) and (1929b).
43. For a GMD critique of the group's view of absolute freedom, see Pan Gongzhan (1930).
44. See editors' afterword, *Xinyue*, vol. 2, no. 3, 1929.
45. Zhang Zhenzhi (1929).
46. Chen Dezheng (1930).
47. Chen Dezheng (1930), p. 6.
48. See Luo Longji (1930c), (1930e), and (1930f).
49. For the Communist critique, see Qu Qiubai (1931) and Peng Kang (1932). Official party history now labels the group anti-Communist and pro-GMD. See, for example, Gao Jun (1990), pp. 545ff.
50. See, for example, Pan Gongzhan (1930). Pan's article was devoted to a criticism of the *Xinyue* group as well as the Leftist Writers Association, but interestingly enough he devoted more space to criticizing the liberals than the radicals. Chen Dezheng (1930) also criticized natural rights for lacking a historical and scientific foundation, p. 37.
51. Zhang Yuanruo (1936), pp. 198–99.
52. Luo Longji (1930f).

53. See Sun Yat-sen (1960). For a brief description of the political ideas of Sun Yat-sen and Chiang Kai-shek, see Fung (2000), pp. 30–50.
54. See especially Chiang Kai-shek (1947), chapter 6, section 3.
55. Reprinted in Cai Shangsi (1983), vol. 2, p. 491.
56. Zhou Fohai (1928), p. 11.
57. Sa Mengwu (1928), p. 3.
58. Zhou Fohai (1928), p. 13.
59. Pan Gongzhan (1930), p. 6; and Chen Dezheng (1930), p. 14.
60. Luo Longji (1930c), pp. 3–7.
61. Pan Gongzhan (1930), p. 5.
62. Pan Gongzhan (1930), p. 5.
63. Luo Longji (1930f).
64. Sa Mengwu (1928), p. 5.
65. Pan Gongzhan (1930), p. 8.
66. Chen Dezheng (1930), p. 22.
67. Zhou Fohai (1928), pp. 11–12.
68. See Pan Gongzhan (1930), p. 5; and Chen Dezheng (1930), p. 14.
69. Pan Gongzhan (1930), pp. 6–7.
70. See also Zhang Yuanruo (1936), p. 206.
71. Peng Kang (1932).
72. Luo Longji in Hu Shi (1930), p. 35, translated in Angle and Svensson (2001), p. 139.
73. Qu Qiubai (1931).
74. See Chen Shuyu (1979) for a collection of primary sources and (1985) for the history of the league.
75. Reported in *Shenbao*, November 1, 1932, reprinted in Chen Shuyu (1979), p. 24.
76. See *Minguo ribao*, November 3, 1932, reprinted in Chen Shuyu (1979), p. 25.
77. See *Shenbao*, December 18, 1932, reprinted in Chen Shuyu (1979), pp. 25–26.
78. See the statutes of the league, reprinted in Chen Shuyu (1979), pp. 3–5.
79. See *Shenbao*, January 18, 1933, reprinted in Chen Shuyu (1979), pp. 26–30.
80. See *Chenbao*, January 31, 1933, reprinted in Chen Shuyu (1979), pp. 32–33.
81. See Fairbank (1982), pp. 72–76.
82. For a full account of these cases and the league's activities, see Chen Shuyu (1979) and (1985).
83. See *Minguo ribao*, February 1, 1933, reprinted in Chen Shuyu (1979), pp. 95–96.
84. According to Yang Quan, one could not separate the struggle against the Japanese from the struggle for civil rights. Quoted in Chen Shuyu (1985), p. 83.
85. See *Shenbao*, May 14, 1933, reprinted in Chen Shuyu (1979), pp. 81–82, and the *China Critic*, vol. 6, May 18, 1933, p. 510.
86. See Chen Shuyu (1985), pp. 89ff; and the *China Critic*, vol. 6, no. 25, June 22, 1933, p. 628; as well the editorial in the *China Critic*, vol. 6, no. 26, June 29, 1933, pp. 638–39.
87. On Dai Li, see Eastman (1974), pp. 74–84, and on the murder, see p. 77.
88. See Song Qingling (1952), p. 73; and the *China Critic*, vol. 6, no. 25, June 22, 1933, p. 628.
89. That the words *minquan* and *renquan* were used interchangeably at this time is shown by the fact that Zhou Enlai, in commemorating Cai Yuanpei in 1940, talked about the League of Human Rights rather than the League of Civil Rights, quoted in Gao Pingshu (1989), p. 329. Others in the 1940s also mistakenly talked about the League of Human Rights, see for example Pan Lang (1941), p. 3145.

90. Speech delivered at the meeting with journalists published by *Shenbao*, December 31, 1932, reprinted in Gao Pingshu (1985), pp. 403–4.

91. Mentioned in an interview in *Shenbao*, February 9, 1933, quoted in Chen Shuyu (1985), p. 29.

92. *Xinwen bao*, February 21, 1933, reprinted in Gao Pingshu (1985), pp. 413–15.

93. It thus seems as if Cai Yuanpei were saying that the idea, although not conceptualized, nevertheless had existed in the Chinese past.

94. Wang Zaoshi would also later share the same fate as Luo Longji during the antirightist campaign. For a collection of Wang's writings and self-criticisms, see Ye Yonglie (1999).

95. Wang Zaoshi (1933).

96. The Communist official history on the league emphasizes the radical and progressive character of the organization, and therefore mainly focuses on the contributions of Song Qingling, Yang Quan, and Lu Xun. Cai Yuanpei is also praised, whereas Hu Shi is strongly criticized and Lin Yutang ignored. See Chen Shuyu (1985).

97. See Song Qingling (1932), p. 1168.

98. See "Chen Tu-hsiu," the *China Critic*, vol. 5, no. 43, October 27, 1932, pp. 1120–21.

99. T. K. Chuan and Lin Yu of the *China Critic* had engaged themselves for the Noulens and signed the petition organized by Song Qingling. Lin Yutang, also a contributor to the magazine, was a founding member of the league.

100. See the editorial, "Civic Liberties Union," the *China Critic*, vol. 5, no. 44, November 3, 1932.

101. Lin Yutang (1932), p. 1157.

102. Reprinted in Chen Shuyu (1985), pp. 150–51.

103. Lin Yutang (1932), p. 1157.

104. Lin Yutang (1933), p. 264.

105. "China League of Civil Rights," the *China Critic*, Vol. 5, no. 52, December 29, 1932, p. 1377.

106. T. K. Chuan (1933a), p. 127. In another of his witty essays, Chuan took "the parlour socialists" to task for only advocating freedom of thought and speech, and ignoring the importance of the right to bread [sic]. This was a rather interesting charge, coming from a liberal as it does, since liberals are usually accused by socialists of having the very same priorities. Chuan wryly pointed out that the freedom of speech the radicals advocated was only the freedom to "shout communist slogans," see Chuan (1933b), p. 1118.

107. See Chen Shuyu (1985).

108. See Zhou Jianren's statement reprinted in Chen Shuyu (1979), p. 159, and Hu Yuzhi, also in (1979), pp. 160–61. On Yang Quan and the *Jinan Hui,* see Yang Xiaofu, reprinted in Chen Shuyu (1979), pp. 165–78.

109. Song Qingling (1952), p. 32.

110. On Zao Taofen, see Chen Shuyu (1979), p. 19. Later, we find Zao Taofen as one of the participants in the human rights movement initiated by Zhou Jingwen in 1941.

111. For Hu Shi's views on the league, see *Minguo ribao*, February 6, 1933, and *Lunyu*, February 16, 1933, both reprinted in Chen Shuyu (1979), pp. 105–6. See also Hu Shi (1933).

112. See Chen Shuyu (1979) for primary sources regarding this incident.

113. See *Shenbao*, March 4, 1933, reprinted in Chen Shuyu (1979), pp. 109–10.

114. See Chen Shuyu (1985), p. 127 and p. 143f; as well as Chen Shuyu (1979), pp. 21–23.

115. Cai's letter is quoted by Tao Yinghui (1995), p. 47f.

116. Quoted by Duiker (1977), p. 123 n. 51, and by Chen Shuyu (1985), p. 134. That the league had become too extreme for many liberals is also evident in the *China Critic*. The

magazine came to believe that a call for civil liberties was futile until people understood them, and therefore urged the league to take on the gradual education of the people. See "The Assassination of Yang Chien," *China Critic*, vol. 6, no. 26, June 29, 1933, pp. 638–39. The magazine also began to gravitate toward a more positive view of the GMD and Chiang Kai-shek during 1933.

117. On the work on a constitutional draft, see Eastman (1974), pp. 159–80.
118. Zhong Yi (1933).
119. Eastman (1974).
120. Zhang Zhiben (1933).
121. Qiu Hanping (1933).
122. For similar views, see also Zhang Ming (1933).
123. On Wu Jingxiong, see Greiff (1985).
124. Wu Jingxiong (1933), p. 45.
125. Wu Jingxiong (1936), p. 106024.
126. Quoted in Greiff (1985), p. 457.
127. Greiff (1985), p. 443.
128. Quoted in Greiff (1985), p. 455.
129. For the discussion on democracy versus dictatorship in general, see Eastman (1974), pp. 141–59, Chen Yishen (1989), and Fung (2000), pp. 114–43. For contemporary summaries of the debate, see Hu Shi (1935a) and (1935c), Chen Zhimai (1935), Ding Wenjiang (1934) and (1935), and Ye Shuheng (1935).
130. On the personal backgrounds of those taking part in the debate, see Chen Yishen (1989), pp. 62–141.
131. Luo Longji (1935). Another long-time democrat, Tao Menghe (1935), also joined the debate.
132. Luo Longji (1935), p. 6.
133. See Li Weichen (1935). See also Ming Xia (1935).
134. Qian Duansheng (1934).
135. Chen Zhimai (1936), p. 106901.
136. Zhang Foquan (1935a) and (1935b).
137. I do not share Eastman's conclusion that the Chinese "were attracted to democracy less because it provided guarantees of individual freedoms than because they were disillusioned with the ineffectiveness of Kuomintang authoritarian rule." See Eastman (1974), p. 153. My analysis on this point is also supported by Fung (2000), pp. 142–43.
138. See, for example, Hu Shi (1935b), Chen Zhimai (1935), Ma Xingye (1937), and Mei Kan (1937).
139. See Zhang Yinlin (1935) and Li Shuqing (1935). Hu Shi (1934) also demanded the release of all those who had been arrested solely for their peaceful expression of thought.

Chapter Eight

Human Rights Debates in Wartime China: Between Individual Freedom and National Salvation

THE CHINA DEMOCRATIC
LEAGUE AND OTHER LIBERAL VOICES

The outbreak of war with Japan in 1937 paved the way for the establishment of the Second United Front between the Nationalists and the Communists. This new situation also led to a temporarily more relaxed political environment. But already by 1939, curtailment of civil liberties and suppression of political opponents surfaced once more; with the outbreak of the Pacific War in 1941, the political repression intensified. During the war years, the Nationalist government continued to be criticized by both liberals and Communists for its curtailment of individual rights, censorship of the press, and arbitrary and illegal arrests of political opponents.[1] The liberals rejected the view that the conduct of war meant that individual rights and freedoms would have to be restricted or sacrificed for the greater goal of national salvation, insisting that it was possible to attain the two goals of liberating the Chinese nation from the Japanese aggressors and of liberating it from the authoritarian, one-party rule of the GMD.

The majority of those discussing human rights during the 1940s were members of the China Democratic League, many of whom had showed a concern about human rights issues early on. Examples include Liu Yazi, who worshipped human rights to such an extent that in 1902 he took the name Renquan; Gao Yihan, who discussed human rights during the May Fourth period; Hu Shiqing, who cofounded the magazine *Renquan* in 1925; Luo Longji, who had written on human rights in *Xinyue*; and Wang Zaoshi, who had been a member of the China League for the Protection of Civil Rights in the early 1930s. But two other members dominated the discussions on human rights in the 1940s, namely, Zhou Jingwen, who launched a "human rights movement" in 1941, and Zhang Junmai, who frequently wrote about human rights in the magazines *Zaisheng* and *Minxian* throughout the 1940s. The members of the league and other liberals mostly focused on human rights violations committed by the GMD but had little experience with or knowledge about the situation in CCP-controlled areas.[2]

In 1941, Zhou Jingwen launched his human rights movement with an article in the magazine *Shidai piping*.[3] Zhou was motivated by a general concern with the human rights' violations committed by the GMD and by a belief that the protection of human rights would enable people to make greater contributions to the war effort. Zhou, and Zhang Junmai after him, was inspired in part by Wells's work to draft a new human rights declaration that would serve as an inspiration during the war and as a manifesto for a future peaceful world.[4] But Zhou also attempted to relate his human rights movement to domestic experiences, in particular the May Fourth Movement.[5] The human rights movement was thus intended to awaken and liberate the Chinese in the spirit of May Fourth.[6] The positive reactions to his first article prompted Zhou to publish a special issue on human rights, some articles of which were also reprinted in book form.[7]

Those writing on human rights in the magazine, although having slightly different views since both liberals and Communists were represented, nevertheless shared some basic assumptions. Like earlier Chinese generations, they defined human rights as those rights that enable one to be a person (*zuoren de quanli*) and without which human existence is impossible. Zhou Jingwen thus talked about the "sacred and inviolable rights to be a person."[8] If a person discarded, or was deprived of his rights, he would be unable to protect his personality.[9] Echoing Chen Duxiu's earlier admonitions, the Chinese people were urged to throw away the shackles of slavery and demand the rights of humans beings.[10] As several of the writers put it: "A human being without human rights is nothing but a commodity or a slave."[11]

The articles in *Shidai piping* were generally not very theoretical and few authors discussed the origin and basis of human rights. Although the majority believed that people enjoyed rights simply by virtue of their humanity, they seem to have rejected the idea of natural rights. Shi Zishan, although agreeing with the above definition of human rights, referred to Ritchie and Burgess, and, like Gao Yihan before him, agreed with Burgess that there were no rights before the establishment of the state.[12] Shi believed human rights to be political rather than natural, although nonetheless arguing that the idea of human rights was indisputably correct and higher and more important than all other ideas. Han Youtong wrote that the question of whether human rights were endowed by nature (*tianfu*) was not within the scope of his article, but that he ventured to assert that human rights were not a favor bestowed by the ruler but rather something obtained by people through their own struggles.[13]

Compared with earlier discussions, the articles in *Shidai piping* reveal a much stronger awareness of the fact that human rights previously had been the privilege of a small minority. Those writing in the magazine stressed that all people should enjoy human rights, not only the bourgeoisie, as had earlier been the case, but ordinary people (*laobaixing*) as well.[14] Human rights, it was argued, belonged to all individuals, regardless of class and position.[15] At the same time, however, some writers could make allowances and exclude traitors from enjoying human rights, thus making rights contingent upon people's support of the war effort.[16] Although civil and political rights continued to be emphasized, it was stressed that economic rights, such as the right to subsistence, were needed in order to enable people to enjoy their rights fully and realize their humanity.[17] And the writers in the magazine criticized earlier human rights declarations in the West for having neglected economic rights.[18]

Those writing in *Shidai piping* believed in universal human rights but were convinced that their human rights movement differed in some crucial respects from earlier ones in the West. They argued that whereas previous ones had been dominated by the bourgeoisie and neglected economic rights, their own movement tried to ensure the human rights of previously neglected groups as well as enlarge the scope to also include economic rights.[19] But while they criticized the fact that people in capitalist countries generally lacked the opportunities and means to realize their civil and political freedoms, they also criticized socialist countries for suppressing these freedoms.[20] Another difference with earlier human rights movements, they believed, was that the new movement not only manifested itself as an internal struggle against feudalism and authoritarianism, thus having as its goal the establishment of democracy and the rule of law, but also took the shape of a struggle against external enemies. Since foreign aggression posed a threat to China, it was believed necessary to link the struggle for human rights to the task of national liberation (*minzu jiefang*).[21] The goal of this external struggle was the liberation of the Chinese nation and victory in the war. Individual human rights would enable the individual to contribute more to the war effort, it was argued, since "a people who does not enjoy freedom within their own country cannot achieve freedom from external enemies."[22] Zhou Jingwen argued that the freedoms of thought and speech were not only necessary for the development of the individual but also for the progress of society and national survival.[23] He and the others writing in the magazine refuted the view that a trade-off existed between different rights, or that individual rights had to be sacrificed in order to secure national rights. They thus dismissed the view that certain rights, such as the freedom of speech, would have to be restricted or curtailed in times of a

crisis or a war.[24] The view that the struggle for human rights could not be separated from the task of national salvation resembles the pre-1911 debate, but it
also shows an affinity with Wells's position during the Second World War.

The GMD rather than the Japanese was the main target of the magazine's critique. The GMD was accused of a whole range of human rights violations, the
first and foremost of which was the closing of independent magazines and the arrest of political opponents.[25] The writers at *Shidai piping* believed that the state was
created by the people and that its task was to protect their human rights; a task
that the GMD did not fulfill.[26] They criticized the one-party system set up by the
Nationalists, and argued that only a democratic government would take the protection of people's human rights seriously.[27] Zhou Jingwen devoted several articles to a discussion and advocacy of constitutionalism, arguing for the establishment of a constitution that would stipulate the protection of people's rights. Zhou
dismissed Wu Jingxiong's view that the Chinese constitutional movement should
have the collective as its starting point and the salvation of the nation as its goal.[28]
He also vehemently objected to the view that the freedom of the individual
would have to be sacrificed for that of the collective.

Some of the articles in the magazine touched upon the relationship between
the concepts of human rights (*renquan*) and people's rights (*minquan*). Zhou
Jingwen, like Luo Longji earlier, argued that people, apart from being citizens,
also were human beings. He contended that human rights were more fundamental than people's rights since they transcended political and national
boundaries.[29] Zhou and the others preferred to speak about human rights
rather than people's rights because they regarded the latter to be more narrow
in character.[30] Duanmu Liang gave an additional explanation as to why they
preferred to talk about human rights, declaring that the term people's rights
had been corrupted by those in power.[31]

Although it was pointed out that the Chinese human rights movement differed from earlier ones in the West, human rights were still believed to be of universal value and application. Nor were there many references to the Chinese tradition or attempts to ground the concept of human rights within Chinese
culture. Pan Lang, for example, believed that although the concept of human
rights in China could be traced to the Mencian idea of providing for the welfare
of the people, it was not until China opened up that it was really accepted, and
he cites the Taiping rebellion as an example of this.[32] No one seems to have questioned the compatibility of human rights with Chinese culture. The only article
briefly touching upon this issue simply pointed out that the reason the Chinese
people's awakening to the concept of human rights had been so late was related
to the emphasis on duties in the Chinese tradition.[33] But the author did not regard this fact as hindering or preventing Chinese people from embracing the
concept of human rights.

During the war years, discussions on human rights, unlike the May Fourth period, were more political- than cultural-oriented. Although there were occasional references to the oppressive cultural tradition, the oppressive political environment commanded people's attention. Chinese intellectuals were generally too preoccupied with the more immediate and pressing task of fighting domestic dictatorship and foreign aggression to have much interest in more theoretical discussions on culture or attacks on Confucianism. But there were also those who, in the face of war and motivated by strong feelings of nationalism, came to take a more positive view of Chinese culture than hitherto had been the case. This cultural interest took different forms. Some scholars such as Liang Shuming tried to build a synthesis of Chinese and Western traditions, whereas the regime launched a more politically motivated National People's Spiritual General Mobilization, an ethics of national salvation that was loosely based on Confucian ideals of loyalty, filial piety, benevolence, and righteousness. The traditional value of obedience to authority was exploited by the GMD to serve the national cause as well as promote unswerving loyalty to the party and Chiang Kai-shek personally.

Although Zhou Jingwen's human rights movement received support from many readers, it failed to influence the political environment. Looking back on the human rights movement three years later, Zhou was forced to conclude that, despite persistent demands over the years for the protection of human rights, violations continued unabated.[34] But advocacy of human rights in *Shidai piping* was not an isolated incident, and human rights demands continued to be raised by others throughout the 1940s. Zhou Jingwen remained on the mainland after 1949 but fled to Hong Kong in 1957, where he wrote a very critical book on his experiences under the CCP and also revived *Shidai piping* for the third time. He continued to publish articles on human rights in the magazine, for example writing on the antirightist movement of 1957 and on the democracy movement of 1978–79.

In March 1941, as a reaction to the growing repression of the Nationalist regime, the League of Chinese Democratic Political Groups was established by representatives of different minority parties.[35] The organization took its final name, the China Democratic League, when it was reorganized as a political party based on individual membership in 1944. During the 1940s, the league played a moderating and mediating role as a "third force" between the CCP and the GMD. But when the GMD broke the agreements laid down at the Political Consultative Conference (PCC) in 1946, many of the league's members became disillusioned with the government. When the league was banned by the Nationalists in October 1947, several of its more radical members left for Hong Kong where they reorganized the league in 1948. The league aligned itself with the CCP, and from 1949 onward, it has continued to exist as one of the eight minor parties on the mainland.

The Democratic League's position on human rights is, not surprisingly, quite similar to those of its members such as Luo Longji, Zhou Jingwen, and Zhang Junmai. Human rights were thus described as sacred and inviolable, and as necessary conditions in order to be a human being.[36] The league emphasized that human rights existed before the establishment of a constitution, which meant that even without a constitution the government had no right to violate people's human rights.[37] Although the league was a staunch defender of civil and political rights, it did not confine itself exclusively to these rights but also advocated economic rights.[38] One of its arguments was that it was vain and empty to only talk about political freedoms to people whose work and livelihood were threatened and unprotected.[39]

During the 1940s, the league repeatedly spoke out against the human rights violations committed by the GMD, demanding freedom of the press and the release of all political prisoners.[40] The league itself was affected by the GMD's repression, as several of its members were harassed and arrested. But the government didn't stop at arrests; it also resorted to political killings. One of the victims was poet and league member Wen Yiduo.[41] Other incidents, such as the one on November 25, 1945, when GMD soldiers opened fire at an antiwar meeting organized by students at the campus of the Southwest Associated University in Kunming, also provoked the league to criticize the government for violating human rights.[42] The league saw these human rights violations as endemic in a one-party dictatorship; only in a democracy would people's human rights be protected.[43] This belief prompted it to try to push the Nationalist regime toward democracy, rule of law, and acceptance of institutionalized political opposition. In its attempts to improve the legal protection of people's human rights, the league in 1946 raised the idea of establishing the Committee for the Protection of People's Freedoms.[44] This suggestion fell on deaf ears, however, and instead suppression of civil and political rights continued, eventually leading to the suppression of the league itself.

Another member of the Democratic League and a strong advocate of human rights was Zhang Junmai.[45] Zhang had studied politics in Japan, where he became a follower of Liang Qichao and established a strong and lifelong interest in constitutionalism and the rule of law. Zhang later also studied in Germany, where he received an academic degree and became an advocate of social democracy and an ardent anticommunist. In 1932, Zhang, Luo Longji, Hu Shiqing, and others, founded the National Socialist Party of China, which, however, later clashed with other democratic parties when it sided with the GMD in 1946. Zhang was very knowledgeable of Western political thought and helped introduce and translate Western works into Chinese. His views on human rights were most probably influenced by Laski. Zhang translated Laski's *A Grammar of Politics* in 1927. But one can also detect a strong German, and particularly Kantian, influence on his stance on human rights. Zhang kept abreast of discussions on human rights in the West and the work in progress in the United Nations on the UDHR. In 1945, he participated in the United Nations Conference on International Organization that adopted the UN Charter, and later through translations and articles in *Zaisheng* provided his readers with information on the work under way to draft a declaration of human rights.[46] Zhang also introduced and translated other discussions on human rights in the West, such as the declaration of human rights adopted by the French *Ligue des droits de l'homme* in 1936, and the human rights manifesto written by Wells in 1940.[47] Zhang was influenced by these declarations, which were fairly radical in nature, and apart from traditional civil and political rights also called for economic rights, such as a right to subsistence.

In his writings Zhang Junmai is rather vague regarding the origin and basis of human rights. On one occasion he wrote that, for the moment, he did not want to make any comments regarding whether human rights (*renquan*) were endowed by nature (*tianfu*) or only created after the establishment of a government, since those holding these two different points of views both acknowledged that people have human rights—which was the main point.[48] He believed, however, that without freedoms of the person, thought, speech, belief, and publication, people would no longer be human beings but mere "cattle."[49] Like other Chinese writers Zhang was of the conviction that human rights were crucial in order to realize and protect one's humanity. On this point Zhang referred to Kant, arguing that the Kantian principle of treating people as an end and not as a means could be said to constitute the philosophical basis of human rights.[50] Zhang defined human rights as rights that are inherent (*tiansheng*) and inalienable (*buke yirang*), in other words rights the government cannot infringe upon.[51] He also stressed that human rights should be enjoyed equally by all people, regardless of race, creed, and beliefs.[52] Zhang took Sun Yat-sen and the GMD to task for limiting rights to those taking the side of revolution. Since all human beings should enjoy equal rights, one could not give rights only to those supporting the revolution and deny them to those who did not.

> It is important to be aware of the fact that [the idea of] human rights refers to the protection of the rights of all people in the country; that is to say, all [people] by virtue of their being human beings should have the same kind of rights. One cannot say that those who participate in the revolution should therefore enjoy human rights, whereas those who do not participate in the revolution should not enjoy any human rights, because the work of the revolution is to establish human rights and not to restrict human rights.[53]

Regarding the content and scope of rights, Zhang Junmai went beyond civil and political rights, emphasizing the importance of economic rights, such as the right to subsistence.[54] Zhang argued that the concept of human rights evolved over time and suggested that it had passed through different stages.[55] Zhang thus took a historical view of human rights, on one occasion talking about two stages of human rights. The first stage was said to have emphasized the individual and was characterized by laissez-faire economics and confined to the national domain. Human rights during the second stage, in contrast, were more social in character, involved economic rights, and had been expanded to the international arena.[56] On another occasion Zhang instead talked about three stages in the development of human rights.[57] The first stage was associated with the early rights struggle in England as manifested in documents such as the Magna Carta, while the second stage was associated with the American and French Revolutions and with philosophers such as Locke. The latest, third stage in human rights thinking, Zhang associated with Franklin Roosevelt's advocacy of the Four Freedoms. Roosevelt's approach signified a widening of the scope of human rights, Zhang believed, from only acknowledging political freedoms to including economic freedoms, and from being an exclusive national affair to becoming a concern for the international community. Zhang pointed out that during the eighteenth and nineteenth centuries, the human rights movement had not paid much attention to whether everybody was really able to enjoy freedom.[58] But from the second half of the nineteenth century onward, and under the influence of different socialist movements, more emphasis had been given to social justice and the equal treatment of people, although Zhang also was acutely aware of the fact that the concept of human rights, for a long period of time, had been under attack by different schools of thought.[59] Zhang saw the recent work to ensure human rights a backing in international law as a direct result of the painful lessons of the Second World War.

In Zhang Junmai's articles published during the 1940s, there are no references to the Chinese tradition, and no attempts to build his advocacy of human rights on traditional concepts or ideas. Zhang only mentions the fact that human rights had been considered of little importance in the Chinese revolution and that Sun Yat-sen, under the influence of the historical school and Benthamite utilitarianism, had turned against the concept of natural rights.[60] He did not provide any explanation for this, nor seek the answer in the Chinese tradition. Later in his life, however, he wrote more on the relationship between human rights and Confucianism, and criticized those, such as Chen Duxiu, who held Confucianism to be identical with despotism and autocracy, and hence incompatible with human rights and democracy.[61] Zhang argued in contrast that there was a strong democratic tradition in China: "From Mencius, who was perhaps the most energetic exponent of democratic rule in the ancient world, to the scholars of the Ming Dynasty, there is in China an unbroken line of thinkers who have espoused the cause of the individual and of his inalienable rights."[62] Zhang also disputed the view that Asia did not recognize the rights of the individual, claiming that this was a misunderstanding. Although there had been no laws that protected human rights in traditional China, Zhang believed that the idea that people should be protected from the tyranny of a despot had existed from time immemorial, which he held to be an idea akin to the concept of human rights.[63]

Zhang Junmai did not content himself with arguing the case of an indigenous democratic tradition, but also ventured to put forward the view that the concept of human rights had originated in China and only later been exported to the West.[64] While Enlightenment philosophers indeed had been inspired by the Chinese classics, Zhang pushed this argument one step further, arguing that the emergence of natural law and natural rights in Europe was due to this Chinese influence.[65] Zhang thus seems to imply that after the export of the concept of human rights (or embryo of human rights thinking) to Europe, it was either lost, or never fully developed in China. He also contended that the Confucian principles of *li* (rites) and *yi* (righteousness) had been established in China in order to prevent strife and thus in many respects were similar in character and fulfilled the same function as the concept of rights in the West.[66]

Zhang's later search for proto-human rights ideas, or precedents in the Chinese tradition, is somewhat difficult to explain in view of his earlier discussions on human rights. Chester C. Tan has suggested that his later belief that roots of democracy could be found in Confucianism was pragmatic in character. It was written "for Americans at a time when, in order to win their support in the struggle against Chinese Communism, it was necessary to convince them that democracy was not impossible in China."[67] The same explanation might apply to his discussions on human rights. Be that as it may, it is obvious that Zhang did not believe that democracy and human rights were exclusively Western concerns or incompatible with Chinese culture.

The issue of human rights continued to come up in connection with discussions concerning the adoption of a constitution, which took off as the war drew to an end. Chiang Kai-shek took the initiative by declaring his intention to convene a national assembly and promulgate a constitution within a year after the end of the war. In 1946, Chiang then unilaterally, and under opposition from the Democratic League and others, convened the National Assembly; a new constitution was adopted the following year. Sporadic discussions on human rights continued during the final years of the 1940s. It is obvious that many Chinese citizens were deeply concerned about the lack of civil and political rights. Politically motivated arrests led to calls demanding the protection of human rights and the immediate release of all those arrested.[68] But many Chinese were also of the opinion that, if people were starving or unemployed, civil and political rights would be of little use if not supplemented with economic rights.[69]

The founding of the magazine *Guancha* in September 1946 can perhaps be taken as the final example of a liberal discussion on human rights in the pre-1949 period.[70] The magazine was edited by Chu Anping, who had studied at Guanghua University in Shanghai between 1928 and 1932 and then come under the influence of Luo Longji. Although Chu never joined the Democratic League, members of the league, such as Zhang Dongsun and Liang Shuming, often contributed to the magazine. The magazine's advocacy of democracy and its critique of political repression was also quite similar in tone to that of the league's; it strongly criticized the government's decision in 1947 to ban the league. During its two years of existence, *Guancha* emerged as the most influential liberal magazine in China, publishing articles very critical of GMD rule, but in December 1948 the Nationalists moved to close down the magazine. After the founding of the People's Republic in 1949, the magazine resumed publication but could no longer continue its independent and liberal stance. Chu Anping later became one of the most prominent victims of the Antirightist Campaign in 1957; he disappeared during the Cultural Revolution, possibly having committed suicide.

In the opening article of *Guancha*, Chu Anping declared that the magazine had set four tasks for itself.[71] The first was the promotion of democracy; the second, the support of all fundamental human rights (*jiben renquan*) and the equality of all persons before the law; the third, to foster political democracy, industrialization, and the growth of a scientific and modern mentality; and the fourth, to promote rationality in the resolution of all types of conflicts and dissuade people from the use of force. The magazine shared the league's liberal conviction that democracy and rule of law was the only road for China. It therefore argued for and practiced peaceful political opposition. In language used many times before, the magazine argued that respect for freedom and human rights was necessary in order to protect people's personality: "Without freedom the people will become a people without personality [*renge*]; a society without freedom turns into a slave society."[72] The magazine showed a particularly strong concern with academic freedom and the freedoms of thought, speech, and the press.[73] Several articles discussed the rule of law, and protested the widespread practice of illegal arrests and disappearances of political opponents.[74]

THE COMMUNISTS ON HUMAN RIGHTS

Not much writing on human rights by the Chinese Communists exists during the pre-1949 period. During the May Fourth Movement, and before becoming full-fledged Marxists, both Chen Duxiu and Li Dazhao had shown an interest in human rights. Toward the end of his life, Chen returned to the issue and again expressed his support of human rights. In the early years of the CCP, interestingly enough, there is not much by way of explicit criticism of the concept of human rights. Only occasionally would Communists, such as Tan Mingqian, criticize the idea of human rights and the fact that the bourgeoisie had only fought for their own rights while disregarding the rights of the proletariat. One of the clearest expressions of a Communist critique in the pre-1949 period is the criticism against Hu Shi and Luo Longji and the *Xinyue* human rights group in the late 1920s. Qu Qiubai and Peng Kang criticized the bourgeois standpoints of these writers and the abstract nature of the concept of human rights, criticisms that were later to become standard fare in the PRC. It is obvious that the idea of universal and abstract human rights are anathema to orthodox Marxists since they do not accept that there can be such a thing as a universal human nature or supraclass rights. This theoretical objection, however, has not prevented Communists from advocating human rights and criticizing the violation of people's rights to freedom of thought, speech, and publication while fighting for power.

In his youth, Mao Zedong expressed a positive view of individualism and attacked Confucianism for suppressing the individual.[75] But, as far as I have been able to find out, he did not then explicitly discuss human rights, or make use of the concept. Calls for freedoms of speech, publication, assembly, and association were, however, quite frequent during the CCP's struggle for power. The First Congress of the CCP, held in August 1921, stressed the importance of struggling for these civil and political freedoms.[76] In its work to organize workers, freedoms of speech, publication, and assembly were also frequently mentioned, together with demands for economic and social rights, such as unemployment relief, limiting the work day to eight hours, and so on. In the Outline of the Constitution of the Chinese Soviet Republic of 1931, freedoms of speech, press, and assembly were all stipulated, although they were denied for so-called reactionaries.[77]

During the war, Mao and the Communists evoked human rights both when attacking the GMD and as a way to unite people in the war against Japan. In their eyes, rights were not innate but enjoyed by people in order to serve specific political ends, namely success in the war against Japan and the revolutionary cause in general. Not everybody could enjoy these rights and freedoms, however; they were confined to those opposing the Japanese aggression. In 1937, Mao wrote that all people, except traitors, should enjoy freedom of speech, publication, assembly, and association, but that these freedoms only could be used in order to fight the Japanese.[78] In the article "On Policy" from 1940, Mao further argued that all capitalists, landowners, workers, and peasants who did not oppose the resistance to Japan should have equal human rights (*renquan*), the right to property, and the right to stand in election, as well as enjoy freedoms of speech, assembly and association, thought and belief.[79] Rights and freedoms were at this time more contingent upon people's correct political stance than their class status per se. In the 1940s, several of the Communist-controlled areas adopted declarations protecting human rights, explicitly using the word human rights (*renquan*).[80] The rights stipulated were predominantly civil and political rights. But following Mao, traitors were excluded from enjoying rights and their exercise was furthermore said to be contingent upon them being used in the struggle against Japan, thus implying that they could not be used to express differing opinions on this issue.

During the 1940s, Mao and the Communists stepped up their verbal attacks on the GMD. The communist press, such as *Jiefang ribao* and *Xinhua ribao*, frequently published articles defending civil and political rights and accusing the GMD of violating them. Political leaders like Zhou Enlai and others also criticized the GMD for violating civil and political freedoms. Zhou, for example, demanded freedom of the person, including the freedom not to be arbitrarily arrested, tortured, and executed, as well as freedom of speech and freedom of association.[81] The release of all "patriotic political prisoners," that is, those fighting the Japanese, was also demanded.[82] The suppression of people's rights and freedoms was particularly objected to since this was believed to obstruct their ability to fight the Japanese.[83] Like Zhou Jingwen in 1941, the Communist press argued that the freedom of the nation would be at risk if people were not free and did not enjoy full rights.

Although the Communists themselves did not subscribe to the idea of inalienable human rights, this did not stop them from making use of wordings such as these when criticizing the GMD. Such an appropriation of the language of human rights demonstrates its rhetorical value in the political debate. The CCP was aware of the liberals' concerns and own references to human rights, and realized that by using the same language it could win their approval and support. Some articles in the Communist press explicitly employed the word human rights. As one article in *Jiefang ribao* stated: "We are not engaging in empty talk on human rights," but will see to it that "human rights are fully protected."[84] It then moved on to express support for freedom of speech, the press, assembly, and association, the rights to receive the most attention in the Communist press.[85] These rights were regarded as the minimum to be enjoyed by people, not to be infringed upon by the government.[86] Although the above-mentioned rights and freedoms were mostly valued from a strictly utilitarian point of view, serving to unleash people's energy and creativity so that they could defend the nation and promote social progress, they were also at times justified on the grounds that they were the hallmark of civilization.[87] Rights and freedoms were also valued since they helped liberate people and turn them into critical and independent-minded individuals.[88] Echoing May Fourth sentiments, one can occasionally find wordings such as these: "[An] individual who loses his right to speak will at the same time lose all his other freedoms. If one loses one's freedom one will be no different from a slave and will not be counted as a citizen."[89]

Despite this affirmation of a whole range of civil and political rights and critique of the GMD, the CCP nevertheless itself violated these very rights in areas under its control. As discussed above, the CCP had laid down the limits of these freedoms so that they could not be used to obstruct or oppose the war effort. Nor did the CCP's advocacy of freedom of speech imply the freedom to criticize the CCP or question socialism. This became obvious during the rectification movement of 1941–44, when purges of political opponents, critical intellectuals, and others took place in Yan'an.[90] The case that received the most attention was that of the writer Wang Shiwei, who was accused of being a Trotskyist and a GMD spy, was arrested, and eventually executed in 1947.[91] One of Wang's other alleged crimes was to have criticized the privilege system and lack of equality in Yan'an in a couple of his essays. This led to charges of his having advocated such things as a classless human nature.[92] In his speech at the Yan'an Forum on Literature and Art in May 1942, Mao Zedong strongly refuted such views and dismissed the existence of abstract love, freedom, truth, and human nature, instead claiming that all these feelings and views were class based.[93] This understanding also shaped the PRC's rights discourse, which similarly rejected the existence of an universal human nature and any supraclass rights.

Mao's selectivity regarding who should enjoy rights and why is also evident in his discussions on the nature of a future Communist-ruled society. According to Mao, only those defined as the people (i.e., those having the right class background and the right political beliefs) should enjoy democracy and freedom of speech, assembly, and association, whereas the enemy was to be deprived of these rights and subject to the dictatorship of the proletariat.[94] After 1949, the Communists abandoned all references to human rights in political discourse, although they still occasionally used the words human rights in issues pertaining to international politics and foreign affairs. But generally speaking, human rights talk now came to be regarded as reactionary and bourgeois. Chinese constitutions over the years have stipulated a variety of citizens' rights, including civil and political rights, such as freedom of speech, freedom of assembly, and so on. But these rights have been more pro forma than real, as well as being confined to those identified as "the people," thus excluding those of a so-called bad class background and with the wrong political opinions. Since rights were given by the government and were not innate, they could also be restricted and denied as the political situation so demanded, as illustrated by the ample and sad examples of post-1949 history.

CHINA, THE UNITED NATIONS, AND THE UDHR

As already mentioned, China took an active part in the drafting of the UDHR and voted in favor of its adoption. It is interesting to note that by the 1940s, the Nationalists, despite their earlier skepticism to human rights talk, had become quite positive to international human rights work. It should, however, be remembered that while the Chinese diplomats were busy promoting human rights abroad, the GMD was violating human rights at home and, as we have seen, facing severe criticism for this from their domestic opponents. One can thus question the GMD's commitment to human rights and wonder whether the new approach did not simply reflect its political needs at the time. The Nationalists needed the help and recognition of the Western powers and may therefore have wanted to appear in a favorable light in their eyes. Contradicting such a conclusion, however, is the fact that China at times went much further in its suggestions on international protection of human rights than most Western governments were prepared to go at the time, although the Chinese voting pattern during the drafting of the UDHR in general closely followed that of the United States.[95] China was very favorably disposed toward developments in international law that promoted strong international organizations. For example, it advocated the compulsory jurisdiction of the International Court of Justice in all legal controversies, which was opposed by both the United States and the Soviet Union. It also paid particular attention to issues of self-determination and racial discrimination, which implied that human rights violations were seen as arising from international injustices rather than domestic ones. Pressure to address them would therefore be put on the international community rather than on national governments, which could be one reason why the Nationalists were more positive toward taking part in international human rights work than answering domestic human rights demands.

China was one of the countries that took part in the preparatory conference on the United Nations at Dumbarton Oaks in Washington, D.C., in 1944. It was represented by diplomats T.V. Soong and V. K. Wellington Koo, who had also represented China at the Paris Peace Conference in 1919 and then supported the Japanese attempt to prevent racial discrimination.[96] China also sent a strong delegation to the UN Conference on International Organization in San Francisco during the spring of 1945 in order to discuss and adopt the UN Charter.[97] It was headed by Soong, the Chinese foreign minister, but also included three members of the minority parties and three independent participants. Zhang Junmai represented the China Democratic Socialist Party; Li Huang, the China Youth Party; and Dong Biwu, the CCP. Among the independent representatives were Hu Shi and Hu Lin, who was the managing director of the liberal newspaper *Dagong bao*. The establishment of the United Nations generally elicited a favorable response in the Chinese press; both the GMD and the CCP supported it.[98] Zhang Junmai, as we have seen, also wrote about these international developments in the human rights field. When the UN Charter was adopted, China received the honor of being the first country to put its signature on the document.

The Human Rights Commission in charge of drafting the UDHR was set up in 1946.[99] It was headed by Eleanor Roosevelt and its two vice-chairs were held by the Chinese representative Zhang Pengjun (P. C. Chang) and the French representative René Cassin.[100] A drafting committee was then appointed consisting of representatives from Australia, Chile, China, France, Lebanon, the USSR, the United Kingdom, and the United States. The first draft outline of the UDHR was written by the Canadian legal scholar John P. Humphrey, director of the Human Rights Division of the UN Secretariat, who drew on texts and drafts presented by different individuals, NGOs, and states. Humphrey's draft was elaborated upon by Cassin, and this draft was then presented to the commission for discussion.

The drafting process was a collaborative effort that engaged not only the drafting committee's members and the Human Rights Commission itself, but also included NGOs and many UN member states. Many countries, including China, also presented their own draft proposals.[101] The drafting went through different stages as the draft passed from the drafting committee to the commission and back, before landing on the table of the General Assembly.[102] Although Humphrey and Cassin put a heavy mark on the first drafts, the final outcome was not a narrowly Western product as has so often been alleged, but was a truly universal text that had been influenced and shaped by many different cultural traditions and societies. The deliberations on the UDHR do not reveal a simple West–East or North–South dichotomy. The different representatives' views were multifaceted and reveal the complexity and diversity of their respective cultures. Cassin, for example, showed a strong communitarian bent and argued for the inclusion of duties, whereas the Lebanese representative Charles Malik, on the other hand, was a Thomist who expressed an essentialist view of human rights and strongly pushed for individual rights against the state.[103]

The Chinese representatives' views were also quite complex in character. While Zhang Pengjun often made conscious references to the Chinese tradition, he was equally prone to refer to Western philosophers. His outlook was quite cosmopolitan in character, revealing a happy blending of Western and

Chinese ideas. It is true, however, that Zhang at times expressed a concern about the Western influence on the draft. When Humphrey was in the process of putting together the first draft he was advised by Zhang to spend some time studying Chinese philosophy.[104] Zhang was also eager to quote Chinese sources in order to show that Chinese traditional philosophy and the concept of human rights were not at odds but actually had much in common. Koo, who also was a member of the Chinese delegation, for his part referred to the fact that the idea of "universal brotherhood" was deeply rooted in China, as exemplified by the thinking of Confucius, Mo Zi, and Sun Yat-sen. But the Chinese representatives also frequently referred to Western eighteenth-century philosophy in their deliberations on human rights at the commission.[105] Zhang would also argue, as did Zhang Junmai later, that the idea of human rights in the West in part had been inspired by Chinese philosophy. "In the eighteenth century, when progressive ideas with respect to human rights had been first put forward in Europe, translations of Chinese philosophers had been known to and had inspired such thinkers as Voltaire, Quesnay and Diderot in their humanistic revolt against feudalistic conceptions. Chinese ideas had been intermingled with European thought and sentiment on human rights at the time when that subject had been first speculated upon in modern Europe."[106]

One of the most heated debates concerning the UDHR was on whether there should be any references to God or natural law in the discussion on the origin of human rights, but in the end neither was mentioned. Article 1 now reads: "All human beings are born free and equal in dignity and rights. They are endowed with reason and conscience and should act towards one another in a spirit of brotherhood." Zhang was strongly against including references to natural law in the UDHR because he felt this was alien to many cultures but he was not alone in taking such a position.[107] Zhang supported the deletion in Article 1 of the words "by nature," which had figured in several draft proposals. He was equally critical of including the phrase "born free," which others suggested; on this point, Zhang eventually had to give in. Zhang's arguments were put forward at an oral intervention at a meeting of the General Assembly on October 9, 1948.

There was no contradiction between the eighteenth century idea of the goodness of man's essential nature and the idea of a soul given to man by God, for the concept of God laid particular stress on the human, as opposed to the animal, part of man's nature. [Zhang] urged that the Committee should not debate the question of the nature of man again but should build on the work of the eighteenth century philosophers. He thought the Committee should agree to a text beginning "All human beings are free"—using "human beings" to refer to the non-animal part of man—as proposed by the Lebanese delegation, and should further agree to delete the words "by nature," as proposed by the Belgian delegation. If the words "by nature" were deleted, those who believed in God could still find in the strong opening assertion of the article the idea of God, and at the same time others with different concepts would be able to accept the text.[108]

Zhang felt that the phrase "all human beings are free" was preferable, as it was sufficiently vague to be acceptable to different cultural traditions.

> The Chinese representative recalled that the population of his country comprised a large segment of humanity. That population had ideals and traditions different from those of the Christian West. Those ideals included good manners, decorum, propriety and consideration for others. Yet, although Chinese culture attached the greatest importance to manners as a part of ethics, the Chinese representative would refrain from proposing that mention of them should be made in the declaration. He hoped that his colleagues would show equal consideration and withdraw some of the amendments to article 1 which raised metaphysical problems.[109]

In view of the fact that many contemporary scholars, as well as the PRC government, seem to believe that economic and social rights somehow would be more acceptable and important to the Chinese people, it is interesting to note that Zhang and other Chinese representatives to the United Nations did not focus on these rights, and at times even seemed reluctant to include them in the UDHR.[110] The draft declaration submitted by China to the Commission on Human Rights on May 3, 1948, thus consisted of ten articles of which only one dealt with economic and social rights. That article stipulated that "Every person has the right to a decent living; to work and leisure, to health, education, economic and social security."[111] At a later stage in the drafting process, China, however, supported the inclusion of rights to food and clothing in the UDHR, but these rights were not originally proposed by China. Zhang would occasionally refer to the Chinese tradition of benevolence when defending the inclusion of these social and economic rights.[112] When the Human Rights Commission later was reviewing the different suggestions and proposals regarding the UDHR, the Chinese representatives stressed, not economic rights, but provisions regarding equality, freedom of conscience, and freedom of speech and expression.[113]

It is also instructive to note that China did not push the issue of duties. Many other countries, such as Latin American countries, and representatives, such as Cassin, spoke more strongly in support of the stipulation of duties in the UDHR than did China.[114] China's view on the role of duties in the declaration was at times a bit ambiguous. Its proposed amendments to the drafting committee text of May 27, 1948, for example, stipulated that the explicit reference to the fact that "the individual owes duties to society," should be omitted, and that one should only keep the more general wording, "the exercise of . . . rights requires recognition of the rights of others and the just requirements of the community in which [one] resides."[115]

Albeit sometimes wavering on the issue of duties, Zhang, however, supported the communal aspect of human rights on a number of other occasions. Cassin had suggested that Article 1 read: "All men are brothers. Being endowed with reason, they are members of one family. They are free and possess equal dignity and rights."[116] Zhang then suggested the addition of the Confucian concept of "two-man-mindedness [*ren*]" to complement the reference to reason and underscore that man also should act in consideration of his fellow human beings. Others approved of Zhang's idea, and the United Kingdom and Lebanese representatives then suggested that the English word "conscience" be used to express the idea of *ren* and added to Cassin's invocation of reason. Zhang also stressed the communal aspect of human rights on another occasion, arguing that: "Stress should be laid upon the human aspect of human rights. A human being had to be constantly conscious of other men, in whose society he lived."[117]

On yet another occasion, Zhang stated his belief that the "aim of the United Nations was not to ensure the selfish gains of the individual but to try and increase man's moral stature. It was necessary to proclaim the duties of the individual, for it was a consciousness of his duties that enabled man to reach a high moral standard."[118] This wording carried strong Confucian connotations. Zhang followed up this statement a day later when he again referred to the draft proposal for Article 1 that included the phrase "in a spirit of brotherhood," and that, to Zhang's mind, was an implicit reference to duties: "A happy balance was struck by the broad statement of rights in the first sentence and the implication of duties in the second. Should Article 1 be taken out of the body of the declaration, it would not claim as much of the reader's attention as it deserved to do; moreover, the various rights would appear more selfish if they were not preceded by the reference to 'a spirit of brotherhood'. Similar reasoning applied to Article 27 [now Article 29 in the UDHR], which contained a statement of duties. Statements of rights and duties should form an integral part of the declaration."[119]

But despite this emphasis on the communal aspect of human rights and, at times, favorable view of duties, Zhang later proposed that the article on man's duties toward his community should be placed near the end of the UDHR. As he then put it, "An article which dealt with the limitations on the exercise of the rights and freedoms proclaimed in the Declaration should not appear at the beginning of the Declaration before those rights and freedoms themselves had been set forth."[120] In the end, only one article in the UDHR mentions duties. Article 29 (1) now reads: "Everyone has duties to the community in which alone the free and full development of his personality is possible."

While the GMD had earlier argued that human rights were inappropriate to China, it was now prepared to stress the universality of human rights and work toward guaranteeing that "all people [were] protected in their inalienable rights."[121] Zhang Pengjun emerged as a strong advocate of universal human rights, arguing that human rights were applicable to all cultures. When the UDHR was put to a vote, China without hesitation also voted in favor; the majority of the abstentions came from communist countries, the exceptions being South Africa and Saudi Arabia.[122] And when UNESCO in 1948 arranged a symposium on the interpretation and justification of human rights from different philosophical traditions, Chung-Shu Lo (Le Zhongshu) voiced the view that human rights not only were compatible with the Chinese tradition, but that many traditional values actually were quite similar in character.[123]

As Twiss has recently argued, Zhang Pengjun had no problem with acknowledging human rights and incorporating them within a Confucian framework.[124] Zhang's and the other Chinese representatives' position during the work on the UDHR reveal a conscious effort to constructively and creatively relate Confucian ideas to the concept of human rights. In this respect, Zhang broke ground with earlier human rights advocates in China who had a tendency to juxtapose human rights and Confucianism. It is interesting to note that since the deliberations on the UDHR, such deliberate efforts to relate human rights to Confucianism have been quite rare in the Chinese human rights debate, one exception again being the GMD in the late 1970s. Zhang's views moreover don't resemble those of some contemporary scholars who lately have tried to discover proto-human rights ideas in the Confucian tradition, or tried to find similarities between Confucian concepts such as *li* and rights. In contrast to others who also refer to traditional values, it should in addition be pointed out that Zhang did not put a priority on socioeconomic rights over civil and political rights or argue that the communitarian Confucian tradition was at odds with an advocacy of individual human rights.

Still, for all of Zhang Pengjun's personal convictions, we should not lose sight of the fact that the GMD had much to gain from presenting Chinese culture as compatible with human rights and took a high moral ground on the issue. By late 1948, the Nationalists had all but lost the civil war against the Communists. It then became politically expedient for the GMD to use human rights critique in the political struggle against the CCP in order to win the support of the so-called Free World. But it was not alone at the time in seeing human rights as a tool with which to fight political adversaries. The United Kingdom also viewed human rights more as a weapon to be used against the Soviet Union than as standards by which it should abide and by which other states would judge its policies.[125]

Until it finally lost its seat in the United Nations to the PRC in 1971, Taiwan continued to raise the issue of human rights violations in the PRC. Taiwan's delegates to the United Nations expressed strong support of the human rights work undertaken by the organization and also took part in the drafting of the two international convenants.[126] They stressed individual rights, and while arguing for the universality of human rights, also emphasized that "the Convenants should not seek to impose, even in good faith, the political, economic, social and cultural concepts of another state or group of states."[127] This is a culturally relativistic position that in fact sounds quite similar to the position of the PRC today. In addition, Taiwan, as the PRC later, put special emphasis on the right to self-determination. After the two human rights convenants were adopted by the UN General Assembly in 1966, they were signed by Taiwan in 1967, but never submitted to the Legislative Yuan. Despite the positive attitude to international work on human rights, however, human rights violations continued under Nationalist rule. Their rule on Taiwan had also begun in an ominous way, when on February 28, 1947, as many as 20,000 people protesting the Nationalist regime were rounded up and killed by GMD troops. After the Nationalists lost the civil war in 1949 and withdrew to Taiwan, martial law was in force on the island until 1987. Throughout these years, political opponents of the GMD were routinely harassed, imprisoned, and even put to death.

CONCLUSION

During the war years both liberals and Communists criticized the GMD for committing serious human rights violations. The frequent demands to respect human rights not only reveal a genuine concern on their part, but perhaps even more—at least in the case of the Communists—the rhetorical value of human rights in political discourse. Despite war and foreign aggression, human rights remained a powerful idea in domestic discourse that could be used as a weapon in political struggles. The new international interest in human rights issues toward the mid-1940s also influenced the Chinese debate. Many Chinese intellectuals, such as Zhou Jingwen and Zhang Junmai, were aware of these international developments and referred to them in their writings; they also took part in international fora to discuss human rights. Not even the GMD, which harbored serious theoretical misgivings regarding the concept of human rights, could remain immune to these developments.

Since Nationalist China participated in international organizations such as the United Nations, it had to address and support the idea of human rights, particularly since it wanted the support of the United States. The GMD therefore chose to forget its earlier, smirking remarks regarding "so-called natural rights." But while the GMD unambiguously endorsed universal human rights, this international acceptance didn't translate into domestic protection and respect of human rights. In this respect, the Nationalists were helped and protected by American policy. After an initial enthusiasm for human rights, American politicians rapidly became more skeptical of the idea, a position that didn't really change until Jimmy Carter became president and elevated human rights to a central issue in American foreign policy. During the Cold War, and thanks to the support of the United States, Taiwan was more or less exempted from human rights critique. Still, the very fact that Nationalist China was diplomatically recognized by the West and allowed to keep China's seat in the United Nations after it lost the civil war, meant that human rights could continue to play a role in the domestic political discourse as political opponents were able to use the concept against the regime. The political development on the mainland under the CCP followed a different trajectory that didn't leave much room for discussions on human rights, as they were dismissed as a bourgeois concept.

NOTES

1. On the political climate and political repression during the war years, see Eastman (1986), and for the civil war, see Pepper (1980). On the suppression of freedom of the press, see Ting (1974).
2. On the intellectuals' critique of the Communists, see Pepper (1980), pp. 199–228.
3. See Zhou Jingwen (1941a). Zhou Jingwen (1908–1985) studied at Waseda University in Tokyo and at the University of Michigan. The magazine *Shidai piping*, a semimonthly, was published in Hong Kong 1938–1941. It was revived after the war and came out in 1947–1949. After Zhou fled to Hong Kong in 1957, it was revived for the third time.
4. For a reference to Wells, see Zhou Jingwen (1941a), p. 2933.
5. See Zhou Jingwen (1941a), p. 2932, and (1941b), p. 2969.
6. Zhou Jingwen (1941c), p. 3014.
7. Readers' reactions were printed in no. 71, and a special issue on human rights was published as no. 73–74, 1941. A book with the title *Where Are Our Human Rights?* containing some of the articles was also published in 1941.
8. Zhou Jingwen (1941d), p. 3089; see also (1940).
9. Shi Zishan (1941), p. 3115.
10. Min (1941), p. 3009.
11. Li Yuan (1941), p. 3233.
12. Shi Zishan (1941).
13. Han Youtong (1941), p. 3127.
14. See, for example, Li Qing (1941), p. 3057.
15. Li Zhangda (1941), p. 3106.
16. Yan An (1941), p. 3244.
17. See Zhou Jingwen (1941b), (1941a), and Lin Huiyu (1941). Min (1941) mentioned the right to subsistence, the right to freedom, and the right to equality. Wen Yu (1941) discussed the right to subsistence, the right to clothing and food, and the right to development. Jin Zhonghua (1941) emphasized that the freedoms of thought and speech were the two most fundamental human rights.

18. See Chen Shaohua (1941), p. 3159.

19. See for example, Pan Lang (1941), p. 3145; and Lin Huiyu (1941), p. 3150.

20. Zhou Jingwen (1940), p. 1746.

21. See Shen Zhiyuan (1941).

22. Bai Peng (1941), p. 3225.

23. Zhou Jingwen (1939a) and (1939b).

24. See, for example, Zhou Jingwen (1941d), p. 3089, and Han Youtong (1941), p. 3127.

25. See, for example, Ji Huang (1941), Shi Zishan (1941), and Shen Zhiyuan (1947).

26. Zhou Jingwen (1940), p. 1744; and Li Yuan (1941), p. 3233.

27. See Zhou Jingwen (1940), p. 1746; Han Youtong (1941), pp. 3125–27; Lin Huiyu (1941), p. 3147; and Bai Peng (1941), p. 3225.

28. Zhou Jingwen (1940), p. 1747.

29. Zhou Jingwen (1941c), p. 3012.

30. Shi Zishan (1941), p. 3117. Occasionally, as in the case of Zhang Youyu (1941) who embraced Sun Yat-sen's Three People's Principles, efforts were made to show that the concepts of human rights and people's rights were more or less identical.

31. Duanmu Liang (1941a), p. 2982.

32. Pan Lang (1941). The Taiping rebellion was also referred to by Chen Shaohua (1941), p. 3159.

33. Qun Xin (1941), p. 3271.

34. Zhou Jingwen (1944), p. 28.

35. The league developed from the Association of Comrades for National Unity founded by Liang Shuming in 1939. On the league, see Zhao Xihua (1992), Seymour (1987), and Fung (2000).

36. For statements by the league referring to human rights, see, for example, the congress report of October 11, 1945, reprinted in ZMTLW, p. 75; a speech by Zhang Lan on January 10, 1946, reprinted in ZMTLW, p. 118; the league's declaration of April 5, 1947, reprinted in ZMTLW, p. 322; and Shi Jing (1947), p. 19.

37. See a speech by the league's Shanghai representative on March 17, 1947, reprinted in ZMTLW, p. 319.

38. For examples, see the league's program of October 10, 1941, reprinted in ZMTLW, p. 8; its provisional draft of September 19, 1944, reprinted in ZMTLW, p. 26; its declaration of July 28, 1945, reprinted in ZMTLW, p. 50; its congress report of October 11, 1945, reprinted in ZMTLW, p. 75; and its declaration of April 25, 1947, reprinted in ZMTLW, p. 321; and Pan Dada (1946), pp. 3–5.

39. See the congress report of October 11, 1945, reprinted in ZMTLW, p. 83, and Zhang Shenfu's speech of January 9, 1946, reprinted in ZMTLW, p. 138. Others during the 1940s also emphasized the importance of economic rights and the right to subsistence. A couple of articles in the magazine *Xianzheng*, for example, argued that if people could not obtain the fundamental right to subsistence (*shengcun quanli*), all other rights and freedoms would become empty talk. In one of the articles, the author criticized the fact that whereas political rights, such as freedom of the person, freedom of speech, freedom of publication, and freedom of assembly were acknowledged, economic rights and "the freedom from want" still had not been recognized by many democracies. He not only drew on Roosevelt's Four Freedoms, but also referred to the principle of people's livelihood (*minsheng zhuyi*) in Sun Yat-sen's Three Principles of the People. Other writers also favored the inclusion of social and economic rights in the constitution. An article in *Xin Zhonghua* in 1944 argued that the

old human rights could no longer satisfy the needs of the contemporary world. The author referred to recent developments in the West where the right to work, right to education, and right to leisure had been recognized in constitutions. See the following articles: Lin Hengyuan (1944), Chen Pokang (1944), and Liu Guansheng (1944).

40. See, for example, its declaration of July 28, 1945, reprinted in ZMTLW, p. 50; its manifesto of October 16, 1945, reprinted in ZMTLW, p. 91; the speech by its Shanghai representative of March 17, 1947, reprinted in ZMTLW, pp. 318–19; and declaration of April 24, 1947, in ZMTLW, p. 321.

41. Wen Yiduo and Li Gongpu were killed on the streets of Kunming within a few days of each other in 1946. On the league's reaction, see, for example, a telegram from Democratic League chairman Zhang Lan to Chiang Kai-shek of July 18, 1946, reprinted in ZMTLW, pp. 198–99. The investigation headed by Liang Shuming on behalf of the league concluded that the assassination had been carried out by the Kunming branch of the GMD. For a description of this incident, see Pepper (1980), p. 144.

42. The students themselves, apart from demanding an end to the civil war and the establishment of a coalition government, demanded the protection of the freedoms of the person, speech, publication, assembly, association, and demonstration. On the student movement that this incident provoked, see Pepper (1980), pp. 44–52.

43. See, for example, the league's declaration of April 5, 1947, reprinted in ZMTLW, p. 322.

44. Hu Jian (1946), p. 8. I do not know if this organization was ever realized. In the same article, it was stated that the Communists had suggested setting up the Committee for the Protection of Human Rights (*Renquan baozhang weiyuanhui*).

45. On Zhang Junmai (1887–1969), see Jeans (1997) and Xue Huayuan (1993).

46. See, for example, the articles translated by Zhang Junmai (1946c), (1946d), and (1946e).

47. See Zhang Junmai (1945) and (1944b).

48. Zhang Junmai (1948a), p. 4. On another occasion, he referred to the controversy on whether rights are natural or historical, but concluded by saying that he would not discuss the issue any further. See (1946a), p. 4.

49. Zhang Junmai (1948a), p. 5.

50. Zhang Junmai (1948a), p. 4.

51. Zhang Junmai (1946b), p. 3. Parts of Zhang's article is translated in Angle and Svensson (2001). A similar statement from the China Democratic Socialist Party can perhaps also be traced to Zhang Junmai's pen. See *Zaisheng*, no. 156, 1947, p. 3.

52. Zhang Junmai (1945), p. 10.

53. Zhang Junmai (1946b), p. 3, translated in Angle and Svensson (2001), p. 198.

54. Zhang Junmai (1944b), (1944c), and (1945). In the first article, he referred to Wells's view that the right to subsistence was the most important of all rights.

55. Zhang Junmai (1946b), p. 4. Lin Huiyu, who had defined human rights as rights bestowed by nature (*tianfu de ziran quanli*), also emphasized that the concept of human rights evolved with society. Lin Huiyu (1941), p. 3147.

56. Zhang Junmai (1944a).

57. Zhang Junmai (1948b), p. 3, and (1946b), p. 3. For an earlier discussion of Roosevelt's Four Freedoms, see also (1944a), p. 6. Others at the time were also influenced by Roosevelt's Four Freedoms. See Chen Pokang (1944) and Liu Guansheng (1944).

58. Zhang Junmai (1948a), p. 5.

59. For example, he mentioned the fact that different schools of thought in the West had refuted the idea of universal human rights on the grounds that such an idea was ahistorical. See Zhang Junmai (1944a), p. 4. See also (1946a), p. 4.

60. Zhang Junmai (1946b), p. 3. .

61. Chang (1952).

62. Chang (1952), p. 52.

63. Chang (1952), pp. 322–30.

64. Zhang Junmai, "The Political Philosophy of Confucianism," reprinted in Cheng Wenxi (1981), p. 386.

65. See Chang (1952), p. 331.

66. Zhang Junmai, "The Political Philosophy of Confucianism," reprinted in Cheng Wenxi (1981), p. 382. Compare with some contemporary scholars who put forward the same views, see chapter 3.

67. Tan (1971), p. 263.

68. Large-scale arrests in connection with a census investigation in February 1947 provoked thirteen professors to publish a statement, later supported by 192 teachers and professors. See Anon., "A Jointly Signed Manifesto of University Professors," *Minzhu ban yuekan*, no. 4, 1947, p. 4. See also Pepper (1980), pp. 141–42.

69. See, for example, Li Xuan (1948), p. 3.

70. On the magazine and Chu Anping, see Pepper (1980), pp. 133–36, and Wong (1993). Chu Anping's collected works, including his writings in *Guancha,* have recently been published in the PRC. See Chu Anping (1998).

71. Chu Anping (1946).

72. Chu Anping (1946), p. 4.

73. See, for example, Luo Zhongshu (1946) and Ge Si'en (1946).

74. See, for example, Li Haopei (1947) and Han Depei (1947). Li mentioned an organization for the protection of human rights founded in Shanghai, the China International Association for the Protection of Human Rights (*Zhongguo guoji renquan baozhang hui*); the same organization is also mentioned in an article in *Zaisheng*. Unfortunately, I have no more information on this organization and its activities.

75. See Schram (1986), pp. 795–96.

76. Reprinted in Saich (1996), p. 15. For another CCP document from the same year also listing these freedoms, see p. 19.

77. Reprinted in Saich (1996), pp. 552–56.

78. See Mao Zedong, "Mobilise All Strength in Order to Struggle for Victory in the War," reprinted in Mao (1991), vol. 2, p. 355.

79. Mao (1991), vol. 2, p. 768.

80. These declarations are reprinted in Dong Yunhu and Liu Wuping (1990), pp. 764–75.

81. See JFRB, March 12, 1944, reprinted in Xiao Shu (1999), p. 8.

82. Mao Zedong "On Coalition Government," reprinted in Saich (1996), pp. 1223–24.

83. XHRB, October 5, 1939, reprinted in Xiao Shu (1999), p. 42.

84. See JFRB, May 26, 1941, reprinted in Xiao Shu (1999), pp. 251–54.

85. See XHRB, March 26, 1944, on academic freedom; and XHRB, February 18, 1946, and JFRB, September 1, 1943 on freedom of the press, reprinted in Xiao Shu (1999), pp. 145–51, pp. 157–59, and pp. 169–75, respectively.

86. See XHRB, January 13, 1946, and XHRB, February 18, 1946, reprinted in Xiao Shu (1999), pp. 260–62 and pp. 266–69, respectively.

87. See XHRB, February 18, 1946, reprinted in Xiao Shu (1999), pp. 157–59.

88. On the aim of education being the cultivation of an independent thinking individual, see XHRB, July 30, 1946, reprinted in Xiao Shu (1999), pp. 221–24. Another article that defended students' rights to freedom of thought held that this was necessary in order to respect their personalities (*renge*) and human rights (*renquan*). See XHRB, June 25, 1944, reprinted in Xiao Shu (1999), p. 210.

89. See XHRB, March 31, 1945, reprinted in Xiao Shu (1999), p. 184.

90. On the rectification campaign, see Teiwes (1993).

91. On Wang Shiwei, see Dai Qing (1994).

92. Dai Qing (1994), p. 106.

93. Reprinted in Saich (1996), pp. 1122–32.

94. See for example Mao Zedong, "On the People's Democratic Dictatorship," 1949, reprinted in Saich (1996), p. 1370.

95. On the Chinese support of American proposals, see Glendon (2001), p. 46,

96. On China's participation in the founding of the United Nations and in its early works; see, in particular, *China and the United Nations* (1959).

97. On the San Francisco Conference, see *China and the United Nations* (1959), pp. 38–62.

98. For Mao's statement in support of the Dumbarton Oaks conference, see Cohen and Chiu (1974), p. 1290.

99. On the drafting of the UDHR, see Humphrey (1984), Lauren (1998), and, in particular, Morsink (1999).

100. Zhang Pengjun (1892–1957) was a brother of the well-known educator and founder of Nankai University, Zhang Boling. Zhang Pengjun received his Ph. D. at Columbia University and his academic career included a stint as professor at Nankai University. Zhang was a member of the People's Political Conference 1938–40, and then embarked upon a diplomatic career that took him to Turkey, Chile, and England. He ended his career as a member of the Chinese delegation to the United Nations.

101. For China's own draft proposal, see UN E/CN.4/AC.1/18, Draft International Declaration on Human Rights, submitted by the Delegation of China to the second session of the Drafting Committee of the Commission on Human Rights on May 3, 1948. Later during the drafting process, China also offered comments and suggestions regarding the drafting committee's text. See UN E/CN.4/102, May 27, 1948, China: Amendments to the Draft International Declaration on Human Rights.

102. For a detailed studies of the drafting process, see Morsink (1999) and Glendon (2001).

103. Some of Cassin's and Malik's articles are found at <www.udhr50.org/history> published by the Franklin and Eleanor Roosevelt Institute [accessed September 6, 2001]. For more on Malik's views, see also Glendon (2001).

104. Humphrey (1984), p. 29.

105. See Morsink (1999), p. 234 and p. 281

106. See *Official Records of the Third Session of the General Assembly* (1948), p. 48.

107. Humphrey (1984), p. 67; and Morsink (1999), pp. 286–87.

108. See *Official Records*, pp. 113–14.

109. See *Official Records*, p. 98.

110. During the second session of the Human Rights Commission, China actually voted against including economic and social rights in the UDHR (again, it took the same side as

the United States), but during the third session, China defended the right to food and clothing. See Morsink (1999), p. 224 and p. 197.

111. See UN E/CN.4/AC.1/18, May 3, 1948. In its own proposed amendments of May 27, 1948, China in addition wanted to substitute the more elaborate and detailed enumeration of social and economic rights with the more vague and simple statement that "Everyone has the right to a decent living; to work and leisure, to health, education, economic and social security." See UN E/CN.4/102, May 27, 1948, China: Amendments to the Draft International Declaration on Human Rights, p. 6.

112. See Morsink (1999), p. 197. At the second session of the Economic and Social Council in June 1946, Zhang had also referred to traditional Chinese values of providing for the welfare of all. Quoted in Glendon (2001), p. 185.

113. Lauren (1998), p. 233.

114. See Morsink (1999), chapter 7.

115. UN E/CN.4/102, May 27, 1948, China: Amendments to the Draft International Declaration on Human Rights, article 2. Such a proposal had been voiced by China already on December 16, 1947. see E/CN.4/77/Annex A.

116. On this discussion, see Morsink (1999), pp. 296–99.

117. See *Official Records*, p. 48.

118. See *Official Records*, p. 87.

119. See *Official Records*, p. 98.

120. Quoted in Morsink (1999), p. 245. Another noncommunitarian action on Zhang's part was his opposition to the inclusion of the word "alone" in Article 29 (1) that had underscored the communitarian bent of this article. Morsink (1999), pp. 246–48. Morsink suggests that Zhang's suggestion could have been because he wanted to curry favor with the United States or because he was unwell at that time.

121. Lauren (1998), p. 167. See also *China and the United Nations* (1959), p. 87. On the Chinese position on human rights in the United Nations generally, see *China and the United Nations* (1959), pp. 185–90.

122. No country voted against the motion, but eight countries abstained, namely Byelorussia, Czechoslovakia, Poland, the Ukraine, the Soviet Union, Yugoslavia, Saudi Arabia, and South Africa.

123. See Lo (1949).

124. Twiss (1998b). While I agree with him that Zhang Pengjun consciously sought to interpret and relate human rights to Confucian ideas, I am more skeptical about his argument that Zhang's views and suggestions led to a marked Confucian influence on the UDHR. Morsink (1999) and Glendon (2001) give a balanced and detailed description of the whole drafting process and the various representatives' and organizations' inputs, and their analyses do not point toward a specific or pronounced Confucian influence.

125. Glendon (2001), p 87, citing Brian Simpson's study on the United Kingdom and human rights.

126. On Taiwan's position on human rights in the 1950s, see *China and the United Nations* (1959), pp. 185–202.

127. *China and the United Nations*, p. 186.

Chapter Nine

The 1950s: Human Rights Debates on Two Sides of the Taiwan Strait

TWO DISCOURSES

The Chinese discourse on human rights continued during the 1950s, but took different forms on the mainland and in Taiwan and Hong Kong under the influence of the different political situations in these societies. Several of the people who had been involved earlier in discussions on human rights retained their interest in the subject and were among the most vocal during this period. While the language of human rights virtually disappeared on the mainland, only to briefly resurface in 1957, it initially was more vibrant in Taiwan where it mainly was discussed in magazines such as *Ziyou Zhongguo*. On the mainland, Luo Longji and Chu Anping, in line with their earlier political convictions, voiced a concern with the CCP's supremacy in political affairs and criticized injustices committed during different political campaigns, but neither of them retained their earlier explicit human rights language. Others during the short-lived period of "blooming and contending" in 1957, more explicitly dressed their critique of the CCP in a human rights garb. After his escape to Hong Kong in the late 1950s, Zhou Jingwei continued to raise the issue of human rights and criticize the CCP in the revived *Shidai piping*.

THE HUMAN RIGHTS DISCOURSE IN THE FREE CHINA MAGAZINE: ANTI-COMMUNISM AND CRITIQUE OF THE GMD

Despite the GMD's highly critical view of human rights before the 1940s, it no longer simply dismissed the concept as inappropriate to China. As discussed in the previous chapter, a representative of the Nationalist government served as the vice-chairman of the committee in charge of drafting the UDHR, and Nationalist China, as a member of the United Nations, voted for its adoption in 1948. Apart from taking part in activities within the United Nations, human rights were also at times celebrated and discussed domestically. On the occasion of the tenth anniversary of the UDHR, for example, several commemorative activities took place, including the issuing of a stamp.[1] Despite this rhetorical support of human rights, human rights violations, including arrests of suspected communist supporters and political opponents, and closures of journals and magazines critical of the regime were frequent in Taiwan up to the lifting of martial law in 1987. But since human rights was a legitimate idea, especially so since Taiwan identified itself with the so-called Free World, it became an effective political weapon that could be wielded by critics of the regime. During the 1950s, ideas of human rights, freedom, and democracy were therefore debated and discussed to a much greater extent in Taiwan than on the mainland.

The magazine *Ziyou Zhongguo* (*Free China*), founded by Hu Shi, Lei Zhen, Yin Haiguang, and others in 1949, was the main vehicle for liberal intellectual and political debate in Taiwan during the 1950s.[2] Lei Zhen, Yin Haiguang, Hu Shi, and Zhang Foquan contributed the majority of the articles on freedom, human rights, and democracy. They were very familiar with Western political thought and their writings reveal little, if any, interest in or influence from traditional Chinese philosophy and thought, in contrast to the contributors to *Minzhu pinglun* (*Democratic Critic*).[3] The *Free China* group at first had fairly close and cordial relations with the Nationalist regime. Lei Zhen was a GMD member who had worked in the Ministry of Education; Yin Haiguang, among other things, had worked at the GMD daily *Zhongyang ribao*; and Hu Shi ended up as Nationalist China's ambassador to the United States. But their support was by no means unconditional, and they also, except in the case of Hu Shi, became more critical of the GMD and its dictatorial system as the years passed.

The *Free China* group advocated an end to the political tutelage period and tried to push the GMD toward democracy. Around 1956 the magazine became more outspoken and critical of the GMD's authoritarian policy and Chiang Kai-shek's personal power. This development was reinforced in 1959 when Chiang decided to amend the 1946 constitution in order to extend his presidency to a third term. Together with activists engaged in local elections, Lei Zhen became involved in plans to establish an opposition party. These activities came to naught, however, and in 1960 Lei Zhen was arrested and the magazine closed down. Lei Zhen was sentenced to ten years in prison and Fu Zheng to six years, while Yin Haiguang lost his position at Taiwan University and eked out a lonely and miserable existence until his death in 1969. Those active in local elections would later become known under the general heading of the *dangwai* (outside-the-party-people) and gradually push Taiwan toward democracy.[4]

The *Free China* group criticized the GMD's sincerity about building democracy and respecting human rights, arguing that one could not fight dictatorship with dictatorship. A major reason for the GMD's defeat on the mainland, they contended, was that it had not practiced democracy. In the struggle against communism, the regime should uphold freedom and democracy; if this was its goal and was what distinguished it from the Communists, it could not very well violate its own goals and principles. Freedom and democracy should not be sacrificed in the struggle against the CCP. As Yin Haiguang put it:

> Human rights cannot be abandoned, no matter what the time, place, situation, or reason, because if we abandon human rights, we will not be complete human beings. . . . [I]nternational communism is the sworn enemy of human rights. Thus, our struggle against communism is being waged to protect human rights. If we say that we must abandon human rights in order to defend human rights, isn't this a contradiction? It is completely ironic that those who oppose communism also should violate human rights.[5]

Although the members of the group, like earlier generations, valued human rights as necessary in order to protect and uphold human dignity, they also saw the struggle for human rights and democracy as a means to oppose the CCP and gain the support of the Free World.[6] In a world where human rights had been placed on the international political agenda through the founding of the United Nations and the adoption of the UDHR, and where the West and East blocs were locked in a political and ideological struggle, the language of human rights attained a new political force and meaning in intellectual and political debates. This new international and political dimension of the human rights discourse was never far from the minds of the *Free China* group.

The Free China Movement, launched with the founding of the magazine, was fiercely anticommunist in character. Its anticommunist stance was evident in the critique of communism in general and CCP rule in particular. The magazine criticized the CCP's dictatorial and nondemocratic rule, as well as its human rights violations. To oppose the Communists was important, but it was not the only goal of the magazine: the ultimate goal was a democratic society in which people enjoyed extensive political and economic rights and freedoms.[7] The fact that the CCP violated human rights was a strong reason why the *Free China* group opposed it.[8] The contributors to the magazine all agreed that democracy was the only political system that would protect the individual's human rights.[9] Communism and dictatorship, in contrast, they described as anathema to human rights.[10] Where democracies respected the existence of inalienable human rights, communism refuted them and instead only talked about citizens' rights (*gongmin quanli*), which, however, were a prerogative for those labeled "the people" (*renmin*), excluding class enemies and other political opponents.

Articles touching upon the subject of human rights and individual freedom appeared from the start in *Free China* but became more frequent after 1953–54. They included both theoretical and historical articles, as well as articles on more political and contemporary issues.[11] In 1958, the magazine celebrated the tenth anniversary of the UDHR by publishing a special issue devoted to the topic of human rights. Yin Haiguang contributed with an editorial, "Do You Want to Be a Human Being?" while another editorial focused on a critique of the CCP's human rights violations. Several articles in the issue gave historical overviews of the development of human rights thinking and the origin of the UDHR. It was pointed out that despite the promulgation of the UDHR, human rights violations continued unabated in many countries, such as South Africa and Indonesia, and that several Western countries also continued to violate human rights in their colonies.[12] Apart from criticizing the situation on the mainland, human rights violations in Taiwan were also brought up for discussion and criticism.[13] These violations included infringement of freedoms of speech, publication, association, and assembly. The fact that political opponents were arbitrarily questioned and arrested was also strongly criticized.

Yin Haiguang's thinking on human rights can be said to be fairly representative of the *Free China* group. Although Yin, in his pre-1949 articles, did not explicitly discuss human rights, he early on criticized the Communists for depriving people of their freedoms of speech, assembly, and association.[14] In his *Free China* articles Yin more explicitly and in greater detail advocated human rights. Yin described human rights as inherent (*guyou de*) in man and not given by the ruler or the state.[15] They were something different from and more general than citizens' rights, originating as they did in human nature. Yin's human rights thinking rested more on a humanitarian than a utilitarian evaluation of rights, even though traits of the latter were ever present. Human rights were necessary in order to be a person (*zuoren*) and to preserve one's humanity and dignity. To respect human rights was to "treat people as human beings" and not as things. It was not enough just to have the means to survive. For an existence worthy of a human being, and in order to live a truly meaningful life, a person's personality had to be respected and nurtured. To this end he needed to enjoy a wide range of civil and political freedoms. Human rights were said to serve as a guideline for how the state should treat people: they should be treated as human beings, not tools, and as ends, not means.[16] Others in the magazine likewise followed the tradition since the late Qing of defining human rights as necessary preconditions in order to realize one's humanity.[17] Zhang Foquan, for instance, wrote several lengthy articles on human rights in the magazine over the years, and in 1954 published the theoretically dense *Freedom and Human Rights*.[18] Zhang, who incidentally had been quite negative to rights talk in the 1930s, emerged as a strong advocate of human rights. He argued forcefully that human rights were inalienable and not bestowed by the state. He furthermore advocated the addition of a bill of rights to the 1946 constitution in order to strengthen the individual's rights against the state.

Discussions regarding the relationship between individual freedom and freedom of the nation appeared time and again in the magazine, with the authors defending the position that the latter would not be promoted by the sacrifice of the former.[19] All of the contributors to the magazine objected to the notion held by Sun Yat-sen and the GMD that individual freedom and human rights had to be sacrificed for the sake of the nation or in times of a national crisis.[20] The *Free China* group instead insisted that the nation was but a tool and that its purpose was the protection of people's freedoms.[21] The fact that the Chinese people in the past had put undue emphasis on the freedom of the nation to the neglect of the freedom of the individual was strongly criticized. Although the *Free China* group was fighting for national freedom, it realized that a free nation might not necessarily protect or respect people's freedom, and therefore emphasized that individual freedom should not be neglected in the struggle for national freedom.[22]

The individualism associated with human rights and hailed by the magazine was not associated with unbridled selfishness.[23] Although the individual constituted the basic unit in society and the state was obliged to respect his or her rights and freedoms, this did not mean that the individual was unconcerned about others; quite the opposite. Humans were social beings whose welfare and happiness were intertwined with and depended upon that of their fellow human beings. This social side of rights was further underlined by the strongly held belief that enjoyment of individual rights was beneficial to society as well. Although Yin Haiguang did not see rights simply as a tool or means for progress or any other national cause, he echoed Mill in the same way as other Chinese writers had done before him when arguing that freedom of thought was necessary for the progress of society.[24] Others also agreed that whereas freedom was necessary for the happiness of the individual and inherent in man's nature, it was in addition beneficial for the progress of society and for the stability of the regime.[25]

The contributors to the magazine mainly focused on civil and political rights. By human rights, Yin Haiguang thus understood freedom of thought, speech, publication, education, association, and religion.[26] Lei Zhen also mostly discussed freedom of belief, freedom of thought, and freedom of speech.[27] The contributors to *Free China* did not write much about economic rights, although they sometimes addressed issues regarding economic freedom and economic

equality.[28] The majority held that democracy and freedom were more important and prerequisites for economic equality.[29] If people lost their political freedoms, Yin Haiguang argued, they would become nothing but slaves and unable
to fight for economic equality.[30]

It is difficult to trace the intellectual and political ideas that shaped the human rights thinking of the *Free China* group. It is obvious, however, that they
all were well versed in Western political thought; numerous references to Western thinkers and Western history appear on the pages of *Free China*. Yin
Haiguang, for example, had been influenced by Fabianism and the British Idealists, such as Green. Green's ethical liberalism was appreciated by Yin, especially
his view of man as a moral agent and his insistence that the function of the
state was to help man perfect his moral character.[31] The *Free China* group, like
Chinese people in the 1930s, were very appreciative of the political thinking
of Laski. Yin Haiguang was also influenced by contemporary Western thinkers
such as Friedrich von Hayek and Karl Popper. On the issue of human rights
he acknowledged that he had been influenced by Zhang Foquan's book *Freedom and Human Rights*, while Zhang was influenced by a whole range of Western philosophers ranging from Locke and Paine to Green and Laski.[32] Zhang
was also quite familiar with the more contemporary human rights literature
and quoted both Eleanor Roosevelt and Maritain, among others.

The writers in the magazine didn't feel any need to seek inspiration and
support in the Chinese tradition but consciously built upon and continued the
May Fourth tradition. The May Fourth heritage of belief in democracy, human
rights, freedom, and science was very much alive and served as a source of inspiration for the *Free China* group.[33] Yin Haiguang believed with Hu Shi that
China should study the West, especially its ideas of democracy, human rights,
and science, and get rid of traditional thinking that was at odds with these
ideas. This unflattering view of the Chinese tradition earned Yin the criticism
of Xu Fuguan and others associated with *Minzhu pinglun* in Hong Kong. But
toward the end of his life, Yin became more interested in Chinese culture, like
Zhang Junmai and others before him, arguing that Chinese culture embraced
a spiritual aspect of life found lacking in the contemporary West. This new interest was perhaps at least partly an outcome of his disillusion and loneliness
during this period of his life. As they grow older many people often have a tendency to return to the religion or traditional values they vehemently rejected
and rebelled against when they were young, and Yin Haiguang might have followed the same kind of trajectory.

The contributors to *Free China* did not dwell on the relationship between
Chinese culture and human rights, nor does it seem that there were any serious doubts regarding their compatibility. As for the question of the origin of
the idea of human rights, Dongfang Jibai went so far as to proclaim that it was

hardly a relevant or interesting topic.[34] To trace its possible Confucian or Western roots was something that he felt could safely be left to a small number of
philosophers; the important thing instead was to give a detailed account of human rights and the various human rights declarations that had been proclaimed
over the centuries. Although several writers expressed critical views of the authoritarian Chinese culture in the spirit of the May Fourth tradition, this did
not shake their belief in the prospects for democracy and human rights in
China.[35]

This being said however, some authors would on occasion voice the opinion that although the idea of rights was foreign to the Chinese, the Chinese
tradition, as exemplified by notions of *ren* and *yi*, nevertheless contained a humanism akin to human rights thinking in the West.[36] Lei Zhen's critique of
communism and its human rights violations was to some extent based on the
fact that its emphasis on class struggle violated fundamental Chinese values,
such as *ren'ai* (kindheartedness), and therefore stood in opposition to human
nature (*renxing*).[37] He also argued that freedom of belief had been respected
throughout traditional China. Others, although not going so far back in the
past, tried to discover early Chinese advocates of human rights. Yin Haiguang,
somewhat surprisingly, mentioned Sun Yat-sen as an early adherent of the concept of human rights.[38] It is, of course, quite possible that such a reverence of
and reference to the Father of the Republic was more pro forma and a conscious attempt to try to legitimize their advocacy of human rights than a reflection of any genuine belief that Sun really had been an advocate of human
rights.

After the closure of *Free China* in 1960, many other liberal magazines and
journals appeared in Taiwan, such as the *Intellectual, Taiwan Political Review*,
and *Formosa*, but the trend steadily went from purely theoretical discussions
toward political activism and electoral campaigning.[39] Human rights demands nonetheless remained a prominent feature of many of these political
activities, and by the late 1970s human rights issues were brought out in the
open in a more pronounced and articulate way. This development was influenced by the fact that human rights had become an important international
issue, with West–East relations through the Helsinki Accords of 1975 and
with the human rights focus of the Carter administration's foreign policy. Political opponents in exile, for example, set up the first Taiwanese human rights
organization, the Formosa Association for Human Rights, in New York in
1976. Around the same time intellectuals again began to publish more academic articles on human rights.[40] In 1979, those behind the magazine *Formosa* then decided to use the occasion of the United Nations Human Rights
Day for a large-scale demonstration. Complete and reliable information on
the demonstration and the violence that erupted between demonstrators and

police is still lacking, but the incident, remembered as the Kaoshiung Incident, ended with the arrest of several of the organizers. Eight of them were later convicted and sentenced to long terms in prison.

In February 1979, the Chinese Association for Human Rights (CAHR) was set up with support from the GMD. The organization was created in the aftermath of the shock caused by the establishment of diplomatic relations between the United States and the PRC. The chairman of the organization, Hang Liwu, was a diplomat and former vice-minister of education, who was quite explicit on the motives behind the establishment of the organization.[41] The fact that human rights had become an important foreign policy goal of the American government convinced him and others that Taiwan, in order to get support from the American people and Congress, had to present itself as an advocate and defender of human rights vis-à-vis the PRC. As one of its tasks, the organization spread information about human rights violations on the mainland, although it also became involved in human rights work at home. Many works criticizing human rights violations on the mainland, however, had been published before that time, both by liberals and GMD people themselves. Another motive behind the establishment of the CAHR was the growing opposition to the GMD and the realization that political opponents had become more apt to use human rights language against the regime. The regime thus wanted to preempt the establishment of independent human rights organizations in Taiwan and itself take the initiative on the issue. People protesting the GMD were increasingly willing to refer to human rights, which became obvious with the Kaoshiung Incident on December 10 later that same year. But it was not until 1984, however, that an independent human rights organization, the Taiwan Association for Human Rights (TAHR), eventually was established in Taiwan.

It is also quite possible that the people behind the CAHR could have been inspired in part by developments on the mainland during the 1978–79 Democracy Wall Movement when human rights slogans, appeals to the outside world, and human rights organizations suddenly appeared. The GMD and various organizations and research institutes associated with it thus voiced their support of the mainland democracy activists and also collected and reprinted their work.[42] In any event, it seems as if more pragmatic considerations and a realization that human rights had become a global issue rather than pure human rights concerns motivated the establishment of the CAHR. (In this respect, then, there are some similarities with the official China Society for Human Rights Studies, set up on the mainland in the aftermath of 1989.) The more pro-independence TAHR, some members of which were involved in the Kaoshiung Incident, came to focus, not surprisingly, more on domestic human rights violations, criticizing the GMD for human rights violations and the CAHR for lending it support. The TAHR also at first had considerable difficulties in carrying out its work, leading a semi-underground existence until 1987; only in 1995 did it become officially registered.

It seems as if references to Chinese culture and attempts to ground human rights in traditional concepts have been more important to the CAHR than to the TAHR.[43] This can perhaps be explained by the former's official association and need to show that the Nationalists were the true heirs and defenders of Chinese culture. If Chinese traditional values were lost on Taiwan, the GMD's claim to rule the whole of China would also be weakened. As in the case of Zhang Junmai, the attempt to find support in tradition might also have been due to a need to show the United States that human rights and democracy were not foreign to the Chinese tradition and that the GMD furthermore was upholding these values. The GMD's invocation of Chinese culture served to legitimize its rule on Taiwan, whereas the pro-independence TAHR, as could be expected, did not have the same need to justify its demands for human rights by referring to Chinese culture, and in fact reacted against the GMD's imposing of tradition and slighting of Taiwan's indigenous culture and history.

For all of their differences, however, the TAHR, the CAHR (which is now largely free from direct control by the GMD), and many other more specialized organizations dealing with child welfare, rights of immigrants, labor rights, and so on, have all contributed to push Taiwan toward democracy during the 1980s and 1990s. The proliferation of civil organizations has been one important factor behind Taiwan's democratization. These organizations have served to promote freedom of speech and association, and also devoted themselves to more concrete human rights violations, such as imprisonment of political opponents, police brutality, and unfair trials, and so on. They have also worked to promote social and economic rights and defended the rights and interests of workers, aborigines, the handicapped, and other socially disadvantaged groups.

THE HUNDRED FLOWERS
MOVEMENT AND HUMAN RIGHTS

After the founding of the PRC, the language of human rights virtually disappeared from the domestic political debate on the mainland. The CCP held that the Chinese people's rights had finally been secured, and human rights could therefore, by definition, no longer constitute a legitimate demand on the government. "Human rights," furthermore, were now explicitly dismissed as a bourgeois slogan, lacking relevance to a socialist society. Instead the CCP used the language of citizen's right when stipulating freedoms of speech, belief, assembly, and association in the constitution, albeit restricting them to those belonging to the category of "the people."[44] Interestingly enough, the language of human rights briefly surfaced in 1957 during the Hundred Flowers Movement. The writings from this period mostly consist of short wall posters that do not elaborate on the more theoretical aspects of human rights, whereas those who wrote more lengthy articles in the official media calling for a strengthening of democracy within the party were careful to stay within the parameters of the official ideology and avoided the word "human rights." The official response, when it came, was harsh and uncompromising: the critics were labeled rightists and their views refuted as reactionary and antisocialist. In the official backlash, the rightists' beliefs in individualism, humanitarianism, and human rights were singled out for further criticism.

In May 1956, Mao Zedong laid down the policy of "letting a hundred flowers bloom" in the field of culture and "a hundred schools contend" in the field of science. This signified a more liberal policy with respect to the arts and the sciences, which revealed that the regime by then felt itself to be in control of the country. In early 1957, discussions within the political leadership concerned the suitability of encouraging nonparty people and members of the democratic parties to speak out in a campaign devoted to a rectification of the party. Toward late February 1957, as a result of his optimistic analysis of the political situation in the country, Mao began to push for a more open and tolerant policy toward nonparty people. In a speech to an enlarged session of China's Supreme State Conference on February 27, entitled "On the Correct Handling of Contradictions among the People," Mao laid down his views on the state of the nation. The speech was not published at the time, and when it finally was published in June, substantial revisions had been made.[45] In the original speech, which circulated among party members, Mao downplayed the threat posed by counterrevolutionaries and warned instead of the threat posed by dogmatists and leftists. The relationship between the working class led by the party and the bourgeoisie would from now on be characterized by unity, not struggle, Mao contended, whereas the relationship between the party and the democratic parties would be one of long-term coexistence and mutual supervision. He argued that the blooming and contending would yield more fragrant flowers, whereas the poisonous weeds would be few and far between, and hence rather harmless. By late April, Mao had managed to get sufficient support for a full rectification movement in which nonparty people were encouraged to speak out against the three evils within the party: bureaucratism, subjectivism, and sectarianism.

It took some prodding, but when people eventually began to speak out, the range and depth of their discontent took the authorities by surprise. During a few weeks in May of 1957, the period of political liberalization culminated with speeches, wall posters, and heated discussions on issues ranging from administrative problems and bureaucratism, to the paramountcy of the CCP in political affairs.[46] The critical views and widespread discontent voiced by different groups revealed that Mao had been overoptimistic in his analysis of the state of people's minds, which prompted the authorities to quickly move against the critics and put a halt to these outpourings. In the revised version of the February speech, which was published in *People's Daily* on June 18, the tone and content had been radically revised. Mao instead warned of revisionism and "right opportunism," which were said to pose a greater threat than those of dogmatism and leftism. The political thaw turned out to be brief, and by early June the so-called antirightist movement was under way. During this movement some 500,000 people were labeled rightists, expelled from their work units and in many cases also sent to labor camps; for some, eventual rehabilitation took more than twenty years. Members of the China Democratic League were among the most prominent victims of the campaign. Zhang Bojun and Luo Longji, two of its vice-chairmen, were accused of forming an alliance opposing socialism and aiming at the overthrow of the party; they have still not been rehabilitated.[47]

Many different groups of people, including workers, minorities, and intellectuals, took advantage of the opportunity to voice their views.[48] Their concerns sometimes differed, but all seem to have reacted to the heavy hand of the party in all aspects of their everyday lives. The intellectuals can be divided into older, liberal thinkers who had a history of speaking out for freedom of speech, such as Chu Anping, Fei Xiaotong, Wang Zaoshi, and Luo Longji, and younger students, such as Lin Xiling and Tan Tianrong. Members of the democratic parties and the older generation of intellectuals were generally quite cautious, whereas some students were often more vehement and direct in their critique, although they stopped short of criticizing socialism. The young students' attitude is interesting since their generation, after all, had come of age in the new society and received a socialist education. After the crackdown, the authorities tried to explain the rightists' "deviant" views by referring to their bad family background and past activities. It was thus charged that of the fifteen members of Peking University Hundred Flowers Society, eleven came from landlord, bureaucrat, and capitalist families.[49] It was also alleged that several of them earlier had been engaged in petty criminal activities. In the case of older intellectuals, their pre-1949 activities and articles were instead taken as proof of long-standing antisocialist views.[50]

Many people had at first been cautious and unresponsive to the party's invitation to criticize bureaucratism and other failures within the party and in society, since they doubted the policy and recalled earlier periods of political relaxation that had come to abrupt ends. It was only with open encouragement at various meetings that they finally began to pour out their pent-up criticism. Students at Peking University and other higher institutions of learning in Beijing led the way as they had done in the past.[51] The first big-character poster at Peking University appeared on May 19, on what became known as the Democracy Wall. Others followed suit and soon the campus was filled with posters and teemed with heated discussions. Tan Tianrong and other students from the department of physics established a Hundred Flowers Society, which published the magazine *Guangchang*.[52] Contacts between different universities and cities also took place. Lin Xiling, for example, who studied at People's University and became the most famous student victim of the antirightist campaign, gave several speeches at Peking University.

The rightists' critique touched upon many different issues.[53] Some pertained to systemic failures, such as the lack of democracy and rule of law, whereas others dealt more with the actual execution of specific policies and the heavy-handedness of certain cadres. Chu Anping's critique of the phenomenon that the "world belongs to the Party" is an example of a more fundamental critique directed at the party's monopoly of power. The fact that party decisions reigned supreme at the expense of legal institutions and the rule of law was also criticized. But many focused on issues closer to home. The intellectuals were particularly concerned about issues regarding the educational system and their professional work. For instance, they criticized the fact that academic learning and professional expertise was not respected enough in society, to the detriment of social and economic progress. They also resented the heavy-handedness of political cadres in educational work and felt themselves mistrusted and at the mercy of party committees. The privileged position of cadres and party members in terms of working and living conditions was also a sore point with many intellectuals and professionals.

The scattered references to human rights in wall posters, speeches, and articles make it impossible to provide a deeper analysis of the understanding of human rights during this period. But the fact that human rights were referred to at all is of some significance. It shows that the language of human rights was not completely forgotten but could still serve as a powerful weapon in political argument. The official reaction to this human rights talk is also quite revealing and indicates that the party was stung by the charge that it was violating human rights. Students at Wuhan University, for example, were later accused of having tried to mobilize people to fight for democracy, human rights (*renquan*), and liberty.[54] To those who made use of the idea of human rights, at least, human rights functioned on a par with other positively loaded words such as democracy and freedom.

The language of human rights was invoked both in connection with more general discussions on the constitution and the legal system and when criticizing past excesses committed during different political campaigns. Many of the writers referred to the stipulation of citizens' rights in the 1954 constitution and argued that these rights were in effect being violated. "The constitution of 1954 stipulates protection of the freedom of the person, and rights such as residence and correspondence, but since [its promulgation] the constitution has been ignored, and incidents of human rights [*renquan*] abuses increased. Among them are limiting the freedom of the person . . . opening of letters, illegal searches of homes . . . illegal detentions, incidents of hanging, beating and controlling people."[55] The student from Peking University who wrote this even called for a bill of human rights in order to protect people's rights and prevent human rights abuses. A student from Wuhan University agreed that the constitution had turned out to be worthless:

> During the campaign to suppress counterrevolutionaries [in 1955] the strange thing was that the constitution proved to be useless. People have no freedom of the person, [their] human rights [*renquan*] are not protected, and [their] dignity of the person is violated. The CCP members do not want any laws, they have nothing but class struggle in their heads. The fact that beatings, killings, and rape occur makes one think about peasant revolutions. We should establish a lawyer's system. Lawyers are a free profession which should not be influenced by any power; lawyers protect the law, human rights, and justice.[56]

The constitution, it was said, was supposed to protect people's human rights, but during the campaign for the suppression of counterrevolutionaries, people's freedom of speech and association as stipulated in the constitution had been grossly violated. People had been arbitrarily accused of "reactionary speech" and of forming "anti-Party organizations."[57]

> [O]ur constitution provides that "freedom of the person of citizens is inviolable." During the campaign for the elimination of counterrevolutionaries in 1955, an untold number of citizens throughout the country were detained by units where they were working. . . . A great many of them died because they could not endure the struggle. No matter how strong the "reasons" were for detaining these citizens to conduct struggles against them, this was, after all, a serious violation of human rights. . . . This is tyranny! This is malevolence![58]

Others criticized the fact that although the constitution stipulated freedom of speech, the press and radio stations were nevertheless controlled by the party.[59] Those voicing views differing from the party, it was charged, risked being labeled counterrevolutionaries and arrested. And whereas the constitution granted people freedom of assembly and association, no meetings could be held or organizations formed without prior approval by the party. As one poster from Tsinghua University put it: "Do we have freedom? We have freedom to shout 'long live.' We don't want the freedom to be wooden men any longer. . . . Give the people the freedom to shout 'long live,' but also give them real freedom to form assemblies and societies. Don't you feel ridiculous when you arrange the May Day parade? Those who fail to join in are regarded as being ideologically backward and it is even suggested that [participation] is a political duty."[60] This poster, one of the fiercest, also argued for the right to leave the country. Others mentioned the freedoms of residence and changing residence, pointing out that peasants in particular were deprived of this right.[61]

Mostly civil and political rights were invoked during the Hundred Flowers Movement. The Hundred Flowers Society at Peking University thus vowed to fight for freedom of the press, speech, publication, assembly, and association.[62] They wanted to abolish censorship of publications and allow private newspapers. Freedom of speech was a particularly treasured freedom.[63] The poet Ai Qing, one of the more prominent rightists, penned the following in defense of freedom of speech: "The constitution is perhaps more meaningful to the poet than to others. It is only with the freedom to speak as he pleases that the poet can transmit the people's will. Then progress is possible. The suppression of free speech is the most brutal of all forms of violence."[64]

Many posters criticized arrests of innocent people and other excesses committed during different political campaigns for serious violations of human rights. Luo Longji had suggested that a committee be set up to investigate injustices committed during the so-called "three-anti" and "five-anti" campaigns and the campaign for the suppression of counterrevolutionaries.[65] Many others also dwelt on this issue in their posters and speeches.[66] They argued that these campaigns had been overly harsh and led to the imprisonment of innocent people. The campaign for the suppression of counterrevolutionaries of 1955, in particular, was heavily criticized. Many argued that the authorities' estimate that counterrevolutionaries constituted 5 percent of the total population had led to the arbitrary labeling of people as counterrevolutionaries in order to meet this quota.[67] The case of Hu Feng, the literary critic who was denounced as a counterrevolutionary in 1955, received a lot of attention and many questioned the decision to label him a counterrevolutionary.[68] The critics demanded his release and the rehabilitation of all innocent people who had been wronged during different movements.[69] They also mentioned other earlier cases of trumped-up charges against innocent men, such as Wang Shiwei in the 1940s and Gao Gang and Rao Shushi in the early 1950s.[70] Some of those who criticized past injustices and the lack of freedom in China were painfully aware that they risked being arrested for doing so.[71]

The fact that those with power could escape sanctioning and had a license to commit all kinds of cruelties was strongly criticized. It was pointed out that whereas "an ordinary person who violated human rights, illegally questioned another person, supervised his movements, and deprived him of his freedom, would be subjected to the sanctioning of the law," political cadres who used the same methods and overstepped their duties would escape legal sanction.[72]

The responsibility for human rights violations was assigned to party officials and the comparisons made were not flattering. One professor from Hangzhou was bold enough to compare the persecution of Chinese intellectuals and others under Mao, not only to earlier Chinese tyrants such as Qin Shi Huangdi, but to the methods used by fascists in Auschwitz and by Stalin in the Soviet Union.[73] Others compared the human rights violations and arrests of people in the PRC to the brutality of the Nationalist regime.[74]

In early June, as mentioned above, the political leadership decided to crack down on the critics. The first indication of the political shift came with the publication of the editorial "What Is This For?" on June 8 in the *People's Daily*. A flurry of statements and articles then followed in the official media with denunciations of those who had criticized the party.[75] Political meetings were called at which these people were publicly criticized and forced to make self-criticisms. Those who were labeled rightists lost their positions and were in many cases also sent to labor camps. Three student leaders in Wuhan who were accused of having led a riot were executed. The main critique of the rightists was that they had opposed the party and the socialist system and wanted to restore capitalism in China. Their advocacy of democracy and rule of law was dismissed as bourgeois and reactionary. The official media also accused the rightists for giving vent to individualism (*geren zhuyi*) and criticized their demands for a free development of people's personalities (*gexing*). They also took some pains to dismiss and reject the concept of human rights and its corollary, humanitarianism (*rendao zhuyi*). Liu Binyan was held up as an example of a rightist who had advocated human rights. He was accused of having mentioned human rights at a forum arranged by the People's Broadcasting Station in Shanghai in 1956. He had allegedly said that after the "three-anti" movement, and in particular during the 1955 campaign for the suppression of counterrevolutionaries, human rights (*renquan*) had been violated and people's dignity (*ren de zunyan*) offended.[76]

In the authorities' attack on human rights, individualism, and humanitarianism, they first of all rejected the idea of a classless human nature.[77] It was argued that people in a class society inevitably would have a class nature and that all talk about a general human nature was empty and false. The rightists' view that human nature was universal in character and transcended class was strongly refuted, as was their belief that humanitarianism was untainted by class feelings. Since people's standpoints in a class society reflect their class position, it was pointed out that those advocating human rights inevitably only had their own bourgeois rights and interests at heart.

[H]umans are marked by class. In a class society, because of people's class position, the interests they represent are different, and so is their thinking, feelings and opinions. People will always have different positions and will protect and struggle for the interests, rights and dignity of their own class. It seems as if the rightists are struggling for the human rights and dignity of all people, but this is in reality deceiving themselves as well as others. In a class society, human dignity, too, is unequal. If there is human dignity of the exploiting class, then there is no dignity of the exploited classes.[78]

The rightists' calls for human rights and human dignity, it was argued, were thus nothing but a sham and a disguise for promulgating the rights of the bourgeoisie, while the CCP claimed to have the interest of all workers and peasants at heart.[79] The party also reacted to charges that it was suppressing people's personalities (*gexing*) through stifling their freedom.[80] To this charge it was retorted that by abolishing the system of the capitalists' exploitation of the proletariat, the party had actually defended and liberated people from suppression. The rightists' calls for the "liberation of the personality," in contrast, was described as a bourgeois ideal that only had the individual in focus and didn't have the interests of the majority at heart.

CONCLUSION

It is not surprising that human rights language stood a greater chance to survive in Taiwan after 1949. The Nationalists, after all, had embraced human rights work in the United Nations and proclaimed themselves to belong to the Free World. This fact was skillfully used, first in the 1950s and then again toward the end of the 1970s, by political opponents who tried to shame and challenge the regime by using the human rights critique against it. At first this mostly manifested itself in the writing of political essays, but later it translated into the establishment of human rights organizations and more concrete human rights work. This development partly reflected the fact that people on Taiwan had much closer contacts with the West and also were more influenced by the globalization of human rights work. Although human rights violations and political imprisonment in Taiwan for political and strategic reasons did not receive much attention from the West during the Cold War, human rights ideas and activism could nonetheless exist and feed on international developments in the human rights field. Still, the very fact that demands for human rights were also raised in the PRC during the 1950s reveals that even in a more hostile environment, and despite being cut off from international human rights work, Chinese people, by their own accord, would raise the issue of human rights. Toward the end of the 1970s, under the influence of domestic political developments and the policy of opening up to the outside world, human rights discussions would resurface on the mainland and gain a new lease on life.

NOTES

1. Zhu Wenbo (1958), p. 19.
2. For general discussions on the magazine and its main contributors, Hu Shi, Lei Zhen, and Yin Haiguang, see Zhang Zhongdong (1990) and Fu Zheng (1992).
3. For a comparison between the two magazines, see Zhang Zhongdong (1990), pp. 213–18. Lei Zhen studied law in Japan and Yin Haiguang studied philosophy at the Southwestern United University in China. On Lei Zhen's political views, see Zhang Zhongdong (1990) and Li Hongxi (1992). On Yin Haiguang's political thinking, see Qian Yongxiang (1990), Lin Yusheng (1990), and Weng Songran (1990).
4. For Taiwan's development towards democracy, see Chao and Myers (1998).
5. Yin Haiguang (1990), vol. 12, p. 761, translated in Angle and Svensson, (2001), pp. 237–38.
6. Yin Haiguang believed that one should attack the Communists at their Achilles heel, that is, their human rights violations; Yin Haiguang (1990), vol. 12, p. 758. Hu Shi argued that if Taiwan struggled for democracy and freedom, its status and support in the world would increase, while Jin Chengyi (1958), p. 28, argued that the same applied to the struggle for human rights.
7. Hu Shi's declaration of the aims of the magazine was reprinted in every issue.
8. See, for example, the editorials in *Ziyou Zhonguo* (1949–1960), vol. 9, no. 9, p. 3, and vol. 10, no. 3, p. 2.
9. Li Jun (1958), p. 22.
10. See, for example, Li Zhongzhi (1951), pp. 13–14.
11. For an article discussing the historical origin of human rights thinking from the Magna Carta onward, see Li Xianglin (1953). And for an article discussing human rights problems in Taiwan, see Cheng Shewo (1954).
12. Zhu Wenbo (1958), p. 17.
13. Zhu Wenbo (1958), p. 17; Wang Jianbang (1958), pp. 24–26; and Yin Haiguang (1990), vol. 2, pp. 759–60.
14. Yin Haiguang (1990), vol. 11, p. 27, see also p. 155.
15. For his most thorough essay on human rights, see Yin Haiguang (1990), vol. 12, pp. 749–62.
16. Fu Zheng (1956).
17. See, for example, the editorials in *Ziyou Zhonguo* (1949–1960), vol. 9, no. 9, p. 3, and vol. 10, no. 3, p. 2; and Long Yi'e (1954), Zeng Xubai (1950), and Xu Guansan (1951).
18. Zhang Foquan (1954).
19. Apart from other texts referred to above, see Luo Hongzhao (1952).
20. Yin Haiguang (1990), vol. 12, p. 761; Li Zhongzhi (1951); and Long Yi'e (1954).
21. See, for example, Xu Guansan (1950), p. 13; Fu Zheng (1992), pp. 359–62; and Yin Haiguang (1990), vol. 11, pp. 397–404.
22. See for example, Xu Guansan (1950), p. 13; and the editorials in *Ziyou Zhonguo* (1949–1960), vol. 9, no. 9, and vol. 10, no. 3.
23. See Li Zhongzhi (1951) and articles cited in the following endnotes.
24. Yin Haiguang (1990), vol. 11, p. 14. One of his arguments for upholding freedom even in times of war was that freedom of speech and academic freedom would be beneficial to the war effort; see also p. 160.

25. Zhang Jinjian (1950).
26. See inter alia Yin Haiguang (1990), vol. 11, pp. 360–61, p. 436, and vol. 12, pp. 749–72.
27. Lei Zhen (1949), p. 11. See also Lei Zhen and Yin Haiguang (1951) on freedom of speech.
28. Some did, however, write more positively on economic rights and economic equality; see Fu Sinian (1949) and Zeng Xubai (1950).
29. Before the launching of the magazine, several of the authors had expressed more of an interest in the issue of economic equality. See, for example, Yin Haiguang (1990), vol. 11, p. 6.
30. Yin Haiguang (1990), vol. 11, p. 211.
31. Yin Haiguang (1990), vol. 11, pp. 200–201.
32. Zhang Foquan (1954), p. 81, p. 107 nn. 21 and 22. It is interesting to note that he earlier had expressed some criticism of Laski's emphasis on rights. See chapter 7 of this book.
33. See Anon., "We Should Implement the Spirit of May Fourth," (1955), p. 3.
34. Dongfang Jibai (1955), p. 28.
35. Xu Guansan (1951).
36. Hu Qiuyuan (1958), p. 15.
37. Lei Zhen (1949), p. 11.
38. Yin Haiguan (1990), vol. 12, p. 754.
39. On these developments, see Chiou (1995) and Chao and Myers (1998).
40. Huang (1976), reprinted in Angle and Svensson (2001).
41. See Hang (1980), pp. 140–41.
42. The Institute for the Study of Chinese Communist Problems published all mainland underground journals it could obtain in a twenty-volume collection, *A Collection of Underground Publications Circulated on the Chinese Mainland*, abbreviated in the following notes as DLDX.
43. See, for example, Hang Liwu (1982) and, in general, the volume published by the *Zhongguo renquan xiehui* (CAHR) in which this article appears. Hang's article is translated in Angle and Svensson (2001).
44. On the constitutional protection of rights, see Edwards (1986) and Nathan (1986b).
45. For a discussion and comparison between Mao's speech and the revised text, see Schoenhals (1986).
46. On the Hundred Flowers and the subsequent antirightist campaign, see MacFarquhar (1960) and (1974), Doolin (1964), Teiwes (1993), and Zhu Zheng (1998). Of late there has been a formidable output of works on the antirightist movement in China, ranging from autobiographical and historical, to compilations of source materials and accounts of the rehabilitation process.
47. On the alliance as a brainchild of Mao, see MacFarquhar (1974), p. 280.
48. Unfortunately, I have not been able to explore their different perspectives and possibly quite different concerns and priorities.
49. See RMRB, July 24, 1957, reprinted in MacFarquhar (1960), p. 137.
50. For an example of such accusations directed against Luo, see MacFarquhar (1960), pp. 289–91.
51. On the movement at Peking University, see Goldman (1962).
52. Articles from the magazine and other writings by rightists such as Tan Tianrong have been published in a three-volume work edited by Niu Han and Deng Jiuping (1998).
53. The rightists' views can be gathered from collections translated and edited by MacFarquhar (1960) and Doolin (1964). For materials in Chinese, see Niu Han and Deng Jiup-

ing (1998), as well as newspapers and booklets published at the time, for example, GDXXYB (1958) and YPYLXJ (1957).

54. Reported in RMRB, August 17, 1957, reprinted in MacFarquhar (1960), p. 145. See also YPYLXJ (1957), p. 59.

55. He Shifen, reprinted in GDXXYB (1958), p. 91.

56. Student quoted in YPYLXJ (1957), vol. 2, pp. 89–90.

57. See Chen Aiwen, reprinted in Niu Han and Deng Jiuping (1998), pp. 100–2; and Zhang Yidun, in Niu Han and Deng Jiuping (1998), p. 121.

58. Reprinted in MacFarquhar (1960), p. 94.

59. See, for example, the views of one student from Beijing Normal University, reprinted in Doolin (1964), p. 49.

60. Poster from Tsinghua University, reprinted in Doolin (1964), pp. 65–66.

61. See the ten-thousand-word letter written by a professor from Hangzhou and sent to Mao. Reprinted in MacFarquhar (1960), pp. 94–96.

62. Mentioned in RMRB, July 24, 1957, reprinted in MacFarquhar (1960), p. 138.

63. See, for example, Yan Wenjie, reprinted in MacFarquhar (1960), pp. 218–19.

64. Ai Qing, "The Spirit of Poetry," translated in Nieh (1981), vol. 2, pp. 63–64.

65. MacFarquhar (1960), pp. 48–49, and (1974), pp. 271–73. The 1950s saw several campaigns, beginning with the three-anti movement in 1951 against corruption, waste, and bureaucratism and the five-anti movement in 1952 directed against bribery, tax evasion, theft of state property, cheating on government contracts, and stealing economic information. Whereas the target of the three-anti movement was government and party officials, the second campaign was directed against businessmen and entrepreneurs. In 1953, a new three-anti movement was launched. A campaign against counterrevolutionaries was carried out from 1950 to 1953, and in 1955 another campaign to eliminate counterrevolutionaries began.

66. See also Chen Xingui of the Democratic League, reprinted in MacFarquhar (1960), p. 223.

67. See professors from Shenyang Normal College, reprinted in MacFarquhar (1960), p. 105; and Jiang Wen reprinted in Niu Han and Deng Jiuping (1998), pp. 103–4.

68. Hu Feng was mentioned by Lin Xiling; see Doolin (1964), pp. 23–29, pp. 38–39, and in a big-character poster written by Luo Lan at Tsinghua University, "The Public Trial of Hu Feng," reprinted in pp. 52–55. See also Liu Qidi "Hu Feng Is Absolutely Not a Counterrevolutionary," reprinted in Niu Han and Deng Jiuping (1998), pp. 113–14.

69. See professor Zhong Yiqun, reprinted in MacFarquhar (1960), p. 111.

70. See a Tsinghua University big-character poster, reprinted in Doolin (1964), pp. 63–65.

71. See Lin Xiling, reprinted in Doolin (1964), p. 28, and a character poster from Tsinghua University reprinted on p. 65.

72. SC, reprinted in Niu Han and Deng Jiuping (1998), p. 190.

73. Reprinted in MacFarquhar (1960), p. 95.

74. Zhou Dajue, reprinted in Niu Han and Deng Jiuping (1998), p. 168.

75. For a selection in English, see MacFarquhar (1960), pp. 277–91.

76. This is reported by Zuo Ai (1957) in *Qingnian bao* in August 1957, and also mentioned in an article in RMRB, July 20, 1957, which is reprinted in MacFarquhar (1960), pp. 73–74. When I asked Liu if he had used the words human rights, he denied this. Be that as it may, the interesting point here is that rightists such as Liu Binyan could be accused of using the words human rights and this was considered to be a powerful and serious accusation.

77. Zhang Size, "The Counterrevolutionary Idea of Human Nature," *Jiefang ribao*, September 13, 1957, reprinted in FYPLWXJ (1957).

78. Zuo Ai, "On Human Dignity," *Zhongguo qingnian bao*, August 18, 1957, reprinted in FYPLWXJ (1957), p. 69.

79. On human rights only being the rights of a small majority in a society characterized by exploitation; see also Zhang Size, "Counterrevolutionary Idea," p. 67.

80. On ideas of *gexing*, see Qun Fang, "Also Discussing the Development of Personality," *Zhongguo qingnian bao*, September 2, 1957, reprinted in FYPLWXJ (1957). See also Li Zheren, "Take a Firm Position in the Struggle against the Rightists," RMRB, September 8, 1957, and Yang Dongchun, "What Kind of Thing Is Liberalism," RMRB, August 4, 1957.

Chapter Ten

The Domestic Challenge over Human Rights: The Democracy Wall Activists and the Official Reaction, 1978–1982

RADICAL RHETORIC, INTERNATIONAL CONFRONTATIONS, AND DOMESTIC POLICY CHANGES

Human rights had no place in the revolutionary ideology of Mao Zedong, although occasional references to human rights were made in the struggle against the Japanese and the Nationalists in the 1940s. In 1965, Mao even ridiculed the concept of human rights. Playing with words, he claimed that all rights originated, not from heaven, but from the people who had bestowed them upon the party.[1] But the term human rights could nonetheless appear in rather surprising contexts during this period. At the height of the Cultural Revolution in 1968, for example, the Yunnan Provincial Revolutionary Committee, reacting to the turmoil and violence in the province, issued a document that forbade arrests, beatings, and violation of people's human rights (*renquan*).[2] Be that as it may, when human rights was mentioned at all after 1949, they were generally dismissed as a bourgeois slogan, as the following quote from Qian Si in 1960 makes clear:

[T]he "human rights" referred to by bourgeois international law and the "human rights" it intends to protect are the rights of the bourgeoisie to enslave and to oppress the labouring people, that is to say, the human rights of the bourgeoisie. Internally, they are used to conceal the encroachment upon rights and freedoms of the labouring people by the bourgeoisie; externally, they provide pretexts for imperialist opposition to socialist and nationalist countries. They are reactionary from head to toe.[3]

Western criticism of human rights violations in other countries was thus denounced as an expression of imperialist aggression. In 1959, the Chinese crushed a rebellion in Tibet, which led to the Dalai Lama's flight to India. When the

United Nations debated the issue, the PRC criticized this as an interference in its internal affairs.[4] But despite its own rejection of human rights as a bourgeois slogan, the PRC would not hesitate at times to proclaim itself to be the true defender of human rights. For instance, it referred to the dismal human rights situation in Tibet before 1951 and declared that it was actually defending the human rights of the Tibetan people. It was the "reactionary elements of the Tibetan upper class," it argued, who had "deprived the Tibetan people of their fundamental human rights and freedoms."[5]

Although human rights was taboo in the domestic discourse, it could nonetheless be referred to and endorsed in foreign policy statements when defending the PRC's own policies and criticizing the West.[6] The PRC thus at times criticized other countries, in particular the Soviet Union and the United States, for violating human rights.[7] This seemingly contradictory position of refuting some human rights concerns as constituting an interference in internal affairs while defending others as legitimate was justified by claiming that "acts of suppressing national movements basically are not a question of a state's internal affairs."[8] The PRC's early human rights rhetoric was related and subordinated to the struggle against imperialism and colonialism and voiced in support of the struggle for national self-determination. It is interesting to note that many of the arguments on human rights in the early 1960s continue to have a prominent place in contemporary human rights rhetoric.

During the 1960s and early 1970s, human rights did not figure in the domestic critique of the regime and the political system. This critique was dressed in a different language, more in tune with the radical rhetoric of the time. Yu Luoke's call for equality at the height of the Cultural Revolution is a good case in point.[9] Yu Luoke reacted against the fact that a person's class status determined his whole future. Those born into a capitalist or landlord family, for example, would come under a cloud of suspicion no matter what their own political views and revolutionary activities. Yu argued that this kind of political and social discrimination violated the principle of equality. All people should enjoy the same rights with respect to education, work, and social and political treatment.[10] Yu advocated an equality of opportunities that would enable children of class enemies to prove their revolutionary fervor. A person's character and political credentials should be decided "not by his birth status, nature, or age, but by his behaviour and whether he was holding high the Red Flag of Mao Zedong Thought."[11] What Yu was advocating was the right of all, regardless of family and class background, to take part in the revolutionary struggle, but it should be noted, not the right to express dissenting views or criticize socialism. Yu does not seem to have questioned the policy that class enemies— those who questioned socialism—should be deprived of their social and political rights. He was simply urging that their children should not suffer from guilt by association. But, at this time, to advocate that the children of class enemies should be able to take part in the revolution was overstepping the acceptable and proved too much to stomach for the regime. After a brief period of a certain fame, Yu was arrested and subsequently sentenced to death; he was executed in March 1970.

Although many who criticized government policies shared the fate of Yu Luoke, others, who went even further in their critique, were spared his end. The most outspoken group, or at least the one that received the most attention in the early 1970s, was the so-called Li Yizhe group, which was brought to public attention through its 1974 wall poster.[12] The group was composed of four people, three of whom contributed a character of their names to form the name Li Yizhe. Li Zhengtian and Wang Xizhe were the most prominent and outspoken of the group, but were later to part ways. Li tried to work within the system and Wang became caught up in the democracy movement of 1978–79. The group consisted of former Red Guards who had become disillusioned with the abuses during the Cultural Revolution and therefore advocated democracy and the development of a socialist legal system. Among other things, they criticized the development of a new class of "red capitalists" who had willfully abrogated their own privileges and denied the masses their right to manage the affairs of the state. The latter right, according to the group, was the most fundamental. They argued that in order to create a true democratic system, people should enjoy the freedoms of speech, press, and association. "The people want democracy; they demand a socialist legal system; and they demand the revolutionary rights and personal rights [*renshen quanli*], which protect the masses of the people."[13] The Li Yizhe group's political outlook and theoretical framework was safely within the folds of Marxism; they believed in socialism and analyzed rights from a class perspective. There was no explicit use of the language of human rights in their writings, and it is highly doubtful whether they believed in absolute freedoms or rights for all, including class enemies. The Li Yizhe group thus had more in common with other earlier socialist critics, such as Yu Luoke, than with many of the later democracy activists.[14]

By the late 1970s, several developments in the PRC served to break the silence on human rights and to bring about a small change in the hitherto negative view. When the PRC became a member of the United Nations in 1971, it also had to become more involved in the organization's work, including human rights work, although its approach at first was hesitant and cautious.[15] By the late 1970s, the international community also finally started to discuss the Chinese human rights record, as information on the horrors of the Cultural Revolution and reports on the democracy activists' views and publications reached the West.[16] This foreign interest and reporting was then relayed to China and contributed to and further spurred both the unofficial and the official debates on human rights.

The new interest in human rights in the PRC, however, was above all due to domestic developments. The death of Mao Zedong and the fall of the Gang of Four and, as a result of these events, the rehabilitation of victims from earlier political campaigns, contributed to a new interest in rebuilding the legal system that had been destroyed during the Cultural Revolution. A new constitution was adopted in 1978 that, on paper at least, guaranteed freedoms of speech, correspondence, and the press, as well as the freedom to demonstrate and strike, and the four great freedoms of speaking out freely, airing one's views fully, holding great debates, and writing big-character posters. Work on a criminal code, which had been interrupted in the 1950s, was also restarted; a criminal code was then promulgated in 1979. Inspired by these developments, a group of young people, today collectively known as Democracy Wall activists, began to raise the issue of human rights in wall posters and magazines in late 1978.[17] This domestic challenge over human rights prompted official China to also tentatively begin to discuss human rights in the national media.

THE DEMOCRACY WALL MOVEMENT

The new, more relaxed and optimistic political atmosphere during the autumn of 1978, which was to culminate with the Third Plenum of the Eleventh Party Congress in December of that year, inspired and encouraged a group of young people. In November 1978 they began to gather at a wall in Xidan, not far from the political center of Tiananmen and Zhongnanhai, to put up big-character posters and debate the political issues of the day. The posters had a wide and varying content, ranging from accounts of personal grievances and persecutions to more general demands for democracy, law and order, and respect for human rights. Their style also varied from passionate and impromptu writings to more elaborate theoretical analyses, from poetry to highly political pieces. Avid readers copied and circulated these posters, which in this way reached a wider readership than would otherwise have been the case, and soon the writers also began to organize themselves and publish their own magazines.[18]

Despite their sometimes divergent views, the democracy activists can be described as a rather homogeneous group. They were mostly young men in their late twenties and early thirties who had come of age during the Cultural Revolution and been shaped by their experiences during that period. Through their experiences, youth, and lack of formal education, they were effectively separated from, and mostly ignored and rejected by, those intellectuals who began to be rehabilitated and restored to their positions in 1978. The older intellectuals were much more circumspect and eager to be entrusted at long last to work within the system.[19] The fact that established intellectuals and professionals did not take part in the democracy movement sets it apart from dissent movements in other socialist countries, such as the Soviet Union and Czechoslovakia, where establishment intellectuals played an important role in various human rights organizations and movements. The democracy activists, although drawing slightly different lessons from the Cultural Revolution, were motivated by the abuse of power, lawlessness, persecution, and poverty they had witnessed during that period. The majority of them had started out as fervent believers in Mao and the party and had thrown themselves heart and soul into the Cultural Revolution, only to come out disillusioned and bruised by the experience. For those like Wei Jingsheng, who had traveled widely in the country, the abject poverty in the countryside came as something of a shock and turned their political worldview upside down.[20] Whereas Wei, as a result of these experiences, turned his back on socialism, the majority of the other activists retained their faith in Marxism. It was thus generally from a Marxist point of view that they criticized the political system. In many respects, then, their critique of the Gang of Four, past power abuses, and lack of democracy and rule of law were shared by the new political leadership, which is one reason the democracy movement was not immediately attacked and suppressed.

Though the Democracy Wall movement originated in Beijing, the first unofficial journal, *Qimeng* (*Enlightenment*), interestingly enough, was published in Guiyang in October 1978. The magazine was put out by the Enlightenment Society, two prominent members of which were the poets Li Jiahua and Huang Xiang. Among the more well-known journals discussing political issues apart from *Enlightenment*, mention should be made of *Zhongguo renquan* (*China Human Rights*), put out by the China Human Rights League headed by Ren Wanding; *Tansuo* (*Exploration*), published by Wei Jingsheng; and *Siwu luntan* (*April Fifth Forum*), with Liu Qing and Xu Wenli as editors. The first three magazines were considerably more radical than *April Fifth Forum* and many of the others. They spoke more strongly in support of human rights and democracy, whereas some of the others were more in accord with the official view and supported the leadership in their reform efforts. Except for *Enlightenment*, all of these magazines were published in Beijing. Beijing was home to at least 55 different Democracy Wall periodicals, while at least another 127 periodicals were published in other parts of the country.[21]

Wei Jingsheng was a rather lonely voice among the Democracy Wall activists in his all-out critique of communism and the party. On March 25, 1979, when Wei published the article "What Do We Want: Democracy or a New Dictatorship?" criticizing Deng Xiaoping, many felt that he had gone too far.[22] *April Fifth Forum* even published an article disputing his critique of Deng.[23] But when Wei was arrested later the same month, *April Fifth Forum* and the other magazines rushed to his defense. Wei's article was written in response to Deng

Xiaoping's critique of the democracy movement. In a speech on March 16 Deng put forward the so-called Four Cardinal Principles according to which all speech and publications should uphold the socialist road, the people's democratic dictatorship, the CCP's leading role, and Marxism-Leninism-Mao Zedong Thought. In this speech Deng also voiced a sharp critique of the Democracy Wall movement's focus on human rights and its use of slogans such as "Oppose Hunger" and "We Want Human Rights." As Deng put it:

> A so-called "China Human Rights Group" has put up a big-character poster urging the U.S. President to "show concern" for human rights in China. Can we tolerate such behaviour which openly calls for foreign intervention in China's internal affairs? A so-called "Thaw Society" has put out a declaration which openly opposes the dictatorship of the proletariat and says this is dividing humankind. Can we tolerate such an open violation of the principle of "freedom of speech" in the constitution?[24]

During the spring, the government gradually curbed the freedom to publish wall posters and arrested several of the more vocal democracy activists. And in November, Wei Jingsheng was put on trial and sentenced to fifteen years imprisonment on charges of counterrevolutionary activities and leaking military secrets to foreigners.[25] These developments did not completely deter others from continuing to publish journals and protest the arrests of their fellow activists. Toward the end of 1979 and in early 1980, many of the journals had been forced to close but others still managed to appear, albeit irregularly. In early 1980, the four great freedoms of speaking out freely, airing one's views fully, holding great debates, and writing big-character posters were deleted from the constitution, further restricting and undermining freedom of speech and publication. The democracy activists had initially been useful for Deng Xiaoping in his attempts to consolidate his power base and push ahead with reforms, but when the increasing boldness and far-ranging scope of some of the critique began to become more of a liability and threaten these reform efforts, Deng did not hesitate to move decisively against the democracy activists.

THE DEMOCRACY WALL ACTIVISTS ON HUMAN RIGHTS

The Democracy Wall activists' concern about human rights was motivated by their personal sufferings during the Cultural Revolution and the general lawlessness of that period. The political developments under way since the fall of the Gang of Four encouraged them to address the issue of human rights and demand their constitutional rights. Nonetheless, the resurfacing of human rights in the political discourse is a bit surprising given the fact that the young democracy activists had been brought up in New China where the idea of human rights was taboo and did not figure in textbooks or in political discourse. The democracy activists were also generally unaware of earlier Chinese generations' discussions on human rights. They, for example, did not know about the scattered writings on human rights that appeared in 1957; in 1978–79 many of the rightists were still in the process of being rehabilitated and were not in touch with the democracy activists. But some democracy activists seem to have been at least vaguely aware of and inspired by earlier calls for human rights. The China Human Rights League, established in 1979, for example, seems to have been partly inspired by the China League for the Protection of Civil Rights of the early 1930s.[26]

Although demands for human rights sprung from specific Chinese problems, in particular the experiences of the Cultural Revolution, they were also in part, or at least for some, inspired by foreign sources and discussions on human rights. The democracy activists thus made frequent references to the French Declaration of the Rights of Man and to the UDHR.[27] Also, through their contacts with foreign journalists who increasingly began to be based in China, they became aware of the work of international human rights organizations, such as Amnesty International. The democracy activists do not seem to have been overly preoccupied with or influenced by traditional Chinese culture in their writings, which is not surprising given the fact that they had grown up exposed to the Communists' attacks on it. They were more attracted to and interested in the West. Some, like earlier Chinese generations, described the West in glowing and widely exaggerated terms as a model of civilization and democracy. China had to learn from the West, they argued, not only in science and technology as the political leadership advocated, but in political ideas such as democracy and human rights.[28] As those of past generations, such as Zou Rong and Chen Duxiu, the democracy activists believed that the ideas of the democratic West could help liberate China from authoritarianism and dictatorship.

> Although the sun of democracy and human rights has risen, we in China can still barely see the light. While most of mankind has already awakened from the bad dream of superstition and dictatorship, we are still sound asleep and suffering nightmares. . . . Today we stand behind the Great Wall looking toward the other side of the sea. We see the blue ocean and a mast that brings peace and friendship. Now it sails with culture and science toward the ancient civilisation of the Orient. With nervous excitement we wait behind the Great Wall and think: "Should we bravely break out of the Great Wall and welcome change, or should we remain dead in our tracks just looking around?". . .This is the demarcation of darkness and dawn. Those who fear brightness and calm can retreat into darkness. Those who welcome the arrival of new days can rush forward in big strides toward the light.[29]

The China Human Rights League, as can be inferred from its name, took a particularly strong interest in the issue of human rights. The organization was established in order to promote the cause of human rights, and its magazine published many articles on the topic. For example, it published a declaration of human rights that included a comprehensive list of nineteen different rights.[30] *Exploration* also carried many articles devoted to the topic of human rights, including Wei's own "Human Rights, Equality and Democracy." The magazine also published some articles that exposed concrete human rights violations, including an exposé of Qincheng No. 1 prison where many high-profile political dissidents had languished in the past, and where Wei Jingsheng himself later was to be incarcerated.[31] It also published an excerpt of Amnesty International's 1978 report on China.[32] The Enlightenment Society took a strong interest in human rights, as witnessed by an open letter to President Carter on the matter. References to human rights also appeared in many of the more literary works published in these magazines, such as short stories and poems; the China Human Rights League even composed a song about human rights.[33]

The democracy activists did not share the official negative view on human rights, but neither were they unanimous in their views nor uncritical of the concept itself. Some were closer to the official position and criticized what they considered to be the extreme views on human rights put forward by the China Human Rights League and the Enlightenment Society. Those advocating human rights were always quick to point out that it was not an exclusively bourgeois idea.[34] They described human rights as a progressive idea and insisted that all oppressed people could make use of it in their struggles for democracy and freedom.[35] In this sense human rights was defended as a universal ideal. There were, however, those who were troubled by the alleged Western overtones of the concept of human rights and felt that by using such a term, they would lay themselves open to attacks by the authorities. They preferred instead to talk about citizen's rights (*gongmin quanli*). Considerations such as these informed Xu Wenli's decision in 1980 to talk about citizen's rights rather than human rights. "The question of human rights is very sensitive to China, so that when vice-premier Deng Xiaoping visited the U.S. he refused to discuss it. For the moment, when China is entering the 1980s, the most that China can take when it comes to protection of human rights is the wording of protection of citizens' rights. . . . Some of us therefore believe that [to refer to the idea of] human rights makes it seem as if one is under the control of Carter."[36] Xu Wenli believed, however, that there were no real differences between citizens' rights and human rights; it was only the latter's problematic connotation in China that made him choose the former words.

Others, such as Wei Jingsheng and Ren Wanding, were not so circumspect and did not shy away from using the term human rights. Nor did they worry overly about being associated with the West or President Carter. Several open letters in fact were composed asking foreigners to pay closer attention to the human rights situation in China. The first such letter was written in March 1977. The writer, a Shanghai intellectual, appealed to President Carter to not forget the suffering of the Chinese people and to support them with the same commitment that he had shown Soviet human rights activists. The poet Huang Xiang, writing under a pen name, wrote a similar letter to Carter in December 1978, which was pasted on the Democracy Wall.[37] But some other Democracy Wall magazines, such as *April Fifth Forum*, agreed with Deng Xiaoping and strongly criticized sending letters to foreigners as unpatriotic.[38]

With the arrests of Wei Jingsheng, Ren Wanding, and Fu Yuehua in the spring of 1979, and Deng's explicit critique of human rights appeals, the concept of human rights seems to have lost some of its attraction and become more of a liability to the democracy movement. Instead, it was the cautious approach of Xu Wenli and others that came to prevail, and talk of people's rights, citizens' rights, and constitutional rights replaced human rights talk.[39] Citizens' rights were not spoken of as inherent, but neither were they regarded as bestowed on the people by the state or the rulers; they were regarded as something won and secured in the constitution by the people themselves. The preference for the language of citizens' rights did not imply a weaker defense of rights, as it was repeatedly argued that these rights could not be interfered with by any individual or organization. Many individual cases, such as the arrests of Fu Yuehua, Wei Jingsheng, Ren Wanding, and Liu Qing were also taken up and criticized in these magazines. They criticized the legal grounds for these arrests and demanded protection of people's legal and constitutional rights.

The Democracy Wall activists who advocated and used the term human rights described them as inherent in human nature. Human rights were demanded since they were regarded as necessary and indispensable for a meaningful and dignified human existence. The struggle for human rights was described as a struggle for the rights to existence, freedom, happiness, and dignity.[40] Or, as it was stated in a poem, "Humans should be like human beings and therefore it is only natural that they should struggle for their inherent and inalienable rights."[41] Others likewise talked about rights as natural, inherent (*sheng ju lai*), and sacred (*shensheng*).[42] Yu Fan, writing in *China Human Rights*, described human rights as rights that one ought to enjoy (*yingyou quanli*), and without which one would no longer be a human being.[43] Echoing earlier writers, he argued that if one did not acknowledge or respect one's own or other people's human rights, one would lose one's human nature. Hua Shi agreed with Yu Fan on this point and went on to argue that human nature was the foundation of human rights.[44] Such a belief in human nature was of course at odds with the official view, according to which there was no such thing as a universal human nature. According to the official understanding, human beings were social beings and, living in a class society, by necessity would have a class character. The focus on class and class struggle, although significantly weakened after 1978, continued to play an important role in the political discourse and therefore strongly influenced discussions on human rights during this period. Yu Fan, it should be noted, did not deny the class character of man, but argued that it was but one aspect of man's human nature. Some other writers more explicitly argued that one had to acknowledge that there existed a supraclass human nature, and that man first of all was an individual person, and only second a class being.[45] Wei Jingsheng also argued that human rights were something that all humans possessed by birthright. Human rights were not endowed by any external force but enjoyed on the basis of one's human nature. This was what was understood by heaven-endowed human rights (*tianfu renquan*) or natural rights (*ziran de quanli*).[46]

The slave trope, a persistent theme in the Chinese rights discourse since the late Qing, was also invoked by the democracy activists. Yu Fan for example emphasized that the enjoyment of human rights distinguished human beings from slaves and beasts.[47] Wei Jingsheng described human rights in similar terms: "[O]nce one loses his human rights [*renquan*], he loses his rights to be a person [*zuoren de quanli*], and what is left to him is nothing but a position of dependency and slavery."[48] Rights are needed since they enable humans to establish an independent and autonomous position in life, whereas without them, a person will become dependent on others and reduced to the position of a slave. A totalitarian system, Wei argued, suppresses human's individuality and is in essence nothing but a slave society. In such a society some people live by enslaving others, while the majority only have the right to live as slaves.[49] *Enlightenment* also described how the Chinese people had lived as slaves without human dignity and human rights since the autocratic rule of Qin Shi Huangdi. Because slavery had deprived people of the right to think, they had become ignorant and passive, and this was said to explain the backward state of the Chinese nation; a conclusion with which both Zou Rong and Chen Duxiu would have agreed. A democratic system, by contrast, would protect people's individuality and enable human beings to live a life in freedom. Wei believed that democracy offered the only escape from enslavement, being the only system that could protect the individual's human rights. Xu Wenli, albeit not using the words human rights, also described rights as necessary for human liberation and development. Discussing the need for political reforms in China, he wrote: "The starting point for all reforms is human liberation, respect for human value and people's rights [*ren de quanli*]. The free development of each individual human being is the precondition for social progress."[50]

Discussions on human nature (*renxing*), the liberation of the individual (*geren jiefang*), and the creation of a new man (*xin ren*) reappeared in the post-1978 period.[51] The Democracy Wall discussions on individual liberation and human nature were also closely linked to their demands for human rights, as they were during May Fourth.[52] It was argued that the Chinese people needed to develop an independent personality, and that to this end they had to get rid of their blind loyalty to authority. The selfless and unquestioning character of Lei Feng, the foremost hero of the Cultural Revolution who went wherever and did whatever the party told him, had to be abandoned. A person who is nothing but a hapless "screw" (as Lei Feng had described himself), could not be said to be a complete human being.[53] Such a mentality thwarts and denies man his individuality and creativity, and, in other words, violates his human rights. Human beings have to be able to think freely and see to their personal interests and should not sacrifice themselves for the public good. In order to develop a personality and become independent, people had to enjoy the freedoms of speech and belief. But in a dictatorship, people would not have any freedom of belief or, differently put, they would only have the freedom to believe in one idea, such as communism, with the result that their spiritual life by necessity would become dull and empty. In such a society, Lu Mang argued, "the individual's highest form of personal life is destroyed and torn down, [and] he loses his purpose of existence."[54] Dictatorship and deprivation of human rights, in other words, was believed to threaten and destroy human dignity and personality.

There was, however, a broad spectrum of views on human rights among the Democracy Wall activists, and some were closer to the official view. Those writing in *April Fifth Forum* and *Science, Democracy, Legality*, in particular, expressed views that were quite similar to those of the liberal establishment intellectuals. These more moderate Democracy Wall activists at times criticized what they regarded as the too-extreme views of Wei Jingsheng, China Human Rights League, and the Enlightenment Society.[55] They were especially critical of the latter's letter to President Carter, arguing that the Chinese people were quite capable of solving their own problems.[56] Like the government, they also dismissed foreign human rights concerns as bogus and criticized the American human rights record. Some of them distanced themselves from the more radical activists out of conviction, whereas others seem to have done so out of tactical considerations, as they were eager not to provide the authorities with a pretext to suppress the democracy movement.[57] They felt that the more radical activists were pushing too far, too fast, and by so doing would undermine the new leadership's reform efforts and any genuine prospects for democracy.[58]

The more moderate democracy activists generally denied that human rights were a monopoly of the bourgeoisie but were careful to make a distinction between the human rights advocated by the bourgeoisie and those advocated by the proletariat.[59] One article in *April Fifth Forum* provided a good overview of the recent critique voiced in the official media.[60] (For details of the official view, see below.) The writer refuted the more extreme critique and based his

arguments for human rights on a humanistic reading of Marxism. He rejected
the critique that the bourgeois origin of human rights should be held against
it, instead emphasizing the progressive and liberating nature of the bourgeois
human rights movement. The author did not address the issue of the class character of rights, an aspect that many democracy activists accepted, such as Yu Fan
cited above, often arguing that there was both a universal and a class dimension to human rights. The author refuted those who dismissed human rights
because they believed that there was no such thing as natural rights, only historical rights. He argued that the epithet "natural" only had been attached to
human rights as a way to elevate their status, but that it was not a crucial aspect. What was important was instead the premise that people were born free
and equal. The author pointed out that even Marx had not disputed the equality of human beings. People were not born unequal: inequality was man-made
and a result of the forces of production. What Marxism disputed—a point the
author agreed with—was the bourgeois belief that human equality could best
be preserved in a private ownership system.

Other writers agreed that the bourgeois view of human rights was biased
and a sham, as it built upon the belief in the sacred right of private ownership.[61]
In this context they also criticized the exploitation of workers in the United
States and the denial of their human rights. Even though these writers acknowledged that people in the West enjoyed many more rights than was previously the case, they believed that the fact that people were still living in a capitalist society, suffering from its exploitations, revealed the shallowness of
human rights in the West compared with socialist states. Whereas people in a
bourgeois society could enjoy some personal and political rights, it was only in
a proletarian democracy that they would be the true masters of society, and
their rights and freedoms fully guaranteed. This understanding also led many
moderate democracy activists to argue with the establishment intellectuals that
different societies would have different human rights conceptions, thus taking
a relativistic position on human rights.[62] Although they did not dispute the language of human rights as such, they believed, in other words, that the proletarian conception would be different from that of the bourgeoisie, or, as one
author put it, that "the proletariat could not sleep in the bourgeois bed of human rights."[63]

Another sensitive issue the article in *April Fifth Forum* addressed was the
question of whether human rights demands were superfluous in a socialist system, and whether they not also implied an open opposition to the CCP—
something that constituted the most serious charge directed against those advocating human rights. The author took great pains to emphasize that advocacy
of human rights did not imply a rejection of socialism. Like many others, both
democracy activists and liberal establishment intellectuals, he pointed out that

the socialist system still was imperfect in China, as exemplified by the gross violations of people's rights during the Cultural Revolution.[64] But he argued that these problems had their roots in remnants of feudalism that had been exploited by Lin Biao and the Gang of Four and had nothing to do with socialism per se. As long as feudal thinking continued to exist, future human rights violations could not be ruled out, which made further vigilance and human rights work necessary, but the fact that human rights violations had and still might take place in China and other socialist societies was not a reason to reject socialism itself.

The human rights discussed and demanded during the democracy movement were predominantly civil and political rights, such as freedom of speech, the press, publication, assembly, association, demonstration, and so on.[65] It is not surprising that the freedoms of speech and publication were high on the democracy activists' list, since these freedoms, after all, are necessary in order to be able to discuss other political and legal issues. Freedom of speech, some argued, was the most fundamental of human rights.[66] Hu Ping thus argued that freedom of speech was necessary for human existence; without it one would be reduced to the level of a slave or a tool.[67] But while freedom of speech was necessary for individual development, it was also seen as crucial for the promotion of truth and beneficial to both society and the government.

The Democracy Wall activists provided lengthy lists of rights, including freedom of speech, freedom to demonstrate, freedom of publication, freedom of belief, and freedom of association.[68] The China Human Rights League in addition listed more concrete rights, such as the right to elect state leaders and the right to attend the National People's Congress (NPC) as observers. It demanded that the system, according to which secret police and party committees could arrest people, should be abolished, and that those arrested for exercising their freedom of speech should be released. It also advocated that minorities should have a right to autonomy. Except in the case of Wei Jingsheng, who was particularly concerned about the situation in Tibet, the democracy activists otherwise did not pay much attention to minority issues. The league also attacked such typical Chinese organizations as the work unit, and advocated that people should have the freedom to chose their own vocation. It also demanded freedom of movement and the right to travel abroad. Economic rights were also invoked by both democracy activists and starving peasants who demonstrated for food and human rights.[69] Several writers dealt with economic issues and welfare reform in their posters and articles, for example calling for improvement of the cramped living conditions of urban citizens.[70] But some explicitly cautioned against limiting human rights to the right to subsistence (*shengcun quan*).[71] Even pets were generally guaranteed a right to subsistence, whereas human beings needed something more than guarantees for a mere physical existence. What separated

human beings from animals was, after all, humans' need for spiritual development and fulfillment, which warranted rights such as freedom of speech, and the
like.

It is evident that the democracy activists, like previous Chinese generations,
valued individual rights, not merely as an end in themselves, but as necessary
preconditions for social progress and modernization.[72] They described human
rights, democracy, and a sound legal system as indispensable if the Four Modernisations were to succeed.[73] This was also the position of Wei Jingsheng, who
argued in his famous article "The Fifth Modernisation," that without the fifth,
namely democracy, the Four Modernisations would come to naught.[74] Wei believed that democracy was the only guarantee that people's rights would be
protected, whereas dictatorships inevitably were the enemy of human rights. In
dictatorships political opponents would be arbitrarily labeled counterrevolutionaries and deprived of their rights and freedoms.[75]

> If the people do not even have the right to express their ideas freely, if there is no free-
> dom of speech, how can one speak of democracy? . . . [I]f there are no different ideas,
> no variety of opinion, and no publications representing dissimilar viewpoints, then
> clearly you have political despotism. . . . Abolishing the people's right of expression un-
> der the pretext of some social phenomena, such as disturbances by a few criminals tak-
> ing advantage of opportunities, is a habitual practice of all new and old dictatorial fas-
> cists.[76]

Socialist countries by definition, Wei argued, did not acknowledge or respect
human rights. Other democracy activists, such as Lu Mang, also believed that
democracy was inseparable from and necessary for the realization of human
rights.[77] The majority of the democracy activists still opted for socialism, however, and only a small minority advocated Western-style political democracy
and the American political system. *Enlightenment* and *China Human Rights* were
especially pro-American in their outlook, but others strongly criticized their
pro-American view and praise of "bourgeois democracy."[78]

The fact that Wei Jingsheng regarded human rights as inherent in man and
universal in character did not mean that he also saw these rights as given for
all time. Wei regarded human rights as historical and relative, and believed that
their content would evolve and expand over time.[79] Human rights were therefore neither absolute nor unlimited. But the limitations surrounding the enjoyment of human rights, Wei believed, would change and diminish as human
beings conquered their environment. Wei thus took a progressive and historical view of rights. Many shared this progressive view of history and belief that
the world, including China, was moving toward a more civilized and just society. One article in *Enlightenment* expressed its belief in universal progress in the
following way: "The enthusiasm for freedom in society today is increasing. We

should model ourselves on those societies which eternally respect the individual's human rights and we need to understand the whole of history. The political system in our country cannot remain unchanged forever, the trend of history has already weakened its foundation. . . . [T]he trend of humankind's development inevitably moves toward democracy and freedom."[80]

The democracy activists generally believed that human rights were universal in character and applicable to China. They disputed the view that because of their bourgeois origin, human rights would be inapplicable to China, instead arguing that demand for human rights was shared by all of humankind. Lu Mang saw the history of humanity as a struggle for human rights against autocrats and tyrants who deprived people of their rights.[81] This belief in universal human rights is also revealed by the many references to the UDHR and other human rights documents.[82] The fact that the PRC then was a member of the United Nations was invoked as a reason that the rights stipulated in the UDHR were valid and should be implemented in China. The democracy activists' only regret was that while the rest of humankind already enjoyed their human rights, the Chinese people were still suffering under dictatorship.[83] The poet Huang Xiang forcefully argued that human rights demands did not differ between people of different nationalities: "Whether to the Chinese people or the American people or the people of any other country in the world, 'human rights' have the same significance. On this planet where humankind lives together there is no distinction as to race, nation, or state boundaries regarding human rights. They are the common desire of all the progressive peoples of our time."[84]

THE VIEW OF HUMAN RIGHTS IN THE OFFICIAL MEDIA

The establishment intellectuals discussing human rights in the official media during 1978–82 were highly circumspect in their writings. They provided a strictly Marxist analysis and mostly confined themselves to an abstract discussion of early natural rights theories, initially virtually ignoring international developments in the human rights field after 1948. Those who voiced a more positive view of human rights were very careful to distance themselves from the Democracy Wall activists. But despite the sensitivity of the issue in the late 1970s, there nevertheless existed some important differences among the establishment intellectuals. Lan Ying, writing in *Shehui kexue*, a more academic magazine, was even so bold as to openly criticize the views of Xiao Weiyun and others writing in the party mouthpiece, *Hongqi*. Xu Bing, writing in *Guangming ribao*, also gave vent to more liberal views. Very few of those writing on human rights today were active during the 1978–82 period. Xu Bing wrote an even more liberal and path-breaking article in early 1989, but since then has not published much on human rights. One of the more conservative scholars in the human rights field, Gu Chunde, who published a quite orthodox article in 1982, has however continued to write on human rights since 1989. Li Buyun, a more moderate scholar on human rights, published a couple of articles in the early 1980s and has been an active and creative contributor in recent debates.

Some of the establishment intellectuals saw discussions of human rights as constituting a direct attack on the regime and simply rejected human rights as a bourgeois slogan that only served the interests of the bourgeoisie.[85] Human rights were seen as nothing but the rights of the bourgeoisie to exploit the laboring masses. According to these writers, those who advocated human rights were opposed to socialism and wanted to restore capitalism in China. Others, however, argued that despite the historical origins of human rights the concept itself was valid, disputing that the bourgeoisie had a monopoly on the idea.[86] They argued that the proletariat could also make use of the language of human rights and claimed that it was possible to formulate a Marxist concept of human rights. These writers believed that the fact that some people had used the slogan of human rights to attack the regime did not undermine the value of human rights as such.[87] Although it was argued that the concept of human rights at the time of its formulation had reflected the interests of the bourgeoisie, many writers nonetheless acknowledged that it had been a progressive idea at the time. Lan Ying went so far as to describe the bourgeoisie's calls for human rights, equality, and freedom as constituting a movement to liberate humankind.[88] And since this was also at the heart of Marxism, advocacy of Marxism and human rights didn't stand in opposition to each other. Such a humanistic interpretation of Marxism, however, was still very rare among establishment intellectuals at the time.

Some writers stressed the rhetorical value of human rights slogans in political struggles and argued that human rights talk could be useful to socialists as a weapon to oppose the bourgeoisie and obtain rights for themselves. But this constituted more of a tactical move than an all-out acceptance on their part. The magazine *Propaganda Trends* acknowledged as much in the following: "[M]arxists have never put forward demands for human rights in isolation, and even less have they placed such demands in [the] first place. Instead, they have used them as supplementary forms of struggle and as strategic slogans, and have brought them into the orbit of, and subordinated them to, the overall struggle of the proletariat and the broad masses of the people for political power."[89] Human rights, according to this understanding, were not and could not be a major or dominant slogan in the socialist struggle.[90] But it was admitted to have been of some limited use to the CCP before 1949, "in order to mobilise the people against imperialism and feudalism."[91] Few articles ventured to give a more extensive overview of earlier, noncommunist discussions of human rights in China. Some, however, mentioned the China League for the Protection of Civil Rights as a progressive organization but criticized Hu Shi's involvement with it and his previous writings on human rights in *Xinyue*.[92]

Quite different views existed on whether the concept of human rights had or would play any role in the PRC after 1949. Whereas Lin Rongnian and Zhang Jinfan argued that the CCP leadership after 1949 had occasionally referred to human rights in different policy statements, others objected to this description.[93] An article in *Guangming ribao* thus argued:

> Since China entered the socialist period, the slogan of human rights has seldom appeared in our Party's documents, in our state laws and in our political life. And this is not difficult to understand because the Chinese revolution has entered a new historical period of the direct elimination of private ownership and classes. Our programmes, slogans, and theoretical articles should use more accurate Marxist formulations rather than stress such slogans as human rights.[94]

But while some writers felt that the idea of human rights had not played and would not play any important role in China, a majority argued that the proletariat could take over this originally bourgeois slogan and give it new content and meaning.[95] The proletarian struggle for human rights, in contrast to that of the bourgeoisie, would aim at abolishing private ownership and the class system and focus on establishing the dictatorship of the proletariat. The logical consequence of such a line of reasoning was that the existence of different economic and political systems would inevitably give rise to different conceptions and interpretations of human rights. This relativistic position on rights would remain a prominent feature of the official discourse; it was elaborated upon and gained in significance in the aftermath of 1989.

Many of the writers who were in favor of adopting the language of human rights were careful to emphasize that one would have to distinguish between people who criticized the Gang of Four for violating human rights and those with "ulterior motives" who used human rights to attack socialism and the dictatorship of the proletariat.[96] It was the motives behind the calls for human rights, rather than human rights appeals as such, that were crucial in their eyes. Most writers believed that with the founding of the PRC, the abolition of exploitation, and the inauguration of public ownership, true human rights had been realized in China. But those more positive to human rights talk did not dispute that human rights problems still continued to exist in the PRC. They emphasized, however, that it was the feudal tradition and the Gang of Four that was to blame and not socialism per se.[97] The new interest in human rights issues among Chinese people were therefore explained with reference to the painful experiences of the Cultural Revolution.[98] These horrors, however, were regarded as aberrations and did not imply any endemic problems with social-ism. The majority believed that with the fall of the Gang of Four, the rehabil-itation of millions of people, and the rebuilding of the legal system, people's rights had been restored and secured, although some were bold enough to ar-gue that people still did not enjoy all rights stipulated in the constitution to the fullest.

Since the enjoyment of rights was believed to be restricted by a society's economic and cultural level, it was argued that the securing of human rights would take a long time in China.[99] China's long history of feudalism and au-thoritarianism, its lack of a democratic tradition, backward economy, and the fact that Chinese socialism had been established in a semifeudal and neocolo-nial state, were said to impede the realization of human rights; similar argu-ments continue to be voiced in the contemporary discourse. It is in a sense in-evitable that the CCP would take a relativistic position on rights. Since man in the Marxist analysis is seen as a social animal, formed by his class interests, it follows that there can be no such thing as universal and supraclass rights. Rights are not absolute or universal, but change with the means of production and the level of economic development.[100] Rights would thus inevitably have a class character in a class society. Whereas rights in a bourgeois society would reflect the interests of the bourgeoisie, rights in a socialist society, on the other hand, would reflect and safeguard the interests of the proletariat. In other words, rights would not, indeed could not, be one and the same in all societies.

This relativistic view of rights is also evident in the analysis of the subject of rights within a given society. Since rights were bestowed by the state on the people, they could be denied to those excluded from the category of "the peo-ple," such as counterrevolutionaries, class enemies and so-called "black ele-ments."[101] The practice of depriving counterrevolutionaries of their political rights was defended as an appropriate and necessary step in order to defend the rights of the great majority, which in fact is an old GMD argument. The more courageous, such as Xu Bing, however, would add that this did not mean that counterrevolutionaries would be deprived of all of their citizens' rights.[102] They could only be deprived of their political rights, and only by the courts, but they would retain their other citizens' rights and should still be treated in a humanitarian way, for example, not being subjected to torture. This was a progressive step from the Cultural Revolution, when counterrevolutionaries were regarded and treated as nonhumans. Xu Bing also argued that whereas human rights was an abstract concept, its concrete manifestation in a given so-ciety took the form of citizens' rights. He furthermore believed that it was le-gitimate to demand rights not already stipulated in the constitution; thus blur-ring the distinction between human rights and citizens' rights. Xu also argued for the right to strike, disputing those who believed that such a right was superfluous in a socialist system with public ownership. This right, however, was removed from the constitution in 1982.

While most writers in the official media during the period 1978–80 limited themselves to a Marxist analysis of the early natural rights idea of the seventeenth and eighteenth century, by 1982 they had begun to discover and study developments in the human rights field after 1948. They especially focused on and appreciated the inclusion of economic and social rights and the right to self-determination alongside the more traditional human rights.[103] These rights were embraced and applauded, as they could be used in the struggle against colonialism, imperialism, and hegemonism. The argument, later to figure so prominently in the official discourse, that the right to self-determination is a precondition to the enjoyment of individual rights, also began to be voiced more widely. Priority was placed on collective and national rights, such as the right to self-determination and development, over individual rights. Another argument, also used before, was the open differentiation between large-scale human rights violations resulting from imperialism and colonialism such as genocide and racial discrimination: in these cases the international community had a right and an obligation to interfere, but in issues pertaining to civil and political rights, which were regarded as an internal affair, the PRC did not permit any interference. This made it possible for China to criticize the Soviet invasion of Afghanistan, the Vietnamese invasion of Kampuchea, apartheid in South Africa, and the Israeli policy against the Palestinians as constituting human rights violations, while at the same time dismissing all criticisms of China as an interference in its internal affairs. China had used this argument already in the 1960s when it had dismissed foreign criticism of the situation in Tibet and, at the same time, criticized the American treatment of Native Americans.[104] In this context it also became expedient to focus on historical injustices committed by the West in order to divert or undermine its critique of China. The PRC thus accused the West for having grossly violated the rights of the Chinese people in the past, for example, by allegedly putting up the sign "No admittance for dogs and Chinese" in a park in Shanghai.[105]

As the PRC became more involved in UN human rights work—it became a member of the UN Human Rights Commission in 1982—it also began to more fully realize the high standing of human rights in international affairs. But this didn't prevent it from expressing some skepticism about the motives behind human rights concerns and criticize the two superpowers for using human rights as a weapon in their ideological and political struggle. "The United States claims that the Soviet Union is violating the fundamental human rights of people in the East European countries. The Soviet Union says that the United States is engaging in a 'propaganda war on human rights,' and has collected materials to denounce the latter for violating human rights. The superpower quarrel over human rights does not show their concern for human rights, but their attempt to dominate the whole world."[106] This skeptical view of the motives behind human rights concerns has also shaped the Chinese critique of Western human rights diplomacy in the post-1989 period.

CHINA AND THE SOVIET UNION: COMRADES IN ARMS ON HUMAN RIGHTS

Despite China's critique of the Soviet Union's position on human rights, it is obvious that they have had much in common, sharing as they have the same Marxist theoretical framework.[107] Both the Soviet Union and China have emphasized the supremacy of economic rights over political rights; collective rights, such as the right to self-determination, over individual rights; and duties over rights. The Soviet Union routinely dismissed Western human rights criticism as an ideological weapon, as well as rejected foreign criticism as an interference in its internal affairs, in this context making frequent references to the supremacy of state sovereignty over human rights; an argument that China also has found useful.[108] Both China and the Soviet Union have furthermore made a distinction between different types of human rights violations. During the 1970s the Soviet Union criticized human rights violations in South Africa, Israel, and Chile, while dismissing Western criticism of its own human rights record.

It is difficult to assess to what extent discussions on human rights in the Soviet Union have influenced the Chinese position, but they were most likely known to the Chinese leadership since articles on human rights by Soviet authors were published in Chinese in the early 1980s.[109] In the early 1990s, more works were translated and Chinese authors themselves also discussed the human rights debates in the former Soviet Union and East Europe and their influences on the demise of communism in these countries.

International developments, such as the adoption of the two human rights covenants by the UN General Assembly in 1966 and a domestic challenge from dissidents in the late 1960s, stimulated discussions on human rights in the Soviet Union. In this context it should be remembered that the Soviet Union, in contrast to China, had abstained from the voting on the UDHR in 1948. The late 1960s and early 1970s saw a gradual and cautious affirmation of human rights among Soviet establishment scholars while, at the same time, dissidents began to use human rights criticism against the regime.[110] As happened later in China, the challenge and initiative on human rights thus came from dissidents. But Soviet dissidents had an advantage over the Chinese in that the Soviet Union was active in the United Nations on the issue of human rights, and its own human rights record early on attracted attention from the West. In contrast to China, the Soviet Union was quick to voice its support of and sign the two major human rights covenants in 1973. But this international commitment did not mean that human rights were respected at home. In 1969, Soviet dissidents founded the Initiative Group for the Defense of Civil Rights, and in 1970 Sakharov and others founded the Moscow Human Rights Committee. After the adoption of the Helsinki Final Act in 1975 and the election of Jimmy Carter as American president in 1977, human rights were brought to the center stage of East–West relations, which further spurred Soviet dissidents in their struggle for human rights. In 1976, encouraged by the Helsinki Final Act, the first Helsinki Watch Group was thus established in Moscow. These developments and the high importance Western governments attached to human rights also prompted official activities in the field of human rights. In the 1970s, the Soviet Union thus began to modify its earlier negative stance on human rights and talk about a "socialist concept of human rights." Research and publication on human rights were initially quite modest, but in 1988 a human rights department was established at a law school, which had been preceded a couple of years earlier by the establishment of a human rights section at the USSR Academy of Science's Institute of State and Law.[111]

Considerable differences of opinion existed among Soviet dissidents on the issue of human rights, which bear some resemblance to those found among Chinese dissidents as well, although Soviet and Chinese dissidents also differed in many ways. Some Soviet dissidents such as Roy Medvedev, who defended human rights from a strictly Marxist perspective, and Valery Chalidze, who was careful to work within the confines of the law and not advocate the overthrow of the regime, reveal positions quite similar to those of the more moderate Chinese democracy activists. Other Soviet dissidents differed with respect to whether they sought inspiration in the West and universal human rights ideas, or whether they looked to tradition. Sakharov thus looked more to the West when criticizing the Soviet political system, whereas Solzhenitsyn was more traditional in his outlook and advanced Russia's own traditions in his critique of the Soviet political system. Wei Jingsheng can be said to bear some resemblance to Sakharov, with the important difference that Sakharov was an established scientist whose outlook was much more sophisticated and cosmopolitan. On the other hand, it is difficult to find any Chinese dissident who, like Solzhenitsyn, has sought inspiration in tradition. Although Soviet dissidents were united in their critique of the human rights violations, they were later to follow quite different paths, and we see the same thing happening among Chinese dissidents. Their common struggle against oppression was what originally united them and made them suppress or ignore underlying individual and political differences, but these differences have generally surfaced as the years passed. The pressure of life in exile as well as social and political changes in their own society have often resulted in breaking this erstwhile and often illusory unity.

CONCLUSION

China's human rights policy underwent a development similar to that of the Soviet Union's but with a considerable time lag because of its isolation during most of the Cold War period and because it was not then a target of Western criticism. Until the end of the Cold War, China was an important card for the West to be played off in the power struggles with the Soviet Union. In the 1970s and early 1980s, the West was eager not to alienate a China that had only recently become a member of the United Nations and thus at long last been incorporated into the international community. China faced a less hostile international environment throughout the 1980s than did the Soviet Union and was more or less exempted from human rights critique. China's knowledge of and participation in UN human rights work gradually grew during the 1980s, but its position on human rights only became more proactive and vocal as a consequence of the fierce criticism it faced in 1989. It seems as if the PRC, when finally taken to task by the international community over its human rights record, reacted more quickly and spent more effort on research on human rights and in pushing its own definition of human rights than the Soviet Union had done.[112] Be that as it may, the PRC's views and strategies nevertheless still continue to exhibit striking similarities to those of the former Soviet Union. Russia and China continue to make use of some of their old arguments and still have somewhat similar positions on human rights issues.[113] Despite their differing political developments since the late 1980s, both countries thus agree on the supremacy of sovereignty rights over human rights and reject humanitarian interference in domestic conflicts.

NOTES

1. Mao Zedong "Speech at Hangzhou," reprinted in Martin, vol. 6, p. 625.
2. I am grateful to Michael Schoenhals who brought my attention to Notice No. 1 of the Yunnan Provincial Revolutionary Committee, 23 August 1968.
3. Reprinted in Cohen and Chiu (1974), vol. 1, p. 609.
4. Chinese statement reprinted in Cohen and Chiu (1974), vol. 2, pp. 1329–32.
5. Cohen and Chiu (1974), vol. 2, p. 1332.
6. See, for example, the 1955 Bandung Communiqué, endorsed by China. It is reprinted in Cohen and Chiu (1974), vol. 1, pp. 123–24.
7. For the role of human rights in Chinese foreign policy, see Nathan (1994).
8. Reprinted in Cohen and Chiu (1974), vol. 2, p. 1333.

9. For a collection of Yu Luoke's own writings, contemporary critique, and reminiscences, see Yu Xiao et al. (1999).

10. In his view on man's equality, Yu seems to have been influenced by Rousseau whom he had read and said he admired. See Yu Luojing in Yu Xiao et al. (1999), p. 324.

11. Yu Luoke in Yu Xiao et al. (1999), p. 69.

12. For information on the group and translations of their work, see Chan, Rosen and Unger (1985).

13. Li Yizhe as translated in Chan, Rosen and Unger (1985), p. 71.

14. See Brodsgaard (1981).

15. For a discussion of China's attitude to human rights work in the United Nations, see Kent (1999).

16. For a good discussion on the West's reluctance to criticize the human rights record in China, see Cohen (1988).

17. For general overviews of the movement, see Huang and Seymour (1980), pp. 1–26; Brodsgaard (1981); and Nathan (1986a).

18. For a discussion of the various unofficial journals, see Chen Ruoxi (1982) and Nathan (1986a). The most complete reprint of these unofficial journals is the twenty volumes published by the Institute for the Study of Chinese Communist Problems, *A Collection of Underground Publications Circulated on the Chinese Mainland*, abbreviated as DLDX. English translations of some of the articles are found in Seymour (1980).

19. On the views on democracy of establishment intellectuals and rehabilitated intellectuals, see Goldman (1994).

20. See Wei's autobiography in Wei Jingsheng (1997).

21. Nathan (1986a), pp. 23–24.

22. Wei Jingsheng, "What Do We Want: Democracy or a New Despotism?" *Exploration*, reprinted in DLDX (1980–84), vol. 1, p. 27. The article is translated in Seymour (1980), pp. 196–200.

23. Published in AFF, no. 9, 1979, reprinted in DLDX (1980–84), vol. 6, pp. 25–30.

24. Deng Xiaoping (1987), p. 19.

25. For the arrests and trials of democracy activists, see Amnesty International (1984).

26. "The Meaning and Present Tasks of the Human Rights Movement," CHR, no. 1, 1979, reprinted in DLDX (1980–84), vol. 2, p. 193. Interestingly enough, they got the name wrong and referred to it as the China Human Rights League.

27. The French declaration was reprinted in PV, no. 6, May 1979, and the UDHR was reprinted in CHR, no. 2, 1979.

28. "China Human Rights Declaration," CHR, no. 1, 1979, reprinted in DLDX, (1980–84), vol. 2, p. 189. An English translation can be found in Seymour (1980), p. 85.

29. Lu Mang, "On Human Rights," reprinted in DLDX (1980–84), vol. 14, p. 299. An English translation can be found in Seymour (1980), p. 126.

30. "China Human Rights Declaration," CHR, no. 1, 1979, reprinted in DLDX (1980--84), vol. 2, pp. 187–90. An English translation is provided in Seymour (1980), pp. 83–86.

31. Wei Jingsheng, "A Twentieth-Century Bastille: Qincheng No. 1 Prison," *Exploration*, no. 3, March 1979, reprinted in DLDX (1980–84), vol. 2, pp. 68–77. An English translation is provided in Seymour (1980), pp. 214–22.

32. *Exploration*, no. 2, 1979, reprinted in DLDX (1980–84), vol. 2, pp. 26–28.

33. One short, Kafkaesque story dealt with the case of Fu Yuehua, who had been abused by her boss and later led peasants in demonstrations. See "A Human Rights Question," PV,

no. 3, 1979, reprinted in DLDX (1980–84), vol. 18, pp. 2–21. For poems, see CHR, no. 1, 1979, reprinted in DLDX (1980–84), vol. 2, p. 201; and SDL, no. 1, 1979, reprinted in DLDX (1980–84), vol. 2, p. 274. See also Ling Bing, "People's Rights," SDL, no. 9, 1979, reprinted in DLDX (1980–84), vol. 14, pp. 4–5; for an English translation see Goodman (1981), pp. 150–51. For the song, see CHR, no. 2, 1979, reprinted in DLDX (1980–84), vol. 3, p. 242. For the literature from the movement in general, see Goodman (1981).

34. For a good overview of this critique and an attempt to defend human rights without straying too far from the official view, see Du Guo, "A View of the Criticism of Human Rights," AFF, no. 13, 1979, reprinted in DLDX (1980–84), vol. 8, pp. 44–49. The text is translated in Angle and Svensson (2001). See also Anon., "The Meaning and Present Tasks of the Human Rights Movement," CHR, no. 1, 1979, reprinted in DLDX (1980–84), vol. 2, p. 193.

35. Yu Fan, "Questions and Answers Regarding the Chinese Society," CHR, no. 1, 1979, reprinted in DLDX (1980–84), vol. 2, p. 206. The text is translated in Angle and Svensson (2001).

36. Interview with Xu Wenli in 1980, reprinted in *Minzhu Zhonghua* (1989), p. 267.

37. Huang Xiang wrote his letter under the pen name *Gongmin* (citizen). For an English translation, see Seymour (1980), pp. 227–39. Another open letter on human rights addressed to Brzezinski also appeared at Xidan in December and is mentioned in Goodman (1981), pp. 64–65.

38. Xu Wenli, "Once More Discussing Whether the US Is a Democratic Paradise," AFF, no. 9, 1979, reprinted in DLDX (1980–84), vol. 6, pp. 17–22. See also, Han Jie, "Also Discussing Human Rights and Democracy," SDL, no. 5, 1979, reprinted in DLDX (1980–84), vol. 10, pp. 138–39; Li Xi, "Socialist Democracy and Human Rights," SDL, no. 5, 1979, reprinted in DLDX (1980–84), vol. 10, p. 144; and the letter from a reader published in the same issue, SDL, no. 5, 1979, p. 187.

39. The magazines *April Fifth Forum* and *Seeking Correctness* carried many articles on constitutional rights and their legal protection. For a representative article, see Hu Fa, "Citizens' Basic Rights Allow No Violation," SC, no. 11, July 1979, reprinted in DLDX (1980–84), vol. 4, pp. 129–32.

40. Yu Fan, "Questions and Answers Regarding the Chinese Society," CHR, no. 1, 1979, reprinted in DLDX (1980–84), vol. 2, p. 203.

41. CHR, no. 1, 1979, reprinted in DLDX (1980–84), vol. 2, p. 201.

42. Hua Shi, "The Human Person, Human Nature, Human Rights," FL, no. 2, 1979, reprinted in DLDX (1980–84), vol. 14, p. 361.

43. Yu Fan, "Questions and Answers Regarding the Chinese Society," DLDX (1980–84), vol. 2, p. 204. Another article described human rights as "rights that one ought to enjoy" (*yinggai xiangyou de quanli*), see "Human Rights? People's Democracy?" SDL, no. 9, 1979, reprinted in DLDX (1980–84), vol. 14, p. 6.

44. Hua Shi, "The Human Person, Human Nature, Human Rights," DLDX, vol. 14, pp. 361–65.

45. See Hou Baochen, "On Human Nature," SDL, no. 5, 1979, reprinted in DLDX (1980–84), vol. 10, pp. 164–67; Hua Shi, "The Human Person, Human Nature, Human Rights," DLDX (1980–84), vol. 14, pp. 361–65; and Jia Wen, "Also Discussing Human Nature and Human Rights," FL, no. 2, 1979, reprinted in DLDX (1980–84), vol. 14, pp. 366–69.

46. Wei Jingsheng, "Human Rights, Equality, and Democracy," *Exploration* no. 3, 1979, reprinted in DLDX (1980–84), vol. 2, pp. 42–43. The full text is translated in Angle and Svensson (2001).

47. Yu Fan, "Questions and Answers Regarding the Chinese Society," DLDX (1980–84), vol. 2, p. 202.

48. Wei Jingsheng, "The Fifth Modernisation," *Exploration* no. 2, 1979, reprinted in DLDX, (1980–84), vol. 2, p. 6. My translation differs somewhat from that in Seymour (1980), p. 64.

49. Wei Jingsheng, "Human Rights, Equality, and Democracy," DLDX (1980–84), vol. 2, p. 49; English translation in Seymour (1980), p. 146.

50. Xu Wenli, reprinted in *Minzhu Zhonghua* (1989), p. 276.

51. The literary magazine *Fertile Land* arranged a symposium in July 1979 at which the demand for a "new man" and the preconditions that were needed in order for man to realize his potentialities as a human person were discussed. See, He Bian (Hu Ping), "A Brief Discussion on the New Man in Literature," and Jiang Feng, "Some Questions Regarding the View and Concept of a New Man," FL, nos. 4 and 5, 1979, reprinted in DLDX (1980–84), vol. 13, pp. 208–11, and 212–20, respectively.

52. See, for example, Hua Shi, "The Human Person, Human Nature, Human Rights," DLDX (1980–84), vol. 14, pp. 361–65; and Jia Wen, "Also Discussing Human Nature and Human Rights," DLDX (1980–84), vol. 14, pp. 366–69.

53. Lei Feng was quoted as having said "I will be a screw that never rusts and will glitter anywhere I am placed."

54. Lu Mang, "On Human Rights," DLDX (1980–84), vol. 14, p. 295, English translation in Seymour (1980), p. 124.

55. For a critique of *China Human Rights League* that did not imply a critique of human rights as such, see Yan Zhen, "Bourgeois Human Rights and Proletarian Democracy," PV, no. 5, 1979, reprinted in DLDX (1980–84), vol. 14, p. 150.

56. See Han Jie, "Also Discussing Human Rights and Democracy," DLDX (1980–84), vol. 10, pp. 138–39; Li Xi, "Socialist Democracy and Human Rights," DLDX (1980–84), vol. 10, p. 144; and a letter from a reader, DLDX (1980–84), vol. 10, p. 187. See also Xu Wenli, "Once More Discussing Whether the US is a Democratic Paradise," DLDX (1980–84), vol. 6, pp. 17–22.

57. For the view that the letter to Carter could destroy the reputation of the Democracy Wall Movement, see a letter from a reader published in SDL, no. 5, 1979, reprinted in DLDX, (1980–84), vol. 10, p. 187.

58. See, for example, Xu Wenli, "An Elementary Discussion of People's Democratic Rights," AFF, no. 7, 1979, reprinted in DLDX (1980–84), vol. 5, p. 9.

59. A few among the democracy activists went even further, and, like the more conservative establishment intellectuals, dismissed human rights as a bourgeois slogan that was used to exploit the workers. See "The Slogan of Human Rights Is Really a Bourgeois Slogan!" SDL, no. 7, 1979, reprinted in DLDX (1980–84), vol. 12, p. 51.

60. See "A View of the Criticism of Human Rights," AFF, no. 13, 1979, reprinted in DLDX, (1980–84), vol. 8, pp. 44–49. For another article which also discussed the official critique of human rights, see Yan Zhen, "Bourgeois Human Rights and Proletarian Democracy," PV, no. 5, 1979, reprinted in DLDX (1980–84), vol. 14, pp. 146–51.

61. See, for example, Li Xi, "Socialist Democracy and Human Rights," DLDX (1980–84), vol. 10, p. 143; and Yan Zhen, "Bourgeois Human Rights and Proletarian Democracy," DLDX (1980–84), vol. 14, p. 147.

62. Han Jie concurred with Deng Xiaoping that there existed different understandings of human rights; DLDX (1980–84), vol. 14, p. 140. See also "Human Rights? People's

Democracy?" DLDX (1980–84), vol. 14, p. 6. This article described abstract human rights as a political illusion.

63. Yan Zhen, "Bourgeois Human Rights and Proletarian Democracy," DLDX (1980–84), vol. 14, p. 148.

64. See also, Han Jie, "Also Discussing Human Rights and Democracy," DLDX (1980–84), vol. 10, p. 138.

65. For enumerations of rights, see, for example, Xu Wenli in *Minzhu Zhonghua* (1989), p. 276; and Xu Wenli, "An Elementary Discussion of People's Democratic Rights," DLDX (1980—84), vol. 5, pp. 4–9. As well as Wei Jingsheng, "A Twentieth-Century Bastille: Qincheng No. 1 Prison," DLDX (1980–84), vol. 2, pp. 68–77; English translation in Seymour (1980), pp. 214–22.

66. Zheng Shiming, "What Kind of Freedom of Speech Do We Want?" HB, no. 1, reprinted in DLDX (1980–84), vol. 19, p. 23.

67. He Bian (Hu Ping), "Freedom of Speech," FL, 1979, reprinted in DLDX (1980–84), vol. 12, pp. 67–115.

68. "China Human Rights Declaration," DLDX (1980–84), vol. 2, pp. 187–90. Lu Mang, "On Human Rights," DLDX (1980–84), vol. 14, pp. 279–300. For English translations, see Seymour (1980), pp. 83–86, and pp. 111–27, respectively.

69. In January 1979, demonstrating peasants carried banners with slogans such as "We Don't Want Hunger," and "We Want Human Rights and Democracy," quoted in Huang and Seymour (1980), p. 19; see also Nathan (1986a), p. 29.

70. Wei Minqing, "They Demand the Right to Rest," BS, no. 6, 1979, reprinted in DLDX (1980–84), vol. 7, pp. 109–13. See also the many articles in *People's Voice* on these topics.

71. Yu Fan, "Questions and Answers Regarding the Chinese Society," DLDX (1980–84), vol. 2, p. 202.

72. See, for example, Xu Wenli, reprinted in *Minzhu Zhonghua* (1989), p. 276, and pp. 278–79, respectively; Wei Jingsheng, "Human Rights, Equality, and Democracy," DLDX (1980–84), vol. 2.

73. "Letter to President Carter," reprinted in Seymour (1980), p. 228.

74. Wei Jingsheng, "The Fifth Modernisation," DLDX (1980–84), vol. 2; reprinted in Seymour (1980), pp. 47–69.

75. Wei Jingsheng, "A Twentieth-Century Bastille: Qincheng No. 1 Prison," DLDX (1980–84), vol. 2, pp. 68–77; English translation in Seymour (1980), pp. 214–22.

76. Wei Jingsheng, "What Do We Want: Democracy or a New Despotism?" DLDX(1980–84), vol. 1, p. 27. For a slightly different translation, see Seymour (1980), p. 197, p. 198.

77. Lu Mang, "On Human Rights," DLDX (1980–84), vol. 14, pp. 279–300; English translation in Seymour (1980), pp. 111–27.

78. Xu Wenli "Once More Discussing Whether the US Is a Democratic Paradise," DLDX (1980–84), vol. 6, pp. 17–22.

79. Wei Jingsheng, "Human Rights, Equality, and Democracy," DLDX (1980–84), vol. 2, p. 43.

80. Shou He, "The Present Democracy Movement," *Enlightenment*, no. 2, reprinted in DLDX (1980–84), vol. 1, p. 237.

81. Lu Mang, "On Human Rights," DLDX (1980–84), vol. 14, p. 279; English translation in Seymour (1980), p. 126.

82. CHR, no. 3, 1979, reprinted in DLDX (1980–84), vol. 3, pp. 258–64.

83. Lu Mang, "On Human Rights," DLDX (1980–84), vol. 14, p. 299; English translation in Seymour (1980), p. 126.

84. "Letter to President Carter," reprinted in Seymour (1980), p. 237.

85. See in particular, Xiao Weiyuan et al. (1979). Parts of the article are translated in Angle and Svensson (2001).

86. See Lan Ying (1979), Wu Daying and Liu Han (1979), Sheng Zuhong (1979), Xu Bing (1979), and Lin Rongnian and Zhang Jinfan (1980). See also "On Human Rights," (1979), p. 74.

87. Lan Ying (1979), pp. 71-75, p. 78. For a translation see Angle and Svensson (2001). For a reference to Ren Wanding's organization, see Anon., "A Summary of the Debate on Human Rights in Domestic Magazines," (1979), p. 77.

88. Lan Ying (1979), p. 72.

89. "On Human Rights," (1979), p. 76. An almost identical formulation is found in Dong Ling and Liu Shi (1979), p. 66.

90. This view was shared by many of the more orthodox writers, including those who were favorably disposed to use the idea of human rights. See also Wu Daying and Liu Han (1979), p. 11.

91. "Notes on the Human Rights Question," BR, no. 45, 9 November 1979, p. 19.

92. Lin Rongnian and Zhang Jinfan (1980), gave a more thorough overview, also briefly mentioning Zou Rong, Sun Yat-sen, as well as Chen Duxiu.

93. Lin Rongnian and Zhang Jinfan (1980), p. 37. The examples given were not particularly extensive or convincing. Dong Biwu, in a statement from 1957, for example, was said to have mentioned that many human rights violations existed in the countryside, without giving any examples, and in the same breath, he named other problems such as begging, robbery, and fighting.

94. "Notes on the Human Rights Question," BR, p. 19.

95. See, for example, Wu Daiying and Liu Han (1979), p. 11.

96. "On Human Rights," (1979), p. 77. See also, "Notes on the Human Rights Question," BR, p. 20.

97. "Notes on the Human Rights Question," BR, p. 20; Wu Daiying and Liu Han (1979), p. 12; and Lan Ying (1979), p. 74.

98. Sheng Zuhong (1979), pp. 19–20.

99. See, for example, Lin Rongnian and Zhang Jinfan (1980), p. 37; Wu Daiying and Liu Han (1979), p. 12; and Lan Ying (1979), p. 74.

100. For a more elaborate discussion on this aspect, see Gu Chunde (1982).

101. For a discussion of the category and language of "non-people" in the PRC, see Schoenhals (1994).

102. Xu Bing (1979).

103. An article in *Guangming ribao* in 1979, however, briefly referred to this new development. See "Notes on the Human Rights Question," BR, p. 17. But a more fully developed view and appreciation of post-1948 developments did not occur until circa 1982; see Shen Baoxiang et al. (1982).

104. See Qian Si, reprinted in Cohen and Chiu (1974), vol. 1, pp. 607-610.

105. "Notes on the Human Rights Question," BR, p. 18.

106. Shen Baoxiang et al. (1982), p. 16.

107. On the Soviet view on human rights, see Brunner (1982) and Toscano (1989).

108. See the critical views of the West expressed by M. S. Gorbachev and V. A. Kartashkin in the 1980s, quoted in Toscano (1989), p. 14. The Soviet Union, like China later, has made frequent references to Article 2 (7) of the UN Charter on domestic jurisdiction; see Toscano (1989), p. 15.

109. For list of publications, see CASS (1992), Han Depei (1995), and Li Lin (1996a).

110. For the Soviet dissidents' struggle for human rights, see Rubenstein (1980).

111. See Quigley (1989). Brunner (1982), however, indicates that quite vibrant human rights discussions and publication activities in the Soviet academia have occurred since the mid-1960s.

112. This is at least the impression one gets when reading Quigley's (1989) account of human rights studies in the Soviet Union. But maybe this difference also is due to the increasing importance of human rights in international politics since 1989.

113. See excerpt of a point agreement published by BBC News, Friday, December 10, 1999, 12:20 GMT, at <www.monitor.bbc.com>.[accessed December 11, 1999].

Chapter Eleven

A Contested and Evolving Discourse: Human Rights Debates since the Late 1980s

LIBERALIZATION AND BACKLASH IN THE LATE 1980s

In the early 1980s, unofficial discussions of human rights were silenced by the arrest of several of the participants of the Democracy Wall Movement. During much of the decade human rights also remained a taboo subject in official discourse. But during this period the PRC, on the other hand, became more involved in international human rights work. It became a member of the UN Human Rights Commission in 1982 and ratified several human rights conventions throughout the 1980s.[1] The PRC's activities in the United Nations, however, reflected particular Chinese considerations and interests. The conventions and declarations to which it chose to accede were mostly conventions that dealt with collective rights or sovereignty issues, such as racial discrimination, slavery, genocide, development, and self-determination. Nonetheless, China also signed and ratified several conventions dealing with individual rights, such as the Convention on the Elimination of All Forms of Discrimination against Women (1980), the Convention against Torture and Other Cruel, Inhuman, or Degrading Treatment or Punishment (1988), and the Convention on the Rights of the Child (1989).

By the late 1980s, the PRC was prepared to acknowledge the importance of international human rights work and openly state its support of such work in domestic fora.[2] In 1986 a spate of articles on the history and significance of the UDHR and the two human rights covenants appeared in the Chinese press, and in 1988 the PRC celebrated the fortieth anniversary of the UDHR with the publication of both articles in the official press and a conference.[3] The Chinese government praised recent developments with respect to the content of human rights. Special emphasis was given to the rights to national self-determination and development, which were proclaimed to be the two most important human rights. These collective rights were also said to be of special importance to Third World countries, which were admonished to "give priority to achieving their collective rights by striving for national independence, safeguarding state and territorial sovereignty, preventing racial discrimination, realising national equality, and developing national economy and culture."[4] While the PRC was prepared to acknowledge that a common standard of human rights existed, it continued to argue that rights would vary with different social and political systems, levels of economic and cultural development, and national customs and habits. Countries should therefore not impose their own standards on other societies or interfere in their internal affairs.

It can be said that the PRC by 1988 had entered a new stage in the debate on human rights.[5] This more affirmative official position encouraged individual scholars, who were emboldened to express more liberal and positive views on human rights. These discussions were also part and parcel of the generally more liberal political climate of late 1988 and early 1989.[6] Views and topics that not long ago had been taboo and met with harsh suppression could be aired more openly, and lively discussions on political reforms and democracy took place. Liberal intellectuals such as Yu Haocheng used the occasion of the fortieth anniversary of the UDHR to voice his support of human rights.[7] Yu argued that criticism of humanism and the concept of human nature, exemplified by the anti-humanitarianism campaign of 1983, explained the earlier negative view of human rights in China. Although Yu affirmed human rights and their universal nature, he nevertheless still proclaimed them to have a class nature. Other scholars were to take the discussion one step further.

Two of the more liberal articles on human rights to be published at that time were written by Xu Bing and Yu Keping.[8] Their views reveal a closing of the gap between the democracy activists of 1978 and the establishment intellectuals. Xu Bing acknowledged that the issue of human rights hitherto had been taboo in the PRC and that there existed many misconceptions regarding the idea. He argued against those who saw human rights as an exclusively bourgeois idea, lacking relevance and application to China. According to both authors, human rights were defined as rights that each human being ought to enjoy (*yinggai yongyou de quanli*) by virtue of his human nature. To violate a person's human rights constituted an attack on his humanity because without rights one would not be a complete human being. Human rights, it followed, were not something given or decided by an individual or a group, presumably not even by the state. They were claims the individual has against the government and society, regarding what the government should and should not do.

Whereas earlier discussions had either tended to prefer citizens' rights over human rights or seen them as identical, Xu Bing and Yu Keping emphasized that human rights were different from citizen's rights in that one could not be deprived of human rights as one could citizen's rights. In contrast to the official debate of the late 1970s, Xu and Yu were also prepared to acknowledge that human rights have a supraclass character. As Xu Bing put it, "To refute the supraclass character of human rights means to emphasise the class character of human rights. To give human rights only to the people and not to enemies results in the complete negation and violation of human rights."[9] Human rights were furthermore regarded as a goal in and of themselves, and not simply as a means toward an end. Yu Keping argued that the progress of a particular society should be evaluated on the basis of its respect for human rights. He divided human rights into fundamental rights, which included the right to existence (*shengcun*), freedom and equality, and social and economic rights. Meanwhile Xu divided human rights into personal rights, which he saw as "the most fundamental rights to be a person [*zuo ren de zui jiben quanli*]," political rights and freedoms, and economic and social rights.

Toward the end of 1988, under the influence of the more liberal political climate, long-time dissident Ren Wanding was inspired to raise the issue of his fellow democracy activists who were still languishing in jail. But it was not until early 1989, however, that human rights became an issue brought out into the open by liberal intellectuals. In early January of that year, Fang Lizhi wrote an open letter to Deng Xiaoping demanding the release of Wei Jingsheng and other political dissidents.[10] Fang referred to the May Fourth Movement and the French Revolution and their ideals of human rights and democracy. Although Fang earlier had taken a strong stance on academic freedom and, in a 1987 interview with a foreign journalist, also expressed concern about Wei's case and the human rights situation in China, it was the first time for him, or any Chinese establishment intellectual, to explicitly and directly take up the cause of political prisoners with the regime.[11] Fang's January letter prompted other Chinese intellectuals to follow suit with similar petitions and open letters. In the letter sent by the poet Bei Dao and thirty-two other intellectuals, mention was made of "a growing trend across the world of respect for human rights." The wording of these petitions and open letters were still relatively mild, however; they described the release of political prisoners as a humanitarian act that would be beneficial for society, rather than taking the government to task for imprisoning people for their views and violating their human rights. Nor did they refer to the UDHR or to the Chinese government's international commitments with respect to human rights.[12]

Later that spring, the Chinese government was faced with a much greater challenge to its political rule as student demonstrations erupted with demands for democracy and an end to corruption.[13] The movement soon spread to involve other groups in society as workers and other citizens joined the ranks of the demonstrators. Besides taking to the streets and occupying public areas, students and workers also began to organize and set up their own independent groups. Their demands for democracy and public accountability were expressed in very general and vague terms. They mainly demanded greater openness on the part of the party and recognition of the legality of their organizations. Freedom of the press and freedom of association were the rights most frequently invoked, although they were generally not referred to as human rights. Slogans such as "Long Live Human Rights!" were chanted, but few posters raised the issue of human rights. Interestingly enough, and somewhat puzzlingly, the students did not take up Fang Lizhi's demand of respect for human rights and the release of political prisoners. Only occasionally did a wall poster, such at the one at Fudan University on April 20, demand the release of all political prisoners.[14]

There were, nonetheless, some instances during the movement when more explicit references to human rights were made in statements and speeches. On several occasions references were made to the May Fourth spirit of democracy, human rights, and awakening of the Chinese people. For example, in the May Fourth Manifesto, read by Wuer Kaixi at Tiananmen Square, the student movement was described as continuing in the spirit of May Fourth, reiterating its calls for democracy and science, and invoking the language of human rights.

> This student movement has but one goal, that is to facilitate the process of modernisation by raising high the banners of democracy and science, by liberating people from the constraints of feudal ideology, and by promoting freedom, human rights, and rule by law. To this end, we urge the government to accelerate the pace of political reform, to guarantee the rights of the people vested in the law, to implement a press law, to permit privately run newspapers, to eradicate corruption, to hasten the establishment of an honest and democratic government, to value education, to respect intellectual work, and to save the nation through science.[15]

A Declaration of Human Rights, published in Beijing around May 20, more explicitly put the focus on the issue of human rights. The declaration stated that all people are born free and equal and enjoy inalienable natural rights, such as the rights to belief, speech, publication, assembly, association, and so on. Those behind the declaration felt that there was a need to make a declaration of people's human rights, "[i]n view of the widespread ignorance and neglect or even apathy toward human rights in Chinese society, in view of several thousand years of cruel interference in and the infringement of human rights by our rulers, and in view of the need to create a new society, a new order, and a new morality."[16] These sentiments are not only reminiscent of earlier demands for human rights in Chinese history, but also similar to the views that Xu Bing expressed earlier the same year within a more academic context.[17]

On the night of June 3 and in the early hours of the following morning, the Chinese government ordered the army to open fire against its own people while "retaking" the streets of central Beijing that students and ordinary citizens had occupied for several weeks. Although no official or reliable figures are available, it is likely that thousands of people were killed in the suppression of the democracy movement. Tens of thousands of people were arrested and many of the student leaders fled the country to continue the democracy movement in exile. The regime defended its actions by describing the movement as a "counterrevolutionary rebellion" and those killed and arrested as "counterrevolutionaries" and "hooligans." But its blatant human rights violations led to an outcry and strong condemnations. For a short period China was treated as an international pariah in the West, as many governments postponed official visits, denied it credits, and imposed sanctions.

THE OFFICIAL APPROPRIATION OF THE LANGUAGE OF HUMAN RIGHTS IN THE POST-1989 PERIOD

In the wake of the crackdown on the democracy movement in 1989, the PRC was confronted with fierce and unprecedented international criticism of its human rights record. Its immediate response was reactive and took the form of highly polemical statements and articles.[18] The standard approach was to dismiss all criticism and argue that the critics were interfering in the PRC's internal affairs. China, like the Soviet Union earlier, tried to make use of selected parts of the UN Charter in order to defend the position that human rights is primarily a domestic issue. As in the past, it was also argued that only gross human rights violations, such as apartheid and genocide, justified actions on the part of the international community, whereas issues pertaining to civil and political rights did not permit any interference. Such a distinction meant that international criticism of the crushing of the democracy movement could be dismissed as constituting unlawful interference. China was quelling a counterrevolutionary rebellion, it claimed, not violating any human rights. But the international criticism also prompted the PRC to move away from a purely reactive stance and develop a more proactive policy on human rights. It thus began to elaborate upon its own distinctive understanding of human rights and moved to appropriate the concept.

During the 1990s, the PRC became more sophisticated in its dealings with the international community over human rights issues. It has used a wide range of methods to defuse and contain human rights critique, including inviting foreign human rights delegations to China, participating in and lobbying international human rights fora, releasing high-profile political dissidents, engaging in bilateral dialogues on human rights, and signing human rights instruments. An important component of China's new human rights policy is its more active participation in and promulgation of its own human rights position at different international and regional fora. Because China's human rights situation, in contrast to the pre-1989 period, has been under scrutiny at the annual meetings of the UN Human Rights Commission, it has become expedient for the PRC to pay closer attention to UN work on human rights. It has lobbied aggressively and effectively to ward off critical resolutions, trying to split the West on the issue and seeking support in the Third World for its no-action motions.[19] The PRC cooperated with ASEAN (Association of Southeast Asia Nations) member states at the Bangkok human rights conference in 1993 and sent a strong delegation to the UN Human Rights Conference that took place in Vienna later the same year.

Apart from work in the multilateral arena, China has also paid particular attention to bilateral exchanges and cooperation in the field of human rights. During the period 1991–94, foreign human rights delegations, both diplomatic as well as more academic, were invited to visit China, and several Chinese delegations were also sent abroad.[20] Since 1997, the focus of China's human rights diplomacy has been on establishing so-called dialogues on human rights with different countries. This is a conscious tactic on the part of the Chinese government to try to split the West. In particular, the PRC wishes to sow discord between the United States and the European Union on the best policy to deal with the PRC over human rights, and it wants to try to undermine any joint activities in the United Nations to censor it. Many countries, including Canada, Australia, and Norway, as well as the European Union, now regularly engage in human rights dialogues with China.[21] These dialogues normally include seminars and discussions on human rights with diplomats and legal experts, but have also included or led to human rights-related cooperation and training of Chinese officials and diplomats.[22]

A closer scrutiny of the PRC's human rights policy reveals that it is actually more the packaging than the content that has changed. Whereas the PRC now takes a more positive, active, and participatory approach to international human rights work and also engages in dialogues with other countries over human rights, domestic critics are treated as harshly as ever before, and no independent human rights organizations are allowed to exist or take part in any of the international work and bilateral dialogues and cooperation programs.

It is, unfortunately, quite difficult to get a clear and complete picture of the background to and deliberations on the new official strategy on human rights within the Chinese administration or on the specific contributions from different institutions and individuals. This being said, however, there is sufficient information available to suggest that the Chinese leadership after 1989 quickly and determinedly set about to formulate a human rights policy that they have since modified and developed as the international environment has changed and their confidence in their own ability to handle the issue has increased. Already in the immediate post–June Fourth period, the Chinese leadership voiced a concern of the use, or abuse, as they preferred to describe it, of human rights slogans during the democracy movement.[23] The students were thus accused of having violated human rights themselves through their illegal strikes and demonstrations. The political leadership was also worried about the fact that the students seemed to harbor a bourgeois understanding of human rights. At a national conference on propaganda in July 1989, President Jiang Zemin himself acknowledged as much: "The so-called 'democracy, freedom and human rights' viewpoint pronounced by the Western bourgeoisie has struck a sympathetic chord among some young intellectuals in our country; it may also be said to be one of the ideological roots which caused the student movement and upheaval. Many young students continue to have a very ambiguous understanding in this area."[24] Jiang concluded that it was of vital importance to promote a Marxist analysis of human rights to counteract these bourgeois influences. The students' interest in human rights and the fact that dissidents in exile united around demands for human rights convinced the Chinese leadership that it was a subject they needed to study more carefully.[25] The government's urgency to grasp the human rights issue was further underlined by the fact that human rights became an important and problematic issue in China's relations with the international community. The political leadership was convinced that the West was using human rights as a weapon in their strategy of "peaceful evolution" aiming to subvert the socialist system in the PRC. To counter this scheme, they decided to put more efforts into human rights work and develop their own strategy on human rights issues.

In November 1989, the Theoretical Office of the CCP Central Propaganda Department gathered a number of scholars to a first meeting on human rights.[26] At subsequent meetings the "urgency" of research on human rights was further stressed. Human rights issues, it was said, could no longer be "dodged"; more research was needed in order to meet the "challenge" of the West. Eight different subtopics on human rights were decided upon and the task to undertake research on them assigned to different departments and institutions, such as the Editorial and Translating Department of Marxism-Leninism-Stalinism Works, Peking University, People's University, the Central Party School, the China Law Association, and the Foreign Ministry, among others. In 1993–94, the result of this work was published in seven volumes by the Sichuan People's Publishing House.[27] This official blessing of research on human rights also inspired other more academic activities. Beginning in 1990, the Chinese authorities have arranged or sponsored several conferences as well as initiated human rights research at different academic institutions and universities.[28] This official support has also been proudly mentioned and acknowledged.

> The Chinese Government actively supports and aids financially the study of human rights. The research subjects aided financially by the State Social Sciences Foundation include a certain number of subjects on human rights. Every year a group of subjects on human rights wins financial aid from the State Education Commission, the Chinese Academy of Social Sciences and local governments. . . . In addition, the China Human Rights Research Fund set up by various social circles collects funds and gives financial aid to research activities on human rights.[29]

Already in March 1989, and partly in response to Fang Lizhi's open letter, several scholars at Peking University had begun to discuss the importance of studying human rights issues.[30] Led by Zhang Zhilian, a leading Chinese scholar of French history, they established the Research Organization for Foreign Issues. Zhang argued that research on human rights was lacking in China but that in the new international environment this was an important issue that Chinese scholars also needed to address. In this context he also suggested that Chinese scholars should investigate human rights violations in other countries. The organization held several conferences, the first in December 1989, and published a newsletter on human rights and its conference papers in book form. In May 1990, the China Historical Materialism Society and China Normal University also gathered scholars to discuss Marxist human rights theories; the following year a conference resulted in the publication of a book.[31] In March 1991, the magazine *Chinese Legal Science* and the China Law Association jointly sponsored an academic conference on human rights. The participants agreed not only to criticize the bourgeois conception of human rights but also to develop a Marxist concept of human rights.[32] After these first conferences several others were held at institutions of higher learning, including an important one at CASS (the Chinese Academy of Social Sciences) in June 1991.[33] Newspapers such as *People's Daily* and *Guangming ribao* also convened special meetings to discuss human rights.

In October 1991, the State Council then published its first White Paper on human rights. This report was an outcome of discussions under way since 1989 among Chinese experts and propaganda officials on how best to handle the human rights issue. Although the White Paper was given ample coverage in the domestic press, it is obvious that it was directed as much to a foreign as to a domestic audience. In this document China described itself as a long-time advocate of human rights, criticized the West for past violations and cruelties toward the Chinese people, and launched its own conception of human rights. The CCP was depicted as having staunchly defended and promoted human rights all along: "Since the very day of its founding, the CCP has been holding high the banner of democracy and human rights." The work to lift people out of poverty and guarantee them their rights as the real masters of the country was described in great detail, while other not so glorious aspects of party history were ignored. Although extensive coverage was given to the right to subsistence, which for the first time was described as the most important right of the Chinese people, political and legal rights were also outlined and discussed. Chinese citizens were said to enjoy extensive and equal political and civil rights as stipulated in the constitution and a number of other laws.

In the aftermath of the White Paper, more conferences were held around the country and human rights became a hot topic in law magazines and other publications. The majority of the articles published during this period were confined to very theoretical and ideological analyses of human rights and did not venture to take on any concrete issues. In November 1991 another meeting on human rights was organized by the CCP Central Propaganda Department. At the meeting, Nie Dajiang, deputy head of the department, emphasized that research on human rights must be within the parameters of Marxism. It should follow "the guidance of Marxist theories and persist in using historical materialist and dialectical materialist outlooks and methodology."[34] The political motives behind the interest in human rights work is quite obvious. In 1992 the Research Institute for Resisting Peaceful Evolution, established after June Fourth and headed by Wang Renzhi, then director of the CCP Central Propaganda Department, put together a report advocating a more offensive strategy on human rights.[35] In the report, human rights were described as a weapon used by the West in order to subvert the Chinese socialist system. In order to resist this "peaceful evolution" and defend China's national sovereignty, more efforts should be put into propaganda work and studies on human rights. The publication of White Papers defending and explaining the Chinese position was regarded as one efficient tool with which to fight foreign criticism. "Now we have released a White Paper, which indicates that we ourselves have taken up the human rights banner and have begun to launch a frontal attack on our own initiative."[36] The State Council has continued to regularly publish White Papers on both more general human rights issues as well as more specific topics, such as prison conditions, the situation in Tibet, religious freedom, and so on; all written with the aim of defending the Chinese human rights record.[37]

In the eyes of the political leadership, human rights research is subordinated to and justified by the need to refute Western critique and protect China's national sovereignty and interests.[38] Some scholars, however, have complained about this politicization of human rights research and called for more academic and independent work.[39] But although more independent and challenging works have indeed emerged within the academic community, the hand of the state still weighs heavily in the field of human rights research.

Several of China's most prestigious universities and research institutes, such as People's University, CASS, and Peking University have set up research institutes or centers on human rights. The works put out by the human rights center at People's University, is, as could be expected, quite conservative in character and close to the official line.[40] The close connection between human rights research and propaganda work is revealed by the fact that the Beijing Municipal Propaganda Bureau commissioned People's University to write a book on human rights. The Human Rights Center at CASS has been very influential and has engaged in a number of different activities in the human rights field, ranging from organizing academic conferences, publishing books on human rights, translating foreign works on human rights, cooperating with foreign institutions, participating in human rights delegations and international human rights conferences and dialogues, engaging in studies and research abroad, and offering proposals and providing information to the political leadership. Scholars at Peking University have likewise published works on human rights and arranged conferences and seminars. Peking University was the first university in China to offer a special course on human rights.[41]

Since the early 1990s, there has been a massive output of publications on human rights in China, especially when compared with previous decades. The number of works is impressive, although many are more political than academic in character and only rehash the official line. More than one thousand articles and probably at least one hundred monographs have been published since 1989.[42] The Sichuan Publishing House alone is said to have employed more than one hundred scholars over three years in order to publish the seven-volume series on human rights that was an outcome of the CCP Central Propaganda Committee meetings, an investment in time and money that gives an indication of the priority placed on such research.[43]

Because NGOs play an important role in contemporary global human rights work, some enjoying observatory status in different UN organs and having a right to present reports and make statements, China has also realized that it is advisable to establish organizations of its own in the field. In 1993, in preparation for the UN Vienna Conference on Human Rights, the China Society for Human Rights Studies (CSHRS) was established.[44] Although the organization ostensibly is independent, its close official connection is revealed by the fact that its first president was a former minister of culture, Zhu Muzhi, who also was head of the CCP Central Committee Foreign Propaganda Small Group in the 1990s. Other officials and former diplomats are also members. The CSHRS has been pushing for international recognition, and in 1998 received NGO observatory status in the United Nations. Since its inauguration, the CSHRS has sent delegations to several countries, participated in international conferences on human rights, arranged conferences itself, as well as published several works on human rights.[45] In 1998, for example, it arranged a big international conference on the fiftieth anniversary of the UDHR and also launched China's first radio series on human rights.[46] One of the organization's main tasks is to refute Western criticism and defend the Chinese government's position on human rights. To that end, for example, it has of late joined in the official denunciation of Falun Gong, an organization that blends *qigong* with Buddhist and Taoist beliefs. It is also actively involved in writing critical pieces on human rights violations in the United States. Since the early 1990s, the publication of the U.S. Department of State's annual human rights reports have met with prompt replies and articles in the Chinese press that outline American human rights problems in a tit-for-tat kind of game. One appendix in the controversial book *China Can Say No*, a widely popular nationalistic work published in 1996 that objected to what it described as the U.S. bullying of China, was written by Yu Quanyu, vice-chairman of CSHRS.[47] In this article Yu described American violations of human rights, using examples of violations of economic and social rights, racism and discrimination of blacks and other groups, widespread violence, and the high incidence of murder.

The issuing of the 1991 White Paper and subsequent White Papers reveal that the Chinese government has come to embrace, or rather appropriate, the language of human rights. The PRC can no longer afford to stand outside the global human rights regime and instead it tries to pose as a defender of human rights. It furthermore tries to imbue human rights with its own content and meaning, leading to the development of what could be called "human rights with Chinese characteristics." China is by no means the only country to have attempted to appropriate the concept of human rights, nor is it a prerogative of governments, as individuals and organizations also are engaged in similar endeavors. Appropriation and contestation over important concepts and ideas is a rather natural and common practice in political discourse. What is important to note for the moment is that such an appropriation reveals that the CCP no longer harbors any doubts as to whether human rights are of relevance to socialist China, or compatible with Marxism.[48] But many aspects of the concept of universal human rights nevertheless continue to pose difficulties for scholars operating within a largely Marxist framework. The political sensitivity of the subject in addition makes academic discussions on human rights highly problematic.

The parameters for the Chinese human rights discourse are still very much set by Marxism although the understanding of Marxism and the Marxist analysis of human rights has changed over the years. Certain theoretical truths remain nonnegotiable even though they have been weakened since the late 1970s. The official position is still that there can be no natural and innate rights relevant for all societies at all times, a view with which many academics concur. But it should be noted that the official discourse now has broken free from the exclusive focus on the class character of human rights that characterized earlier debates. It is openly acknowledged today that human rights also have a universal dimension, even though it is still argued that human rights inevitably will have a class character in a class society.[49] The general position is thus to acknowledge that human rights are both universal and particular in character.[50]

A crucial assumption in the 1991 White Paper, one which has been reiterated both before and since, is that, due to "differences in historical background, social system, cultural tradition and economic development, countries differ in their understanding and practice of human rights." From this premise the conclusion is drawn that it is "neither proper nor feasible for any country to judge other countries by the yardstick of its own mode or to impose its own mode on others."[51] This assumption and its conclusions are open to dispute in many ways. First of all, it deliberately ignores the question of domestic differences over human rights: governments and political opponents generally do not share the same view, and even within the establishment and the political opposition divergent views can exist. It also ignores the fact that there actually is a universally accepted human rights standard that countries, including China, have agreed upon despite all their differences, and that it therefore is perfectly acceptable for countries to criticize others that do not meet this standard. It furthermore begs the question whether, to the extent that different understandings of human rights really exist, this would rule out or make criticism from outsiders nonpermissible.

The Chinese political leadership has made the definition of the content and scope of human rights its own prerogative and monopolizes the debate. It has thus abrogated the right to decide which human rights are more in tune with China's "cultural traditions" and level of economic development. The official relativism, it should be noted, is more premised upon economic than cultural or historical differences. This is not surprising since China's official position, after all, builds upon a Marxist analysis and understanding of rights. The following quote from the Sichuan People's Publishing House series on human rights makes this abundantly clear:

> Marxism opposes the view of an idealist historical humanitarianism which [sees] human rights as absolute and abstract, and advocates [the view] that human rights are historical, concrete, and relative; in the final analysis they are conditioned by the socioeconomic level of development. [Marxism] emphasises that since every country's social system, economic conditions, cultural traditions, and values are different, there cannot exist any absolutely universal human rights or completely identical human rights standards.[52]

Although cultural traditions are referred to here, the main thrust behind both the official position and that of many Chinese scholars is that it is the level of economic development that determines and restricts human rights in a given country.[53] This understanding implies that rights are premised upon whether it is possible to implement the right in question; in other words, that one cannot have a right unless the necessary economic resources exist for its implementation.

Even though China takes a relativistic approach to human rights, this has not hindered it from criticizing others for violating human rights. In doing so, however, China undermines and violates its own principles, acting as if human rights were universal in character after all. China has criticized the United States for not living up to its own values as put forward in the American Declaration of Independence, an appropriate approach of a relativist. But by also criticizing the United States for violating rights held dear by China, such as economic and social rights, it is judging a society on values exogenous to it since the United States has not signed the ICESCR—something that a good relativist should never do. Following its own logic, China could thus be accused of "imposing" its own human rights standard on the United States. By issuing reports criticizing the United States, China also undermines its own argument that the publication of reports on other countries' human rights records constitute an interference in their internal affairs.[54] China's references to international conventions when criticizing other countries' human rights record reveal that it has come to accept the international regime on human rights and the universal application of these conventions, at least when it serves its own purposes, which once again undermines its relativistic position.[55]

THE RIGHT TO SUBSISTENCE

Since the early 1990s, the right to subsistence figures prominently in the contemporary official discourse. The Chinese government regards this right as the most fundamental of all human rights and argues that it must be prioritized at China's present stage of development.[56] It also accuses the West (read the United States) of neglecting economic and social rights. But economic and social rights have been on the agenda of a wide range of Western philosophers and political thinkers since the seventeenth century and, more recently, scholars such as Henry Shue have also argued for a right to subsistence.[57] Furthermore, a vast majority of Western countries have signed the ICESCR; the notable exception being the United States. Economic and social rights thus have deep, if complex, roots in the West. Nor should the CCP get the credit for having invented or been the first to have propagated a right to subsistence in China. As discussed in chapter 6, it seems as if Gao Yihan and Dai Jitao could have been among the first in China to talk about such a right. It is at least possible to say that the term entered the Chinese political lexicon some time after 1920, and that it continued to play a prominent role in human rights discourse until 1949. The CCP, as far as I can tell, did not explicitly use the term "right to subsistence" in the pre-1949 period, nor did it figure in the official discussion on human rights during the late 1970s and early 1980s, when the most important rights instead were said to be the rights to development and self-determination.[58] It was only with the 1991 White Paper that the right to subsistence was highlighted as the single most important right for the Chinese people. Dong Yunhu, a young scholar from the Central Party School who also participated in the drafting of the white paper and since has played a prominent role in the CSHRS, has been credited as being one of the scholars responsible for the concept as it exists in its current incarnation.[59]

Even before the publication of the 1991 White Paper, the official rhetoric stressed that it was more important to be able to "eat one's fill and dress warmly" and to receive medical care and education, than to engage in "empty human rights sloganeering."[60] The first official mention of the right to subsistence as the most important human right occurred in meetings held by Jiang Zemin and Li Peng with former American President Carter in April 1991.[61] In some of the more theoretical works, the right to subsistence is interestingly enough traced to Western philosophers, although it is emphasized that the Chinese understanding is different from these Western predecessors. The right to subsistence is thus traced to Thomas Aquinas and also found to be related to the right to life found in the writings of Locke and stipulated in the American Declaration of Independence.[62] It is also seen as owing much to the developments of social rights in revolutionary France and to the Soviet Declaration of Rights of the Exploited Laboring People of 1918. Anton Menger, a socialist who wrote on the right to subsistence in the 1890s, is also mentioned in this context. In its more modern incarnation, the right is seen as hailing from developments after the Second World War and to have precedents both in the 1966 ICESCR and in the 1981 African Human Rights Charter. No mention is made, however, of contemporary Western scholars such as Henry Shue.

It is worth noting that the right to subsistence is described in quite different terms in the contemporary official discourse than was the case in the pre-1949 debates. In contrast to these, the term is now given a more collectivistic and nationalistic interpretation. Although it is said that the subject of the right can be both individuals and collectives, it is often described as a collective right on a par with and encompassing the rights to development and self-determination. The rights to national independence and state sovereignty are said to be prerequisites for guaranteeing the right to subsistence of the Chinese people.[63] As a collective right, the right to subsistence refers to the rights to survival and protection from extinction of a nationality or a state.[64] When the right to subsistence pertains to individuals, it refers to economic and social rights, both those needed in order to protect life and those needed to uphold life.[65] To more liberal writers the right to subsistence not only refers to the securing of food and clothing but also encompasses the total development and well-being of the individual. They would include the following rights within the right to subsistence: the right to life and the right to respect; the right to the means to uphold life, including property; the right to work, including the rights to leisure and protection; the right to economic support; the right to development, such as the right to education; and the rights to environment, health, and peace.[66] Even Chen Zhishang, a more conservative scholar, would argue that the right to subsistence is not limited to economic rights.[67] Chen also dismisses as a misunderstanding the view that China only focuses on the right to subsistence to the neglect of political and civil rights. The fact that China still is a relatively poor country that has emerged from a long period of imperialist encroachment and wars, is a reason why the right to subsistence at the present time is the most important right in China. But Chinese writers tend to describe this right as the most important right for all developing countries, hence, not only for China. They furthermore contend that as these societies develop and people's basic subsistence is guaranteed, other rights, such as civil and political rights, come to the fore. Such an understanding builds upon a general belief that the level of economic development shapes and restricts the level and extent of human rights enjoyed in any given society.

THE ACADEMIC DISCOURSE

As already hinted at above, it is becoming increasingly obvious that one has to distinguish between the official rhetoric on human rights and the more academic discussions taking place in China.[68] In this context one must of course bear in mind the political constraints under which academic research operates, particularly in such a politically sensitive field as human rights. Not surprisingly, most academic writings are highly theoretical and abstract in character and refrain from addressing the actual human rights situation in China. It would seem as if, to date, mostly legal scholars and philosophers have been engaged in research on human rights. Political scientists and historians, for example, have not yet contributed much to the field.

The establishment intellectuals are not a homogeneous group but can tentatively be divided into conservatives, neo-authoritarians, moderates, and liberals, although this crude categorization hides important differences on specific aspects of human rights within the different groups as well as overlooks similarities between them.[69] Keeping this in mind, it could be said that among the conservative scholars are academics such as Chen Zhishang at Peking University and Gu Chunde at People's University.[70] These people take a more pronounced Marxist view of human rights. But although they still tend to emphasize the class character of human rights, they no longer dismiss human rights as a mere bourgeois slogan. Neo-authoritarians such as He Xin and political cadres such as Wang Renzhi, former head of the CCP Central Committee Propaganda Department, are particularly concerned about what they call the "human rights diplomacy" of the West, and thus tend to see human rights as a weapon used by the West to contain China.[71] But such a view, however, is quite common among many others as well.

The largest group of the establishment intellectuals would be what one could call the moderates, a wide group of people including Li Buyun and others at CASS.[72] More liberal scholars would include Xu Bing, formerly at CASS; Zhang Wenxian of Jilin University; Liu Junning, also formerly at CASS; and possibly Xia Yong at CASS. These scholars generally stress that human rights are moral rights and accept that they at least partly spring from the common nature of human beings, which leads them to emphasize their universal character. They also tend to put more emphasis on rights than on duties, and regard civil and political rights as equally important to economic and social rights. They furthermore generally tend to interpret rights in more individualistic terms. Several of them, such as Xin Chunying, Li Shenzhi, and Liu Junning, are also very critical of so-called Asian values.

Not surprisingly, these different groups of scholars also show quite different intellectual influences. Most establishment intellectuals writing on human rights are still influenced by, or at least pay lip-service to Marxism. A minority of scholars, such as Xia Yong, try to put forward a synthesis between Western ideas and more traditional Confucian ideas, but even they cannot escape the constraints of Marxism. Although there are more references to international human rights literature today than in the early 1980s, many writers still seem to be rather unfamiliar with both Western and non-Western literature on the topic. The younger generation of Chinese scholars, however, is generally more up-to-date as well as active in translating Western works. In the 1998 CASS human rights encyclopedia, Western twentieth-century scholars who have their own entries are Maritain, Lon Luvois Fuller, John R. Rawls, Martin Luther King Jr., Dworkin, and Robert Nozick; a fairly eclectic selection of scholars and activists.[73] Several works by Western scholars have also been translated during the 1990s, either as excerpts and brief selections or complete works.[74] Examples from the latter category include books by Milne, Henkin, Humphrey, R. J. Vincent, Thomas J. Buergenthal, and Donnelly.[75] CASS and Peking University have published books on human rights in cooperation with foreign institutions that include contributions by both Chinese and foreign scholars.[76] Several compilations of international documents and conventions on human rights have also been published since 1989.[77]

Among the rather diverse group of Western scholars introduced to the Chinese readership, we find both universalists, such as Henkin and Donnelly, and relativists, such as Milne. Although some of them, like Cranston, object to economic and social rights as human rights, the majority of the others take a fairly positive view of these rights. And whereas Donnelly, for example, is critical of collective rights, many of the others, such as Roland Rich, Gillian Triggs, and Ian Brownlie, are more positive to such rights.[78] Politically these writers range from liberals (Cranston, Henkin) to personalists (Maritain), social-democrats (Donnelly), and socialists (Eugene Kamenka). Generally speaking, it can be said that Chinese scholars have been most influenced by Western scholars who advocate economic and social rights, acknowledge collective rights, voice moderate relativism, as well as express a critique of some aspects of the mainstream human rights position in the West.

Milne, a less well-known human rights scholar in the West, is one who has received the most attention in China. He was also among the first Western scholars to be translated after 1989; one article was published in 1991. The fact that two groups of scholars, unaware of each other it seems, chose to translate his 1986 work *Human Rights and Human Diversity*, is quite interesting and revealing. Some chapters were also included in the Sichuan People's Publishing House's two volumes on Western human rights ideas as part of their seven-volume series. In addition, in 1993 another short translation of Milne's work appeared under the misleading title "Opposing the Idea of Human Rights." Milne's ideas have also been discussed in the volume edited by Han Depei, and by Xia Yong in his works. The interest in Milne is beyond doubt partly due to the fact that he, in contrast to many other Western scholars, takes a more relativistic position on human rights.[79] It is obvious that such a view and other aspects of his thinking, as discussed below, are congenial to that of many Chinese scholars. But it also should be pointed out that Milne's views on human rights are influenced by Kant and the British Idealists, and, as we recall from earlier chapters, these thinkers' views deeply influenced previous generations of Chinese intellectuals, which could help explain the contemporary interest in Milne.

Milne's starting point is the Kantian categorical imperative, according to which the human person should be treated solely as an end and not as a means. In order to be an autonomous person the individual needs certain rights.[80] All human beings, it follows, are entitled to the same kind of concern and equal treatment. This proposition leads Milne to advocate a universal minimum standard of human rights applicable to all societies. These aspects of Milne's thinking have inspired Chinese scholars such as Xia Yong to describe human rights as moral rights. But other aspects of Milne's thinking, such as his somewhat negative and skeptical view of the UDHR, have also been quite crucial and explain his popularity.

Milne takes quite a relativistic view of human rights. This is revealed in his critique of the UDHR, which he argues reflects the influence of Western liberal democracies. Many of the rights stipulated in the UDHR, he claims, would not be applicable or relevant in non-Western societies. This critique is not surprisingly noted and shared by all his Chinese commentators.[81] Milne argues that the moral and social diversity in the world gives rise to different values and that, therefore, rights that belong to all human beings cannot exist. His rejection of natural rights and insistence on the social embeddedness of rights is also met with sympathy by Chinese establishment intellectuals.[82] Since Milne is no Marxist, he does not, like the Chinese scholars, stress the importance of economic differences or argue that in a class society people's rights would be class based, but focuses on the moral and social diversity in the world. He does not reject the existence of a common morality, however, from which he deduces certain universal human rights, but, like most Chinese scholars, prefers to speak about the joint existence of a particular and a common morality.

Among the universal human rights that cannot be morally forfeited, according to Milne, are the rights to life, to justice in the form of fair treatment, to aid, to freedom from arbitrary interference, to honorable treatment, to civility, and, in the case of children, to care, whereas he denies that the right to property is a universal human right. Despite his belief in this commonality of human rights, Milne holds that the particular form these rights take inevitably will vary between different societies. Milne furthermore argues that an outsider should not judge or impose his own standards on other communities but would have to abide by the maxim: When in Rome, do as the Romans. Of particular interest in the Chinese context is also Milne's rejection of foreign interference in cases of human rights violations.[83] Milne's refutation of outside critique thus fits well with the official Chinese view that the West is imposing its human rights standards on the rest of the world and thus its critique of such behavior.[84]

CONTROVERSIES IN THE ACADEMIC DISCOURSE ON HUMAN RIGHTS

The Chinese academic debate has run high on some of the very same issues that have also been hotly debated in the West, namely, the basis and origin of rights, the subject of rights, and the content and scope of rights. Quite different views regarding the nature and origin of human rights exist among Chinese scholars today. Some like Xu Bing and Yu Keping take an essentialist view and hold that human rights are the rights that humans ought to enjoy by virtue of their humanity, without which human existence is impossible or would be incomplete. Or, as others would put it, "The source of human rights is the nature and dignity of the human person. . . . If he cannot enjoy these rights and freedoms, he cannot be said to live a human life."[85] Xia Yong likewise argues that "human rights are the rights to which you are entitled as long as you are a human being."[86] And according to Li Lin, human rights are founded upon human nature (*renxing*), personality (*renge*), and humanitarianism (*rendao*).[87] Humans possess human rights solely by virtue of their being humans and this separates them from animals. Human rights therefore transcend nation, class, race, sex, age, and belief. In this context, Li also criticizes the situation under the Cultural Revolution, when the concept of human rights was rejected and people were treated differently depending on their political status.[88] Xu Xianming similarly speaks about fundamental rights (*jiben quanli*) as those which separate human beings from animals.[89] The idea of human rights, he argues, arose in opposition to enslavement and the practice of "not treating people as human beings." Human rights are essential for human existence: they serve to guarantee and protect people's personality, dignity, and independence, and prevent their enslavement.

Few establishment scholars, however, are prepared to speak of human rights as completely innate or derived from human nature since they base their analysis on historical materialism and regard human nature as being shaped by social and economic relations.[90] Li Buyun, who also defines human rights as "the rights which man ought to enjoy by virtue of his human nature [*benxing*]," thus argues that human nature is both natural and social in character.[91] Li offers a quite elaborate definition of human rights and divides them into those rights one ought to enjoy by virtue of one's humanity, or one's due rights (*yingyou quanli*), for short; one's legal rights (*fading quanli*); and the actual rights that are realized in society (*shiyou quanli*). Li's definition of human rights is shared by other contemporary scholars and has become quite widespread and accepted.[92]

Li Buyun thus acknowledges that human rights are something more than, and above, legal rights. The fact that they are not bestowed by anybody but are due to humans, he claims, explains how the concept has become a weapon of the oppressed and the weak. But although these due rights existed before the implementation of law, they are not natural in the sense that they are innate or unrelated to the specific conditions of one's society. His concept of "due rights," Li contends, is different from the Western idea of natural rights, which ignores the social character of man. In this context, he seems to lean toward a needs-based theory of human rights according to which human rights are needed in order to satisfy man's needs and realize his humanity.[93] Li Buyun believes that a gap often exists between people's due rights and their legal rights in society, as well as a gap between their legal rights and the rights actually enjoyed. He attributes these gaps to several factors, such as a lack of a democratic and legal tradition, low human rights consciousness, a low level of economic development, and so on.[94] Although Li's concept of due rights seems to imply that rights exist regardless of their legalization or realization, actual rights are still relative to the level of development. Building on the proposition that people's due rights are constrained by the level of development, Li argues that, as human societies develop and contacts between them intensify, they tend to become more alike. In the process, the particularistic character of human rights progressively becomes weaker and their universality more pronounced.[95] This optimistic and progressive view of human society and development could very well be described as a convergence theory of human rights, which opens up the possibility of a consensus on human rights.

Li Buyun's definition of human rights as due rights that are not necessarily matched with legal rights in society lends itself to the view that human rights are a kind of moral rights. Other scholars have also more explicitly defined human rights as moral rights. Zhang Wenxian and Xia Yong both describe human rights as moral rights, albeit rights that should be transformed into legal rights. The acknowledgment that a gap or difference between human rights and legal rights can exist has also paved the way for distinguishing human rights from citizens' rights. Li Buyun argues against an identification of human rights with citizens' rights on the grounds that this would deprive people without citizenship, such as refugees, of their rights.[96] Li Lin also strongly emphasizes that human rights and citizens' rights are different and that the former stand above the latter.[97] Human rights are not granted but are possessed by human beings on the basis of their humanity, irrespective of acknowledgment by the law. Citizens' rights, on the other hand, are granted by the law and can be changed, deprived, or annulled. These distinctions between human rights and citizens' rights are not far from those put forward by Luo Longji in the 1920s. Some conservative scholars, however, continue to prefer the term citizens' rights to human rights.[98]

Although the official position places special emphasis on duties, many scholars take a more rights-oriented position. Before 1989, several legal scholars voiced the opinion that the strong emphasis on duties and neglect of rights in the past were detrimental to Chinese society. Zhang Wenxian argues that to strengthen people's rights would liberate the Chinese people from their authoritarian heritage and promote a civic consciousness, a view quite similar to those held in the early twentieth century.[99] Li Lin joins Zhang in this critique of the earlier one-sided emphasis on duties.[100] To affirm and respect the individual as a rights-bearing agent, he claims, is not only beneficial for the development of the individual but for society as a whole. Other scholars have also highlighted the importance of rights in order for humans to become autonomous individuals.[101] In view of the often assumed duty orientation of the Chinese society, it is also interesting to note that this characteristic is not borne out in some recent examinations of the Chinese people's attitudes toward their rights and duties. In a survey undertaken by CASS in the early 1990s, in answer to the question, "As a citizen, what do you think about the current situation of your enjoyment of rights and fulfilment of duties?", 37.22 percent of the peasants responded: "I feel that I have enjoyed few rights, but that I have undertaken too many duties"; while 15.95 percent chose: "I feel that I have no rights, only undertake duties."[102] Urban citizens were even less satisfied. This, albeit limited, survey shows that Chinese people are not as uninterested in their rights, or as duty-oriented as many persist in believing them to be.

Chinese scholars in general seem to accept the division of human rights into three generations or stages. Among human rights are civil and political rights, and economic and social rights. They pay particular attention to collective rights, the third generation, such as the right to development and the right to self-determination. They also tend to criticize the West for only focusing on the former and ignoring the two latter generations.[103] Whereas in the official discourse, priority is often placed on social and economic rights, scholars have voiced slightly different views on this issue. Zhang Wenxian, for example, argues that civil and political rights are as important as social and economic rights and refuses to see any either-or choice between them.[104] Sun Zhe also argues against the tendency to emphasize economic rights to the neglect of civil and political rights.[105] He criticizes the notion that the Chinese people would only be interested in material matters, but not freedom, respect, and self-development. Sun, in addition, refutes the view that China's special national conditions would make the right to subsistence the most relevant and urgent right for the Chinese people.

Liu Junning is even more explicit on this issue.[106] He first of all criticizes the tendency to view the right to subsistence from a narrow, nationalistic perspective and not from the perspective of the individual. To Liu's mind, it is the individual who should be in focus and not a collective, such as the nation. The right to subsistence should furthermore have as its goal the individual's total well-being and development, not solely the issue of securing food and clothing. If it does not include respect for individual freedom and dignity, human rights would be no different from animal rights. Liu also criticizes the view that the individual's rights and freedoms would have to be curtailed in the name of stability or development. There is no need to curtail political rights, he argues, as they are necessary to promote economic rights and development. An interesting survey conducted by the China Politics and Law University in 1992 also shows that not all Chinese share the official definition of, or priority for human rights. A mere 9.6 percent of those asked understood human rights to be confined to the rights to food and subsistence, whereas 33.3 percent defined human rights as political rights and freedoms that the government should not infringe upon, and 50.8 percent defined human rights as those stipulated in the UN Charter and other human rights conventions that protect human dignity and common interests.[107]

Regarding the purpose of human rights, Xu Bing and Yu Keping in 1989 voiced the opinion that human rights were an end rather than a means. They related human rights to human nature and saw them as necessary in order for a person to be a complete human being and live a dignified life. Others have expressed themselves in similar terms during the 1990s.[108] They argue that if a person is deprived of his rights he will no longer be a human being but a mere slave. Human rights, in other words, are needed in order to affirm the meaning, value, and dignity of human existence and realize individual autonomy.[109] Li Lin and others have also tried to relate human rights to the Marxist struggle for the liberation of humankind.[110] Since the purpose of human rights is to secure the full and free development of the individual, human rights would be perfectly acceptable to Marxists. Such a humanistic reading of Marx is similar to that of some of the democracy activists in the late 1970s. More utilitarian arguments are also often voiced in the debate. Zhang Wenxian, for example, points out that the enjoyment of rights is not only beneficial to the interests of the individual but also to the interests of society as a whole.[111] If people do not actively, enthusiastically, and creatively use their rights to political participation, freedom of speech, scientific research, and so forth, there will be no prospect for democracy, economic development, scientific progress, or literary accomplishments. But in general, Chinese scholars do not simply value human rights as a means for social progress and national modernization but see them as necessary for human existence and development.

CHINESE DISSIDENTS ON HUMAN RIGHTS

Since 1989, the human rights consciousness among Chinese citizens and dissidents has grown, as manifested in their open letters and petitions to the political leadership and attempts to establish independent human rights organizations. Generally speaking, however, Chinese dissidents have not contributed much by way of theoretical writings on human rights. This is only natural since they are activists who do not spend their time in the ivory towers of academia. Furthermore, in contrast to establishment intellectuals, they have had neither the time nor the resources at their disposal to enable them to engage in more theoretical work or elaborate on an alternative to the official conception of human rights. Although human rights is no longer a taboo subject in China, unauthorized discussion or organizing still leads to persecution.

During the 1990s, the Chinese political leadership was flooded with waves of petitions demanding respect for human rights and release of political prisoners. This development has no doubt been influenced and encouraged by both Fang Lizhi's open letter, the active dissident community set up abroad after June Fourth, and the new international interest in human rights issues in China since 1989. In March 1989, inspired by Fang Lizhi's open letter, Human Rights in China (HRIC) was founded by Chinese scholars in the United States, the first organization of mainland dissidents abroad devoted to the human rights cause.[112]

Chinese dissidents remaining on the mainland were not silenced by the 1989 crackdown but could soon be heard calling for a reversal of the official verdict of June Fourth as a counterrevolutionary rebellion, political reforms, respect for human rights, and so forth. Political activism has been somewhat cyclical in character, as periods of open dissent inevitably have led to increased repression. But once the political climate has been relaxed somewhat, new demands and open activism have resurfaced. After the releases of some well-known democracy activists, 1993–94 saw the emergence of increased activism, including several attempts at political organization. In 1993, for example, dissidents from Beijing, Shanghai, and Wuhan founded Peace Charter, modeled on the Czechoslovakian human rights organization, Charter 77. In 1994, seven influential intellectuals, scientists, and writers issued "An Appeal for Human Rights," which called on the authorities to respect human rights. Several attempts by democracy activists to establish independent human rights organizations also occurred in 1993–94. In Xi'an, Ma Shaohua and others founded the Human Rights Defense Movement.[113] At the same time in Shanghai several long-time dissidents, who had set up the Shanghai Human Rights Association in 1978, tried to get the organization officially registered, and another Shanghainese activist, Bao Ge, applied for official registration for the Voice of Human Rights.[114] All these attempts came to naught, however, as the authorities immediately cracked down and imprisoned the initiators. Wei Jingsheng, who had been released in September 1993, was rearrested in April 1994 as the authorities began to worry about increasing activism and contacts between dissidents. Wei's arrest set off another wave of political repression, but despite this, many still openly protested his arrest.

Another spate of activism occurred in 1995; this time more in the form of petitions and open letters than attempts to found political organizations and human rights groups.[115] In February, two petitions addressed the issue of legal and political reforms, whereas two petitions in May called for the release of prisoners of conscience and the realization of tolerance in China in view of the United Nations' 1995 Year of Tolerance. Relatives of those killed during June Fourth, who in 1993 had begun to break their silence, sent a letter to the NPC demanding an open inquiry into the killings. When Wei Jing-sheng was sentenced to a long prison term in December 1995, which was fol-lowed the next year by a number of harsh sentences meted out to other po-litical dissidents, people became more cautious and refrained from open activism. Toward late 1997, however, inspired and encouraged by China's sign-ing of the ICESCR and Jiang Zemin's visit to the United States, some dissi-dents again became emboldened to speak out. The spring of 1998 saw the emergence of the most liberal period since 1989, as both academics and dis-sidents openly engaged in debates on political and legal reforms. In 1998, long-term dissidents Qin Yongming and Xu Wenli tried to set up a human rights organization, the China Human Rights Monitor. Due to their involve-ment later that year in founding China's first large-scale opposition party, the China Democratic Party, they were arrested toward the end of the year as an-other period of repression set in; they were quickly sentenced to twelve and thirteen years' imprisonment, respectively. The crackdown on the China Democratic Party continued in 1999 and 2000, at the same time that many other political dissidents, labor activists, and religious believers were impris-oned and brought to trial. In the spring of 1999, Falun Gong emerged as the biggest threat against the regime since 1989, when some 10,000 of its mem-bers demonstrated in central Beijing. They wanted official recognition for their organization but, instead, the group was banned. Since 1999 several of its leaders have been sentenced to long terms in prison, although the regime de-fends its crackdown by arguing that it is protecting people against a danger-ous "cult" that endangers their lives.

Chinese citizens' invocation of the language of human rights is part and par-cel of the globalization of human rights and feeds on growing and strength-ened contacts with the international community. It has also in part been stim-ulated, or provoked, by the Chinese government's own references to human rights, publishing of White Papers, and signing of the two human rights covenants. In 1991, while still serving his 1979 prison sentence, Wei Jingsheng penned his reactions to the Chinese government's recent discussions on human rights.[116] Wei forcefully and ingeniously rebutted a number of arguments used by the government, including the view that human rights is an internal affair, that different cultures and societies have different human rights concepts, and that economic rights supersede all other rights. China's first White Paper, issued later the same year, provoked further reactions from dissidents at home and abroad. A group of Chinese citizens in Beijing who tried to organize a politi-cal party, the Liberal Democratic Party of China, immediately published a statement demanding the release of political prisoners and respect for the UDHR. Although they regarded the government's new talk about human rights as opportunistic and insincere, they were nevertheless prepared to see it as a step forward and they capitalized upon this development in order to push the human rights issue.

> Amid a wave of condemnation both at home and abroad, the CCP authorities were compelled to issue a "White Paper on Human Rights" in China. It is not difficult for those who know the real facts to expose the lies and quibbles in the "White Paper." Nevertheless, this is still a great victory for the people in the international community and at home who work for the democratic cause in China. . . . [W]e also hope that the "White Paper" is a positive posture of the CCP authorities for improving the human rights situation in China as a result of the concern and pressure exerted at home and abroad.[117]

Those behind the statement were soon arrested and received some of the harshest sentences handed out in the post–1989 period.[118] As with the 1991 White Paper, the 1997 and 1998 signing of the ICESCR and ICCPR also unleashed a flood of petitions and declarations from the dissident community that made use of the government's official recognition of human rights. In 1998, for example, a group of intellectuals issued two human rights declarations, one dealing with civil and political rights and the other with social and economic rights.[119]

The universality of human rights is generally stressed by Chinese citizens and dissidents. At the World Conference on Human Rights in Vienna in 1993, Chinese human rights NGOs outside of China made a joint statement declaring their commitment to the universality and indivisibility of human rights. "Human rights has already become the common idea of the international society. No government should be allowed to use the pretext of specific cultural, historical, or national situations to deny international standards and put forward [a standard] for itself. Likewise, civil and political rights and economic and social rights are interdependent and mutually supportive. No government can arbitrarily emphasise one group of rights to the detriment of the other."[120] Fang Lizhi has also defended the idea that human rights is a universal concept applicable to all societies, strongly refuting the argument that its so-called uniqueness would render human rights invalid in China, or that China's human rights concept would be different from that of other societies.[121] Fang draws a parallel between the government's claim that "China has its own standard of human rights" to earlier dynasties' claims that "China has its own astronomy."[122] To Fang's mind, these claims are equally preposterous.

Wei Jingsheng has likewise criticized the view that China, because of its history and national conditions, would have a different concept of human rights.[123] In his 1991 letter to Jiang Zemin and Li Peng, Wei strongly refuted the official view that different human rights standards apply to different societies, arguing that human rights are "rights with which every person is born."

Liu Qing, the chairman of Human Rights in China, also argues against the government's claim that human rights standards vary between different societies.[124] Liu discusses human rights in terms of "those basic rights that make a person a person," showing affinity with earlier pre-1949 discussions but also with some of the more liberal establishment intellectuals in the 1990s.

One petition on the occasion of the sixth anniversary of June Fourth underscores this prevalent belief in the universality of human rights in no uncertain terms: "Respecting individual freedom, equality and dignity, and guaranteeing indivisible, inalienable, inviolable human rights, are the marks of social progress, mutual concern and human dignity."[125] In 1998, several intellectuals and relatives of June Fourth victims published two human rights declarations that made a strong case for the belief in inherent and universal human rights. "The primary basis of our appeal is the recognition that human rights are innate, that everyone is born free. This freedom belongs to each of us, regardless of race, colour, sex, language, religion, political or other views, nationality or class origin, wealth, birth or other identity; it is inalienable, and non-negotiable; in exercising our own freedoms and rights, each of us should respect and refrain from obstructing others in their equal enjoyment of such rights."[126] According to Wang Ming, another democracy activist, freedom of speech is an innate, sacred, and inviolable right. To lose the right of freedom of speech is a disgrace and the greatest misfortune to befall a human being. "In fact, absolute freedoms like freedom of speech are minimum conditions for every individual's pursuit of happiness. Even though a person who enjoys freedom of speech will not necessarily be happy, a person who loses this kind of freedom will absolutely not attain happiness. Freedom of speech is like the air and water on which we depend for our existence: we cannot do without it even for an instant."[127]

Although Chinese dissidents sometimes also give more utilitarian justifications of rights, describing them as necessary for social progress, their utilitarianism is much less pronounced than that found in the official discourse, nor is it central to their defense of human rights. It is not surprising that Chinese dissidents, in contrast to official China and many establishment intellectuals, defend the universality of human rights. This provides them with greater protection, as they can seek moral and legal authority outside and above the Chinese legal system.

People such as Wei Jingsheng, Hu Ping, Wang Ming, and Yang Zhou all see freedom of thought and speech as basic and crucial for the enjoyment of all other rights and freedoms.[128] But Chinese dissidents generally tend to pay equal attention to civil and political rights and economic and social rights. Liu Qing refutes the argument that a trade-off exists between civil and political rights, on the one hand, and the right to economic development, on the other hand. At the same time, Wei Jingsheng ridicules the Chinese authorities' claim that the right to subsistence is the greatest human right. As he sarcastically puts it: "If feeding the people and keeping them from starving or freezing to death constitutes the greatest respect for human rights, then consider the feudal lords and slave owners. The fact that slaves and serfs were kept from starving or freezing to death could prove that the slave owners had protected 'the greatest human right' as you have done."[129] The gap between the Chinese rhetoric on economic rights and the much bleaker reality has also led some Chinese citizens to use the regime's own rhetoric against it. They thus criticize the Chinese government for failing to deliver the promised goods. As a group of laid-off workers phrased it in a letter to Jiang Zemin in 1997, using words quite similar to that of Wei: "You said that human rights in China are [*sic*] the right to eat rice. This is an arbitrary justification for the sake of political agenda. This is not human rights, but rather animal rights. Anyway, according to your interpretation, when tens of millions of workers are deprived of their right to eat rice, doesn't this amount to the loss of their human rights?"[130] Statements such as these reveal that Chinese citizens are creatively reworking and making use of the official rights talk to "talk back" to the regime.

Dissidents put the responsibility for the human rights violations in China squarely on the Chinese government and the totalitarian political system. They believe, with earlier generations, that democracy is essential in order to promote and protect human rights. Occasionally, however, some blame for the current situation is also assigned to the Chinese tradition. One of the 1998 human rights declaration stated that

> China is a country with a long history and tradition. Bound by a firmly established system of imperial power and a hierarchical structure for several thousand years, we Chinese people have always had a relatively weak sense of individuality, individual rights and freedoms. We have to acknowledge that this is not a virtue of our race, but a failing. . . . For this reason, our whole nation needs to conduct a self-examination, so as to fundamentally change the out-dated concept of giving supremacy to the so-called interests of the nation and the collective while blurring the value of the individual into the whole, and to allow the independent personality of citizens to arise.[131]

This all-out critique of the Chinese tradition in the manner of May Fourth should not be taken to mean that the signatories believe that the Chinese tradition prevents or rules out the realization of human rights in China. Instead of referring to and building upon Confucian or other indigenous concepts when defending their human rights, Chinese dissidents are more prone to reject traditional values and seek inspiration in the international human rights regime. In this respect they have more in common with the May Fourthers and latter-day human rights advocates on Taiwan than with some neo-Confucians.

It is obvious that their critique of tradition, vehement as it often is, springs from despair over the present situation and is informed by opposition to the current regime. But also, it should be noted, it is a result of the party's own relentless critique of Chinese culture in the past. In the case of Taiwan, advocacy of human rights and critique of Chinese culture has also sometimes gone hand in hand. One example is that of Bo Yang, an ardent critic of Chinese culture, (in)famous for his book, *The Ugly Chinaman*, who also is a known and respected defender of human rights. Bo Yang, who spent ten years in prison, has founded an organization that aims to promote human rights education, as he believes that the Chinese people lack a deep-rooted human rights consciousness.

In the case of the mainland, traditional values are not so firmly associated with the power holders since the CCP's recent turn to tradition is only partial and highly ambivalent. But the rejection of tradition and adoption of an outward-looking strategy is part and parcel of a well-established and ingrained political repertoire that is shared by human rights activists in other countries. That being said, however, there are those who find some support for human rights in tradition.[132] It is possible that references to traditional values could become stronger in the Chinese human rights discourse once the political situation changes, or if the CCP tries to appropriate the language of traditional values still further. Although critique of the tradition still takes place on both sides of the Taiwan strait, it is no longer so central or so fierce as in the past, since Chinese tradition today is more distant and no longer influences people's lives to the same extent. The main foe of the human rights advocates is not Chinese culture but totalitarian power holders and their apologists.

CONCLUSION

Since the late 1980s, human rights has become an accepted, if still contested, concept in Chinese political discourse. The CCP has now adopted the human rights language and uses it against its own critics. But although it attempts to control and dominate the debate, it inevitably faces challenges at home and from abroad. The CCP also risks becoming a prisoner of its own human rights rhetoric, as Chinese citizens have been quick to exploit the new situation and raise charges of human rights violations against it.

Not only are ordinary citizens and dissidents challenging the regime over human rights, establishment intellectuals are also expressing views that sometimes diverge from the officially sanctioned discourse. Even though the contemporary discourse is influenced by international developments in the human rights field and today's specific political concerns, certain themes and discussions nevertheless closely resemble earlier Chinese discussions. It is, for example, interesting to note that Xu Bing, Yu Keping, Li Buyun, and Zhang Wenxian all agree with earlier generations that human rights can be defined as those rights that enable a human being to be a person, and closely relate the idea of human rights to notions of human dignity and self-autonomy.

The wide range of opinions on human rights among establishment intellectuals can be gathered by juxtaposing two events that took place in late 1998, on the fiftieth anniversary of the UDHR. (It should be remembered that only ten years earlier the anniversary was celebrated in the PRC for the first time.) In October, the CSHRS arranged a major international conference on human rights.[133] The Chinese participants were officials and quite conservative scholars who have long promoted more orthodox Marxist views on human rights and often are called upon to defend the official position, including defending the crackdown on Falun Gong. The conference received ample coverage in the Chinese media and was also graced by the presence of Vice-Premier Qian Qichen and officials from the Information Office of the State Council, which is responsible for issuing the official White Papers on human rights. Many of the scholars at the conference, such as Dong Yunhu and Gu Chunde, have played important roles in the official debate on human rights. Although they voiced their support of the UDHR and hailed it as a benchmark in the history of humankind, they also gave vent to some critiquing of its "historical limitations." They criticized its heavy emphasis on rights at the expense of duties, individual rights at the expense of collective rights, and civil and political rights at the expense of economic and social rights. They furthermore stressed that the universality of human rights has to be balanced with the particularity of human rights, which vary according to different traditions and economic conditions. The participants also emphasized that national sovereignty is the sine qua non for all human rights and argued that human rights concerns cannot be used as an excuse to interfere with a country's national sovereignty.

In December 1998, CASS, for its part, arranged a small roundtable workshop to discuss human rights that drew quite a different group of people.[134] These scholars proffered more liberal views on human rights, which tellingly illustrates how far the human rights discourse has moved since the late 1970s. The participants, inter alia, voiced a critique of Asian values, questioned the argument that the right to subsistence should be narrowly focused on food and clothing, emphasized the importance of civil and political rights, described human rights as an end in themselves, as well as demanded that human rights not be limited to the level of rhetoric but also put into practice. The range of issues and often quite liberal views were significant and remarkable. Especially noteworthy is the absence of the earlier all-pervasive Marxist rhetoric and reference to the class character of human rights. Most writers, although still accepting that human rights also have a particular nature, had no problem with acknowledging that human rights are, after all, are universal in nature. They complained about the fact that despite the gross human rights violations committed during the Cultural Revolution, human rights for a long time afterward continued to be regarded as a suspect idea.[135] Whether human rights then were rejected or simply not discussed at all, the discussion had later moved on to the position that national sovereignty is above and more important than human rights, while the major issue in the contemporary official discourse was found to be the universality versus the particularity of human rights, with the majority stressing the latter aspect.[136] Some of the scholars ventured the view that the debate on human rights in the PRC, despite many promising signs of late, still had a long way to go. What was needed, many of the participants agreed, was more work on the actual protection of human rights and less talk on their particularity.

Recently, scholarly attention has partly shifted away from purely theoretical discussions to research on the PRC's adjustment to international human rights law in view of acceding to the two human rights covenants.[137] But the discussions on human rights among establishment intellectuals continue to remain oddly divorced from concrete human rights problems in China, in contrast to the much less theoretically inclined discussions among Chinese dissidents.

NOTES

1. For China's international activities in the human rights field, see Kent (1999).
2. Quoted in State Council (1991), p. 80. See also Guo Shan (1987).
3. In 1986 articles appeared in, for example, *Zhongguo fazhi bao*, December 15 and 17, 1986, and *Shijie zhishi*, no. 23, 1986. For the UDHR references, see Wei Min, "Discussing Some Questions Regarding Human Rights. Commemorating the 40th Anniversary of the Adopting of the Universal Declaration of Human Rights," RMRB, December 3, 1988, and "Human Rights Importance Noted," CD, December 7, 1988.
4. CD, December 7, 1988.
5. Some Chinese scholars speak of three stages, identifying 1978, 1988, and 1989 as key turning points; see Li Lin and Zhu Xiaoqing (1992), pp. 375–79. Zhou Wei (1995) talks about two periods, pre-1989 and post-1989; the latter period is further divided into 1989–90 and the period after 1990, p. 83.
6. On these debates, see Goldman (1994).
7. Yu Haocheng published his article in *Shijie zhishi* in 1988 and later (1995) elaborated on his view on human rights.
8. Xu Bing (1989) and Yu Keping (1989).
9. Xu Bing (1989), p. 9.
10. For Fang Lizhi's and the other's letters, see Fang Lizhi (1990), pp. 242–43, pp. 305–8.
11. See interview with Tiziano Terzani in Fang Lizhi (1990), p. 207, p. 212.
12. In an essay published in the *New York Review of Books* on February 2, 1989, Fang, however, criticized the Chinese government for not endorsing the two UN human rights covenants; see Fang (1990), p. 252.

13. For a useful account of the movement, see Calhoun (1995).

14. On file with the author.

15. Reprinted in Han Minzhu (1990), pp. 136–37.

16. Reprinted in Ogden (1992), pp. 280–81.

17. "For historical reasons, our country's people are fairly unfamiliar with ideas of human rights. It is necessary to develop a widening, deepening and continuing movement of enlightenment on human rights ideas," Xu Bing (1989), p. 10.

18. For examples, see articles in RMRB, August 25, November 26, December 8, 1989; and January 12 and 25, 1990.

19. See Kent (1999).

20. The Australians led the way, sending one delegation in 1991 and another in 1992. France, the United Kingdom, Switzerland, and Sweden also sent delegations. Chinese human rights delegations have visited the United Kingdom, France, and Sweden, among other countries.

21. For a discussion on the Chinese new strategy of dialogues in the human rights field, see HRIC (1998).

22. For a brief overview of these projects, see Mellbourn and Svensson (1999).

23. See Shi Yun, "Who Is the Real Defender of Human Rights?" RMRB, July 7, 1989. The article is translated in Angle and Svensson (2001).

24. Quoted in FBIS-CHI-91-177, September 11, 1992, p. 28. See also Dong Yunhu and Liu Wuping (1990), p. x.

25. See description in an internal report on human rights, discussed more below, and reprinted in FBIS-CHI-91-177, September 11, 1992, p. 27.

26. I am not sure if this was the first meeting. For information on this and other meetings of the Central Propaganda Department, see Guo Daohui (1998), pp. 695–700.

27. The volumes are *The Human Rights Theory of Marxism*, *Western Human Rights Theories* (2 volumes), *Developing Countries and Human Rights*, *The View of Human Rights of Socialist and Democratic Socialist Parties*, *The Building of Human Rights in China*, and *Human Right Treaties and Laws from Different Countries in the World*.

28. The first projects were led by Gu Chunde, People's University; Xia Yong, CASS; and Xu Xianming, Shandong University.

29. State Council (1996).

30. Zhang Zhilian (1995), pp. 356–69.

31. Feng Zhuoran and Gu Chunde (1992).

32. On this conference, see Rao Fang (1991).

33. On the CASS conference, see Li Lin et al. (1991), and on the People's University conference, see Yang Xiaoqing (1991). For a list of different conferences in 1991–92, see Report of the Second Australian Human Rights Delegation to China (1992), pp. 94–95.

34. Report from Xinhua, reprinted in FBIS-CHI-91-218, November 12, 1991, pp. 25–26.

35. See the confidential reports published by *Dangdai*, a Chinese magazine in Hong Kong, and reprinted in FBIS-CHI-91-121, June 23, 1992, pp. 32–36; FBIS-CHI-92-141, July 22, 1992, pp. 14–17; and FBIS-CHI-91-177, September 11, 1992, pp. 26–29.

36. FBIS-CHI-91-121, June 23, 1992, p. 15.

37. Translations of full texts of several White Papers on human rights can be found on the Internet at <www.chinaguide.org/e-white/>[accessed July 14, 2001].

38. For such an understanding, see also Zhou Jue's preface to Dong Yunhu and Liu Wuping (1993), p. 5.

39. See Li Lin (1993), pp. 230–31.

40. One of those active at the center is Gu Chunde, who since 1982 has written quite conservative pieces on human rights. For the groups' activities, which up to 1996 included the publication of seven books, see Gu Chunde, "Theoretical Research on China's Human Rights," BR, March 4–10, 1996.

41. The first course took place in the spring of 2000. Other universities nowadays also teach human rights in their courses on international law. The Nordic human rights centers are involved in organizing courses in human rights for Chinese teachers and publishing course materials to be used for teaching human rights. Plans are also under way to establish a master's program in human rights law.

42. See the 1995 Chinese White Paper, see <www.chinaguide.org/e-white/> [accessed July 14, 2001]. For information on the titles, see bibliography lists in CASS (1992), Han Depei (1995), and Li Lin (1996a).

43. Zou Sicheng (1995), pp. 36–37.

44. See "Zhu Muzhi on Human Rights," BR, 16–22 June 1997.

45. For information of the activities of CSHRS, see its Web site at <www.humanrights -china.org/> [accessed September 9, 2001].

46. For the conference, see page 289 of this chapter. For information on the radio series, see Ma Chenguang, "Series on Human Rights Broadcast," CD, December 9, 1998.

47. See Song Qiang et al. (1996), pp. 345–55.

48. For summaries of the Marxist view on human rights, see Li Lin et al. (1991), Ji Tongwen (1992), Zhang Guangbo (1990), and Chen Zhishang (1997).

49. Li Lin (1993), p. 229.

50. See Liu Nanlai (1994), pp. 6–15; Xia Yong (1994), pp. 918–19; and Sun Jicheng (1993), pp. 55–64, among others.

51. State Council (1991), p. ii, p. 85.

52. This is the general foreword of the series published by Sichuan People's Publishing House; see, for example, the volume edited by Liu Nanlai (1994), p. 2.

53. Guo Jisi (1991), p. 19.

54. The American reaction to the Chinese report in 1997 is also worth noting in this respect. Nicholas Burns, the State Department spokesman, reportedly said: "I don't think . . . we need to listen to lectures from authoritarian countries about our human rights performance because we are the world's champion of human rights." This reveals that the debate on human rights, unfortunately all too often, is corrupted by self-serving political rhetoric and the employment of double standards.

55. Yu Quanyu, for example, advocates the use of UN standards when judging other countries' human rights records. He also criticizes America for not having signed some UN conventions; see Song Qiang et al. (1996), p. 347, and p. 354.

56. See State Council (1991).

57. Shue (1980). In this context it is interesting to note that J. R. Vincent's book *Human Rights and International Relations*, which made use of Shue's concept of a right to subsistence, was translated into Chinese in 1998. However, I have not seen any references to Shue in the Chinese discourse.

58. See RMRB, December 3, 1988.

59. For his views, see Dong Yunhu and Liu Wuping (1993), pp. 11–35.

60. See, for example, Guo Jisi, "Opposing Using the Human Rights Issue as an Excuse to Interfere in Internal Affairs," RMRB, January 12, 1990, p. 7.

61. See "Top Leaders on Human Rights Issue," BR, April 22–28, 1991, p. 7. *Shengcun quan* was translated here as "the right of existence." In *The Human Rights Encyclopedia of China*, published by CASS in 1998, it is still translated as "the right to exist."

62. See Xu Xianming (1992) and CASS (1998).

63. State Council (1991), pp. 7-8.

64. Dong Yunhu and Liu Wuping (1993), p. 14.

65. Dong Yunhu and Liu Wuping (1993), p. 13.

66. Xu Xianming (1992), pp. 46–48.

67. Chen Zhishang (1997), p. 170.

68. For overviews of discussions on human rights in the 1990s, see Li Lin and Zhu Xiaoqing (1992), Chen (1993), Shih (1993), Keith (1993), Zhou Wei (1995), and Weatherley (1999).

69. Shih (1993) prefers to divide them into those who are pro-human rights, those who are anti–human rights, and those who take a more eclectic middle position, whereas Sullivan (1998) talks about Neo-Maoists, reform-Leninists, developmentalists, and universalists.

70. For representative works, see Feng Zhuoran and Gu Chunde (1992), and Chen Zhishang (1997).

71. See He Xin (1996), vol. 1, pp. 310–24. For Wang Renzhi's group, see FBIS report quoted in note 35 above.

72. Their views can be gathered from CASS (1992) and Li Lin (1996a).

73. For a discussion on Western human rights scholars, see Shen Zongling in CASS (1998), pp. 88–93; this is more or less a reprint of an article he wrote in 1992. Shen discuss Maritain, Kamenka, Gewirth, Finnis, Feinberg, D. D. Raphael, Harro von Senger, Hohfeld, Cranston, Donnelly, Milne, Henkin, Evan Laurd, D. P. Forsythe, and others. In a work published by Wuhan University in 1995, brief summaries of the ideas of Maritain, Léon Duguit, and Dworkin are presented, with more extensive discussions on the thinking of Maritain, Rawls, Nozick, Dworkin, and Milne. Han Depei (1995).

74. In the two volumes on Western conceptions of human rights published by the Sichuan People's Publishing House, the twentieth-century scholars who are partly translated are Allan S. Rosenbaum, Forsythe, Gewirth, Cranston, Carl Wellman, Morton Winston, Milne, Maritain, von Senger, Roland Rich, Gillian Triggs, Warren L. Holleman, Henkin, Rawls, Dworkin, Peter Stein, Francesco Capotori, Felix Ermacora, Hersch Lauterpacht, L. F. Damrosch, B. G. Ramcharan, and Brownlie.

75. To my knowledge, few works by Western authors were translated before 1989 although some Russian authors were. The following are a sample of articles that I have been able to identify; the year within parentheses refers to year of publication in China: Henkin (1981) and (1988), Milne (1991), Forsythe (1991), B. G. Ramcharan (1991), Damrosch (1991), Cranston (1992), Dworkin (1992), Vincent (1992, two articles), David Gillies (1992), H. T. Dickinson (1993), Milne (1993), Vincent (1993), Henkin (1993), Henkin (1999), Andrew J. Nathan (1999), Peerenboom (1999), and Hart (1999). Interestingly enough, two different translations exist of Milne's *Human Rights and Human Diversity*, one published in 1991 and the other in 1995. Humphrey's *The International Law of Human Rights* was published in 1992; Konstantin U. Chernenko, *Human Rights in Soviet Society*, published in 1992; Buergenthal, *International Human Rights in a Nutshell*, published in 1995; Henkin, *The Age of Rights*, published in 1997; C. G. Weeramantry, *Human Rights and Scientific Technological Development*, published in 1997; Vincent, *Human Rights and International Relations*, published in 1998; Edward H. Lawson, *Encyclopaedia of Human Rights*, published in 1997; Katarina Tomasevski, *Human Rights in Population*

Policies, published in 1998; and Asbjörn Eide and Gudmundur Alfredsson, *The Universal Declaration of Human Rights—A Commentary*, published in 1999. Some of these works have been published with funding from foreign organizations, such as the Ford Foundation and the Raoul Wallenberg Institute of Human Rights and Humanitarian Law.

76. See Baehr et al (1996), and Mendes and Traeholt (1997).

77. In the early 1960s, one volume with human rights texts and declarations was published and in 1989, another was published. The first after 1989 was Dong Yunhu and Liu Wuping (1990), and since then several others have followed.

78. Rich, Triggs, and Brownlie contributed articles in Crawford (1988).

79. See Xia Yong (1992), pp. 250–51, for a discussion on Milne's relativism and appreciation of his stress on the social diversity and critique of the Western human rights concept.

80. Milne (1986b), p. 125. Compare also: "To be totally dependent for one's treatment upon the caprice of other people is not to share with them the status of fellow human beings. It is to be a slave, or at best a domestic pet," p. 131. Such phrasings, and other aspects of his thinking, reveal an affinity with the British Idealists, about whom Milne also has written (1986a).

81. Wei Shaoying in Han Depei (1995), p. 342; Xia Yong (1992), p. 242. This is also mentioned in the introduction to the 1991 translation of Milne's book.

82. Wei Shaoying in Han Depei (1995), p. 346; Xia Yong (1992), pp. 246–50.

83. See Wei Shaoying in Han Depei (1995), p. 347f.

84. On the West's human rights standard not applying to China, see Xia Yong (1992), p. 243.

85. Dong Yunhu and Liu Wuping (1993), p. 4.

86. Xia Yong (1992), p. 199.

87. Li Lin (1996b).

88. Li Lin (1996b), p. 44.

89. Xu Xianming (1991). Xu argues that fundamental rights also could be called human rights, civil rights, constitutional rights, and so forth; while the name is different, its meaning would be the same.

90. See Shen Zongling (1992a), pp. 19–20; and Chen Zhishang (1997), pp. 163–67.

91. Li Buyun's 1991 article in which he first elaborated this view was later published in CASS (1992). See Li Buyun (1992), p. 3. See also his later works (1996a), p. 4, and (1998), p. 481.

92. Zhang Wenxian (1992).

93. See, in particular, Li Buyun (1996a), p. 4, and (1996b), pp. 16–17.

94. See in particular Li Buyun (1996a), pp. 13–14.

95. See Li Buyun (1996a), p. 7, and (1998), p. 484. For a similar view, see Guo Daohui (1992).

96. See Li Buyun (1992).

97. Li Lin (1996b).

98. Zhang Guangbo (1990), p. 17.

99. Zhang Wenxian (1992). On Zhang's view of rights, see also Chen (1993).

100. Li Lin (1996b), p. 45.

101. See the discussion in Chen (1993), p. 131.

102. Gao Hongjun (1995), p. 40.

103. See, for example, Shen Zongling (1992b).

104. Zhang Wenxian (1992).

105. Sun Zhe (1992), p. 219.

106. See Liu Junning's comments at a roundtable discussion on human rights arranged at CASS in December 1998 and reprinted in *Gongfa*, no. 1, 1999, pp. 324–27.

107. See Gong Xiangrui (1993), p. 282.

108. Zou Pingxue in Han Depei (1995), p. 352, and pp. 362–63. See also Xu Xianming (1991).

109. Zou Pingxue in Han Depei (1995), p. 362. This is also the view of Gong Pingxiang, see Chen (1993), pp. 132–33. See also Dong Yunhu and Liu Wuping (1993), pp. 4–5.

110. See Li Lin (1996b), p. 38 and p. 46; and Li Buyun (1996a), p. 14.

111. Zhang Wenxian (1992), p. 40.

112. For a personal account of the founding of HRIC, see Fu Xinyuan, "Searching for Answers," *CRF*, Summer 1999.

113. See Ma Shaohua, "Witness: A Human Rights Activist Inside China's Detention Centers," *CRF*, Spring 1995.

114. For information on these two organizations, see the profile of Yang Zhou in *CRF*, Winter 1995, and the profile of Bao Ge in *CRF*, Summer 1996.

115. For an account of the 1995 wave of open letters and a sample of them, see Xiao Qiang, "Letters from Citizens. The Development of a Chinese Human Rights Movement," *CRF*, Summer 1995.

116. Wei Jingsheng (1997), pp. 164–76.

117. "Rights Statement Posted at Beijing University," written by the Liberal Democratic Party of China. The text was originally published in *Ming pao*, November 16, 1991, and translated by the Foreign Broadcasting Service, in FBIS-CHI-91-222, November 18, 1991, pp. 22–23. It is reprinted in Angle and Svensson (2001).

118. They were rounded up in 1992, and in 1994 they were tried and sentenced to prison terms ranging between three and twenty years.

119. These declarations are reprinted in *CRF*, Spring 1999, and can also be found at <http://www.hrichina.org> [accessed September 7, 2001].

120. Reprinted in *CRF*, Fall 1993, p. 40.

121. See Fang Lizhi (1990), p. xlii, p. 247, p. 258, pp. 262–66, and p. 290.

122. Fang Lizhi (1990), p. 264.

123. Wei Jingsheng (1997), pp. 164–76.

124. See Liu Qing (1995).

125. Reprinted in *CRF*, Summer 1995, p. 13.

126. Reprinted in *CRF*, Spring 1999, and can also to be found at <http://www.hrichina.org>.

127. Wang Ming, "A Citizen's Declaration of Freedom of Speech," *CRF*, Spring 1997; translation modified by myself. The Chinese original is found on <http://www.hrichina.org>.

128. Hu Ping (1998) is one of the few Chinese dissidents who refrains from talking about economic and social rights as human rights at all. The article is translated in Angle and Svensson (2001). For Yang Zhou's views, see Mark Goellner's interview with Yang in *CRF*, Winter 1995.

129. Wei Jingsheng (1997), p. 171.

130. Quoted in Leung (1998), p. 12.

131. Reprinted in CRF, Spring 1999, also can be found at <http://www.hrichina.org>.
132. Few Chinese dissidents discuss the Chinese tradition at all. Yang Zhou, however, on one occasion stressed that the value of the human being was an important element of traditional thought. See Mark Goellner's interview with Yang in CRF, Winter 1995, p. 15.
133. Conference papers were rapidly available at CSHRS's home page at <www.humanrights-china.org/>. Several articles on the conference were also published in the Chinese media, including *China Daily* and *People's Daily*; see CD and RMRB, October 21 and 22, 1998. Dong Yunhu later published his paper as an article in *People's Daily*; see Dong Yunhu, "The 50th Anniversary of the UDHR," RMRB, December 10, 1998 <www.snewb.com/pdhome> [accessed March 20, 2000].
134. See "Notes at a Meeting Commemorating the 50th Anniversary of the UDHR," *Gongfa*, no. 1, 1999, pp. 323–49.
135. Comments by Guo Daohui, *Gongfa*, p. 328.
136. Comments by Zhang Zhiming, *Gongfa*, p. 328.
137. China signed the ICESCR in 1997 and the ICCPR in 1998. It ratified the ICESCR in February 2001 but has yet to ratify the ICCPR, a process that is widely expected to take much longer and be more complicated.

Chapter Twelve

The Chinese Human Rights Debate: Conclusion and Prospects

HISTORY AND HUMAN RIGHTS: THE QUESTION OF TRUTH, JUSTICE, AND HISTORICAL MEMORY

This work has shown that Chinese people, contrary to what many skeptical voices would have us believe, have been engaged in vigorous debates on human rights throughout the twentieth century. The idea of human rights could move people to such an extent that, like Liu Yazi, they even adopted the name Renquan. Chinese people have not only been engaged in academic debates, but also in more concrete human rights struggles against successive rulers' suppression of their rights and freedoms. In order to protect their rights, people have published magazines, launched movements, established organizations, and written petitions and open letters, all devoted to human rights. Apart from the most recent Chinese activities in the field of human rights, however, most of these past debates and activities are relatively unknown and forgotten today. One of the aims of this study, therefore, has been to uncover and recover the truth about past human rights work and encourage others to explore this forgotten history further and in greater depth.

I have already raised the spectre of relativism on many occasions in this book so it is fitting that I confront it one final time. Is it possible to write a true and objective historical work and, if not, do we have to accept that historical writings inevitably are relative, reflecting only the standpoint and prejudices of the historian and writer in question? For what purpose and with what intentions do people write about history, and whose history do they write? Historical writings, as Joyce Appleby, Lynn Hunt, and Margaret Jacob have emphasized, are at best only provisional in character and should be undertaken with both modesty and civility.[1] This being said, however, not all historical writings are equally valid or acceptable. We have to be alert to the fact that history can be manipulated, invented, and rewritten to suit the needs and interests of certain individuals, groups, political parties, or states, as shown, for example, in the official human rights historiography and discourse in the PRC.

Historical writings, I believe, should attempt to make those people heard who have been silenced or prevented from telling their own accounts of the past. As historians we have a responsibility not to speak for, as this would be presumptuous, but to listen to and record the voices of those who are forgotten or suppressed. In this work I have tried to give different Chinese voices a fair hearing and I have also done my best to recover history, not invent or rewrite it.

All historical work inevitably touches upon issues of truth and representativity, and in no case is this more evident than in work on human rights. For victims of human rights violations it is necessary that the truth about these violations be uncovered and acknowledged in order to restore their dignity and worth. But human rights violators are not interested in trying to understand or uncover the truth and often try to deny or cover up past and present human rights violations, in the process attempting to rewrite history to suit their own needs and interests. Societies ruled by a government that is not only responsible for past human rights violations but also continues to commit new ones tend to be very cautious and circumspect when it comes to discussions of human rights issues. In this respect they are walking a tightrope since the new international human rights regime inevitably forces them to talk the talk of human rights.

A new government or a government in a society that has gone through a transition from an authoritarian to a democratic political system has more opportunities and also some political interest in making a clean break with the past. But societies in this latter category often choose different approaches when dealing with the past and with past human rights violations. These differences are due to a number of factors, including social and cultural differences, differences in vision and outlook among the political leadership, the nature of the human rights abuses in question, how distant they are in time, as well as the impact of the international community on the society in question. In order to accomplish a successful transition to democracy, a society has to make a clean break with past policies and human rights abuses, but this doesn't mean that the past should be ignored or forgotten. While victims have a "right to know," governments and society in general must shoulder the corresponding "duty to remember." Members of a society need to know about its past, including past human rights violations and human rights debates, in order to ensure a future in which human rights are upheld and protected. /

There have been quite heated debates within the human rights community on which approach is best when dealing with past human rights abuses, and no general model exists that applies to all societies and all situations. It is, however, customary to call for accountability and divide it into two phases. The first is the truth phase during which human rights violations are disclosed and acknowledged. The second is the justice phase during which those with the highest level of responsibility are prosecuted and punished for their crimes. In order to deal with past human rights violations and ensure their nations' political reconstitution, many new democracies have set up so-called truth and justice commissions; witness the case of South Africa. What is of concern to me here is the truth phase, since what happened and why is a central question to historians. Historical studies help us understand the reasons for human rights violations and provide us with tools that prevent them from reappearing in the future. While this book hasn't dealt with human rights violations per se, it has nonetheless been concerned with issues of truth, justice, and historical memory. Historical studies of human rights debates are valuable, indeed indispensable I would contend, for human rights activists intent on promoting a sustainable and viable human rights culture.

Whereas past human rights abuses and failures to protect human rights provide negative lessons that are important to heed, human rights struggles, both those that failed and those that eventually succeeded, provide valuable positive examples for contemporary human rights activists. In order to promote a viable human rights culture, as in China, it is important to be able to build upon and take pride in one's own history and traditions in this respect, otherwise human rights risk being regarded as a foreign idea imposed upon and alien to the society in question. In this context it is crucial and worthwhile to know about earlier human rights debates in one's own society. As shown in this work, China has a rich and long history of indigenously motivated debates on human rights that dates from the late Qing dynasty. Although these debates inevitably were constrained by and reflected the social and political conditions at the time, and human rights didn't have a high standing in international discourse until after the Second World War, they can be built upon and provide valuable perspectives to contemporary debates. The Asian values debate has tellingly revealed how dangerous it is to lack a firm knowledge of the history of domestic human rights debates and human rights struggles. It should be remembered that nondemocratic governments advocated Asian values and took upon themselves the task to define and write their history, whereas local NGOs, in contrast, embraced the universality of human rights and provided a different account of the history of these Asian societies. The work of indigenous human rights NGOs clearly demonstrates the extent to which human rights have been embraced, which reveals how mistaken the belief in specific Asian values is. This once more alerts us to the important fact that human rights discussions and dialogues must be truly pluralistic and include people from all walks of life, not only government officials.

The PRC and Taiwan, not surprisingly, have approached the past in different ways, which reflect their different political developments. But although the two societies differ in crucial respects we can also find certain similarities. Taiwan has successfully completed the transition from authoritarian to democratic rule, which explains why it now more readily addresses past human rights violations. But even in Taiwan the process has been rather slow and cautious in comparison with other countries that have gone through a similar democratic transition. Taiwan has not set up any truth and justice commission, and research into past human rights violations has also been fairly underdeveloped.[2] It is only during the past five or six years that Taiwanese scholars have begun to research in greater depth human rights violations that occurred during the February 28 Incident in 1947 and the White Terror period. The official approach has been one of acknowledging and apologizing for past human rights violations rather than bringing those responsible to justice. Truth and the restoration of dignity to victims of persecution have thus been regarded as more important than accountability and justice brought about through criminal prosecutions. A near universal consensus seems to exist in Taiwanese society on this policy initiated by the GMD and continued by the Democratic Progressive Party (DPP); in any case, few voices have been heard calling for more thorough investigations of past human rights violations that would also include the prospect of criminal prosecutions.[3]

Already during the Nationalists' last years in power, before DPP's victory in the 2000 presidential election, certain steps were taken by the government to acknowledge and apologize for past human rights violations. These included public apologies by the president to the victims of these violations, the erection of a monument on Green Island in honor of political prisoners who had been imprisoned there, the establishment of a park in commemoration of the victims of the February 28 Incident, and the adoption of laws to provide human rights victims with compensation. The new administration headed by Chen Shuibian has taken over and embraced this policy of public acknowledgments of past violations and the restoration of the dignity of those victimized rather than attempt any criminal prosecutions. In several speeches the new administration has thus stressed the importance of acknowledging past human rights abuses and also apologized for them, even though they occurred during GMD rule. To mark International Human Rights Day in 2000, the government, for example, made a public apology to one hundred representatives of political victims and their families and conferred so-called human rights souvenir badges on them. As the spokesperson of the presidential office put it: "The badge symbolises both Taiwan's farewell to the dark age of political oppression and its striding toward an era of human rights."[4]

To publicly acknowledge past human rights violations is an important gesture that reveals that they are not acceptable in the new society and is a strong statement of the new government's commitment to human rights. In this respect, the DPP of course has an edge over the GMD, as its members themselves have been victims of human rights violations, whereas the GMD, at least initially, had some difficulties in convincing the public of its sincerity, as it had been the perpetrator of human rights violations itself.

In October 2000, the new administration established the President's Advisory Group on Human Rights. In a speech at the group's first meeting, Chen Shuibian addressed the issue of historical memory by quoting Bo Yang's words: "Past mistakes and evil acts can be understood, tolerated, and forgiven, but should not be forgotten."[5] Chen went on to say that those who forget past human rights violations risk repeating these wrongdoings, arguing that it is essential to record and reflect upon the past in order to create a new society in which human rights are respected. In his speech Chen also mentioned earlier human rights debates and struggles in Taiwan and emphasized that it was necessary to continue and develop this domestic human rights tradition. At a memorial ceremony on the fifty-fourth anniversary of the February 28 Incident, Chen further acknowledged the importance of uncovering the truth of human rights violations in order for reconciliation to take place: "Only when the truth of the incident has been revealed, will all the relatives of the victims be able to put the emotions of sadness and hatred behind them."[6] Whereas one of the relatives reportedly said: "We will accept apologies from [the] oppressors and forgive them, but we have to find out who those oppressors were first." To uncover and record the truth is thus widely seen as crucial for the process of reconciliation in Taiwanese society. The argument that the truth about the past needs to be uncovered and made public has also recently been used to motivate the opening of archives and encouraging of research into human rights violations.[7]

It is, however, somewhat ironic to note that Taiwan lags behind the PRC when it comes to human rights research institutes and the publication of works on human rights and international law. The first human rights research center in Taiwan was set up at Soochow University as late as December 2000, while the PRC, as we have seen, began to establish human rights research centers at several important institutions of higher learning in the early 1990s.[8] The PRC has also been much more active in the field of human rights publications, whereas few works to date have been published in Taiwan.[9] This fact by itself doesn't tell us much about the state and quality of human rights research, and even less of course about the actual human rights situation in each society. Lest there be any doubts, Taiwan far surpasses the PRC when it comes to respect for human rights. The fact that for a long period of time Taiwan has had a number of independent and very active human rights NGOs speaks volumes; it is these kinds of organizations that have been crucial for protecting human rights and that have helped push Taiwan toward democracy. The PRC currently lacks independent human rights organizations, and academic research motivated by mere strategic considerations in effect do little to actually promote and protect human rights; it only reveals that the PRC has been quick to realize the need to engage in human rights research in order to refute foreign criticism. Although the GMD, during the late 1970s, had realized the political importance of human rights work and to this end established its own human rights organization, much as the CCP did in 1993, it didn't have the same urge as the CCP to encourage human rights research since it was more or less immune to human rights criticism during the Cold War, which at least partly helps explain the lack of human rights research centers in Taiwan.

After the death of Mao Zedong and the fall of the Gang of Four, the new political leadership of the PRC turned its back on class struggle and embarked on an ambitious program of economic reforms and opening up to the outside world. The earlier political campaigns were declared to have been mistaken, or at least excessive, and their victims began to be rehabilitated.[10] In some cases it was a question of a posthumous clearing of a person's name, while in others it entailed releasing people from prison and giving them back their positions and previous jobs. The focus was on officially clearing people's names, which in some important cases was taken care of at a ceremony held by the work unit or the party committee, or else announced in the media. But in most cases it was more of a low-keyed event in which an official, terse statement of rehabilitation was handed over to the victim in question. In some cases people who had been imprisoned or fired were handed back the equivalent of their accumulated salary over the years, but in no case was it a proper compensation. Nor was the CCP prepared to engage in general public apologies for past misdeeds or erect monuments to the memory of those who had been wrongfully imprisoned or killed during different political campaigns. For example, the party turned a deaf ear to writer Ba Jin's suggestion to open a museum dedicated to the Cultural Revolution.

Apart from the Gang of Four, which was held responsible for 34,800 deaths during the Cultural Revolution, no one has been indicted for the violations committed during the Cultural Revolution or during other political movements and campaigns. Instead of seeing past human rights violations as endemic of the political system and the responsibility of the party, the responsibility for the Cultural Revolution was assigned to four people. The question of accountability was highly problematic and sensitive, but the party needed some scapegoats in order to exonerate itself. Deng Xiaoping and others who came to power in the late 1970s were victims of the Cultural Revolution but they had themselves been in charge of and responsible for campaigns in the 1950s, which explains the leadership's reluctance to investigate and assign responsibility for these campaigns. Thus, the antirightist campaign is described as excessive but is not regarded as a complete mistake, and therefore a handful of people have still not been rehabilitated. Although the CCP has victimized people it is also the CCP, often the very same people, that has rehabilitated them, and people are expected to thank the CCP. The party believes that after acknowledging past mistakes and correcting them, the past is best forgotten. The impossibility for the PRC to make a clean break with the past is also due to the fact that the one-party system itself hasn't changed.

The question of truth and accountability is of course even more problematic in the case of recent human rights violations. The crackdown on the 1989 democracy movement is thus still described as correct and the movement itself as a counterrevolutionary rebellion. The authorities have not made public the number of people killed and imprisoned, nor have they allowed any independent investigations. The lack of freedom of speech and association makes it difficult, if not virtually impossible, for people to expose human rights abuses and achieve accountability. People who dare to challenge the official silence on human rights abuses by gathering information on prisoners of conscience or privately commemorating June Fourth, for example, inevitably risk imprisonment for their activities.[11] But despite the difficulties and the official wrath they face many Chinese citizens nonetheless continue to expose and commemorate human rights violations. Family members of those killed during the crushing of the democracy movement of 1989 have formed a group known as the Tiananmen Mothers that campaigns for a public inquiry and an end to impunity for those responsible for the killings and other human rights violations. The Tiananmen Mothers have asked China's Supreme People's Procuratorate to initiate a criminal investigation into the killings to determine the legal responsibility and they have also recently brought a lawsuit in the United States against former Premier Li Peng for his role in the crackdown.[12]

The party's ambivalent position on past political campaigns and human rights violations is also evident in its representation of and writings on PRC history. The party suffers from selective historical amnesia and attempts to rewrite party history and prevent others from telling their alternative versions of this history. Research on violations committed during different political campaigns is not only quite sensitive but also very difficult to access since archives are closed to scholars.

The PRC's incorporation in the international human rights regime and its own changed position on human rights, however, has necessitated a revision and rewriting of party history to make it seem more supportive of human rights. Numerous articles and books have recently appeared that try to demonstrate that the CCP and political leaders such as Mao Zedong have been staunch defenders of human rights all along.[13] The CCP is described as having liberated the Chinese people and restored their human rights. According to the 1991 White Paper: "The situation in respect to human rights in China took a basic turn for the better after the founding of the People's Republic of China. Greatly treasuring this hard-won achievement, the Chinese government and people have spared no effort to safeguard human rights and steadily improve their human rights situation, and have achieved remarkable results. This has won full confirmation and fair appraisal from all people who have a real understanding of Chinese conditions and who are not prejudiced." But, as is obvious from this quote and the rest of the White Paper, in order to portray the CCP as having respected human rights since coming to power, party historians have had to ignore and keep silent on many violent aspects of party history.

It is possible to come up with documents that show that human rights, to some extent and in certain periods, have figured in party rhetoric, but it is more difficult, if not impossible, to show, de facto, that the CCP also has always protected human rights; in any event, it requires a highly selective memory. And although it is true that the party, for example, used human rights slogans in its struggle against the GMD in the 1940s, the strategic reasons for such a position have not been fully acknowledged or addressed. The party, furthermore, is not always appreciative of others' attempts to resurrect party texts and statements that entail demands for human rights. In 1999, for example, when a collection of articles on democracy and human rights from different party newspapers published in the 1940s was reprinted, the book was rapidly forbidden.[14] The Chinese authorities were quick to realize that the publication of the book was intended as a reminder to the party that it had not lived up to its high-sounding promises to respect human rights and that it was an attempt to use the party's own words against it.

While there have been some, albeit very selective, efforts to mention the party's pre-1949 human rights rhetoric, the party has been silent on its position in the post-1949 period. It is obvious that it doesn't want to admit or discuss its highly critical views from the late 1970s, when human rights were dismissed as a bourgeois slogan. In the contemporary human rights debates there are few references to more liberal, non-CCP debates on human rights. The *Xinyue* group and the China League for the Protection of Civil Rights are both well known and discussed in standard works on history—the former criticized and the latter praised—but other discussions remain largely forgotten. Alternative and dissenting voices simply don't make it into the official historiography on human rights except as targets of criticism.

Chinese dissidents quite naturally have a different understanding of PRC history and the party's culpability in past and present human rights violations.

A group of Chinese dissidents, writing in reaction to the 1991 White Paper, thus presented a strikingly different historical account of CCP rule.

> Since the CCP became a ruling party, it has imposed a bureaucratic-monopoly, military and police rule on China to exercise comprehensive autocracy over the Chinese people politically, economically, and culturally, and deprive the Chinese people of the basic human rights which they should have enjoyed a long time ago. From the large-scale persecution of the intellectuals in 1957 to the ten-year catastrophe of the Great Cultural Revolution which started in 1966, and to the massive massacre and persecution of the pro-democracy activists in 1989, the crime of the CCP authorities of exercising autocracy has triggered the hatred of all Chinese people, including the majority of those fair-minded Communist Party members with a conscience. The perverse acts of the CCP authorities have brought poverty and sufferings to the Chinese nation.[15]

The people who wrote this account were rapidly arrested and sentenced to long terms in prison. A regime genuinely concerned about human rights issues would have responded to their claims rather than simply silencing them.

CONCEPTUAL AND POLITICAL CHANGES

The fact that nations, interest groups, and individuals seek to describe themselves as human rights defenders and justify their own actions in terms of human rights is one measure of the power of the human rights concept today. The globalization of the human rights discourse has forced many erstwhile critics to adopt and appropriate the language of human rights, although by so doing they unwittingly invite others to use it against themselves.

The Chinese people's position on human rights has shifted over the years depending on their political convictions, the political situation, and the status of the concept itself in domestic and international discourse. There have been fierce contestations between the concept of human rights and other political concepts, although today it seems as if human rights has won out against concepts such as people's rights and other more revolutionary slogans. In their choices between different concepts people have been motivated by the positive effects these would provide. People often try to challenge old concepts or make use of new ones in reaction to ingrained political concepts used by the power holders. In the 1940s, for example, many people preferred to talk about human rights because they felt that the concept of people's rights had been corrupted by the GMD. They tried to escape the ideological constraints of the language of those in power and therefore reached out for and claimed a new language for themselves. To reach out for a universal concept such as human rights is particularly attractive and effective when trying to seek the moral high ground against domestic adversaries.

From the start, fierce political contestations surrounded the concept of human rights in China. Opponents to those in power have always been ready to adopt the language of human rights. In the early twentieth century many progressive Chinese individuals thus referred to human rights in their struggle for a new, modern China. To them the language of human rights carried a strong connotation of progress and civilization. The strategy of those in power has been much more ambivalent, but more often than not they have rejected or simply ignored the concept of human rights. Before 1948 they could afford to do so since human rights then didn't have much status in the world in general. But the establishment of the United Nations and the gradual development of a strong international human rights regime forced first the GMD and later the CCP to adopt and appropriate the concept of human rights.

The Chinese human rights discourse has its immediate background in domestic concerns and political contestations, but it is obvious that it also has been shaped and inspired by international developments in the human rights field. This was evident already in the 1940s, although the globalization of human rights didn't take off until the late 1970s. Until the 1970s, the PRC was fairly immune to human rights talk since it stood outside of the UN system and therefore could afford to reject and dismiss it. But since that time the PRC has been incorporated into the international human rights regime with the result that international developments, to an ever greater extent, shape and influence the Chinese human rights discourse.

The CCP's position on the concept of human rights has, as we have seen, shifted over the years and been somewhat ambivalent in character. In the pre-1949 era there were times when it more or less completely dismissed human rights for being a mere bourgeois slogan, while at other times it made good use of it for strategic reasons, as a tool in the struggle against political adversaries. In the late 1920s, the CCP thus dismissed human rights as an excessively abstract concept not fitting a revolutionary society. Luo Longji's critique of such a position deserves to be repeated, as it is equally valid today as it was when it was penned in 1929.

> There are some people . . . who have deceived themselves into saying that human rights is an "abstract term." They use slogans like "starving and unable to eat, freezing, and unclothed" to claim that the human rights movement cannot be compared to the reality of the materialist, class revolution. Those people have completely failed to realise what human rights are. Of course human rights encompass clothing and food; they also include many things still more important than clothing and food. Consider, after all, that if in his day Germany had enjoyed complete freedom of thought, speech, and publication, Marx would not have had to flee to London's British Museum in order to write *Das Kapital!* Those who criticise human rights as an abstract term have completely failed to realise what human rights are.[16]

Although the times have changed and the CCP no longer dismisses human rights outright, they continue to argue that food and other social and economic rights are more important than civil and political rights, such as the freedom of speech. Developments in international human rights work, however, have lent more support to Luo Longji's views: In order to be a human being and live a meaningful life we need to enjoy a whole range of rights, and these rights are furthermore to be regarded as being both interdependent and indivisible.

The CCP has at times made skilful use of the human rights concept purely out of strategic considerations. The Communists' theoretical objections to human rights did not prevent them from advocating human rights and criticizing the violation of people's rights to freedom of thought, speech, and publication while fighting for power against the Nationalists in the 1940s. Such an appropriation of the language of human rights reveals its rhetorical value in political debate. This strategic appropriation of human rights talk has also been acknowledged by the CCP itself. It has thus argued that it was a useful tool before 1949 "in order to mobilise the people against imperialism and feudalism."[17] In the 1940s, as in the 1990s, the CCP has realized that human rights talk can yield some political benefits as well as confuse its critics. The PRC's membership in the United Nations in 1971 and increasing involvement in the international human rights regime since then has paved the way for an acceptance of sorts of the concept of human rights. Human rights are at least no longer regarded as taboo or inappropriate to a socialist country, which however, doesn't mean that human rights are no longer a sensitive topic.

Hu Ping, a Chinese dissident living in exile in New York, has made a concise summary of the CCP's recent turnabout and appropriation of the concept of human rights.

As late as the mid-1980s, the CCP still took the position of completely rejecting the concept of human rights, dismissing it as a "bourgeois concept." Since then, the CCP's attitude towards human rights has gradually changed. During the past few years, the Chinese authorities have accepted the concept of human rights and agreed to sign the two UN covenants on human rights, namely the International Covenant on Economic, Social and Cultural Rights and the International Covenant on Civil and Political Rights. However, this does not mean that the debate surrounding the concept of human rights has already subsided. At present, the basic strategy of those opposing human rights is to accept the expression "human rights" but twist its contents, so that they can resist the genuine demands of human rights.[18]

What we are witnessing today both with respect to the human rights concept in China and in the world in general is what conceptual historians would call a *demokratiserung* (democratization) and *politiserung* (politicization) of the human rights concept.[19] The former process refers to the fact that political concepts once only intelligible to and used by a small elite gradually tend to become familiar to and taken up by broader groups of people. If human rights was once a concept only known and invoked by a few Chinese intellectuals, such days are long since gone, as the globalization of the human rights language has now irreversibly reached China. The high visibility of human rights in the official discourse inevitably has repercussions and inspires citizens to challenge the government over the definition and understanding of the concept.

Governments expect that by appropriating the human rights language they will also be able to control and defuse the human rights issue. But this is not always such an easy task and the policy can easily backfire. The Chinese political leadership's own invocation of human rights has not only resulted in a strengthening of the governments' own grasp of the issue, which was the original intention, but it has also opened a veritable Pandora's box as more Chinese citizens and scholars have taken the opportunity to independently explore the issue. Most alarming from the governments' point of view must be the fact that Chinese citizens increasingly dare to invoke the language of human rights against the regime. Chinese citizens are creatively reworking and making use of the official rights talk to rebuke the regime while, at the same time, supporting their own demands by referring to China's international commitments in the human rights field. As Wei Jingsheng quite aptly has described this development:

> Human rights have already been accepted globally as a standard of conduct. . . . Even autocratic states, even countries where slavery is practised, have had to pay lip service to the acceptance and respect of human rights principles. This attitude creates favorable conditions for those who fight for human rights, freedom and democracy and it gives the people who suffer persecution growing encouragement to fight for the rights which belong to them.[20]

Politiserung is understood to be the process whereby certain political concepts easily become susceptible to use as propaganda slogans and weapons of abuse in conflicts among different groups of people or between governments. Human rights is one of the political concepts in the post–Second World War period that has come to have such a positive ring that all regimes, including authoritarian ones, have begun to talk the talk of human rights. This has led many of them to set up their own human rights organizations or human rights commissions in order to take the initiative on the issue. Philip Alston has called attention to this new strategy of dictatorial regimes to portray themselves as the true defenders of human rights.[21] Examples abound of countries trying to get on the human rights bandwagon in order to preempt human rights critique. In order to portray itself as a human rights defender, Nigeria, for example, decided to set up the National Human Rights Commission in 1996 after it had been condemned by Western governments for the execution of the author, poet, and playwright, Ken Saro-Wiwa.[22] China's human rights policy in the 1990s also fits Alston's description very well; witness the founding of the CSHRS in 1993.

The *politiserung* of the human rights concept in the PRC is also revealed by the prominent role played by the party propaganda machinery in the official appropriation of human rights. The institutionalization of the Chinese human rights discourse and the rapid development of research on human rights is quite remarkable, especially when compared with many other countries that also face human rights critique. The Chinese government's appropriation of the concept of human rights and its new human rights policy has not been random or unplanned but is the result of a conscious effort that combines the forces of foreign ministry officials, propaganda officials, and researchers at various departments and institutions. In some respects it has been quite ingenious and successful, whereas in other cases its dependence on Marxist jargon makes it look out-of-date and less convincing. Since the human rights policy targets both a domestic and a foreign audience the packaging and the arguments sometimes differ depending on the audience in mind. With respect to the foreign audience, the Chinese Foreign Ministry has been quite successful in preventing critical resolutions from being adopted at the United Nations and in gathering support for its human rights position from other Third World countries. Toward the late 1990s, it also managed to split the West on the issue of whether resolutions in the United Nations were useful and the best way to deal with China over human rights. The PRC's invocation of the particularity of human rights not only finds strong resonance in the Third World but among cultural relativists in the West as well. As for the domestic audience, the government has an advantage in that it monopolizes the debate and is able to prevent other voices from being heard, but its human rights vision nevertheless has not gone unchallenged. The conscious nationalistic dressing of the official human rights discourse, as discussed below, however, has made it more palatable to ordinary Chinese than would perhaps otherwise have been the case.

The Chinese authorities have made ample use of a whole new range of methods and institutions to push its own vision of human rights and defend its human rights record. It has, for example, issued White Papers, set up human rights research centers and organizations, and engaged in extensive publication drives and propaganda efforts through the use of newspaper, radio, television, and the web. One important aspect of the new Chinese human rights policy has been the issuing of a number of White Papers over the years since 1991. These White Papers have been addressed more to a foreign than a domestic audience even though at least initially they were prominently displayed in the domestic media. They not only attempt to refute Western criticism and attack its conception and stance on human rights but also portray the CCP as a defender of human rights. Another important rhetorical device during the past years has been to challenge and criticize the human rights record of Western governments, in particular that of the United States, using the West's own human rights rhetoric against it, and in this context also making ample use of, and finding support in, international conventions. When criticizing other countries the State Council in addition often quotes information obtained from international human rights organizations, which it normally doesn't regard as very reliable. The weakness of the official human rights policy is that it is inherently self-contradictory and inadvertently touches upon problems that exist in China itself. [23] While the PRC continues to argue that criticism of the Chinese human rights record constitutes interference in its internal affairs as well as an imposition of foreign values, it undermines its own relativistic position by criticizing other countries.

The recent crackdown on the Falun Gong movement is a particularly good example of the official appropriation of the concept of human rights. While the regime earlier would simply dismiss human rights criticism as an interference in its internal affairs, it now portrays itself as the true defender of human rights.[24] It has, for example, focused on cases of suicides and refusals to seek medical treatment among alleged Falun Gong believers and describe the movement and its leader as discarding people's lives and itself as defending people's right to life. By banning an evil cult, which is what Falun Gong is declared to be, the Chinese government claims that it is actually protecting freedom of religious belief, not suppressing it as the critics would contend.[25] At the fifty-seventh session of the United Nations Human Rights Commission, which took place in March 2001, a government-sponsored organization, the China Anti-Cult Association, demonstrated outside the UN offices carrying banners calling for human rights against "evil cults" that reportedly had been signed by more than one million Chinese people.[26] This is not only an interesting example of an appropriation of the concept of human rights but also of the methods of international human rights organizations that have long been in the habit of demonstrating and collecting signatures in defense of human rights.

REPRESENTATIVITY AND HUMAN RIGHTS

Although the PRC now is taking an active part in the international human rights regime and human rights research at home is encouraged and supported, there is still no room for independent human rights organizations, and domestic critics continue to be harshly treated. The contemporary human rights discourse is dominated and monopolized by the regime, which raises the problem of representativity. Human rights work in China today is a predominantly top-down affair. It is more of an issue between the Chinese government and foreign governments than an issue between the government and its people. The government wants "dialogue" with the West but is obviously less interested in dialogue with its own people. Since the actual violator of human rights generally is the state, the fact that it also is the sole agent in the debate on human rights as well as a self-proclaimed defender of human rights undermines its credibility on human rights issues. The protection of human rights in any given society depends on the existence of a human–rights–conscious citizenry who are willing and capable to defend their own rights and to this end are free to establish real NGO's that supervise the government and safeguard human rights. There is no lack of courageous Chinese citizens trying to do precisely this, but when they do, they are without fail harassed and arrested by their own government.[27] There is a need for a genuinely pluralistic discourse on human rights in China that would include ordinary citizens, workers, peasants, women, and minorities, and not only representatives of the government and its apologists.

However, one should not draw the conclusion that the Chinese dissident community is a homogeneous group, or the only genuine Chinese voice. The majority of Chinese dissidents, or at least those known to and able to present their views in the Western media, are well-educated and urban-based elites whose lives and concerns sometimes are very remote from that of ordinary workers and peasants. And although they often address issues of concern to the two latter groups or seek contact with them, this is sometimes done in a paternalistic and condescending manner.

CULTURE AND UNIVERSALITY

It seems as if references and attempts to ground human rights in traditional concepts often would have been more important in official human rights rhetoric than among ordinary citizens who criticize their governments for human rights violations. This was obviously the case with respect to the Asian values debate, but many other societies also exhibit similar tendencies.[28] In China, this tendency has been most obvious in the case of the GMD, while the CCP still harbors a more ambivalent attitude toward Chinese culture and Confucianism. Since the 1930s, the Nationalists have thus seen themselves as the true heirs and defenders of Chinese culture. In their human rights discussions of the 1940s and the late 1970s we find conscious attempts to relate human rights ideas to Confucian ideas and concepts. Since Confucian values were appropriated by the regime in power and thus

came to carry an authoritarian stigma, opponents of the regime were more comfortable with and attracted to a universal human rights discourse that stood above
and beyond culture. It is not surprising, for example, that the pro-independence
Taiwan Association for Human Rights did not try to justify its demands for human rights by referring to Chinese culture but sought support in international
human rights documents.

Although the PRC, beginning in the 1990s, often has argued that the Western view of human rights does not fit the Chinese cultural and historical background, there is not much by way of more concrete discussions on which aspects
of Chinese culture render the Western concept of human rights infeasible in
China, or on attempts to formulate a human rights theory based on indigenous
concepts. Nor have mainland dissidents attempted to explore or justify their human rights demands with references to tradition. One explanation to this could
be that traditional ideas and Confucian values for so long have been denounced
and rejected by the regime that this conceptual repertoire has been lost on the
mainland. It has been more natural for dissidents to reach out to universal human rights documents, especially so since human rights now constitute an important part of international law. The rejection of tradition and adoption of an
outward-looking strategy is also part and parcel of a well-established and ingrained political repertoire that dates from the early twentieth century. Still, I
would not completely rule out the prospects of a liberal reading and interpretation of the Chinese tradition that could be used by critics to challenge the current regime on the mainland, but to date there is little in the of such attempts.
However, Liu Junning, the critic of Asian values whom we met in an earlier
chapter, has lately presented a more liberal reading of Confucianism that could
point in just such a direction.

NATIONALISM AND HUMAN RIGHTS

The contemporary human rights debate in China is not only a domestic affair
but also has a strong international dimension, as human rights now is a hotly
debated and contested topic in China's bilateral and multilateral relations.
Whereas the Chinese government is confronted with human rights critique
from dissidents and political opponents at home and abroad, it also faces critique from foreign governments and international human rights organizations.
Although the PRC now, to some extent at least, is prepared to acknowledge
that human rights is a universal concern that outsiders also have a right to raise,
and itself takes part in bilateral and multilateral human rights work and cooperation, it, like most other governments, is very sensitive to foreign criticism,
which it sees as malicious and ill-intentioned. In the PRC's rhetoric on human

rights we not only encounter an authoritarian regime intent on defending its own hold on power but also a government that tries to ride the tide of a growing nationalism. The Chinese government thus tries to divert attention from its own responsibilities and human rights violations by invoking a powerful language of national humiliations and imperialist bullying. To this end it portrays China as a victim of foreign aggression stretching back in time to the Opium War, Japanese aggression, and Cold War hostilities, while more recent events, such as the NATO bombing of 1999 and the American spy plane affair of 2001, are seen as proof of continuing Western aggression toward China.

China also accuses the West of hypocrisy over human rights since the West itself has long been engaged in violations of human rights. It finds it expedient to focus on historical injustices committed by the West in order to defuse and undermine the West's critique of China. The PRC thus accuses the West for having grossly violated the rights of the Chinese people, for example, by allegedly putting up the sign "No admittance for dogs and Chinese" in a park in Shanghai.[29] It also tries to point out and reveal the hypocrisy of the West's human rights concerns by looking at more current policies. After the NATO bombing of the Chinese embassy in 1999 in Belgrade, the three Chinese journalists killed were thus proclaimed to have died while defending freedom of speech and publication. Their killing was described as a gross violation of human rights and the West's concern for freedom of speech as a sham.

Foreign human rights criticism is thus dismissed as both hypocritical and an affront to nationalist sentiments. The West's human rights diplomacy is said to aim to subvert the socialist system of China, suppress its economic development, and establish Western hegemonism.[30] The Chinese governments' policy since about 1997 has been to emphasize that it wants dialogue (*duihua*) not confrontation (*duikang*) on human rights. But all human rights criticism and venting of differing opinions are described as confrontational and anti-Chinese (*fan Hua*); attempts at securing resolutions in the UN Human Rights Commission critical of the Chinese human rights record, for example, are routinely labeled anti-Chinese.[31] This choice of words consciously plays on nationalistic feelings and serves to give the Chinese people the impression that human rights criticism per definition is anti-Chinese in character. The rise of nationalism in China in the 1990s and the official exploitation and encouragement of these nationalist sentiments is a cause for concern. One should not underestimate the fact that Western human rights criticism in these circumstances can be regarded as an affront to national pride. China's failure in 1993 to get the Year 2000 Olympics was for many a turning point, which led some to refute human rights as a ploy used by the West against China. Such a line of thinking was first most explicitly formulated in the 1996 book *China Can Say No*, by Song Qiang et al. Many Chinese people, in addition, feel that it is unfair that the West now criticizes

China's human rights record, since the human rights situation after all was much worse during the 1960s and 1970s.

The regime is not always able to control or route nationalism in the directions it deems most profitable, and many nationalistic outpourings are also regarded as problematic by the regime, such as, for example, those pertaining to the issue of the Diaoyutai islands and compensation to comfort women abused during the Japanese occupation. On these points dissidents have sometimes tried to exploit nationalism by presenting themselves as more patriotic than the government itself. Under the cover of nationalism some Chinese dissidents also used the 1998 killings of ethnic Chinese in Indonesia to protest this violation of human rights. The Chinese government's own belated response on this issue was motivated by this outburst of nationalism, whereas its initial silence had been due to a profound uneasiness to criticize Indonesia, because it has so strongly championed the view that human rights criticism is an interference in a country's internal affairs.

It is obvious that dissidents at times can take a position akin to that of the government, especially when nationalistic feelings are involved. Some, for instance, share the official view that sovereignty rights are more important than or stand above human rights. In the wake of the NATO bombing of the Chinese embassy, heated discussions on the relationship between sovereignty rights and human rights broke out among Chinese students and dissidents abroad.[32] This incident made some of them, like their government, question the sincerity of the West with respect to human rights. Nationalism more than human rights concerns also seems to have motivated some of those Chinese who protested the violence against ethnic Chinese in Indonesia. The issue of Tibet and other minority areas pose another challenge to Chinese human rights activists as many of them have not paid much attention to minority rights issues and show little understanding of and interest in the human rights violations in these areas.

Thus, one has to be aware of the fact that there is a very real risk that Chinese people could become alienated from the idea of human rights because of the hypocrisy and inconsistency of the West's human rights policy and the Chinese government's own exploitation of nationalistic sentiments.

CONCLUDING REMARKS: THE CHINESE HUMAN RIGHTS DISCOURSE IN THE TWENTY-FIRST CENTURY

Since 1987 Taiwan has steadily moved toward becoming a full-fledged democracy. It held its first presidential election in 1996, and at its second election in 2000, saw the peaceful transfer of power from the GMD to the DPP. Human rights activism and human rights organizations have figured quite prominently in this development toward democracy. Although the human rights situation significantly improved after martial law was lifted in 1987, the struggle for human rights has not abated. To many people on Taiwan, the fact that Taiwan since 1971 has stood outside the UN human rights regime is a cause of concern. In recent years individuals and organizations have tried to promote human rights education in schools and in society at large. In December 1999, twenty-two Taiwanese NGOs formed a coalition to work toward establishing a National Human Rights Commission.[33] In his inaugural presidential address, the new president, Chen Shuibian, endorsed establishing such an institution and generally took a strong position on human rights. Shortly after taking office Chen set up an Advisory Group on Human Rights that would work toward establishing a human rights commission. The new administration has also realized that commitment to human rights and a more active human rights policy could promote its international position and be a means toward international and diplomatic recognition. To this end, for example, it has recently announced that Taiwan should aim toward ratifying the two UN-sponsored human rights covenants and make human rights an integrated part of its development aid policy.[34]

Although the PRC still has a long way to go compared with Taiwan, it should be remembered that it has traversed quite a lot of ground in a very short time. After all, not long ago human rights were dismissed outright as bourgeois and irrelevant to China. But since the late 1970s, the official view on human rights has gradually changed as a result of both domestic and international developments. More than anything else, however, the events of 1989 finally placed human rights on the official agenda. Chinese officials, establishment intellectuals, dissidents, and ordinary citizens are today engaged in fierce debates over human rights both among themselves and with the international community.

The picture that emerges as the PRC enters the twenty-first century is complex and somewhat contradictory. On the one hand, the PRC shows an increasing acceptance, or appropriation, of the language of human rights, while, on the other hand, human rights violations nevertheless continue unabated. This new, more positive and proactive human rights policy manifests itself in China's incorporation in the international human rights regime and its ongoing bilateral dialogues and cooperation on human rights issues with foreign governments. Revisions of domestic laws and the signing of the ICESCR and the ICCPR, on paper at least, have significantly strengthened the rights of the individual. But human rights rhetoric is one thing and human rights protection quite another. Whereas the PRC in 1998 signed the ICCPR, thus presenting the world with an image of commitment to human rights, the same autumn also saw a deterioration of the human rights situation that intensified as the twentieth century drew to its close. In a 2000 White Paper on human rights that traced developments in the human rights field over the past fifty years, entitled *Fifty Years of Progress in China's Human Rights*, the Chinese government glossed over past and present human rights violations, instead presenting an upbeat picture of the Chinese human rights situation.[35] The paper focused exclusively on legal and constitutional stipulations of rights and freedoms, but failed to mention the discrepancy between rights on paper and rights in reality. It also explained away any shortcomings by arguing that China still was a developing country limited by its "semi-colonial, semi-feudal" past and backward economy.

It is impossible to predict what lies ahead but it is possible that the State Council's own prediction that "China's human rights situation will see unwavering improvement" will come true. What is beyond doubt, however, is that the CCP will continue to face challenges over its human rights vision and political rule. The human rights issue will most definitely not disappear from either the domestic or the international agenda in the foreseeable future.

NOTES

1. For a discussion about truth and historical writings, see Appleby, Hunt, and Jacob (1995).

2. It should be acknowledged, however, that Taiwan's transition to democracy has been more gradual than in many other countries and took place under and was guided by the former one-party regime. For a general discussion of democratic transitions in Taiwan and elsewhere, see Diamond, Plattner, Chu, and Tien (1997). And for human rights in political transitions, see Hesse and Post (1999).

3. For one such, rather isolated, voice, see Phyllis Hwang, "History Is Not the Rights Judge," *Taipei Times*, October 7, 1999, <www.taipeitimes.com> [accessed March 1, 2001].

4. Quoted in Liu Shao-hua, "Rights Drive to Take Center Stage," *Taipei Times*, December 7, 2000, <www.taipeitimes.com> [accessed December 27, 2000].

5. See Chen Shuibian, "*Zongtong chuxi 'Zongtong fu renquan zixun xiaozu chengli dahui' zhici* (Address by President Chen Shuibian on establishing the President's Advisory Group on Human Rights) <http://web.oop.gov.tw/> [accessed October 24, 2000]. The address is translated in Angle and Svensson (2001).

6. "228 [February 28 Incident] Victims Demand Truth," *Taipei Times*, March 1, 2001, <www.taipeitimes.com> [accessed March 1, 2001].

7. On this, see articles in the Taiwanese press, for example, "Chen Opens Records from 228 [February 28] Incident," *Taipei Times*, February 28, 2001, <www.taipeitimes.com> [accessed March 1, 2001].

8. On the history of the establishment of the center and its purpose, see Hawang (2001).

9. Many Taiwanese human rights activists have also complained about this lack of work on human rights; see Peter Huang (2001).

10. Of late, several works have appeared in China that discuss this process of rehabilitation after 1978. See, for example, Dai Huang (1998).

11. In 1996 Li Hai was sentenced to nine years in prison for gathering information on those imprisoned in 1989, and in 2000 Jiang Qisheng was sentenced to four years for suggesting peaceful activities in commemoration of June Fourth, to cite but two examples.

12. For further information on the Tiananmen Mothers' struggle for accountability, see <www.hrichina.org> [accessed September 7, 2001].

13. See, for example, Liu Zhongheng and Tan Shuangchuan (1998).

14. Xiao Shu (1999).

15. See statement of the Liberal Democratic Party of China, FBIS-CHI-91-222, November 18, 1991, pp. 22–23. Text originally published in *Ming pao*, November 16, 1991. Reprinted in Angle and Svensson (2001).

16. Luo Longji in Hu Shi (1930), p. 35, translated in Angle and Svensson (2001), p. 139.

17. "Notes on the Human Rights Question," BR, no. 45, November 9, 1979, p. 19.

18. Hu Ping (1998), translated in Angle and Svensson (2001), pp. 424–25.

19. Richter (1995).

20. Wei Jingsheng (1998).

21. See Alston (1990), p. 6.

22. For a fascinating account of Nigeria, see Obe (2001).

23. China has thus criticized the use of the death penalty in the United States for being extremely arbitrary and targeting poor people. The fact that mentally retarded persons and juveniles have been sentenced to death is also deplored. The Chinese also draw attention to cases of miscarriages of justice and the execution of innocent people, and criticize the low level of public defenders. But the same kind of criticism could also be voiced with the respect to the use of the death penalty in China, although China, it should be acknowledged, in contrast to some states in the United States, explicitly forbids the imposition of the death penalty on minors below the age of eighteen.

24. Although this is indeed a new development that has become more pronounced during the past few years, in 1989 the PRC also partly defended its crackdown on the democracy movement in these terms. It argued that the students themselves were violating human rights by striking and thus interfering with other people's lives and work. See Shi Yun (1989), translated in Angle and Svensson (2001).

25. Examples of this line of reasoning can be found inter alia on the television program *Jinri shuo fa*, which on March 22, 2001, discussed Falun Gong from a human rights perspective. The host had invited as a guest Liu Nanlai, a human rights expert from the human rights center at CASS. A transcript of the program can be accessed at the Web site of *Zhongguo jiancha ribao*, <www.jcrb.com.cn> [accessed April 16, 2001]. And for a news item with a similar message addressed to a foreign audience, see "Freedom of Religion Progressing," CD, February 21, 2001, <www.chinadaily.net.cn> [accessed February 24, 2001].

26. "Group Demonstrates against Cults," CD, March 21, 2001, <www.chinadaily.net.cn> [accessed March 21, 2001]. One cannot help but note that in the PRC itself the freedom to demonstrate is hardly respected.

27. For information and updates on human rights work among ordinary Chinese citizens, see Human Rights in China's (HRIC) Web site at <www.hrichina.org> [accessed August 24, 2001].

28. There are some exceptions to this, as we have seen earlier in this work. Buddhism and Islam, in contrast to Confucianism, are living religions. Many Buddhists including Aung

San Suu Kyi and the Dalai Lama, and Muslim activists have had more reason to relate their human rights demands to traditional concepts and ideas.

29. For an early use of this myth in discussions on human rights, see "Notes on the Human Rights Question," BR, no. 45, November 9, 1979, p. 18. For a thorough discussion on the sign and its uses in argument, see Wasserstrom (2000).

30. This is evident of many articles in the more recent political discourse. See "A Comment on the South-North Dispute on Human Rights," in RMRB, March 17, 1997.

31. See, for example, the article "Another Example of Using Human Rights to Create Confrontation—Criticising the Chinese Section in the Human Rights Report of the American State Department," in RMRB, March 14, 1997. And for the latest example, see the reaction after the voting at the 2001 annual meeting of the United Nations Commission on Human Rights (UNCHR) in RMRB, April 19, 2001.

32. See articles published in *Beijing zhi chun* during 1999.

33. For a discussion of the work of Taiwanese human rights organizations to this end, see Mab Huang (2001).

34. The new administration's human rights diplomacy was outlined by Hung-mao Tien, minister of foreign affairs, at the International Conference on National Human Rights Commissions held in Taipei, January 2–4, 2001, and organized by Soochow University. His speech can be found at <www.mofa.gov.tw/emofa/20010102.htm> [accessed January 15, 2001].

35. Information Office of the State Council of the PRC, "Fifty Years of Progress in China's Human Rights," February 2000 <www.chinaguide.org/e-white/> [accessed July 14, 2001]. Since then a new White Paper, "Progress in China's Human Rights Cause in 2000," has been published; it can also be found on the same Web site. The White Paper was published in CD, April 10, 2001.

Glossary

ben: root 本
benfen: duties; one's natural position and duty 本分
benwei: duties 本位
benxing: human nature 本性
buke duo: inviolable 不可夺
buke fan: inviolable 不可犯
buke gerang: inalienble 不可割让
buke paoqi: inalienable 不可抛弃
buke paoqi de quanli: inalienable rights 不可抛弃的权利
buke qinfan: inviolable 不可侵犯
buke yirang: inalienable 不可移让
buke zhuangrang: inalienable 不可转让
chenmin: subjects 臣民
chouxiang: abstract 抽象
dangwai: outside of the party 党外
duli renge: independent personality 独立人格
fading quanli: legal rights 法定权利
faxian le ren: discovery of man 发现了人
fazhi guo: a country with rule of law 法治国
feiren de shenghuo: inhuman lives 非人的生活
fu tianfu zhi renquan: restore one's human rights 复天赋之人权
fu guo li min: to enrich the country and benefit the people 富国利民
genyuan quanli: original rights 根原权利
geren de quanli: the rights of the individual 个人的权利

geren duli zizun zhi renge: individual personality of independence and self-respect 个人独立自尊之人格
geren jiefang: liberation of the individual 个人解放
geren zhuyi: individualism 个人主义
gexing: personality 个性
gongde: public morality 公德
gongmin quanli: citizen's rights 公民权利
gongli: universal principle 公理
gongquan: public rights 公权
gongxin: public morality 公心
gongyong: function 公用
guyou (de): innate; inherent 固有的
guyou zhi quanli: innate rights 固有之权利
guyou zhi renge: innate personality 固有之人格
guyou zhi ziyou quan: innate freedom 固有之自由权
guojia quanli: rights of the nation 国家权利
guojia quanti: the whole nation 国家全体
guomin: citizen; citizenry 国民
guomin quanli: national's rights 国民权利
guomin zhi ziyou you yu tianfu: citizen's freedom is endowed by nature 国民之自由由于天赋
guoquan: rights of the nation; power of the nation 国权
jiben quanli: fundamental rights 基本权利
jiben renquan: basic human rights 基本人权
jiazu zhuyi: clanism; familism 家族主义
jingji: economics 经济
jiu ziji: salvation of the individual 救自己
jiuguo: salvation of the nation 救国
jiuren: salvation of humankind 救人
juedui: absolute 绝对
junquan: rights of the ruler 君权
laobaixing: the ordinary people 老百姓
li: rites 礼
li: interest; benefit 利
liang min: respectable person 良民
liyi: interest 利益
lizhi: reason 理智
lunli: morals 伦理
minquan: people's rights; people's sovereignty; people's power; civil rights 民权

minsheng: people's livelihood 民生
minzu jiefang: national liberation 民族解放
nanquan: men's rights 男权
nüquan: women's rights 女权
pingdeng: equality 平等
pingdeng quan: equality; right to equality 平等权
pingmin zhengzhi: democracy 平民政治
pingquan pai: school of equal rights 平权派
qiangquan: rights of the strongest 强权
qiangquan pai: school of the rights of the strongest 强权派
qinggan: feelings 情感
quan: rights; power 权
quanheng: weigh; balance 权衡
quanli: rights 权利
quanli: power; might 权力
quanshi: might 权势
quanwei: authority 权威
ren: benevolence; humaneness 仁
ren sheng er ju lai de: born with; innate 人生而俱来的
rendao: humanitarianism 人道
rendao zhuyi: humanitarianism 人道主义
ren de quanli: people's rights 人的权利
ren de zunyan: people's dignity 人的尊严
renge: personality; human dignity 人格
renmin: the people 人民
renmin de quanli: people's rights 人民的权利
renmin yingyou zhi quanli: rights that people ought to enjoy
人民应有之权利
renquan: human rights 人权
renquan re: human rights fever 人权热
renquan zhi shou chu yu tian, er renquan zhi li ze zai yu ren: human rights
are given by nature, but their realization depends on man
人权之受处于天而人权之立则在于人
renquan zhi xuanbu: human rights declaration 人权宣布
renshen quanli: personal rights 人身权利
renxing: humanity; human nature 人性
shehui: society 社会
shenfen: dignity 身分
shenquan: divine rights 神权
shensheng: sacred 神圣

shensheng buke qinfan renquan: sacred and inviolable human rights 神圣不可侵犯人权

sheng ju lai: inborn; innate; inherent 生俱来

sheng ju lai de ziran quanli: innate natural rights 生俱来的自然权利

shengcun quan: right to subsistence 生存权

shenghuo bixu pin: necessary things in life 生活必须品

shengming: life 生命

shiren ziran quan: natural rights of humans 是人自然权

shiyou quanli: actual rights 实有权利

sixiang jiefang: liberation of thought 思想解放

suowei tianfu renquan: so-called natural rights 所谓天赋人权

tian: Heaven; Nature 天

tian sheng ren er ren yi ziyou pingdeng zhi quanli: people are born with rights to freedom and equality 天生人而人以自由平等之权利

tianfu: innate; endowed by nature; endowed by Heaven 天赋

tianfu de quanli: natural rights 天赋的权利

tianfu de ziran quanli: natural rights 天赋的自然权利

tianfu nanquan: natural rights of men 天赋男权

tianfu renquan: natural rights; human rights 天赋人权

tianfu zhi quanli: natural rights 天赋之权利

tianfu ziyou quan: liberties; freedoms; human rights 天赋自由权

tianli: justice 天理

tianquan: natural rights 天权

tianran quan: natural rights 天然权

tianran zhi pingdeng: natural equality 天然之平等

tianran zhi quanli: natural rights 天然之权利

tiansheng: inherent; innate; natural 天生

tiansheng de guoyou quanli: natural and innate rights 天生的固有权利

tianxing: nature 天性

wanquan ren: complete human being 完全人

weili: power 威力

wenming: civilized; civilization 文明

wo guoren zhi da bing, dan zhi you ji er bu zhi you ren: our people's major ill is that they only know about themselves and not about others 天我国人之大病单知有己而不知有人

wu: task 务

xiangyou quanli: due rights 享有权利

xin ren: new man 新人

yi: justice; righteousness 义

yi quanli wei li: rights as power 以权利为力

yi quanli wei liyi: rights as interests 以权利为利益
yi quanli wei ziyou: rights as liberties 以权利为自由
yi renlei de zige er yingxiang de quanli: rights that one ought to enjoy on the
basis of one's humanity 以人类的资格而应享的权利
yi shou hui wo tianfu zhi quanli: restore our natural rights
以受回我天赋之权利
yipan sansha: a sheet of loose sand 一盘散沙
yiqie liyi zhi shi: all beneficial things 一切利益之事
yiwu: duties 义务
yinggai yongyou de quanli: rights that one ought to have 应该拥有的权利
yingxiang zhi quanli: rights that one should enjoy; due rights 应享之权利
yingyou quanli: rights that one ought to enjoy 应有权利
yong bu momie de renquan: eternal human rights 永不磨灭的人权
you yingxiang zhi quanli: rights that one should enjoy; innate rights
有应享之权利
yuanquan: original rights 原权
zeren: responsibility 责任
zheng quan zhi shidai: an age of struggling for rights 争权之时代
zhengquan: political rights 政权
zhi: duties; obligations 职
zhi you ji, er bu zhi you qun: only know about oneself and not about
others 知有己而不知有群
zhuren: master 主人
zichan jieji kouhao: bourgeois slogan 自产阶级口号
zigui: self-esteem 自贵
zijue: self-consciousness 自觉
ziran quanli: natural rights 自然权利
ziran zhi quanli: natural rights 自然之权利
ziyou: freedom; liberty 自由
ziyou quan: freedoms; liberties; right of freedom 自由权
zizhi: self-rule 自治
zizhu zhi quan: right to self-mastery 自主之权
zizhu zhi renge: personality of self-mastery 自主之人格
zizun: self-respect 自尊
zui zhong renquan, zun ziyou: respect human rights and freedom the most
最重人权尊自由
zunxin ziyou: freedom of belief 尊信自由
zuoren: to be a person; acting as people; humanity 做人
zuoren de quanli: the rights to be a person 做人的权利

zuoren de zui jiben quan: most fundamental rights to be a person
做人的最基本权

Bibliography

ABBREVATIONS OF MAGAZINES, NEWSPAPERS, AND OTHER WORKS

AFF	April Fifth Forum (*Siwu luntan*)
BR	Beijing Review
BS	Beijing Spring (*Beijing zhi chun*)
CD	China Daily
CHR	China Human Rights (*Zhongguo renquan*)
CRF	China Rights Forum
DLDX	*Dalu dixia kanwu huibian* (A collection of underground publications circulated on the Chinese mainland)
FBIS	Foreign Broadcasting Information Service
FEER	Far Eastern Economic Review
FL	Fertile Land (*Wo tu*)
FYPLWXJ	*Fan youpai lunwen xuanji* (A collection of antirightist articles)
GDXXYB	*Gaodeng xuexiao youpai yanlun xuanbian* (A collection of rightist speech from schools of higher education)
HB	Heavy Bells (*Chen zhong*)
JFRB	Liberation Daily (*Jiefang ribao*)
PV	People's Voice (*Renmin zhi sheng*)
RMRB	People's Daily (*Renmin ribao*)
SC	Seeking Correctness (*Qiushi bao*)
SDL	Science, Democracy and Law (*Kexue, minzhu, fazhi*)
XHRB	*Xinhua ribao*
YPYLXJ	*Youpai yanlun xuanji* (A collection of rightist speech)
ZMTLW	*Zhongguo minzhu tongmeng lishi wenxian* (Historical documents of the China Democratic League)

WEB SITES

China Society for Human Rights Studies
Human Rights in China <www.hrichina.org>
White Papers published by the State Council of the PRC*Zhongguo jiancha ribao* <www.jcrb.com.cn>

WORKS IN WESTERN LANGUAGES

The bibliography is divided into one section with publications in Western languages and one with Chinese-language material. Anonymous works are listed chronologically under Anon.

Alitto, Guy S. 1986. *The Last Confucian: Liang Shu-ming and the Chinese Dilemma of Modernity*. Berkeley: University of California Press.

Alston, Philip. 1990. "The Fortieth Anniversary of the Universal Declaration of Human Rights: A Time More for Reflection than for Celebration." In *Human Rights in a Pluralist World: Individuals and Collectivities*, ed. Jan Berting. London: Meckler.

———. ed. 1995. *Human Rights Law*. Aldershot, U.K: Dartmouth Publishing Co.

Ames, Roger T. 1988. "Rites as Rights: The Confucian Alternative." Pp. 199–216, in *Human Rights and the World's Religions*, ed. Leroy. S. Rouner. Notre Dame: University of Notre Dame Press.

———. 1997. "Continuing the Conversation on Chinese Human Rights." *Ethics & International Affairs* 11:177–205.

Amnesty International. 1984. *China: Violations of Human Rights and Prisoners of Conscience and the Death Penalty in the People's Republic of China*. London: Amnesty International.

Angle, Stephen C. 1998. "Did Someone Say 'Rights'? Liu Shipei's Concept of Quanli." *Philpsophy East and West* 48, no. 4 (October): 623–51.

———. 2002. *Human Rights and Chinese Thought: A Cross-Cultural Inquiry*. New York: Cambridge University Press.

Angle, Stephen C., and Marina Svensson. 2001. *The Chinese Human Rights Reader: Documents and Commentary, 1900–2000*. Armonk, NY: Sharpe.

An-Na'im, Abdullahi Ahmed, ed. 1995. *Human Rights in Cross-Cultural Perspectives: A Quest for Consensus*. Philadelphia: University of Pennsylvania Press.

Appleby, Joyce, Lynn Hunt, and Margaret Jacob. 1995. *Telling the Truth About History*. New York: Norton.

Arendt, Hannah. 1973. *The Origins of Totalitarianism*. New York: Harcourt Brace Jovanovich.

Aung San Suu Kyi. 1991. *Freedom from Fear and Other Writings*. New York: Penguin.

Ball, Terence, James Farr, and Russell L. Hanson, eds. 1989. *Political Innovation and Conceptual Change*. Cambridge, U.K.: Cambridge University Press.

Bastid-Bruguière, Marianne. 1990. "The Influence of Jean-Jaques Rousseau on Chinese Political Thought before the 1911 Revolution." In *China and the French Revolution: Proceedings of the International Conference in Shanghai, 18–21 March 1989*, ed. Zhang Zhilian. Oxford, U.K.: Pergamon.

Bauer, Joanne R., and Daniel A. Bell. 1999. *The East Asian Challenge for Human Rights.* Cambridge, U.K.: Cambridge University Press.

Beahan, Charlotte L. 1975. "Feminism and Nationalism in the Chinese Women's Press, 1902–1911." *Modern China* 1, no. 4: 379–416.

Baehr, P. R. et. al., eds. 1996. *Human Rights: Chinese and Dutch Perspectives.* The Netherlands: Kluwer Law International.

Beetham, David. 1995. "Introduction: Human Rights in the Study of Politics." *Political Studies* 43:1–9.

Beijing Review (weekly magazine). 1979.

Bell, Lynda S., Andrew J. Nathan, and Ilan Peleg, eds. 2001. *Negotiating Culture and Human Rights.* New York: Columbia University Press.

Bennett, Adrian. 1967. *John Fryer: The Introduction of Western Science and Technology into Nineteenth-Century China.* Cambridge, Mass.: Harvard University Press.

Benton, Gregor. 1998. *Chen Duxiu's Last Articles and Letters, 1937–1942.* Honolulu: University of Hawaii Press.

Berlin, Isaiah. 1969. *Four Essays on Liberty.* Oxford, U.K.: Oxford University Press.

Bickers, Robert A., and Jeffrey N. Wasserstrom. 1995. "Shanghai's 'Dogs and Chinese Not Admitted' Sign: Legend, History and Contemporary Symbol." *The China Quarterly*, no. 142 (June): 444–66.

Biggerstaff, Knight. 1961. *The Earliest Modern Government Schools in China.* Ithaca, N.Y.: Cornell University Press.

Bloch, Ernst. 1987. *Natural Law and Human Dignity.* Cambridge, Mass.: MIT Press.

Bloom, Irene. 1998. "Fundamental Intuitions and Consensus Statements: Mencian Confucianism and Human Rights." Pp. 94–116 in *Confucianism and Human Rights*, ed. Wm Theodore de Bary and Tu Weiming. New York: Columbia University Press.

Bobbio, Norberto. 1996. *The Age of Rights.* Cambridge, U.K.: Polity.

Boorman, Howard L. 1967. *Biographical Dictionary of Republican China.* New York: Columbia University Press.

Booth, Ken. 1999. "Three Tyrannies." Pp. 31–71, in *Human Rights in Global Politics*, ed. Tim Dunne and Nicholas J. Wheeler. Cambridge, U.K.: Cambridge University Press.

Braisted, William Reynold. 1974. *Meiroku Zasshi. Journal of the Japanese Enlightenment.* Cambridge, Mass.: Harvard University Press.

Brodsgaard, Kjeld Erik. 1981. "The Democracy Movement in China 1978–1979: Opposition Movements, Wall Poster Campaigns, and Underground Jounrals." *Asian Survey* 21, no. 7 (July).

Bruun, Ole, and Michael Jacobsen eds. 2000. *Human Rights and Asian Values: Contesting National Identities and Cultural Representations in Asia.* Surrey, U.K.:Curzon Press.

Burgers, Jan Herman. 1992. "The Road to San Francisco: The Revival of the Human Rights Idea in the Twentieth Century." *Human Rights Quarterly* 14, no. 4 (November): 447–77.

Calhoun, Craig. 1994. *Neither Gods nor Emperors. Students and the Struggle for Democracy in China.* Berkeley: University of California Press.

Chan, Anita, Stanley Rosen, and Jonathan Unger, eds. 1985. *On Socialist Democracy and the Chinese Legal System: The Li Yizhe Debates.* Armonk, N.Y.: M. E. Sharpe.

Chan, Joseph. 1999. "A Confucian Perspective on Human Rights for Contemporary China." Pp. 212–237, in *The East Asian Challenge for Human Rights*, ed. Joanne R. Bauer and Daniel A. Bell. Cambridge, U.K.: Cambridge University Press.

Chang, Carsun. 1952. *The Third Force in China.* New York: Bookman Associate.

Chang, Hao. 1971. *Liang Ch'i-ch'ao and Intellectual Transition in China 1890–1907.* Cambridge, Mass.: Harvard University Press.

Chang, P'eng-yüan. 1968. "The Constitutionalists." In *China in Revolution. The First Phase, 1900–1913,* ed. Mary Clabaugh Wright. New Haven, Conn.: Yale University Press.

Chang, Wejen. "Confucian Theory of Norms and Human Rights." Pp. 117–41, in *Confucianism and Human Rights,* ed. Wm Theodore de Bary and Tu Weiming. New York: Columbia University Press.

Chanock, Martin. 2000. "'Culture' and Human Rights: Orientalising, Occidentalising and Authencity." Pp. 15–36, in *Beyond Rights Talk and Culture Talk. Comparative Essays on the Politics of Rights and Culture,* ed. Mahmood Mamdani. New York: St. Martin's.

Chao, Linda, and Ramon H. Myers. 1998. *The First Chinese Democracy. Political Life in the Republic of China on Taiwan.* Baltimore, Md.: Johns Hopkins University Press, 1998.

Chen, Albert H.Y. 1993. "Developing Theories of Rights and Human Rights in China." Pp. 123–49, in *Hong Kong, China, and 1997: Essays in Legal Theory,* ed. Raymond Wacks. Hong Kong: Hong Kong University Press.

Chen Ruoxi. 1982. *Democracy Wall and the Unofficial Journals.* Berkeley: Center for Chinese Studies, Institute of East Asian Studies, University of California.

Chen Shuibian, "*Zongtong chuxi 'Zongtong fu renquan zixun xiaozu chengli dahui' zhici* (Address by President Chen Shuibian on Establishing the President's Advisory Group on Human Rights)" <http://web.oop.gov.tw/> [accessed October 24, 2000]. Translated in Stephen C. Angle and Marina Svensson, eds. *The Chinese Human Rights Reader: Documents and Commentary, 1900–2000.* Armonk, N.Y.: Sharpe, 2001.

Chen Xiaomei. 1995. *Occidentalism. A Theory of Counter-Discourse in Post-Mao China.* New York, Oxford University Press.

Chen Zhishang. 1997. "Philosophical Foundations of Human Rights in China: A Marxist Perspective." Pp. 161–82, in *Human Rights: Chinese and Canadian Perspectives,* ed. E. P. Mendes and A-M Traeholt. Ottawa: Human Rights Research and Education Center, University of Ottawa, 1997.

Cheng, Chung-ying. 1979. "Human Rights in Chinese History and Chinese Philosophy." *The Comparative Civilizations Review,* no. 1:1–20.

Chiang Kai-shek. 1947. *China's Destiny.* New York: Macmillan.

Ch'ien Tuan-Sheng. 1961. *The Government and Politics of China.* Cambridge, Mass.: Harvard University Press.

China and the United Nations. 1959. Report of a study group set up by the China Institute of International Affairs. New York: Manhattan Publishing Co.

China Critic (magazine). 1932–1933.

China Daily (newspaper). 2001.

China Rights Forum (magazine). 1995–2001.

Chiou, C. L. 1995. *Democratizing Oriental Despotism: China from 4 May 1919 to 4 June 1989 and Taiwan from 28 February 1947 to 28 June 1990.* London: St. Martin's.

Chow Tse-tsung. 1960. *The May Fourth Movement: Intellectual Revolution in Modern China.* Cambridge, Mass.: Harvard University Press.

Chuan, T. K. 1933a. "Useful Hints to Editors." *China Critic* 6, no. 5 (2 February).

———. 1933b. "A League for Animal Rights." *China Critic* 6 (16 November).

Clapton, Roger W., and Tsuin-Chen Ou, ed. 1973. *John Dewey: Lectures in China 1919–1920.* Honolulu.

Claude, Richard Pierre, and Burns H. Weston. 1992. *Human Rights in the World Community: Issues and Action*. Philadelphia: University of Pennsylvania Press.

Clausen, Sören. 1995. "Current Western Perceptions of Chinese Political Culture." Pp. 446–87, in *Cultural Encounters: China, Japan, and the West*, ed. Sören Clausen, Roy Starrs, and Anne Wedell-Wedellsborg. Aarhus, Denmark: Aarhus University Press.

Cohen, Jerome Alan, and Hungdah Chiu. 1974. *People's China and International Law: A Documentary Study*. 2 vols. Princeton, N.J.: Princeton University Press.

Cohen, Paul A. 1978. "Christian Missions and Their Impact to 1900." Pp. 543–90, in *The Cambridge History of China*. Vol. 10, *Late Ch'ing, 1800–1911*, pt. 1. General editors Denis Twitchett and John K. Fairbank. Cambridge, U.K.: Cambridge University Press.

———. 1984. *Discovering History on China: American Historical Writing on the Recent Chinese Past*. New York: Columbia University Press.

Cohen, Paul. A., and Merle Goldman ed. 1990. *Ideas Across Cultures. Essays on Chinese Thought in Honor of Benjamin I. Schwartz*. Cambridge, Mass: Harvard University Press.

Cohen, Roberta. 1987. "People's Republic of China: The Human Rights Exception." *Human Rights Quarterly* 9:447–549. Reprinted in *Occasional Papers/Reprint Series in Contemporary Asian Studies*, no. 3. School of Law University of Maryland, 1988.

Cook, Rebecca J. ed. 1994. *Human Rights of Women: National and International Perspectives* Philadelphia: University of Pennsylvania Press.

Copper, John F., et al. 1985. *Human Rights in Post-Mao China*. Boulder, Colo.: Westview Press.

Cranston, Maurice. 1973. *What are Human Rights?* New York: Taplinger.

Crawford, James, ed. 1988. *The Rights of People*. Oxford, U.K.: Clarendon Press.

Dagger, Richard. 1989. "Rights." Pp. 292–308, in *Political Innovation and Conceptual Change*, ed. Terence Ball, James Farr, and Russell L. Hanson. Cambridge, U.K.: Cambridge University Press.

Dai Qing. 1994. *Wang Shiwei and "Wild Lilies": Rectification and Purges in the Chinese Communist Party 1942–1944*. Armonk, N.Y.: M. E. Sharpe.

Davis, Michael C., ed. 1995. *Human Rights and Chinese Values: Legal, Philosophical, and Political Perspectives*. Hong Kong: Oxford University Press.

De Bary, Wm. Theodore. 1986. "Human Rites: An Essay on Confucianism and Human Rights." Pp. 109–32, in *Confucianism: The Dynamics of Tradition*, ed. Irene Eber. New York: Macmillan.

———. 1988. "Neo-Confucianism and Human Rights." Pp. 183–98, in *Human Rights and the World's Religions*, ed. Leroy. S. Rouner. Notre Dame: University of Notre Dame Press.

———. 1998. *Asian Values and Human Rights: A Confucian Communitarian Perspective*. Cambridge, Mass.: Harvard University Press.

De Bary, Wm. Theodore, and Tu Weiming. 1998. *Confucianism and Human Rights*. New York: Columbia University Press.

Dikötter, Frank. 1992. *The Discourse of Race in Modern China*. Hong Kong: Hong Kong University Press.

Dirlik, Arif. 1989. *The Origins of Chinese Communism*. New York: Oxford University Press.

———. 1991. *Anarchism and the Chinese Revolution*. Berkeley: University of California Press.

Deane, Herbert. 1955. *The Political Ideas of Harold J. Laski*. New York: Columbia University Press.

Diamond, Larry, Marc F. Plattner, Yun-han Chu, and Hung-mao Tien. 1997. *Consolidating the Third Wave Democracies, Regional Challenges*. Baltimore, Md.: Johns Hopkins University Press.

Donnelly, Jack. 1985. "Human Rights and Development: Complementary or Competing Concerns?" in *Human Rights and Third World Development*, ed. Ved P. Nanda and George W. Shepherd. Westport, Conn.: Greenwood Press, 1985.

———. 1989. *Universal Human Rights in Theory and Practice*. Ithaca, N.Y.: Cornell University Press.

———. 1997. "Conversing with Straw Men While Ignoring Dictators: A Reply to Roger Ames." *Ethics & International Affairs* 11:207–13.

———. 1999. "Human Rights and Asian Values: A Defense of 'Western' Universalism." Pp. 60–87, in *The East Asian Challenge for Human Rights*, ed. Joanne R. Bauer and Daniel A. Bell. Cambridge, U.K.: Cambridge University Press.

Doolin, Dennis J. 1964. *Communist China: The Politics of Student Opposition*. Stanford, Calif.: Hoover Institution on War, Revolution, and Peace, Stanford University.

Dooling, Amy D., and Kristina M. Torgeson. 1998. *Writing Women in Modern China: An Anthology of Women's Literature from the Early Twentieth Century*. New York: Columbia University Press.

Du Gangjian, and Song Gang. 1995. "Relating Human Rights to Chinese Culture: The Four Paths of the Confucian Analects and the Four Principles of a New Theory of Benevolence." Pp. 35–56, in *Human Rights and Chinese Values: Legal, Philosophical, and Political Perspectives*, ed. Michael C. Davis. Hong Kong: Oxford University Press.

Duara, Prasenjit. 1995. *Rescuing History from the Nation: Questioning Narratives of Modern China*. Chicago: University of Chicago Press.

Dudden, Alexis. 1999. "Japan's Engagement with International Terms." Pp. 165–91, in *Tokens of Exchange: The Problem of Translation in Global Circulations*, ed. Lydia H. Liu. Durham, N.C.: Duke University Press.

Duiker, William J. 1977. *Ts'ai Yüan-p'ei: Educator of Modern China*. University Park, Penn.: Pennsylvania State University.

Dunne, Timothy, and Nicholas Wheeler, eds. 1999. *Human Rights in Global Politics*. Cambridge, U.K.: Cambridge University Press.

Dworkin, Ronald. 1977. *Taking Rights Seriously*. London: Duckworth.

Eastman, Lloyd E. 1974. *The Abortive Revolution: China under Nationalist Rule, 1927–1937*. Cambridge, Mass.: Harvard University Press.

———. 1986. "Nationalist China during the Sino–Japanese War 1937–1945." Pp. 547–608, in *The Cambridge History of China*. Vol. 13, *Republican China 1912–1949*, pt 2. Cambridge, U.K.: Cambridge University Press.

Eber, Irene. 1986. *Confucianism: The Dynamics of Tradition*. New York: Macmillan.

Edwards, Louise. 1994. "Chin Sun-ts'en's A Tocsin For Women: The Dextrous Merger of Radicalism and Conservatism in Feminism of the Early Twentieth Century." '*Jindai Zhongguo funü shi yanjiu* [Research into the History of Women in Modern China],' no. 2:117–40.

Edwards, R. Randle, Louis Henkin, and Andrew J. Nathan. 1986. *Human Rights in Contempoarary China*. New York: Columbia University Press.

Emmerson, Donald K. 1995. "Singapore and the 'Asian Values' Debate." *Journal of Democracy* 6 (October): 95–105.

Etzioni, Amitai. 1995. *Rights and the Common Good: The Communitarian Perspective*. New York: St. Martin's.

Fairbank, John K. and Ssu-yü Teng, 1954. *China's Response to the West: A Documentary Survey 1839–1923*. Cambridge, Mass.: Harvard University Press.

Fairbank, John K. 1982. *Chinabound: A Fifty-Year Memoir*. New York: Harper and Row.

Fang Lizhi. 1990. *Bringing Down the Wall: Writings on Science, Culture, and Democracy in China.* New York: Norton.

Feigon, Lee. 1983. *Chen Duxiu: Founder of the Chinese Communist Party.* Princeton, N.J.: Princeton University Press.

Feinberg, Joel. 1980. *Rights, Justice, and the Bounds of Liberty: Essays in Social Philosophy.* Princeton, N.J.: Princeton University Press.

Finnis, John. 1980. *Natural Law and Natural Rights.* Oxford, U.K.: Clarendon.

Fogel, Joshua A., and Peter G. Zarrow, eds. 1998. *Imagining the People: Chinese Intellectuals and the Concept of Citizenship, 1890–1920.* Armonk, N.Y: Sharpe.

Foreign Broadcasting Information Service (FBIS), China Daily Report. Washington D.C.

Foot, Rosemary. 2000. *Rights Beyond Borders: The Global Community and the Struggle over Human Rights in China.* Oxford, U.K.: Oxford University Press.

Freeden, Michael. 1991. *Rights.* Buckingham, U.K.: Open University Press.

Frey, R. G. 1984. *Utility and Rights.* Oxford, U.K.: Basil Blackwell.

Friedman, Edward, ed. 1994. *The Politics of Democratization: Generalizing East Asian Experiences.* Boulder, Colo.: Westview.

Fukuyama, Francis. 1992. *The End of History and the Last Man.* London: Penguin.

Fukuzawa Yukichi. 1969. *An Encouragement of Learning.* Tokyo: Sophia University.

Fung, Edmund S. K. 2000. *In Search of Chinese Democracy: Civil Opposition in Nationalist China, 1929–1949.* Cambridge: Cambridge University Press.

Furth, Charlotte. 1970. *Ting Wen-chiang: Science and China's New Culture.* Cambridge, Mass.: Harvard University Press.

Galston, William A. 1991. "Practical Philosophy and the Bill of Rights: Perspectives on Some Contemporary Issues." Pp. 215–65, in *A Culture of Rights: The Bill of Rights in Philosophy, Politics, and Law—1791 and 1991,* ed. Michael J. Lacey and Knud Haakonssen. Cambridge, U.K.: Cambridge University Press.

Galtung, Johan. 1994. *Human Rights in Another Key.* Cambridge, U.K.: Polity.

Gasster, Michael. 1969. *Chinese Intellectuals and the Revolution of 1911: The Birth of Modern Chinese Radicalism.* Seattle: University of Washington Press.

Gewirth, Alan. 1982. *Human Rights: Essays on Justification and Applications.* Chicago: University of Chicago Press.

Ghai, Yash. 1995. "Asian Perspectives on Human Rights." Pp. 54–67, in *Human Rights and International Relations in the Asia Pacific,* ed. James T. H. Tang. London: Pinter.

Gipoulon, Catherine, 1989–1990. "The Emergence of Women in Politics in China, 1898–1927." *Chinese Studies in History* 32, no. 2:46–67.

Glendon, Mary Ann. 1991. *Rights Talk: The Impoverishment of Political Discourse.* New York: Free Press.

———. 2001. *A World Made New: Eleanor Roosevelt and the Universal Declaration of Human Rights.* New York: Random House.

Goetsky, Rubin, and Ervin Laszlo, eds. 1970. *Human Dignity—This Century and the Next: An Interdisciplinary Inquiry into Human Rights.* New York: Gordon and Brech.

Goldman, René. 1962. "The Rectification Campaign at Peking University: May–June 1957." *China Quarterly* 12 (October–December): 138–53.

Goldman, Merle. 1994. *Sowing the Seeds of Democracy in China: Political Reform in the Deng Xiaoping Era.* Cambridge, Mass.: Harvard University Press.

Goodman, David S. G. 1981. *Beijing Street Voices: The Poetry and Politics of China's Democracy Movement.* London: Marion Boyars.

Greiff, Thomas E. 1985. "The Principle of Human Rights in Nationalist China: John C. H. Wu and the Ideological Origins of the 1946 Constitution." *China Quarterly*, no. 103:441–61.

Green, T. H. 1986. *T. H. Green Lectures on the Principles of Political Obligation and Other Writings*, ed. by Paul Harris and John Morrow. Cambridge, U.K.: Cambridge University Press.

Grieder, Jerome B. 1970. *Hu Shi and the Chinese Renaissance: Liberalism in the Chinese Revolution, 1917–1937*. Cambridge, Mass.: Harvard University Press.

———. 1981. *Intellectuals and the State in Modern China: A Narrative History*. New York: Free Press.

Griswold Jr., Charles L. 1991. "Rights and Wrongs: Jefferson, Slavery, and Philosophical Quandaries." Pp. 144–214, in *A Culture of Rights: The Bill of Rights in Philosophy, Politics, and Law—1791 and 1991*, ed. Michael J. Lacey and Knud Haakonssen. Cambridge, U.K.: Cambridge University Press.

Guo Jisi. 1991. "On Human Rights and Development Right." In *China: Issues and Ideas (3), China and Human Rights*. Compiled by *Beijing Review*.

Guo Shan. 1987. "China's Role in the Human Rights Field." *Beijing Review*, nos. 5 and 6.

Hamrin, Carol Lee, and Timothy Cheek, ed. 1986. *China's Establishment Intellectuals*. Armonk, N.Y.: Sharpe.

Han Minzhu. 1990. *Cries for Democracy: Writings and Speeches from the 1989 Chinese Democracy Movement*. Princeton, N.J.: Princeton University Press.

Harrell, Paula. 1992. *Sowing the Seeds of Change: Chinese Students, Japanese Teachers, 1895–1905*. Stanford, Calif.: Stanford University Press.

Harrison, Lawrence E., and Samuel P. Huntington. 2000. *Culture Matters: How Values Shape Human Progress*. New York: Basic.

Hart, H. L. A. 1979. "Between Utility and Rights." In *The Idea of Freedom*, ed. Alan Ryan. Oxford, U.K.: Oxford University Press.

Haskell, Thomas L. 1987. "The Curious Resistance of Rights Talk in the 'Age of Interpretation.'" *Journal of American History* 74, no. 3 (December): 984–1012.

Hawang, Shiow Duan. 2001. "A Center for the Study of Human Rights at Soochow University." Paper presented at the International Conference on National Human Rights Commissions, Promoting and Protecting Human Rights, Taipei, 2–4 January. Organized by the Department of Political Science, Soochow University.

He Zhaowu. 1990. "The Concept of Natural Rights and the Cultural Tradition." *Chinese Studies in Philosophy* 21, no. 4 (Summer): 3–33

Henkin, Louis. 1978. *The Rights of Man Today*. Boulder, Colo.: Westview Press.

———. 1986, "The Human Rights Idea in Contemporary China: A Comparative Perspective." Pp. 7–39, in *Human Rights in Contempoarary China*, ed. R. Randle Edwards, Louis Henkin, and Andrew J. Nathan. New York: Columbia University Press.

Hesse, Carla, and Robert Post, eds. 1999. *Human Rights in Political Transitions: Gettysburg to Bosnia*. New York: Zone Books.

Hill, Thomas E. 1973. "Servility and Self-Respect." *The Monist* 57: 87–104.

Horne, Thomas A. 1988. "Welfare Rights as Property Rights." Pp. 107–31, in *Responsibility, Rights, and Welfare: The Theory of the Welfare State*, ed. J. Donald Moon. Boulder, Colo.: Westview.

Howard, Rhoda E. 1995a. "Dignity, Community, and Human Rights" Pp. 81–102, in *Human Rights in Cross-Cultural Perspectives: A Quest for Consensus*, ed. Abdullahi Ahmed An-Na'im. Philadelphia: University of Pennsylvania Press.

———. 1995b. *Human Right and the Search for Community*. Boulder, Colo.: Westview.

HRIC (Human Rights in China). 1998. *From Principle to Pragmatism: Can "Dialogue" Improve China's Human Rights Situation?* New York: HRIC.

Hsiung, James C., ed. 1986. *Human Rights in East Asia: A Cultural Perspective.* New York: Paragon.

Huang, Mab. 1979. "Human Rights in a Revolutionary Society: The Case of the People's Republic of China." In *Human Rights: Cultural and Ideological Perspectives*, ed. Admantia Pollis and Peter Schwab. New York: Praeger.

———. 2001. "Drafting a Bill for a National Human Rights Commission: Taiwan, 2000." Paper presented at the International Conference on National Human Rights Commissions, Promoting and Protecting Human Rights, Taipei, 2–4 January. Organized by the Department of Political Science, Soochow University.

Huang, Mab, and Seymour, James D. 1980. Introduction. Pp. 1–26, in *The Fifth Modernization: China's Human Rights Movement, 1978–1979*, ed. James D. Seymour. Stanfordsville, N.Y.: Human Rights Publishing Group.

Huang, Peter. 2001. "The Paradox of Taiwan's Human Rights Conditions." Paper presented at the International Conference on National Human Rights Commissions, Promoting and Protecting Human Rights, Taipei, 2–4 January, organized by the Department of Political Science, Soochow University.

Huang, Philip C. C. 1998. "Theory and the Study of Modern Chinese History: Four Traps and a Question." *Modern China* 24, no. 2 (April): 183–208.

Hudson, Yeager, and Creighton Peden, eds. 1993. *The Bill of Rights: Bicentennial Reflections.* Lewiston, N.Y.: Edwin Mellen Press.

Hufton, Olwen. ed. 1995. *Historical Change and Human Rights: The Oxford Amnesty Lectures 1994.* New York: Basic.

Human Rights Watch. 1993. *Indivisible Human Rights: The Relationship of Political and Civil Rights to Survival, Subsistence, and Poverty.* New York: Human Rights Watch.

Humphrey, John P. 1984. *Human Rights and the United Nations: A Great Adventure.* Dobbs Ferry, N.Y.: Transnational Publishing.

Hunt, Lynn. 1996. *The French Revolution and Human Rights: A Brief Documentary History.* Boston: Bedford/St. Martin's.

———. 2000. "The Paradoxical Origin of Human Rights" Pp. 3–17, in *Human Rights and Revolutions*, ed. Jeffrey N. Wasserstrom, Lynn Hunt, and Marilyn B. Young. Lanham, Md.: Rowman & Littlefield.

Huntington, Samuel P. 1993. "The Clash of Civilizations." *Foreign Affairs* 72, no. 3 (Summer): 22–49.

Huston, James H. "The Bill of Rights and the American Revolutionary Experience." Pp. 62–97, in *A Culture of Rights: The Bill of Rights in Philosophy, Politics, and Law—1791 and 1991*, ed. Michael J. Lacey and Knud Haakonssen. Cambridge, U.K.: Cambridge University Press.

Hwang, Phyllis. "History Is Not the Rights Judge," *Taipei Times*, October 7, 1999, <www.taipeitimes.com> [accessed March 1, 2001].

Ip, Hung-Yok. 1994. "The Origins of Chinese Communism." *Modern China* 20, no. 1 (January).

Jeans, Roger B. ed. 1992. *Roads Not Taken: The Struggle of Opposition Parties in Twentieth-Century China.* Boulder, Colo.: Westview.

———. 1997. *Democracy and Socialism in Republican China: The Politics of Zhang Junmai (Carsun Chang), 1906–1941.* Lanham, Md.: Rowman & Littlefield.

Jellinek, Georg. 1895. *Die Erklärung der Menschen-und Bürgerrechte.* Leipzig: Duncker & Humblot.

Jenner, W. J. F. 1998. "China and Freedom." Pp. 65–92, in *Asian Freedoms: The Idea of Freedom in East and Southeast Asia*, ed. David Kelly and Anthony Reid. Cambridge, U.K.: Cambridge University Press.

Judge, Joan. 1996. *Print and Politics: 'Shibao' and the Culture of Reform in Late Qing China*. Stanford, Calif.: Stanford University Press.

Kagan, Richard Clark. 1969. *The Chinese Trotskyist Movement and Ch'en Tu-Hsiu: Culture, Revolution and Polity. With an appended translation of Ch'en Tu-Hsiu's Autobiography*. Ph.D. diss., University of Pennsylvania.

Kausikan, Bilahari. 1993. "Asia's Different Standard." *Foreign Policy*, no. 92 (Fall): 24–41.

Keenan, Barry. 1977. *The Dewey Experiment in China: Educational Reform and Political Power in the Early Republic*. Cambridge, Mass.: Harvard University Press.

Keith, Ronald. 1993. "The New Relevance of Rights and Interests: China's Changing Human Rights Theories." *China Information* 10, no. 2 (Autumn): 38–61.

Kelly, David, "The Chinese Search for Freedom as a Universal Value." Pp. 93–119, in *Asian Freedoms: The Idea of Freedom in East and Southeast Asia*, ed. David Kelly and Anthony Reid. Cambridge, U.K.: Cambridge University Press.

Kelly, David, and Anthony Reid. 1998. *Asian Freedoms: The Idea of Freedom in East and Southeast Asia*. Cambridge, U.K.: Cambridge University Press.

Kent, Ann. 1993. *Between Freedom and Subsistence: China and Human Rights*. Hong Kong: Oxford University Press.

———. *China, the United Nations, and Human Rights—The Limits of Compliance*. Philadelphia, University of Pennsylvania Press.

Kim Dae Jung. 1994. "Is Culture Destiny? The Myth of Asia's Anti-Democratic Values." *Foreign Affairs* 73, no. 6 (November/December): 189–94.

Kolakowski, Leszek. 1983. "Marxism and Human Rights." *Daedalus* 112, no. 4 (Fall).

Kuo, Thomas C. 1975. *Ch'en Tu-Hsiu (1879–1942) and the Chinese Communist Movement*. South Orange, N.J.: Seton Hall University Press.

Kuper, Adam. 1999. *Culture: The Anthropologist's Account*. Cambridge, Mass.: Harvard University.

Kwok, D. W. Y. 1998. "On the Rites and Rights of Being Human." Pp. 82–93, in *Confucianism and Human Rights*, ed. Wm. Theodore de Bary and Tu Weiming. New York: Columbia University Press.

Lacey, Michael J., and Knud Haakonssen. 1991. *A Culture of Rights: The Bill of Rights in Philosophy, Politics, and Law—1791 and 1991*. Cambridge: Cambridge University Press.

Lan, Hua R., and Vanessa L. Fong, eds. 1999. *Women in Republican China: A Sourcebook*. Armonk, N.Y.: Sharpe.

Laski, Harold. 1948. *A Grammar of Politics*. London: Allen & Unwin.

———. 1949. "Towards a Universal Declaration of Human Rights," Pp. 78–92, in *Human Rights, Comments and Interpretations*. A Symposium edited by UNESCO with an introduction by Jacques Maritain, New York: Wingate.

Lauren, Paul Gordon. 1998. *The Evolution of International Human Rights: Visions Seen*. Philadelphia: University of Pennsylvania Press.

Leary, Virginia A. 1995. "Postliberal Strands in Western Human Rights Theory: Personalist-Communitarian Perspectives." Pp. 105–32, in *Human Rights in Cross-Cultural Perspectives: A Quest for Consensus*, ed. Abdullahi Ahmed An-Na'im. Philadelphia: University of Pennsylvania Press.

Lee, Eliza. 1995. "Human Rights and Non-Western Values." Pp. 72–90, in *Human Rights and Chinese Values: Legal, Philosophical, and Political Perspectives*, ed. Michael C. Davis. Hong

Kong: Oxford University Press.

Leung, Trini W.Y. 1998. "Labour Unrest in China in the 1990s. Labour Fights for Its Rights." *China Perspectives*, no. 19 (September/October).

Lewis, Bernard. 1975. *History—Remembered, Recovered, Invented*. Princeton, N.J.: Princeton University Press.

Leys, Simon. 1986. *The Burning Forest*. New York: Holt.

Lin Yü-sheng. 1972. "Radical Iconoclasm in the May Fourth Period and the Future of Chinese Liberalism." In *Reflections on the May Fourth Movement: A Symposium*, ed. Benjamin I. Schwartz. Cambridge, Mass.: Harvard University Press.

———. 1979. *The Crisis of Chinese Consciousness: Radical Antitraditionalism in the May Fourth Era*. Madison: University of Wisconsin.

Lin Yutang. 1932. "For a Civic Liberty Union." *China Critic* 5, no. 44 (3 November).

———. 1933. "On Freedom of Speech." *China Critic* 6, no. 10 (9 March).

———. 1936. *A History of the Press and Public Opinion in China*. London: Oxford University Press.

Lindholm, Tore. 1995. "Prospects for Research on the Cultural Legitimacy of Human Rights: The Cases of Liberalism and Marxism." Pp. 387–426, in *Human Rights in Cross-Cultural Perspectives: A Quest for Consensus*, ed. Abdullahi Ahmed An-Na'im. Philadelphia: University of Pennsylvania Press.

Liu, Lydia H. 1996. *Translingual Practice: Literature, National Culture, and Translated Modernity—China, 1900–1937*. Stanford, Calif.: Stanford University Press.

———. 1999. "Legislating the Universal: The Circulation of International Law in the Nineteenth Century." Pp. 127–164, in *Tokens of Exchange: The Problem of Translation in Global Circulations*, ed. Lydia H. Liu. Durham, N.C.: Duke University Press.

Liu Shao-hua, "Rights Drive to Take Center Stage," *Taipei Times*, December 7, 2000, <www.taipeitimes.com> [acccessed December 27, 2000].

Liu Xiaobo. 1995. "Chinese Patriotism Driven by Inferiority Complex." Orignally published in the magazine *Kaifang*. Translated and reprinted in Foreign Broadcasting Information Service, Daily Report China FBIS-CHI-95-041 (March 2), Washington, D.C.

Lo, Chung-Shu. 1949. "Human Rights in the Chinese Tradition." Pp. 186–90, in *Human Rights, Comments and Interpretations:* A symposium edited by UNESCO with an introduction by Jacques Maritain, New York: Wingate.

Lubot, Eugene. 1982. *Liberalism in an Illiberal Age: New Culture Liberals in Republican China, 1919–1937*. Westport, Conn.: Greenwood.

Luo Yanhua. 1997. "Human Rights Research from an East and Southeast Asian Perspective." Pp. 311–38 in *Human Rights: Chinese and Canadian Perspectives*, ed. E. P. Mendes and A-M Traeholt. Ottawa: Human Rights Research and Education Center, University of Ottawa, 1997.

Lust, John. 1968. *Tsou Jung: The Revolutionary Army. A Chinese Nationalistic Tract of 1903*. Paris: Mouton and Co.

McCloskey, H. J. 1984. "Respect for Human Moral Rights versus Maximizing Good." In *Utility and Rights*, ed. R. G. Frey. Oxford, U.K.: Basil Blackwell.

McDonald, Michael. 1995. "Should Communities Have Rights? Reflections on Liberal Individualism." Pp. 133–61, in *Human Rights in Cross-Cultural Perspectives: A Quest for Consensus*, ed. Abdullahi Ahmed An-Na'im. Philadelphia: University of Pennsylvania Press.

MacFarquhar, Roderick. ed. 1960. *The Hundred Flowers Movement*. London: Stevens and Sons.

———. 1974. *The Origins of the Cultural Revolution 1: Contradictions among the People, 1956–1957.* London: Oxford University Press.

MacIntyre, Alasdair. 1981. *After Virtue.* Notre Dame: University of Notre Dame Press.

Mackie, J. L. 1984. "Rights, Utility, and Universalization." In *Utility and Rights,* ed. R. G. Frey. Oxford, U.K.: Basil Blackwell.

Mahbuubani, Kishore. 1995. "The Pacific Way." *Foreign Affairs* 74, no. 1 (January/February): 100–111.

Maritain, Jacques. 1947. *The Rights of Man and Natural Law.* New York: Scribner.

———. 1952. *Man and the State.* Chicago: Chicago University Press.

Martin, Helmut. ed. *Mao Zedong Texte: Sechster Band, 1965–1976. Teil 2.* Carl Hanser Verlag.

Martin, Kingsley. 1953. *Harold Laski (1893–1950): A Biographical Memoir.* London.

Martin, Rex, and James W. Nickel. 1980. "Recent Works on the Concept of Rights." *American Philosophical Quarterly* 17, no. 3 (July): 165–80.

Martin, Rex. 1986. "Green on Natural Rights in Hobbes, Spinoza and Locke." Pp. 104–26, in *The Philosophy of T. H. Green,* ed. Andrew Vincent. Aldershot, U.K.: Gower.

Masini, Federico. 1993. "The Formation of Modern Chinese Lexicon and Its Evolution toward a National Language: The Period from 1840 to 1898." *Journal of Chinese Linguistics.* Monograph Series no. 6.

Mast III, Herman, and William G. Saywell. 1974. "Revolution Out of Tradition: The Political Ideology of Tai Chi-t'ao." *Journal of Asian Studies* 34, no. 1 (November): 73–98.

Meienberger, Norbert. 1980. *The Emergence of Constitutional Government in China (1905–1908).* Bern: Peter Lang.

Meisner, Maurice. 1967. *Li Ta-Chao and the Origins of Chinese Marxism.* Cambridge, Mass.: Harvard University Press.

Mellbourn, Anders, and Marina Svensson. 1999. *Swedish Human Rights Training in China: An Assessment.* Stockholm: Sida.

Mendes, E. P., and A-M Traeholt, eds. 1997. *Human Rights: Chinese and Canadian Perspectives.* Ottawa: Human Rights Research and Education Center, University of Ottawa.

Mendus, Susan. 1995. "Human Rights in Political Theory." *Political Studies* 43:10–24.

Menger, Anton. 1899. *The Right to the Whole Produce of Labour: The Origin and Development of the Theory of Labour's Claim to the Whole Product of Industry.* London: Macmillan.

Milne, A. J. M. 1986a. " The Common Good and the Rights in T. H. Green's Ethical and Political Theory." Pp. 62–75, in *The Philosophy of T. H. Green,* ed. Andrew Vincent. Aldershot, U.K.: Gower.

———. 1986b. *Human Rights and Human Diversity: An Essay in the Philosophy of Human Rights.* London: Macmillan.

Mill, John Stuart. 1985. *On Liberty.* London: Penguin.

Morsink, Johannes. 1999. *The Universal Declaration of Human Rights: Origins, Drafting, and Intent* Philadelphia: University of Pennsylvania Press.

Müller, Sven-Uwe. 1997. *Konzeptionen der Menschenrechte im China des 20. Jahrhunderts.* Hamburg: Mittelungen no. 274, Istitut der Asienkunde.

Müllerson, Rein. 1997. *Human Rights Diplomacy.* London: Routledge.

Narramore, Terry. 1985. "Luo Longji and Chinese Liberalism 1928–32." *Papers on Far Eastern History,* no. 32:165–95.

Nathan, Andrew J. 1986a. *Chinese Democracy: The Individual and the State in Twentieth Century China.* Berkeley: University of California Press.

———. 1986b. "Political Rights in Chinese Constitutions." Pp. 77–124, in *Human Rights in Contempoarary China*, ed. R. Randle Edwards, Louis Henkin, and Andrew J. Nathan. New York: Columbia University Press.

———. 1986c. "Sources of Chinese Rights Thinking." Pp. 125–64, in *Human Rights in Contemporary China*, ed. R. Randle Edwards, Louis Henkin, and Andrew J. Nathan. New York: Columbia University Press.

———. 1994. "Human Rights in Chinese Foreign Policy." *China Quarterly*, no. 139 (September): 622–43.

Neier, Aryeh. 1993. "Asia's Unacceptable Standard." *Foreign Policy*, no. 92 (Fall): 42–51.

Ng, Margaret. 1995. "Are Rights Culture-Bound?" Pp. 57–71, in *Human Rights and Chinese Values: Legal, Philosophical, and Political Perspectives*, ed. Michael C. Davis. Hong Kong: Oxford University Press.

Nicholson, Peter P. 1990. *The Political Philosophy of the British Idealists: Selected Studies*. Cambridge: Cambridge University Press.

Nickel, James W. 1987. *Making Sense of Human Rights: Philosophical Reflections on the Universal Declaration of Human Rights*. Berkeley, Calif.: University of California Press.

Nieh, Hualing. 1981. *Literature of the Hundred Flowers*. New York: Columbia University Press.

Nordahl, Richard. 1995. "A Marxian Approach to Human Rights." Pp. 162–87, in *Human Rights in Cross-Cultural Perspectives: A Quest for Consensus*, ed. Abdullahi Ahmed An-Na'im. Philadelphia: University of Pennsylvania Press.

O'Brien, Kevin J. 1996. "Rightful Resistance." *World Politics* 49, no. 1:31–55.

Obe, Apoola Modupe Ogunsola. 2001. "Working with and Monitoring the National Human Rights Commission: The Experience of Nigeria." Paper presented at the International Conference on National Human Rights Commissions, Promoting and Protecting Human Rights, Taipei, 2–4 January. Organized by the Department of Political Science, Soochow University.

Official Records of the Third Session of the General Assembly, Part 1, Social, Humanitarian, and Cultural Questions, Third Committee, Summary Records of Meetings 21 September–8 December, 1948. Lake Success, N.Y.: United Nations.

Ogden, Suzanne P. 1982. "The Sage in the Inkpot: Bertrand Russell and China's Social Reconstruction in the 1920s." *Modern Asian Studies* 16, no. 4: 529–600.

———. 1992. *China's Search for Democracy: The Student and the Mass Movement of 1989*. Armonk, N.Y.: Sharpe.

Okin, Susan Moller. 1981. "Liberty and Welfare: Some Issues in Human Rights Theory." Pp. 230–56, in *Human Rights. Nomos XXIII*, ed. J. Roland Pennock and John W. Chapman. New York: New York University Press.

"On Human Rights." 1979. Originally published in the Chinese magazine *Xuanchuan*, translated and reprinted in *Chinese Studies in Philosophy* 28, no. 1 (Fall): 74–76.

Ono Kazuko. 1989. *Chinese Women in a Century of Revolution, 1850–1950*. Stanford, Calif.: Stanford University Press.

Otter, Sandra M. Den. 1996. *British Idealism and Social Explanation: A Study in Late Victorian Thought*. Oxford, U.K.: Clarendon.

Our Voice: Bangkok NGO Declaration on Human Rights. 1993. Reports of the Asia Pacific NGO Conference on Human Rights and NGOs' Statements to the Asia Regional Meeting, published by Asian Cultural Forum on Development, Bangkok.

Paltiel, Jeremy T. 1997. "Cultural and Political Determinants of the Chinese Approach to Human Rights." Pp. 25–73, in *Human Rights: Chinese and Canadian Perspectives*, ed. E. P.

Mendes and A-M Traeholt. Ottawa: The Human Rights Research and Education Center, University of Ottawa.

——. 1998. "Confucianism Contested: Human Rights and the Chinese Tradition in Contemporary Chinese Political Discourse." Pp. 270–96, in *Confucianism and Human Rights*, ed. Wm. Theodore de Bary and Tu Weiming. New York: Columbia University Press.

Paine, Thomas. 1985. *Rights of Man*. New York: Penguin.

Patterson, Orlando. 1995. "Freedom, Slavery, and the Modern Construction of Rights." Pp. 131–78, in *Historical Change and Human Rights: The Oxford Amnesty Lectures 1994*, ed. Olwen Hufton. New York: Basic.

Peerenboom, R. P. 1993. "What's Wrong with Chinese Rights?: Toward a Theory of Rights with Chinese Characteristics." *Harvard Human Rights Journal* 6: 29–57.

——. 1995. "Rights, Interests, and the Interest in Rights in China." *Stanford Journal of International Law* (Summer): 359–86.

——. 1998. "Confucian Harmony and Freedom of Thought: The Right to Think Versus Right Thinking." Pp. 234–60, in *Confucianism and Human Rights*, ed. Wm. Theodore de Bary and Tu Weiming. New York: Columbia University Press.

Pepper, Suzanne. 1980. *Civil War in China: The Political Struggle 1945–1949*. Berkeley: University of California Press.

Perry, Elizabeth J., and Mark Selden, eds. 2000. *Chinese Society: Change, Conflict, and Resistance* London: Routledge.

Pittau, Joseph. 1967. *Political Thought in Early Meiji Japan 1868–1889*. Cambridge, Mass.: Harvard University Press.

Pollis, Admantia. 1992. "Human Rights in Liberal, Socialist, and Third World Perspective." Pp. 146–56, in *Human Rights in the World Community: Issues and Action*, ed. Richard Pierre Claude and Burns H. Weston. Philadelphia: University of Pennsylvania Press.

——. 1996. "Cultural Relativism Revisited: Through a State Prism." *Human Rights Quarterly* 18, no. 2:316–44.

——. 2000. "A New Universalism." Pp. 9–30, in *Human Rights: New Perspectives, New Realities*, ed. Admantia Pollis and Peter Schwab. Boulder, Colo.: Rienner.

Pollis, Admantia, and Schwab, Peter, eds. 1979. *Human Rights: Cultural and Ideological Perspectives*. New York: Praeger.

——. 2000. *Human Rights: New Perspectives, New Realities*. Boulder, Colo.: Rienner.

Preis, Ann-Belinda S. 1996. "Human Rights as Cultural Practice: An Anthropological Critique." *Human Rights Quarterly* 18, no. 2 (May): 286–315.

Price, Don. 1990. "Constitutional Alternatives and Democracy in the Revolution of 1911." In *Ideas Across Cultures: Essays on Chinese Thought in Honor of Benjamin I. Schwartz*, ed. Paul Cohen and Merle Goldman. Cambridge, Mass: Harvard University Press.

Pusey, James Reeve. 1983. *China and Charles Darwin*. Cambridge, Mass.: Harvard University Press, 1983.

Pye, Lucian. 1988. *The Mandarin and the Cadre: China's Political Cultures*. Ann Arbor: University of Michigan, Center for Chinese Studies.

Quigley, John. 1989. "Human Rights Study in Soviet Academia." *Human Rights Quarterly* 11, no. 3:452–58.

Rakove, Jack N. 1991. "Parchment Barriers and the Politics of Rights." Pp. 98–143, in *A Culture of Rights: The Bill of Rights in Philosophy, Politics, and Law—1791 and 1991*, ed. Michael J. Lacey and Knud Haakonssen. Cambridge, U.K.: Cambridge University Press.

——. 1971. *Declaring Rights: A Brief History with Documents*. Boston: Bedford Books.

Rankin, Mary Backus. 1971. *Early Chinese Revolutionaries: Radical Intellectuals in Shanghai and Chekiang, 1902–1911.* Cambridge, Mass.: Harvard University Press.

———. 1975. "The Emergence of Women at the End of the Ch'ing: The Case of Ch'iu Chin." Pp. 39–66, in *Women in Chinese Society,* ed. Margery Wolf and Roxane Witke. Stanford, Calif.: Stanford University Press.

Raz, Joseph. 1986. *The Morality of Freedom.* Oxford, U.K.: Clarendon Press

Renteln, Alison Dundes. 1990. *International Human Rights: Universalism versus Relativism.* Newbury Park, Calif.: Sage.

Report of the Second Australian Human Rights Delegation to China, 8–20 November 1992. 1993. Canberra: Australian Government Publishing Service.

Reynolds, Douglas R. 1993. *China, 1898–1912: The Xinzheng Revolution and Japan.* Cambridge, Mass.: Harvard University Press.

Richardson, Michael. 1997. "Asian Nations Rally against U.S. over Rights." *International Herald Tribune,* 30 July.

Richter, Melvin. 1964. *The Politics of Conscience: T. H. Green and His Age.* London: Weidenfeld and Nicolson.

———. 1995. *The History of Political and Social Concepts: A Critical Introduction.* New York: Oxford University Press.

Robison, Richard, ed. 1996. *Pathways to Asia: The Politics of Engagement.* St Leonards, Australia: Allen & Unwin.

Rodan, Garry, and Kevin Hewson. 1996. "A "Clash of Cultures," or the Convergence of Political Ideology?" Pp. 29–56, in *Pathways to Asia: The Politics of Engagement,* ed. Richard Robison. St Leonards, Australia: Allen & Unwin, 1996.

Rorty, Richard. 1993. "Human Rights, Rationality, and Sentimentality." Pp. 111–34, in *On Human Rights: The Oxford Amnesty Lectures 1993,* ed. Stephen Shute and Susan Hurley. New York: Basic.

Rosemont Jr. Henry. 1988. "Why Take Rights Seriously? A Confucian Critique." Pp. 167–82, in *Human Rights and the World's Religions,* ed. Leroy S. Rouner. Notre Dame: University of Notre Dame Press.

———. 1998. "Human Rights: A Bill of Worries." Pp. 54–66, in *Confucianism and Human Rights,* ed. Wm. Theodore de Bary and Tu Weiming. New York: Columbia University Press.

Rosenbaum, Alan S., ed. 1980. *The Philosophy of Human Rights: International Perspectives.* Westport, Conn.

Rouner, Leroy S., ed. 1988. *Human Rights and the World's Religions.* Notre Dame, Ind.: University of Notre Dame Press.

Roy, Denny. 1994. "Singapore, China and the 'Soft Authoritarian' Challenge." *Asian Survey* 34, no. 3 (March): 231–42..

Rubenstein, Joshua. 1980. *Soviet Dissidents: Their Struggle for Human Rights.* Boston: Beacon.

Russell, Bertrand. 1922. *The Problem of China.* London: Allen & Unwin.

Ryan, Alan. 1995. *John Dewey and the High Tide of American Liberalism.* New York: Norton.

Saich, Tony. ed. 1996. *The Rise to Power of the Chinese Communist Party.* Armonk, N.Y.: Sharpe.

Sandel, Michael. 1984. *Liberalism and its Critics.* New York: New York University Press.

Schachter, Oscar. 1983. "Human Dignity as a Normative Concept." *The American Journal of International Law* 77. Reprinted in Philip Alson ed. *Human Rights Law.* Aldershot, U.K: Dartmouth Publishing Co. 1995, pp. 848–54.

Schmale,Wolfgang, ed. 1993. *Human Rights and Cultural Diversity*. Goldbach, Germany: Keip.
Schoenhals, Michael. 1986. "Original Contradictions—On the Unrevised Text of Mao Ze-dong's 'On the Correct Handling of Contradictions Among the People." *Australian Journal of Chinese Affairs*, no. 16 (July): 99–112.
———. 1994. "'Non-People' in the People's Republic of China: A Chronicle of Terminological Ambiguity." *Indiana East Asian Working Paper Series on Language and Politics in Modern China*. Paper no. 4 (July). Bloomington: East Asian Studies Center, Indiana University.
Schram, Stuart. 1986. "Mao Tse-tung's Thought to 1949." Pp. 789–870, in *The Cambridge History of China*. Vol. 13, *Republican China 1912–1949*, pt 2. Cambridge, U.K.: Cambridge University Press.
Schwarcz,Vera. 1986. *The Chinese Enlightenment: Intellectuals and the Legacy of the May Fourth Movement of 1919*. Berkeley, Calif.: University of California Press.
Schwartz, Benjamin. 1951. "Ch'en Tu-Hsiu and the Acceptance of the Modern West." *Journal of the History of Ideas* 12, no. 1 (January).
———. 1964. *In Search of Wealth and Power:Yen Fu and the West*. Cambridge, Mass.: Harvard University Press.
Sen, Amaratya. 1999. *Development as Freedom*. Oxford, U.K.: Oxford University Press.
Seymour, James D. ed. 1980. *The Fifth Modernization: China's Human Rights Movement, 1978–1979*. Stanfordsville, N.Y.: Human Rights Publishing Group.
———. 1987. *China's Satellite Parties*. Armonk, N.Y.: Sharpe.
Shain, Barry Alan. 1994. *The Myth of American Individualism:The Protestant Origin of American Political Thought*. Princeton, N.J.: Princeton University Press
Shapiro, Ian. 1986. *The Evolution of Rights in Liberal Theory*. New York: Cambridge University Press.
Shen Baoxiang et al. 1982. "The Question of Human Rights in the International Realm." *Beijing Review*, no. 30 (26 July): 13–17, 22.
Shih, Chih-yu.1993. "Contending Theories of 'Human Rights with Chinese Characteristics.'" *Issues and Studies* 29, no. 11 (November): 42–64.
Shklar, Judith N. 1980. *Political Thought and Political Thinkers*. Chicago: Chicago University Press.
Shue, Henry. 1980. *Basic Rights*. Princeton, N.J.: Princeton University Press
Shute, Stephen, and Susan Hurley, eds. 1993. *On Human Rights:The Oxford Amnesty Lectures 1993*. New York: Basic.
Shweder, Richard A. 2000. "Moral Maps, 'First World' Conceits, and the New Evangelists." Pp. 158–72, in *Culture Matters: How Values Shape Human Progress*, ed. Lawrence E. Harrison and Samuel P. Huntington. New York: Basic.
Song Qingling. 1932. "Madame Sun's Statement on Civic Liberty." *China Critic* 5, no. 44 (3 November).
Spar, Fredric J. 1992. "Human Rights and Political Engagement: Luo Longji in the 1930s." Pp. 61–81, in *Roads Not Taken:The Struggle of Opposition Parties in Twentieth-Century China*, ed. Roger B. Jeans. Boulder, Colo.: Westview.
Spiegelberg, Herbert.1970. "Human Dignity: A challenge." Pp. 39–64, in *Human Dignity—This Century and the Next:An Interdisciplinary Inquiry into Human Rights*, ed. Rubin Goetsky and Ervin Laszlo. New York: Gordon and Brech.
Stammers, Neil. 1995. "A Critique of Social Approaches to Human Rights." *Human Rights Quarterly* 17, no. 3:488–508.
State Council of the People's Republic of China. 1991. *Human Rights in China*. Beijing: State Council of the People's Republic of China.

Stetson, Brad. 1998. *Human Dignity and Contemporary Liberalism.* Westport, Conn: Praeger.

Strauss, Leo. 1953. *Natural Right and History.* Chicago: University of Chicago Press.

Strzelewicz, Willy. 1983. *De mänskliga rättigheternas historia.* Stockholm: Ordfronts förlag.

Sullivan, Michael J. 1999. "Developmentalism and China's Human Rights Policy." Pp. 120–43, in *Debating Human Rights: Critical Essays from the United States and Asia*, ed. Peter van Ness. London: Routledge.

Sun Yat-sen. 1960. *San Min Chu I: The Three Principles of the People.* Translated by Frank W. Price. Taipei.

Suzuki Shuji. 1996. "Terminology Surrounding the 'Tripartite Separation of Powers.'" Paper presented at the East-West Center Conference on Confucianism and Human Rights, Honolulu, Hawaii. Translated by Joshua A. Fogel.

Svarerud, Rune. 2000. 'Jus gentium sinese. The Earliest Chinese Translation of International Law with Some Considerations Regarding the Compilation of *Haiguo tuzhi*.' *Acta Orientalia* 61: 203–37.

Sweet, William. 1993. "Individual Rights, Communitarianism, and British Idealism." Pp. 261–77, in *The Bill of Rights: Bicentennial Reflections*, ed. Yeager Hudson and Creighton Peden. Lewiston, N.Y.: Edwin Mellen Press.

Taipei Times (newspaper). 1999–2001. <taipeitimes.com>.

Tan, Chester C. 1971. *Chinese Political Thought in the Twentieth Century.* New York: Doubleday.

Tan, Kevin Y. L. 1996. "What Asians Think about the West's Response to the Human Rights Debate." *Human Rights Dialogue* 4 (March): 3–4.

Tang, James T. H. 1995. *Human Rights and International Relations in the Asia Pacific.* London: Pinter.

Tao, Pao Chia-lin. 1994. "The Anti-footbinding Movement in Late Ch'ing China: Indigenous Development and Western Influence." *Jindai Zhongguo funü shi yanjiu* (Research into the History of Women in Modern China), no. 2:141–78.

Teiwes, Frederick C. 1993. *Politics and Purges in China.* Armonk, N.Y.: Sharpe.

Tesón, Fernando R. 1985. "International Human Rights and Cultural Relativism." Pp. 42–51, in *Human Rights in the World Community: Issues and Action*, ed. Richard Pierre Claude and Burns H. Weston. Philadelphia: University of Pennsylvania Press, 1992. First published in *Virginia Journal of International Law* 25, no. 4.

Tien, Hung-mao. 2001. "Human Rights: The Future of Taiwan's Diplomacy." Speech given at the International Conference on National Human Rights Commissions in Taipei on January 2–4, sponsored by Soochow University. <www.mofa.gov.tw/emofa/20010102.htm> [accessed January 15, 2001].

Ting, Lee-hsia Hsu. 1974. *Government Control of the Press in Modern China 1900–1949.* Cambridge, Mass.: Harvard University Press.

Toscano, Roberto. 1989. *Soviet Human Rights Policy and Perestroika.* Lanham, Md.: University Press of America.

Tu Wei-ming, ed. 1994. *China in Transformation.* Cambridge, Mass.: Harvard University Press.

Tuck, Richard. 1979. *Natural Rights Theories: Their Origin and Development.* Cambridge, U.K.: Cambridge University Press.

Tucker, John Allen. 1996. "Confucianism and Human Rights in Meiji Japan." Paper presented at the East-West Center Conference on Confucianism and Human Rights, Honolulu, Hawaii.

Twiss, Sumner B. 1998a. "A Constructive Framework for Discussing Confucianism and Human Rights." Pp. 27–53, in *Confucianism and Human Rights*, ed. Wm. Theodore de Bary and Tu Weiming. New York: Columbia University Press.

———. 1998b. "Confucian Contributions to the Universal Declaration of Human Rights: A Historical and Philosophical Persepective." Paper presented at an academic seminar, Perceptions of Being Human in Confucian Thought, Beijing, June.

UN E/CN.4/77/Annex A. Commission on Human Rights. Second Session. Draft International Declaration on Human Rights. December 16, 1947.

UN E/CN.4/AC.1/18. Draft International Declaration on Human Rights, submitted by the Delegation of China to the second session of the Drafting Committee of the Commission on Human Rights, May 3, 1948.

UN E/CN.4/102. Commission on Human Rights. China: Amendments to the Draft International Declaration on Human Rights, May 27, 1948.

UNESCO. ed. 1949. *Human Rights, Comments, and Interpretations.* A Symposium edited by UNESCO with an introduction by Jacques Maritain. New York: Wingate.

Van Ness, Peter. 1999. *Debating Human Rights: Critical Essays from the United States and Asia.* London: Routledge.

Vasak, Karel. 1977. "A 30-Year Struggle." *The UNESCO Courier*, November. Paris: UNESCO.

Vincent, Andrew, ed. 1986. *The Philosophy of T. H. Green.* Aldershot, U.K.: Gower.

von Senger, Harro. 1993. "Chinese Culture and Human Rights." Pp. 281–333, in *Human Rights and Cultural Diversity*, ed. Wolfgang Schmale. Goldbach, Germany: Keip.

Wacks, Raymond. ed. 1993. *Hong Kong, China, and 1997: Essays in Legal Theory.* Hong Kong: Hong Kong University Press.

Wakabayashi, Bob Tadashi. 1984. "Kato Hiroyuki and Confucian Natural Rights, 1861–1870." *Harvard Journal of Asiatic Studies* 44:469–92.

Waldron, Jeremy. 1985. *Theories of Rights.* Oxford, U.K.: Oxford University Press.

———. 1987. *Nonsense upon Stilts, Bentham, Burke, and Marx on the Rights of Man.* London: Methuen.

Wang Guangwu. 1991. *The Chineseness of China: Selected Essays.* Hong Kong: Oxford University Press.

Wang Jisi. 1996. "Civilizations: Clash or Fusion?" *Beijing Review* (January 15–21): 8–12.

Wang, Y. C. 1966. *Chinese Intellectuals and the West.* Chapel Hill: University of North Carolina Press.

Wang Zheng. 1999. *Women in the Chinese Enlightenment: Oral and Textual Histories.* Berkeley, Calif.: University of California Press.

Wasserstrom, Jeffrey N. 1992 "Afterword: History, Myth, and the Tales of Tiananmen. " Pp. 244–80, in *Popular Protest and Political Culture in Modern China*, ed. Jeffrey N. Wasserstrom and Elizabeth J. Perry. Boulder, Colo.: Westview, 1992.

———.1997. "History and the Debate Over Human Rights in China." *The Chronicle of Higher Education* (24 October).

———. 2000. "The Chinese Revolution and Contemporary Paradoxes." Pp. 19–40, in *Human Rights and Revolutions*, ed. Jeffrey N. Wasserstrom, Lynn Hunt, and Marilyn B. Young. Lanham, Md.: Rowman & Littlefield

Wasserstrom, Jeffrey N., and Elizabeth J. Perry, eds. 1992. *Popular Protest and Political Culture in Modern China.* Boulder, Colo.: Westview.

Wasserstrom, Jeffrey N., Lynn Hunt, and Marilyn B. Young, eds.. 2000. *Human Rights and Revolutions* Lanham, Md.: Rowman & Littlefield.

Weatherley, Robert. 1999. *The Discourse of Human Rights in China: Historical and Ideological Perspectives.* London: Macmillan.

Wei Jingsheng. 1997. *The Courage to Stand Alone: Letters from Prison and Other Writings.* New York: Viking.

———. 1998. "A Handful of Pennies." <www.indexoncensorship.org> January 16 [accessed March 20, 2000].

Wells, H. G. 1940. *The Right of Man, or What are We Fighting For?* London: Secker and Warburg.

Westbrook, Robert B. 1991. *John Dewey and American Democracy.* Ithaca: Cornell University Press.

Weston, Burns H. 1992. "Human Rights." Pp. 14–30, in *Human Rights in the World Community: Issues and Action,* ed. Richard Pierre Claude and Burns H. Weston.

Weston, Timothy B. 1998. "The Formation and Positioning of the New Cultural Community, 1913–1917." *Modern China* 24, no. 3 (July): 255–84.

White Papers. Published by the State Council of the PRC, <www.chinaguide.org/e-white/>.

Wilson, Richard A., ed. 1997. *Human Rights, Culture, and Context: Anthropological Perspectives.* London: Pluto.

Wong Young-tsu. 1993. "The Fate of Liberalism in Revolutionary China: Chu Anping and His Circle, 1946–1950." *Modern China* 19, no. 4 (October): 457–90.

Woo, Peter K. Y. 1980. "A Metaphysical Approach to Human Rights from a Chinese Point of View." Pp. 113–24, in *The Philosophy of Human Rights: International Perspectives,* ed. Alan S. Rosenbaum. Westport, Conn.

Wright, Mary Clabaugh. ed. 1968. *China in Revolution: The First Phase, 1900–1913.* New Haven, Conn.: Yale University Press.

Xiao Qiang. 1995. "Letters from Citizens. The Development of a Chinese Human Rights Movement," *China Rights Forum* (Summer).

Yanabu Akira. 1996. "The Concept of Right." Paper presented at the East-West Center Conference on Confucianism and Human Rights, Honolulu, Hawaii. Translated by Joshua A. Fogel.

Yu Haocheng. 1995. "On Human Rights and Their Guarantee by Law." Pp. 93–115, in *Human Rights and Chinese Values: Legal, Philosophical, and Political Perspectives,* ed. Michael C. Davis. Hong Kong: Oxford University Press.

Yü Ying-shih. 1994. "The Radicalization of China in the Twentieth Century." Pp. 125–50, in *China in Transformation,* ed. Tu Wei-ming. Cambridge, Mass.: Harvard University Press.

Zakaria, Fareed. 1994. "Culture is Destiny: A Conversation with Lee Kuan Yew." *Foreign Affairs* 73, no. 2 (March/April): 109–26.

Zarrow, Peter. 1988. "He Zhen and Anarcho-Feminism in China." *The Journal of Asian Studies* 47, no. 4 (November): 796–813.

———. 1990. *Anarchism and Chinese Political Culture.* New York: Columbia University Press.

———. 1996. "Chen Duxiu: Human Rights and Politics in the New Culture Movement." Paper presented at the East-West Center Conference on Confucianism and Human Rights, Honolulu, Hawaii.

———. 1998. "Introduction: Citizenship in China and the West." Pp. 3–38, in *Imagining the People: Chinese Intellectuals and the Concept of Citizenship, 1890–1920*, ed. Joshua A. Fogel and Peter G. Zarrow. Armonk, N.Y: Sharpe.

Zhou Wei. 1995. "The Study of Human Rights in the People's Republic of China." Pp. 83–96, in *Human Rights and International Relations in the Asia Pacific*, ed. James T. H. Tang. London: Pinter.

Zhu Feng. 1999. "Human Rights Problems and Current Sino-American Relations." Pp. 232–54, in *Debating Human Rights: Critical Essays from the United States and Asia*, ed. Peter van Ness. London: Routledge.

Zou Sicheng. 1995. "Series on Human Rights Studies Published." *Beijing Review* 38, no. 46 (November 13–19): 36–37.

Zylstra, Bernard. 1968. *From Pluralism to Collectivism: The Development of Harold Laski's Political Thought*. Amsterdam.

WORKS IN CHINESE

Anon. 1901. 《原国》 [The Origin to the Nation]. 《国民报》, No. 1. Reprinted in Zhang Nan and Wang Renzhi, eds. Vol. 1:1, pp. 63–65.

Anon. 1901. 《二十世纪之中国》 [Twentieth-Century China]. 《国民报》, No. 1. Reprinted in Zhang Nan and Wang Renzhi, eds. Vol. 1:1, pp. 65–71.

Anon. 1901. 《自由不死》 [Freedom Cannot Die]. 《国民报》, No. 1.

Anon. 1901. 《天赋权与强权之说》 [The [Two] Schools of Heaven-Granted Rights and Rights of the Strongest]. 《国民报》, No. 1.

Anon. 1901. 《议论一致之弊》 [The Harm of Identical Opinions]. 《国民报》, No. 1.

Anon. 1901. 《自由之民》 [A Free People]. 《国民报》, No. 3.

Anon. 1901. 《说国民》 [On Citizens]. 《国民报》, No. 2. Reprinted in Zhang Nan and Wang Renzhi, eds. Vol. 1:1, pp. 72–77.

Anon. 1901. 《中国灭亡论》 [The Extinction of the Country]. 《国民报》, Nos. 2, 3, and 4. Reprinted in Zhang Nan and Wang Renzhi eds. Vol. 1:1, pp. 78–89.

Anon. 1901. 《人民论》 [On People]. 《开智录》, Nos. 4, 5, and 6.

Anon. 1903. 《权利篇》 [On Rights]. 《直说》, No. 2. Reprinted in Zhang Nan and Wang Renzhi, eds. Vol. 1:1, pp. 479–84.

Anon. 1903. 《为外人之奴隶于为满洲政府之奴隶无别》 [There Are No Differences between Being the Slaves of the Foreigners and of the Manchus]. 《童子世界》, No. 24, 2 May. Reprinted in Zhang Nan and Wang Renzhi, eds. Vol. 1:2, pp. 526–27.

Anon. 1903. 《国民教育》 [The Education of Citizens]. 《湖北学生界》, No. 3.

Anon. 1903. 《论中国之前途及国民立尽之责任》 [On China's Future and the Responsibilities of the Citizens]. 《湖北学生界》, No. 3. Reprinted in Zhang Nan and Wang Renzhi, eds. Vol. 1:1, pp. 459–66.

Anon. 1903. 《痛黑暗世界》 [A Dark Age]. 《湖北学生界》, No. 4.

Anon. 1903. 《敬告同乡学生》 [A Call to My Fellow Students]. 《湖北学生界》, No.5.

Anon. 1903. 《论中国合群当自地方自治始》 [On China's Unity Starting from Local Self-Government]. 《汉声》, No. 7–8.

Anon. 1903 《纪十八世纪末法国之乱》 [Recording the chaos in France at the end of the eighteenth century]. 《游学译编》No. 4, 1903.

Anon. 1903. 《奴痛》 [The Bitterness of Slavery]. 《湖北学生界》,No. 4.

Anon. 1903. 《箴奴隶》 [Admonishing Slaves]. 《国民日日报汇编》, October, 1904. Reprinted in Hu Weixi ed. (1994), pp. 76–91.

Anon. 1904. 《论侵人自由与放弃自由之罪》 [On Violating Other's Freedom and Renouncing One's Own]. 《女子世界》, No. 2.

Anon.1904. 《论自由必先具裁制之力》 [In Order to Talk about Freedom One Must First Have the Ability of Control]. 《时敏报》. Reprinted in Zhongyang yanjiu yuan jindai shi yanjiu suo, ed. 《近代中国对西方及列 强认识资料汇编》,Vol. 5:2.

Anon.1904. 《祝苏报馆之封禁》 [The Closure of Subao]. 《江苏》, No. 4.

Anon. 1905. 《世界将来大势论》 [On the Future Major Powers in the World]. 《广益丛报》, No. 73.

Anon. 1906. 《说权利》 [On Rights]. 《申报》.Reprinted in 《东方杂志》, Vol. 3, No. 4, pp. 6333–8.

Anon. 1906. 《论君主立宪政体之性质》 [On the Character of Monarchic Constitutionalism]. 《北洋学报》. Reprinted in Zhongyang yanjiu yuan jindai shi yanjiu suo 《近代中国对西方及列强认识资料汇编》, Vol.5:2.

Anon. 1906. 《国民义务辨》 [A Distinction of People's Duties]. 《南洋日日官报》. Reprinted in 《东方杂志》, Vol. 3, No. 4.

Anon. 1906. 《论国人宜知政法之大要》 [What Our Citizens Ought to Know about Politics and Law]. 《时报》, 29 March. Reprinted in 《东方杂志》, Vol. 3, No. 5.

Anon. 1906. 《集会结社之自由及其限制》 [The Freedoms of Assembly and Association and Their Restriction]. 《时报》, 17, 18, 19, and 20 November.

Anon. 1906. 《论中国人失其自觉心之危》 [The Danger of the Chinese Having Lost Their Consciousness]. 《时报》, 13 and 14 December.

Anon. 1906. 《论救中国必先培养国民之公德》 [In Order to Save China It Is First Necessary to Develop the Public Morality of the People]. 《东方杂志》, Vol. 3, No. 7.

Anon. 1907. 《论中国社会之缺点》 [On the Weak Points of the Chinese Society]. 《津报》. Reprinted in 《东方杂志》, Vol. 4, No. 8.

Anon. 1907. 《论国民法律上之地位》 [The Legal Status of Citizens]. 《时报 3 and 4 July.

Anon. 1907. 《论生命权》 [On the Right to Life]. 《时报》, 2 August.

Anon. 1908. 《帝国主义之结果》 [The Results of Imperialism]. 《新世纪》, No. 63. Reprinted in 《近代中国对西方及列强认识资料汇编》, Vol. 5:2, pp. 1307–09.

Anon. 1908. 《论国民之热心权利》 [On Citizens Enthusiasm for Rights]. 《时报》, 29 April.

Anon. 1919. 《关于民国建设方针的主张》 [On the Policy of the Construction of the Republic]. 《星期评论》, No. 2, 15 June.

Anon. 1920. 《新思潮之新人生观》 [The New View of Life]. 《北京大学学生周刊》, No. 1.

Anon. 1920. 《就来的三自由》 [The Coming Three Freedoms]. 《北京大学学生周刊》, No. 1.

Anon. 1920. 《敬告教职员诸君 [A Call to Teachers and Staff]. 《北京大学学生周刊》, No. 1.

Anon. 1920. 《我们的新宗教》 [Our New Faith]. 《北京大学学生周刊》, No. 5.

Anon. 1920. 《自由的代价》 [The Price of Freedom]. 《北京大学学生周刊》, No.16.

Anon. 1924. 《北京的言论自由》 [The Freedom of Speech in Beijing]. 《现代评论》, Vol. 1, No. 6.

Anon. 1925. 《发刊词》 [Foreword]. 《人权》, No. 1, August.

Anon. 1925. 《人权的保障在那里？》 [Where Is the Protection of Human Rights?]. 《现代评论》, Vol. 2, No. 39, pp. 147–48.

Anon. 1926. 《又一个人权问题》 [Another Human Rights Question]. 《现代评论》, Vol. 3, No. 64.

Anon. 1947. 《个大学教授联名宣言》 [A Jointly Signed Manifesto of University Professors]. 《民主半月刊》, No. 4, p. 4.

Anon. 1947. 《我们对于政府压迫民盟的看法》 [Our View on the Government's Suppression of the Democratic League]. 《观察》, Vol. 3, No. 11, p. 3.

Anon. 1953. Editorial, 《从反共义士的行动看出自由民主的真价值》 [Seeing the Value of Freedom and Democracy from the Actions of the Righteous Fighters Against Communism]. 《自由中国》, Vol. 9, No. 9.

Anon. 1953. Editorial, 《自由日谈真自由》 [Talking about Real Freedom on Freedom Day]. 《自由中国》, Vol. 10, No. 3.

Anon. 1954. Editorial, 《要谈谈什么？》 [What Shall We Discuss?]. 《自由中国》, Vol. 12, No. 4.

Anon. 1955. Editorial, 《我们要贯彻「五四」精神》 [We Should Implement the Spirit of May Fourth?]. 《自由中国》, Vol. 12, No. 9.

Anon. 1979. 《国内报刊关于人权问题的讨论综述》 [A Summary of the Debate on the Issue of Human Rights in Domestic Magazines]. 《社会科学》, No. 3, pp. 76–78.

Awuleituo. 1901. 阿勿雷脱 《欧洲近代哲学》 [European Modern Philosophy] in 《国民报》, No. 1.

Bai Peng. 1941. 百鹏 《人权运动的重要性及其展开》 [The Importance and Development of the Human Rights Movement]. 《时代批评》, No. 73/74.

Bo Yangzhong. 1907. 伯阳重 《人权宣言论》 [On the Declaration of Human Rights].

CASS. 1992. 中国社会科学院法学研究所编[Legal Institute of CASS, ed.].
《当代人权》 [Contemporary Human Rights]. Beijing: 中国社会科学院出版社.
———. 1998. 《中国人权百科全书》 [The Human Rights Encyclopedia of China].
Beijing: 中国大百科全书出班社.

Cai Shangsi, ed. 1983. 蔡尚思《中国现代思想史资料简编》 [A Concise Edition of
Materials in Modern Chinese Thought]. 浙江人民出版社.

Chang Yu. 1910. 长舆《立宪政治与舆论》 [The Establishment of Constitutional Rule
and Public Opinion]. 《国风报》, No. 13, 17 June 1910. Reprinted in Hu Weixi, pp.
205–12.

Chen Dezheng. 1930. 陈德徵《人权论及其他》 [Human Rights and Other Subjects].
Shanghai: 上海特别市党部宣传部

Chen Duxiu. 1903. 陈独秀《安徽爱国会拟章》 [A Draft for the Anhui Patriotic
Society]. 《苏报》 7 June. Reprinted in Ren Jianshu et al., Vol. 1, pp. 17–19.
———. 1914. 《爱国性与自觉性》 [On Patriotism and Consciousness]. 《甲寅杂
志》, 1 (4):1–6 (10 November). Reprinted in Ren Jianshu et al., Vol. 1, pp. 113–19.
———. 1915a. 《法兰西人与近世文明》 [The French and Modern Civilization]. 《新
青年》, Vol. 1, No. 1, 15 September. Reprinted in Ren Jianshu et al. Vol. 1, pp. 136–39.
———. 1915b. 《敬告青年》 [A Call to Youth]. 《新青年》 Vol. 1, No. 1, 15
September. Reprinted in Ren Jianshu et al. Vol. 1, pp. 129–36.
———. 1915c. 《东西民族根本思想之差异》 [The Fundamental Difference in
Thinking between Orientals and Westerners]. 《新青年》, Vol. 1, No. 4, 15
December. Reprinted in Ren Jianshu et al. Vol. 1, pp. 165–69.
———. 1915d. 《今日之教育方针》 [The Direction of Today's Education]. 《新青
年》, Vol. 1, No. 2, 15 October. Reprinted in Ren Jianshu et al., Vol. 1, pp. 140–46.
———. 1915e. 《一九一六年》 [The Year 1916]. 《新青年》, Vol. 1, No. 5.
Reprinted in Ren Jianshu et al., Vol. 1, pp. 170–74.
———. 1916a. 《宪法与孔教》 [The Constitution and Confucianism]. 《新青年》,
Vol. 2, No. 3, 1 November. Reprinted in Ren Jianshu et al., Vol. 1, pp. 224–29.
———. 1916b. 《孔子之道与现代生活》 [Confucianism and Modern Life]. 《新青
年》, Vol. 2, No. 4, 1 December. Reprinted in Ren Jianshu et al., Vol. 1, pp. 230–37.
———. 1916c. 《袁世凯复活》 [The Rebirth of Yuan Shikai]. 《新青年》, Vol. 2, No.
4, 1 December. Reprinted in Ren Jianshu et al., Vol. 1, pp. 238–40.
———. 1918. 《人生真义》 [The Real Meaning of Life]. 《新青年》, Vol. 4, No. 2,
15 February. Reprinted in Ren Jianshu et al., Vol. 1, pp. 345–47.
———. 1919a. 《新青年》罪案之答辩书 [A Reply on the Case of New Youth].
《新青年》, Vol. 6, No. 1, 15 January. Reprinted in Ren Jianshu et al., Vol. 1,
pp. 442–43.
———. 1919b. 《旧党的罪恶》 [The Crime of the Old Parties]. 《每周评论》, Vol. 11,

2 March. Reprinted in Ren Jianshu et al., Vol. 1, pp. 493–95.

———. 1919c. 《人种差别待遇问题》 [The Question of DifferentialTreatment of Races]. 《每周评论》, No. 12, 9 March. Reprinted in Ren Jianshu (1993), Vol. 1, pp. 496–97.

———. 1919d. 《北京市民宣言》 [A Manifesto of the Citizens of Beijing]. 9 June 1919. Reprinted in Ren Jianshu et al., Vol. 2, pp. 25–26.

———. 1919e. 《我们究竟应当不应当爱国》 [Should We Really Love the Country?]. 《每周评论》, No. 25, 8 June. Reprinted in Ren Jianshu et al., Vol. 2, pp. 22–24.

———. 1919f. 《实行民治的基础》 [The Foundation of Implementing Democracy]. 《新青年》, Vol. 7, No. 1, 1 December. Reprinted in Ren Jianshu et al., Vol. 2, pp. 28–39.

———. 1919g. 《法律与言论自由》 [The Law and Freedom of Speech]. 《新青年》, Vol. 7, No. 1, 1 December. Reprinted in Ren Jianshu et al., Vol. 2, pp. 43–44.

———. 1919h. 《新青年》宣言 [The Manifesto of New Youth]. 《新青年》, Vol. 7, No. 1, 1 December. Reprinted in Ren Jianshu et al., pp. 41–42.

———. 1920a. 《劳动者底觉悟》 [The Workers' Conciousness]. 《新青年》, Vol. 7, No. 6, 1 May. Reprinted in Ren Jianshu et al., Vol. 2, pp. 135–37.

———. 1920b. 《我的意见》 [My Opinions]. 《新青年》, Vol. 7, No. 6, 1 May. Reprinted in Ren Jianshuet al., Vol. 2, pp. 138–44.

———. 1920c. 《民主党与共产党》 [Democratic Party and Communist Party]. 《新青年》, Vol. 8, No. 4, 1 December. Reprinted in Ren Jianshu et al., Vol. 2, pp. 219–20.

———. 1921a. 《如何才是正当的人生》 [What Should Be Called a Proper Life]. 《广东群报》, 24 January. Reprinted in Ren Jianshu et al., Vol. 2, pp. 265–66.

———. 1921b. 《妇女问题与社会主义》 [The Woman Question and Socialism]. 《广东群报》, 31 January, 1 February. Reprinted in Ren Jianshu et al., Vol. 2, pp. 267–70.

———. 1929. 《致中央常委同志信》 [Letter to the Comrades in the Central Committe]. 5 August. Reprinted in Ren Jianshu et al., Vol. 3, pp. 33–57.

———. 1940a. 《给连根的信》 [A Letter to Lian Gen]. 1 July. Reprinted in Ren Jianshu et al., Vol. 3, pp. 547–49.

———. 1940b. 《给西流的信》 [A Letter to Xi Liu]. September. Reprinted in Ren Jianshu et al., Vol. 3, pp. 552–58.

———. 1940c. 《我的根本意见》 [My Fundamental Views]. 28 November. Reprinted in Ren Jianshu et al., Vol. 3, pp. 559–63.

Chen Pokang. 1944. 陈伯康《确定并保障人民的经济权利》 [Stipulating and Protecting People's Economic Rights]. 《宪政》, No. 4, pp. 20–26.

Chen Qixiu. 1919. 陈启修《庶民主义之研究》 [Research onDemocracy]. 《北京大学月刊》, Vol. 1, No. 1, pp. 25–32.

Chen Shaohua. 1941. 陈绍华 《从人权运动谈到中山先生的三民主义》 [Discussing

Sun Yatsen's Three People's Principles from the Point of View of the Human Rights Movement]. 《时代批评》, No. 73/74.

Chen Shuyu. 1979. 陈漱渝 《中国民权保障同盟》 [The China Leagu for the Protection of Civil Rights]. Beijing: 中国社会科学出版社.

———. 1985. 《中国民权保障同盟》 [The China League for the Protection of Civil Rights]. Beijing: 北京出版社.

Chen Tianhua. 1982. 陈天华 《陈天华集》 [Chen Tianhua's Collected Works]. Changsha: 湖南人民出版社.

Chen Yishen. 1989. 陈仪深 《独立评论的民主思想》 [The Idea of Democracy in the Independent Critic]. Taipei: 联经出版事业公司.

Chen Zhimai. 1935. 陈之迈 《民主与独裁的讨论》 [The Discussion on Democracy and Dictatorship]. 《独立评论》, No. 136, pp. 4–11.

———. 1938. 《民治主义的演变》 [The Change in Democracy]. 《东方杂志》, Vol. 33, No. 17, pp. 106895–901.

Chen Zhushan. 1925a. 陈筑山 《人权的人生观》 [The outlook on life in human rights]. 《人权》, No. 2, September.

———. 1925b. 《人权的社会观》 [The Outlook on Society in Human Rights]. 《人

Cheng Shewo. 1954. 成舍我 《「人权保障」与「言论自由」》 [The Protection of Human Rights and Freedom of Speech]. 《自由中国》, Vol. 12, No. 6, pp. 8–11.

Cheng Wenxi, ed. 1981. 程文熙 《中西印哲学文集》 [A Collection of Chinese, Western and Indian Philosophy]. Taipei: 学生书局

Chu Anping. 1946. 储安平 《我们的志趣和态度》 [Our Aspiration and Stance]. 《观察》, Vol. 1, No. 1, pp. 3–4.

———. 1998. 《储安平文集》 [Chu Anping's Collected Works].Shanghai: 东方出版中心.

Chu Hong-Yuan. 1995. 朱源 《同盟会的革命理论—民报个案研究》 [The Revolutionary Theory of Tongmeng hui: A Case Study of Min bao]. Taipei: Academia Sinica, Institute of Modern History, 2d ed.

Da Wo. 1903. 大我 《新社会之理论》 [A Theory of a New Society]. 《浙江潮》, Nos. 8 and 9. Reprinted in Zhang Dan and Wang Renzhi, eds. Vol. 1:2, pp. 509–16.

Dalu dixia kanwu huibian (DLDX) 1980–1984. 《大陆地下刊务汇编》 [A Collection of Underground Publications Circulated on Chinese mainland]. Taipei: 中共研究杂志社编印, Vol. 1–20.

Dai Huang. 1998. 戴煌 《胡耀邦与平反冤假错案》 [Hu Yaobang and the Rehabilitation of Unjust, False, and Misjudged Cases]. Beijing: 中国文联出版公司.

Deng Xiaoping. 1987. 邓小平 《坚持四项基本原则》 [Uphold the Four Cardinal Principles]. Reprinted in 中共中央书记处研究室, ed. 《坚持四项基本原则反对资产阶级自由化》 [Uphold the Four Cardinal Principles, Oppose Bourgeois

Liberalization] Beijing: 人民出版社.

Ding Chuwo. 1904. 丁初我《女子家庭革命说》 [A Theory on Revolution of the Women's Family]. 《女子世界》, No. 4. Reprinted in Zhang Nan and Wang Renzhi, eds. Vol. 1:2.

Ding Shouhe, ed. 1982. 丁守和《辛亥革命时期期刊介绍》 [An Introduction to Periodicals from the Period of the Xinhai Revolution]. 5 vols. Beijing: 人民出版社.

Ding Wenjiang. 1934. 丁文江《民主政治与独裁政治》 [Democracy and Dictatorship]. 《独立评论》, No. 133, pp. 4–7.

———. 1935. 《再论民治与独裁》 [More on Democracy and Dictatorship]. 《独立评论》, No. 137, pp. 19–22.

Dong Ling and Liu Shi. 1979. 东岭、柳石 《「人权」口号的由来及其阶级实质》 [The Origin and Class Character of the Slogan Human Rights]. 《实线》, No. 7, pp. 64–66.

Dong Yunhu and Liu Wuping, eds. 1990. 董云虎、刘武萍《世界人权约法总览》 [World Documents of Human Rights]. Chengdu: 四川人民出版社.

———. 1993. 《世界人权约法总览续编》 [Supplement to World Documents of Human Rights]. Chengdu: 四川人民出版社.

Dongfang Jibai. 1955. 东方既白《介绍张佛泉著「自由与人权」—论个人与社会》 [Introducing Zhang Foquan's Work "Freedom and Human Rights": On the Individual and Society]. 《自由中国》, Vol. 13, No. 12, pp. 28–30.

Du Wei (John Dewey). n.d. 杜威《杜威在闽讲演录》 [A Record of Dewey's Lectures in Fujian]. The Educational Bureau of Fujian.

Du Qingfeng. 1904. 杜清封《男女都是一样》 [Women and Men Are Equal]. 《女子世界》, No. 6.

Duanmu Liang. 1941a. 端木良《论人权运动》 [On the Human Rights Movement]. 《时代批评》, No. 70.

———. 1941b. 《人权运动行动性》 [The Character of the Human Rights Movement's Activities]. 《时代批评》, No. 73/74.

FYPLWXJ. 1957. 《反右派论文选集》 [A Collection of Antirightist Articles], 湖北人民出版社编辑. Edited by the Hubei People's Publishing House, Wuhan.

Fen Min. 1911. 愤民《论道德》 [On Morality]. 《克复学报》, Nos. 2 and 3. Reprinted in Hu Weixi (1994), pp. 254–62.

Feng Banggan. 1902. 冯邦干《法律平谈》 [On Law]. 《新民丛报》, No. 4.

Feng Zhuoran and Gu Chunde, eds. 1992. 冯桌然、谷春德 《人权论集》 [A Collection on Human Rights]. Beijing: 首都师范大学出版社.

Feng Ziyou. 1900. 冯自由 《论演说之源流及其与国民之关系》 [On the Origin of the Theory of Evolution and Its Significance for Citizens]. 《开智录》, No. 1.

———. 1906. 《录中国日报民生主义与中国政治革命之前途》 [A Record on Zhongguo ribao on Democracy and the Future of the Chinese Political Revolution].

《民 报》, No. 4.

———. 1928. 《中华民国开国前革命史》 [A Revolutionary History before the Founding of the Republic of China]. Taipei: 世界书局 1984 (1928).

Fu Sinian. 1949. 傅斯年《自由与平等》 [Freedom and Equality]. 《自由中国》, Vol. 1, No. 1, pp. 9–10.

Fu Zheng. 1956. 傅正《国家要把人当人》 [The Country Should Treat People as Human Beings]. 《自由中》, 1 October.

———. 1992. 《自由中国的时代意义》 [The Meaning of the "Free China" Period]. In 《台湾民主自由的曲折历程》 [The Tortuous Course of Democracy and Freedom in Taiwan]. Taipei: 自立晚报文化出版部 pp. 349–69.

GDXXYB. 1958. 《高等学校右派言论选编》 [A Collection of Rightist Speech from Schools of Higher Education]. Beijing: 中共中国人民大学委员会生会主义思想教育办公室.

Gao Hongjun. 1999. 高鸿钧《中国公民权利意识的演进》 [The Awakening of Consciousness of Rights among Chinese Citizens]. In Xia Yong (1999), pp. 43-106.

Gao Jun, ed. 1990. 高军《中国现代政治思评要》 [A Critical Appraisal of Modern Chinese Political Thought].

Gao Pingshu. 1985. 高平叔《蔡元培政治论著》 [A Collection of Cai Yuanpei's Political Works]. Shijiazhuang: 河北人民出版社.

———. 1989. 《蔡元培与民权保障》 [Cai Yuanpei and the Protection of Civil Rights]. In 《论蔡元培—纪念蔡元培诞辰120周年学术讨论会文集》 [On Cai Yuanpei: Proceedings from an Academic Conference Commemorating Cai Yuanpei's 120th Anniversary]. Beijing:旅游教育出版社.

Gao Ruiquan ed. 1995. 高瑞泉《向着新的理想社会—李大钊文选》 [Moving toward a New Ideal Society: A Collection of Li Dazhao's Works]. Shanghai: 上海远东出版社.

Gao Yihan. 1915a. 高一涵《共和国家与青年之自觉》 [On the Republic and Young People's Consciousness]. 《新青年》, Vol. 1, Nos. 1, 2, and 3.

———. 1915b. 《民约与邦本》 [The Social Contract and the Basis of the Nation]. 《新青年》, Vol. 1, No. 3, 15 November.

———. 1915c. 《国家非人生之归宿论》 [The State Is Not the Ultimate Goal of Life]. 《新青年》, Vol. 1, No. 4, 15 December.

———. 1916a. 《戴雪英国言论自由之权利论》 [Dicey on the Right to Freedom of Speech in England]. 《新青年》, Vol. 1, No. 6, 15 February.

———. 1916b. 《乐利主义与人生》 [Utilitarianism and Life]. 《新青年》, Vol. 2, No. 1, 1 September.

———. 1918a. 《近世三大政治思想之变迁》 [On the Changes in Three Great Political Thoughts in the Modern World]. 《新青年》, Vol. 4, No. 1, 15 January.

———. 1918b. 《读弥尔的自由论》 [Reading Mill's On Liberty]. 《新青年》, Vol.

4, No. 3, 15 March.

———. 1920. 《欧洲政治思想小史》 [A Brief History of Western Political Thought]. Shanghai: 中华书局.

———. 1921. 《省宪法中的民权问题》 [The Question of People's Rights in the Provincial Constitutions]. 《新青年》, Vol. 9, No. 5, 1 September, pp. 609–15.

———. 1922. 《我国宪法与欧洲新宪法之比较》 [A Comparison of Our Constitution and the New Constitutions in Europe]. 《东方杂志》, Vol. 19, No. 22, November.

———. 1925a. 《平民革命的目的与手段》 [The End and Means of People's Revolution]. 《现代评论》, Vol. 3, No. 53, pp. 2–3.

———. 1925b. 《军阀与言论集会的自由由》 [The Warlords and Freedom of Speech and Assembly]. 《现代评论》, Vol. 3, No. 55.

———. 1926a. 《卢梭的民权论和国权论》 [On Rousseau's Theory of People's Rights and National Rights]. 《东方杂志》, Vol. 23, No. 3, February, pp. 66169–80.

———. 1926b. 《革命军与言论自由》 [Revolutionary Army and Freedom of Speech]. 《现代评论》, Vol. 3, No. 64, pp. 224–25.

———. 1929. 《我的共产嫌疑的证据》 [Proofs Regarding My Suspected Communist [Sympathy]]. 《现代评论》, Vol. 6, No. 146, pp. 846–848.

———. 1930. 《政治学纲要》 [An Outline of Political Science]. Shanghai: 神州光社刊.

Gao Yuan. 1919. 高元 《民主政治与伦常主义》 [Democracy and the Confucian Hierarchical System]. 《新朝》, Vol. 2, No. 2, 1 December.

Ge Si'en. 1946. 葛思恩 《新闻自由的低潮》 [On the Low Tide of Press Freedom]. 《观察》, Vol. 2, No. 16, pp. 8–10.

Gong Fazi. 1902a. 攻法子 《国民主义》 [Nationalism]. 《译书汇编》, Vol. 2, No. 9.

———. 1902b. 《英人之权利思想》 [The English View of Rights] and 《日人之权利思想》 [The Japanese View of Rights]. 《译书汇编》, Vol. 2, No. 9.

Gong Xiangrui, ed. 1993. 龚祥瑞 《法治的理想与现实》 [The Ideal and Reality of the Rule of Law]. Beijing: 中国政法大学出版社.

Gongfa 《公法》 [Public Law Review]. Vol. 1, 1999.

Gu Chunde. 1982. 谷春德 《略论姨庬橙巳岀说》 [A Brief Outline of the Idea of "Natural Rights"]. 《红旗杂志》, No. 7, pp. 32–36.

Guang Sheng. 1917. 光升 《中国国民性及其弱点》 [The Chinese National Character and Its Weaknesses]. 《新青年》, Vol. 2, No. 6, February.

Guo Daohui. 1992. 郭道晖 《论人权的阶级性与普遍性》 [On the Class Character and Universality of Human Rights]. In CASS, pp. 66–76.

———. 1998. 《法的时代呼唤》 [Epochal Call for Law]. Beijing: 中国法制出版社.

Han Depei. 1947. 韩德培 《人身自由的保障问题》 [On the Question of the Protection of the Freedom of the Person]. 《观察》, Vol. 3, No. 11, pp. 5–7.

———. 1995. 《人权的理论与实践》 [The Theory and Practice of Human Rights]. Wuhan: 武汉大学出版社.

Han Ju. 1903. 汉驹 《新政府之建设》 [The Foundation of a New Government]. 《江苏》, Nos. 5 and 6 1903. Reprinted in Zhang Dan and Wang Renzhi, eds.Vol. 1:2, pp. 579–93.

Han Youtong. 1941. 韩幽桐 《人权运动与民主政治》 [The Human Rights Movement and Democracy]. 《时代批评》, No. 73/74.

Hang Liwu. 1982. 杭立武 《人伦民权与人权》 [Human Relationships, People's Rights, and Human Rights]." In Chinese Association for Human Rights, ed., 《人权论文选辑》 [Selected Essays on Human Rights]. Taipei.

He Qi, and Hu Liyuan. 1994. 何启、胡礼垣 《新政真诠》 [The Interpretation of the New Policies]. Shenyang: 辽宁人民出版社.

He Siyuan. 1920. 何思源 《布尔塞维克主义》 [Bolshevism]. 《新朝》, Vol. 3, No. 2.

He Xin. 1996. 何新 《中华复兴与世界未来》 [The Resurgence of China and the Future of the World]. Chengdu: 四川人民出版社.

He Yimin. 1991. 何一民 《论辛亥革命前近代知识分子人权意识的觉醒》 [The Awakening of an Understanding of Human Rights among Modern Intellectuals before the Xinhai Revolution]. In Hu Weixi (1991), pp. 64–83.

Hen Hai. 1906. 恨海 《满政府之立宪问题》 [The Problem of the Manchu Government Establishing a Constitution]. 《复报》, No.1. Reprinted in Zhang Nan and Wang Renzhi, eds. Vol. 2:1, pp. 546–51.

Hu Jian. 1946. 胡剑 《祇有人民自己组织起来才能保障人民的自由。论人民自由保障委员会的组织》 [People's Freedom Can Only be Protected if People Organize Themselves. Discussing the Committe for the Protection of People's Freedom]. 《民主周刊》, Vol. 3, No. 3.

Hu Ping. 1998. 胡平 《言论自由是第一人权》 [Freedom of Speech is the Foremost Human Rights]. 《世界周刊》, 25 October.Translated in Angle and Svensson [2000].

Hu Qiuyuan. 1958. 胡秋原 《世界人权宣言之渊源及其意义》 [The Origin and Meaning of the Universal Declaration of Human Rights]. 《自由中国》, Vol. 19, No. 11, pp. 10–16.

Hu Shi. 1918. 胡适 《易卜生主义》 [Ibsenism]. 《新青年》, Vol. 4, No. 6, June. Reprinted in 《胡适哲学思想资料选》 [A Selection of Materials on Hu Shi's Philosophy]. Shanghai: 华东师范大学出版社, 1981, pp. 155–71.

———. 1920. 《争自由的宣言》 [Manifesto for the Struggle for Freedom]. 《东方杂志》, Vol. 17, No. 16, August.

———. 1921. 《杜威先生与中国》 [Dewey and China]. 《东方杂志》, Vol. 18, No. 13.

———. 1929a. 《人权与约法》 [Human Rights and the Provisional Constitution]. 《新月》, Vol. 2, No. 2, pp. 1–8.

———. 1929b. 《我们什么时候才可有宪法？》[When Will We Have a Constitution?]
《新月》, Vol. 2, No. 4, pp. 1–8.

———. 1929c. 《新文化运动与国民党》 [The New Culture Movement and the
Guomindang]. 《新月》, Vol. 2, Nos. 6 and 7.

———. 1930. 《人权论集 》 [A Collection of Essays on Human Rights]. Shanghai:
新月书店.

———. 1933. 《民权保障》 [Protection of Civil Rights].《独立评论》, No. 38, 19
February, pp. 2–5.

———. 1934. 《汪蒋通电裏提起的自由》 [The Mention of Freedom in the
Telegrams of Wang Jingwei and Chiang Kai-shek]. 《独立评论》, No. 131, pp. 4–5.

———. 1935a.《从民主与独裁的讨论里求得一个共同政治信仰》[Searching for a
Common Faith in the Debate on Democracy versus Dictatorship]. 《独立评论》,
No. 141.

———. 1935b.《个人自由与社会进步》 [Individual Freedom and the Progress of
Society]. 《独立评论》, No. 150, pp. 2–5.

———. 1935c. 《一年来关于民治与独裁的讨论》 [A Year-Long Debate on
Democracy and Dictatorship]. 《东方杂志》, Vol. 32, No. 1, pp. 98499–507.

———. 1992. 《四十自述》 [Autobiography at Forty]. Shenzhen: 海天出版社.

Hu Shiqing. 1925. 胡石青《我们为什么要主张人权？》 [Why Do We Advocate
Human Rights?] 《人权》, No. 1, August.

Hu Weixi, ed. 1991. 胡伟希《辛亥革命与中国近代思想文化》 [The Xinhai
Revolution and Modern Chinese Thought and Culture]. Beijing: 中国人民大学
出版社.

———. 1994. 《民声－辛亥时论选》 [People's Voice: A Collection of Works from the
Xinhai Period]. Shenyang: 辽宁人民出版社.

Hua Lin. 1913. 华林《人权进化观》 [The Evolutionary View of Human Rights].
《东方杂志》, Vol. 10, No. 1, 19 January.

Huai Jiang. 1906. 怀姜《立宪驳议》[A Critique of Constitutionalism]. 《复报》,
No. 5. Reprinted in Zhang Nan and Wang Renzhi, eds.Vol. 2:1, pp. 555–57.

Huang Kunjin. 1980. 黄坤锦《人权概论》 [An Introduction to Human Rights].
Taipei: 嵩山出版社.

Ji Huang. 1941. 冀潢《人权运动与抗战》[Human Rights and the War of Resistance].
《时代批评》, No. 73/74.

Ji Tongwen. 1992. 吉同文 《试论马克思主义人权观的几个理论问题》 [Exploring
Some Theoretical Questions Regarding the Marxist View of Human Rights]. 《政法
论坛》, Nos. 1, and 2, pp. 2–10, and pp. 1–10.

Jian He. 1908. 健翮《论政府束缚言论自由. [The Government' Curtailment
of Freedom of Speech]. 《时报》, 19 and 20 January.

Jian Hongyi. 1907. 剑虹一《论国之责任》 [On the Country's Responsibility]. 《云南

杂志》. Reprinted in 《东方杂志》, Vol. 4, No. 8.

Jin Chengyi. 1958. 金承《纪念人权节应把台湾建为保障人权模范省》 [In Order to Commemoroate Human Rights Day, Taiwan Should Be Made Into a Model Province of Human Rights Protection]. 《自由中国》, Vol. 19, No. 11, pp.27–28.

Jin Zhonghua. 1941. 金仲华《保障舆论与保障人权》 [Protect the Media and Human Rights]. 《时代批评》, No. 73/74.

Kang Baiqing. 1919. 康白情《人权之贼》 [The Enemy of Human Rights].
《少年中国》, Vol. 1, No. 4, October, pp. 416–17.

Kato Hiroyuki. 1901. 《物兢论》 [On Struggle]. 《译书汇编》, Nos. 4, 5, and 8.

———.1903. 《人权新说》 [A New Theory of Human Rights]. Tokyo: 译书汇编社.

Lan Ying. 1979. 蓝瑛《人权从来就是资产阶级的口号吗？》 [Will Human Rights Always Remain a Slogan of the Bourgeoisie?] 《社会科学》, No. 3, pp. 71–75, p. 78.

Lei Fen. 1906. 雷奋《宪法界说》 [On the Limits of the Constitution]. 《宪政杂志》, No. 1. Reprinted in 《时报》, 17 and 18 December.

Lei Zhen. 雷震《独裁，残暴，反人性的共产党》 [A Communist Party That Is Dictatorial, Ruthless, and Opposes Human Nature]. 《自由中国》, Vol. 1, No. 1, pp. 11–13.

Lei Zhen. 1989. 《雷震全集》 [Lei Zhen's Collected Works]. 桂冠图书股份有限公司, Vol. 13 and Vol. 17.

Lei Zhen, and Yin Haiguang. 1951. 《言论自由的认识及其基本条件》 [The Understanding of Freedom of Speech and Its Fundamental Preconditions]. 《自由中国》, Vol. 5, No. 7, p. 3.

Li Buyun. 1992. 李步云《论人权的三种存在形态》 [On the Three Modes of Existence of Human Rights]. In CASS, pp. 3–15.

———. 1996a. 《社会主义人权的基本理论与实践》 [The Fundamental Theory and Practice of Human Rights in Socialism]. In Li Lin, pp. 1–14.

———. 1996b. 《人权的两个理论问题》 [Two Theoretical Questions Regarding Human Rights]. In Li Lin, pp. 15–23.

———. 1996c. 《个人人权与集体人权》 [Individual Human Rights and Collective Human Rights]. Li Lin, pp. 77–91.

———. 1996d. 《中国人权的体制保障》 [The System of Protection of Chinese Human Rights]. In Lin Lin, pp. 140–49.

———. 1998. 《人权》 [Human Rights]. In CASS, pp. 481–84.

Li Dazhao. 1916a. 《民彝与政治》 [The People's Will and Politics]. 《民彝》创刊号, 15 May. Reprinted in Gao Ruiquan (1995), pp. 18–39.

———. 1916b. 《宪法与思想自由》 [The Constitution and Freedom of Speech].
《宪法公言》, No. 7, 1916. Reprinted in Gao Ruiquan (1995), pp. 62–68.

———. 1917a. 《自然的伦理与孔子》 [Natural Ethics and Confucius]. 《甲寅》日刊, 4 February. Reprinted in Gao Ruiquan (1995), pp. 73–74.

———. 1917b. 《大亚细亚主义》[Pan-Asianism]. 《甲寅》日刊,18 April.
Reprinted in 《李大钊文集》.

———. 1918a. 《东西文明根本之异点》 [The Fundamental Differences between
Eastern and Western Civilizations]. 《言治》季刊, Vol. 3, 1 July. Reprinted in
Gao Ruiquan (1995), pp. 150–64.

———. 1918b. 《法俄革命之比较观》 [A Comparison between the French and the
Russian Revolutions]. 《言治》季刊, Vol. 3, 1 July, 1918. Reprinted in Gao
Ruiquan (1995), pp. 164–67.

———. 1919a. 《劳动教育问题》 [The Labor Education Question]. 《晨报》,
14 and 15 February. Reprinted in Li Dazhao (1984), Vol. 1.

———. 1919b. 《战后之妇人问题》 [The Postwar Woman Question]. 《新青年》,
Vol. 6, No. 2, 15 February. Reprinted in Li Dazhao (1984).

———. 1919c. 《危险思想与言论自由》 [Dangerous Thinking and Freedom of
Thought]. 《每周评论》, No. 24, 1 June. Reprinted in Gao Ruiquan (1995), pp.
190–92.

———. 1922. 《宗教与自由平等博爱》 [The Relationship between Religion and
Freedom, Equality and Fraternity]. Reprinted in Gao Ruiquan (1995), pp. 392–94.

———. 1984. 《李大钊文集》[Li Dazhao's Collected Works]. Beijing: 人民出版社.

Li Haopei. 1947. 李浩培《法治实行问题》 [The Implementation of the Rule of Law].
《观察》, Vol. 2, No. 12, pp. 3–6.

Li Hongxi. 1992. 李鸿禧《雷震之宪法学者像素描》 [A Sketch of Lei Zhen as a
Constitutional Scholar]. In 《台湾民主自由的曲折历程》 [The Tortuous Course of
Democracy and Freedom in Taiwan]. Taipei: 自立晚报文化出版部, pp. 1–27.

Li Huaxing, and Wu Jiaxun, eds. 1984. 李华兴、吴嘉勋 《梁启超选集》 [A Selection
of Liang Qichao's Works]. Shanghai: 上海人民出版社.

Li Jun. 1958. 李钧《如何保障基本人权》 [How to Protect Fundamental Human
Rights]. 《自由中国》, Vol. 19, No. 11, pp. 22–23.

Li Lin. 1993. 李林《人权研究述评》 [An Analysis of Research on Human Rights].
《中国法学研究年鉴１９９１》 [1991 Year Book of Chinese Legal Research].
Beijing: 中国政法大学出版社.

———. 1996a. 《当代人权理论与实践》 [The Theories and Practice of Human Rights
in Our Time]. Changchun: 吉林大学出版社.

———. 1996b. 《作为道德权利的人权与作为法律权利的公民权》 [Human Rights
as Constituting Moral Rights and Citizens' Rights as Constituting Legal Rights]. In
Li Lin, pp. 36–48. Li Lin et al. 1991. 李林《以马克思主义为指导深入研究人权理论
— 人权理论研讨会综述》 [Human Rights: A Summary of a Research Meeting on
the Theory of Human Rights]. 《法学研究》, No. 5, pp. 13–22.

Li Lin, and Zhu Xiaoqing. 1992. 李林、朱晓青《十一届三中全会以来人权问题讨
论概要》 [An Outline of the Discussions of Human Rights since the Third Plenum of

the 11th Central Committe]. In CASS, pp. 375–79.

Li Qing. 1941. 李青《论人权运动与我们当前的任务》[On the Human Rights Movement and Our Present Task]. 《时代批评》, No. 72.

Li Shenzhi. 1995. 李慎之《亚洲价值与全球价值》[Asian Values and Global Values]. 《东方》, Dongfang, No. 4.

Li Shucheng. 1903. 李书城《学生之意争》[The Students' Debate]. 《湖北学生界》, No. 2. Reprinted in Zhang Dan and Wang Renzhi, eds. Vol. 1:1.

Li Shuqing. 1935. 李树青《逮捕学生 言》[On the Arrest of Students]. 《独立评论》, No. 143, pp. 4–5.

Li Weichen. 1935. 李微尘《独裁勃兴的原因与它的弱点》[On the Reason for the Sudden Rise of Dictatorship and Its Weakness]. 《宇宙旬刊》, No. 4, pp. 7–17.

Li Xianglin. 1953. 李祥麟《基本人权溯源》[The Source of Fundamental Human Rights]. 《自由中国》, Vol. 10, No. 3, pp. 10–12, p. 26.

Li Xuan. 1948. 黎玄《民主政治的真谛》[The True Significance of Democracy]. 《再生》, No. 203.

Li Yonghui. 1995. 李永辉《这地方，怎一个"亚洲"了得》[This Place. What Asia.] 《东方》, Dongfang, No. 4.

Li Youning, and Zhang Yufa, eds. 1975. 《近代中国女权运动史料》[Historical Materials on the Movement for Women's Rights in Modern China]. Taipei: Biography Literary Publishing Company.

Li Yuan. 1941. 李原《论人权运动》[On the Human Rights Movement]. 《时代批评》, No. 73/74.

Li Zhangda. 1941. 李章达《人权的释义和今日—中国所迫切需要的人权保障障》[The Meaning of Human Rights: China Urgently Needs the Protection of Human Rights]. 《时代批评》, No. 73/74.

Li Zhongzhi. 1951. 李中直《个人与国家》[The Individual and the State]. 《自由中国》, Vol. 5, No. 6, pp. 12–14.

Lian Shi. 1907. 炼石《女权平议》[Discussion of Women's Rights]. 《中国新女界杂志》, No. 1. Reprinted in Li Youning and Zhang Wufa, eds. Vol. 1, pp. 430–33.

Liang Qichao. 1899–1902. 梁启超《自由书》[Notes on Freedom]. Reprinted in Liang Qichao (1978).

———. 1899. 梁启超《爱国论三。论民权》[On Patriotism, Part Three: People's Rights]. 《清议报》, No. 22.

———. 1901a. 《中国积弱溯源论》[The Origin of China's Weakness]. 《清议报》, No. 80. Reprinted in Li Huaxing and Wu Jiaxun, eds. (1984), pp. 140–47.

———. 1901b. 《国家思想变迁异同论》[On the Development of Ideas on State and Their Differences and Similarities]. 《清议报》, Nos. 94 and 95. Reprinted in Li Huaxing and Wu Jiaxun, eds. (1984), pp. 184–93.

———. 1901c. 《霍布士学案》[A Study of Hobbes's Thought]. 《清议报》,

No. 96, 97.

———. 1902a. 《论学术之势力左右世界》, [On the World Being in the Power of Science]. 《新民丛报》, No. 1. Reprinted in Li Huaxing and Wu Jiaxun, eds. (1984), pp. 269–76.

———. 1902b. 《论立法权》 [On Legislative Power]. 《新民丛报》, No. 2, 1902. Reprinted in Li Huaxing and Wu Jiaxun, eds. (1984), pp. 296–303.

———. 1902c. 《保教非所以尊孔论》 [To Protect the Faith Is Not to Respect Confucius]. 《新民丛报》, No. 2. Reprinted in Li Huaxing and Wu Jiaxun, eds. (1984), pp. 304–13.

———. 1902d. 《论政府与人民之权限》 [On the Limits between the Government and the People]. 《新民丛报》, No. 3. Reprinted in Li Huaxing and Wu Jiaxun, eds. (1984), pp. 1315–20.

———. 1902e. 《乐利主义泰斗边沁之学说》 [The Doctrine of Bentham, Master of Utilitarianism]. 《新民丛报》, Nos. 15 and 16.

———. 1902f. 《敬告我同业诸君》 [A Call to Those in the Same Business]. 《新民丛报》, No. 17. Reprinted in Li Huaxing and Wu Jiaxun, eds. (1984), pp. 334–39.

———. 1902–1903. 《新民说》 [The New Citizen]. Reprinted in Liang Qichao (1978).

———. 1978. 《饮冰室专集》 [Collected Works from the Ice-Drinker's Studio]. Taipei: 台湾中华书局, Vol. 3.

Liang Shiqiu. 1929a. 梁实秋 《论思想统一》 [On Unifying Thought]. 《新月》, Vol. 2, No. 3.

———. 1929b. 《孙中山先生论自由》 [On Sun Yatsen's View of Freedom]. 《新月》, Vol. 2, No. 9.

Liang Shuming. 1994. 梁漱溟 《中国文化要义》 [Essence of Chinese Culture]. Hong Kong: 三联书店.

Liang Xihua, ed. 1982. 梁锡花 《胡适秘藏书信选》 [A Selection of Hu Shi's Private Letters]. Taipei: 远景出版社, Vol. 1.

Lin Hengyuan. 1944. 林亨元 《五五宪草人民基本权利之研讨》 [A Discussion on People's Fundamental Rights in the May Fifth Constitutional Draft]. 《宪政》, No. 11, pp. 30–32.

Lin Huiyu. 1941. 林晦予 《人权与人权运动》 [Human Rights and the Human Rights Movement]. 《时代批评》, No. 73/74.

Lin Keyi. 1922. 林可彝 《天坛宪法应该怎么样改正》 [How to Amend the Temple of Heaven Draft Constitution]. 《东方杂志》, Vol. 19, No. 21, November.

Lin Qiyan. 1989. 林启彦 《步向民主_中国知识分子与近代民主思想》 [Moving toward Democracy: Chinese Intellectuals and Modern Democratic Thought]. Hong Kong: 中华书局.

Lin Rongnian, and Zhang Jinfan. 1980. 林榕年、张晋藩 《谈人权问题》 [On the Human Rights Issue]. 《学习与探索》, No. 1, pp. 30–37.

Lin Yusheng. 1990. 林毓生《殷海关先生阐释民主的历史意义与中国民主理论发展的前景》 [Yin Haiguang's Exploration of the Historical Meaning of Democracy and the Prospects for the Theoretical Development of Chinese Democracy]. In Wei Zhengtong et al., pp. 214–24.

Liu Guansheng. 1944. 刘冠生《人民的健康权利—论五五宪草人民权利章》 [People's Right to Health: On the Chapter of People's Rights in the May Fifth Constitutional Draft]. 《新中华》, Vol. 2, No. 9, pp. 15–17.

Liu Guangjing. 1994. 刘广京《晚清人权论初探—兼论基督教思想之影响》 [A Preliminary Study of the Ideas on Human Rights in the Late Qing Period—With Comments on the Influence of Christian Thought]. 《新史学》, Vol. 5, No. 3, September, pp. 1–23.

Liu Junning. 1998. 刘军宁《什么是"亚洲价值观"》 [What Are Asian Values?]. 《澳港信息日报》, 29/8–4/9. Reprinted in Angle and Svensson (2001).

Liu Nanlai, ed. 1994. 刘楠来《发展中国家与人权》 [Developing Countries and Human Rights]. Chengdu: 四川人民出版社.

Liu Qing. 1995. 刘青《人权民主与中国》 [Human Rights, Democracy, and China]. China Rights Forum, Summer, pp. 37–41.

Liu Qingpo, ed. 1986. 刘晴波《杨度集》 [Yang Du's Collected Works]. Changsha: 河南人民出版社.

Liu Shipei. 1907a. 刘师培《人类均力说》 [On the Equality of Mankind]. 《天义报》, No. 3. Reprinted in Zhang Nan and Wang Renzhi, eds. Vol. 2:2.

Liu Shipei. 1907b. 刘师培《无政府主义之平等观》 [The Egalitarianism of Anarchism]. 《天义报》, Nos. 4, 5, and 7. Reprinted in Zhang Nan and Wang Renzhi, eds. Vol. 2:2.

Liu Wenjuan. 1993. 刘文娟《试论五四时期人权思想的演变》 [An Exploration of the Development of the Idea of Human Rights during the May Fourth Period]. 《华中师范大学学报》, No. 1, pp. 83–88.

Liu Yazi. 1904. 柳亚子《哀女界》 [The Pitiful World of Women]. 《女子世界》, No. 9. Reprinted in Zhang Nan and Wang Renzhi, eds. Vol. 1:2.

———. 1907. 柳亚子《立宪问题》 [Problems of Constitutionalism]. 《复报》, No. 8. Reprinted in Wang Jing and Wang Xuezhuang, eds. Vol. 1, pp. 80–83.

Liu Zhongliang, and Tan Shuangquan, eds. 1998. 刘仲良 谭双泉《中国共产党人权理论与实践研究》 [Research into the CCP's Human Rights Theory and Practice]. Changsha: 湖南人民出版社.

Long Chuan. 1903. 泷川《公法上之人格》 [Personality in Public Law]. 《政法学报》, Vol. 3, No. 5.

Long Yi'e. 1954. 龙一谔《民主必需有个人自由》 [Democracy Need Freedom of the Individual]. 《自由中国》, Vol. 13, No. 2, pp. 10–12.

Luo Hongzhao. 1952. 罗鸿诏《国家自由与个人自由》 [Freedom of the Nation and

Freedom of the Individual]. 《自由中国》, Vol. 8, No. 1, pp. 5–6.

Luo Jialun. 1919a. 罗家伦《妇女解放》 [The Liberation of Women]. 《新朝》,
Vol. 2, No. 1, 30 October.

———. 1919b. 《近代西洋思想自由的进化》 [The Evolution of Freedom of
Thought in the Modern West]. 《新朝》, Vol. 2, No. 2, 1 December.

Luo Longji. 1929a. 罗隆基《论人权》 [On Human Rights]. 《新月》,
Vol. 2, No. 5. Reprinted in Hu Shi (1930), pp. 33–73.

———. 1929b. 《告压迫言论自由者》 [A Warning to Those Who Suppress
the Freedom of Speech]. 《新月》, Vol. 2, Nos. 6 and 7.

———. 1930a. 《论共产主义_共产主义理论上的批评》 [On Communism:
A Theoretical Critique of Communism]. 《新月》, Vol. 3, No. 1, pp. 1–22.

———. 1930b. 《我的被捕的经过与反感》 [My Experience and Reactions to
Having Been Arrested]. 《新月》, Vol. 3, No. 3, pp. 1–17.

———. 1930c. 《人权不能留在约法里？》 [Human Rights Cannot Be
Incorporated into the Provisional Constitution?] 《新月》, Vol. 3, No. 7, pp. 3–7.

———. 1930d. 《对训政时期约法的批评》 [On Criticism of the Provisional
Constitution of the Political Tutelage Period]. 《新月》, Vol. 3, No. 8, pp. 1–26.

———. 1930e. 《我们不主张天赋人权》 [We Are Not Advocating Natural
Rights]. 《新月》, Vol. 3, No. 8, pp. 4–6.

———. 1930f. 《人权释疑》 [The Definition of Human Rights]. 《新月》,
Vol. 3, No. 10, pp. 5–10.

———. 1930g. 《我们要什么样的政治制度》 [What Kind of Political System Do
We Want?] 《新月》, Vol. 2, No. 12.

———. 1932. 《罗隆基政治论文》 [A Collection of Luo Longji's Political Works].
Shanghai: 新月书店.

———. 1935. 《我对中国独裁政治的意见》 [My Opinions on Chinese Dictatorship].
《宇宙旬刊》, No. 3, pp. 1–11.

Luo Mingda, and He Hangzhou. 1993. 罗明达、贺航洲《论人权的个体属性》
[On the Individual Attribute of Human Rights]. 《政法论坛》, No. 1, pp. 56–61.

Luo Yanhua. 1998.罗艳华《东方人看人权－东亚国家人权观透视》 [Asians Look at
Human Rights. A Perspective on Asian Nations View on Human Rights]. Beijing:
新华出版社.

Luo Zhongshu. 1946. 罗忠恕《学术自由与文化进展》 [Academic Freedom and
the Progress of Culture]. 《观察》, Vol. 1, No. 12, pp. 8–10.

Ma Junwu. 1903a. 马君武《论赋税》 [On Taxes]. 《新民丛报》, No. 27, 12 March.
Reprinted in Mo Shixiang, ed., pp. 93–99.

———. 1903b. 《唯心派巨子黑智儿学说》 [The Idealist Hegel's Theory].
《新民丛报》, No. 27, 12 March. Reprinted in Mo Shixiang, ed., pp. 99–107.

———. 1903c. 《茶余随笔》 [Jottings at Leisure]. 《新民丛报》, No. 27, 12

March. Reprinted in Mo Shixiang, ed., pp. 108–13.

———. 1903d. 《论中国国民道德颓落之原因及其救治之法》 [On the Reason for the Decline of People's Morality in China and on the Way Remedy It]. 《新民丛报》, No. 28. Reprinted in Mo Shixiang, ed., pp.128–35.

———. 1903e. 《弥勒约翰之学说》 [John Stuart Mill's Theory]. 《新民丛报》, Nos. 29, 30, and 35. Reprinted in Mo Shixiang, ed., pp. 135–52.

———. 1903f. 《论公德》 [On Public Morality]. 《政法学报》, No. 1. Reprinted in Mo Shixiang, ed., pp. 152–61.

———. 1906. 《帝民说》 [On People's Sovereignty]. 《民报》, No. 2. Reprinted in Mo Shixing, ed., pp. 227–30.

———. 1911. 《敬告共和国之军政府》 [A Call to the Republic's Military Government]. 《民立报》, 24 November. Reprinted in Mo Shixing, ed., pp. 243–244.

Ma Xingye. 1937. 马星野 《言论自由与政府的新闻政策》 [Freedom of Speech and the Government's Press Policy]. 《国闻周报》, Vol. 14, No. 12, 1937, pp. 3–8.

Ma Zuyi. 1900. 马祖毅 《中国翻译简史》 [A Brief History of Chinese Translations]. 中国对外翻译出版社 1984.

Mai Menghua. 1900a. 麦孟华 《说权》 [On Rights]. 《清议报》, No. 44, 1900, pp. 1–4.

———. 1900b. 《说奴隶》 [On Slaves]. 《清议报》, No. 69, 1900.

Mao Zedong. 1965. 毛泽东 《在杭州会议上的讲话》 [Speech at Hangzhou], December 21, 1965, from 《毛泽东思想万岁》 [Long Live Mao Zedong Thought]. Reprinted in Helmut Martin, ed. Mao Zedong Texte. Sechster Band, 1965–1976. Teil 2. Carl Hanser Verlag.

———. 1991. 《毛泽东选集》 [Mao Zedong's Selected Works]. Shanghai: 人民出版社, Vol. 1–4.

Mei Kan. 1937. 梅凯 《给我自由！》 [Give Me Freedom!]. 《国闻周报》, Vol. 14, No. 15, 1937, pp. 5–7.

Min. 1941. 民 《人与奴之争》 [The Struggle between Man and Slave]. 《时代批评》, No. 71.

Minzhu Zhonghua. 1989. 《民主中华—中国民运文集》 [Democratic China: A Collection from the Democracy Movements]. Hong Kong: 远东事务评论社.

Ming Xia. 1935. 鸣夏 《我对民治的意见》 [My Opinions on Democracy]. 《宇宙旬刊》, Vol. 2, Nos. 8 and 9, pp. 1–4, and pp. 3–6.

Mo Shixiang, ed. 1991. 莫世祥 《马君武集 1900–1919》 [Ma Junwu's Collected Works, 1900–1919]. Wuhan: 华中师范大学出版社.

Nai Xuan. 1903a. 耐轩 《立宪论》 [On Constitutionalism]. 《政法学报》, Vol. 3, Nos. 1 and 2.

———. 1903b. 《政法之友》 [The Friend of Politics and Law]. 《政法学报》,

Vol. 3, No. 4.

Ning Shupan and Chen Kuangshi. 1984. 宁树潘、陈匡时《评开智录》
  [An Evaluation of Kai zhi lu]. 《复旦学报》, No. 3, pp. 22–28.

Niu Han and Deng Jiuping, eds. 1998. 牛汉、邓九平《原上草—记忆中的
  反右派运动》[Grass on the Plateau: The Antirightist Movement in Memory].
  Beijing: 经济日报出版社.

Pan Dada. 1946. 潘大达《对于宪草中人民权利的检讨》[A Self-Criticism of
  the Chapter on People's Rights in the Constitutional Draft]. 《民主周刊》, Vol. 3,
  No. 4, pp. 3–5.

Pan Gongzhan. 1930. 潘公展《对于争自由的认试》[The Understanding of the
  Fight for Freedom]. 《新生命》, Vol. 3, No. 7.

Pan Lang. 1941. 潘朗《论现阶段的人权运动》[On the Present Stage of the
  Human Rights Movement]. 《时代批评》, No. 73/74.

Peng Kang. 1932. 彭康《文化运动与人权运动》[The Cultural Movement and
  the Human Rights Movement]. 《新思潮》, No. 4, February. Reprinted in Cai
  Shangsi, ed. (1983), Vol. 3, pp. 101–117.

Peng Ming, ed. 1988. 彭明《中国现代史资料选辑》[A Selection of Materials
  on Modern China's History]. Beijing: 中国人民大学出版社, Vol. 3 (1927–1931).

Pu Man. 1906. 扑满《革命横议》 [A Discussion on Revolution]. 《民报》, No. 3.

Qian Duansheng. 1934. 钱端升《民主政治乎？机权国家乎？》[A Democratic
  or a Totalitarian Government?]. 《东方杂志》, Vol. 31, No. 1.

Qian Shifu.1948. 钱实甫《民权论在政治学中的地位》 [The Position of
  People's Rights in Political Science]. 《东方杂志》, Vol. 44, No. 8.

Qian Yongxiang. 1990. 钱永祥《殷海光先生的民主观与民主的两个概念》
  [Yin Haiguang's Two Concepts of Democracy]. In Wei Zhengtong et al. 韦政通
    《自由民主的思想与文化》 [The Ideas and Culture of Freedom and
    Democracy]. Taipei: 自立晚报社文化出版部, pp. 1–18.

Qiu Hanping. 1933. 丘汉平《宪法上关于人民之权利规定之商榷》
    [A Discussion on the Stipulations of People's Rights in the Constitution].
    《东方杂志》, Vol. 30, No. 7, April.

Qu Qiubai. 1931. 瞿秋白《中国人权派的真面目》 [The Real Feature of the
  China Human Rights Group]. 《布尔什维克》 Vol. 4, No. 6. Reprinted in Cai
  Shangsi, ed. (1983), Vol. 3, pp. 35–41.

Quan Liang. 1903. 权量《宪政平议》[A Discussion on Constitutionalism].
  《湖北学生界》, No. 2.

Qun Xin. 1941. 群心《人权运动之管
  Rights Movement]. 《时代批评》, No. 73/7.

Rao Fang. 1991. 饶方《一项重要的法学研究课题—如何开展人权与法制文题
的理论研究座谈会综》 [A Very Important Subject in Legal Research:

A Summary of a Conference on How to Develop Research on Human Rights and the Legal System]. 《中国法学》, No. 3, pp. 5–6.

Ren Jianshu, Zhang Tongmo, and Wu Xinzhong, eds. 任建树、张统模、吴信忠 《陈独秀著作选》 [A Selection of Chen Duxiu's Collected Works]. Shanghai: 上海人民出版社, Vol. 1–3.

Renmin ribao 《人民日报》

Sa Mengwu. 1928. 萨孟武 《以党治国》 [Party Rule of the Country]. 《新生命》, Vol. 1, No. 4.

Saneto Keishu. 1982. 实藤惠秀 《中国人留学日本史》 [A History of Chinese Students in Japan]. Hong Kong: 中文大学出版社.

Sato Shinichi. 1992. 佐藤慎一 《一八九_年代的「民权」论—以张之洞和 何启的论争为中心》 [The Discussion on People's Rights in the 1890s: Focusing on the Debate between Zhang Zhitong and He Qi]. Reprinted in Xu Zhengxiong (1992), pp. 106–130.

Shang Yi. 1922. 尚一 《近代妇女运动发生的途径》 [The Development of the Modern Women's Movement]. 《东方杂志》, Vol. 19, No. 18, September.

Shen Qichang. 1907a. 沈其昌 《法界微尘录》 [An Account of the Boundaries of the Law]. 《法政学报》, No. 1.

———. 1907b. 《法》 [Law]. 《法政学报》, No. 6.

Shen Xiangyun. 沈翔云 《复张之洞书》 [A Reply to Zhang Zhitong]. Reprinted in Zhang Nan and Wang Renzhi, eds., Vol. 1:2, pp. 764–775.

Shen Zhiyuan. 1941. 沈志远 《人权运动与民族解放》 [The Human Rights Movement and National Liberation]. 《时代批评》, No. 73/74.

———. 1947. 《坚决争取人权的永久保障》 [Firmly Fight for the Lasting Protection of Human Rights]. 《时代批评》, No. 85.

Shen Zongling. 1992a. 沈宗灵 《人权是什么意义上的权利》 [What Kind of Rights are Human Rights]. In CASS, pp. 16–22.

———. 1992b. 《二战西方人权学说的演变》 [The Development of Human Rights Studies in the West since the Second World War]. 《中国社会科学》, No. 5, pp. 57–70.

Sheng Zuhong. 1979. 盛祖宏 《人权与法制》 [Human Rights and the Legal System]. 《民主与法制》, No. 2, pp. 19–20.

Shi Jing. 1947. 史靖 《人民的权利》 [People's Rights]. 《民主半月刊》, No. 4, pp. 18–19.

Shi Weihuan. 1922. 史维焕 《我国宪法应明定国民之生存权》 [Our Constitution Should Explicitly Lay Down the Right to Subsistence]. 《东方杂志》, Vol. 19, No. 21.

Shi Zishan. 1941. 师子山 《人权运动的理论和工作》 [The Theory and Work of

the Human Rights Movement]. 《时代批评》, No. 73/74.

Si Hui. 1906. 死灰《国民势力与国家之关系》[The Relationship between
People's Power and the Country]. 《云南杂志》, No. 2.

Shi Yun. 1989. 史云《谁是人权的真正捍卫者》[Who Is the Real Defender
of Human Rights]. 《人民日报》 July 7. Translated in Angle and Svensson (2001).

Song Qiang, et al. (1996). 宋强《中国可以说不》 [China Can Say No].
Beijing: 中华工商联合出版社.

Song Qingling. 1952. 宋庆龄《为新中国奋斗》[The Struggle for the New
China]. Beijing: 人民出版社.

Su Qing. 1989. 苏青《结婚十年正续》[Ten Years of Marriage and Its Sequel]. Shanghai:
上海书店.

Sun Jicheng. 1993. 孙纪成《人权初论》[A Rudimentary Discussion on Human
Rights]. Kunming: 云南人民出版社.

Sun Lou. 1910. 荪楼《宪法大纲刍议》[My Humble Opinion on an
Outline of a Constitution]. 《民声》, No. 1, May. Reprinted in Hu Weixi
(1994), pp. 213–32.

Sun Zhe. 1992. 孙哲《新人权论》[A New Theory of Human Rights]. Zhengzhou:
河南人民出版社.

Sun Zhongshan. 1981. 孙中山《孙中山全集》[Sun Yat-sen's Collected Works].
Beijing: 中华书局, Vol. 1.

Tan Mingqian. 1920. 谭鸣谦《现代民治主义的精神》[The Spirit of Modern
Democracy]. 《新朝》, Vol. 2, No. 3, 1 April, pp. 586–90.

Tan Ruqian. 1980. 谭汝谦《中国译日本书综合目录》[A Comprehensive Catalogue
of Works Translated from Japanese into Chinese]. Hong Kong: 中文大学出版社.

Tang Wenquan and Sang Bing, eds. 1990. 唐文权、桑兵《戴季陶集 1909-1920 》
[Dai Jitao's Collected Essays, 1909–1913]. Wuhan: 华中师范大学出版社.

Tang Youren. 1925. 唐有壬《什么是反革命？》[What Is the Meaning of
Counterrevolutionary?] 《现代评论》, Vol. 2, No. 41, pp. 196–97.

Tao Menghe. 1924. 陶孟和《言论自由》 [Freedom of Speech]. 《现代评论》,
Vol. 1, No. 19, pp. 4–7.

———. 1935. 《民治与独裁》 [Democracy and Dictatorship]. 《国闻周报》,
Vol. 12, No. 1, pp. 1–4.

Tao Yinghui. 1995. 陶英惠《胡适与蔡元培鸭讣™共同经历真相的探讨》
[Hu Shi and Cai Yuanpei: A Discussion on the Real Facts of Their Common
Experience]. In 《郭廷以先生九秩诞辰纪念论文集》. Taipei: Academia Sinica,
Institute of Modern History, Vol. 1.

Wang Ermin. 1983. 王尔敏《中国近代之人权醒觉》[The Recognition of
Human Rights in Modern China]. 《香港中文大学中国文化研究所学报》,
No. 14, pp. 67–83.

———. 1995a. 《晚清政治思想史论》 [A History of Political Thought in the Late Qing]. Taipei: 台湾商务印书馆.

———. 1995b. 《中国近代思想史论》 [A History of Modern Chinese Thought]. Taipei: 台湾商务印书馆.

Wang Jianbang. 1958. 王建邦《请政府切实保障人权！》 [Requesting the Government to Conscientiously Protect Human Rights]. 《自由中国》, Vol. 19, No. 11, pp. 24–26.

Wang Jing and Wang Xuezhuang, eds. 1989. 王晶、王学庄《柳亚子选集》 [Liu Yazi's Selected Works]. Beijing: 人民出版社.

Wang Jingwei. 1905. 汪精卫《民族的国民》 [Citizens of the Nation]. 《民报》, Nos. 1 and 2. Reprinted in Zhang Nan and Wang Renzhi, eds., Vol. 2:1, pp. 82–114.

———. 1906a. 《希望满洲立宪者盍听诸》 [Hoping that the Manchu Constitutionalists Will Listen]. 《民报》, No. 3.

———. 1906b. 《驳新民丛报最近之非革命论》 [Criticizing Xinmin congbao's Latest Nonrevolutionary Theory]. 《民报》, No. 4. Reprinted in Zhang Nan and Wang Renzhi, eds., Vol. 2:1.

Wang Shi, ed. 1986. 王《严复集》 [Yan Fu's Collected Works]. Beijing: 中华书局.

Wang Shijie. 1924. 王世杰《现代之出版自由》 [Modern Freedom of the Press]. 《东方杂志》, Vol. 21, No. 1, January.

Wang Xiaoqiu. 1992. 王晓秋《近代中日文化交流史》 [A History of Cultural Exchange between China and Japan in Modern Times]. Beijing: 中华书局.

Wang Zaoshi. 1933. 王造时《自由之战争》 [The War of Freedom]. 《自由言论半月刊》, No. 2.

Wei Fang. 1922. 惟方《我对于国宪的三个建议》 [My Three Opinions on the Constitution]. 《东方杂志》, Vol. 19, No. 21, November.

Wei Zhengtong et al. 1990. 韦政通《自由民主的思想与文化》 [The Ideas and Culture of Freedom and Democracy]. Taipei: 自立晚报社文化出版部.

Wen Yu. 1941. 文俞《青年与人权》 [Youth and Human Rights]. 《时代批评》, No. 73/74, p. 3221.

Weng Songran. 1990. 翁松燃《殷海关先生的民主观》 [Yin Haiguang's View of Democracy]. In Wei Zhengtong et al., pp. 228–53.

Wu Daying and Liu Han. 1979. 吴大英、刘瀚《对人权要作历史的具体的分析》 [It Is Necessary to Make a Historical and Concrete Analysis of Human Rights]. 《法学研究》, No. 4, 1979, pp. 9–13.

Wu Jingxiong. 1933. 吴经熊《三民主义和法律》 [The Three Principles of the People and the Constitution]. In Wu Jingxiong, 《法律哲学研究》. Shanghai: 上海法学编机社.

———. 1936. 《中华民国宪法草案的特色》 [The Characteristics of the Constitutional Draft of the Republic of China]. 《东方杂志》, Vol. 33, No. 13.

Wu Jingxiong and Huang Gongjue. 1937. 吴经熊、黄公觉《中国制宪史》 [A History of the Chinese Constitutions]. Shanghai: 商务印书官.

Wu Pinjin. 1923. 吴品今《人权论之真谛》 [The True Significance of theTheory of Human Rights]. 《东方杂志》, Vol. 20, No. 18, September, pp. 55949–52.

Wu Yu. 1917. 吴虞《儒家主张阶级制度之害》 [The Harm of the Confucian Hierarchial System]. 《新青年》, Vol. 3, No. 4, 1 June.

Wu Yue. 1906. 吴越《吴越君献身意见书》 [The Intellectual Testament of Wu Yue]. 《复报》, No. 2.

Xia Yong. 1992. 夏勇《人权概念起源》 [The Origin of the Concept of Human Rights]. Beijing: 中国政法大学出版社.

———. 1994. 《中国法律年鉴１９９４》 [China Legal Yearbook 1994]. Beijing: 中国法律年鉴出版社.

———. ed. 1999a. 《走向权利的时代》 [Toward a Time of Rights]. Beijing: 中国政法大学出版社.

———. 1999b. 《论和女士及其与德、赛先生之关系－写在"五四"运动八十　周年》 [On Ms He and Her Rrelations with Mr De and Mr Sai: Written on the Occasion of the Eightieth Anniversary of May Fourth]. 《公法》, Vol. 1, pp. 42–54.

Xian Jie. 1906. 县解《论社会革命当与政治革命并行》 [On Why Social and Political Revolutions Should Be Carried Out Simultaneously]. 《民报》, No. 5.

Xiao Jiabao and Liu Yingqi. 1994. 萧家保、刘英琪《中国百年人权史》 [China's One-Hundred-Year Human Rights History]. Shenyang: 辽宁人民出版社.

Xiao Shu. 1999. 笑蜀 [The Heralders of History—the Solemn Promises of Half a Century Ago]. 《历史的先声半个世纪前的庄严承诺》. Shantou: 汕头大学出版社.

Xiao Weiyun et al. 1979. 肖蔚云《马克思主义怎么样看匀巳尸问题》 [On the Marxist View of the Issue of Human Rights]. 《红旗杂志》, No. 5, pp. 43–48.

Xin Chunying. 1996. 信春鹰《亚洲国家的人权观》 [The Human Rights View of Asian Countries]. In Li Lin, ed., pp. 340–54.

———. 1999. 《亚洲价值观与人权一场没有结语的对话》 [Asian Values and Human Rights: A Diaologue without Conclusion]. 《公法》, No. 1, pp. 167–81.

Xin Hua. 1904. 新华《论中国无国权》 [On China Having No National Rights]. 《东方杂志》, Vol. 1, No. 5.

Xinyue 《新月》

Xiong Yuezhi. 1994. 熊月之《西学东渐与晚清社会》 [The Dissemination of Western Learning and Late Qing Society]. Shanghai: 上海人民出版社.

Xiong Yuezhi. 1989. 熊月之《略论五四时期的人权思想》 [A Brief Discussion of Human Rights Thinking during the May Fourth Period]. In

《五四运动与中国文化建设—五四运动七十周年学术讨论会论文选》
[The May Fourth Movement and the Reconstruction of Chinese Culture—
Selected Articles from an Academic Conference on the Occasion of the Seventieth
Anniversary of the May Fourth Movement]. Beijing: 社会科学文献出版社, Vol. 1,
pp. 435–46.

Xu Bing. 1979. 徐炳《论人权与公民权》[On Human Rights and Citizens' Rights].
《光明日报》19 June.

———. 1989. 《人权理论的产生和历史发展》[The Origin and Historical
Development of the Theory of Human Rights]. 《法学研究》, No. 3, pp. 1–10.

———. 1992. 《人权与宪政》[Human Rights and Constitutionalism]. In CASS,
pp. 180–92.

Xu Guansan. 1950. 许冠三《西方文明的挑战》[The Challenge of Western
Civilization]. 《自由中国》, Vol. 2, No. 6, pp. 11–13.

———. 1951. 《民主中国的障碍在那里？》[Where Are the Obstacles to a
Democratic China?]. 《自由中国》, Vol. 4, No. 9, pp. 13–14.

———. 1953. 《我所了解的自由》[My Understanding of Freedom]. 《自由中国》,
Vol. 8, No. 2, pp. 9–12.

Xu Xianming. 1991. 徐显明 《"基本权利"析》[An Analysis of "Basic Rights"].
《中国法学》, No. 6, pp. 23–28.

———. 1992. 《生存权论》[On the Right to Subsistence]. 《中国社会科学》,
No. 5, pp. 39–56.

Xu Yucheng. 1907. 许玉成《金匮许玉成女士对于女界第一次演说稿》
[An Outline of Xu Yucheng's First Speech to Women]. 《中国新女界杂志》,
No. 5. Reprinted in Li Youning and Zhang Wufa, Vol. 1, pp. 444–50.

Xu Zhengxiong. 1992. 许政雄 《清末民权思想的发展与歧异—以何启、胡礼垣为
例》[The Development and Different Meanings of the Theory of People's Rights at
the End of the Qing: The Example of He Qi and Hu Liyuan]. Taipei:文史哲出版社.

Xue Hong. 1908. 雪鸿《立宪国之人民》[People in a Constitutional Country].
《时报》, 11 May.

Xue Huayuan. 1993. 薛化元《民主宪政与民族主义的辩证发展—张君劢思想研
究》[The dialectical development of constitutional democracy and nationalism: a
study of Zhang Junmai's Thought]. Taipei: 稻禾出版社.

Xue Jinjiang. 1903. 薛锦江《二十世纪之中国》[Twentieth-Century China].
《童子世界》, No. 25. Reprinted in Zhang Nan and Wang Renzhi, eds. Vol. 1:2.

YPYLXJ. 1957. 《右派言论选集》[A Collection of Rightist Speech]. Edited by the
propaganda department of the CCP's Hubei provincial secretariat,
中共湖北省委宣传部.Wuhan: 湖北人出版, Vol. 1 and 2.

Ya. 1904. 亚《磨剑室读书记》[Book Reviews from the Room Where Swords Are
Sharpened]. 《江苏》, Nos. 9 and 10.

Ya Cui. 1903. 亚粹《论法治国》 [On a Country Ruled by Law]. 《政法学报》, Vol. 3, No. 1.

Ya Sheng. 1904. 亚牲《论全寿造国民母》[On the Creation of the Nation's Mothers]. 《女子世界》, No. 7. Reprinted in Zhang Nan and Wang Renzhi, eds., Vol. 1:2.

Yan An. 1941. 雁庵《人权译义》 [The Definition of Human Rights]. 《时代批评》, No. 73/74.

Yan Cunsheng. 1992. 严存生《论人权的主体》[On the Subject of Human Rights]. In CASS, pp. 49–65.

Yang Dusheng. 1903. 杨笃生《新湖南》 [New Hunan]. Reprinted in Zhang Nan and Wang Renzhi, eds., Vol. 1:2, pp. 612–48.

Yang Xiaoqing. 1991. 杨晓青《人权理论研究座谈会综述》 [A Summary of a Conference on Human Rights Research]. 《中国法学》, No. 4, 1991, pp. 46–47.

Ye Lin. 1919. 叶麟 《无强权主义的根据及无强的社会略说》[The Foundation of Anarchism and an Account of an Anarchist Society]. 《新朝》, Vol. 1, No. 3, 1 March.

Ye Shengtao. 1919. (Ye Shaotao) 叶绍钧《女子人格问题》《女子人格问题》 [The Question of Women's Personality]. 《新朝》, Vol. 1, No. 2, 1 February.

Ye Shuheng. 1935. 叶叔衡《民治与独裁的争论与调解》 [The Debate between Democracy and Dictatorship and a Mediation between the Two]. 《独立评论》, No. 140, pp. 5–12.

Ye Yonglie. 1999. 叶永烈《王造时—我的当场答复》[Wang Zaoshi: My on the Spot Reply]. Beijing: 中国青年出版社.

Yin Haiguang. 1990. 殷海光《殷海光全集》 [The Collected Works of Yin Haiguang]. Taipei: 桂冠图书公司, Vol. 11 and 12.

Yu Danchu. 1987. 俞旦初《美国独立史在近代中国的介绍和影响》 [The Introduction and Influence of the History of American Independence in Modern China]. 《世界历史》, No. 2, pp. 60–81.

Yu Keping. 1989. 俞可平《人权引论—纪念法国'人与公民权利宣言'问世200周年》 [An Introduction to Human Rights: Commemorating the 200th anniversary of the French Declaration of the Rights of Man and the Citizen]. 《政治学研究》, No. 3, pp. 30–35.

———. 1992. 《人权与马克思主义》 [Human Rights and Marxism]. In CASS (1982), pp. 152–67.

Yu Xiao et al. 1999. 徐晓《遇罗克遗作与回忆》[Posthumous Works and Recollections of Yu Luoke]. Beijing: 中国文联出版社.

Yu Yingshi. 1992a. 余英时《国际人权标准与中国人权状况，国际研讨会论文集》 [Proceedings from an International Conference on the International Standard of

Human Rights and the Situation of Human Rights in China]. New York: Human Rights in China.

———. 1992b. 《国文化与现代变迁》 [Chinese Culture and Modern Change]. Taipei: 三民书局.

Yuan Sun. 1904. 辕孙《落西亚虚无党》 [Russian Nihilism]. 《江苏》, No. 4. Reprinted in Zhongyang yanjiu yuan jindai shi yanjiu suo, ed. 《近代中国对西方及列强认识资料汇编》, Vol. 5:2.

ZMTLW. 1983. 《中国民主同盟历史文献》 [Historical Documents of the China Democratic League]. Beijing: 文史资料出版社.

Zeng Qi. 1920. 曾琦《法兰西文明特点的一斑》 [The Special Characteristics of the French Civilization]. 《少年中国》, Vol. 2, No. 4, October, pp. 64–70.

Zeng Xubai. 1950. 曾虚白《「自由」「民主」「社会」三主义合论》 [On the Combination of the Three Isms of Freedom, Democracy, and Socialism]. 《自由中国》, Vol. 2, No. 5, pp. 14–16.

Zhang Baixi. 1904. 张百熙《新定学务纲要》 [New Regulations on Educational Policy]. Reprinted in Zhongyang yanjiu yuan jindai shi yanjiu suo, ed. 《近代中国对西方及列强认识资料汇编》, Vol. 5:1.

Zhang Foquan. 1933. 张佛泉《论国民政治负担》 [On the Political Burden of the People]. 《国闻周报》, Vol. 10, No. 33, pp. 1–8.

———. 1934. 《我们对于政治应取的态度》 [Our Attitude to Politics]. 《独立评论》, No. 131, pp. 6–9.

———. 1935a. 《论自由》 [On Freedom]. 《国闻周报》, Vol. 12, No. 3, pp. 1–10.

———. 1935b. 《个人自由与社会统制》 [Individual Freedom and the Control of the Society]. 《国闻周报》, Vol. 12, No. 28, pp. 1–12.

———. 1954. 《自由与人权》 [Freedom and Human Rights]. Taipei: 台湾商务印书馆. Reprinted in 1993.

Zhang Guangbo. 1990. 张光博《坚持马克思主义的人权观》 [Uphold a Marxist View on Human Rights]. 《中国法学》, No. 4, pp. 10–17.

Zhang Jinjian. 1950. 张金鉴《个人自由底社会价值》 [The Social Value of Individual Freedom]. 《自由中国》, Vol. 2, No. 7, pp. 10–11.

Zhang Junmai. 1944a. 张君劢《两时代人权运动概论》 [An Outline of the Human Rights Movement's Two Different Ages]. 《民宪》, No. 9, pp. 3–7.

———. 1944b. 《威尔斯氏政治思想及其近作人权宣言》 [H. G. Well's Political Thought and His Human Rights Manifesto]. 《民宪》, No. 10, pp. 4–13.

———. 1944c. 《人民基本权利三项之保障》 [The Protection of the People's Three Fundamental Rights]. 《新中国日报》, 1 March. Reprinted in 《再生》, Vol. 5, No. 10, 1964.

———. 1945. 《法国人权协会之人权宣言》 [The Human Rights Manifesto of the French Association for Human Rights]. 《民宪》, No. 12, pp. 9–12.

———. 1946a. 《国家为什么要宪法》 [Why Does the Country Need a Constitution?]. 《再生》, No. 123.

———. 1946b. 《人权为宪政基本》 [Human Rights Are the Basis of the Constitution]. 《再生》, No. 125.

———. 1946c. 《国际人权法案》 [A Draft of an International Law on Human Rights]. 《再生》, No. 128, pp. 2–3.

———. 1946d. 《人权经济自由联合国》 [Human Rights, Economy, Freedom and the United Nations]. 《再生》, No.141, pp. 7–8.

———. 1946e. 《国际人权宣言诸问题》 [Questions Regarding the Universal Declaration of Human Rights]. 《再生》, No. 142, pp. 9–10.

———. 1948a. 《民主政治的哲学基础》 [The Philosophical Basis of Democracy]. 《再生》, No. 240.

———. 1948b. 《宪法人权章之意义》 [The Meaning of the Human Rights Chapter in the Constitution]. 《再生》, No. 246.

Zhang Ming. 1933. 张铭 《人权原则新义》 [The New Meaning of the Principle of Human Rights]. 《新中华》, Vol. 1, No. 8, pp. 51–52.

Zhang Nan and Wang Renzhi, eds. 张丹、王忍之 《辛亥革命前十年间时论选集》 [A Selection of Materials from the Ten-Year Period before the Xinhai Revolution]. Beijing: 三联书店.

Zhang Shenfu. 1919. 张申府 《危险思想？》 [Dangerous Thinking?]. 《新青年》, Vol. 6, No. 5, May, pp. 551–53.

Zhang Wenxian. 1992. 张文显 《论人权的主体与主体的人权》 [On the Subject of Human Rights and Human Rights Subjects]. In CASS, pp. 35–48.

Zhang Yiding. 1981. 张彝鼎 《中外人权思想之比较》 [A Comparison of Chinese and Western Views on Human Rights]. Taibei: 中央文务供应社发行.

Zhang Yinlin. 1935. 张荫麟 《论非法捕捉学生》 [On the Illegal Arrest of Students]. 《独立评论》, No. 143, pp. 4–5.

Zhang Youyu. 1941. 长友渔 《人权运动与三民主义》 [The Human Rights Movement and the Three People's Principles]. 《时代批评》, No. 73/74, pp. 3102–05.

Zhang Yuanruo, 1936. 章渊若 《章力生政法论文集》 [A Collection of Zhang Lisheng's Works in Politics and Law]. Shanghai.

Zhang Zhenzhi, ed. 1929. 张振之 《评胡适反党义著》 [Criticizing Hu Shi for Violating the Party Spirit]. Shanghai: 光明书局.

Zhang Zhiben. 1933. 张知本 《宪法草案委员会之使命及草案中应行研究之问题》 [The Mission of the Constitutional Draft Committte and the Questions in the Draft which Ought to Be Studied]. 《东方杂志》, Vol. 30, No. 7, April.

Zhang Zhilian. 1995. 张芝联 《从『通鉴』到人权研究》 [From "Tong jian" to Human Rights Research]. Beijing: 生活岫潦獒新知三联书店.

Zhang Zhongdong. 1990. 张忠栋《胡适、雷震、殷海光—自由主义人物画像》
[Hu Shi, Lei Zhen, and Yin Haiguang: Protraits of Liberals]. Taipei:
自立晚报社文化出版部.

Zhao Xihua. 1992. 赵锡骅《民盟史话1941-1949》[A History of the
Democratic League, 1941–1949]. Beijing: 中国社会科学出版社.

Zhen. 1907a. 真 (Li Shizeng)《祖宗革命》[Revolution of the Ancestral System].
《新世纪》, Nos. 2 and 3. Reprinted in Hu Weixi, ed. (1994), pp. 141–47.

———. 1907b. 《三纲革命》[Revolution of the Three Cardinal Guides].
《新世纪》, No. 11. Reprinted in Hu Weixi, ed. (1994), pp. 148–55.

Zhen Gui. 1903. 斟癸《新名词译义》[Translations of New Concepts].
《浙江潮》, No. 2.

Zheng Hangsheng and Gu Chunde. 1994. 郑杭生、谷春德《人权史话》
[A Historical Narrative on Human Rights]. Beijing: 北京出版社.

Zhina Zi. 1903. 支那子《法律上人民之自由权》[People's Legal Rights and
Freedoms]. 《浙江潮》, No. 10.

Zhong Jiu. 1919. 仲九《德莫克拉西的教育》[Democratic Education]. 《教育潮》,
Vol. 1, No. 1, pp. 19–27.

Zhong Yi. 1933. 仲逸《民权与宪法》[Civil Rights and the Constitution].
《东方杂志》, Vol. 30, No. 5, March.

Zhongguo renquan xiehui. 1982. Chinese Association for Human Rights, ed.,
《人权论文选辑》[Selected Essays on Human Rights]. Taipei.

Zhou Fohai. 1922. 周佛海《自由和强制—平等和独裁》[Freedom and Force —
Equality and Dictatorship]. 《新青年》, Vol. 9, No. 6, 1 July.

———. 1928. 《民权主义的根据和特质》[The Basis and Particulars of the Doctrine
of Popular Sovereignty]. 《新生命》, Vol. 1, No. 2.

Zhou Jingwen. 1939a. 周鲸文《战时言论自由的重要及言论界的责任》
[The Importance of Freedom of Speech during the War, and the Responsibility of
the Media]. 《时代批评》, No. 4, pp. 109–13.

———. 1939b. 《争取抗战的言论自由》[Struggle for the Freedom of Speech to
Resist Japan]. 《时代批评》, No. 27, pp. 1155–6.

———. 1939c. 《论抗战中的宪政运动》[The Constitutional Movement during
the War]. 《时代批评》, No. 34.

———. 1939d. 《抗战期中为何需要宪政》[Why We Need a Constitutional
Government during the War]. 《时代批评》, No. 37, pp. 1590–95.

———. 1940. 《中国需要怎样的宪法》[What Kind of Constitution Does China
Need?] 《时代批评》, No. 41, pp. 1744–66.

———. 1941a. 《展开人权运动》[Launch a Human Rights Movement].
《时代批评》, No. 69, pp. 2931–4.

———. 1941b. 《用人权运动纪念五四》[To Use the Human Rights Movement to

Commemorate May Fourth]. 《时代批评》, No. 70.

———. 1941c. 《人权运动的理论与实际》 [The Theory and Practice of the Human Rights Movement]. 《时代批评》, No. 71.

———. 1941d. 《人权运动纲领》 [The Program of the Human Rights Movement]. 《时代批评》, No. 73/74.

———. 1944. 《论身体自由与法律威信》 [On Freedom of the Person and the Prestige of the Law]. 《民宪》, No. 8.

Zhu Wenbo. 1958. 朱文伯《理论与事实崖™谈人权保障问题》 [Theory and Practice—An Informal Discussion on the Protection of Human Rights]. 《自由中国》, Vol. 19, No. 11, pp. 17–19.

Zhu Zheng. 1998. 朱正《1957年的夏季–从百家争鸣到两家争鸣》 [The Summer of 1957: From the Hundred Schools of Contending to the Two Schools of Contending]. Zhengzhou: 河南人民出版社.

Zhu Zhimin. 1989. 朱志敏 in 《论五四时期的平民主义思潮》 [On Ideas of Democracy in the May Fourth Period]. 《今代史研究》, No. 2.

Zhu Zhuang. 1904. 竹庄《论中国女学不兴之害》 [On the Harm of Not Promoting Schools for Women in China.]. 《女子世界》, No. 3, 1904. Reprinted in Zhang Nan and Wang Renzhi, eds., Vol. 1:2.

Ziyou Zhongguo. 《自由中国》, 1949–1960.

Index

Xiao Weiyun, 247
Xin Chunying, 276
Xin qingnian (magazine). See *New Youth*
Xin shiji, 120
Xingqi pinglun, 148, 149
Xinmin congbao, 72, 109
Xinyue (magazine), 160–61, 197, 249, 304; CCP critique of, 166, 170; GMD critique of, 116–169; views on human rights, 160–66. *See also* Hu Shi; Luo Longji
Xu Bing, 247, 250–51, 262–63, 276, 278–79, 282
Xu Fuguan, 218
Xu Wenli, 237, 240, 241, 242, 284
Xu Xianming, 279
Xu Yucheng, 103
Xu Zhimo, 160, 162

Ya Cui, 110–11
Yan Fu, 72, 87, 90, 92, 101, 114, 118
Yan'an, 160, 199
Yang Du, 100, 117
Yang Dusheng, 103, 114, 120
Yang Quan, 171, 172, 175, 176
Yang Tingdong, 85
Yang Zhou, 286
Ye Shengtao, 137, 144
Yin Haiguang, 214, 215, 216, 217, 218, 219
Yishu huibian, 72, 85, 86, 87, 114
Yu Dafu, 171
Yu Fan, 241, 242, 244
Yu Haocheng, 262,
Yu Keping, 262–63, 278–79, 282
Yu Luoke, 234–35
Yu Quanyu, 271
Yuan Shikai, 141, 151
Yunnan zazhi, 107, 113

Zaisheng (magazine), 188, 193
Zao Taofen, 171, 175

Zhang Baixi, 109
Zhang Bojun, 223
Zhang Dongsun, 196
Zhang Foquan, 162, 180, 214, 216–17, 218
Zhang Jinfan, 249
Zhang Junmai (Carsun Chang), 162, 187, 202, 206, 218, 221; view on Chinese culture, 194–95; view on human rights, 193–94; Western influences on, 192–93
Zhang Pengjun (P. C. Chang), 201–5
Zhang Shenfu, 145
Zhang Shizhao, 132
Zhang Yuanruo, 166
Zhang Wenxian, 276, 280, 281, 282
Zhang Xiruo, 179
Zhang Zhiben, 177
Zhang Zhidong, 83
Zhang Zhilian, 268
Zhang Zixun, 151
Zhejiang chao, 72, 81, 99, 108, 112
Zhi shuo, 90
Zhong Yi, 177
Zhou Enlai, 84, 198
Zhou Fohai, 138, 168, 169
Zhou Jianren, 171, 175
Zhou Jingwen, 188–91, 192, 198, 206
Zhu Muzhi, 270
Zhuang Zi, 172
Ziyou Zhongguo. See *Free China Magazine*
Zou Rong, 63, 239, 242; anti-Manchu sentiments of, 112, 115–16; on human rights, 100, 107, 111; influenced by the American revolution, 86; on slave mentality of the Chinese people, 101
zuoren (to be a person, acting as people, humanity): in Confucian thought, 104; and enjoyment of human rights, 41, 104, 162, 137, 168, 173, 180, 188, 216, 242, 263

About the Author

Marina Svensson is assistant professor in the Department of East Asian Languages and research associate at the Centre for East and Southeast Asian Studies, Lund University, Sweden. Her research focuses on political and institutional changes in China, the theory and practice of human rights, and issues related to the protection of the Chinese cultural heritage. She is coeditor of *The Chinese Human Rights Reader* (2001).